THE BRIDE OF THE LAMB

THE BRIDE OF THE LAMB

Sergius Bulgakov

Translated by

Boris Jakim

WILLIAM B. EERDMANS PUBLISHING COMPANY
GRAND RAPIDS, MICHIGAN

T&T CLARK
EDINBURGH

Published jointly 2002
in the United States of America by
Wm. B. Eerdmans Publishing Co.
255 Jefferson Ave. S.E., Grand Rapids, Michigan 49503
www.eerdmans.com
and in the U.K. by
T&T Clark Ltd
59 George Street
Edinburgh EH2 2LQ
Scotland
www.tandtclark.co.uk

Printed in the United States of America

06 05 04 03 02   7 6 5 4 3 2 1

Library of Congress Cataloging-in-Publication Data

Bulgakov, Sergei Nikolaevich, 1871-1944.
[Neviesta Agntsa. English]
The bride of the lamb / Sergius Bulgakov;
translated by Boris Jakim.
p.   cm.
Includes bibliographical references.
ISBN 0-8028-3915-0 (pbk. : alk. paper)
1. Theology, Doctrinal.
2. Russian Orthodox Church — Doctrines.
I. Title.

BT75.3.B8513 2002
20'.19 — dc21
2001040383

British Library Cataloguing-in-Publication Data

A catalogue record for this book is available from the British Library
ISBN 0 567 08871 5

Contents

Contents

SECTION II
The Church, History, and the Afterlife

SECTION III
Eschatology

Contents

Translator's Introduction

1

And the angel said: "Come hither, I will show thee the bride, the Lamb's wife. And he carried me away in the spirit to a great and high mountain, and showed me that great city, the holy Jerusalem, descending out of heaven from God, having the glory of God" (Rev. 21:9-11).

As Sergius Bulgakov makes clear, the Bride of the Lamb is the Church, but she is the Church of the "new heaven and new earth," which appears after all the old barriers and separations have been abolished.

The new Jerusalem signifies the transfigured and glorified world. The world is reconnected with the paradise planted by God, with all that grows in it, including the mysterious tree of life and the tree of the knowledge of good and evil. But the time for such knowledge is past: good and evil in their duality and struggle have been transcended. There is no more evil. But there is also no more good, in its relativity. Only the tree of life remains, which has vanquished death.

The city of God, the Church, the Bride of the Lamb, is the final goal of all natural and historical life, of all of humanity's creative energies and activities. The city of God also represents the goal and conclusion of Sergius Bulgakov's magnum opus, *The Bride of the Lamb*.

2

Father Sergius Bulgakov (1871-1944) is the twentieth century's most profound Orthodox systematic theologian. Born into the family of a poor provincial priest, Bulgakov had a strict religious upbringing and entered the seminary at a young age. But owing to a spiritual crisis, in the direction of materialism and atheism, he did not complete his seminary studies. He chose, instead, to follow a secular course of study, which led to his matriculation at the University of Moscow, where he specialized in political economics.

This marked the beginning of his relatively short-lived Marxist period. In 1901, after he defended his master's dissertation, *Capitalism and Agriculture* (1900), Bulgakov was appointed professor of political economy at the Polytechnical Institute of Kiev. During his years there (1901-6), he underwent a second spiritual crisis, this time in the direction of idealist philosophy and the religion of his youth.

Influenced first by the philosophies of Kant and Vladimir Solovyov, and then by the great Orthodox theologian Pavel Florensky, Bulgakov gradually began to articulate his own original sophiological conception of philosophy. This conception was first worked out in his *Philosophy of Economy*, for which he received his doctorate from the University of Moscow in 1912. Later, in *The Unfading Light* (1917), he gave his sophiological ideas definite philosophical shape.[1] Following this, Bulgakov's intellectual output was, for the most part, theological in character. Indeed, his personal religious consciousness flowered in the following year, and he accepted the call to the priesthood, receiving ordination in 1918.

These years of internal crisis and growth in Bulgakov's personal life paralleled the tumultuous period in Russian political and social life that climaxed in the October Revolution of 1917 and the subsequent Bolshevik ascendancy. In 1918 Bulgakov left Moscow for the Crimea to assume a professorship at the University of Simferopol. But his tenure was short-lived, owing to Lenin's banishment in 1922 of more than one hundred scholars and writers deemed incurably out of step with the official ideology.

Bulgakov left the Soviet Union on January 1, 1923, traveling first to Constantinople and then to Prague. Finally, having accepted Metropolitan Eulogius's invitation both to become the dean of the newly established Saint Sergius Theological Institute and to occupy the Chair of Dogmatic Theology, he settled in Paris in 1925. Here, until his death (and

---

1. Later in this introduction I will discuss sophiology in some detail in the context of Russian religious thought as a whole.

some might say "transfiguration")[2] in 1944, he was to make his most fruitful and lasting contributions to Orthodox thought.

During the theologically most productive period of his life, Bulgakov produced six books, grouped into two trilogies. The works of the so-called little trilogy, *The Friend of the Bridegroom* (1927), *The Burning Bush* (1927), and *Jacob's Ladder* (1929), are efforts to capture the glory, the uncreated, sophianic light streaming from John the Baptist, the Mother of God, and the holy angels. The great trilogy, with the general title *On Divine Humanity*,[3] consists of volumes on Christology (*The Lamb of God*, 1933), pneumatology (*The Comforter*, 1936), and ecclesiology and eschatology (*The Bride of the Lamb*, published posthumously, 1945).

3

Modern Russian religious thought[4] started in the 1840s with the Slavophiles, especially Aleksei Khomiakov (1804-60) and Ivan Kireevsky (1808-56). This group introduced the key idea of sobornost (derived from the Russian *sobirat'*, to gather, and related to *sobor*, council). Sobornost was considered by Khomiakov to be embodied in the Church as a divinely inspired fellowship. It is community in love, communion in the spirit, the free union of the faithful in the pure heart of the Church.

The religious thought of the Slavophiles was developed by the greatest nineteenth-century Russian philosopher, Vladimir Solovyov (1853-1900). Two of Solovyov's key ideas had an enormous influence on the development of Russian religious thought in general and on Bulgakov in

---

2. His disciple Sister Joanna Reitlinger describes in a memoir how, during the illness that was to cause his death, those who surrounded Father Sergius saw him in a state that can only be described as a transfigured one: an intense light shone from his face and a profound peace descended upon all who were present. See *Sergius Bulgakov: Apocatastasis and Transfiguration*, translated, edited, and with an introduction by Boris Jakim (New Haven: Variable Press, 1995).

3. These are not really three volumes of a single, unified work. Bulgakov's studies of Christ and of the Holy Spirit are, of course, interdependent, but his great work on the Church, *The Bride of the Lamb*, is complete in itself and can be read independently of the other two.

4. By modern I mean a thought that diverges from the rote teachings of an ecclesiastical scholasticism and that takes into account the findings of contemporary science and philosophy. This "modern" thought does not thereby cease to be religious or even Orthodox, that is, of the Orthodox Church.

particular. These are the notions of Divine-humanity and Sophia. Divine-humanity is rooted in the Creed of Chalcedon, which defines the dual nature of Christ, divine and human, and expresses the process whereby man cooperates with God, leading to the transfiguration of humanity and fusing the entire human community into a heavenly Church without barriers between denominations. This process has its central focus in the Incarnation of God in Christ.

Solovyov's second central idea is that of Sophia, the Wisdom of God. He identifies Sophia with the world soul considered as the active principle that progressively exemplifies in the created world the eternal all-uniting idea in the Logos. Sophia is also identified with the goal of this process, with that which is produced, that is, with spiritualized humanity, the community of persons united in Divine-humanity. Sophia is depicted as the eternal ideal proto-image of humanity (the image of God in man), as the world soul actively engaged in actualizing this prototypical image, and as the fully developed divine-human organism. She is portrayed both as the active principle of the creative process and as its realized goal, the kingdom of God, the society of those participating in Divine-humanity.

These key ideas of Divine-humanity and Sophia, together with the idea of sobornost, served as the ferment that gave rise to the great Russian religious renaissance of the beginning of the twentieth century. Influenced by the Slavophiles, by Solovyov, and by Dostoevsky, figures like Nikolai Berdyaev (1874-1948), Lev Shestov (1866-1938), Vasily Rozanov (1856-1919), Andrey Bely (1880-1934), Viacheslav Ivanov (1866-1949), S. L. Frank (1877-1950), Pavel Florensky (1882-1937), and Bulgakov produced a modern religious philosophy unparalleled in depth and beauty. It is from this soil that Bulgakov's sophiology and his own doctrine of divine-humanity grew.[5]

Developed in such works as *The Philosophy of Economy, The Unfading Light,* and the trilogy on Divine-humanity (of which *The Bride of the Lamb* is the third part), Bulgakov's sophiology is an attempt to bring Eastern Orthodox dogmatics into the modern period. By this I mean that, continuing the work of Solovyov, Bulgakov seeks to carve out a greater role for man in the preparation of our salvation and in the transfiguration of creation, than previously allowed by official Orthodox doctrine. But Bulgakov's sophiology is a return to true Orthodoxy, for it is rooted in the feat of the God-man, who received from the Father the power of salvation

5. Bulgakov once stated that sophiology is nothing but the full elucidation of divine-humanity.

and transfiguration. Man is not a passive participant in the vast eschatological process that is taking place. By virtue of the divine-humanity, he is a crucial actor in these events.

4

The Bride of the Lamb, Bulgakov's last major theological work, is the greatest sophiological work ever written. A masterpiece of mystical theology, it is the crowning glory of Bulgakov's theology (and one of the crowning glories of twentieth-century Christian theology in general), the most mature development of his sophiology.

In his preface, Bulgakov indicates that the theme of this work is the doctrine of the Church, ecclesiology, understood in all its breadth and depth as sophiology. It examines the various aspects of creaturely being, from its natural and fallen state to its glorified and transfigured state.

The first section of the work treats the nature of created beings and the relationship between the Creator and creation. The creation of the world "out of nothing," creaturely freedom, and the interaction of God with creaturely freedom are the specific aspects considered. The nature of the Church is examined next, with emphasis on hierarchy, sacraments, and grace. The interaction between God and human history is also addressed.

Perhaps the book's most profound chapter follows: a discussion of death and the afterlife, which is perhaps based on Bulgakov's near encounters with death during severe illnesses and on the visions he had at these times. Eschatology is the subject of the final section, as is fitting. The parousia, the transfiguration of the world, the universal resurrection, and judgment and separation are all examined, as is the question of the eternity of hell and the possible salvation of the fallen angels.

The entire work is imbued with the presence of the Divine Sophia; it is permeated with her light, as it were. Man is created in the image of God and is thus expressive of the Divine Sophia, who is humanity's prototype. Upon the creation of the universe, Sophia in God, who serves as the principle of Trinitarian self-revelation, manifests herself as creaturely Sophia in humanity and in the cosmos. Through Sophia, Divine and creaturely, a link is found to express the belonging of the world to God, who is its source and also its ultimate end. Humanity itself in this way is likewise a Divine-humanity both in its foundation and in its finality.

Let me quote a key passage from *The Bride of the Lamb*, which, I think, expresses the crux of Bulgakov's sophiology: "The Incarnation, in which all human beings are co-resurrected in glory together with Christ, makes [the] sophianic proto-image of every human being [the image of God in man: see Gen. 1] transparent and clear. Resurrection in glory is therefore the definitive sophianization of man through the manifestation in him of his proto-image. In this sense, resurrection in glory is the manifestation of the Divine Sophia in the creaturely Sophia, the completion of creation. . . . The image of the resurrected human being . . . is his proper eternal image in God, hitherto hidden and obscure, but manifested in its power and glory in resurrection" (p. 451 of the present edition).

5

And when all are resurrected, when the images of all men become transparent and clear, they will all be in the New Jerusalem. And in the New Jerusalem, "God shall wipe away all tears from their eyes, and there shall be no more death, neither sorrow, nor crying, neither shall there be any more pain: for the former things are passed away" (Rev. 21:4).

The new creation, the new heaven and new earth, will demand a new love in God, in Christ and the Holy Spirit, in the Divine Sophia. The sophianicity of creation, which is the living and permanent self-revelation of God in creation, will be the basis for the unification of love for God and love for the world in the union of the Divine Sophia with the creaturely Sophia.

The great city, the holy Jerusalem, descending out of heaven from God, is the Bride of the Lamb. And the angel said (to John the seer of mysteries and perhaps to Father Sergius as well): "'Come hither, I will show thee the bride, the Lamb's wife.' And he carried me away in the spirit to a great and high mountain, and showed me that great city, the holy Jerusalem, descending out of heaven from God, having the glory of God."

•   •

Bulgakov's original Russian text could have used a little editing: I have excised three essay-length "addenda"[6] and an almost book-length "excursus"

---

6. These addenda comprise "On the Question of the Apocatastasis of the Fallen Spirits (in connection with the doctrine of St. Gregory of Nyssa)" (this essay was published in Jakim's translation of *Sergius Bulgakov: Apocatastasis and Transfiguration*).

on Augustinianism and predestination, which probably should have been published separately. I have also excised an excursus on salvation in chapter 5 and one on the biblical doctrine of the final fate of sinners in the section on eschatology. The original Russian volume contains copious and complicated notes, many of them with long quotations in Latin. For the sake of readability, I have taken out some of the notes and shortened others, leaving ellipsis points in square brackets ([. . .]) where I have removed material. Translator's notes are marked by the abbreviation "Trans." Translations of foreign phrases are given in brackets following the phrase.

.   .

I must acknowledge my esteemed colleague, the late Constantin Andronikof, the greatest French translator of Russian religious thought: I have been able to untwist many a thorny passage of *The Bride of the Lamb* by referring to his excellent translation into French, published as *L'Épouse de l'Agneau* (Editions l'Âge d'Homme, Lausanne, 1984).

6

Bulgakov refers to a number of his own works. I give bibliographic information and their Russian titles below. In the body of the notes I give only the English title and appropriate page numbers.

Russian transliterations of the works of other authors are given only the first time the work is cited.

Bulgakov's Books

Two Cities: An Inquiry into the Nature of Social Ideals (Dva grada: Issledovaniia o prirode obshchestvennykh idealov), Moscow, 1911.

The Philosophy of Economy (Filosofiia khoziaistva), Moscow, 1912. (Translated into English by Catherine Evtuhov, Yale University Press, 1999.)

The Unfading Light: Contemplations and Speculations (Svet nevechernii: Sozertsaniia i umozreniia), Moscow, 1917.

The Burning Bush: An Essay in the Dogmatic Interpretation of Certain Features in the Orthodox Veneration of the Mother of God (Kupina neopalimaia: Opyt dogmaticheskogo istolkovaniia nekotorykh chert v pravoslavnom pochitanii Bozh'ei Materi), Paris, 1927.

Jacob's Ladder: On the Angels (Lestvitsa Iakovlia: Ob angelakh), Paris, 1929.
The Icon and Its Veneration (Ikona i ikonopochitanie), Paris, 1931.
On the Gospel Miracles (O chudesakh Evangel'skikh), Paris, 1932.
The Lamb of God (Agnets Bozhii), Paris, 1933.
The Comforter (Uteshetel'), Paris, 1936.
The Philosophy of the Name (Filosofiia imeni), Paris, 1953.

Bulgakov's Articles

"Apocalypse and Socialism" *(Apokaliptika i sotsializm)* in *Two Cities.*
"Hypostasis and Hypostatizedness" *(Ipostas' i ipostasnost')* in the Collection
    in Honor of P. B. Struve, Prague, 1925.
"The Eucharistic Dogma" *(Evkharisticheskii dogmat)*, *Put'*, Paris, 1930.
"Judas Iscariot: The Traitor-Apostle" *(Iuda Iskariot Apostol-Predatel')*, *Put'*,
    1931.
"The Holy Grail" *(Sviatoi Graal')*, *Put'*, Paris, 1932. ("The Eucharistic
    Dogma" and "The Holy Grail" have been translated into English by
    Boris Jakim in *The Holy Grail and the Eucharist*, Lindisfarne Books,
    Hudson, N.Y., 1997.)
"Hierarchy and the Sacraments" *(Ierarkhiya i tainstva)*, *Put'*, Paris, 1935.
"The Problem of Conditional Immortality" *(Problema uslovnogo bess-
    mertiya)*, *Put'*, Paris, 1936-1937.
"Chapters on Trinity" *(Glavy o Troichnosti)*, *Trudy Pravoslavnogo Bogoslov-
    kogo Instituta v Parizhe*, I, II.

Other Works

Migne's *Patrologia Graeca* is abbreviated as PG; his *Patrologia Latina* is abbreviated as PL.

To the Reader

The work offered to the reader's attention is the third and concluding volume of a theological trilogy devoted to the study of *Divine-humanity,* a fundamental truth of Christianity. In the general plan of this trilogy, as it was conceived about ten years ago, the first and second volumes are devoted to the divine nature. *The Lamb of God* (1933) is devoted to christology, and *The Comforter* (1935) is devoted to pneumatology. The third and final volume is devoted to anthropology. In this final volume we consider the various aspects of creaturely being, from its natural and fallen state to its glorified and transfigured state. Thus, the theme of this work is the doctrine of the Church, ecclesiology, understood in all its breadth and depth as sophiology. This third volume necessarily includes eschatology, which concludes the doctrine of Divine-humanity and contains its most general and final truths. This is therefore the most important part of this trilogy on Divine-humanity. Indeed, such is its importance for the author, who now submits it for discussion by the Church.

Let me say a few words about the external fate of this book. It was finished by 1939; however, the great cataclysm experienced by the world caused a long delay in its publication. The trials of those years, both personal and general, naturally became for me a verification by life of the beliefs that find their profession here. In connection with this I must say that I now unhesitantly submit this book to the publisher in the form in which it was originally written.

What else can I say? The truths contained in the revelation of Divine-humanity, particularly in its eschatological aspect, are so unshakable and universal that even the most shattering events of world history, which we are now witnessing, pale and are nullified in their ontological significance in the face of these truths insofar as we perceive these events in the light of that which is to come. And that which is to come is the Church in its power and glory, together with the transfiguration of creation. The heart and the soul, the personal center of creation, is the Virgin Mother, the "Wife and Bride of the Lamb." She is also "the holy city, new Jerusalem, coming down from God out of heaven, prepared as a bride adorned for her husband . . . the tabernacle of God . . . with men" (Rev. 21:2-3).

And in the face of this Coming Church, the prayer of faith, love, and hope should cry out again and again in one's heart: "And the Spirit and the bride say, Come! And let him that heareth say, Come! . . . He which testifieth these things saith, Surely I come quickly! Amen. Even so, come, Lord Jesus!" (Rev. 22:17, 20).

11/24 June 1942
St. Sergius Theological Institute, Paris

SECTION I

The Creator and Creation

CHAPTER 1

The Creation of the World "Out of Nothing"

1. Cosmism

In the Christian understanding of the relation existing between God and the world, it is first necessary to exclude two polar opposites: pantheistic, or atheistic, monism on the one hand and the dualistic conception of creation on the other. According to the monistic doctrine, the world is self-sufficient and can be understood from itself. In the depths of its immanence it realizes the fullness of itself, for there it contains the hidden roots of its own being. The substance of the world is its unique and final foundation. However we understand it, whether materialistically as matter or energy, or spiritualistically as a spiritual monad or system of monads, common to all forms of monism is this self-enclosedness and self-sufficiency of the world, and its absoluteness in this sense. This worldview is essentially cosmotheism, speculative or mystical, or simply atheism, which denies the existence of a divine being above the world or in the world.

This worldview denies the very problem of the *origin* of the world, since one cannot speak of the origin of an absolute being. This being is eternal, even if its fullness is realized only in time. Here, it can be a question of the relation of noumenal and phenomenal being, substance and the empirical. In general, there is room for all kinds of distinctions within this self-enclosed worldview. Thus, different forms of monism are possible — from the mystico-poetical perception of the world to its prosaically empirical, mechanistically materialistic conception. Here, one can even have the development of a mysticism that is capable of assuming not only a poetic but even a subjectively religious form. However, the monistic worldview too is atheistic, insofar as it does not recognize the supramundane, transcendent God, closes itself off from Him in autonomous being, and thus loses the true idea of the world. The true idea of the world exists only in the *relation* of the world to the supramundane divine principle.

Because different layers or depths can be distinguished in immanent being, pantheism can fail to be conscious of itself in its cosmotheism as an atheism. History knows religiophilosophical systems that were considered to be profoundly religious, both by their own adepts and by their successors. Stoicism and especially Neoplatonism, Brahmanism and Buddhism, and modern theosophy and anthroposophy are examples of such systems. These doctrines have the common and distinctive feature that the idea of the *creation* of the world by the supramundane God is alien to them. They sometimes admit the creation of the world, but only in the sense of its self-formation, through its higher powers ("hierarchies") in relation to the lower ones. They speak of the emergence of a number of worlds within the depths of a single cosmic whole. This is a cosmic evolution whose origin is unknown but which, in its "avatars," is proceeding to infinity. But this auto-evolution of the world does not change anything in the fundamental *cosmism* of this worldview. The main feature distinguishing it from Christian cosmology is the absence of the idea of the createdness of the world, and this absence is, of course, rooted in the denial of the existence of the Creator. The fundamental relation between the Creator and creation, with the entire complex problematic this relation implies, is absent in pantheism. For pantheism, the world is self-evident and does not need an explanation for itself.

2. Dualism

At the opposite pole to cosmism or cosmotheism is dualism. Dualism is characterized by the recognition of the createdness of the world. However, for dualism the world is created not by one creator but by two: "Nature was created together by a white god and a somber black god." The conception of this second principle has its roots in morality and theodicy. It comes from the need to explain the evil and imperfection in the world, but a metaphysical or ontological theme is also important here. Insofar as it is not-God, even though it has its foundation in God as its Creator, the world cannot do without a point of reference or support outside of God or alongside God.

It is this point that lies at the basis of the world's extra-divine being. What we find here is a peculiar application of the law of identity, which is negatively expressed in the law of contradiction (and the law of the "excluded middle"). In the fullness of His divine being, God is only God. He is enclosed and as if limited in His being by His own divinity. There is thus no place in divinity for the world in its separateness. What remains for the world is to search for *pou stō*, an ontological place for itself (Plato's *ekmageion*) outside of or alongside divinity. This leads to the postulate of a certain divine altero-being, a second god, whose face is wholly turned toward the world. This second divinity is conceived either in various mythological images of the original mother-matter, Tiamat, whatever the character of these concrete mythological images may be in different religions, or in dualistic ditheism, which recognizes two not only different but, in a certain sense, even opposite gods, gods who fight against and complement each other; for example, Ormuzd and Ahriman in the Persian religions. We find the same thing in gnostic doctrines. It is easy to see the religious absurdity of such a dualism, which is only a masked form of atheism: Two gods are not gods, for they mutually annul each other. Inherent in the idea of God is absoluteness and, thus, uniqueness. If alongside the first god there must necessarily be a second, this means that the first is not a god. The idea of two gods (not resembling in any way the doctrine of the divine tri-unity, or the Holy Trinity) is an expression of a poverty of thought, of thought that has come to a dead end and seeks a way out of this dead end in the absurd. For this reason there is not a single significant philosophical system that is dualistic. Even polytheism, insofar as it is a heno-polytheism (Olympus), appears to be a higher worldview than dualism with its dead-end character. In polytheism we have the idea of the *multiplicity* of the divine world, which in its fullness becomes a kind of multi-unity, a divine pleroma. The fundamental lie of polytheism consists in the illegitimate hypostatization of the rays of this pleroma as gods; however, when polytheism is understood as creaturely hierarchies or as an intelligent heaven it receives a relatively legitimate interpretation. On the other hand, dualistic atheism is a kind of subjugation to satanism, where the prince of this world, the black god, pretends to occupy a place alongside God.

But this second principle can also be understood as a "place" for the world, Plato's *ekmageion* or *chōra*, where the world can find existence for itself alongside God's absoluteness. The world does not want to become nothing in the face of this absoluteness, but instead seeks its own *something*. It finds this *something* in a kind of anti-god or minus-god. But a minus is only a minus and remains a minus. If a minus wants to transform its own no-thing into a something, it borrows this something from the fullness of divine being, submerges itself in this being, and in a certain sense merges with the latter. Or conversely, it wants to draw the divine being into itself, into its own being. It wants to oppose itself to the fullness of divine being. But divine being is indivisible and cannot be a part of itself. Therefore, it is not possible to take from this being a part of it.

In other words, ditheism is unrealizable. Every system of dualism falls apart from internal contradiction, is ontological nonsense, which one does not have to take into account in the general problematic of the world. It is impossible to accept that God exists and that, alongside Him and besides Him, there exists a pseudo-divine principle, a "second god," expressly directed at the world. We can simply neglect this philosopheme (or theologeme).

But let us affirm the legitimacy and even the inevitability of the striving, expressed here, to find a special place for the world, to protect it in its own being from the fullness of divine being and thereby to save ourselves from pantheism, which sometimes ambushes us not only on the path of cosmotheism but also on the path of theism. It is necessary for the world to find its own place, so that it would be possible to juxtapose and, in a certain sense, even to oppose the world to God, to *distinguish* ontologically God and the world. However, the conclusion that we can draw from the impossibility and contradictoriness of dualism remains only negative: There is no place and can be no place of its own or independent ground for the world which would belong to it alone. If there is such a place, it must be established by God, for there is nothing that is outside of or apart from God and that in this sense is not-God.

This idea is expressed in the dogmatic formula that the world *is created by God* "out of nothing." Of course, one should not conceive this "nothing" as some *something* existing before the creation of the world as its necessary material or at least as the possibility of the origination of the world. To conceive "nothing" as some *something*, as some metaphysical nebulosity, as some sort of *me on*, or some sort of noncreaturely, or more precisely, precreaturely (but already tending to creatureliness) "freedom" is to open the door to dualism with all its annihilating contradictions. The nothing out of which the world is created is precisely a *not*-something, the pure *not* of ontological emptiness.

In other words, the formula that the world is created by God out of nothing has, first of all, a negative meaning: No extra-divine ground of creation exists. This formula expresses only the content of the idea that the world *is created* by God (the "analytic" judgment in Kant's sense). According to Pseudo-Dionysius, God also created nothing,[1] giving it being in creation. In this sense we must distinguish two nothings without confusing them: (1) the precreaturely or noncreaturely nothing, or the pure ontological zero, emptiness, which is conceived by us only through logical repulsion, the negation of all being in a certain "illegitimate judgment" (as Plato calls it); and (2) the ontic, creaturely nothing, *me on*, which permeates creation, so to speak. This *me on* is just a *mode* of this creaturely being, but in this sense it *is*.

3. The Sophianicity of the World

Do we not return, through a consistent overcoming of dualism, to a certain *divine* monism, which is, as it were, the antipode of pantheistic, or theocosmic, monism? If the latter proclaims that all is the world and that there is nothing outside the world or higher than the world, the former antithetically proclaims that all is God and only God, that there is no place and can be no place for being outside of or alongside God, and that there is therefore no world and can be no world. In the history of thought this conclusion is the usual final result of religiously colored pantheism: All is atman, the divine breath, divinity. There seems to be no way out for thought from this antithesis. A way out can be found only by transferring the question to another plane, *metabasis eis allo genos*, from the static to the dynamic plane. The world relates to God not as equal to Him, not as a mode of being coordinated with Him, but (if one can say this) as a heterogeneous mode of being. The world is *created* by God; it is His creation. The world's existence is a special *modality* of being. This being is one; it is precisely divine being. And for the world there is no other ground, or "place," of being except this createdness by God, except this special mode of divine being. And the fact that the world is created out of nothing means only that the world exists in God and only by God, for the world does not have within itself the ground of its own being. In itself, the world is groundless; it is established on top of an abyss, and this abyss is "nothing."

The world is created. Instead of the problematic of a special place for the world, a place that is the world's own, the problematic of a second god or altero-god, who does not exist, we have the fullness of the problematic of *creation*, which determines both the being of the world and its relationship with God, the directedness of the world toward God, for createdness is precisely this relationship. It is necessary to understand the nature or

---

1. Cf. my book *The Unfading Light*, the chapter on the creaturely nothing.

character of this relationship. We enter here into the domain of Christian revelation, for the createdness of the world can only be an object of faith and a content of revelation. This truth about the world lies beyond the world. As relating to God, this truth cannot be established by the power of human thought, which, as such, remains immanent to the world. In this sense, this truth is a limit to thought. Nevertheless, this truth can be grasped at the boundaries where it touches the world.

Thus, one must first of all try to understand the idea of *createdness* in its essential features, in both its positive and its negative aspects. Therefore, a general preliminary question arises: Is the world created by God, or does it have its own being and thus does not need to be created?

a. Platonism

This idea of the createdness of the world serves as the foundation of the doctrine of the world in revelation and is already expressed in the first, foundational chapters of the first book of the Bible, Genesis. This idea is also an element of certain pagan doctrines, although with inevitable dualistic additions and distortions. But this idea was alien and even repellent to ancient philosophy. First of all, it plays no role in Plato's theory of ideas as it is expounded in such fundamental dialogues as *Phaedrus,* the *Symposium,* and the *Phaedo.* Ideas represent the world of the genuinely existent, hovering above and duplicating the empirical world, as it were. This is the sophianic photosphere above the world, the eternal, Divine Sophia, Divinity without God. Contraposed to the Divine Sophia is the creaturely Sophia, the same ideas but submerged in nothing, in becoming, and thus finding themselves in a defective state. (In fact, this state is so defective that there arises the difficult question whether all the images of being can have corresponding ideas.) Thus, the world of becoming looks into the heaven of ideas and (though with refractions) reflects this heaven in itself. But how can one cross this abyss that separates the heaven of ideas from the empirical vale? How can one overcome this ontological *hiatus?* Platonism[2] has no answer to this question, and it is precisely this separa-

---

2. Even if one were to understand ideas as living beings (Florensky) and to transform thereby the world of ideas into an Olympus of hierarchies or essences, such a polytheism could not tell us how these gods find their way into the world and how the multiplicity of ideas is unified. In any case, the hierarchical Olympus too needs its Zeus, but Plato does not have one.

tion of the ideal, intelligible ground of the world from the world itself, this *hiatus,* that Aristotle has in mind in his critique of Platonism.

b. Aristotelianism

Ideas exist not in things but above and outside things. They exist as abstract shadows, to which Aristotle opposes the same ideas but ones that are essentially connected with being *in concreto,* as goal-causes, energies, entelechies.[3] Aristotle does not deny the truth of Platonism in the teaching of ideas, but he wishes to complete it or to completely unfold it. (Of course, new difficulties arise for him during this attempt at unfolding.) In Plato's *Timaeus,* we have something like an attempt to complete Platonism. This work speaks of the creation of the world by a demiurge, who creates while looking at ideas, made up of different combinations. In its philosophical incompleteness, the *Timaeus* is like a torso without a head and face, and the mythological images in which its most fundamental themes are expressed do not aid the understanding but rather hamper thought. The *Timaeus* appears to discuss creation, but who is the creator? Is he a god or is he a "demon," an intermediary being, only a demiurge? There is no direct answer to this question. In the *Timaeus,* we find a certain positive definition of the relationship between the Divine Sophia (ideas) and the creaturely Sophia, as if in answer to Aristotle's reproach that they are separated. But the fundamental question of their connection in the One Primordial Principle, or God, is not posed. As in Plato's other works, we have only Sophia, divinity without God, ideas without anyone who has them, inasmuch as the demiurge is not God. Platonism remains only an abstract sophiology, unconnected with theology. Owing to this limitation it dialectically does not hold together, despite the fact that it is unique and a work of genius. It inevitably slides either into subjective (transcendental) idealism (which is where recent critical philosophy places it) or into Aristotelian monism. The latter is a kind of portal leading into Christian theology, but only a portal, not a building. As a *sophiological* system, Aristotle's metaphysics, despite his polemic with Plato, can be understood as a variant of Platonism. Although Aristotelianism is not free of the claim of being a theology, we have in Aristotle's philosophy only a system of sophiological cosmology, though the latter is expounded in theological

---

3. Aristotle reproaches Plato for the fact that his ideas do not explain motion; they are principles, not causes.

9

expressions. God and the world merge to the point of indistinguishability in this philosophy, are substantially identified. The transcendent is not distinguished from the immanent, insofar as the latter transcends into the former and is its lower state. In this sense, that is, in the light of Christian doctrine, Aristotle's entire system is theologically ambiguous and even contradictory.

According to Aristotle the world is motion, which, with its series of local movers or causes, has neither beginning nor end. *The world is eternal* (*Phys.* VIII, 252 a 5-24). The motion could not have had a beginning, since a beginning assumes a preceding motion for itself. This leads to the postulation of a prime mover that, being the source of all motion, is itself unmoved, unmoved eternity, *aiōn* (*Met.* X, 1072 b 29-30). The unmoved mover is God, *actus purus,* the simple substance, a kind of eternal proto-essence, *zōon aidion ariston* (Met. X, 1072 b 29). Thought is this substance's primary and sole activity — the thought of thought, *autos ara noei eiper esti ti kratiston kai estin hē noēsis noēseos noēsis* (X, 1074 b 34-5), with the identity of thought and the object *(to auton nous kai noeton).* The prime mover moves by the power of love, as its object, *kinei hōs erōmenon,* and motion is an act of eternal love. That which is moved directly moves everything else by the prime mover *(kinoumena de alla kinei).* The prime mover is good, the object of desire and understanding, the "first desired"; it is identical with the first understood. "The unmoved mover moves, while remaining without motion and immobile. All the energy must be in that which is moved, and only the act must be in the mover. The prime mover touches, itself remaining unmoved. Between God and the world there is not contact but connection. God moves the world as a desired but inaccessible goal, a being which is all perfection and the goal to which all beings tend" (*Eth. Nic.* X. 1178 b 12). Without examining Aristotle's system in its strong and weak points, let us only characterize his fundamental idea of the eternity of the world in God. For Aristotle, eternity is equivalent to the necessity of the absolute and unconditional existence of the world.[4]

Aristotle's entire system is marked by the limitations of antiquity. First of all, it does not contain the creation and createdness of the world and therefore the doctrine of God the Creator (together with the corresponding problematic). Second, Aristotle's system is essentially impersonalistic, since the absence of the idea of the person generally characterizes Hellenism in its entirety: The Prime Mover, God, is not a Person. The Prime Mover is a kind of *it, to erōmenon, to agathon.* It is true that life, *to*

---

4. *De coelo* I, 12, 282 a 25.

zōon, is attributed to it, but this definition does not lead thought to personalism.

All this defines Aristotle's system as a monistic cosmism, a hierarchical cosmotheism, with an unmoved mover at its basis. This unmoved mover, divinity, is the entelechy of the world, the world's highest being or foundation. The unmoved mover is identical with the world, though it differs from the world in the mode of its being. This system poses a danger to Christian theism precisely because of this its ambiguity, which, as we shall see, places its stamp on the doctrine of Thomas Aquinas and the subsequent Thomism, which philosophically are steeped in Aristotelianism. Aristotle makes the supreme principle of the world, the prime mover, so transcendent that it appears to be separated from the world, above it. But at the same time, this principle is only the world, although taken to its highest power. Aristotle's theology therefore has a cosmological character, and his cosmology passes into theology. Strictly speaking, his theocosmism has a real place neither for God nor for the world, because it does not really distinguish between them. The world continues into God, so to speak, and God descends to the world, is immanent in it, as its (impersonal) foundation. Aristotle's doctrine of the *eternity* of the world in space and time corresponds to this duality. This eternity can simultaneously and with equal justice be understood both as bad infinity, or indeterminate and in this sense unlimited spatiality and temporality, and as the supratemporality and supraspatiality of the Absolute.

In general, as a doctrine of God, Aristotle's system cannot be translated into the language of Christian theology and expressed in the terms of this theology. (This was attempted in the system of Thomism, though not to the great benefit of Christian theology.) To this one should add that, in Aristotelianism, the relation between the prime mover and the moved world is interpreted on the model of a causal relation: God is the *cause* of the world (Thomism defines the Creator's relation to creation in the same sense). But this definition attests only to the absence in Aristotle of the idea of the world's creation. This idea is replaced by the idea of God's all-permeating causality. This postulation of a causal connection existing between God and the world even further reinforces the Aristotelian theocosmism, the theory that God is immanent to the world. God is only one of the causes of the world and in the world, although He is the first cause. This cause has an indissoluble connection with the world. But this proposition can also be reversed: the world is inseparable from God, as God's manifestation.

This fateful ambiguity of Aristotelianism can be understood and

11

thus overcome only in the light of sophiology, which alone is capable of giving it a Christian coefficient and thus including it in Christian theology. Aristotle's cosmology is nothing but a sophiology, but a sophiology that is deprived of its trinitarian-theological foundation. This sophiology is a doctrine of divinity without God and apart from God, of divinity in place of God, in the capacity of God. We have said the same thing about Platonism as a theory of self-existent ideas, of Divine Sophia in herself.[5] The entire difficulty and, in a certain sense, the impotence and indefensibility in this form of Plato's theory of ideas consist in the separateness of the Divine Sophia from the creaturely Sophia as well as in the ungroundedness of the world of ideas. This world is not unified; it is not even subsumable in a higher unifying principle. The world therefore turns out to be only a speculative projection of pagan polytheism. (It remains so in Father Pavel Florensky's interpretation of ideas as spiritual entities.) This feature, the separateness of ideas from concreteness, that is, from the world, makes them a doubling of the world in abstraction, a transparent overlayering of reality with mirror reflections.

This point became the focus of Aristotle's critique of Platonism. To the fleshless abstractions of ideas he opposed their entelechic being, saturated with concreteness. What Aristotle did was transpose ideas from the domain of the Divine Sophia to the domain of the creaturely Sophia. He proclaimed the being of the latter *without* the former, as if in separation from it. He thus reduced ideas to the empirical, taken only in the category of universality (which would also require special explanation).

This replacement of the Divine Sophia by the creaturely Sophia, with both principles affirmed in their isolatedness and one-sidedness, can scarcely be considered a real achievement. Aristotle's critique of Plato's theory of ideas does not represent an overcoming of the one-sidedness of this theory, because this critique exhibits another kind of one-sidedness. In the theory of ideas, Platonism and Aristotelianism represent a *dialectically* connected thesis and antithesis, which mutually condition each other but are hardly capable of replacing each other, as Aristotle thought. Plato and Aristotle are both right, and both wrong, in their one-sidedness of thesis and antithesis. They each postulate a synthesis, which is not contained in their theories but which must be found beyond and above them. It is true that ideas concretely exist only in things, that is, in the world, but their existence cannot be exhausted by this mode of their actualization. Otherwise, they would be extinguished in the darkness of the empirical.

5. See *The Unfading Light,* the chapter on Plato's doctrine.

But their light shines in darkness and is not comprehended by it, because this light penetrates into the darkness from the heights. The creaturely Sophia is the manifestation and reflection of the heavenly Sophia. Nevertheless, sophiology, as the doctrine of the *supramundane* principle of the world, must incorporate these great sophianic insights of ancient thought. The dialectic of Platonism and Aristotelianism in the theory of ideas is synthesized in the Christian revelation of the divine-creaturely, or divine-human, character of being, of the sophianicity of creation.

But Sophia, as well as sophianicity, cannot be conceived outside of a relation to the One to whom this Sophia belongs as His self-revelation and revelation, that is, to the Personal, Trihypostatic God. Divinity belongs to God, who *has* divinity and in this sense *is* divinity. But, in itself, divinity *is not* yet the personal God. Divinity is different from Him, although it is contained in Him, inherent in Him. But this connection of God and Sophia, without separation but also without identification (just as hypostasis and ousia are indivisible but not identical), was not known outside of revelation, in paganism. Aristotle's philosophy turns out to be impotent and becomes tangled in sophiological contradictions in the further development of the doctrine of the creaturely Sophia. The chief defect, *prōton pseudos,* of Aristotle's religiophilosophical system lies in this identification of God with divinity, or Sophia (who is taken in her creaturely aspect). From this come the ambiguity of Aristotelianism and its swings. Its main difficulty as well as its inconsistency consists in the fact that it is equally incapable of really connecting or really distinguishing God and the world. On the one hand, self-evident for Aristotle is the divine, sophianic foundation of the world, which he raises in its being to the supramundane divinity. Not knowing the personal God and therefore not having the source of the true knowledge of Sophia, Aristotle identifies the world with God on the basis of the sophianicity of the world, the presence of the Divine Sophia in the creaturely Sophia. One then gets, as a speculative expression of the sophianicity of the world, pantheism or, more precisely, theocosmism, the identification of God and the world.

But Aristotle also naturally attempts to *distinguish* God and the world. However, he is utterly unable to achieve this differentiation since his philosophy lacks the idea of the *personal,* self-subsistent God, connected with the world as the Creator with his creation. It is precisely this connection that simultaneously unites and separates God and the world. Although the prevailing intuition of Aristotelianism in sophiology leads it to the preferential recognition of the creaturely Sophia, this judgment too must be significantly qualified. One can even say that what is characteristic for Aristotle is precisely the nondistinction or confusion, to the point of identification, of the Divine Sophia and the creaturely Sophia. Aristotle's idea of the unmoved mover can be likened to the line of the horizon where the earth and sky meet and appear to join.

In the final analysis, Aristotle identifies God and the world, since the principle of the world's motion issues directly from the prime mover, the supramundane God. For Aristotle, the creaturely Sophia is the ontological combination of the energetic hierarchies of being, ascending from potentiality to reality and bearing in themselves, as the internal, "entelechic" law of their development, the sophianic seeds of being *(to kath holon),* the ideal in the real. The substrate of reality is the dark *hule,* the principle of creaturely actualization in becoming, which more or less corresponds to Plato's *me on.* In the language of Christian revelation, this corresponds to the land "without form and void, *tohu vabohu*" (Gen. 1:2), that is, summoned into being "out of nothing" by God's command — as *me on* from *ouk on.* But this multiple and relative being, which is defined energetically as motion, presupposes a mover and what is moved. The prime mover, or the absolute prime being, remains unmoved. That is, it has primordial eternity (and not just a derivative eternity, which is what the world it moves has). This prime mover has supramundane, nonmaterial, spiritual being. It is self-thinking, absolute thought, the supreme good, love, divinity. This principle clearly corresponds to the Divine Sophia, to divinity as the foundation of the world. However, because of the absence of theology in Aristotle, the Divine Sophia is identified with the hypostatic God, but at the same time she merges with the world, as its supreme potency.

Thus, all that both Plato and Aristotle (each in his own way and in his own language) have to report about the divine or sophianic foundation of the world is true as an intuition of human philosophy. However, this foundation remains uncomprehended and unexplained in its special nature as Sophia or divinity in relation to God. Sophia is directly equated with God here, and sophiology is considered to exhaust both theology and cosmology. Plato and Aristotle are both sophiologists, but they are unable to complete their sophiologies in a theology. Indeed, they do not even have a theology. In this they are burdened by the limitedness of paganism. Olympus, the intelligent heaven, beautiful and perfect humanity, is nothing else but the pagan projection of Divine Sophia, Divine-humanity, which was given philosophically in Platonism (and later in Neoplatonism) and Aristotelianism. All this is the old testament in paganism, and it is precisely in its sophiology that antiquity comes closest to Christianity and can find a place for itself in Christian theology. But only the *plenitude* of truth allows us to see that implenitude which fatally leads to distortion. Sophiology can be justified not in itself but only *in connection with* theology, when the former occupies its proper place in the latter, but does not supplant it, which is exactly what we see in the speculation of antiquity.[6] From abstract sophiology as such one cannot perceive the most essential and decisive elements of the problem of God and the world in their interrelationship; nor can one perceive the connection of the Divine Sophia and the creaturely Sophia where they are different and also where they are identical; nor can one understand the Divine Sophia's relation to the personal God who reveals himself in the world. At the same time, both ancient philosophy and ancient religion attested so powerfully and authentically to the *sophianicity* of the world that this cannot be forgotten in the history of thought and has become an inalienable part of Christian theology. This contribution of ancient philosophy has been understood only partially and has not yet been illuminated in its full significance.

c. Patristics

In the early patristic literature, that is, in the apostolic and apologetic writings, we do not encounter a theological system except in St. Irenaeus. This literature is therefore devoid of the sophiological problematic, a problematic that became possible only when such theological systems appeared, beginning with Origen. In Origen, we already have the beginnings of sophiology, although they are obscured by his identification of Sophia (Prov. 8:22-32) with Logos, who for Origen is also a demiurge in a certain sense. This is the source of Origen's subordinationism.[7] This is the price he pays for the fundamental sin of his theology, namely, the failure to differentiate Sophia in God. (This failure had a fateful influence on further patristic logology, which took the path marked out by Origen's confusion.) This failure automatically produces, so to speak, the failure to distinguish the Divine Sophia from the creaturely Sophia; and this leads to the subordinationist distortion of the dogma of the Holy Trinity. The

---

6. Stoicism, as the most pantheistic system of antiquity, commits the greatest sin in this respect. On the one hand it approaches materialism or gnosticism, while on the other hand it approaches the direct identification of divine and cosmic being. Stoicism does not even observe that distinction between the Divine and the creaturely Sophia which we find in Plato and Aristotle.

7. See my book *The Comforter*, chap. 1.

need to link God with the world, and also to differentiate Him from the world, is satisfied here by the fact that Logos is considered as a second, lower God, who can serve as the intermediary between God and the world. The absence of sophiology is compensated by and also punished by the confusion of sophiology with logology. Logos as the second hypostasis is not identical with Sophia, the nonhypostatic divinity in God; Sophia here is the self-revelation of the entire Holy Trinity. This one-sidedly logological conception of Sophia contains the *prōton pseudos,* the primordial defect, of all patristic sophiology, which was thus forced to fit the entire sophiological problematic into logology and even christology. A good example of this confusion is the sophiological christology of St. Athanasius, who in the exegesis of Proverbs 8 is forced to distinguish, in terms of the Divine and the creaturely Sophia, two aspects of Christ: before or outside the Incarnation and after the Incarnation.[8] In the open and consistent subordinationist Tertullian (just as in Arianism), the Logos, or the Son, gets a purely instrumental interpretation as the means to the creation of the world. Here, the *de facto* significance of Sophia is attributed to the Logos. In the case of such an identification, the question of the difference between the Divine and the creaturely Sophia becomes hopelessly confused.

But logological sophiology does not exhaust the entire content of the patristic doctrine of Sophia. Next to this main current, a second stream arises, which can be called *applied* sophiology. That is, among a number of fathers (St. Gregory the Divine, St. John of Damascus, St. Maximus the Confessor, Pseudo-Dionysius, and St. Augustine), we encounter the doctrine of the prototypes, paradigms, or ideas of creaturely being in God. Clearly discernible here is a certain, direct or indirect, influence of Platonism and Aristotelianism, as if a kind of reminiscence of them. The doctrine of the ideal proto-ground of the world, or of the entelechies of the world, seeps into patristics and occupies a place *next to* christology (even a place next to christological sophiology).

In connection with this there arises a fundamental question, which, however, is not understood as such in patristics itself, and therefore does not find an answer for itself there: the question of how one should properly understand the relation of these prototypes of the world to Logos, and then to the Divine Sophia and the creaturely Sophia. In particular, do these ideas have a divine and eternal character? Do they refer to divine being? Or are they created ad hoc, so to speak, as the ideal foundation of the

---

8. See the patristic excursus in my book *The Burning Bush.*

world, as "heaven" in relation to "earth"? In other words, is it a question here of the Divine Sophia or of the creaturely Sophia? All these questions and uncertainties *do not have a precise and clear answer* in the appropriate patristic texts, just as, in general, patristic thought *does not distinguish* these elements of the problem. For a full understanding of patristic sophiology, it is, of course, essential to consider both of these currents: logological sophiology, on the one hand, and the theory of ideas in their mutual *interrelation and harmonization,* on the other. But there are insufficient grounds for a definitive interpretation of these doctrines in one sense or the other. Patristic sophiology remains essentially unfinished in this question, and therefore different interpretations of it are possible.

In the first place, these divine ideas of the world can be equated with the Divine Sophia, since the Divine Sophia includes the ideal *all,* the ontic seeds of Logos. By a creative act these seeds are implanted in "nothing" and form the foundation of the being of the creaturely world, that is, the creaturely Sophia, who also shines with the light of eternity in the heavens, in the Divine Sophia. In the Divine Sophia, these seeds belong to the self-revelation of divinity in the Holy Trinity or to the divine world, whereas in the creaturely world they are its divine goal-causes, or entelechies. As ideas of the intelligent cosmos, they belong to Logos. As being, life, beauty, they are a revelation of the Holy Spirit. In the Divine Sophia, these seeds of being are the bi-unitary self-revelation of the Father in the Son and the Holy Spirit. The main trait of these prototypes of creaturely being is that they are *not* created, but have a divine, eternal being proper to them. This is the uncreated heaven, the glory of God. But these prototypes, or ideas, can also be considered as *created* by God as the prototypes of the world *before* creation, as it were. They ontologically precede creation but are connected with it. This is that heaven about which it is said: "In the beginning God created the heaven and the earth" (Gen. 1:1). Here, heaven can mean not only the angelic world as a specific *part* of creation but also the intelligent world of creaturely proto-essences. If one calls this too Sophia (of course, with violence done to terminology), one would then have to say that Sophia is created, and that in general only the creaturely Sophia exists, although she is not an independent part of this created world but only its plan. This is indeed the understanding of some theologians, though for us this idea of a solely creaturely, *ad hoc* created Sophia contains a number of irreconcilable contradictions and dogmatic absurdities. In particular, it introduces changeability into the very essence of God. God in creation is different from God before creation: He creates something new even for himself, namely, the creaturely Sophia.

17

The two alternatives are mutually exclusive, even though both thrust themselves upon us or, at any rate, can be admitted in the interpretation of patristic sophiology, which thus can be likened to a torso without a head. That is, patristic sophiology is unfinished and imperfectly clarified; it is a kind of sophiological ambiguity.

This unfinished character of the sophiology leads to a lack of fundamental clarity in the patristic cosmology. One cannot say that the sophiological theme is completely absent in patristics. We know that it can be found in a number of doctrines. But this theme does not achieve completeness, remains in an "ante-Nicene" indeterminacy, so to speak. There is no doubt that this is partly a result of that confusion of this theme with christology which was an indirect consequence of the Arian disputes and bears the traces of Arianism's confusion of these two problems. As a result, the dogma of the creation of the world also remains incomplete. This dogma is disclosed from the side of the trihypostatic revelation in it of the three persons of the Holy Trinity. But this separateness of the persons is not synthesized in unisubstantiality and unisophianicity with reference to the one act of creation and the unity of the world in Sophia.

In Eastern theology, the development of theology after St. John of Damascus is broken off in connection with a general stagnation of thought. Thought is squandered on a fruitless, scholastically schismatic polemic with Rome concerning the procession of the Holy Spirit. The sophiological-cosmological problematic lies dormant for six centuries.[9] Byzantine theology once again approaches this question in St. Gregory Palamas's doctrine of energies, which is essentially an unfinished sophiology. The fundamental idea of Palamism is that, alongside God's transcendent "essence," there exists His manifold revelation in the world, His radiation in "energies," as it were. But Palamas's doctrine of essence and energies is not brought into connection with the dogma of the Trinity, in particular with the doctrine of the three hypostases as separate persons and of the Holy Trinity in unity. The fundamental idea of Palamism concerning the multiplicity and equi-divinity of the energies in God discloses *polypoikilos sophia tou theou,* "the manifold wisdom of God" (Eph. 3:10). Palamas considers the energies primarily in

---

9. One could give a sophiological interpretation to the works of St. Symeon the New Theologian — in his theology and especially his hymns. Consciously, the sophiological problem was foreign to him, but his inspiration and profound understanding of man's deification make his doctrine a sophiological one.

18

the aspect of *grace,* the supracreaturely "light of Tabor" in the creaturely world. But these energies have, first of all, a world-creating and world-sustaining power which is a property of Sophia, the Wisdom of God, in both of her forms: the Divine Sophia, the eternal proto-ground of the world, and the creaturely Sophia, the divine force of the life of creation. The sophiological interpretation and application of Palamism are yet to come in the future. By accepting Palamism, the Church has definitely entered onto the path of recognizing the sophiological dogma. But the theological realization of this recognition still requires a long path of intellectual labor. Essential here is the connection with onomadoxy,[10] which has recognized the divine reality and power of the divine-human name of Jesus and, in general, the power of the name of God in the world. It is not by chance that onomadoxy is linked with Palamism. However, these particular applications of sophiology do not yet go to the root of the sophiological problem.

d. Western Theology (Thomas Aquinas)

Various themes are united and intertwined in Aquinas's theology: Aristotelianism and Platonism, Augustinian and scholastic dogmatics. Therefore, a precise characterization of this complex doctrine is scarcely possible. Depending upon which of these elements is emphasized, the system of Thomism is seen in one primary color or another. The theology of Thomas Aquinas is not so much a synthesis as a meeting of different, not always unifiable, influences.

In the first place, the influence of Aristotle, the *"philosophus,"* is obvious in the most fundamental, initial definitions, those which concern the relation between God and the world. As his point of departure Thomas Aquinas takes not the Christian dogma of the personal, trihypostatic God, but Aristotle's impersonal divinity. The trihypostatic dogma is added later, and this is done without influencing the fundamental cosmological conception, which is rather based on the purely Aristotelian relation of God and the world. To be sure, this relation is *complicated* by the doctrine of the Creator and creation, but it is not determined by this doctrine.

We see already in the initial definition (*Summa Theologica,* [*S. Th.*] I, qu.

---

10. Literally "glorification of the name" (Russian *imiaslavie),* onomadoxy is the theory that the name of God has divine reality. — Trans.

2, a. 3) that God is understood by Aristotle as *the prime mover, primus motor:* "*necesse est devenire ad aliquod primum movens, quod a nullo movetur* [it is necessary to have recourse to some prime mover, who is moved by nothing]." To this is added the concept of *causa efficiens* [efficient cause]: "*necesse est ponere aliquid quod sit per se necessarium, non habens causam necessitatis aliunde, sed quod est causa necessitatis aliis* [it is necessary to posit something that is necessary in itself, not having a cause of necessity outside itself, but that is the cause of necessity for other things]." This cause is "*causa esse, et bonitatis et cujuslibet perfectionis* [the cause of being and of goodness and of every sort of perfection]." And this is "*aliquid intelligens, a quo omnes res naturales ordinantur ad finem: et hoc dicimus Deus* [some intelligent being by whom all natural things are directed to their end; and this being we call God]." Thus, in this deduction of the existence of God or "its proofs" from the existence of the world, the existences of God and the world are essentially and indivisibly coordinated and merged. These existences differ in *degree* of perfection but not in essence. This is very reminiscent of the fundamental Aristotelian scheme concerning the prime mover, who is *actus purus,* free of all potentiality, and who, by virtue of his absolute actuality, sets the world in motion while remaining unmoved himself.

Connected with the influence of Aristotelianism on Aquinas's doctrine is a question typical for the latter, namely, the question of the world's *eternity.* Aquinas returns to this question several times, at different periods of his life. His final conviction (in *S.Th.* I, qu. 46, a. 1) is that, speculatively, this question remains open, and only faith, on the basis of revelation, decides that the world is not eternal: "*mundum non semper fuisse sola fide tenetur et demonstrative probari non potest . . . mundum incoepisse est credibile, — non autem demonstrabile, vel scibile* [by faith alone do we hold, and by no demonstration can it be proved, that the world did not always exist. . . . That the world began to exist is an object of faith, but not of demonstration or science]" (a. 2). In this fideism, with reference to a question which for Aquinas was an object of philosophical inquiry, one cannot fail to see indirect evidence of the influence of Aristotle's teaching, which Aquinas was prevented from recognizing by his acceptance of the Christian dogma of the creation of the world in time. But, theoretically, Aquinas admits the possibility that the world does not have a beginning. Although he submits in this question to the dogmatic prescription of the Church, he in fact refuses to actualize this prescription in his thought or to speculatively justify it. On the contrary, theoretically, he fully admits the possibility of the eternity of the world. Here in Aquinas we have a compromise between Moses and Aristotle, a compromise that is unconvincing for Aquinas himself as a theologian and philosopher, and that exposes in this question his hidden or unconquered Aristotelianism.

The influence of Aristotelianism is even more pronounced in the further definition of the relation between God and the world as the relation between the prime mover and that which is moved, between cause and effect. Here, it is typical that this relation is defined without reference to the relation between the Creator and creation. It is defined statically, so to speak, not dynamically. Here we come to a highly interesting question, the question of what can be called sophiology in Aquinas. We note that Aquinas reproduces the ancient, pre-Christian, Platonic-Aristotelian sophiology, with all its limitations and contradictions (see above). In some of its features, this construction is similar to Spinoza's pantheism: *Deus sive natura* [God or nature] or *natura naturans* [nature being fully nature]. Reminiscent of such similarity is the following general definition of the relation between *Deus* (in the impersonal Aristotelian sense) and the world *(omnes res)*: *"Deus est in omnibus rebus, non quidem sicut pars essentiae, vel sicut accidens, sed sicut agens adest ei in quod agit. Cum autem Deus sit ipsum esse per suam essentiam, oportet quod esse creatum sit proprius effectus eius, sicut ignire est proprius effectus ipsius ignius. Unde oportet quod Deus sit in omnibus rebus et intime* [God is in all things; not, indeed, as part of their essence, nor as an accident, but as an agent is present for that upon which it works. Now since God is very being by his own essence, created being must be his proper effect, as to ignite is the proper effect of fire. Hence, it must be that God is in all things, and innermostly]" (*S.Th.* I, qu. 8, a. 1). "[*Deus*] *est in omnibus, per potentiam in quantum omnia eius potestatis subduntur: et per praesentiam in omnibus in quantum omnia nuda sunt et aperta oculis eius: est in omnibus per essentiam, in quantum adest omnibus ut causa essendi* [God is in all things by his power, inasmuch as all things are subject to his power; he is by his presence in all things, as all things are bare and open to his eyes; he is in all things by his essence, inasmuch as he is present for all things as the cause of their being]" (a. 3). God in the world, or the world in God, is a gradation of images of being in the descending or ascending perfection of different steps of being, depending on the degree of nonbeing or imperfection that is added in. God sees himself in himself, but he sees what is other than himself not in this other but in himself *(alia autem a se videt non in ipsis, sed in se ipso)*, inasmuch as his essence contains a resemblance of the other to himself *(similitudinem aliorum ab ipso)* (*S.Th.* I, qu. 14, a. 5). The multiplicity of creaturely being results from its imperfection, *defectus*.

This purely pantheistic, Aristotelian definition of the relation between God and the world is further supplemented and complicated by the Christian doctrine of the *creation* of the world by God *ex nihilo* (qu. 45 sq.). But the two series of ideas do not form an organic unity. The doctrine of the Holy Trinity is already introduced in the idea of creation. It is characteristic, however, that creation too is defined by the pantheistic term *emanatio* [emanation]: "all being emanates from the universal cause . . ." (qu. 45, a. 1), just as *"voluntas Dei est causa rerum* [the will of God is the cause of things]" (qu. 19, a. 4). Things preexist *(prae-existunt)* in God, not only insofar as there is commonality between them but also insofar as they differ, in both the divine mind *(intellectus)* and the divine will *(velle)*. It follows that, just as *"scientia Dei est causa rerum* [the knowledge of God is the cause of things]" (qu. 14, a. 8), so *"voluntas Dei est causa rerum"* (qu. 19, a. 4). *"Deus per intellectum suum causat res, cum suum esse sit suum intelligere; unde necesse est quod sua scientia sit causa rerum, secundum quod habet voluntatem conjunctam* [God causes things by his intellect, since his being is his act of understanding; and hence his knowledge must be the cause of things, insofar as his will is joined to it" (qu. 14, a. 8).

One should note that Aquinas uses both *intellectus* and *voluntas* without any reference to the personal God. Strictly speaking, he uses these terms not with reference to *Deus* but with reference to *Deitas*. In his doctrine of the world in relation to God, Aquinas introduces yet another notion that remains sophiologically unclarified, the notion of *alia a Deo* [that which is other than God]. He introduces it twice: in the doctrine of the divine reason and in the doctrine of the will. In this doctrine, he establishes a twofold principle, namely that *"scientia Dei est causa rerum"* (qu. 14, a. 8) and that *"voluntas Dei est causa rerum"* (qu. 19, a. 1). As regards divine knowledge, he establishes that *"necesse est Deum cognoscere alia a se* [it is necessary that God know things other than himself]" (qu. 14, a. 5). God's knowledge in relation to created things is like an artist's knowledge in relation to his works. But, in God's knowledge, it is not the case that these things exist from all eternity *(ab aeterno)* and, although God's knowledge is eternal, it does not follow that the creations are eternal (qu. 14, a. 8). Aquinas also distinguishes between two modes of divine knowing: in relation to that which exists in the present, past, and future *(scientia visionis* [knowledge of vision]) and in relation to that which is only possible but which never was and will never be *(scientia simplicis intelligentiae* [knowledge of simple intelligence]). This is a highly obscure and arbitrary distinction, which admits in God an abstract, unreal thinking of bare possibilities, contrary to the fact that God's thoughts are also his deeds. This is pure anthropomorphism.

22

From the distinction in God of *velle se* and *alia a se* [to will himself and things other than himself] it follows that, in the former, God *vult se ut finem* [wills himself *as* an end], whereas in the latter he wills *alia vero ad finem* [the others *to* an end] (qu. 19, a. 2). Here, God wants himself, his grace, with necessity, whereas, on the contrary, *alia* is not *necessarium absolute* but *necessarium ex supposito* [the other is not absolutely necessary but necessary by supposition] (a. 3), as a means to a necessary goal. "God's will is the cause of things, and God acts by will, not by necessity" (a. 4). "Since God's being is the understanding of himself, his action preexists in him, *effectus secundum modum intelligibilem* and *per modum voluntatis* [effects after the mode of intellect and after the mode of will]. For his inclination [*inclinatio*] to action consists in the fact that what is perceived by the mind refers to will, and will is therefore the cause of things" (a. 4), whereas God's will itself "does not by any means have causes" (a. 5).

This doctrine, according to which God's knowledge necessarily causes the existence of things while his will freely causes this existence, with both the one and the other being the cause of things, is not one of the clearest and most consistent parts of Aquinas's doctrine. This is essentially a scheme of sophiology that is utterly obscured by the fact that, instead of being related to the trinitarian doctrine of the Personal God, it is developed impersonalistically, as a doctrine of will and mind in divinity. The most unclear point refers to the idea of *alia a Deo in Deo*. Such a principle, which, on the one hand, is "other" than God and, on the other hand, belongs to him, can only be the Divine Sophia, as the self-revelation of God in himself, which has being in itself (though not for itself), as a nonhypostatic Divinity. The distinction between *Deus* and *alia a Deo* therefore refers to hypostasis and hypostatizedness, to God and Divinity.

A further distinction is made between the self-revelation of divinity in God and that in the creaturely world, between the Divine and the creaturely Sophia. But Aquinas starts to clarify this distinction from the middle, so to speak, and, what is most crucial here, his entire analysis is damaged by Aristotelian impersonalism in the doctrine of divinity. However, Aristotle does not conceive for an impersonal God a will, which in general is inseparable from *personal* being. For Aristotle, God is only a "thinking" of himself, for which there cannot be any *alia a se* or any *velle*. This entire conception of Aquinas's, inspired by Christianity, is a torso without a head. The doctrine of the trihypostatic God appears here only *after* this doctrine of the divine knowledge and will and of their relation to created things. The early chapters of the *Summa* are written "from Aristotle," with an admixture of Christian dogmatics, while the second part is

23

devoted to this dogmatics but receives its foundation from Aristotelianism. Aquinas's sophiology is completely insufficient on this point; we find lack of clarity and ambiguity here precisely with reference to whether his doctrine of the world should be understood only sophiologically, if only in the sense of the ancient Platonic-Aristotelian sophiology (cf. qu. 44, a. 1), or whether it should be understood theologically, in the sense of *Christian* dogmatics. This ambiguity is not overcome but is only externally set aside by the doctrine of the creation of the world.

Aquinas's sophiological thematic receives its fullest expression in his *doctrine of ideas.* He first expounds this doctrine in the context of the general doctrine of God, after the doctrine of *scientia Dei,* as its development (qu. 15). The doctrine of ideas is therefore *not* brought into a connection with the doctrine of the Holy Trinity, does not belong to the trinitarian doctrine, but refers, so to speak, to the pre-trinitarian or extra-trinitarian (more Aristotelian than Christian) doctrine of God as mind, *noesis.* The question of ideas is examined in three aspects: (1) Do ideas exist? (2) Are they multiple? (3) Do they refer to all that is known by God? The question is openly posed in the spirit of Platonism, which is thereby brought into the very heart of Christian philosophy. Having established the necessity of accepting ideas (*idea greca, latina forma dicitur* [what is called the idea in Greek is called the form in Latin]), Aquinas defines them in the spirit of Plato as "*formae aliarum rerum praeter ipsos res existentes* [the forms of other things, existing in addition to the things themselves]" (qu. 15, a. 1). Thus, ideas are defined in relation to their supramundane *(praeter)* being and in relation to things or the world *(mundus).*

"*Quia mundus non est casu factus, sed est factus a Deo per intellectum agente* (cf. qu. 46 a. 1; see below), *necesse est quod in mente divina sit forma ad similitudinem cuius mundus est factus. Et in hoc consistit ratio ideae* [As then the world was not made by chance, but by God acting by his intellect, as will appear later (qu. 46, a. 1), there must exist in the divine mind a form to the likeness of which the world was made. And in this the notion of an idea consists]." In this sense, God is *prima causa exemplaris omnium rerum* [the first exemplary cause of things]. "For the production of any thing a specimen *[exemplar]* is necessary, so that the action would accord with a definite form. An artist produces a definite form in matter according to a specimen at which he looks; this specimen either is outside or is perceived by thought inside. . . . This definition of forms goes back, as to the first principle, to divine wisdom, which conceived *[excogitavit]* the harmony of all" (qu. 46, a. 1).

It is then asked whether ideas in God are multiple. If we accept this multiplicity, does it not follow that multiple things, which arise in time, determine the eternity of God? Referring to St. Augustine, Aquinas responds that *"necesse est ponere plures ideas* [it is necessary to posit several ideas]" (qu. 16, a. 2). The ideas of what has been made exist in the thought of the maker as that which is understood and not as forms of that *by which* it is understood. *"Plures ideae sunt in mente divina ut intellectae ab ipsa* [many ideas exist in the divine mind, as things understood by it]" (ibid.). God can know his essence not only as it is in itself but also to the extent that it is perceived according to a certain image of resemblance in creatures. "Every creature has its own image, according to which it receives a likeness of the divine essence. . . . An idea expresses the divine essence not to the extent it is an essence but to the extent it is the likeness or reason *[ratio]* of one thing or another. Thus, since there exist multiple images received from a single essence, accordingly one speaks of multiple ideas." Thus, Aquinas distinguishes a single proto-source in God from the multiplicity of ideas in creation, Divine Sophia from creaturely Sophia, so to speak. *"Deus autem non solum intelligit multas res per essentiam suam, sed etiam intelligit se intelligere multa per essentiam suam. Sed hoc est intelligere plures rationes rerum, vel plures ideas esse in intellectu eius, ut intellectas . . . huiusmodi respectus, quibus multiplicantur ideae, non causantur a rebus sed ab intellectu divine comparante essentiam suam ad res* [Now not only does God understand many things by his essence, but he also understands that he understands many things by his essence. And this means that he understands the several types of things; or that many ideas are in his intellect as understood by him. . . . Such relations, whereby ideas are multiplied, are caused not by the things themselves but by the divine intellect comparing its own essence with these things]" (a. 2). Further, Aquinas distinguishes ideas, first, as the *exemplar* according to which all arises from God in time, and, second, as all that is known by God, although it is not realized at any time, but in the whole as that which is known by God *"secundum propriam rationem* [according to their proper type]" and even *"per modum speculationis* [in a speculative manner]" (a. 3). What a strange, contradictory, and unreal notion of abstract "speculation" in God.

All of these additional clarifications, according to which not only the actual world but also its never-realized possibilities, as well as God's "speculations," are included in the idea of God, unnecessarily complicate and tangle the "exemplary" character of ideas. In general, one can say that, on the one hand, Aquinas's doctrine of ideas that have their foundation in God and act in the world must be understood sophiologically as a doctrine of the Divine Sophia and the creaturely Sophia in their identity and difference, but that at the same time this doctrine is also an unfinished and underclarified combination of Platonism and Aristotelianism with Christian dogmatics. This doctrine is not brought into any connection with the trinitarian dogma and bears the stamp of intellectualism in the doctrine of God, which is in general typical of Aquinas. The interpretation of ideas is also constrained by instrumentalism, owing to which the very being of ideas (or at least their distinction) in God is connected with the existence of the world of things, and not vice versa. Dubious is the inclusion in ideas of thoughts of God that never become a reality (contrary to Aquinas's own principle that *scientia rerum est causa rerum*).

A particular obstacle for the sophiological interpretation of the doctrine of ideas is that same general principle which is expounded in other works of Aquinas and is the guiding principle of his entire scholastics. That is, the world that is created by God is understood here not as unique in its design and perfect ("it was good"), after the creation of which God "rested . . . from all his work" (Gen. 2:2). Rather, it is understood as imperfect, as only one of many possible types of worlds, so to speak. This supposition not only shakes the principles of healthy cosmology and anthropology (including christology) but also introduces an element of irrational accident and arbitrariness in the relation of the Creator to creation. In any case, we get a quantitative noncorrespondence of ideas and things. The domain of ideas is larger than the domain of things; Divine Sophia does not coincide in content with creaturely Sophia. But then does not the existence of such never-actualized ideas (which, after all, according to Aquinas himself, are understood originally as the prototypes of things) lose its *raison d'être*? And, most importantly, the significance of ideas in general in the life of divinity itself remains completely indeterminate if there is no correspondence between *scientia rerum* and the general *scientia Dei*. In general, Aquinas's entire doctrine of ideas has a random and indeterminate character, and taken sophiologically, it is unfinished. Sophiology is not only a doctrine of ideas as the prototypes of things but primarily a doctrine of the self-revelation of the Holy Trinity, and only subsequently of the revelation of the Holy Trinity in creation. In Aquinas we have a Platonism that is supplemented by Aristotelianism, and this combination is mechanically, inorganically, brought into Christian theology.

The treatise on creation (qu. 44) is *"de processione creaturarum a Deo et de omnium entium prima causa* [on the procession of creatures from God, and on the first cause of all things]." This work establishes that all that exists in one way or another is from God (a. 1) and has being not from itself but from its participation in him *(participens esse)*. And "it is necessary to suppose that even the proto-matter is created from the universal cause of that which exists" (a. 2). Creation is the work *"proximae et universalissimae causae quae est Deus* [of the most proximate and most universal cause, which is God]" (qu. 45, a. 5), and *"creare est proprie causare sive producere esse rerum* [to create is, properly speaking, to cause or produce the being of things]" (qu. 45, a. 6). It is *"emanatio totius entis a causa universali, quae est Deus* [the emanation of all being from the universal cause, which is God]" (a. 1), and this "emanation" we call "creation." Thus, the creative act is, on the one hand, defined in the spirit of emanative pantheism, while, on the other hand, it is wholly subsumed under the category of causality: God is the universal proto-cause. How can this idea be applied in relation to the trihypostatic God? Since creation belongs to God according to his being *(secundum suum esse)*, it follows that *"creare non est proprium alicui personae, sed commune toti Trinitati* [to create is not proper to any one Person, but is common to the whole Trinity]," that is, apart from hypostatic distinction. According to the general impersonalism of Aquinas's theology, which deduces the being of the hypostases solely from the distinctions and relations in divinity, the participation of individual persons in this causality takes place only *"secundum rationem suae processionis* [according to the nature of their procession]." "God is the cause of things through his mind and will; he is like an artist in relation to the things he produces. An artist creates through the word born in his mind and through the love of his will *(per amorem suae voluntatis)*, which relates to something. Thus, God the Father established creation by his Word, which is the Son, and by his love, which is the Spirit. Therefore, *processiones personarum sunt rationes productionis creaturarum in quantum includant essentialia attributa quae sunt scientia et voluntas* [the processions of the Persons are the types of the production of creatures inasmuch as they include the essential attributes, knowledge and will]" (a. 6).

"In different creations in which there are mind and will, representation *[repraesentatio]* of the Trinity in an image *[per modum imaginis]* is found insofar as in them the conceived word and the emanating love are found" (a. 7). Thus, the creator of the world is, strictly speaking, the impersonal Aristotelian divinity. This divinity has mind and will and therefore establishes a foundation in itself for hypostatic distinctions. Causal emanativity in the understanding of the act of creation finds its disclosure here.

God is the *causa exemplaris* of all things (qu. 44, a. 3). This notion of "exemplary cause"[11] is subsequently clarified in the sense that for the pro-

---

11. Cf. in general Théodore Régnon, *La métaphysique des causes d'après Saint Thomas et Albert le Grand*, Paris, 1906.

duction of any thing an *exemplar* is needed, as a determinate form contemplated by a master and realized in matter. "The definition of these forms has, as its first principle, divine wisdom, which conceived *[excogitavit]* the order of the universe, which consists in the multiplicity of things. One must therefore say that the divine wisdom contains the images *[rationes]* of all the things about which we spoke above in qu. 15, 1, i.e., ideas, the exemplary forms of existence in divine thought. Although they become multiple in relation to things, these exemplary forms do not really differ from the divine essence *[non sunt alia a divina essentia]* as it is perceived differently in different cases. Thus, God himself is *primum exemplar omnium* [the first exemplar of all things]" (a. 3). That is all that we find in Aquinas concerning the connection of the doctrine of ideas with his doctrine of creation. As we can see from the foregoing, Aquinas identifies ideas, the divine essence, and God without any intermediate links, so that the *raison d'être* for a special doctrine of ideas even becomes incomprehensible. The fundamental ambiguity of Aristotelianism, which is not overcome in Aquinas's theology but is only complicated by a mechanical connection with Christian dogmatics, is once again clearly exhibited here. To understand creation not only in its foundation in God but also in its creaturely originality, to link creation's being with divine being while distinguishing between these two beings, this task does not enter into Aquinas's Aristotelianism.[12]

Other scholastic theologians (Bonaventura, Duns Scotus) serve up other versions of the doctrine of ideas. This doctrine is also being developed as the normative one in contemporary Catholic theology.[13]

Thus, we have seen that, with regard to God's creation of the world,

---

12. This trait of Thomism is also reproduced in contemporary expositions, where *being* categorically precedes hypostasis and, in general, is the most elevated and generalizing category for both the divine entity and creaturely entities. See, for example, Garrigou-Lagrange, *Dieu, son existence et sa nature,* Paris, 1933.

13. To be sure, Catholic theology does not establish a direct relation between the doctrine of ideas and sophiology, although this relation is essentially evident. Here, this doctrine is incompletely clarified and developed; it is not related to general sophiology, although it is expounded as if it were self-evident. Ideas have their ultimate ground in the divine essence, and their immediate ground in the intellect. In God's essence there is a "model," a "copy," as it were, i.e., the Word: "it translates divine being for God" (Garrigou-Lagrange, op. cit., supra n. 12). This essence is one and simple. To the unity of ideas *ex parte Dei* corresponds their multiplicity *ex parte connetatorum.* Ideas are rooted in the Word. Ideas are effective in creation not in themselves but only in combination with the divine will. [. . .]

the patristic and the scholastic doctrines converge in the necessity of accepting the prototypes, paradigms, or ideas of creaturely being in God. But both doctrines are incomplete and lack sufficient clarity, because both of them lack a sophiology. How should one understand the very being of these prototypes or ideas in relation to God, as well as in relation to the creaturely world? Do they have only an instrumental significance for the creation of the world and in this sense a creaturely character? Or do they refer to the self-determination of God himself in relation to creation, as the *"causa exemplaris"* (according to Aquinas's teaching)? But in both cases an accidental character is attributed to ideas, thereby introducing the same nuance of *accident* in the self-determination of God Himself as well. To this corresponds a similar nuance of accident in the origination of the world. Patristics did not sufficiently examine several questions: To what degree is the creation or noncreation of the world possible? To what degree is the creation of other worlds possible? And, consequently, to what degree can these other worlds be created differently from the existing world? Instead, patristics affirmed only the general notion of the creation of the world by God's free will, in contradistinction to the necessity that reigns in divinity's internal self-determinations (such, for example, is St. Athanasius the Great's statement of the question in his christology). From the fact that the world, which originates on the basis of freedom, can originate or not originate, be or not be (freedom is equated here with unmotivated noncausality), one must also conclude that ideas, or prototypes, of the world have a precarious character, a contingent existence. Patristics does not directly draw this conclusion, since, in patristics, the content of the idea of creation is not sufficiently analyzed. But, in scholastic theology, there is a certain comparative deepening of this question, and this deepening is in the direction of precariousness. To be sure, scholastic theology does not directly conclude that ideas have a contingent, or instrumental, character, but, as we already know, it affirms that the existence of this world is only *one* of the possibilities, alongside which other worlds or other states of this world are possible. The element of accident or divine arbitrariness is brought into the very heart of the dogma of the creation of the world. And this occasionalism must also be extended to the divine precondition of the world, the world's idea, which divine Wisdom "conceives" [*excogitavit*] ad hoc.

The distinction between the internal necessity of God's being and the free determination of God's will to creation is defined as the opposition between necessity in the willing of that which touches upon the natural properties of God (in particular, *"bonitatem suam Deus ex necessite vult"*:

qu. 19, a. 3) and freedom in that which touches upon will as the cause of things, where God acts by will, not by the necessity of nature (a. 4). In this case, *liberum arbitrium* is attributed to God (a. 10). God's will does not have a cause (a. 5). This statement of the question is essentially unsophiological. In this statement, *liberum arbitrium* as the indeterminacy of the divine will is brought into God's being. And there is no reason *not* to extend it to ideas in God.[14] We do not yet know what these ideas signify in themselves. Do they have a direct relation to divinity's own life, or only to the creaturely world, for the necessity of its creation? We observe an oscillation between these two directions.

But in order to define the real significance of these ideas one must conceive them as divine life, the self-revelation of God in Divine Sophia, or as the divine world, which exists in God for God himself. Only from this conception can one obtain a foundation for creation. Without this, theology is doomed to that occasionalism which characterizes it in both the East and the West, in both the Western scholastics and the scholastic theology of the Eastern church that has been nourished by Western scholastics. We find an anthropomorphism in the acceptance of this dishonorable doctrine of accident and arbitrariness in God. A distinction is made in God himself between necessity and freedom, with freedom understood as the presence of different possibilities that are equally unmotivated, for freedom is without cause. Here, the anthropomorphism consists in the distinction (and even the opposition) in God between freedom and necessity, on the model of the one that has place in the limited being of creatures. The life of the *creaturely* spirit is really determined both by the free self-positing of *personal* being and by natural *givenness*, which is overcome in the personal being. This givenness can be internal as well as external: the internal limitedness by natural necessity and the external conditionedness by human will. The antinomic conjugacy of freedom and necessity invariably determines creaturely life, and the very distinction and opposition between the two finds its origin here. The self-positing of the will, *liberum arbitrium,* refers to freedom, whereas the determination of the will refers to necessity. This opposition is overcome, although never removed, in creaturely life, where self-positing is combined with positing through givenness, when there is a harmony between the two. But, when there is no disharmony, this opposition is experienced as contradiction and bondage to necessity. Freedom is the creaturely spirit's highest

---

14. For some reason this is done by L. Schwane in *Dogmengeschichte der mittleren Zeit,* 182-83. He attributes eternal necessity *per se* to ideas.

achievement, although freedom is incapable of leaving its self-contained repose except by touching givenness. This correlation and conjugacy of freedom and givenness spawns the presence of different *possibilities,* which are actualized or not actualized in the self-creativity of creaturely life. *Possibility* is the fundamental category for this synthesis.

But this copositing and opposition of freedom and necessity are permissible only for creaturely limitedness. They do not exist for God as Absolute Spirit. In Him, all is equally necessary and equally free. Therefore, the very distinction in God between necessity and freedom that we find in Aquinas and, under the influence of Western scholastics, in Eastern theology as well does not hold here. This distinction brings into divinity the element of accident and arbitrariness, that occasionalism which is not appropriate to God's magnificence and absoluteness. To the idea of different and manifold *possibilities* in God, actualized and unactualized, we must oppose the idea of the *uniqueness* of the ways of God, a uniqueness that excludes all other, unactualized possibilities. To be sure, creation differs from God's own being. In Himself, God differs from Himself as the Creator and Almighty, but this distinction does not refer to the opposition of freedom and necessity and is not determined by them. God posits His own natural being in absolute freedom, which is united with the absoluteness of this being's content as the only possible and, in this sense, necessary content. But one can say the same thing about God's creative act, which finds an absolutely sufficient ground in His essence and, in this sense, is just as necessary a self-determination of God as His being, though *in another way.* The notion, freely accepted by Aquinas and others, that God, by virtue of this "freedom" of His, could have refrained from creating the world must be rejected as not appropriate to His essence. If God created the world, this means that he *could not have refrained from creating it,* although the Creator's act belongs to the fullness of God's life and this act contains no external compulsion that would contradict divine freedom.

And if one can speak of the *will* to creation in God, this will, as synonymous with freedom, is not an anthropomorphic will, which can desire or not desire, but the divine will, which invariably and absolutely desires. In general, the distinction between God's being and His creation, defined according to the feature of freedom and understood in the sense of different *possibilities,* must be completely eliminated, for such a distinction does not exist. Having in himself the power of creation, God cannot fail to be the Creator. As the scholastics point out, God's *goodness* is already sufficient ground for this. "None is good, only God," and God cannot be completely not good, or good only to a limited extent, by virtue of which He

31

could have abstained from creation. This goodness is the same sort of "necessity" in God as His own being, to which goodness belongs. The world's "creation" is not something *extra,* not some *plus* to God's proper life. This creation enters into the divine life with all the force of "necessity," or of the freedom that, in God, is completely identical with "necessity." And it is completely inappropriate to speak of the *liberum arbitrium* of the creation or non-creation of the world in God in this "extra" sense.

This entire discussion concerns the fundamental defect of Western theology in general and of Thomism in particular. This theology is characterized by an anthropomorphism that distinguishes intellect and will in the one life of God and defines them in terms of completely opposite features. One must say simply that *will* in the sense in which Aquinas uses it, as the absolute causelessness of indeterminism but, at the same time, as connected with the divine mind, does not exist in God at all. In the one, simple being of God, there is no place for acts of willing and therefore for a willing will, which appears in us only because of our defectiveness and limitedness, when we desire to heal or overcome this defectiveness. In this sense, one can say that, for the divine fullness and autonomy of God's will, *there is nothing to desire,* for this will has all. This all must be understood in the sense that this fullness, *freely* experienced, is divinity's own self-determination.[15] To this all refers not only God's very being with all its "properties" but also God's self-determination as the Creator. We must also distinguish in God's being His creative act, but we cannot isolate this act as an arbitrary action of God, as a kind of caprice that did not have to be. Therefore, this entire auxiliary construction with the distinction and partly the opposition of *substantia* and *voluntas* must be rejected as an illegitimate anthropomorphism in the doctrine of God.

In connection with the foregoing, in turning to the question of ideas in God, we must point out that their very character in Thomism should be understood in connection with the occasionalistic interpretation of creation. This intensifies the nuance of their *instrumental* significance: God has them not according to Himself but with reference to the creation of the world, so to speak: *"quia mundus non est casu factus, sed est factus a Deo per*

---

15. Is it not this character of divine freedom, in its contradistinction from creaturely freedom, that is remarked by St. John of Damascus? In his *Exposition of the Orthodox Faith,* 3, 14 (p. 1041), he writes that "it is necessary to know that freedom is spoken of in different senses. It is spoken of in one sense in relation to God, in another sense in relation to angels, and yet in another sense in relation to human beings. For in relation to God this word must be understood in a *supernatural* sense."

intellectum agente, necesse est quod in mente divina sit forma ad similitudinem cuius mundus est factus. Et in hoc consistit ratio ideae [as then the world was not made by chance, but by God acting by his intellect, there must exist in the divine mind a form to the likeness of which the world was made. And in this the notion of an idea consists]" (qu. 15, a. 1).

To be sure, even with this interpretation one cannot completely deprive ideas of their sophiological meaning. In any case, the aspect of the *creaturely* Sophia is expressed in ideas. But this significance of ideas is taken here in an extremely limited sense, since the creaturely Sophia cannot be understood outside the connection with the Divine Sophia as the face the Divine Sophia turns to the world. Outside of this connection, ideas receive a limited and "accidental" character, as it were, as the plan of the world, its preliminary blueprint: *"quia mundus non est casu factus."* Ideas are ontologically suspended in the air; they are situated somewhere between God and the world. They are only blueprints, not being itself. They do not have reality in the world's being, although they are called to being (out of nonbeing?) for the sake of the world. And this fundamental sophiological ambiguity in Thomism prevents one from answering the fundamental question of cosmology: What is the world in God and what is God in the world?

e. "Creation Out of Nothing"

We have seen how difficult it was for ancient philosophy, patristics, and scholastics, in a different sense but to an equal degree, to coordinate divine and creaturely being, God and the world. This difficulty consisted in the need to simultaneously unite and separate, identify and oppose, two modes of being: divine-absolute and creaturely-relative. It was thought that there were two ways to overcome this difficulty: (1) the pantheistic identification of these two modes of being, where the world is God and the substance of the world is divine; and (2) their opposition as God's eternal being and being created "out of nothing." These two conceptions were most often combined in the same theologeme: the world in its highest potentiality was raised to divine being (the Stoics, Plato in part); or it was considered as God's emanation (Neoplatonism); or divinity was understand as the world's cause and substance. In Thomism we have a characteristic unification of the two themes. On the one hand, the world is an emanation of divinity, which is present in things *in time*. On the other hand, it is created in the order of divine freedom, where divinity *"est causa rerum"* in its *scientia* and *voluntas*. These two unconnected and somewhat contradictory series of thoughts, taken more from Aristotle's philosophy than from Christian revelation, represent two postulates of cosmology, which, indeed, must be developed in the latter. That is to say, cosmology must first *connect* the world with God and overcome the world's isolation. And, secondly, it must *separate* and distinguish the world from God. It is necessary to avoid both the Scylla of pantheism, in which the world is in danger of sinking in the ocean of divinity, and the Charybdis of abstract cosmism, in which the world's being loses its connectedness with divinity. That is the task of Christian cosmology. The attempt to connect the world with God by the category of causality is the answer to these questions that can be encountered in various currents of patristic and scholastic thought: God is the prime mover, or first cause, while the world is what is moved, or the effect. In connection with the use of this category, "proofs of God's existence" arise which constitute the foundation of Thomism[16] in the past and in the present.

But this conception of God as the "first" cause of the world represents an age-old misunderstanding, which must be eradicated from both philosophy and theology. First, the idea of the *prime* mover and *first* cause contains a contradiction that Aristotle and his Christian followers evade sophistically, by speaking of an *unmoved* mover or an *uncaused* cause. Here, the idea of a mover that transmits its energy in a series of infinite motions is replaced by a qualitatively different idea, *immobility*, as the foundation. In the face of this *anabasis eis allo genos,* the idea of the mover loses its positive meaning. A certain verbal self-deception occurs, caused by the need to *begin* a motion or to refer it to some fixed point. But, in this case, motion cannot be explained on the basis of the motion itself. This self-deceiving *transcensus* occurs under the guise of motion that is immanent to the world. The attempt to find a *perpetuum mobile* ends in failure. This self-deception produces the fundamental obscurity and ambiguity of both Aristotelianism and the Thomism that is based on Aristotelianism. The distance, the difference, between God and the world is erased and eliminated. Here, the world is God, but only at the lower levels of self-revelation. This notion is fully articulated in Hegelianism. We have the same thing with reference to the category of causality in connection with the definition of the relation between God and the world. It is indisput-

16. See, for example, Garrigou-Lagrange's work *Dieu, son existence et sa nature,* which is wholly based on the conviction that God cannot be proved from creation; also, Régnon, *La métaphysique des causes d'après Saint Thomas et Albert le Grand.*

able that, in the series of the world's causes, we do not encounter God *as one of them.* Here, Laplace's saying is valid that, in the empirical arena, the observer has no need of the "hypothesis of God." Newton's principle is applicable: *hypotheses non fingo* [I do not make up hypotheses]. The strength of the causal series lies in its continuity, and if a gap were to occur at only a single point, this series would be atomized into world dust. (This is equally valid whether we understand this series subjectively as the form of categorial synthesis or objectively as the power of the world's becoming.) *Ex nihil nihil fit* is the axiom of causality. By laying a free, or uncaused, cause at the basis of the causal series, we explode this series from within, for uncaused causality is not a cause, and one should not play with sophisms.

The causal series is infinite with a bad infinity; it cannot be interrupted or stopped anywhere. In general, both causality and motion (which is only a particular form of causality) belong to the world of discursive being and are incapable of leading beyond it except at the cost of self-negation and contradiction. Causality causes and is caused, just as a mover moves and is moved. They both belong to the world of uninterrupted, unruptured, *unitary* being, continuous in motion and in causal connection. On these paths it is not possible to transcend the world, to rise above the world, just as in time and space we deal with beginninglessness and infinitude. We can sooner admit infinite circular motion, a kind of *ewige Wiederkehr,* whose phantom tormented Ecclesiastes as well as Nietzsche, than an uncaused cause. To see God as the cause of the world, or as its prime mover, is either to distort the idea of cause into its opposite or to diminish God, making him immanent to the world, linking him with the world into a single, common God-world being, which we have in Aristotelianism. The category of first cause and prime mover is not suitable for determining the relations of God and the world. God is *not* the cause of the world, for, being above the world, he does *not* belong to the world's being. One could sooner ask whether God belongs to *being* at all, at least in the sense in which being is proper to the world. To measure God by the world and its categories is to assert pantheism. God is not present in the world's being; he cannot be known by the world's means. The possibility of atheism is already given in this self-enclosedness and self-being of the world, and God's being is affirmed only by *faith,* leading us beyond and freeing us from the world's being. "Through faith we understand that the worlds were framed by the word of God, so that the visible came from the invisible" (Heb. 11:3). We do not understand this through knowledge according to the category of causality.

We must point out a general defect of the Aristotelian-Thomistic theology: The doctrine of God as the prime mover, or first cause, of the world is completely unconnected with the divine Person. Divinity, the only divinity that Aristotle knows and the *de facto* divinity of Aquinas's doctrine of the world's creation, is impersonal in this theology. (The personal properties of individual hypostases are introduced in Aquinas later and do not have a determining significance for this question.) The impersonal divinity can also be viewed under the category of causality and motion. But God's Person, who is a Doer, not a cause, does not fit at all into this category. The fateful abuse of abstractions in this case consists in the fact that subsumed in one and the same category of causality are both the impersonal mechanism of the world and personal acts and relations that are *not* mechanical and therefore are not subordinate to the law of causality. The problem of the difference between the personal God and the impersonal mechanism of motion and causality is not posed at all in the case of a causal interpretation. A cause, like a mover, is always mechanical; they are both subordinate to the mechanical law of the conservation of energy.

But if the idea of the prime mover and the first cause as immanent to the world is incapable of leading us beyond the world and explaining it *not* from itself, do we have any choice but to recognize the world as understandable in itself, as not requiring explanation, as self-sufficient? But that too is impossible, because of the relativity, or (what is the same thing) the discursivity, of the world's being. To this relativity corresponds the "bad infinity" of the world's causal connection and motion. Neither thought nor feeling is capable of being satisfied with this bad infinity with its "physical" antinomies of beginning and beginninglessness, causedness and causelessness (Kant). Being thus satisfied would be tantamount to anchoring oneself in emptiness. Thought seeks a sufficient ground for the world, which would be free of the mirage of exitless causality and the *perpetuum mobile* of motion. Truly, in our spirit there exists the postulate of *freedom* from causality or from the infinite course of motion, a postulate that is expressed in the contradictory idea of prime mover and first cause. But the language of these categories is also completely powerless to express this thought in connection with *positive* (and not only negative or bad) infinity.

To determine the actual relation between God and the world, another category must be used, a category for which there is no place in the immanence of the world. This category must be used to perform the *metabasis eis allo genos* that preserves both the positive connection between God and the world and the ontological distance between them. This category is not cause, or motion, but *creation* and *createdness*. God is not the cause, or mover, of the world. He is the world's *Creator* (as well as the world's Preserver and Provider, about which below), and the world is God's *creation*. Philosophical and theological usage often does not notice the entire essential distinction between these categories; on the contrary, creation and createdness are usually understood to signify only a special form of causality, to correspond to a specific mode of the latter. Translating the language of creationism into the language of causality, people say and think that the createdness of the world signifies the world's *causal* dependence upon God, whereas what actually exists here is a difference that approaches oppositeness. Such a translation is contraindicated already by the fact that, in his relation to the world, God the Creator is above and outside the causality that exists in the world itself. In *this* sense, God is not the cause of the world but its Creator, just as the world is not an *effect* of divine causality but God's creation. God and the world are not related as cause and effect by analogy to the mechanical causality of the world (*post hoc, propter hoc* and *causa aequat effectum* [the cause equals the effect]). They are linked in another way, by another connection, which we will now examine more closely.

It is first necessary to point out that the idea of creation, in contradistinction to causality, is *personal* and presupposes a personal God. The idea of causality or the prime mover does not include creation and in a certain sense even excludes it, insofar as the latter is personal whereas causality, or motion, is mechanical and impersonal. Of course, God's act of creation remains, like God Himself, transcendental to human comprehension, but this act does become accessible to human comprehension by virtue of divine revelation, even if only "through a glass darkly," in its bare ontological outline. Before examining this outline, let us consider an *analogy* for this which exists in the modes of human creaturely creativity. Human creativity is limited, and this limitedness must be removed as inappropriate to God's creativity. Human creativity is partial and limited in its very conception, and it is constrained in the means that it needs and that condition it. It is therefore also constrained by givenness and is not free of givenness. Nevertheless, human creativity has certain features that distinguish it from causal, mechanical connection, as something *sui generis*. Specifically, in contradistinction to causality, human creativity transcends itself and reflects upon itself: it is characterized by the self-revelation of the creator in his creation. Something new appears here which is not causally conditioned, and at the same time it is connected with its creator, as belonging to him. Above this relation there breathes the spirit of creative freedom, overcoming (even if only in part) dead necessity. Causality is dead; creativity is alive and life-bearing. Causality can be included in creativity but only as subordinate to its goals and plans. For, in itself, mechanical causality is blind and empty, in the sense that creative novelty is absent from it. Creativity is guided by a task, a goal; it is exemplary (*causa exemplaris* according to the ill-chosen expression of scholastic theology), entelechic.

Of course, one can also consider creativity as a particular form of causality and thereby annul its originality. But this would be a completely arbitrary and forced identification. Creativity does not stop being itself, does not lose its originality, just because one applies to it a logical Procrustean bed, that is, a category that does not capture its nature, that is not appropriate to it.

Thus, God is not the cause of the world, just as the world is not His effect, is not connected with Him in a causal connection. God is the Creator of the world, and the world is God's creation. The relation of the Creator to creation is essentially different from that of cause to effect. It must be understood as such in both of its terms, in relation to both the creativity of the Creator and the createdness of creation.

The world is created by God out of nothing. That is the dogmatic formula that must now be analyzed in all its terms.

(1) The Creator

God is self-subsistent and self-sufficient, the consubstantial and indivisible Trinity in Unity and Unity in Trinity. This consubstantiality of God's nature is eternally revealed in God as the Divine Sophia, Truth in Beauty, the ideal-real life of God, the divine *world*. This world possesses divine noncreaturely suprabeing, for it is the being in and for itself of the divine trihypostatizedness itself. This world cannot be understood only as a subjective representation or an unreal metaphor. On the contrary, the world must be understood as an essence, with all the force of ideal reality that is proper to God's being. In this sense, it must be understood not as a "property," not even as the property of properties, but as *to ontos on,* self-subsistent being. It is not an instrumental plan, *causa exemplaris,* as the combination of ideas conceived with reference to the world's creation. Rather, it is God's own life, inseparable from *personal* divinity, as His self-revelation. For a correct comprehension of the Divine Sophia, as the divine world, as divinity in God, it is extremely important to understand her in connection with the divine hypostases in the Holy Trinity. As divinity, Sophia is nonhypostatic (is not a "fourth hypostasis"), but she is eternally

38

hypostatized in the Holy Trinity and never exists nonhypostatically or extrahypostatically. She *belongs* to the divine trihypostatic Person as this Person's life and self-revelation. She exists *in herself, but not for herself.* She exists for the hypostatic God. The Divine Sophia contains the entire fullness of divine being, but she does not exist in isolation from the divine trihypostatic Person. Divinity belongs to the personal God.

At the same time, as God's self-revelation, the Divine Sophia is a principle that is immeasurably greater than only the combination of divine ideas that are conceived for the creation of the world (Thomas Aquinas) and bear in such an instrumentality the mark of randomness and incompleteness. The Divine Sophia is God's *exhaustive* self-revelation, the fullness of divinity, and therefore has absolute content. There can be no positive principle of being that does not enter into this fullness of sophianic life and revelation. The divine All belongs to the Divine Sophia; she is the all-unity of the divine All. Any vacillations about various *possibilities* in God or the distinction between "*scientiae visionis* [knowledge of vision]" and "*scientiae simplicis intelligentiae* [knowledge of simple intelligence]" (*Summa Theologica* 1, qu. 14, a. 8) must be removed. All that can be conceived exists in the fullness of God in the Divine Sophia, with all the force of reality. Every idea, element, or atom of being contemplated by the thought of the divine Word and illuminated by the life-giving power of the Holy Spirit is contained in the Divine Sophia. And to this multiplicity of fullness belongs the connection of multi-unity, all-unity. The unity does not revoke, swallow up, or weaken the multiplicity; nor does the multiplicity annul the unity. Sophia is integral wisdom and all-wisdom, all in all and unity in multiplicity. This connection is revealed to our creaturely comprehension, first of all, as an ideally logical connection, a logical cosmos of ideas, mutually dialectically reflecting and revealing one another; and as a real, living connection of one life, manifested and revealing itself at all points and in all forms in being, as in a body, which has different but equally vital members living in harmony. The Divine Sophia (also known as the divine world) is therefore a *living* essence in God. However, she is not a "hypostasis" but a "hypostatizedness,"[17] which belongs to the personal life of the hypostasis, and because of this, she is a living essence. One must, once and for all, overcome the deadening abstractness that is afraid of realism in thought and prefers the abstract nominalism of "properties" to essences. One must understand that the sophianic *All* belongs to God's life, enters into and participates in God's life, divinely lives. And if that is

17. See my article "Hypostasis and Hypostatizedness."

the case, then the connection of all-unity that is known by us as ideal-real is, in divine reality, the connection of *love*. The logic and beauty of creation are God's *love,* love's power of the cross of the mutual sacrificial self-renunciation of the hypostases, as well as the kenosis of *all*, through which this *all* finds itself in its fullness and glory. God is love. This refers not only to the mutual personal love of the hypostases of the Trinity but also to divine life, to the self-revelation of God, the Divine Sophia. She is also love, first because she is the *object* of the love of the divine hypostases, to which she responds in her own way, although *not* hypostatically. In this nonhypostatic love, she unites herself, surrenders herself, and reveals herself in the proper life of the divine hypostases. But, in herself as well, she is love, as the ideal-real connection of the *all*. In this divine *all*, there is nothing that is not permeated with the power of love: "And there is nothing in nature that is not full of love," as the poet said. Logic and aesthetics are also full of love, for a mutual connection of love between Truth and Beauty exists in the Divine Sophia. Love is all-unity, integral wisdom, cosmic altruism. The divine world in itself is an organism of love, a ladder of descending and ascending love.

To be sure, thus understood, the Divine Sophia, as the divine world that has love as the foundation of its being, cannot be conceived in categories of causal necessity, which are so carelessly and unreflectively applied here in theology (especially in Thomism, which applies them systematically). Truly, one should ask oneself: Is love freedom or necessity? The answer is that it is, to the highest degree, both freedom and necessity, though not in their opposition or differentiation, but in their unity and identity. For, truly, love contains both the greatest necessity and the greatest freedom. Love is free, self-originating volition, which has in itself its own indestructible and inalienable foundation. Love is the bliss of self-identity, which completely overcomes altero-being, whether in enslavement to necessity or in the self-willfulness of freedom. Divine love is absolute; it does not have anything *outside* itself but includes everything in the totality of God's life. Therefore, divine love unites in itself unconditional groundedness or necessity with unconditional creative freedom. Unfreedom in love would be a contradiction. And this fullness of love in the divine world has no place for greater or lesser, for the inevitable or the merely possible. All is included in it by the power of fullness and is made equal by the power of love. Therefore, there is also no place here for the distinction of many or different worlds, merely possible or real, necessary or unnecessary, perfect or defective. There exists one absolute divine world, *one* Divine Sophia as the *Principle* in God, his life and self-revelation.

However, all of these definitions are insufficient to understand the Divine Sophia in relation to the divine trihypostatic hypostasis (Trinity in Unity and Unity in Trinity). Sophia must also be understood in the sense of *creative* self-determination, the supra-eternal *creative act* of the Holy Trinity, the self-creativity of the Holy Trinity, the *actus purus* in God. Self-positing and, in this sense, self-creativity is, in general, proper to the person. It was given to Fichte, in his *Ich-Philosophie,* to understand the initial personal act, I's very I-ness, as self-positing *(Thathandlung).* But Fichte's insight remained limited because, from this self-positing, he excluded *natural* self-determination (for Fichte, nature in *I* exists only as *not-I,* the limit to *I,* in the extreme case as *äussere Anstoss),* while including only pure I-ness. However, nature does essentially enter into the creative self-positing of *I,* for outside of nature, there is nothing for *I* to posit in itself in order to live. Abstract I-ness is insufficient for this. It can be likened to a source of light that is separated from the space that is to be illuminated and that therefore has nothing to illuminate. However, a spirit is a natural *I,* not an abstract one. It is submerged in its own natural self-determination: *I* lives in its own nature and reveals itself in it.

This self-revelation in creaturely life has two aspects: a passive aspect, which depends on what is given; and an active, creative, or rather self-creative aspect. This is explained by the fact that the creaturely *I,* having nature as the givenness of this entire world, does not possess nature fully and is therefore even possessed by nature to a certain extent. The creaturely *I* is nontransparent for itself and thus remains imperfectly known. The creaturely I is revealed for itself only in the progression of time. But even such a partial self-revelation cannot remain only passive. It necessarily contains elements of creativity and, therefore, self-creativity. A spirit is the creator in its own life, and creativity is its own element. But this creative nature of a spirit is obscured in this case by its creaturely limitedness, by its dependence upon the given, which has for the spirit the force of a fact, not an act. And this factuality of life contradicts the actuality of the spirit, paralyzes this actuality, although it cannot completely annihilate it, for spirit is creativity, life is creativity, the perception of the world is creative, and personality itself as I-ness is the originally creative, self-determining, and self-positing energy.

But all these limitations fall away in relation to the divine Spirit. The divine Spirit is *actus purus,* absolute actuality, free of all givenness. This actuality does not have any factuality or thingness alongside itself, in itself, or for itself. Rather, all its life, it realizes, as self-affirmation, a supra-eternal *act.* In our theology there exist certain ossified formulae that fundamentally contradict this divine self-creative actuality. This includes the usual dogmatic formula relating to the Holy Trinity: God "has" three persons and one nature. The formulation that God has three persons is imprecise if it is not also stated that God himself is a trihypostatic person. But we can ignore this imprecision; it will not necessarily lead to incorrect conclusions. But the formula that the Holy Trinity *has* one *nature* is, in this form, unsatisfactory in general. For what do this "nature" and this "has" signify? "Nature" in this case is invariably understood to mean the external factuality of things, specifically, a kind of single given of nature belonging to the three persons of divinity. In order to explain how one should understand the content of this "nature" as the self-revelation of divinity in its life, that is, as the Divine Sophia, no further step is taken, of course. Thus, only the concept of nature as the combination of divine "properties" or as some force of things, givenness in general, remains. However, "nature," to be sure, is divinity itself, God's own life in its self-revelation. In no wise is it a property of this life to be a fact or a givenness of things. On the contrary, this life is divinity's eternal *act.* God's nature is thoroughly transparent for God. In God's light there is no darkness, and God's Spirit probes everything, even the depths of God.

God's nature is, in this sense, the creative self-positing of divinity, God's personal — trihypostatic — act. This act is the Divine Sophia, the self-positing and self-revelation of the Holy Trinity. As such, she is the divine world, possessing all the force of being, even though this being is nonhypostatic. It is important to understand here that, in the sense of the personal self-positing of God, she is the creative act of the divine trihypostatic person, God's *supra-eternal creative act,* in which each of the hypostases acquires its hypostatic self-determination.[18] Only on the basis of such a conception of the divine nature, or Sophia, as God's self-creative act can we wholly overcome the rationalistically reified concept of God and think of him not statically, but dynamically, as *actus purus.*

18. To be sure, creative act and self-creative act do not mean here the appearance out of nothing or, in general, the production of some new thing, hitherto nonexistent. Such is the so-called creation out of nothing, which refers to God's creation of the world as well as to creaturely creative activity. God's self-creative act signifies God's self-positing, a spiritual actuality that excludes all givenness or thingness. God *has* nature (or Sophia). This does not mean that nature is given to him like a thing or fact. Rather, He himself posits nature in himself and, by positing it, He has it in his supra-eternal actuality. This is by no means a creation out of nothing; rather, it is, if one can thus express it, creation of oneself out of oneself. See expositions of this question in the chapter on Sophia in *The Unfading Light,* and in *The Lamb of God,* chap. 1: "The Divine Sophia" (pp. 112-40).

Thus, God's being is the supra-eternal act of the Trinity's self-affirmation, realized in Sophia. This act issues from the triune hypostatic center which, as such, is the hypostatic self-affirmation and encompasses God's being, the divine world, the eternal fire of God's love. And this act returns to this center in the eternal cycle of God's life, which has no origin and is not subject to change, but which, from all eternity, *is and is generated*: a flame of divine fire feeding itself, the Burning Bush, burning but not consumed.

God's self-revelation in the Divine Sophia, or the divine world, is a perfect and adequate act of divinity's life, which is nonhypostatic ("natural") in its own content but trihypostatic in its procession and self-affirmation. This life is inseparable from the three hypostatic centers of the trihypostatic divinity. It is the personal life of God, "the life and lives" of Trinity in Unity and Unity in Trinity, according to the expression of the Great Canon of St. Andrew of Crete.

(2) Creation

Only the divinity of the existent God *is*, and there is nothing apart from and outside of divinity. This axiom of the religious consciousness is directly opposite to the nonreligious, immanent consciousness for which being belongs only to the world and, consequently, there is no God. One can choose only between these two possibilities: only divinity or only the world. *Tertium non datur.* This fallacious third possibility, according to which both divinity and the world primordially coexist on an equal footing, opposing each other or combining in different proportions, must be wholly excluded. But, in fact, it is precisely this kind of conception that, semiconsciously, most often has dominion over the minds of men. But this conception directly contradicts the doctrine that God created the world *out of nothing*, and that therefore there is nothing except divinity itself. "Out of nothing" means, after all, that there is no matter or force that could contain the possibility of the world and could assure for the world a place *alongside* God, *outside of* or *apart from* God. The existent God has being, that is, essence and existence. The trihypostatic Person of God has His own nature or His own divine world, and all belongs to this life and world. Therefore, the assertion that there is nothing apart from God is only a negative expression of this positive conception. In fact, such an extra-divine nothing simply does not exist. It is by no means the limit to divine being. Divine being is limitless. Nothing is by no means like an ocean that flows around this being. Rather, it is divinity itself that is an ocean without any shores. A limit is only a postulate of our thought concerning relative, bounded existence, but not concerning the absolute, limitless being of God. Absolute nothing, *ouk on,* simply does not exist; it is a "conditioned reflex" of our thought, not more. And if we believe that the world is created out of nothing, then, in the positive sense, this can mean only that God created the world out of Himself (to use Metropolitan Antonii Khrapovitsky's bold expression). The whole power of the world's being belongs to Divinity. This power is divine: "in him we live, and move, and have our being" (Acts 17:28); "for of him, through him, and to him, are all things" (Rom. 11:36).

It is impossible to imagine that, *before* creation, there "was" a nothing that was like a kind of emptiness, a sack into which, later, upon creation, all the forms of being were poured. Such a state of divine being *before* or *outside* the creation of the world simply did not exist and could not have existed, just as there was no such emptiness and no such sack. The very idea of the *being of nothing,* to whatever emptiness we reduce the *minimum* attributed to it, is contradictory and negligible, and one must free oneself from this logical fetish. *Nothing* "before" creation simply never existed, and any attempt to *begin* creation with a *nothing* that supposedly preceded it degenerates into a contradiction. Even if one could seek the *beginning* of creation, it would have to be perceived not outside, not in time or in space, but inside, in the character of creaturely being and, in the last analysis, in divine being. The guiding and self-evident principle here is the consciousness that the absolute nothing, *ouk on,* does not exist at all, that it is only a negative gesture of thought, a *minus* as such, abstracted from every concrete application. Only the relative nothing, *me on,* exists. This nothing is included in the state of the relative being of creatures, in the context of this being, as a kind of half-shadow or shadow in the latter. In this sense, one can, following Pseudo-Dionysius, say that God also created nothing. And the analysis of the idea of creation necessarily includes this notion of the "creation of nothing" as a characteristic feature of the creative act.

One must include the world's creation in God's own life, coposit the creation with God's life, correlate God's world-creating act with the act of His self-determination. One must know how to simultaneously unite, identify, and distinguish creation and God's life, which in fact is possible in the doctrine of Sophia, Divine and creaturely, identical and distinct.

The roots of the world's creation lie in God's eternity. It is usually considered that the world's creation is something nonessential, additional, and as if accidental in God's being. It is thought that God did not have to become the Creator, that He does not need the world, that He could remain in the solitude and glory of His magnificence (cf. Thomas Aquinas and the scholastics; see above). Corresponding to this is the confused notion that God supposedly began to be the Creator in a time that preceded the time of his being *before* creation. An effort is then made to draw a distinction between the "necessity" of God's own, natural being and the non-necessity of creation, the "freedom" of God in relation to creation. But all such attempts to measure God's being by time, namely before and after creation, or to define different modes of necessity and freedom in God, as well as their degree, are exposed as absurd, as contradicting God's eternity and unchangeability. In general, the intention, in God Himself, not only to distinguish but also to separate and even to oppose God in Himself and the Creator is wholly fallacious. God's all-simple essence is one and unchanging, and if God is the Creator, He is the Creator from all eternity.

This direct identification of the Creator and God is indisputably confirmed by Scripture. The scholastic intricacies that aim to distinguish in God God Himself from God in necessity and freedom, God from the Creator, are utterly alien to Scripture. However difficult it may be for theological thought to unite and identify these two determinations, this difficulty cannot be the basis for arbitrary abstracting, for the separation in God of His being and creativity, contrary to His self-identity and simplicity. Once it is *given* that God is also the Creator, and that the Creator is God, our thought must be governed by the inclusion of creation in God's own life, and this inclusion must be on completely equal principles of divine necessity in freedom or of freedom in necessity. This means that the world's being must be included in God's own life, must be correlated with this life, must be understood not only in its own being for itself, but also in its being in God, in divine being. In the contrary case, we fall into an unconscious dualism, more or less pronounced and consistent, according to which the world, as an autonomous principle of being, exists alongside God, limiting Him. To be sure, such a coexistence of the world with God is characteristic of the world's being (see below) in the latter's permitted, God-given autonomy. However, this is God's work in the world. In a certain sense, this is a self-determination of intra-divine life, not a special, independent principle of being, existing alongside God.

Thus, God is both God in Himself and the Creator, with a completely equal necessity and freedom of His being. In other words, God cannot fail to be the Creator, just as the Creator cannot fail to be God. The plan of the world's creation is as co-eternal to God as is His own being in the Divine Sophia. In *this* sense (but only in this sense), God cannot do without the world, and the world is necessary for God's very being. And to this extent the world must be included in God's being in a certain sense. (But by no means does this inclusion signify the crude pantheistic identification of God and the world, according to which God is the world and only the world.)

The creation of the world is, first of all, a self-positing of God, which exists in God together with His sophianic self-revelation. In essence, the creation cannot, of course, differ from this sophianic self-revelation. The creation of the world is included in God's sophianic self-positing and consists in the fact that the Divine being in Sophia receives *another being in the world*. The Divine Sophia exists in a dual mode: in her own mode, which belongs to her in eternity; and in the creaturely mode, as the world. Only such an identification of the two modes of Sophia, with their simultaneous differentiation, can explain why, although God is the Creator, this does not change his divinely sophianic being or introduce in the latter a non-divine or extra-divine principle. The introduction of such a principle in God is impossible and contradictory, for no such non-divine and extra-divine being exists as the "nothing" out of which, according to the generally accepted formula, the world is created.

For this reason, we must consider inadmissible and contradictory the anthropomorphic principle that God "freely" (i.e., in the sense of the absence of necessity, not compulsory but inner necessity, of course), or accidentally, as it were, created the world, and that the world therefore did not have to be created. Without mentioning the fact that it is impossible to admit anthropomorphic occasionalism in God's being, an occasionalism according to which God supposedly can create or not create the world, can be or not be the Creator, there exists a positive foundation for the creation of the world, which is grounded in the very fact of the world, in the presence of the world's being in God's being. In what sense does God need the world, as the Creator needs his creation? In what sense is the very being of the world connected with God's being? In what sense does the world's being have a necessary foundation in God's being? In other words, can God not be the Creator?

Of course, one must first eliminate the false notion that the world somehow completes God's being and in this sense is necessary to God Himself. God's being is absolute in its fullness, both in hypostatic self-positing and in natural-sophianic ground. The divine person is exhaustively disclosed in the Holy Trinity, and nothing can be added to or subtracted from this person.[19] Likewise, God's nature is *the fullness of divin-*

19. See my article "Chapters on Trinity."

ity. It is exhaustive, "positive infinity," the concreteness of the divine world, all-unity, the ideal cosmos, quickened in beauty. Nothing can be added to God's fullness, and such an addition is not even conceivable, for there is nothing besides God, nothing outside of God.

However, this exhaustive character of God's being does not refer to the *mode* in which this being is possessed. This mode can be twofold. It can correspond not only to the hypostatic God's own life in Himself through His own nature, but also to God's being in Himself, which is non-hypostatic (though not extra-hypostatic) as the self-sufficient divine world, the Divine Sophia. To be sure, this distinction can be conceived only in abstraction. God's nature is always hypostatized in the Holy Trinity and never becomes extra-hypostatic. But this does not prevent God's nature from having nonhypostatic being in itself, in its sophianic originality, as the *content* of the divine world. We must recognize the equal power and reality of the being of the hypostases and the nature in God, where they are seen as inseparable, but without absorbing one other. The personal-subjective and natural-objective elements in the life of divinity do not annul, reduce, or limit each other. And since God is love, which has different modes, both hypostatic and nonhypostatic, the hypostases and the nature in God are united. But they are also distinguished and are realized as different realities of love. On this basis, the nature, Sophia, in God, being connected with the hypostases or hypostatized by them, has at the same time its own being. The aforesaid merely serves to unfold the content of the dogma that God has a trihypostatic hypostasis *and* a nature, all of this bearing the stamp of God's absoluteness, of exhaustive fullness. In this sense (but not *only* in this sense), God's being is necessary and unchangeable in its fullness, although this ontological necessity is united with free self-positing and self-creation. Freedom in God is wholly identical to necessity, and vice versa. In this self-positing, God lives in Himself, by the fullness of His divine life, all-satisfied and all-blissful, in the inner interrelationship of the hypostases, without any relation to anything outside of Himself, for nothing exists outside of God. God is *one* in his holy trihypostasizedness. He is identical to Himself from all eternity.

To be sure, the creaturely mind is not given the power to penetrate into the depths of God's life, to discover, with means of its own, what is contained in these depths. However, the creaturely mind is given the power to understand what is revealed to it by God Himself concerning divine reality. This reality includes the creation of the world by God, and this creation should be understood on the basis of what has been revealed to us about God's life. The fact of God's creation of the world certifies

47

that there is a place for the world in the divine life. Of course, in this fact we must also see a manifestation of divine omnipotence, but the latter must be understood not abstractly, not outside of ontological relationships (as a *deus ex machina*), but in the framework of specific ontological relationships, in accordance with the nature of things. It must be understood not as accidental in the sense of being arbitrary, but as essential, as a necessary self-positing of God. In the creation (or the non-creation) of the world by God, one must see in this sense not arbitrariness but necessity, the free necessity of love. The world is "freely" created by God, for both the world and God. The world could not have been not created. There is no chance in the world's being; the world's being is included in the very being of God, although in another way than His own ontic content.

The trihypostatic God has the divine world in and for Himself. But the being of this divine world contains yet another mode of its *being in itself*: as *content* that is independent of its belonging to God. The divine world belongs not only to God's being, being hypostatized in it. The divine world also exists in itself, in its nonhypostatic being, precisely as a determinate content of the divine cosmos, as the *world*. And this dual character of the being of the divine world in God also lays the foundation for the two modes of the world's being in itself: as the *divine* world, which enters into hypostatic life, and as the *world,* which contains the entire fullness and richness of its own being. And to this corresponds that self-determination by which the hypostatic God, eternally possessing this divine world as His own nature, *releases* it from the depths of hypostatic being into *self-being,* makes it the cosmos in the true sense, *creates* the world "out of nothing," that is, out of Himself, out of His own divine content. In other words, creation is, first of all, an act of God's own self-determination, God's action in Himself. It is audacious and impious to ask whether God could have not created the world, for it is meaningless to introduce the caprice of chance where all is illuminated by the light of God's face and only divine reality exists.

Instead of indulging in such empty conceptualizing, one should concentrate on understanding the *positive* foundation in God for creation. This is the foundation that, unique and freely necessary, determines the entire life of God, and outside of it nothing can be conceived in God. This foundation is *love.* God is love, and the creation of the world is the action of God's love, its self-revelation. God is love, and love is God's ontological self-determination, a self-determination that is not monotonously impoverished but multifariously diverse. Different in its mode is the love of each of the hypostases for the other hypostases: the love of the Holy Trinity for its nature, Sophia; the love of Sophia for the Holy Trinity; and the love of God for His creation and the love of creation for God. But all of it is love. God is love, and the creation of the world is love. And the world's being is thereby included in God's love. And if that is the case, if it is included in God's love by God Himself, then who can exclude it from God's love, impiously thinking that God does not have to love in *this* way and can do without *this* kind of love, thinking that, for God, *this* kind of love is superfluous and accidental? Who will be so audacious and impious as to limit God's love, to differentiate in it what is necessary from what is not necessary, what is essential from what is not essential, what is ontological from what is accidental? Is not the very idea of *such* a differentiation wrongly conceived and impious? We are given and directed to differentiate the *modes* of love, but not love itself, which is equally necessary and equally free (but not capriciously arbitrary) in *all* its aspects. It is equally "necessary" for the God who is Love to love in Himself, in the Holy Trinity, in His nature, and in creation.

God is the Creator and the Creator is God. That is the axiom of revelation. And this is the case not in the sense that God, *in addition to* being God, is also the Creator, though he did not have to be such. Rather, God is the Creator by virtue of the inner necessity of His nature, divine love, because God is love, which is exhaustive and includes all its modes, and in particular love for creation. One can say that God is the Creator just as essentially as He is the Holy Trinity, the Father, the Son, and the Holy Spirit, that He is God having His nature, having his creation. God's self-determination as the Creator enters into the inmost depths of the divine being.

We can also take the following step in defining the mode of the love of God as the Creator. We know that the Trinity's love is mutually sacrificial as a mutual renunciation of the hypostases. Each hypostasis finds itself and realizes itself in the others in this renunciation. Therefore, the Trinity's love can be understood in this sense as a supra-eternal kenosis, but a kenosis that is overcome for each of the hypostases in joint trinitarian love, in the all-blissfulness of this love.

The relation of the hypostases of the Trinity to God's nature, Sophia, is just as kenotic as their interhypostatic self-determination, since the Divine Sophia herself, in her content as the divine world, is the kenotic self-positing of the three hypostases. This self-positing is realized in a single act of divine self-determination,[20] and in this act this kenosis of the hypostatic acts is overcome in the joy of perfect divine being. This tri-

---

20. See *The Lamb of God, The Comforter,* "Chapters on Trinity."

49

hypostatic kenosis of love is manifested in yet *another* way in the relation of God to the divine world in the act of creation. Here, the Holy Trinity in Unity, or the Unity in Trinity, renounces, as it were, in its sacrificially kenotic love the possession of the divine world for itself and allows this world to have its own being. The Trinity in Unity has, or posits, this world outside itself, in separateness from itself, precisely as the world, as nonhypostatic self-being. To be sure, ontologically, there can be no such separation of the world from God, "for in him we live, and move, and have our being" (Acts 17:28), and, from all eternity, the divine world belongs to God, existent in the Holy Trinity, as His self-revelation. But "in creating the world," in giving it self-being, God does not take away from it the divine force of its being. Rather, he posits the world outside Himself, as it were, releases it from Himself into divinely extra-divine and even non-divine being. This precisely means that God *creates the world*. This creation is, first of all, God's own self-determination in His own being.

Thus, the Divine Sophia is not only the divine "project" of the world (its "ideas"). She is much more. She is the very *foundation* of the world, and the divine world is the essence of the creaturely world. The creaturely world does not contain any ontological novelty for God. Revealed in this world are the same words of the supra-eternal Word that make up the ideal content of the Divine Sophia, the life of God: "All things were made by him; and without him was not any thing made that was made" (John 1:3). It is strange to think that the Word could have had special words for the creation of the creaturely world above or beyond the content that He Himself establishes for the divine world. This is the same Word of God that sounds in the universe, in the heavens: "both *ano* and *kato*" (according to a hermetic expression). And this is the same life-giving power of the Holy Spirit that clothes the words of the Word with life and beauty. One and the same Spirit of God gives them being. It is necessary to affirm and understand with all one's power this identity of the divine and creaturely world, or (what is the same thing) the identity of the Divine and the creaturely Sophia, in their essence, and thus the *eternal*, uncreated, divine foundation of the world in God.

More difficult than to accept this identity of the foundation of the divine and creaturely world is to understand the entire *difference* between the Divine and the creaturely Sophia. The creaturely world has the attribute of createdness, which simultaneously unites in itself not only divinity but also non-divinity and even extra-divinity. In what way can non-divine and extra-divine being, creation, find a place for itself in God and in the divinity of His life? The foundation for this being consists in God's goodness, in the power of love as God's very being: "Only God is good." This love is realized in God in all its fullness and possibilities. Among these realized possibilities is the kenotic sacrifice of God's love that is expressed in the positing, alongside divine being, of creaturely, non-divine being, given to itself. God loves himself with divine love not only in His own life in the Divine Sophia but also in the life of the world, that is, in the life of the same Sophia but freed, as it were, from the hypostatized being in God, in her non-hypostatic being. This, once again, is what *creation* is: by virtue of it God, having His divinity as God in His Sophia, is also the Creator in His creation. The first definition is inseparably connected with the second. One should not diminish the second definition, the definition of God as the Creator, in comparison with the first, as some sort of accidental, secondary definition, which does not have a ground in itself. The second definition is just as supra-eternal and necessary as the first. God as Love in His eternity is both the Creator and God in His own life. The two are identical and cannot be separated. God cannot not be the Creator, just as the Creator cannot not be God. By one and the same eternal divine act, God is both God and the Creator. The diminution and relativization of God's definition as the Creator undeniably reflect the relativity of the being of creatures and the subordination of tHis being to temporality. Therefore, it is so important to understand creatures and creation not only in their temporal-creaturely being but also in their divine-eternal foundation, that is, to understand them as Sophia, as the creaturely Sophia who has her foundation in the Divine Sophia and in that sense is identical to her.

The act of divine self-determination by which God gives His own nature, or the Divine Sophia, nonhypostatic, autonomous, and, in this sense, extra-divine being, thereby annulling, as it were, her inclusion in His hypostatic being, is a mystery of divine life. In its *how*, this mystery is unfathomable for both human beings and angels, for creatures in general. Only God's Spirit knows God's depths, which forever remain inaccessible for creatures. However, in its *what*, in the very fact of creation, in its power and even in its contours, this mystery becomes accessible to creatures, insofar as it is turned toward the life of creatures and even determines this life. Let us try to capture these contours.

The "creation of the world" should be understood, first of all, as a supra-eternal act of God's self-determination, an act that belongs to God's eternity. This creation is not subject to time (contrary to the de facto view of theology). Rather, it is eternal with all of God's eternity, as eternal as the Holy Trinity and its self-revelation in the Divine Sophia, as eternal as God's life. The trihypostatic God has His natural life as the divine *and* the creaturely Sophia, as *ousia* and creation, as self-revelation in absolute, hypostatized being and in relative, extra-hypostatic being. What does creation mean, first of all, in relation to divine being? Here, we must again recall the enigmatic dogmatic formula of the creation of the world out of *nothing.* In what way and in what sense can God, who possesses all the fullness of absolute being, enter into contact with *nothing,* nonbeing (which, however, is inseparably *connected* with being as its shadow in relativity)? Clearly, this is possible *not* in God's own being but only in His being that has acquired its own self-being as the creaturely Sophia. Separated from the trihypostatic Person of God, the creaturely Sophia necessarily realizes her content as such in all its multiplicity, a multiplicity, however, that is united by the power of "integral wisdom." The creaturely Sophia begins to *belong to herself* in all the richness of her content, in all its multiple themes. The multiplicity and multiformity of the divine cosmos appear in her with necessity not only as harmony and accord but, first and foremost, as the actualized potency of potencies. She is differentiated in herself, and the fullness of the multiplicity of divine ideas, or ontic forces, as themes of creation becomes actual for her. But multiplicity, real and realizing itself, also appears (not in its unity but in its differentiation) as a genuine *diversity,* which presupposes not only delimitation but also the limitedness of each special mode of being. This limitedness does not exist and cannot be realized in God's own life, insofar as it has not only a natural character but also a personal one, is wholly transparent for the Trinity of hypostases, is permeated with their light. But this limitedness manifests itself with necessity, insofar as its reality is posited according to itself, as if outside this hypostatic light. Into this being enters the principle of multiple limitedness *(omnis definitio est negatio),* that is, nonbeing. Multiple being is replaced, so to speak, by *nonbeing.* And the nothing arises in which, out of which, and given which God created the world.

This *nothing* is included in fullness as multiplicity. On the one hand, it is the ontological shadow of multiplicity (of course, in no wise containing evil but only bearing witness to richness), a combination of light and shadow, as it were. On the other hand, it is a special color in the spectrum of being into which the all-encompassing white light of integral wisdom is differentiated. One can say that the creaturely Sophia plays with her own rays, is clothed in their rainbow. Note the biblical symbol: "I do set my bow in the cloud, and it shall be for a token of a covenant between me and the earth" (Gen. 9:13). The rainbow is a token of the covenant between God and the "earth," that is, creation. It is the creaturely face of the Divine Sophia, white light in the play of colors. Difference in unity, multiplicity in connectedness, cannot be a heap of atoms of being. It can only be a kind of ontological hierarchy, in which each individual member of being finds itself in connection with the all, in the concreteness of subordination to the whole. The diversity of the world is not chaos, but *cosmos,* the cosmic hierarchy of ideas and beings. Their difference or manifestation corresponds to the acts of creation, whose sequence is determined by the mode of their concrete connectedness. In this creation, each sophianic order of ontic ideas, or ideal realities, acquires being: Plants grow; birds fly in the air; fishes swim in the water; the earth is populated with animals; and God's command is addressed to all: "be fruitful and multiply."

We do not set for ourselves here the task of the exegesis of the Six Days of Creation, Genesis 1–2, in their particulars. It is essential to understand the foundation of the Six Days as the manifestation of the sophianic content of the "beginning." To be sure, the expression "in the beginning" (Gen. 1:1) in no wise should be understood as a "condition of time" applied to God himself. Such a conception is clearly absurd and anthropomorphic, since God is above temporal determinations. Such an impossible and contradictory conception would be equivalent to interpreting John 1:1 in terms of temporal relationships: "In the beginning was the Word." Genesis 1:1 does not signify that God *began* to create at a certain moment of time, and that this beginning in time was the creation of the heaven and the earth. Even if we refer this "beginning" not to God but to the temporality of the world and creation, one cannot avoid here the application of time also to God, who thereby begins the time of creation. Here, *beginning, principium, bereshith* signifies not time but the Divine Sophia as the foundation of creation. Here, "in the beginning" signifies "by the principle, on the basis of the principle," that is, of the divine world. A semantic commentary necessarily not only complements but is more important than a philological commentary, in view of the difficulty, or even the impossibility, of literally interpreting this text.

The world is the altero-being of the Principle, the creaturely mode of the divine being. Eternity becomes the foundation for temporal-spatial multiple being. In the creaturely world, the divine world is clothed in *becoming;* it is not, but becomes. Becoming being is an alloy of the divine "principle" with *nothing.* Nothing is the proper foundation of the autonomous being of creation as the condition of its becoming. *Nothing arises in creation* insofar as the Principle is separated from the divine hypostases in the "creation" of the world. Nothing is the world's *privilegium odiosum* in becoming. Nothingness thus makes up the autonomous being of cre-

53

ation,[21] which, at the same time, through its ontological foundation in God, is becoming divinity. But what, in itself, is this *nothing?* Do not some people attribute to this nothing its own being, a kind of ontological independence or "freedom," *alongside* God's being? Such an absolutization of *nothing,* set alongside God, as a principle parallel to or independent of Him, and therefore given from outside even for Him, limiting Him, is an absurdity, since such an absolutization annuls the absoluteness of God's being. This introduces a kind of dualism that places this nothing alongside God. But *nothing* "in itself" simply does not exist. It is an empty metaphysical hole, a bottomless abyss, in which there is no content, and especially no supracreaturely or equidivine freedom. *Nothing* acquires significance, "arises" only in connection with being (just as a zero placed to the right of an integer leaves its null state and becomes a number). In this sense, one can truly say that *nothing* is created by God together with creation. Acquiring potential being, *ouk on* becomes an existent *me on.* In this capacity, by being included in created, relative being, nothing really becomes, in a certain sense, the foundation of creaturely freedom and creativity, bears in itself the *possibility* of the being of creatures, is Plato's *ekmageion,* the container, or potency, of creaturely being.

This actualization of potential being is connected with nothing, which thus, precisely in its nothingness, genuinely establishes a basis for creaturely creativity in freedom. But this freedom is nonetheless empty; it does not contain anything in itself. And the *theme* of this freedom and of the creativity connected with it is given in the divine entelechy of creaturely being, and this theme is thus given the task of "free" self-actualization or self-disclosure. Freedom in nothing is, in this sense, created by God, as is nothing itself, which arises in the altero-being of the divine world. Therefore, nothing is not absolute; it does *not* exist *by* itself and *for* itself; it is a *relation,* and appears only in relative being. Nothing is not a *something.* It is only a *how,* not a reality but a possibility of the real. It is the spring that moves apart the positive elements of being and introduces selfhood and "freedom" for them. As a result, creaturely freedom too, arising in and out of nothing, does not contain anything positive in itself. Nothing is only a zero or zeroes for an infinite series of numbers, and in its integral this series is the Divine Sophia. Nothing is a modus of reality. "Creation of the world out of nothing" is therefore a divine act, which is, first of all, a divine self-determination. God posits Himself as the Creator. This means that He has His divine world in a twofold way: as Sophia and as creation, or (which is

21. See *The Unfading Light,* the chapter on the creaturely nothing.

the same thing) as the Divine and the creaturely Sophia. The Divine Sophia exists in eternity, in a unitary integral act, whereas the creaturely Sophia is submerged in temporality and becoming, in "nothing." God in the Holy Trinity creates the world: the Father, as the Beginning or Principle, posits the world by his sophianic self-revelation ("in the Beginning") in the Son and the Holy Spirit. The hypostatic creative act proceeds from the Father. The Son and the Holy Spirit are "hands" as it were: "All things were made by him (the Word)" by the Holy Spirit.[22]

The patristic and scholastic conception of the sophianicity of creation comes down to the recognition of prototypes, *proorismoi,* in God. "Ideas," or "prototypes," are, so to speak, the *plan* of creation sketched out by the Creator. This metaphor *imprecisely* expresses the real relation between the Divine and the creaturely Sophia, God and the world. The *connection* between the divine and the creaturely world is indisputably affirmed here, but it is characterized insufficiently. The difference between the two worlds must be understood as being much more profound than only the relation between a plan and its realization. Although creatures exist by the power of God and their being is affirmed in God, they nevertheless form a different and special world, a world that is *new* in a certain sense. Ideas in this sense are *not* images or prototypes *according to* which creaturely things are formed. Rather, they are the very seeds of being, implanted in the "meonal" half-being of becoming.

The multi-thematic character of being, which is contained in the divine world of the integrally wise multi-unity, is decomposed here into a multiplicity of becomings. Succession in time and connectedness in space are included here. A peculiar new life arises, a new self-creativity of the creaturely Sophia by the powers of the Divine Sophia. Creation should not be understood as a copy, or imprint, of the Divine Sophia, as a simple repetition of the Divine Sophia's "prototypes." That would be a sign of the miserliness of the Divine Sophia, not of her generosity. Creation also could not be a copy of the Divine Sophia because of the inaccessibility and unrepeatability of the divine prototypes. The relative novelty of the world compared with its divine "Principles" consists in the fact that the world has a certain self-creativity based on the divine forces implanted in it. In this sense, one could say that creation is *directly* created by the Divine Sophia according to God's "command." God, positing the Divine Sophia as the foundation of creation, makes her the power of creaturely being in its originality. "In the *Beginning* [in the Divine Sophia] God created the

22. See *The Comforter,* chaps. 4, 5.

heaven and the earth," that is, the entire fullness of creation. He released his own nature into the freedom of creativity in nonbeing, called to being.

The relation between the divine principle of the world and creation is defined not according to the mode of repetition but according to the mode of creativity. However, it is defined thematically, and thus not according to the mode of causality as a succession of causes and effects, but according to the themes of their creative realization. If, in eternity, the Divine Sophia possesses the whole unfathomability and inexhaustibility of God's being as her content, then the world in its creative realization also possesses the power of creaturely eternity with the infinity and inexhaustibility of its self-creativity. One can and must say that, in creation, there is nothing and can be nothing that does not have a seed, theme, or foundation in the Divine Sophia, that is asophianic and that therefore is *new* for God Himself. But, at the same time, one can say that, in creation, there is nothing that *is not new in its own way* for the world, always new, for the entire being of the world bears the stamp of self-creativity. There are two modes of eternity. The first is the eternity of the unchangeable, immobile divine peace, fullness, absoluteness, integral wisdom, *aeternitas*. The second is creaturely eternity, *aeviternitas*, infinity, not "bad" or contentless infinity, but good infinity, for full of content and creative. These two modes of eternity are not separated from each other; rather, they are connected in such a way that eternal life enters into, is revealed, in the life of infinity, not annulling but filling the latter. Every element of creation has from God its own theme or character, is eternally given and given as a task to itself. But it is also included in the world, with the universality of its being, which bears the stamp of God's eternity. God is eternal; creation is infinite, although it is not beginningless, for it has a beginning in God's eternity. God's life, by a single eternal act, exists in the heavens, in Sophia, but it is manifested and, in this sense, created in time. God lives not only in Himself by His own life, but also outside Himself, in the becoming world.[23]

f. The Eternity of Creation and the Temporality of Its Being

The usual exposition of the doctrine of God's creation of the world includes the temporality of the world, namely, its appearance "in the beginning," at the beginning of time, at its first hour, day, or instant. But the

---

23. See the exposition of this question in *The Lamb of God*.

very expression "in the beginning of time" involves an obvious contradiction or confusion. Time flows; it does not know a *first* moment or, in general, any beginning. Every segment of time presupposes preceding and succeeding moments; it is included in the *flow* of time. This logical contradiction of the idea of the beginning of time was shown by Kant in his first, physical, antinomy, according to which the mind in relation to time necessarily unites both poles of the antinomy: namely that time has and does not have an end and a beginning. This is an obvious indication that time *in abstracto* does not exist. Only the concrete, filled temporality of creaturely being, which is measured by time, exists. Time is only the measure of temporality, but, as its quantity, it does not exist in itself and therefore cannot begin or end as such (just as distance is the measure of spatiality, which has only a concrete filling but does not exist *in abstracto,* and which therefore, like time, knows neither beginning nor end). The abstract idea of infinite or finite time as such is a forced transformation of concrete arithmetic into abstract algebra, where the force of concrete being is attributed to the algebraic signs. Time does *not* begin in the sense that some sort of emptiness, the absence of time, exists beyond this beginning. Time presupposes the being of time, existent temporality. Therefore, the idea of the *beginning* of time tacitly presupposes some sort of timeless, supratemporal being, in which time can appear as the temporal dimension. Therefore, Genesis 1:1, if one rejects the contradictory interpretation of "in the beginning" with reference to time, signifies precisely an extratemporal and supratemporal act of creation: "In the Beginning God created the heaven and the earth."

All this compels us, rejecting the widespread conception of the origin of the world in time before which there supposedly was nothing (not even time itself), to explore the question of the relation of time and eternity in creation. Aristotle had already considered this question, in connection with the pantheistic bias of his philosophy, and he resolved it by affirming the *eternity* of the world. (The idea of the createdness of creation in general remained alien to his pagan and limited theology and the cosmology that was connected with the latter.) In Christian theology, if we do not count Origen, the notion of the eternity of the world appears, under the influence of Aristotle, in Thomism and in Aquinas's[24] pantheistic biases that have their origin in Aristotelianism. However, Aquinas's last word on this ques-

---

24. The idea of the eternity of the world appears among the Arabic Aristotelians, but it encounters decisive opposition among the majority of the scholastics (Albert the Great, Bonaventura, Henry of Ghent, et al.).

tion reduces, as we have seen, to the indecisive affirmation that there is no speculative need to recognize the world either as eternal or as having its origin in time. Therefore, it is necessary to follow revelation, which attests to the origin of the world in time. (That is also the opinion of Duns Scotus.) Biases in the direction of the admissibility of the eternity of the world or, at least, in the direction of recognizing its possibility exist also in contemporary Thomism. The decisive thing here is the testimony of revelation (understood, to be sure, in favor of time: "in the beginning").[25]

These investigations are not definitive, but they make impossible the naive conception of the beginning of the world in time, at a certain moment of time, after which empty time is filled with the world's being. Apart from the contradictoriness of such an idea of time, time is thereby introduced in God's very being. God *begins* to be the Creator only together with the creation of the world. This admits *change* in the life of God Himself, which is obviously inadmissible. God is eternal as the Creator too. Therefore, we must conceive the creation of the world as an act of eternity, as God's eternal self-determination, His action "in the *Beginning*," not "in the *beginning*," for no "in the beginning" exists for God. The Creator creates the world in His divine eternity, and the world is eternal by God's eternity. However, we must at once qualify this self-evident proposition with reference to the *world*. The falseness of Aristotelianism's doctrine of the world's eternity consists in its pantheistic *equating* of God and the world, of divine and cosmic being. In the absence of the very idea of creation this identification is inevitable and the only thing that is possible. But it becomes wholly inadmissible because of the abyss that exists between the Creator and creation, for the Creator is eternal, whereas creation is temporal, and the temporality of becoming is the very nature of creation.

The Creator creates the world in eternity. His creative word, uttered once before the ages, sounds through all the ages. Translating this into the language of time, one can say that God always creates the world. But this translation is imprecise, since *always* does not exist for eternity, whereas eternity exists for and determines *always*. God's creative act, which creatures describe as successively occurring in time, is, for God,

---

25. The most remarkable Catholic writer on this question is A. D. Sertillanges. See his "La creation" (*Revue Thomiste*, 1928) and "L'idée de création dans St. Thomas d'Aquin (*Revue des sciences philos. et theol.*, 1907). Cf. his *Foundation of Thomist Philosophy*. See also Gilson, *The Philosophy of St Thomas Aquinas*, Cambridge, 1929; Durantel, "La notion de la création dans St. Thomas" (*Annales de Philos. chrét.*, 1912); Fr. M. Sleszek S.J., "Die Auffassung des St. Th. V. A. in seiner Summa Theologiae von der Lehrer des Aristoteles über die Ewigkeit der Welt" (*Phil. Jaehrb.* 35).

above and beyond all time. "My Father worketh hitherto, and I work" (John 5:17). This act is God's general *relation* to Himself as the Creator, or God's relation to His own life both in Himself and in creation, in the creative act. In this sense, eternity belongs to creation, and therefore the world for God is co-eternal with Him. For creaturely, temporal being, the translation of this eternal being of the world in God into the language of temporality is inadmissible, and any attempt at such a translation will fall short. The path *per negationem simplicem* is applicable here. *None* of the limitations of temporality connected with the *movement* of time from the past through the present into the future exist for eternity. From a height one can survey with a single gaze the plan of a city as a whole. Likewise, for eternity, the differences of time, with the limitedness and incompleteness of each moment, do not exist. Both the past and the future are equally the "present" in God's eyes.[26]

In God and for God, all is eternal, all belongs to eternity. But, in the life of creation, all is necessarily united with the temporality of creation. The creaturely world does not know eternity with its immobile repose. This world belongs to temporality and becoming. Divine knowledge, seeing creation in eternity, sees it above time. For human temporal, discursive knowledge, this mode of divine knowledge is inaccessible, transcendent. It is not characterized by becoming. The world is seen here in its fullness, as the creaturely mirror of eternity. That which is not present, that which has passed or not yet come, is supratemporal for God, and, in this sense, it abides eternally, enters into God's life as its creaturely reflection. The souls of people who have died and the souls of those who have not yet been born, of those who have not yet existed for the world, as well as all the ages of ages of cosmic events, together with the deification of the world through the Incarnation and Pentecost, the parousia and the transfiguration of the world, in which God will be all in all — all this is present in exhaustive fullness as a *single act* in God's eternity, as if participating in God's repose, in the sabbath of absolute being. "And on the seventh day God ended his work which he had made; and he rested on the seventh day from all his work which he had made" (Gen. 2:2; cf. Heb. 4:10).

But if becoming does not exist for God's eternity but only the repose of fullness exists for it, does this not mean that time and all that happens in it, creaturely being, is illusory, for only eternity exists? But the fact is

26. In St. Augustine we find the opinion that, in God, there exists only the real, in connection with the world's eternity or noneternity. [. . .] See *De diversis questionibus* 83, qu. 17 *(de Scientia Dei)*, Migne, PL 40, 17.

that temporality has all the force of reality *("let there be"),* and this reality of temporal being is rooted in nothing else but eternity. This constitutes the peculiar antinomic character of creatureliness. The temporal of the world is eternal for God, and the eternal in God exists in temporality in creation. The temporal is fundamentally eternal, and the eternal is revealed to temporality.

Thus, God Himself in His immobile eternity, in the eternal rest of the actuality of his *aeternitas,* remains wholly transcendent for creaturely experience, although He is present in and postulated by this experience as its very foundation. Creation has in itself a divine foundation and its own creaturely, becoming being, and the two are indivisible. Creation would stop existing if it were deprived of its immobile, eternal, divine foundation in the higher world. But this foundation shines in the half-darkness of creaturely becoming, is revealed to creation. This antinomic conjugacy of eternal and temporal being, like the becoming of creation, wholly corresponds to the identity and distinction of the Divine and creaturely Sophia in God and the world. The world as the creaturely Sophia lives by the Divine Sophia, by the fullness and glory of God's world. The Divine Sophia is present in God's world as the intelligent heaven, as eternal power and divinity. The creaturely Sophia is not another Sophia expressly created with and for the world. She is only a special *mode* of the being of the Divine Sophia, the revelation of the Divine Sophia in the creaturely Sophia. Having its foundation in the Divine Sophia, the world is not created but eternal, by this eternity of its foundation. But the world is also created and belongs to temporal being, for, in it, as the creaturely Sophia, the Divine Sophia acquires the mode of her being — not only in the eternal life of God in God and for God in His triune hypostases, but also by herself, in her becoming. In relation to essential fullness, this becoming is, like temporality in relation to eternity, a diminished, kenotic state. The creaturely Sophia is, in this sense, the kenosis of the Divine Sophia. God's creation of the world is a kenotic act in divinity, first in the general sense that God, by placing alongside His absoluteness the relative being of creation, kenotically places Himself into a correlation with the latter by the voluntary sacrifice of love for it. Insofar as He is the Creator and Provider, He becomes correlative to the world, receives this correlativeness into the depths of His self-determination. This is a hypostatic kenosis.

But this kenosis has also its sophianic expression: Positing alongside His divine world the becoming world, or the creaturely Sophia alongside the Divine Sophia, God realizes kenosis in His own life, whereby Sophia becomes in "nothing" or is created out of "nothing." Of course, Sophia as a nonhypostatic but natural mode of divine being cannot determine herself to kenosis. She can be determined to it only by God's hypostatic creative act. By virtue of this hypostatic act she is diminished to becoming, and this kenosis then becomes the state of her being, her own, although passively received, kenosis. The truth of which Platonism had a premonition in its differentiation as well as in its identification of ideas in divine and creaturely being is fully disclosed in Christian revelation. The Divine Sophia and the creaturely Sophia are not two but one, although in two modes of being: as ideal reality belonging to eternity and as the entelechic character of creation in the autonomous being of the created world. As a result of the unity of Sophia in her two modes, the world is both created and not created, belongs to temporality in its being and to eternity in its foundation. That is the second antinomy of creatureliness, disclosed in creation itself.

After the foregoing and on the basis of it, we must show and forcefully affirm the *temporality* of creation, its emergence and life in time *for itself* or, what is the same thing, *the reality of time* for the world. This affirmation corresponds to the generally accepted dogmatic proposition that "the world is created in time." The reality of time for creation itself is not diminished but is precisely grounded by the rootedness of temporality in eternity, a rootedness that overcomes illusionism, or subjective idealism, in relation to time. *Time* is real because it has eternity itself as its content. The temporal contains the temporal and the eternal. The temporal will be consumed by fire in the last separation of "nothing" from the sophianic reality of the world. But this will not be the dissolution of the world, the termination of the world's being in itself, the loss of the world's autonomous being. Rather, it will be the harmonization of creaturely being, of *creaturely eternity,* which nevertheless differs from eternal being. The creaturely Sophia will be maximally identified with the Divine Sophia, without, however, being submerged in, or swallowed up, by the latter. She will preserve her own creaturely nature.

How should one conceive this differentiation of the Divine Sophia and the creaturely Sophia in their relation to God? It can be expressed in the following formulae: God *has* Divine Sophia. She belongs to God, and she herself in this sense *is* God, His eternal power and divinity, the *uncreated* divine essence.[27] In contrast, the creaturely Sophia, or the world,

---

27. There is a perfect analogy here with St. Gregory Palamas's doctrine: The divine energy, like the divine *ousia,* is God, although one cannot say that God, in His trihypostatizedness, is energy or even *ousia.* Rather, He *has* them. An irreversible proposition of identity results: God is Sophia as Divinity, but Sophia or Divinity is not the hypostatic God.

belongs not to God, but to herself. She is created (or more precisely, is eternally being created) by God, is God's creation. Although she is grounded in divine power and is capable of limitless deification, she is *not* God (even in her limit). She is created; she is the *creaturely* Sophia. But what does *creation* mean?

Above, we opposed creation and causation. The Creator is not the "first" cause of the world or the "prime" mover. In general, He is not the cause, or mover, of the world, because he is above the world, does not belong to the world, is not connected with it, not even by a causal connection. God's connection with the world is creative, not causally mechanical. Between creativity and causality there is the difference that, in causality, cause is adequate to effect *(causa aequat effectum),* whereas in creativity there is no such adequacy. Creativity summons to being something *new,* and in this sense uncaused. The world, created by God, does not have a cause; a cause is, in general, an intramundane category, which presupposes the presence of the world's being. The world is created in the creative freedom of God. Its creation must be understand as the action of this freedom, the intradivine relation of God to Himself, and only thence to the world in creation. Creation is a divine correlation, arising in the dual mode of the possession of Sophia: in the eternal divine world and in the creaturely world. This dual possession is proper to God: along with the fact that He divinely has Sophia in His own being, He also creates the world, has it as the creaturely Sophia. The attribute of creatureliness is precisely the extra-divinity of the world's being, the abiding of creatureliness in "nothing," that is, not in God but in itself, or more precisely, for itself.

The entire positive force of the creaturely world's being is divine, is Sophia in her creaturely mode, for, in itself, "nothing" has no force of being. The being of the creaturely world, its origination, is, first of all, an act in God Himself, His self-determination, resulting in the origination of creaturely being, of the world. As such an *ontological prius,* the act of creation in God, as divine self-determination, precedes creation itself, which is, first of all, the imparting of the image of the Divine Sophia to the creaturely Sophia. This creation in God evidently occurs in God's own eternity. And this eternal, supratemporal, and extra-temporal act of creation in Sophia lies at the basis of the creation of the world in the strict sense, that is, in the sense of being as temporal becoming.

In God as *actus purus,* all His self-positings in the divine Ousia-Sophia are actual. God not only has His self-revelation, but He accomplishes it supra-eternally, posits Himself in His own creative life. Not only is this self-positing in God's life His own act, but the positing of Sophia as creaturely, or the creation of the world, is also a creative act of God, both in relation to the trihypostatic God Himself and in relation to sophianic creation. In the first sense, God is the Creator who, with the participation of all three persons of the Holy Trinity, *Himself* creates the world, positing Himself as its Creator differently for each of the hypostases, in accordance with their place in the Divine Sophia. But God is the Creator not only in relation to Himself as the Subject of the world-creating act but also in relation to the world as its object. In other words, He creates the creaturely Sophia; He forms the creaturely world by the power of the Divine Sophia. The Divine Sophia is not simply released, so to speak, into the freedom of autonomous being, by God's negative act of abstaining from the possession of her. In God there is no place for any passivity; all is creatively active in Him. And the relation of God to the creaturely Sophia, her very presence along with the Divine Sophia, as a special mode of the latter, is God's *action* upon His own nature. In the language of St. Gregory Palamas, it is the radiation of the energies of the creaturely Sophia from the darkness of the transcendental unfathomability of the divine Ousia-Sophia. And these lightnings illuminate the night of pre-being, of "nothing."

In his relation to the creaturely Sophia, God does not abandon or reject her, for she is His own self-revelation. He has her, as He has the Divine Sophia, but in another way. Allowing her autonomous being, he "creates" her together with the world. The uniqueness of the creaturely Sophia, or the world, consists in the fact that *uncreated* forces and energies, submerged in nothing, receive a creaturely, relative, limited, multiple being, and the universe comes into being. The world as the creaturely Sophia is uncreated-created. Ontologically the world consists of the Word's words, of divine ideas. It lives by God's life-giving power; it is joined together by the divine "let there be." That is the world's divine, uncreated ground in eternity. But this ground lays a foundation for being *in itself,* that is, for creaturely being not in God but *alongside* Him, in the reality of creaturely life in contradistinction to divine life. This power of being is actually and creatively conferred by God, and this mysterious self-positing of God, which is inaccessible to the understanding of creatures, is what is called creation, *to create.* Creation in the precise sense of the word is, first of all, the imparting of the image of the Divine Sophia to the creaturely Sophia, "a prologue in heaven," "co-being" in Sophia. And this co-being refers wholly to God's eternity. It is "in the Beginning God created," making His own life and nature the beginning of creaturely being. God did not want to limit Himself to His own fullness but provided a place for relative, creaturely being. He manifested His life not only in the absoluteness of the Divine Sophia but also in the becoming of the creaturely Sophia. The reception of the image of the Divine Sophia by the creaturely Sophia is the common source of particular creation, which determines the genres and themes of creation. God creates from this Beginning, that is, in the last analysis, out of Himself, or (which in this case is the same thing) "out of" nothing.

The creaturely Sophia, as the heavenly face of the world's being, already contains the entire fullness of creation, just as the spring earth already contains all the seeds that will issue forth sprouts in their time. The creaturely Sophia connects and contains all. She is the universe containing the *all* of creaturely being and linking it in a cosmic connection. In *this* sense, the creaturely Sophia is the *soul* of the creaturely world, its supracreaturely wisdom, the divine instinct of creaturely being, the guardian angel of creation, the very substance of creatureliness, submerged in nothing.

This positing of the Divine Sophia as the principle of the creaturely Sophia already constitutes a *pre-creation* of the world, or its *first*, preliminary and original, creation, so to speak. This *heavenly creation* (if one is permitted to use this expression) is defined in Scripture through the expression: "in the *Beginning* God created." And this corresponds to the positing of the Divine Sophia as the creaturely Sophia. Such is the eternal, pre-temporal creation of the world in God, which is then followed by its creation in the world. This is precisely what is recounted in the Six Days of Creation section of Genesis, and what, in general, is revealed by Scripture.

But, in connection with this, we must ask the following preliminary question: How should one understand the relationship between the first, heavenly or ontological, creation, that is, the self-positing of God as the Creator, the revelation of the Divine Sophia in the image of the creaturely Sophia, and the disclosure of the creaturely Sophia in the world through its creation? Is the second included in the first to such an extent that it becomes unnecessary in the special form of particular creations, or is the one co-posited parallel with the other, revealed and fulfilled in the other? In other words, how should one understand the relationship between the heavenly pre-creation of the world and its creation in the Six Days? Is a special creation of the world necessary if its foundation, the creaturely Sophia, already exists?

It is undeniable that, in the creaturely Sophia, the entire fullness of creaturely being already exists in its foundation, *pre*-exists ontologically. And, in a particular creation, nothing can be created that would in this sense be *new*, that would be an addition to this supra-eternal foundation of the world, its heavenly theme: "What is above is also below." All particular creation is only a development of the general sophianic theme of creation. Not to accept this would be to open the door wide to all kinds of contradictions. In particular, it would be to admit change in God Himself, who, in the creation of the world, would then presumably create something new for Himself as well and would therefore change with this creation.

However, just as a theme differs from its execution and variations, so the heavenly *pre*-existence in the creaturely Sophia differs from the concrete being of its images in and for themselves. Particular creation produces the *multiplicity* of the images of creaturely being, which are connected and contained in the one world soul, the creaturely Sophia. She must liberate her *all* in the universe, actualize her possibilities, her content in fullness, and this is done in the Six Days of Creation. In the biblical text (Gen. 1), we discern two stories of the creation of the world. The first refers to the *reality* of being in general, which contains the whole fullness of being. This is *tohu vabohu*, "the earth [that] was without form, and void; and darkness was upon the face of the deep." This is the *power* of being, its element, which has being in itself, in its own formlessness: "Darkness was upon the face of the deep," but it already had above itself the luminous "heaven" of the angelic world, the living ideal prototypes of being. Here, it is essential to remark a feature of this elemental turbulence of the ancient "chaos," *tohu vabohu*, in which the self-creativity of the creature, the participation of the "earth" in its own creation, begins to operate. It is highly important to remark this feature in order to understand God's creative act.

The creation of the world in the Beginning gives autonomous being to the creaturely Sophia, takes her out of God's life and into her own, though, of course, it does not annul her sophianic nature, that is, her rootedness in divinity. In this first and, so to speak, fundamental act of creation, the creaturely Sophia, as the world soul, also becomes the potency of the all, the "earth," from which sprouts grow, animal life issues, and the human body is formed. This foundation has life, and this life-giving principle is imparted to this foundation by the Spirit of God: "The Spirit of God moved upon the face of the waters" (Gen. 1:2), warming the cold of nothing with his life-giving breath. This foundation contains the "seminal logoses" of being, though in a potential formlessness. The real multiplicity of diverse creatures, which characterizes the universe and is unified by the world soul, appears in the second creation, the Six Days. In this second creation, the universe is created by a series of God's creative acts (which, of course, include an uncountable number of individual, particular creations). To characterize this creative act one must first note that it already presupposes the presence of a universal creative potency: the "earth." This is not creation out of nothing. It is creation out of proto-matter. It is birth from the proto-mother who is summoned to participate in her own way in creation: The earth *responds* to the creative summonses of the Creator that are addressed to her. This general idea of the "earth's" responsive participation in creation by her own self-creativity is directly expressed in Scripture in the story of the world's creation beginning with the third day (though in the preceding days as well, in the separation of the waters by the firmament and in the separation of the waters from the dry land, and even in the creation of the light with its separation from the darkness, one can already infer the participation of the "earth,"[28] which is created even before the light). "And God said, Let the earth bring forth grass . . . and the earth brought forth grass" (Gen. 1:11-12). "Let the waters bring forth abundantly the moving creature that hath life, and fowl that may fly above the earth in the open firmament of heaven. And God created great whales, and every living creature that moveth, which the waters brought forth abundantly" (vv. 20-21). This characteristic combination of the two ideas (1) "and God created" and (2) "which the waters brought forth abundantly" undeniably bears witness to a certain interaction in creation between the creating God and the earth (water) that brings forth abundantly, like *natura naturans,* from which *natura naturata* arises. One must add that this general and fundamental creative determination gives to the earth the *power* to realize creation in numberless births and is indeterminate in duration: "And God blessed them, saying, Be fruitful, and multiply, and fill the waters in the seas, and let fowl multiply in the earth" (v. 22).

The same thing is repeated in relation to the animal world: "And God said, Let the earth bring forth the living creature after his kind . . . and it was so. And God made the beast of the earth after his kind" (Gen. 1:24-25). Here, one sees the same identification, or at least the same unification, in one act of creation of the birth-giving power of the earth and the creative action of God. One sees *God-creatureliness* (if one can use this expression) in separate acts of creation. *Natura naturans* is created first, full

---

28. The same thing can be said about the creation on the fourth day: of lights in the firmament of heaven to measure time and "to give light upon the earth" (Gen. 1:15, 17).

of powers for all possible acts of separate being. Then, in it and on its foundation, different species of *natura naturata* are created. But, here, it is a question not of chronological alternation, in which each successive moment expels the preceding one, but of the ontological coexistence of the "earth," that is, of the creaturely Sophia, the proto-mother and proto-source of creatures, with her different species. The "earth" is Plato's *me on,* in which are submerged the "ideas" of the Divine Sophia, ideas realized in the becoming, *genesis,* of creaturely being. "Earth" presupposes "heaven"; the creaturely Sophia presupposes the Divine Sophia. The symbolic language of Genesis 1 expresses this in the story of two different creations, before the Six Days and of the Six Days.

All of creation is generalized and brought to a focus in man; the Six Days is the story of man's creation. In man's creation, the interaction of the Creator with creation is expressed in a special way, differently from the other creations. That is, what we have here is God's direct hypostatic participation in the communication of His image to man, or (what ontologically is the same thing) God's breathing the breath of life into man. The testimony that "God formed man of the dust of the ground" (Gen. 2:7) is also directly relevant here. The same earth that, according to Scripture, accomplished birth-giving, creative acts *prior to man* now communicates the fullness of its birth-giving powers to man, and he therefore recognizes in her his "mother earth."

It goes without saying that the Six Days are only a schema of creation. Creation consists not of "six" acts but of an infinite number of acts. Here this infinite number is generalized into six groups. These groups include *all* creation, the universe, all the possibilities of creaturely being that have been actualized, are being actualized, and will be actualized. The potential riches of the world are uncountable and unfathomable, just as the Divine Sophia, the divine power that reveals itself in creation, in the creaturely Sophia, is unfathomable. The Six Days also express the general idea that creaturely being in its infinite variety is *hierarchical,* has an internal connectedness, and finds its culmination in man. The universe is man ("Adam-Kadmon"), connecting and containing all. The Six Days are the story of the world as the story of man, the story of the creation of the world for man, for the purposes of man, having man in view.

It may be asked: What is the relation of the *first* creation of the world in the creaturely Sophia, or the pre-creation, to the subsequent creation, to the Six Days? Should one understand them as separate and successive acts, or does the successiveness refer only to their depiction? As is well known, the opinion that the world was created in a *single* act (St. Augustine) exists in patristics: the Six Days are conceived as the story of this single creation told in separate acts. (This opinion is also held by Clement of Alexandria, Origen, St. Athanasius of Alexandria, and, to some extent, by St. Basil the Great and St. Gregory of Nyssa.) There are therefore no exegetical or theological obstacles to merging these two creations to the point of indistinguishability. But, in relation to the Creator, this identification of all the separate creative acts receives a special significance with reference to God's eternity. In divine eternity, there is neither separateness nor successiveness of time. All the creative acts that we conceive separately and successively exist unified in God. They are included in God's self-determination as the Creator, in His supratemporality. There is a *single* divine creation, the creaturely Sophia, in whom there is no place for succession and alternation, in whom there is only all-unity.

We now approach the most difficult problem in the understanding of creation, that of the unification in it of temporality and eternity. In God there is no temporality, whereas in the world there is only temporality. But God relates Himself to this world, which is subordinate to temporality, from His eternity. How should one understand this relation? Does it mean that temporality is an illusion, a maya that veils eternal being from the weak eyes of creation, and therefore does not really exist? But it would then turn out that our entire existence is an illusion, that God created an illusory world by a self-deception. This blasphemous idea contradicts the healthy philosophy of creation: The world must be recognized as having all the fullness of reality given to it by the Creator; the world is *ens realissimum* by its sophianicity. As the creaturely Sophia, the world is real with the reality of divinity, in which it finds the foundation of its being. To seek to overcome the antinomy of eternity and temporality on the path of the annihilation or negation of the reality of temporal being is to fall into acosmism and to reject the power of God's creation. Its power consists in the fact that, by an act of creative love existing from all eternity, God places becoming being alongside His eternity and the creaturely Sophia alongside the Divine Sophia. God the Creator abides by His life in Himself, that is, in the Divine Sophia. But He also abides "outside Himself," in the creaturely Sophia. Therefore, we must conceive these two modes of God's life, in eternity or in Himself and outside Himself or in temporality, as united in the *one* life of God as one God. God's being in the creaturely Sophia as the Creator is His assumption of temporality, or becoming, into His life as the sacrifice of divine love for creation. In creation, divine eternity passes into temporality in a way unfathomable for creatures. Static being passes into becoming being. That which always exists in God's eternity but does not become or arise in this eternity becomes and arises in the world, in creation, in its life, development, becoming. Temporality is the "moving image of God's eternity." Insofar as the world is turned toward God and is the emanation of His glory or the Divine Sophia, it is not created in time but simply belongs to God's eternity. Insofar as the world is the *creaturely* Sophia, becoming being, it is created for time and its life belongs to time. Temporality is the form of its being, outside of which it simply does not exist.

If one takes these antinomically conjugate relations only statically, no special difficulty in the simultaneous acceptance of both terms of the antinomy arises. But a special difficulty does arise when these relations are understood dynamically. God as the Creator, positing the temporal world and relating to this world, subjects himself to temporality. The entire Bible, beginning with the Six Days of Creation and ending with the Apocalypse, is the story of the revelation of God in time, in which He lives together with man, as it were. And both the Incarnation and the Pentecost bear the stamp of temporality. If one reads the sacred story with unprejudiced, naive eyes, it is impossible to avoid the impression that God participates *together with* man in the history of the world and is, in general, Himself subject to temporality, and precisely this gives to the world and history all the reality that they possess. It might appear that creation imposes its proper form, temporality, upon God as well, who in the kenosis of His love for creation accepts this form for Himself. It is impossible to think this away and to say that temporality in God's life is only apparent for creation, and that in fact *nothing real* corresponds to temporality, for that would be to deprive creation of all ontological reality. For what would remain of creation if one were to take away from it this unceasing contact with divinity? But, at the same time, one cannot deny that, precisely owing to their mere temporality, creatures have only limited knowledge of themselves and of God. Nevertheless, one cannot go to the extreme of completely separating temporality from eternity as a certain absolute *"durée,"* for such a thing is inconceivable and does not exist. On the contrary, eternity is the tacit presupposition of temporality, as it were, its ontological bottom, onto which it cannot descend, but which it can touch. Without this "bottom," the very reservoir of temporality could not exist.

The antinomy of eternity and temporality is the foundation of creation's existence. Creaturely life itself is an antinomy, wherein lie its fire, force, and interest. Eternity is accessible to creatures only *through* temporality and the overcoming of temporality. For God, eternity is His own life, whereas temporality is an image of divine being that is perfectly transparent for and adequate to eternity, an image proper to Him not in itself but only in relation to creation. Temporality is real for God with all the reality of creation, which is posited by God Himself. But this is God's kenosis for the sake of creation, not God's own life but the life of extra-divine (in the sense clarified above) creation, to which God condescends in His love, as if taking off his eternity and putting on temporality. But this "taking off" is only a kenotic act, which does not weaken or annul all the force of eternity, of God's own life, for, along with the latter, God also lives for the world.

Aristotle's question, Is the world eternal or not? was addressed by several scholastics (Thomas Aquinas and the Thomists), who "got around" it to some extent by transferring it to the dogmatic domain. This question inevitably arises in the doctrine of the world, but it was posed by the aforementioned scholastics incompletely and incorrectly, that is, non-antinomically. For Aristotelianism the antinomy of temporality and eternity does not exist, insofar as, pantheistically, no distinction is made between God and the world as the Creator and creation. Thomas Aquinas and the Thomists alternately take either the one or the other side of the antinomy and, philosophically postulating the eternity of the world, dogmatically and practically affirm its temporality. The fullness of the truth compels us to affirm both the one and the other: The world is eternal in God, for in Him all is eternal, as in its eternal prototype, the Divine Sophia; and the world exists, as such, as a creation, in temporality or becoming. The two are incompatible abstractly-logically, but, ontologically, they mutually condition each other.[29]

Hitherto we have spoken only of *temporality,* which, in itself, is not yet time, although it presupposes time as the mode of its existence or becoming. We must now translate what belongs to temporality into the language of *time.* Time and temporality must first be distinguished in the appropriate manner. Even though it is, so to speak, a function of temporality, time is not identical with temporality. Time is the abstract *measure* of temporal being; however, it is not the *unique* measure, for it can have different units of measurement. There can be several times, as different modes of creaturely or temporal being. There is angelic time (perhaps with differentiation of orders in the assembly of angels) and human time

---

29. Scholastic philosophy, in contemporary Thomism, considers the "logical" laws of contradiction and the excluded middle, as well as deductions from these laws, as the supreme criterion, which weighs and proves God's very being. The insufficiency of these "laws" and their inapplicability to the original principles of being are obvious.

(with differentiation of times into epochs). What is fundamental here is the determination of temporality as becoming, for which time is the form or measure. Therefore, in general, one must speak *not of the beginning of time* (which is what is usually done) but *of the emergence of temporality,* where time appears in a derivative manner, by a kind of reflex as it were. Should one speak of God's creation of the world *in* time or of his creation of time itself?

In itself, time does not exist. It is the "subjective form" of temporality, just as temporality, in turn, is a mode of becoming, of becoming eternity or becoming being. As a measure, time does not have its own being; it is functional, that is, it originates from the function of measurement. Time is created with temporality and is included in the character of temporal being. In the symbolism of the Six Days of Creation, time is created only on the "fourth day," that is, it is implanted in the fullness of already existing creaturely life. "And God said, Let there be lights in the firmament of the heaven to divide the day from the night; and let them be for signs, and for seasons, and for days and years" (Gen. 1:14) — of course, for man. Time is created and exists for the one who, by his nature, has the consciousness and knowledge of time in the temporality of becoming being.

Time is a *relation* within becoming, creaturely being. By definition, this relation is characterized by the conjugacy of each of its moments with the preceding and succeeding ones, for such is the connectedness of becoming. In this sense, time, conceived as a measure, can neither begin nor end; it is sick with subjective "bad infinity," forward and backward, in both directions. In this connection, time is similar to the idea of the atom, which cannot stop being divided and attain the limit of true indivisibility. With equal necessity an atom presupposes a quantity both greater and smaller than itself, for there is no limit to measure and measurement. Between an atom of any minimality and zero lies a whole infinity of divisions, for an atom precisely is divisibility itself, indivisible in its wholeness.

The same thing can be said about space as the measure of spatiality. Every spatial unit borders on or is surrounded by space and cannot be isolated from the latter, but must necessarily be included in it. At the same time, every measure or unit of space is, in itself, a whole spatial world, which can be divided without limit. In general, a *limit* or a real unit of space is only a *practically* determinable quantity, which finds a place for itself in spatiality but cannot be theoretically measured. In the last analysis, such a quantity signifies *motion* as the becoming of the incompleteness of being, which *nothing* surrounds on all sides and permeates in all its pores.

71

The practical measure of temporality has for us a more direct significance, for we live in it, *counting* time. For our "practical reason," temporality is something abstract, existing above or below time, as it were, and time is a concrete, real quantity. The net of time that we cast over life (the way a latitude-longitude grid is cast over the globe of the continuous, indivisible earth) makes life pass in time for us, whereas in fact there exists a single integral (but becoming) being, the integral of time. Something occurs that is completely analogous to the apparent motion of the sun around the earth, contrary to its actual immobility as the earth moves. Returning to our discussion of the *beginning* of time, we must separate two different questions that are usually confused: (1) Does temporality as becoming have a beginning and does time as the measurement of temporality have a beginning? (2) Does the world have a temporal beginning that can even be measured and precisely determined, namely, 5508 years from the creation of the world to the birth of Christ?

It is obvious that time as measurement can, by its very concept, have neither beginning nor end. If we speak of the end of some period of time, we do this in a language of practical anthropomorphism, to signify the accomplishment of certain events. Time *flows*, and to this fluidity, *durée*, no beginning or end can be attributed. Abstract time exists only for mathematics, just as abstract space exists only for geometry. But neither time nor space exists outside things themselves. The question of the beginning of time can therefore be posed only in the following sense: Does temporality itself have a beginning? There is no time in God's eternity. God's eternity is *not* measured by time, just as, in general, it is not measured by anything, for only creaturely, relative, becoming being is measurable. God's eternity is transcendent to creation, and no measure of creatureliness is, in general, applicable to this eternity. On the contrary, measurability is an essential property of creaturely becoming, for becoming is a kind of ontological movement, or change, *from* and *to*, which is defined by measure. However, all this refers to particulars *within* the limits of becoming, but not beyond these limits; in differentials, but not in integrals. Is it appropriate to include becoming itself in the content of what is becoming, or, on the contrary, must we presuppose the existence of becoming for the very possibility of individual *acts* of becoming, whereas, as such, it is both *beginningless* and endless? One must say that, in this case, *beginninglessness* in no wise means *eternity*, in no wise is identical with eternity. If we have characterized creation as beginningless, this does not mean that it is uncreated, that it possesses the unchangeable eternity of divine being. Eternity is *not* measurable by time, either negatively or positively. To define eternity as beginninglessness or endlessness is an anthropomorphism that does not know how to deal with the idea of eternity except by expressing it in terms of temporality, although with a minus, that is, by expressing it apophatically.

Although eternity contains the foundation for temporal, becoming being, it should not be understood as beginninglessness. In other words, the beginninglessness of the world does not yet mean that it has an eternity equivalent to that of divinity. On the contrary, its beginninglessness can be combined, and really is combined, with its createdness. According to the Church's dogma, the world is *created* by God. But this dogma does not say that the world has a beginning in time (this is a false interpretation of the biblical "in the Beginning"). We cannot attribute a beginning to the created world in the sense that "there was a time when the world did not exist" (which was seen as the characteristic feature of creatureliness by Arius and the Arians as well as by the anti-Arians). This would be to introduce time and change in the very life of the Creator. It would be to assert that there was a time when God was not the Creator, but that He began being the Creator only at a certain moment of time. But God *never began* being the Creator, for He is such eternally. In this sense, the world is not created *in* time in the sense of a definite moment of time or a beginning. It is created *for* time, and its being is not its own. Rather, its being is given to it. The world is beginningless in time; in fact, time itself receives its beginning *in the world,* in the temporality or becoming of the latter.

It behooves us to precisely understand this idea of the beginninglessness of the creaturely world, which, however, exists only in and together with time. Beginninglessness in time signifies a certain relation to time and expresses an aspect of creaturely being, the aspect of *temporality* as the foundation of time, but a foundation that, itself, does not belong to time. This is creaturely eternity, *aeviternitas,* which precisely by its directedness at and its connectedness with time, differs from the supratemporal eternity of God, *aeternitas.*

The world does not have a beginning in time, but it is *created* out of nothing. The world appeared not in time (for it was created by God) but for time. Therefore, its beginninglessness is not supratemporal in the sense of eternity, but all-temporal. It is considered generally accepted that the world will never end and that emptiness, empty time, will never engulf the world's being. Infinity in the direction of the end is therefore considered to correspond to the world's ontic foundation; however, this is not admitted in relation to the world's temporal beginningless. Here, one fails to see that the recognition of endlessness is only another form of the recognition of beginninglessness. If, at one end of time, the world is not subordinate to the power of time and is not submerged in the post-ontic void, then, at the other end, it is indeed submerged in this void, insofar as one recognizes that the world begins in time. One therefore recognizes *time that is prior to creation,* uncreated, empty, hollow time, a nothing that *existed* even prior to creation and did not need to be created together with the world (as some church fathers actually teach).[30] It is clear that the very conception of the creation of the world in time, a conception that gives time primacy over creation and thereby establishes its absoluteness, disintegrates into a contradiction that cannot withstand the critique of lucid thought. This conception can survive only in the lowlands of naive mythology.

Thus, the beginninglessness of creation signifies *not* the eternity of creation but only the fact that it has no beginning *in* time, since time exists only in creation, as the measure of temporality. The idea of the beginning of creation in time is internally contradictory, for, in itself, time does not exist, does not begin and does not end. Time is a function of creaturely being, which, having its sophianic root in supratemporality, exists as becoming in time. If time, being a function or measure, is nonetheless conceived and understood as a reality, this is done in a subjectively anthropomorphic sense, analogously to the way the measure of a day is determined by the apparent motion of the sun around the earth. Such anthropomorphisms, consisting in the reification of time, must, in religious philosophy, be *translated* from this subjective language to a language appropriate to the nature of things, even if this language has no practical usefulness. In such a translation, one must first establish that there is no absolute beginning of time, for time never begins. It is only a gap between *before* and *after,* but it cannot be realized without *before* or *after,* and cannot arise out of nothing and disappear in nothing. Therefore, there is also no beginning of the world in time, just as there is no end of the world in time. This is a simple misunderstanding. Our consciousness's need to conceive the beginning and the end of the world in time is, so to speak, a logical illusion, which is as unreal as the line of the horizon, though vision cannot do without this line.[31]

---

30. Namely, they teach that God also created nonbeing, that is, evidently, in its relation to being.

31. Patristics more than once posed the question: What was God doing *before* the creation of the world, or before the first day of creation? This question inevitably arises in connection with that anthropomorphic conception of God's creation which does not hesitate

Createdness is not connected with time. Rather, it is what posits time. Createdness is not a temporal act, but a supratemporal one. It is the ontological relation between the Creator and creation,[32] between the Divine and creaturely Sophia. Createdness does not need time and is not subsumed in time. Temporality, or becoming, is not time, but the foundation of time. However, temporality is realized only in time, which, in this sense, is the *form* of temporality. Temporality is the creation that leaves the hands of the Creator, and, as such, it belongs to eternity. But, for itself, temporality is realized only in time. Creation is becoming, but it is not *emergence out of nothing*, with a pretemporal beginning of time. There is no emptiness of pretemporality in which time would have begun. Every state of being, whatever its character, already bears time within itself, occupies in time a certain point, which is necessarily coordinated in a system of points, is determined not by itself alone but by at least two other points: the preceding one and the succeeding one. Time cannot begin, just as it cannot end.

The same thing must be said about space, which, like time, is a function of spatiality. Every point of space is coordinated with a whole system of coordinates, and, without them, outside of them, it simply does not exist. Therefore, space is the internal relativity of spatiality and, like time, space can neither begin nor end. The idea of an endless, that is, absolute, independent, space is internally contradictory, and it is internally contradictory in two directions, in the direction of positive endlessness in the sense of limitlessness, or nonrelativity, and in the direction of the infinitesimal, or zero. Every space is measurable and is a measure. In itself, the question of the existence of space as such, its closedness or limitedness, is

---

to introduce time in the divine life itself. Creation is thus viewed as something new in God, as something that hitherto did not exist in him, as a change in God himself. The answers given to this question were more or less evasive. Augustine avoided answering by joking angrily that, before creation, God was thinking up punishments for idle questioners. But this question is by no means an idle one; rather, it is completely inevitable given an anthropomorphic conception of God's creation of the world. Gregory the Theologian's answer was that God was contemplating his own Wisdom, as the ensemble of prototypes of the world to come. Here, the Divine Sophia and the creaturely Sophia (or the world) are directly linked, but this ontological link between proto-image and image, ground and consequent, cannot, of course, be expressed in terms of a succession in *time*. Scholastic writing did not advance this question. A certain positive approach to the problem can be found in the system of John Scotus Erigena, in the doctrine of *natura naturans* and *natura naturata*, but the question is obscured and even distorted by the general pantheism of his system.

32. This is precisely how Sertillanges defines it in a number of his works.

an unreal one. In this sense, space can be likened to a sphere that, on the one hand, is closed and does not have an exit, whereas, on the other hand, it allows all kinds of motion inside itself. The sphere can expand or contract, but inside it a constant correlation of points, that is, of space, remains. Mathematics represents this relation by conventional symbols, but the real content of these symbols is nevertheless only a *relation*.

But if time is a functional relation, a subjective form of creaturely being, is not the very reality of time (and of space) in the life of creatures abolished? Did we not say previously that time has all the reality that belongs to creation as the creaturely Sophia posited to being by God's creative act? But such an understanding touches not the *reality* of time but only its special character. Reality is strictly proper not to time but to creation, while time only expresses this reality or life of creation. Reality belongs here not to time as a measure but to what it measures and expresses. The temporality and spatiality of being cannot actualize themselves otherwise than in change or becoming. In other words, reality is possessed not by time as an empty form, which as such a form simply does not exist, but by that which fills it or is measured by it. And this suffices to recognize the relative reality of time itself.[33]

33. Temporality is realized in time as a succession of moments, the following one supplanting the preceding one. Of course, these moments, or atoms of time, have a conditionally pragmatic character: Time can be measured in seconds and hours, or in years and centuries, and all measures have their justification but are not absolute. An object measured by time is temporal being, *durée*, mobility, flux as such. However, absolute flux stops existing for us as time; it turns into its opposite; its flow stops, as it were. This mode of temporality corresponds to the perception of temporality as a single, integral act, in which all things are synthesized and nothing is lost, in which all things become simultaneous, as it were, not sequential. The fragmentation of being into separate atoms, corresponding to separate moments of time, is thereby exposed to be relative. In reality, time *flows* as a continuous stream; there are no ontological pores or voids between the separate atoms of time. At the basis of times and seasons lies a supratemporal single being, unfolding before us its panorama in time. That which has flashed by in the film of the wheel of time and disappeared in nonbeing, as it were, is, in fact, preserved and exists as individual and successive pages of the *book of life*. This book can be read not only in its separate pages but also as a whole (see Rev. 20:12, 15; 3:5; 13:8; 21:27). This is God's "eternal memory," of which our human memory is a pale reflection. This "eternal memory" overthrows the power of Chronos with his scythe and bears witness to the supratemporality of life. In this integral synthesis, a human life is perceived in its entirety: this is how, so it is said, it is seen at the hour of death. And this is how all-human temporal being will be seen at the Last Judgment. In general, human life has two dimensions: horizontal and vertical, sequential and fixed, fragmented and integral.

A final question arises: From the point of view developed here how should one view the story of the creation of the world in time? How should one understand the days of creation in their succession? Does not the aforesaid contradict direct revelation?[34] However, we know that patristics too has no single definitive tradition concerning this question and resists giving a literal interpretation to the figurative language of Genesis 1–2. And it cannot be otherwise when all the details of the biblical narrative are closely examined. In this anthropomorphic story of the creation of the world, of the creation of temporality itself or becoming being, the succession of days should most plausibly be understood *not* chronologically but ontologically, as the differentiation of the *internal* hierarchy of creaturely being, its successive steps. On top of this ladder stands man, the center of creation, the image and likeness of God. Man is the supreme goal of creation, and this goal is therefore realized at its end. This is the internal structure of the world as the creaturely Sophia, of all-embracing, universal being, which receives from the Creator its *let there be*, both in general and in all the particular forms of being. The biblical story represents a kind of ontological catalogue of creation, its table of contents, in which there is an ontological succession. Of course, this catalogue is sketched out in Genesis only in its most general and basic features, in the language of sacred poetry, but its significance is precisely such. It is a kind of sacred hieroglyph, written in the mysterious runes of an ancient epoch, in its language. The brief schemata of the first chapter of Genesis are focused or generalized[35] into a single point in Genesis 2:1-2: "Thus the heavens and the earth were finished, and all the host of them. And . . . God ended his work which he had made."

It is therefore inappropriate and even strange to see in Genesis a kind of scientific or even historical account of how the work of the creation of the world in time was accomplished, or to engage in the vanity of a subtle scholarly apologetics that seeks to defend or interpret creation as a succession in time, which in essence is not even spoken of here. This tale needs not a scholarly apologetical interpretation, but an ontological, anthropological, and finally a literary interpretation. In the language of this sacred poetry, the "days" of creation, long or short, passing rapidly or

34. It is known that Thomas Aquinas did not consider rationally provable the idea of the createdness or noncreatedness of the world in time. Nevertheless, he took the origin of the world in time as an article of faith, although (like Sertillanges) he did *not* attempt to give it a rational expression.

35. Here we intentionally set aside the whole *critical* problem of original sources, for it does not have a decisive significance for the dogmatic understanding.

long-lasting, simply lose their significance as measurements of time. Thus, the "first" day of the Bible, which, however, is "preceded" by a kind of general extratemporal creation of heaven and earth,[36] does *not* signify the beginning of time. From the world, from within creaturely being, it is impossible to conceive the state of nothing before being, the state of emptiness which *"preceded"* the being of the world and with which its "first" day began. By this precedence this emptiness is already *included* in being, as though anticipating it. What precedes becomes full of the force of being from what follows. This pre-temporal emptiness already is not nothing, just as the succeeding beginning of time is already not a beginning. This beginning cannot in general be separated from the series it begins. In this series, it is already not a beginning, but only a preceding term, a term included in the chain of continuous being. And if we attempt to take one more step, that is, to step *beyond* the beginning, to seek the beginning of the beginning, this attempt will then always encounter the same sort of failure. Out of being it is impossible either logically or ontologically to leap into nonbeing; its sphere is closed. Therefore, an absolute *beginning* is something inconceivable or simply an illusion. The axiom of our contemplation is that, for every given being, one can find or conceive a being preceding it, and therefore it itself cannot be the first, or beginningless, beginning. From this it follows once again that the world does not have a beginning in time, and its origin must be sought only in the fact that it is created supratemporally or, more precisely, from all eternity. In this sense, it is incorrect to think that the world of the "first day of creation" contains *only* light, and that therefore the world in its being "begins" with light, so that the "beginning" of the world is located where there is as yet no light. Light coexists with the works of the other days of creation, although in a certain, ontological, sense it is the first of these works, the *a priori* of creation, as it were. The fullness of creation includes *all* the days of creation together, and each of them equally lacks a beginning except that sole Beginning which is the Divine Sophia for the creaturely Sophia.

The world is created for time, but not in time, and in time the world has neither beginning nor end. But, *as created*, it has a beginning in the *Beginning*. The world is not self-sufficient, for it presupposes God's creative act as the foundation of its being as the creaturely Sophia. This act is supratemporal, for it refers to God's eternity. But temporal being, and time itself, arise precisely by virtue of this act. Insofar as the world is the

---

36. It goes without saying that to understand the expression "in the beginning" as applying to time, as is usually done, is totally inadmissible.

creaturely Sophia, uniting in herself the divine principle of Sophia and creatureliness, it is an essential antinomy. It is eternal-temporal, uncreated-created being, in which God's power pierces the icy emptiness of *nothing*. Just as God Himself has the unity of the images of the Divine and creaturely Sophia in *one* Sophia, so the creaturely world of temporal being has the unity of time and eternity, *becoming eternity*. The latter has neither a temporal beginning nor a temporal end, for eternity is capable of being reflected only in the entire *fullness* of temporality, and not in its separate parts. Therefore, it *requires* endlessness, which has beginninglessness as its counterpart. Beginninglessness not only does not contradict createdness; it corresponds to createdness.[37]

4. The World Soul and Its Hypostases

The world is a creaturely multi-unity, and the world soul is the creaturely Sophia. This must first be understood on the basis of the general definition of creatureliness. In relation to the Divine Sophia, creatureliness is diminution and limitation, kenosis. The world's autonomous being, its creation "out of nothing," is purchased only at the price of such limitation. Creatureliness is the loss of the Divine Sophia's "integrity" through her submergence in the multiplicity, temporality, and relativity of particular being. Because of this, the world's sophianicity loses the clarity and self-evidentness of its manifestation; the chaotic element, raised by cosmic storms, its waves thrashing furiously, is unleashed. This element also manifests itself as the vegetative force that fills the world with an uncountable number of species of the vegetative world, and as the energy that gives birth to an uncountable diversity of animals. The world is a ladder of life with many steps. There is no place for dead matter in the world; only different states of life exist in it. This boundless variety of life does not tear the world apart into disconnected atoms, which pour into the

---

37. One should note that Scripture uses the notion of eternity in relation to temporality (and time) in two senses: first to express the divine ground of creation, the ontological base of temporality, which the latter covers and which is accessible only through it; and, second, to express the infinity of time. These are two *different* aspects, which can be distinguished but should not be confused. For example, the expression "eternal life" should be distinguished from (in fact, is opposite to) the expressions "eternal fire" or "eternal torment." The first aspect corresponds to immobility and depth, the second to becoming, changeability, "bad infinity," that is, to precisely what is not characteristic of eternity. Cf. *The Lamb of God:* "Eternity and Time," pp. 153-56.

abyss of the void, as it were. This void is neutral, neither separating nor connecting. But the *world* exists, as a positive unity to which all these species of being *belong*. It exists as the image of the "integrity" that is being sought and found. This unity is not *only* the sum of separate forms of mundane, creaturely being (although it *is* their sum), and it is not only one of the many particular types of this being. This unity exists above or at the foundation of this form as the unifying force, real center, and plan of the world, as the world's idea and formative energy. And this unifying force, this cosmourgic potency, is nothing else but the creaturely Sophia herself, who is the image of divine being, the force of "integrity." She is, in this sense, the world's soul and entelechy, who is being actualized, or *becoming*, in the world. She is the life of the world.

To correctly understand this doctrine of the creaturely Sophia as the world soul, one must make several distinctions and dispel some common misunderstandings.

We are speaking about the soul of the world, *not* its spirit. The difference between soul and spirit consists in the fact that the soul is *not* hypostatic, whereas the spirit is. Sophia is not a hypostasis; and neither is the world soul. The soul corresponds to the spirit's nature. The soul lives and is hypostatized by the spirit (and, in this sense, the soul is not the spirit's hypostasis but its hypostatizedness, or more precisely, its hypostatizability). In this sense, although the world is not spirit, it is correlative to spirit as its life, as the source and content of this life. In this respect, the world soul is a connected, organic multi-unity. It is not only a content (= multi) but also a connection (= unity). The world soul is the creaturely Sophia.

But can one speak of a "soul" with reference to the divine world, the Divine Sophia, and precisely with reference to the divine life? One cannot speak of it directly, for the soul belongs to the divided multi-unity that has fallen from the state of integrity and that the soul unites. But, in the divine integrity, there is no place for unification, for there is no division. Sophia is the "body of God" in its integrity, as the self-revelation of God and the glory. Therefore, the most that can be said about Sophia is that she is the eternal foundation for the soul of the world, the soul of the soul.[38] But, strictly speaking, the concept of the soul corresponds only to the creaturely Sophia in her relation to the world.

---

38. In the Office of St. Sophia, Wisdom of God, we read in the concluding prayer: "unfathomable and all-praised Wisdom of God, illustrious Sophia . . . *the soul of virgins*. . . ." There is added a logological interpretation of Sophia in the *given* context: "that is to say, the only begotten son, the Word of God."

The world soul is not only a unifying, "logical" principle, in which all the forms of creaturely being acquire their meaning, connectedness, and cosubordination, their proper place on the ontological (and, in this case, also logical) ladder of being. It is also the life-giving principle. It is life given by the Giver of Life, the Holy Spirit. This significance of the world soul is noted in the Old Testament interpretation of blood, about which it is said that it is the soul of animals, not excluding man. "For the soul of every body is its blood" (Lev. 17:14).[39] From this comes the Old Testament symbolism of sacrificial blood and the whole meaning of the New Testament Blood, which poured into the world, giving life to it, as its new soul, its "New Testament" soul.[40]

But blood belongs only to the living, animate, or rather, animal world, including man. In what sense is blood the seat of the world soul? Clearly, the principle of "blood" must be understood in a broader sense than only the blood of animals. The fact that the whole world, without exception, is animated by the world soul signifies that it participates in *life*. "God did not create death" (Wisdom 1:13); therefore, He did not create anything dead. What we consider dead, or rather nonorganic, contains the principle of life, even if only at its lowest levels, in its dark state. This idea can be understood in a twofold sense. First, it signifies that in all the stages of being there is a living principle. To capture this principle is the task of both natural science and "occult" knowledge (the power to know the language of this "flame of things" is given not only to poets but also to various kinds of occultism, irrespective of their religious or even antireligious coefficient).[41] Second, all creaturely matter is capable of being quickened and of participating in life through living beings: the angels, who have knowledge of the elements, man, and even animals. The boundary between the living and the dead in nature is mobile. Nature is constantly being quickened, humanized by man, becoming the periphery of his body.[42]

The conclusion follows that the world soul lives and unifies the entire world without any exception. It is the world's inner entelechy.

39. This is a literal translation from the Russian Bible. — Trans.

40. See my articles "The Eucharistic Dogma" and "The Holy Grail."

41. The Church boldly and openly confesses this thought *not* only in its symbology of things (colors, metals, materials, etc.) but also in the direct summons to all the elements of the world to glorify and praise the Lord. Would it be appropriate to address such a summons to *dead* nature, and is such a phraseology suitable if it is devoid of direct meaning?

42. See my book *The Philosophy of Economy.*

Nevertheless, it would be dangerous to limit our knowledge of the creaturely world to its *soul* alone, to the creaturely Sophia, which is the creaturely image of the Divine Sophia. The creaturely Sophia is becoming the image and likeness of the Divine Sophia. (Image and likeness in this case precisely correspond to the idea of entelechy: The image is the foundation and the given, as the ideal, uncreated image of creation in Sophia. The likeness is the becoming of this image, through which the image is realized in the creaturely world, ascending from potentiality to actuality.) However, this significance of the creaturely Sophia as the world soul kenotically diminishes her with respect to her prototype in the Divine Sophia, not only because of the creatureliness that throws her into the state of becoming, but especially because she falls out of the fullness of hypostatic life in which the Divine Sophia lives in the Holy Trinity. The creaturely Sophia as the world soul is extrahypostatic or nonhypostatic. She loses the place in the fullness of the life of the spirit that belongs to her as nature, as predicate in relation to subject. She is subjectless, does not belong to anyone, is without master, as it were. As such, she is deprived of the fullness of creaturely being that is postulated by her as the soul of the creaturely world and consists in hypostatizedness. Introduced into extra-divine being through the creation of the world "out of nothing," the creaturely Sophia is thus taken out of divine hypostatizedness. This necessarily leads one to ask whether the creaturely Sophia remains in this extra-hypostatic, impersonal being, or whether she is hypostatized, but in an extradivine manner, whereby she receives her own creaturely hypostases, which would correspond to her creaturely image.

It is clear that this is postulated by the fullness of the image and likeness of God, which belong to creation not only in its natural being but also in its hypostatization *in the image and likeness of God,* which is mentioned in the Genesis account of the creation of man. Image and likeness in creation necessarily include in their fullness not only sophianic nature but also hypostasis as the subject of the latter; and in the creation of the world, the creaturely Sophia receives her own hypostatization from God. In this sense, she belongs to herself; by her multihypostatic person she faces the divine Trihypostatic Person. How can one understand her multihypostatic person in relation to her nature?

The question consists in this: Along with creaturely nature which, as the creaturely Sophia, is created by God out of or upon the foundation of the Divine Sophia, the hypostatization of this creaturely-sophianic world is not yet given by its sophianicity itself as such. The creaturely world is hypostatized by an act other than its creation. This act unites hypostasis to nonhypostatic being and makes the latter hypostatic. As for creaturely being in itself, its ability to become hypostatized comes from its character as the creaturely Sophia. The Divine Sophia is hypostatized from all eternity by the Holy Trinity in its hypostases. Hypostatic being is an attribute of the Divine Sophia; she presupposes it in herself. But having been taken out of the Holy Trinity and having lost the hypostatization that she had in the Holy Trinity, how can she regain or in some sense restore this hypostatization? The creation of a hypostasis or hypostases, as such, is not yet included in the creation of the natural world. The creation of hypostases is therefore a special, additional or parallel act, alongside the creation of the world. Revelation gives us a direct indication of this duality or parallelism in the Genesis reference to the council held within the Holy Trinity concerning the creation of man "in our image, after our likeness" (Gen. 1:26), in contradistinction or in addition to the general creation that took place over the Six Days or just on the Sixth Day, which includes the creation of man. There is a further indication in the story of Genesis 2:7: "the Lord God formed man of the dust of the ground, and breathed into his face the breath of life, and man became a living soul." Both of these passages of Genesis are full of profound meaning, which it is our task to show.[43]

There is a radical difference between the creation of the world as *nature* for the human spirit in its sophianicity and this hypostatic spirit itself. This difference is expressed, first of all, in the fact that the spirit cannot be created like nature, impersonally, by the direct command or self-determination of God in Sophia: "God said: Let there be such and such," with all these separate creative acts being united in a single accomplishment: let the Divine Sophia be creaturely, and let the creaturely world be grounded in the divine world. Personal being — the human spirit and (what in this case is the same thing) the angelic spirit — is not created in *this* way. In her pleroma, in the infinite multiplicity of the rays of her spectrum, the Divine Sophia contains possibilities or themes for *individualities* that are different but nevertheless capable of being encompassed in the same world. However, such an *individuality* is not yet personality, but only its "substrate" or possibility. One can say that the individuality in a living being is the body-animating *soul* as a special form of creaturely life. Amoebas, and even plants, have individuality. The entire

43. There is no narrative of the creation of the angelic spirits in the Bible. There is but mention of the mere fact of their creation. So, we must have recourse to our own human speculations, relying on an assumed analogy between angels and human beings.

animal world has individuality, not only its species but also in its particular specimens. The highest degree of individuality and complexity is attained by man, in his psychic being. This is what the apostle Paul means
by "natural man." Even though man stands at the top of the organic ladder, he shares individual being with all its steps. And the foundation for
this individuation — not only in the negative sense *(omnis definitio est
negatio)* but also in the positive sense — consists in a specific theme, a
special color, sound, or word: an idea in creation as it is given from all
eternity in Sophia.

In this sense, individuality is sophianic, and therefore it is not person, personality, or personal spirit, insofar as Sophia herself is not a
hypostasis, but a hypostatizedness, though she is eternally hypostatized
by the divine hypostases. She cannot communicate to creation what is not
proper to her. Natural individuality is given by nature, but the creaturely
Sophia herself must yet be hypostatized. This hypostatization can only be
accomplished by a personal act, by a revelation of the divine Person, the
Holy Trinity, in the creaturely Sophia, in the world. The creation of the
world therefore consists of two acts and necessarily has two sides: the creation of creaturely nature as the creaturely Sophia and the creation of
new, creaturely persons, capable of hypostatizing this nature, of being the
subjects of the creaturely Sophia. This act of creation of personal spirits
refers not to Sophia but to the very Person of God. And if the world is created "out of nothing," that is, "out of" the Divine Sophia through her reception of becoming, then the creaturely hypostases, the spirits that
hypostatize the world, are directly created by God out of Himself: Out of
Himself God "breathed" a living soul, created man "in His image," gave
him a hypostasis. The force of this figure should not be diminished by re-
interpretations; it directly contains the idea that the human spirit, personality, has not a creaturely but a *divine* origin, even though it is created,
that is, even though it is determined to being for creatures or in connection with the creation of the world.

This contrasts with natural creaturely being, which also has something divine, insofar as it is the creaturely Sophia, and divine powers act in
it. In a certain sense, the creaturely Sophia does *not* repeat the Divine
Sophia but is the combination of creative variations on the theme of the
Divine Sophia. However, the Divine Sophia is the creaturely Sophia's
entelechy and inwardly determines her; and by reason of this sophianicity
of hers, she *is* Sophia, even if in a pale translation into the language of
creatureliness. Although personality (the personal spirit) lives in the
creaturely Sophia and has her as its own "nature" or the world, it does *not*

itself belong to Sophia, but is given to her as her subject. This constitutes the positive difference between the Divine Sophia and the creaturely Sophia. The former is hypostatized by the Divine Person, belongs to God, whereas the latter is entrusted to creaturely, human persons (as well as angelic ones), is independently hypostatized by them. The place of the Divine Person in the creaturely Sophia is allotted to man, and this hypostatization of hers fully constitutes the definitive creation of the world, the world's autonomous being and belonging to itself. The creaturely Sophia, who is only a hypostatizedness, not a hypostasis, is hypostatized just like the Divine Sophia. The creaturely Sophia, though, is hypostatized by the human person, whereas the Divine Sophia is hypostatized by the Divine Person from all eternity. In *this* sense, the creaturely world is a cosmo-anthropic world, or man is a microcosm. The humanness of the world is revelation's fundamental and generalizing truth about creation. Man was created on the "last day," "after" the rest of creation, which was therefore assumed to exist already and to include him in order that he possess the "earth" and "have dominion" over creation. And he received from God "the image of God," that is, a hypostatic spirit, which possesses its own nature and fullness of life in this image. Or, as man is usually called in the language of patristics, he is a "creaturely god."

Thus, having the creaturely Sophia as his nature, as the source and foundation of his life, the creaturely god, man, received also his own personal spirit. Now the question arises: Can a personal spirit, to whom self-positing is proper (I am I or, simply, I am in my self-belonging), be created? Can *I*, a subject, be *not-I*, an object, even if only for the Creator Himself? Insofar as *I*'s very being, its life in its nature, is connected with creation, the stamp of creatureliness lies even upon *I*'s very origination, if in fact it has originated. But it has originated. To be sure, this origination occurs *not* in time, for *I* itself looks down from its height at time, is for time an immobile sun, illuminating its movement. However, the creaturely *I* exists *for* and *in* time, is connected with *temporality*. But, despite this, it is free of the discursiveness of time, composed of a series of separate moments or determinations, and is not at all exhausted by them. The creaturely *I* is never free of time but always belongs to it, is correlative to time, directs its light projector at time.

The creaturely *I* is qualified by *temporality*, as a potency of time. This supratemporal-temporal character of *I* constitutes's *I*'s antinomy, which discloses, with reference to temporality, the general antinomy of the uncreatedness/createdness of the human *I*. (The same antinomism can also be noted in the relation of the creaturely *I* to spatiality: Although personal self-consciousness, or the creaturely spirit, is not connected with place, is not found in space, yet it looks at space and surveys it, as if encompassing it in itself. Personal self-consciousness is present in the spatiality that is proper to creaturely being.)

In the fullness of the divine image given to man, his nature, that is, the world as belonging to man, is sophianic, and this sophianicity of the world in man belongs, of course, to the fullness of the divine image. However, the human personality itself, *I,* is *not* sophianic, but is added to sophianicity, is implanted in sophianicity, as its subject, or hypostasis. The human personality is in conformity with the divine Personality and is its image. God repeated Himself in the human personality, and, as it were, was reflected in the latter. And the reflected image received life and being, became a person. This is the limiting formula for the expression of God's creative act in relation to the human person. God reflected Himself in His images; He repeated and multiplied Himself in them. The creaturely image is not a mere reflection that does not have its own being. It *does* have its own being; it is also a person.

This self-positing of God in His living images is unfathomable for creatures, as is the creation of the world in Sophia. Here, we once again have a limiting concept for our thought, which gropes along in half-darkness, feeling for its own roots, sunk simultaneously in divinity and in nothing. The antinomy that arises as a result of this groping cedes its place either to the Luciferian *Ich-Philosophie,* for which the human I is as divine as God's, or alone is divine, uniquely divine, absolute in its autonomous being and self-sufficiency, or to nihilism, which takes our personal self-consciousness to be a reflex (of what and how?) or an illusion, in general, a function corresponding to nonpersonal, natural, even material being. It is not noticed here that between personal and nonpersonal being, between I and not-I (more precisely, extra-I), lies an abyss that is wholly insuperable for thought. Nothing can explain the appearance of I in not-I, just as nothing can explain the sinking and disappearance of I in not-I. Although, empirically, I's being is connected with temporality, and the sun of I appears both to rise from and to set in nonbeing beyond the horizon, yet I's own self-consciousness, its quality of I as such, does not know anything about this appearance and disappearance. I is conscious of itself as supratemporally existing, as rising in this fixed I-ness as if in eternity and not containing any destiny of time. Therefore, toward the fact, empirically known by it, of its pre-being or nonbeing, with interruptions in time, our I's attitude is inwardly invincible *bewilderment* or questioning. It knows about this outwardly and admits it in some way, but does not assimilate or postulate it. This is a manifestation of the contra-dictoriness and limitedness of our being in this aeon, which can be defeated and removed only in the future aeon of immortality. Only immortality will remove the very possibility of I's "disappearances," whether in death or before birth. Only immortality will definitively reveal I's supratemporal nature.

Thus, the creation of the human (and likewise angelic) spirit or person belongs to the "council of the Holy Trinity." It belongs to the Divine Subject — not, of course, in separation from his nature or the Divine Wisdom, in this sense not antisophianically or asophianically, but on the basis of a supra-eternal unity with the Divine Wisdom. But this takes place face to face, with a concentration on the personal principle. God the Creator must be understood here not only as the Creator of the world in Sophia, but also as the Creator of His own living images, persons, according to His image in its trihypostatic character. In the creation of the world, God repeats His own being in Sophia, as it were. He repeats His nature, the Divine Sophia, in the creaturely Sophia, or in the world. In the creation of persons, of hypostatic spirits, human and angelic, God repeats Himself, as it were, creates *co-I's* for Himself in his hypostatic image, breathing into them the breath of His own divine life. He creates co-gods for Himself, "gods by grace." This creation is transcendent and unfathomable for the human understanding inasmuch as it takes place beyond our being, and our very being is conditioned by God's creative act. But our thought is capable of encompassing the idea of the *living participation* of the creaturely I in the divine spirit, a kind of commonality of life that is accessible, if only to an infinitesimal degree, to creatures. The roots of a person's being are submerged in the bottomless ocean of divine life and get their nourishment from this life. Here, these roots are the infinitely small in the infinitely great. They are like the reflection of the rays of the great divine light. This relationship can still be encompassed by creaturely thought, which is simultaneously conscious of both the limitedness and the boundlessness of the creaturely spirit.

But what creaturely thought cannot encompass, what transcends it, is the *origin* of the creaturely I, insofar as the latter has an origin at all. However, can the creaturely I really have an origin, or is it the case that our I, bearing the stamp of eternity, does not have an origin at all? In fact, the creaturely I is conscious of itself as not having been originated and as not being originated, but as self-positing and self-sufficient. This testimony of I, its self-witness, cannot be doubted or invalidated, because it is the basis of all self-evidence. This basis does not have a higher court above it, and in this sense it is unassailable by criticism. *I am* also means *I exists;* this is a closed circle of the self-positing: *I am existent.*[44]

In this sense, I is its own self-lighted sun, a being that is illuminated with its own light, the subject of all possible predicates, connected with them by a copula.[45] But this self-positing, this I-ness, encounters a boundary in *not-I,* in the nontransparence and, in this sense, the givenness of the latter. I is an addition to *not-I,* as it were. *Not-I* determines I by entering into I's I-ness and thus exposing I's limitedness. Thus, in itself, I bears witness both to its self-positing, to its non-origination, to its being from itself, and to its origination, its createdness. I is internally contradictory, and this is not a logical but an ontological contradiction, an antinomy. Both terms of the antinomy must be taken into account in the doctrine of I. Even if I is created, that is, originated *not* from itself, but from somewhere outside, it could not have been created like a thing, without being asked, so to speak. Rather, it must have been drawn to its own creation, through self-positing. I must have been asked to agree to its own being. But, together with this, I must have been created by God's omnipotence.

Our reason cannot admit a *both-and* here. It can admit only an *either/or,* for the one appears to exclude the other. But we must take as our guide not this testimony of discursive thought, which does not tolerate contradictions and is afraid of antinomies, but precisely this self-witness of our consciousness. And our consciousness proclaims with certainty that, in the creation of I, I itself was *asked* to agree to be, and this agreement was I's self-positing, which resounds in I supratemporally, as the witness of its own belonging to itself. From the emptiness of *nothing* there resounds this *yes of the creature* that is asked whether it consents to exist. In this sense, *nothing* truly turns out to be the receptacle of creaturely freedom, even if in a negative sense. One must conclude that, if this *yes* were absent, creation too would not exist, and this failed creation, the *ouk on* not becoming the *me on,* would sink into the emptiness of *nothing,* would abide in nonbeing, for all positive being originates from its proto-source, the Creator. Nothing gives its "answering" *yes* by the power and energy of the divine act of creation.

---

44. Descartes' *cogito ergo sum* (more precisely, "I am thinking") is based on a proposition that is tautological in content but ontological in essence: *I am I,* or *I am,* or *I is, exists.* This ontological openness of *I* for *is* already implies the possibility of all and any predicative being for *I: I* is A, B, and so on. But, in the fact of its existence, *I* is self-evident.

45. See my manuscript work on names, the chapter on personal pronouns. [This work was published posthumously as *The Philosophy of the Name,* Paris, 1953. — Trans.]

But there is the positive act of the creation of the human (and angelic) hypostases, of the communication of the power of being to them: "God created man in his own image, in the image of God created he him" (Gen. 1:27). And this verse is preceded by another verse about the same thing: "And God said, Let us make man in our image, after our likeness" (1:26). Here, the plural *includes the multihypostatic character* of man, represents him as a tribe, a race, a family, a multi-unity bound by love, in the image of the Holy Trinity. This "our" also indicates the real *conformity* of the creaturely I to the divine hypostases. Adam became "as one of us, to know good and evil" (3:22) not only in his fall. He was created "as one of us," as a hypostatic image of God, as a *co-I* of the Holy Trinity, as the creaturely — and in this sense the "fourth" — multihypostatic human hypostasis, which is called to have and is capable of having a *personal* relationship with God. Genesis 1:27 says: "God created man in his own image, in the image of God created he him; male and female created he them." Insofar as the image of God necessarily refers also to the creaturely hypostases, it is realized hypostatically not in *one* but in two (and more) persons, in male and female. More precisely, we have here, first of all, a *hypostasis* in general, a personal I, without distinction as to whether this pure I-ness is given to male or female. As I, the divine hypostases are not distinguished among themselves and equally enter into the triunity of the trine *I*. But, not being distinguished in their common I-ness, the hypostases have personal features *(gnōrismata hupostatika)*. The First, Second, and Third Hypostases are the Father, the Son, and the Holy Spirit, respectively. However, in the complete human image we have only two hypostases that have personal features: male and female.

Thus, first of all, why are there two, not three, who, in their combination, compose man: "God created man in his own image"? Is it not because the hypostasis of the Father remains transcendent to creation, although this hypostasis is the Creator *par excellence*?[46] Is it not perhaps precisely by virtue of this, since creation is accomplished by the Father through the sophianic self-revelation of the hypostases of the Son and the Holy Spirit? The Father reveals Himself both in the Divine Sophia and in the creaturely Sophia, in creation, through the Second and Third Hypostases, the *two* revealing hypostases. But does this not correspond, in the manifestion of man as one humankind, to the fact that he has not

---

46. See the chapters about the Father and about creation in *The Comforter*, as well as the corresponding chapter in *The Lamb of God.*

three but two images ("male and female created he them")? These two images therefore correspond to the Second and Third Hypostases.

But, here, we encounter a new difficulty: In both Scripture and the patristic literature the Logos is usually considered as the heavenly man, who as the new Adam gives his image to the earthly man. Thus, the old Adam bears in himself the image of the new Adam, though distorted by sin. This explains the humanization of the Logos, the Second Hypostasis. But revelation forces us to unite to this proto-image of the human image of God also the female, Eve, evidently in the image of the Third Hypostasis, who, although He Himself is not humanized, descends into the world upon man. This Hypostasis descends upon the Ever-Virgin, who is in fact called the second Eve by analogy with the second Adam. Thus, humankind is hypostatized not by one and not by three but by two hypostases, which are in the appropriate relationship to each other — both in eternal proto-images in the Holy Trinity and in creaturely images in man. In the Holy Trinity, the hypostasis of the Word reveals the Father, while the hypostasis of the Holy Spirit accomplishes this revelation, manifesting His beauty or glory. In this sense, the revelation of the Third Hypostasis "depends" on the Second, follows the Second, does not precede it (in the ontological sequence).

Conversely, the revelation of the Second Hypostasis "depends" on the Third, for without the Third the Second does not have power and life. This analogy holds also with reference to the male and female hypostases, of which the male has primacy, both in the order of creation, and in being the chief: the woman is "taken out of Man" (Gen. 2:23), but the man (the male) "shall cleave unto his wife" (2:24) so that together "they shall be one flesh" (2:24), that is, one humankind.[47] Given birth in the fulfillment of God's commandment of multiplication, children of the male and female sexes reproduce only the male and female structure of the spirit and do not introduce anything new in the original typical dual-unity of man.

Thus, we are led to conclude that the male hypostasis exists in the image of the hypostasis of the Logos, while the female hypostasis exists in

---

47. As we, in fact, read in the Apostle: "the head of every man is Christ; and the head of the woman is the man; and the head of Christ is God.... [A] man ... is the image and glory of God: but the woman is the glory of the man. For the man is not of the woman; but the woman of the man. Neither was the man created for the woman; but the woman for the man.... Nevertheless neither is the man without the woman, neither the woman without the man, in the Lord. For as the woman is of man, even so is the man also by the woman; but all things of God" (1 Cor. 11:3, 7-9, 11-12).

the image of the hypostasis of the Holy Spirit. By no means is the inverse conclusion valid, the conclusion that the Logos and the Holy Spirit respectively are the male and female hypostases in divinity itself. We have no grounds and no need for such a conclusion: it would be an unnecessary anthropomorphism. The only thing we can say is that, in translation into the language of creation or with reference to man, the qualities of the Second and Third Hypostases correspond to, are analogous to, are parallel to (but by no means identical to) the male and female principles in it. This corresponds to the fundamental fact that the Son of God was humanized into the male nature, while the hypostatic descent of the Holy Spirit took place into the female nature of the Most Holy Mother of God.

Thus, the two hypostases that reveal God the Father in the Divine Sophia, the sophianic hypostases, are proto-images of the creaturely human hypostases. The hypostasis of the Logos is multiplied in the male hypostases; it is their multi-unity or center, as it were. The hypostasis of the Holy Spirit is multiplied in the female hypostases and forms their multi-unity or center. Each of the creaturely hypostases has a supra-eternal proto-image in the Second and Third Hypostases, respectively. How can one better understand this correlation, this reflection of the proto-images in the images?

The following consideration can help us here. Every creaturely hypostasis is not only a person, a personal center, *I*, but also an individuality. In other words, every creaturely hypostasis has its own special qualitative character or qualifiedness. Personality and individuality are connected but not identical. The difference consists, first of all, in the fact that a person is in a certain sense an absolute subject, which is not limited by anything in its subjectivity, in its ability to hypostatize all manner of content into its personal life (or I-ness). This Godlikeness of the personal self-consciousness can be taken so far as to reject the very difference between image and Proto-image, divine and creaturely I-ness. God says His **I**, addressing man (and angel) as *I* (or, what in this case is the same thing, as *thou*), and man, on his part, also addresses God. Imperceptible in this address is the difference between the I of the Proto-image and that of the creature, between the Heavenly Sun and its reflection in the image. Only in its creaturely origination and dependence does the creaturely I differ from its Creator.

But the whole difference between the divine and the creaturely I appears in connection with their qualifiedness. This difference can be expressed in the following way: The divine I is *not* individual; it is universal; it is qualityless, for it is omni-qualitative; it is not qualified in any way, for it qualifies everything. It is simple, so that for creatures this simplicity can be expressed only apophatically, though not in a negative but in a positive sense: White light is not a color, but is the foundation of all colors, and in this sense it is not the negation of coloredness. On the contrary, every color is not only a certain positive determination, but also a negative, limiting determination. The color red is not only red; it is also not green, not gray, and so on. Some of these colors coexist with red as complementary to it, while others are wholly alien to red. In a word, *omnis definitio est negatio.* Apart from becoming, creaturely multiplicity is characterized by partiality, fragmentedness, outwardly manifested diversity. It has its inner foundation in multi-unity, although it exists, first of all, as a multiplicity of individually qualified being. This individuality of personal being is not its supreme and definitive determination. On the contrary, this being is subordinate to the power of integrity, of unity in the whole, where one's soul must be "lost" before it can be saved, where the corn of wheat must die before it can bring forth fruit. This being becomes fully itself when it *loses* its individuality. This individual, qualified ray, which hitherto has shined only in its own color, now begins to shine with the light of the pleroma and participates in the wholeness in which God is all in all.

However, the creaturely hypostasis receives its original being only on the basis of its proper personal qualifiedness, on the basis of a definite personal character. This hypostatic qualifiedness, as the theme of personal being, *belongs* to the fullness of the all-hypostatic hypostatizedness, the divine pleroma; it is given and proposed as a task by the latter. In this sense, even the proper *I* of the creature does not belong to the creature, is not the creature's self-creation in "freedom" as something new in God and for God. However, at the same time, this principle of qualified personal being is assimilated by the person itself, is the work of the person's hypostatic self-positing.

We approach here what is most mysterious in the act of God's creation of the person (human or angelic). God eternally is and, in this sense, has Himself in the Holy Trinity: three hypostases from all eternity exhaustively realize the divine hypostatic triunity. There are three hypostases, not more and not less. The sacred number three expresses the fullness of the hypostatic principle in God. In this sense (but only and precisely only in this sense) these three hypostases in God *necessarily* belong to the proper divine being. Any "fourth," creaturely hypostasis is *un*necessary, redundant. It would be a self-repetition of God, which in no wise can be said about the hypostases of the Trinity. But God possesses the creative power to repeat Himself hypostatically, to extend the domain of hypostatic being beyond trinity, to reflect himself in a fourth hypostasis or in the "fourth" creaturely hypostases, created and in this sense non-divine. The hypostatic divine love, in which the divine hypostases sacrificially deplete themselves, in their triunity realizing themselves in the suprapersonally personal life of the Holy Trinity,[48] is *not* limited by this absolute act of trinitarian self-positing. This love is capable of transcending itself, its proper limits, into the emptiness of the creaturely *nothing*, also into its hypostatic life. This love is capable, so to speak, of loving nothing, as the "place" of the creation of the creaturely hypostases, by a creatively ecstatic love, and of hypostatically multiplying. The words of God addressed to man during creation, "be fruitful and multiply" (Gen. 1:28), have, in relation to other creatures, the force of command and blessing of the omnipotence (see 1:22). But, with reference to man as the image of God, they express not only a blessing command addressed to man, but also God's own action and self-determination, the progression of the Holy Trinity itself into the domain of the creaturely-hypostatic being of the "fourth," creaturely hypostases.

This wholly special divine activity in the creation of the creaturely hypostasis is expressed in the language of the second chapter of Genesis as follows: God "breathed into his nostrils the breath of life" (2:7). This "breathed" symbolizes an act — inexpressible in human language — of God's ecstatic love, which transcends its own limits to call creation to personal being. God bends down, as it were, over the abyss of nothing and, reflecting in this abyss His hypostatic all-person, calls creaturely hypostatic persons to being. And these reflections are filled with life and light up with inner light. And, in answer to God's call to being, they respond by the many-voiced choir of the multihypostatic angelic-human *I*: Out of the abyss of nothingness creaturely I's call out to the Creator by their own I's to the divine Thou, which answers them as the divine I. The dialogue of the Creator with hypostatic creation begins. "Out of the depths [of nonbeing] have I cried unto thee, O Lord. Lord, hear my voice" (Ps. 130:1-2).

We have already pointed out above[49] that the creation of *personal* being necessarily differs from the creation of natural being, for natural being is created on the basis of the Divine Sophia, whereas the image of the divine hypostasis is created in personal being. The creation of the person necessarily includes not only the divine call to being (more precisely, the

48. See the "Chapters on Trinity."
49. Also see *The Burning Bush* and *The Lamb of God*.

93

divine positing of hypostatic being beyond divinity as an act of God's creativity) but also the answering (or "simultaneous") self-positing of the creaturely hypostasis, or I's consent to its positing by God. For I's creation is precisely this call to self-positing, which is I's very life. God's creative act, calling the creaturely I to being, is included, is actualized, in I's proper self-positing, because it can have no other mode of actualization. I is precisely the self-positing I. I's being is its self-positing, which is the work of freedom, and cannot be accomplished by coercion, even if on the part of God's omnipotence. In *this* sense, I's creation is also a *self-creation.* Man coparticipates with God in his own creation or, more precisely, God includes this creation in His own act.

This mystery of the image of God in the human hypostasis is not subject to further comprehension. It is a limit to our self-consciousness and self-knowledge. It is necessary here to exclude the possible temptation of human self-deification, the deification of emptiness or *nothing* as freedom. The self-positing of the creaturely I, which we analytically isolate as a special act or moment of creation, acquires force only in God, in the act of His hypostatic self-revelation, the positing of His image outside Himself, in the creation of the hypostases. But the limits to God's creative act must be extended to such an extent that, in the content of this act, in its "how," there could be included not only passive createdness, obedient to the creative *let there be,* but also the creature's own answer, the creature's active acceptance of this *let there be.* This is the special extravagance of God's love, which transmits its own creative will to the created creation, asking the latter about its will to self-creation, and includes creation's *yes,* its creative self-positing, in its own creative act. God *creates* man through man himself, but here the Creator is nevertheless God and not man, and therefore there are no grounds to speak of proper human self-creation.

But at the same time, God, creating in His own image a hypostatic being to whom the gift of freedom is given, includes this freedom in the very creation of this being. What is free is created in freedom; it is a thing at no instant of its existence. Freedom arises freely and out of freedom. If the creaturely understanding cannot fathom the mode of this free creation, and it seems to us a *contradictio in adjecto,* then not less contradictory must seem the appearance of freedom *after* creation in its creaturely bearer. How can freedom *begin,* and can it begin? Can an object to which thingness is proper acquire freedom, and is this more understandable than the idea that it is originally created in freedom? No! Freedom does not arise and does not begin. It is beginningless and genuinely bears the image of God's beginninglessness: creaturely freedom is in the image of divine freedom. This means that creaturely freedom is *not* created but is included in God's creative act itself. In other words, creaturely freedom is not an object of creation, but creation itself, a divine-human creative act. Creaturely freedom radiates from the eternal light of God's freedom, and in this sense it is supramundane or supracreaturely. Thus, in man as a hypostatic spirit (as well as in angels) we have the case of yet one more ontological antinomy: that of creatureliness-noncreatureliness, eternity-temporality, which protects the garden of God's creation.

But freedom in man's creation is not limited to the hypostatizedness, the self-positing of I together with the creative act of I's creation by God. It is not limited to I-ness. In the Holy Trinity, the hypostases are equi-hypostatic I's, personal centers of divine self-consciousness. At the same time, they are qualified by hypostatic attributes and in this sense are different, so that I-ness and hypostatic qualifiedness form a hypostasis only when combined. There is a similar relation in the creaturely hypostatic images, in human hypostases. They too have equal I-ness, but they also are different, for they are individually qualified.

What is this individual qualifiedness and to what does it refer? In the first place, as we already know, two types of persons, which together express the image of God in man, are fundamentally separate: male and female ("male and female created he them" [Gen. 1:27]), who are created in the image of the hypostases of the Son and the Holy Spirit. We can recognize this distinction, even if we cannot express it clearly in word and thought. Although the male and female principles are equally personal and, in this sense, both equally form an I, the timbre of the male I is different from that of the female I. This is a self-evident fact. Neither the male nor the female I comprises any composition of the two elements. Male and female I's are equally immediate and simple; they are not a composition, mixture, or addition. Each is a simple ray, though the two rays are different.

But by virtue of this simplicity and immediacy of self-positing, I necessarily includes its male or female qualification, which is further expressed in all of life, in the entire spiritual image of one I or another. The self-positing of the creaturely I already has a male or female voice. There are only two possibilities of I in God's creative act, in which I is created in the image of God, male and female. And if we recognize as certain the fact that the creaturely I participates in its own creation through self-positing, we must necessarily admit a definite qualifiedness in this self-positing. God creates not an abstract I in general but a concrete — male or female — I, and this creative call from above receives a creaturely answer from below, so to speak, from within creation, from creation's determinate image.

But this does not exhaust the concrete qualifiedness of the creaturely I, for the latter, besides the quality of the male or female principle, is also characterized by individuality, according to the general order of the male or female gender. The individuality proper to creatureliness, in contradistinction to the divine supra-individuality or all-individuality, is determined not only positively, by the presence of one feature or another, but also negatively, by the absence of all the other possible features, i.e., by limitation. As an individual, every person is a definite ray in a rainbow, occupying its place in the whole, calling one thing to itself, while repulsing another. Every person has his own theme of being which does not repeat other themes, although it is consonant with them. This theme is God's thought about creation, about its place in the sophianic pleroma. All of these themes, whose possibility is implanted in the "integrity" of the Divine Sophia, become "substrates," or hypostases, in personal being. And there cannot be a hypostasis without a specific theme, or an empty I, so to speak, an I that does not have its own individually colored nature.

Thus, we must come to the conclusion that the creation of a person includes not only I-ness as such, and not only its male or female qualifiedness, but also its specific, individual *theme,* which both distinguishes the person from the whole and unites the person with the whole. This theme is *given* by God, enters into His creative act. But with reference to this theme we must extend the postulate of creative freedom as self-positing. In this case, this freedom is expressed in the mode of the personal *acceptance* of one's own theme in one's own self-positing, in the personal adoption of this theme by a free, self-creative act. Being free, this acceptance, or adoption, can have different degrees of fullness, this difference not having any other cause than self-positing. For *liberum arbitrium,* freedom, is uncaused. Thanks to the presence of freedom, God's creative acts relative to personal creaturely beings, unified in divine fullness and perfection, nevertheless differ in their acceptance through the creaturely freedom of self-positing. These acts can differ in character, so to speak, causing the creaturely hypostases to be not only empirically but also metaphysically different.[50]

---

50. This primordial difference, which precedes and determines empirical being, is spoken of in Rom. 9:10-13: "when Rebecca also had conceived by one, even by our father Isaac (for the children being not yet born, neither having done any good or evil . . .), it was said unto her, The elder shall serve the younger [Gen. 25:23]. As it is written, Jacob have I loved, but Esau have I hated" [Mal. 1:2-3].

Freedom accompanies them from their very appearance in being, and they enter being *differently,* in a state of greater or lesser conformity to their proper theme or even in a certain resistance to this theme. However, this does not change the theme of being, which remains the same even when it is distorted. What is essential here is that although this is not a temporal and historical act but a supratemporal and supra-empirical one, it nevertheless constitutes the premise, the basis, of all our being. History is the manifestation of ontology. It presupposes and is coordinated with ontology. Here there can arise the problem of the relation of this "intelligible," ontological character to that empirical character in which the former is freely manifested. In Schopenhauer's opinion, freedom is entirely exhausted by this ontological character, for it does not undergo change but is only manifested in the empirical world. However, this opinion lacks sufficient grounds, and it cannot be confirmed empirically. Free self-positing, as an intelligible character, is determined *for* time and, although it is extra-temporal or supratemporal, it is *not above* time. A human person is one and lives in time, in which he becomes himself. This becoming embraces both the meta-empirical world and the empirical world. The free self-positing that is accomplished in the meta-empirical world is developed in empirical causality. Therefore, there is an interaction here, an osmosis, not a mere coexistence of two planes of being. (The problem of evil and original sin must be understood in connection with this, about which below.)

Thus, the image of God in human hypostases is determined by the divine hypostases of the Logos and the Holy Spirit, which hypostatize the pleroma, the Divine Sophia, from which the creaturely Sophia also acquires her image. These two hypostases differ, as hypostatic centers, in their *how*, but not in their *what*; and in this sophianicity of theirs, in the pleroma, both hypostases contain all of their creaturely images. They are *all-hypostases,* or more precisely, the one proto-image of any hypostatizedness, which in itself is thereby transparent for the Logos and the Holy Spirit. This proto-image is precisely the one true hypostasis. All humankind in the male image is the one hypostasis of Christ, is Christ; it finds its hypostases in Christ's hypostasis, reflects and is reflected in His hypostasis. All humankind in the female image is the hypostasis of the Holy Spirit, which is revealed, becomes transparent, in the image of the Mother of God and, in *this* sense, is manifested in Her hypostasis. These two images of human all-hypostatizedness are united in one creaturely Divine-humanity, just as in the heavens, in the Holy Trinity, they are united in one Heavenly Divine-humanity. Insofar as a man "loses his soul for my sake," he becomes Christ, is united with Him. Also, he who does the will of the Father in heaven "is [his] Mother and [his] brothers."

The law of the identification of different things, which is love, operates here. When love is extinguished, the personality is asserted in Luciferian manner by its opposition and resistance to the Proto-image. The little I, the creature, enclosing itself in the icy emptiness of imaginary grandeur, wants to be a big I that is equal to or even greater than God. But the actual reality and content of the little I are nevertheless determined by the fact that it is only an image of the Proto-image, its reflection, a reflection with a minus sign attached to it, so to speak. However, this connection and dependence remain known to this self-consciousness, which is thereby doomed to all-devouring envy. The hypostatic fall, characteristic of Lucifer and his host, is therefore hypostatic envy, envy directed at its own Proto-image; Lucifer is, in this sense, the proto-antichrist.

The question arises: How can one reconcile this dual-unity of the human hypostasis in Christ and the Mother of God, or the Logos and the Holy Spirit, with the Scripture's testimony that in Jesus Christ "there is neither male nor female" (Gal. 3:28)? One must first indicate that, in this case, it is a question, strictly speaking, not of a hypostasis, male or female, but of humanity, of human nature, as such, which in holy baptism is clothed in Christ, becomes Christ's humanity by the power of His humanization or incarnation. Of course, this power of Divine-humanity is directly connected precisely with Christ's humanization, which is accomplished by the Holy Spirit and in this sense is inseparable from the Third Hypostasis. However, the difference remains that the Third Hypostasis is the incarnating hypostasis, while the hypostasis of the Logos is the one that is incarnated. Therefore, in the broad sense, baptism is accomplished in the name of the Holy Trinity, while, in the direct sense, it is the being clothed in Christ, just as the Church is, first of all, the body of Christ, the incarnation of God, but also the temple of the Holy Spirit, Pentecost. However, the work of our salvation is centered in Christ, our life in Christ, and Christ's life in us, which is a work of the Holy Spirit. And in the light of this life-in-Christ of *all* of humankind, the difference between male and female does not hold.

However, a hierarchical relationship with the primacy of the male principle also holds with regard to the hypostases in man. The fact of the matter is that, in the Holy Trinity too, it is the Son who is the hypostatic image of the Father, and the Holy Spirit rests upon the Son, putting its stamp upon Him. The hypostasis of the Holy Spirit is transparent for the hypostasis of the Son; it does not manifest anything different or new, but only what is already revealed (the Holy Spirit "reminds" one of the words of Christ). In this sense, one can say that the hypostasis of the Word is the hypostasis that has *content*, while the hypostasis of the Spirit is the hypostasis that *operates* or *accomplishes*. But the latter is nevertheless second, not first, in the pair of hypostases that reveal the Father. Likewise, in the creation of the human being in the image of God, the male hypostasis is first, while the female hypostasis is derivative of the male hypostasis, or, in any case, correlative and additional, as it were, with respect to the male hypostasis. The female is created ontologically *after* the male, "from his rib." This same relation can be found in connection with the divine Incarnation: "For the husband is the head of the wife, even as Christ is the head of the church" (Eph. 5:23). In this sense, the name of the husband is, in a certain sense, the name of the wife as well (which is expressed by the genius of language in the wife's taking the husband's name). And so, the hypostatic image of the male remains fundamental, guiding, for the hypostatic image of the female. In this sense, all of humankind has *one* all-human hypostasis, one all-hypostatic name: Christ, who in the Incarnation was indivisibly united with the Mother of God.

This positive all-unity of the hypostases is realized in the Church. On the one hand, the Church is the *multi*-unity of all the individual hypostases. On the other hand, it is a multi-*unity*, in which the individuality of many hypostases is extinguished by the power of sacrificially humbling love. Here, both hypostatic centers simultaneously receive power. In love for Christ there is neither male nor female. All find their hypostasis in Christ, so that "not I, but Christ liveth in me" (Gal. 2:20). And, in this love for Christ, the character of the love of the Lord's Servant, the Mother of God, is revealed. This character consists in the fact that She "humbles" herself both empirically and ontologically, stops being for Herself, becomes transparent for the hypostasis of the Son, reveals this hypostasis, as is proper to the Third Hypostasis, the Holy Spirit, in the supra-eternal love in the Holy Trinity. The Holy Spirit's hypostatic character, as hypostatic love, consists in the fact that its hypostasis does not exist, as it were, despite the fact that, or precisely because, it is such. The Church is the body of Christ, but it is also the temple of the Holy Spirit. Christ is "imaged" in the Church by the power of the Holy Spirit. Thus, all the hypostases are submerged in the all-unitary, but bi-unitary, hypostasis of the Church of Christ. By virtue of the Holy Spirit one name is inscribed upon all: Christ, but Christ made incarnate by the Holy Spirit, Jesus-Mary, the all-human being and the divine human being, the uncreated Proto-image of the human being and the created image of God.

Does this difference between the male and female principles in humanity not erase that which belongs to the fullness of the image of God in it? If Christ is the all-hypostasis for all of humankind, does this not annul all of the female hypostases? Conversely, if the Church as all-humankind finds itself in fullness only in Jesus-Mary, do not the male hypostases thereby lose their significance? One must answer no to both of these questions. The fact of the matter is that hypostatic characters or names are never simple or unitary; rather, they consist of two elements, one of which is primary, while the other is an overtone, as it were. Such are the proper hypostasis and name of Logos-Christ, and of the Holy Spirit in Mary. This dual-unity is preserved in unity. The male nature is hypostatized in Christ in His relation to the Church, as the head of the body of Christ, while the female nature is hypostatized in relation to Him as the Bridegroom of the Church: "Thee, my Wife, I love." There are two relations here: centrifugal and centripetal. And both are necessarily united in each human hypostasis; however, they are united in different tonalities, with the love of Christ for the Church, or of the Church for Christ, being dominant.

To the characterization of the creaturely hypostases it is necessary to add the following feature. In the Divine Sophia the nature of divinity is perfectly transparent for the divine hypostases and is completely hypostatized by them. In this case, one can say that, in divinity, no boundary of being exists between nature and hypostasis, although this does not exclude all the reality of nature and hypostasis in their difference. In creaturely being there exists not only this difference but also the noncoincidence in fact of hypostatic being and the hypostatizedness of nature: in the human being, the nature of the world is *not* completely hypostatized by the human hypostasis; the hypostatized domain is very limited, although it is subject to unlimited expansion and the ceaseless humanization of nature. Hypostatic being and natural being oppose each other here as distinct spheres of being, although they can, in their limit, coincide and be identified; however, they are still far from this state.

The question is asked, How are these separate modes of creaturely being mutually determined in the creaturely Sophia?

In the first place, one must completely eliminate the idea that the domain of non-hypostatized, natural being is completely alien to hypostatization, is a kind of dead matter, of an essentially different nature from all that lives and is hypostatically alive. In general, there is nothing in creation that is absolutely dead; God did not create death. There are only different degrees of life on the way to its complete triumph and the complete hypostatization of being. Although it is alien to hypostatic life, "dead" or, more precisely, not-yet-hypostatized nature contains the potential of hypostatization. In this potential sense, it can belong (and in a certain, though minimal, degree, already belongs) to a hypostasis. Nevertheless, till now it abides in a state of de facto autonomy, as it were, in the fullness of its proper, natural, nonhypostatized being. This being has a certain natural, though not hypostatic, center in the *world soul*, which is nothing else but the creaturely Sophia not yet fully actualized in creaturely hypostases. This is the instinctive wisdom of nature, its inner entelechic character, which in its infallibility surpasses the conscious, hypostatic understanding of individual human hypostases. Here, we have a special form of subconscious life (in the sense of the absence of a hypostatic center of consciousness) and also unconscious life. It is not just a mechanical causality but also an inner purposefulness, which is already a sign, a manifestation of life. One can say that, in this sense, nature as *natura naturans* tends to the fullness of its realization in *natura naturata*. It ascends to hypostatization in a twofold way: naturally in the world soul and consciously in the life and creative effects of creaturely hypostases. This duality is characteristic for the current state of the creaturely world, when the soul is not yet brought into full connection with spirit. This is not that final and definitive state of the future age, of glorified being, when God will be all in all. But even now when the creature is "subject to vanity not willingly, but by reason of him who hath subjected the same in hope," and it yearns for "the glorious liberty of the children of God" (Rom. 8:20-21), the connection between nature and man, as the logos of the world and its hypostasis, remains, for it is unbreakable. However, as long as this connection is only a potential one, the world remains divided and incomplete.

It is necessary to distinguish hypostasis (or hypostatizedness) from lack of consciousness or lack of feeling. Only with hypostasis do we have fullness of being, the life of the person in its proper nature, the living and vital I. This refers only to beings that have spirit, that is, to human beings and to angels. But even hypostatizedness as such, which does not have a spiritual-hypostatic center, is not deprived of its own peculiar life and does not belong to dead matter (which in general does not exist). Nature knows a series of diverse images of life, which correspond to different degrees of hypostatizedness. Such in general is the organic world, from plants to animals, from the lower levels of the animal world to the higher. Animals have souls, although they are deprived of spirit, and the Bible says that the animal soul, the living principle, is in the blood. Animals have not a personality but an individuality, a qualified center not only of generic but also of individual being, insofar as they have a living soul. On the one hand, this soul is the principle and function of the life of the genus; on the other hand, it is a certain quasi-personal center. In animals, this center differs from the human center in that it lacks a personal, supranatural spirit. But it does contain the entire apparatus of life with its energy. Animalness is natural creaturely vitality as such, and it is always individual. Of course, the principle of the genus, the life of the genus, is expressed in animals with much greater force than in human beings, and in this sense animals are more impersonal than human beings. But a genus consists of individuals, and a being that is only generic, that is not individualized, does not even exist. Individuals differ from one another even if they are members of the same genus.

Thus, the world soul moves genera either like a dark instinct, the inner law of being in its different forms, or like the life of individuals who have spontaneity of movement, which is the lower kind of creaturely freedom and self-creativity. In the first case, we have the more immediate manifestation of Wisdom in creation, of divinity in nature, which astonishes us by an infinite abundance of forms, the inexhaustibility of life, and the wise purposefulness of all things. However, a question remains: Can this manifestation of Divine Wisdom in creation be recognized as absolute or adequate to such an extent that an equals sign can be placed between the ideas of Wisdom and the laws of nature? The answer is no. The ideas of Wisdom, the reason of nature, its infallible instinct, shine refractedly in the creaturely world and are manifested in this world with a certain limitation and even distortion. This limitation is due to the general limitedness of all the aspects of creation, a limitedness that is associated with their multiplicity and diversity, realized through the actualization of *nothing;* a limit, *peras,* is thus imposed upon being with its different aspects. By becoming individualized and thus delimiting itself from the others, each of these aspects becomes limited in its own being. The world soul *becomes* together with the world itself, as if again arising out of nonbeing. From the state of sophianic potentiality, the world soul is actualized in creation. The world soul must overcome the inertia of nonbeing, the stagnant mass of *tohu vabohu,* the invisible and formless earth, which creaturely being originally is. To this inertia one must add the direct resistance of the darkness of chaos to the light of sophianicity. All the paths of natural being changed as a result of the fall of Adam, who had been called to be the architect of this being and the organizer of the world according to the image of its sophianicity. All creation groans, awaiting its liberation through the sons of men. (This question will be fully examined below in connection with the general question of evil in the world and in man.)

Let us go further: The world soul actualizes itself through the lower creaturely freedom of the animal world and, in general, of the entire living world, a freedom that nevertheless characterizes the spontaneity of the movements and actions proper to this world. The spontaneous movement of the amoeba and the regal movements of the lion and tiger represent different degrees of creaturely freedom, but only in the psychic and individual, not spiritual and personal, domain. This spontaneity is established by God's creative act, the creation of "a living soul." This spontaneity is characterized by levels and nuances not only of genera and species but also of individuals, in the peculiar creativity of the life of animals. The sophianicity of creation is realized in the animal world both as instinct in the direct generic sense, by virtue of which, for instance, birds fly away and return at specific times and from and to a specific place; and as individual self-determination in the life of individuals, where a certain will and mind of the animals already operate. The animal world is already called to build the world, and insofar as it is individual, this world is called to freely follow and actualize its own laws in nature.

Here, with the individuality of a given species and individual, there is mixed (even more than in generic being) a certain qualifiedness of this species and individual with possible contaminations of evil. On this score we have the testimony of biblical zoology, both of a positive and of a negative character, from the serpent of Eden, which, being "the wisest of beasts," was capable of receiving the suggestion of the evil spirit, to Balaam's ass, capable of seeing the angel of the Lord (Num. 22:23-27), as well as the ass upon which the Lord rode into the holy city. The ability of animals to enter into communion with man, from almost direct conversation with him to obedience to him, shows that animals participate in the world soul not only in its necessity but also in its creaturely freedom. But the creaturely world is headed only by man, in the fullness of his spiritual and creative freedom.

5. The Eternity and Temporality of Man

In connection with the doctrine of the eternity of the world in God and the temporality of the world for itself (i.e., its createdness), the question of the temporality and eternity of man arises. The two are imprinted in human consciousness with equal clarity. On the one hand, "all flows" in this consciousness, whereas a stopping of time signifies the termination of life, death. But with the same certitude a human being knows about himself, about his I, that it did not come into being, for it *exists* supratemporally. A human being has an astonishing intuition not only about himself but also about his neighbor, his *co-I*. When a human being is born into the world, this occurs in time, at a specific moment of time, a calendar date, but this is accompanied by our consciousness that the newborn has always existed and only just now has appeared in the world, that in general he exists supratemporally. That is the usual intuition of parents regarding their children. They cannot allow there was a time when their children did not exist. This same intuition is, in general, applicable to all whom we love and recognize by love. This intuition bears witness to the depth in which being is rooted in eternity.

How should one conceive this relation of the eternal and unchangeable, the Creator, with creaturely hypostases, who are not only objects of creation but also hypostatic centers upon which God's love reposes? Here, one must first distinguish the angelic world from the human world. According to the doctrine of the Church, which does not provoke any misunderstanding in this connection, *all* the angels are created by a single creative act, simultaneously. The fullness of the angelic world, *all* its hypostases, was called together to a being that, as a result of the absence of death in the spiritual world, will never confront one of the fundamental boundaries of temporality: an end by death. In this sense, this being is, if not eternal, at least infinite. Of course, the absence of successive individual acts of occurrence in time, analogous to births in humankind, also frees the angelic consciousness from the *special* sense of temporality that characterizes human beings. In this sense, the perception of the eternal ground of its being is closer and more natural to the consciousness of the angelic world than to humankind.

Enormously important for us is the fact that the angelic world is given as full and finished in the instantaneous creation of this world. The creation of this world does not go beyond this, and we thus conclude that the *number* of angels is finite, determinate, limited. But this finiteness is not connected with any external boundary or limit, beyond which God's omnipotence, wisdom, and love grow weak and are nullified. Clearly, there can be no such weakening. Rather, this boundary expresses the fact that this world is internally finished or full, which in no wise requires bad infinity or unlimitedness. Otherwise, the angelic world would run the risk of lacking fullness or of being unfinished. And if our faith teaches us the contrary, this means that not only a negative ("bad") finitude but also an actual, positive finitude is possible, that a finite infinitude or an infinite finitude is possible, at least in the angelic world.

Such a positive, finite infinitude is, in general, revealed to us through the creation of the world, in which the divine *all* is implanted. But this *all* is realized in a definite, limited period of time ("the six days of creation"), and is implanted in definite, limited forms, or modes, of being. Otherwise, the world could not have been fully created, fully finished. And the divine sabbath could not have come, just as it would not have been said: "Thus the heavens and the earth were finished, and all the host of them. And on the seventh day God ended his work which he had made" (Gen. 2:1-2). The divine fullness is therefore combined not with an infinity that is powerless to exhaust itself and in this sense is genuinely bad, but with a determinate completeness, which is nevertheless characterized by an inexhaustible depth of eternity, by an eternal life realized in creaturely temporality. By virtue of this combination, every atom of being, however small it might be, potentially contains its entire actual infinity, which is manifested not only in the static profile of its being but also in its dynamic, energetic realization.

Thus, we can admit neither that the angelic world lacks fullness nor that it is unfinished (the fall of part of the angels does not change anything in the original fullness of this world). We thus conclude once again that this fullness is compatible with the fact that this world is finished. We can express this idea in another way by saying that a finitely infinite world has *the potential of being created*, and that the idea of this does not contain an ontological contradiction, which would be inevitable if its fullness were not in general encompassable in finite forms. The very creation of the creaturely world would then be an ontological absurdity, an impossibility. The creaturely image of divine fullness encompasses in its formedness and (in this sense) limitedness, or finitude, the potentiality of divine infinity. This is realized, evidently, not by virtue of the determinateness or formedness of each of its parts, since every boundary is opposed to and repelled by fullness, but by virtue of actual integrity, that is, the dynamic interpenetration of all by all, divine integrity. Every creaturely spirit is a window opening onto the entire divine universe; it communes with the divine nature by which it lives. And, in this sense, this nature is as if its own nature. The individuality of its hypostatic image, *gnōrisma hupostatikon*, does not fragment but multiplies this all-unity, and each of these multiple images can be penetrated by the others by virtue of mutually hypostatic love. "Individuality" here is not limitedness in the sense of *omnis definitio est negatio*. Rather, it is manifold, positive difference, which must be finished, cannot fail to be finished. Otherwise, the very fullness of perfection would turn out to be unfinished.

In this sense, every creaturely (in this case angelic) hypostasis, not as an "individuality," a limitedness, but as a hypostatic center of the *all*, is already sufficient ontologically to encompass and realize in itself the fullness of being in its own nature. But it is insufficient for itself, since it is enclosed in its hypostatic I-ness, which necessarily requires for itself, for its own actualization, hypostatic love, the "multiple eyes" of the being of multiple hypostases, hypostatic multi-unity in the image of the Holy Trinity, imprinted in every creaturely spirit. The hypostasis must, in any case, *not* be single; there must be *many* hypostases.

But what determines this multi-unity or number of angels, and can this number be determined or, so to speak, exhausted? The guiding principle in the discussion of this question must be the Proto-image for all the creaturely hypostases, that is, triadicity, one in trinity. All-unity, as the self-revelation of the divine nature, or Sophia, is joined together through the unity of the divine hypostasis, "one in Trinity." But this unity is not only one in Trinity but also Trinity in one, and in this sense it is a multi-unity; however, it is not a single hypostasis, but three hypostases, although joined together in unity. This number of the multiplicity, three, as a necessary aspect of the divine threeness, is a *determinate* and therefore a limited number. The divine immeasurability, or absoluteness, is therefore hypostatized not by an infinite number of divine hypostases (an idea that is both blasphemous and absurd) but by *three* hypostases. Consequently, the immeasurability of life does not require such an immeasurability of the number of hypostases but is compatible with a determinate number or measure. This immeasurability is an actual, exhaustible, utterly transparent, realized infinity.

It goes without saying that *three* hypostases, not more and not less, in their concrete mutual being, correspond only to the Holy Trinity. This aspect of the Holy Trinity is not repeated in creatures, whose hypostases are not trinely multiple, but simply multiple. Creatures take this property of nonuniqueness, of multiplicity, of multi-hypostatizedness from the trine Proto-image, but without taking the trinity that is proper only to divinity. One feature of the divine triunity nevertheless remains proper to creatures: The multiplicity of creaturely hypostases is not a bad infinity, which cannot exhaust itself and reach an inner limit. Rather, it is definite and exhaustible. The angelic world is *fully* created in all its hosts and therefore has a finite number. We must postulate that this concrete number of the angelic multiplicity, or multi-unity, is not determined by an arbitrary and random stopping at some number, is not broken off by an ellipsis, but that its value is determined by the *inner* integrity of the angelic world, by the fact that this world is a finished one. This *angelic number* is unknown to us, at least in the life of this age, where we see only through a glass darkly. But even now we know that such a number exists, and therefore the angelic world is an inwardly finished whole, not a bad infinity. In this we see the guiding idea for the perception of positive, and not only negative, infinity, however this idea may be realized in the philosophy of mathematics or general ontology. A finite number of elements is capable of encompassing an infinite, unlimited, absolute content, or eternity itself. Eternity is not an *apeiron,* a disorganizedness, or formlessness; on the contrary, it presupposes *peras,* concrete organizedness, form.

When one compares the angelic and human multi-unities, the first difference that one observes is that the angelic number is complete, the multi-unity is finished, whereas the human number is *not yet* complete but is continuing to increase. Humankind has a beginning but does not yet know an end. The humankind that has existed or exists is only a fragment in relation to that which will exist. And there are no direct data on the basis of which one can determine what part of the whole has already been realized and what part remains unrealized. If one considers the problem empirically, on the basis of demographic data which show the unprecedented growth of population and its greater density precisely in our time, we are led to conclude that probably only a small part of humankind has been realized, whereas its greater part will be realized in the future. It is therefore not difficult to conclude that humankind as a whole does not yet exist. Therefore, when we speak of the integral Adam, who was assumed by the new Adam, the God-man, into his manhood, then this integral assumption is in fact empirically impossible because of the absence of the reality of this integral Adam. What is accessible to empirical assumption is only a fragment of the whole, perhaps not the most important fragment, and in any case not the largest fragment. The rest of humankind remains unassumed, and what follows then from St. Gregory the Theologian's maxim, "What is not assumed is not redeemed"?

This theory of fragmentary humanity, in which its empirical phenomenon is equated without qualification with its ontological determination, leads to serious misunderstandings in the domains of Christian anthropology, christology, and soteriology.

If one limits oneself solely to this empirical understanding of humanity, one inevitably arrives at the conclusion that the incarnation of Christ with the assumption of *all* of human nature was unrealizable and impossible nineteen centuries ago and is unrealizable and impossible at the present time. For this assumed humankind inevitably turns out to be *pars pro toto* in the empirical understanding, whereas the assumption of the integral Adam is necessarily presupposed here. True, the attempt is made to escape from the inevitability of such a conclusion by referring to Christ's assumption of the human *nature* not in the aspect of man *(anthrōpos)* but in the aspect of humanity *(anthrōpotēs)*. Even though the abstract concept of nature, separated from hypostatic concrete being, very conveniently fits into Aristotle's schemata of *prōte* and *deutera ousia* ("first and second nature"), in which "nature" can be understood separately from hypostasis, this concept in fact is an abuse of an abstraction.

No human *nature* exists that has being wholly independent of hypostatic concretization, as if *prior to* or *outside of* it. Humanity as nature is found only in the fullness and presence of hypostases. Nature and hypostasis can be separated or opposed only in abstraction *(en epinoia);* and in itself, this separation or opposition does not correspond to any reality. Humanity is a multi-unity with one nature but multiple hypostases; it is not an indefinite and unfinished series, with ellipsis points indicating continuation, but the unity of this series, its integral. Therefore, the following question arises inevitably: Does this humanity exist and has it ever existed? (And to this another question is inevitably added: Will it in fact ever exist as a whole, as a fullness?) In general, does the one "old" Adam exist and, consequently, does the integral new Adam exist? These are the aporias to which empiricism in anthropology leads, an empiricism that, in theology, has found expression in abstract creationism, in the doctrine that God creates a new soul during the birth of each man, continuing a creation that apparently was not completed in the "Six Days." Leaving aside all other difficulties encountered in the development of this theory, let us note the chief one. According to this doctrine, humanity is still being created and does not yet exist as a whole. Consequently, the Incarnation of God is also impossible. Or the Incarnation must be understood in a crudely mechanical manner. Such an understanding was attributed — wholly undeservedly — to Apollinarius and consisted in the view that assumption applied only to the human body, the bones and muscles, together with the "soul." Here, it remains completely unclarified whether this assumption is just the de facto assimilation of only certain material elements of the human body (and soul), or whether it acquires a general significance, namely that of the assumption of the *entire* human nature. But, if this is the case, one must try to understand how and in what sense this assumption of the elements of the human bodily and psychic nature is equated with the assumption of the human nature in its entirety, of the whole old Adam.

This question has never been posed and never been discussed in theology, and the absence of such a discussion is, in general, an *anthropological* lacuna in christology. Dogmatically, the Chalcedonian formula with the doctrine "perfect in humanity . . . truly man . . . consubstantial with us according to humanity *[teleion en anthrōpotēti, anthrōpon alēthōs . . . homoousion hēmin kata tēn anthrōpotēta]*" contains precisely this idea — not concerning the de facto, only ad hoc assimilation of given elements of the human body or of the human nature in general, but precisely concerning the assumption of the "perfect" humanity and "consubstantiality" with us in this sense. This idea can also be found in patristic theology. But the significance of this homoousian relation of Christ to all humanity has remained unclarified in theology, particularly as regards the applicability of this idea to the entire human multi-unity.

One must first clarify the general premises of this homoousianism. If one does not limit oneself just to the external identification of the de facto assumption of human corporeality with that of the integral or "perfect" *(teleion)* humankind,[51] but rather searches for the ontological meaning of this homoousian definition, one must admit that an integral humanity does exist. The possibility of its being thus assumed exists. Consequently, this possibility is not contradicted by the fact that humanity is multiple and unfinished in time. In some sense, humanity exists independently of these limitations of time, or supratemporally. The assumption of the integral humanity signifies not the abstract assimilation of certain human properties, corporeal and psychic, but the concrete assumption of me, you, them. In general, humanity does not exist abstractly and impersonally. It exists only as mine, yours, ours, theirs. It consists of the totality of all particular human persons. The Lord took His humanity not from impersonal nature but from each of us *personally.* He thus became one with His humanity, introducing it into His own hypostatic being. And only on this basis can it be said: "Christ lives in me."

But that is not sufficient. Humanity is not only hypostatic multiplicity but also hypostatic multi-unity; it is the integral Adam. Adam is

51. This thought finds its fullest expression in Gregory of Nyssa: "Man created in the image of God is nature as a whole. . . . He is created by God's omnipotent Wisdom not as part of a whole but as the integral nature, existing in him at once" (*De opificio hominis,* c. 22, PG 44, 204-5). "The plenitude of humankind is included as one body by the providential power proceeding from God" (c. 16, 181-85).

not only a certain human person but also the human multi-unity, the all-person, in the image of the one but trihypostatic God. Adam, like every human person in Adam, exists not only in and for Himself but also *together* with others, as a member of a multihypostatic all-unity. Empirically, this higher reality penetrates into and is realized in our consciousness only weakly and in a limited way, although man, as a generic being, is never capable of fully leaving behind this generic self-consciousness. Ontologically, this personal-generic self-consciousness is determined from the depths of man's being and constitutes the very foundation of his person. Just as Adam is the "progenitor" of the *whole* human race and bears in himself *all* of humanity, is connected with all of humanity, so the sons and daughters of Adam all bear him in themselves and are, in this sense, Adam himself in his multi-unity.

Therefore, humanity, like each individual human being, must not be understood as a series of individual units, attached one to the other by virtue of a kind of similarity (that would be heretical homoiousianism instead of orthodox homoousianism). It must be understood only as a whole: the entire natural Adam lives in every human being. Every person is a point on the surface of this sphere, connected by a radius to the center. The whole and a particular variant, the genus and an individual, exist with one existence, are inwardly one. The historical chain of individual human lives with all its diversity manifests the multiplicity of the genus; far from abolishing the multi-unity, it even presupposes it. Thus, each human individual, being a generic being, is at the same time personal and *all-human*. Such, naturally and first of all, is the first man, Adam. In this sense, Genesis 1:27-28 speaks of the creation of man in general, or of the all-man. It does not speak of the creation only of a particular person: "God created man in his own image, in the image of God created he him; male and female created he them. And God blessed them, and God said unto them, Be fruitful and multiply, and replenish the earth, and subdue it." Compare Genesis 2:7: "And the Lord God formed man of the dust of the ground, and breathed into his nostrils the breath of life." Here, the entire second chapter speaks of the all-man or man in general. Only in chapter 3, after the fall, does the particular man Adam appear, and then Eve (3:8-9, 12, 17, 20-21).

Only in connection with this all-humanity of every man can one understand the idea of original sin as the fall precisely of the all-man, and, in him, the fall of every particular man. Original sin, as damage undergone by the whole human nature, can be understood only in relation to the all-man, taken in his generic all-unity H, not only as the aggregate or sum of the individuals h^1, h^2, h^3, h^4, . . . h^m, h^{m-n}. . . .

Original universally human sin therefore presupposes the existence of the all-man and the all-humanity. As in the case of the Incarnation, *pars pro toto* is inadmissible here. Original sin cannot be understood only as a combination of separate events that occurred in the past, occur in the present, and will occur in the future. This kind of atomistic understanding annuls the idea of a generic, universal sin and replaces it with a series of individual, unconnected falls.[52]

To be sure, this does not annul the individual principle proper to every hypostasis; nevertheless, this principle is antinomically connected with the generic principle. Every person not only has certain universally human traits, or participates in humanity. Every person is also an all-man: *homo sum et nihil humani a me alienum esse puto* (I am a man and nothing human is foreign to me). That is the fundamental anthropological axiom which lies at the basis of the idea of original sin and God's incarnation and, finally, redemption. For the latter also necessarily presupposes the existence of an integral all-humanity, which is redeemed by Christ in its entirety and not only in its individual parts or persons. One should not think that first only the generations living before Christ are redeemed, and that the generations living after Him up to our own day are redeemed next, but that those generations that are not yet born are not yet redeemed but will participate in redemption only later. They, like every human being, in their freedom accept or do not accept, accomplish or do not accomplish, redemption for themselves, a redemption which, nevertheless, is given to *all* humanity once and for all. The new Adam redeemed the whole old Adam and in this sense replaced him with himself. And no *pars pro toto*, or series of successive and partial redemptions, could correspond to this task, which is a universal one.

Thus, if the existence of the all-man as the fullness and all-unity of humanity constitutes the dogmatic presupposition of the fundamental Christian dogmas — original sin, the Incarnation, with all its consequences, and redemption — we must consider it as a dogmatic problem. What does this premise signify? Clearly, at its basis we find the idea that, although this all-humanity is not given to us in empirical experience, in

---

52. Besides being insufficient in general as regards sin, the conception, common in patristics, of original sin as a hereditary illness introduces the idea of the *universal man* only in a roundabout way, heredity already being a principle that links individuals into a generic unity; and it must be understood precisely on the basis of this ontological presumption.

the succession of generations or persons, it nevertheless exists, although outside the empirical world. Humanity is born and arises in individual persons or generations *in* history, but all-humanity exists *above* history. How can one understand this supratemporal being, which transcends creaturely being, being that was drawn "out of nothing" by God's creative act? Can man's being be conceived as above its empirical manifestation in the world?

In order to understand this relation we must return to the fundamental thesis of the doctrine of creation, namely, that God's creative act necessarily unites in itself the aspects of eternity and temporality. In God as the Creator, all of His actions in relation to the world, or His creative acts, are eternal with divine eternity, and if we wish to express this with reference to time, it is necessary to say that they are supratemporal. They are free of the limitations of the present, past, and future, of all becoming, the only form in which life and the world exist for creation. In them, all is given in the one act of all-unity and all-fullness. Although creation does not have the eternity of divinity itself, for it is called to being out of the extra-divine "nothing" and is created, yet in God or for God it is supratemporal, possesses *creaturely eternity,* for time does not limit God. Only God can freely limit Himself by temporality in order to be correlative to creation, in the divine kenosis of the creative act. It necessarily follows from this that God, in Himself or for Himself, creates the world and its focus, man, by a single supratemporal act, and not successively and gradually, as it might appear when we look at the successive birth of generations with the supposed creation of new souls. If we suppose this, the very creation of the world in humanity would have to be recognized as unfinished, as continuing to the very end of the world. The time for the divine sabbath, for God's accomplishment on the seventh day of all His works, has not yet come, contrary to the direct testimony of Scripture. But this supposition is, as we have already seen, compatible neither with the Incarnation nor with redemption.

The eternal aspect of the creative act reveals in God himself the character of creation in all its fullness. God sees as existent even what has not yet occurred, for, in Him and for Him, it supra-eternally *is* as the creaturely Sophia. But in relation to time this supra-eternity of creation signifies its *supratemporality* in the sense that, for God, creation exists in a certain integral of all-temporality, whereas for creatures it is the unfurling scroll of the time of empirical being. This supratemporality is realized in the life of creatures, for they are created for time, but in a certain supratemporal mode of being. For humanity in particular, this signifies that, although, in earthly being, human generations are born and thus appear in time, as it were, this is possible only on the basis of the supratemporal creation of all of them. The integral Adam, humanity in its totality, is supratemporal, but he is also created by God for time, as Man, or the All-man.

By no means does this signify a doctrine of the preexistence of souls or reincarnation, a doctrine which has been rejected by the Church, for here there is no *"pre"* which would belong to temporal succession and which would be postulated beyond the limits of our time. Let us repeat, one creation of the whole Adam in the whole fullness of multiple hypostases is accomplished by God *not* in time but *for* time, supra-temporally, though not extra-temporally. This creation is given, so to speak, to time for the empirical realization of this creative act for our creaturely being.[53] As regards their supratemporal root, human souls do not differ, despite their successive appearance in time. If we translate this idea into the language of time, we can say, although with inevitable inac-curacy, that all human souls are simultaneous or equi-temporal, even though they are hetero-temporal in empirical being. Precisely in this supratemporal root of theirs they belong to the one integral Adam; they are the one all-man, to whom both the Incarnation and the redemption refer.

Thus, we distinguish the creation of man in time from his *supra-temporal creation*, his being for God, his rootedness in eternity, in which God equally knows the past, present, and future. All the human hypostases, both those who are already born and those who are yet to be born, are present before the face of God. Therefore, appearance in time does not contain anything new for God, anything that does not exist supratemporally; and *creation in time* is the realization of supratemporal-ity. Man himself is sufficiently conscious of this supratemporality of be-ing, which is revealed in time. Herein lie the mystery and root of creaturely freedom as its self-determination to being, a self-determination that is not abstract but concretely qualified. Every human person is also created as an individual; that is, he has his own face, his own ontological theme, his own special character of being. And this self-positing contains not only the ac-ceptance of one's theme of being but also its special form, for this form contains a greater or lesser mastery of one's theme, in different modes; a

---

53. We have already had occasion to develop this idea in connection with the doc-trine of original sin in *The Burning Bush*, to which we refer the reader. This dual origin of man, in time and in divine eternity, is also reflected in the duality of his self-consciousness, which simultaneously belongs to both realms.

greater or lesser giftedness or genius with which this theme is treated. Genius is the *what* in every human being, while talent is his *how*. God gives to every human being the gift of ontological genius, the gift of one's own theme of being (the "talent" or "talents" in the Gospel parable). In God, no one is ungifted; all are gifted. However, this giftedness consists not only of being given a gift but also of the mode of the reception of this gift, again according to the Gospel parable: one person multiplied what was given to him; another buried it in the earth. This mode of reception is actualized in the unfolding of creaturely being in time, in empirical life, but it is also pre-actualized in supratemporal self-positing.

Every personal theme, we must conclude, not only can be realized differently in earthly, creaturely life but can be received differently outside of or "prior to" this life. Therefore, to one person five talents are given; to another two are given; whereas to a third only one is given. Strictly speaking, they are not given but *taken* according to the proper freedom of each. In principle, each gets an equal amount, although in different gifts, for God has no favorites.[54] It follows that, in the "last judgment" (if one combines the parables that concern it in the "little Apocalypse" of Matthew 25 with the parables of the talents and of the ten virgins), the thing judged depends not only on empirical freedom, accomplishment in time, in earthly creaturely life, but also on supratemporal freedom, self-positing, creaturely self-determination. These two modes of self-positing — above time and in time — are only different aspects or modes of one and the same act.

Man's supratemporal self-determination in relation to empirical being allows one to understand both the universality of original sin and the fact that it is received personally, though in different measures depending on the person.[55] Entering into a world that is burdened by universal sin, a human being makes it his own by an act of *personal* acceptance, which can differ from individual to individual, so that different persons enter into the world with different burdens of sin, as it were. A human being's earthly fate, the time and circumstances of his appearance and life in the world, are also determined in accordance with this supramundane self-determination of every human being by God's wisdom, unfathomable for us within the limits of this world. Earthly life is "preceded" by a prologue in heaven. Meta-empirical foundations are revealed in the empirical world; a noumenal char-

54. See the complex antinomics of Rom. 9.
55. This question is examined in *The Burning Bush* in connection with the problem of the relation between the Mother of God and original sin.

acter is revealed in the empirical character. Man is created by God's original call to being, but, in the fulfillment of this call, a place is made for creaturely freedom. To this extent man is also his own creator. Herein lies the divine-human mystery of the man's existence, and in this sense man is a noncreaturely-creaturely being, created and self-creating.

But man also belongs to noncreaturely-creaturely being in another sense (cf. *The Lamb of God*). In creating man out of the earth, as the supreme and universal image of all creation, God "breathes" into him a living soul from His own being, as if sharing Himself, His own life, with him. Man, intended to become "a god by grace" or a "created god" (let us ignore the apparent contradiction in this combination of words), in a certain sense is already divine even according to creation, although this is combined in him — without separation and without confusion — with the creatureliness of his natural being. In calling man to life, God goes out of Himself, as it were, to breathe into him a "living soul." More than that: by an ecstatic act of creative, self-renouncing love, God multiplies the hypostases outside and, as it were, above trinity, gives life to His hypostatic images, or repetitions, as it were. God hypostatically lives outside of Himself. The one God in the Holy Trinity, He condescends to participate in the multiplicity of hypostases in creaturely images.

These hypostases, without being God, are divine — not only by the nature of their spirit breathed into man by God but also by their hypostatic "faces," as living reflections of the trinitarian God. As existent in Himself, God is the Holy Trinity, consubstantial and indivisible. But as the Creator, God is not only the Holy Trinity. He lives not only in Himself but also in hypostatic multiplicity outside of and apart from Himself, as it were. This "apart from" signifies that, although, ontologically, the creaturely hypostases are only reflections of the divine hypostasis, they also exist for and in themselves, "apart from" God, are different from Him. They say "thou" to Him, and he answers creation with a *thou*, is hypostatically correlative with it. What results is a kind of altero-being of the divine hypostasis, however contradictory the very notion of such a being might appear, for a hypostasis is precisely autonomous being, being in and for itself. However, what we have here are reflections of the divine hypostasis that wholly depend in their being on this hypostasis, belong to it as images of the Proto-image. But precisely for this reason they are ontologically not equal to it, but only similar to it. Therefore, by themselves they are not capable of *multiplying* the divine hypostases, of transforming the Trinity into a quaternity or pentity. Although they have autonomous being, being for themselves, and to this extent also being by themselves, yet, ontologically, in the very ground of their being they are only divine reflections. We are brought to such antinomies of created-uncreated being by the analysis of man's being, both in the aspect of the creaturely-divine nature of his spirit and in the aspect of his creaturely-divine hypostasis.

One must evidently say the same thing regarding the angelic spirits. They too are creaturely and divine, created and uncreated, by analogy with human beings, with the difference, of course, that they lack bodies, taken from the earth, and in this sense are fleshless spirits.[56] Their natural life is realized only through their participation in the divine nature, inasmuch as, unlike human beings, they do not have a proper nature. The angelic hypostases, like the human ones, are images or reflections of the divine hypostases, which receive their own being for themselves.

The following doubt can arise here: Does not this conception of the created hypostatic spirits, human and angelic, as creaturely-noncreaturely images or reflections of the divine hypostatic spirit lead to a certain identification of these spirits with the divine hypostatic spirit? Or does it not lead at least to a convergence of the divine and creaturely hypostases that obliterates the very distinction between Creator and creatures, between the hypostases of the Trinity and the creaturely hypostases? But convergence is not yet identification, and a connection is not yet an equation. Between the hypostasis of the Creator, the Holy Trinity, and the creaturely hypostases there remains the insurmountable difference that, in the triadicity of its hypostases, the Holy Trinity is revealed and exists in itself and for itself, in its inner natural life, in an absolute manner, in the exhaustive fullness of self-sufficiency. For Himself, for the fullness of His being, God does not need any other being, and therefore cannot receive anything into His being from outside. In fact, no such "outside" even exists. Outside of God there is nothing, and about this nothing one cannot even say that it exists as a certain, even negative, boundary of the divine being. It simply does not exist, just as no such boundary exists.

Nothing is *no* thing, not some something. Its existence can be posited only by an effort of abstraction, which in vain attempts to apply to God that shadowy, limiting significance of *nothing* which the latter receives in the creaturely world. In this sense, nothing also belongs to the relative being of the created world; particular images of *nothing* flit by like shadows and half-shadows, reflected from being. But absolute nothing, which could be juxtaposed with or opposed to divine being, simply does not exist. Absolute nothing is not something; there is no place for it even

---

56. See my book *Jacob's Ladder: On the Angels.*

in thought, into which it penetrates only by separating itself out of its fusion with the being of the world "created out of nothing." Only God exists and there is nothing besides God. In this sense, creation "out of nothing" does not complete or supplement God's being in any way. All things that are positive in creation belong to divinity, even though divinity receives in creation extra-divine being, another being, which precisely constitutes creation and creatureliness. Translated into the language of sophiology, this means that, by virtue of its sophianicity, all creation has a noncreaturely-creaturely character, for the positive force of its being is the creaturely Sophia as the image of the Divine Sophia. This expressly refers to what constitutes the focus of being, the "concentrated" world, that is, to man, and especially to the human spirit as the living image or repetition of the divine hypostases.

An anthropological occasionalism often arises in the understanding of the relation of the Creator to creation. The questions are asked: Can God not be the Creator? Does he have the freedom to create the world or not to create it? Is the creation of the world only an episode, so to speak, in the divine life, an episode that did not have to be? Or, on the contrary, did it have to be? The following kind of childish argument is naively added to this question: If the world is an empirical accident that did not have to be, then we, creatures, should be even more grateful to the Creator than if the world had to be created and God had to be the Creator of the world, that is, if God were connected with the world by a relation of necessity.

God is, of course, the Creator from all eternity, and the one thing is inseparable in Him from the other. To separate the two even in abstraction is to allow that God did not have to be God and that He did not have to actualize His love and the power of His divinity. But this ontological necessity does not have anything compulsory in it that would limit God's freedom. That is the crux of the matter. In general even the very opposition and differentiation of freedom and necessity, as they exist in the relative being of creatures, should not occur with reference to God, for, in God, freedom is also necessity, and vice versa. In God, there is no givenness which would have the character of compulsory necessity, for His entire life is free self-affirmation. But, in this freedom, there is no room for any arbitrariness: God's self-affirmation absolutely exhausts and is exhausted by His life. In this sense, the life of the Holy Trinity in itself and the life of the Holy Trinity outside itself, as the Creator, are equally free and necessary. This does not remove the ontological difference between the being of God in and according to Himself, the life of the Holy Trinity, and the life of God outside of Himself in creation, either in content or in significance. The first is the Proto-image; the second is the image. The first is absolutely autonomous; the second is derivative.

However, one canot separate the being of God in Himself from His self-revelation outside of Himself in creation; and one cannot allow that God started being the Creator only "at a certain moment of time" of His being (as if He were subject to time), and did not have to be the Creator at all. God is the Creator from all eternity. However, for God the creation of the world is a kenosis, a sacrificial love, which truly must evoke the creature's gratitude and praise, regardless of whether this creation had to be or did not have to be. Even in human relationships, does the sacrificial love of their father or mother evoke a different answering feeling in children depending on whether they think this love is necessary and inevitable? And even more inappropriate is it for the creature to measure the divine love that is bestowed upon it. Love is a living unity of freedom and necessity and, despite all the ontological difference with regard to character and object, both God's love for Himself in the Holy Trinity and the Creator's love for creation manifest Love as such: God is Love.

Returning to the question of the creation of man within the framework of general creation, we must distinguish two aspects of this question: the aspect of directedness at eternity, at the Creator, and the aspect of directedness at creation itself. God is the Creator, and His entire creation, having its focus in man, exists, first of all, not for and in itself, but in God and for God, in a manner, of course, that is appropriate to God's eternity. Although God creates for time, so that creation is an image of the being of the divine principles in becoming, or temporality, God does not thereby become subordinate to and limited by time. For God, creation has a supratemporal aspect and exists above time. This supratemporal existence is not characterized by succession in time and thus by partialness and alternation. This means that God knows and has His creation by a single all-embracing act, which for creatures is disclosed only in temporal succession. In this sense, one must accept with necessity that the creative act by which God establishes being contains *all* humanity, the integral Adam in the present, past, and future: integral humanity supratemporally *is* in God and for God. Therefore, its appearance in time is possible only in individual persons and generations.

In this creative act, we necessarily distinguish a supramundane aspect directed at God, and an aspect directed at creation: the Divine and the creaturely Sophia. All created things have a supra-eternal, *uncreated* proto-image in the Divine Sophia. In particular, such a proto-image of the creaturely Adam and of the whole human multi-unity is "the heavenly man," humanity in God, which is precisely the Divine Sophia, the Father's self-revelation in the Son and the Holy Spirit. This is the absolute heavenly humanity, which is not created and does not belong to the creaturely world except as its proto-image. This proto-image in the Divine Sophia is the foundation for creaturely being, which is becoming in time — as the creaturely Sophia. However, though she receives creaturely being, she does not thereby become separated from God. To allow this is to allow the possibility of a second principle of being alongside God; it is to fall into dualism with all its contradictions. Although she actualizes herself in time, the power of time, which extends to this mode of her revelation, does not extend to God Himself, as a limitation.

Even though, in creation, God is directed at time, so that by the creative act he establishes temporality, giving a place, alongside Himself, also to independent temporal being, yet, He Himself, as the Creator, has a supratemporal, or extratemporal, relation to the creature. All times and seasons are joined together in this all-temporal supratemporality. God knows the entire being of the world at all its moments, but He Himself does not belong to time. He does, however, give time a place in the creative act, and, in this sense, He creates time. Creaturely, becoming being therefore has a supratemporal root. It is affirmed by the Creator in the act of His creation. With reference to man this signifies that *all* of humanity, the integral Adam, exists in and for God; but for itself and for creation in general, this all-humanity is actualized in time.

Consequently, in every human being and in all of humankind, that which exists above or beyond time, as its deep basis, is distinguished from creation's temporal life, which is composed of a succession of current moments. Thus, we have two modes of human self-determination: (1) before time or on the eve of time (this does *not* mean *in eternity,* for eternity belongs only to uncreated, i.e., divine being) and (2) in temporal becoming. The two modes are connected, inasmuch as they belong to one becoming being in its original ("noumenal") and empirical self-determination. They are the prologue before time (which, however, already takes place in creaturely temporality) and temporal being itself. In the creaturely Sophia, ontology must therefore be distinguished from history, and supratemporality from time. But the history remains ontological, and the ontology is directed at and presupposes the history.

Thus, although the Creator posits temporality and, with it, time in the life of creation, He is not limited by time. Temporal succession in creation therefore exists only for man, not for God. In particular, this is also applicable to the creation of man, who, although he is born in history, originates in the one creative act of God, through the creation of the integral humankind. For God, humankind appears not as an aggregate, or sum, of human individuals, who first appear in time, but as an integral multi-unity, the all-human organism in all its fullness. Only by belonging to and being originally included in this organism do human individuals and generations acquire being in time. There *is as yet no* integral humankind in time, for it is still only appearing, but it does exist in supra-temporality, which is whence this appearance comes. In relation to this original existence, humankind does *not* differ from the assembly of angels, though, empirically, this assembly was fully created by a single act and is therefore not subject to multiplication. The two worlds are correlative: "What is above is also below." In "heaven," in the angelic world, the fullness of earthly being is already sketched out and given.

That the origination of the hypostases of the angelic world differs from that of the hypostases of the human world does not change the fact of their correlation. There is an aspect in which the unity of the creative act is manifested even more strongly and fully in relation to humanity than in relation to the angelic world. The angels are a *choir*. They realize the fullness of angelhood in the assemblage of angelic orders and individual angels. Although an angelic "nature" does not exist, yet, along with individual and hierarchical distinctions, the *particularity* of the existence of angels is real. They can resemble one another, and in this sense one angel repeats another as it were; however, this establishes between them neither a generic unity nor, thus, an identity, the latter being proper to humanity. About each individual man as a generic being, it can be said that he is not only an individual but also a man in general, a universal man, that all-humanity exists in him, although in an individual form. But this cannot be said about angels, for an all-angelhood that would be analogous to all-humanity does not exist. In this sense, angels are a choir, a harmonious multiplicity, not a multi-unity. Thus, what is ontologically necessary for the realization of the fullness of the angelic assembly is their creation in exhaustive fullness, the creation of the entire choir by an integral act rather than by successive and partial origination, as in the case of humanity, where through the succession of births, however, neither all-humanity nor all-unity is destroyed. As in other respects too, humanity thus more fully expresses the image of the Divine Sophia in the creaturely Sophia, for Sophia is ontological integrity, the wisdom of the whole, where each part is ontologically connected with and, in this sense, equal to the whole, whereas in the angelic choir, integrity is realized in the form of fragmented rays, interconnected but not interpenetrating.

Even though it exists in angels, the image of God is revealed in its fullness only in man.

Keeping in mind this *pre*-createdness of *all* of humanity in the fullness of its multi-unity "prior to" its birth in time, we must necessarily conclude that there exists an *integral* humanity with a definite, finite number of individuals, analogous to that of the angels. The bad infinity of successive generations and the unfinished and indefinite character of humanity resulting from this bad infinity are thereby overcome. There is a "human number," and it is finite, like the angelic number.

Here we again encounter the general aporia that we previously encountered with regard to both the angelic and the human world: Can the number of human beings, as well as the number of angels, be finite? In general, does not finitude belong to that relative and limited being which does not correspond to the divine fullness or pleroma, the pleroma of the Church? This question has a paradoxical character, which consists in the fact that, if the human number were infinite, God could never have finished the world, and the life of the future age, after the universal resurrection, could never begin. We are brought to this paralysis of thought by the idea of bad infinity as applied to the divine fullness.

We find an original application of this idea in connection with the problem of the eternity or non-eternity of the world in scholastic theology: Against the eternity of the world it is argued[57] that, if the world is admitted to be eternal, the number of human souls born would turn out to be infinite, and that this is impossible. To be sure, the doctrines of the eternity of the world and of the infinite number of creaturely souls do not coincide, since even in the case of the infinite duration of the world it is possible that only a finite number of souls would be born. The question consists not in this but in whether the divine fullness that is proper to humanity is capable of being reflected in a definite, finite number of human hypostases. We have already posed this question with reference to the number of angels, a number already definite and finite at their creation, according to revelation.

The guiding consideration for deciding this question is the fact that *fullness* belongs to the nature of the hypostatic spirit, and this fullness is experienced as infinite, inexhaustible depth, creaturely eternity, *aeviternitas*. In its hypostatic multi-unity, this fullness presupposes the diversity and therefore the multiplicity of individual modes, but by no means is this

---

57. Such an argument against the Averroists, the Arabic Aristoteleans, is presented by Bonaventura: Sent. 11 bis, p. 1, art. 1, qu. 2, ad *Sed. oppositum,* 5.

multiplicity a bad infinity, incapable of ending, of exhausting itself. Such a bad infinity would be precisely *lack of fullness*. Bad infinity is by no means synonymous with self-enclosed, self-sufficient eternity, with which it is sometimes equated (e.g., in eschatological discussions of "eternal" bliss and "eternal" torments, although it is obvious that two different modes of "eternity" are distinguished and opposed here; see below). Bad infinity would indicate only that creaturely being cannot encompass fullness. On the contrary, exhaustive fullness is realized not in bad infinity, in which it cannot be realized, but in a definite number of hypostatic centers. The governing Proto-image here is the Holy Trinity, where precisely three hypostases, not one or two, and not four or more, express, hypostatize the divine fullness. The same thing holds in the angelic world, although the number of angels and the inner justification of this number in relation to the fullness of angelic life are not revealed to us and remain unknown.

It is likewise with multiple human hypostases in relation to human fullness. This number too must be definite and therefore finite. We do not yet know this number, or its justification, but there is such a number. This is the "human number," human fullness. It is not important at what moment it will be realized in time, in empirical reality, but that moment of realization will come. Moreover, in nature, there are no repetitions of what bears the stamp of individuality and is a person. Only generic beings of the animal world, which are deprived of personality, are infinite with bad infinity. Being different specimens of their species and genus they, although empirically distinct, ontologically repeat one another. Individual immortality, personal eternity, is unnecessary and impossible for them, since there is no personality here. The fullness of the life of the genus and species is only a natural fullness; the multiplicity of individuals does not belong to it. In contrast, human fullness is a nature that is qualified in persons, who, being connected among one another, manifest human fullness in the image of the heavenly humanity of the Divine Sophia. If humanity were really subject to bad infinity, incapable of exhausting itself, it would even be incapable of setting such a task before itself. Humanity would then turn out to be completely subordinate to time; it would belong completely to creatureliness. But humanity has its own fullness, as a spiritual body, as an organism, as "Adam-Kadmon." Therefore, it belongs to eternity, though to creaturely eternity, which is realized in time.

These considerations lend support to the proposition that humanity is supratemporally created as a whole, by a single creative act, with the participation of creaturely self-positing. It is to this supratemporal being that the personal self-determination of every human being belongs, both in relation to himself, that is, to his own theme, and in relation to original sin, in relation to humanity and to the whole world. This self-determination is hidden in silence. It manifests itself only in the case of the empirical appearance of every man as a certain "predetermination" of him in this sense. Therefore, meta-empirically, the one integral humanity, Adam, *exists;* and it is possible for this integral humanity to determine itself in relation to the world and in relation to God. Its self-determination in relation to the world is original sin; its self-determination in relation to God is realized in the Incarnation and the redemption. This is the uncreated-created, divine-cosmic being that is the true intermediary — *metaxu* — between God and creation: Divine-humanity. All of creation has in God a supratemporal foundation and through this foundation participates in eternity, for the creaturely Sophia is the image of the Divine Sophia. And, in *this* sense, humanity too, as the center of the world, originates from God's eternity, though in its creatureliness it is subject to becoming or creaturely temporality, which knows *before* and *after*. This dynamic unity is present in man, for every person is not only an individual but *also* an all-man in his supratemporality. But, in the world, this unity is actualized only in the succession of time, whose focus is, of course, the birth of the new Adam, the true God-man: "When the fullness of the time was come, God sent forth his Son" (Gal. 4:4), for time is the moving image of eternity (Plato), eternity in becoming.

CHAPTER 2

Creaturely Freedom

In considering freedom, one must first take into account the extraordinarily wide range of meanings of this concept and therefore the great imprecision with which the term is used. As a result, the meaning of *freedom* can change within the scope of a single discussion. It is a kind of logical chameleon, and this has a fatal effect on the final conclusions. The primary reason for this chameleon character of the concept of freedom is that it does not have a positive content. It is inevitably correlative to something, expresses not *what* but *how*. In this sense, freedom is not an ontological substance but only a modality, which differs in different cases of its manifestation, depending both on its object and on its specific relation to its object. This is the main difficulty in interpreting freedom and the reason for endless misunderstandings concerning this question.

In itself, freedom is empty; it does not exist in and for itself as such. Nor is it a magician's hat, into which one can put or out of which one can pull all kinds of things. Freedom in general does not exist; only the freedom of something, in something, from something, to something, or for something, exists. Freedom is only a *predicate,* which can be predicated in relation to different concepts or essences, and it is more negative or delimiting than positive in its application. Taken as such, outside of relations that determine it positively in individual cases, freedom is simply a fiction of abstraction, a function turned into *res,* a modality taken for a reality. In this sense, freedom is completely analogous to the category of nothing, as the pure and absolute *not,* to negation. *Not* as such does not exist except in logical abstraction; it is definable only in repulsion from being, as a modality of negation. This bodiless shadow comes to life only when it drinks the living blood of reality. It then comes to life as delimitation, thus acquiring existence on a foreign body. A pre-creaturely or non-creaturely *nothing* simply does not exist. And "creation out of nothing" signifies only the absence of any foundation for the creation of the world except God Himself, for there is only God. Similarly, freedom *before* or *outside* of that which is the subject or object of freedom also does not exist except in logical reflection or ontological fiction. Freedom is characterized by modality and therefore relativism, and the concept of absolute freedom is a *contradictio in adjecto.*

I am saying all this not to diminish the significance of freedom (nor that of *nothing*) in being, but to remove certain preliminary misunderstandings and logical illusions, to put things in their place. On the contrary, the practical significance of freedom as a modality cannot be exaggerated. Just as, in the world of creaturely being, or becoming, *nothing* becomes a positive reality and even a force, so freedom is the breathing of the creaturely world. Therefore, the true definition of freedom must be sought in relative being, with reference to creaturely freedom, which, for practical purposes, is synonymous with freedom in general.

However, just as, in general, creation cannot be understood in and from itself without ascending by thought to the Creator and to its heavenly proto-image, so creaturely freedom must be understood on the basis of the relation that exists between the Divine and creaturely Sophia. If the true domain of freedom in its multifarious manifestations belongs precisely to the creaturely Sophia, its source must be sought in the Divine Sophia, and the problem of creaturely freedom in general is one of the fundamental problems of sophiology.

In what sense is the concept of freedom applicable to divinity, and what does it signify in this case? If one does not mythologize freedom, turning it into a kind of mythical being, but sees in it a relation or mode of being, then, clearly, the concept of divine freedom can be defined only by relations that exist within divine life. Is there a place here for freedom as such, as distinct from or opposed to *unfreedom* (which is qualified by different concepts, but most frequently as divine necessity)? Or is there no place here for such mutual limitation and opposition, since freedom and necessity are identical in God, so that they cannot be distinguished (nor, especially, opposed) except by abstracting thought?

Since the concept of freedom gets its positive content only depending upon that to which it is applied, we can distinguish it in relation to the divine hypostases in the Holy Trinity, in relation to the divine *physis* or Ousia and Sophia, God's essence and self-revelation, and finally in the relation of the Creator to creation.

Creaturely freedom is necessarily a play of light and shadow: The rays of freedom must be reflected from a wall which is its boundary, just as the I in Fichte's system requires a not-I in order to posit itself. Autonomous being collides here with what is given, and the self-positing of freedom reflexively appears only in connection with or as dependent upon unfreedom. Creaturely freedom is always relative or, what is the same thing, modal. This freedom is correlative with necessity.

But in God or for God there is no necessity or boundary. Therefore, there is no place here for *relative* freedom of the sort that exists in the creaturely world. In relation to God, the very use of the word *freedom* is imprecise and incorrect, for God is higher than freedom understood in relation to unfreedom, or necessity. He is supra-freedom, for which freedom as correlative to necessity does not exist, just as, in this sense, He is also supra-necessity. If we wish to express this idea in creaturely language, we would have to say that God is wholly freedom, or (what is the same thing) wholly necessity. Therefore, it is incorrect to apply to divine life these two concepts that are polar and antithetical in the creaturely world.

Freedom in creation is, first of all, connected with the *personal* principle. As *autonomous being,* the person is synonymous with freedom, as actuality or self-positing. Without this, the person does not exist. Personal self-positing is synonymous with life: The person is a living principle; the person is alive, and freedom is a function of life. The personal God is the living God: "As truly as I live, all the earth shall be filled with the glory of the Lord" (Num. 14:21). And if one speaks of freedom, or more precisely of supra-freedom, in God, one should first see it in the Divine Person, the divine I. But as Fichte showed convincingly, the creaturely I is, in its freedom, connected with necessity, with not-I, which reflects and limits it. On the other side, the creaturely I is limited by another I, the *co-I,*[1] thou, he. . . . The creaturely I is not absolute; its very freedom is unfree, confined within certain boundaries. Only the Divine Person is free and absolute, for it is the Holy Trinity, in which I and Thou are contained in one trinitarian Person. This Person has itself wholly in itself, and it does not require a co-I outside itself. Therefore, its autonomous being, or freedom, is sufficient unto itself.

What is the power that grounds and actualizes this freedom, frees it from limit or necessity? This power is the intrahypostatic love of the Holy Trinity. God *is* Love, and this definition of Revelation is applicable, first of all, to the divine trihypostatic Person. In the mutual love of the three

1. Cf. "The Chapters on Trinity."

127

hypostases, the hypostatic principle is exhaustively revealed and hypostatic limitation is overcome. In revelation, it is said not that God is freedom but that He is love. Therefore, He is higher than freedom in its indissoluble connection with necessity. In love, there is no place for freedom and necessity; there is only freedom, as free necessity. In love, there is also no place for personal self-assertion, although there is a place in it for personal self-revelation. Love is beyond freedom and necessity, because perfect fullness belongs to divine love. In divine love, all is given in order to gain all. "That which thou sowest is not quickened, except it die" (1 Cor. 15:36); "whosoever will lose his life for my sake shall find it" (Matt. 16:25).

The Holy Trinity, the Divine Person, is therefore free from freedom, above freedom. The Holy Trinity is Suprafreedom, which is love. But God is not only Person-Love; He also has His nature, which, as ousia or *physis,* is the root and depth of divine being and which, as Sophia, is its self-revelation in God. In the creaturely spirit, nature is givenness or unfreedom. It is necessity that is realized in the freedom of the person. For itself, the creaturely spirit is the unity of subject and object or predicate, and this duality is the presumption of a freedom that is thus connected with givenness and limitation. There is no such duality or limitation in divinity, for God's nature is a perfectly transparent self-positing of the trihypostatic Person. God's nature is fullness, in which neither what is given nor what is proposed exists. Being perfectly transparent, God's nature is thoroughly hypostatized by the divine hypostasis, belongs to the divine I, and in this sense is in no wise separated from this I, although it is distinct from it. God's nature does not violate or limit the divine freedom; nor, therefore, does it reflect it. The nature is vitally fused with the person here, although it is ontologically distinct from it.

God's nature is not only the silent, bottomless depth of Ousia, but also the speaking, self-manifesting Sophia. The trihypostatic person reveals itself in Sophia. Sophia is the thoroughly transparent bottomless abyss of the divine nature. Is Sophia a given that limits divinity and introduces in divinity the dialectic of freedom and necessity? No! For Sophia is the self-revelation of intrahypostatic love; she is love. Sophia is the self-positing of mutually self-sacrificing hypostases; she is completely permeated by hypostatic love, which is not negative freedom, reflected from necessity, but positive freedom, suprafreedom. Sophia is God's love for Himself in his self-revelation. She too loves God, though not with a hypostatic love. But love dissolves in itself all givenness, all necessity. God is love — positive freedom, suprafreedom, not only in the hypostatic but also in the natural and sophianic aspect. God is love not only as God but also as divinity.

We arrive at the paradoxical conclusion that, in God, there is no place for freedom, although the source of freedom for creatures is found in Him. Belonging to all that is created out of nothing, freedom is the ontological privilege precisely of creatures. And, by virtue of this connection with creatureliness, freedom is as much a gift of heaven as a *privilegium odiosum*. The character of this privilege is expressed both in the possibility of free agreement with one's genuine givenness, through obedience to God's commandment, and in disobedience with respect to this commandment, the possibility of which is revealed in the serpent's temptation: "Ye shall be as gods, knowing good and evil" (Gen. 3:5). Creaturely willfulness is bared here with the possibility of choice and, in general, the appearance of different possibilities.

However, as a preliminary, we must distinguish in the divine life that which belongs to God in Himself from that which belongs to Him as the Creator of the world, in creation. The concept of necessity and freedom as they are given in the creaturely world is usually introduced in connection with this distinction. That in God which belongs to Him Himself — His trihypostatizedness and nature, or His own being — is usually considered as necessity in Him, whereas that which refers to creation (and therefore God's creative act, His self-determination) refers to freedom *(liberum arbitrium)*, nonnecessity. That is, it is considered as something that did not have to be and as having a lower ontological rank. Such is the formulation of this problem from St. Athanasius the Great to Thomas Aquinas.

From the point of view noted above this entire distinction is a complete misunderstanding. On the one hand, divinity's proper life, which is qualified here as necessity, is also absolute freedom, for in God, who is Love, there is, in general, no place for necessity which is distinct and separate from freedom. To be sure, this freedom does not have anything in common with the arbitrariness and randomness of *liberum arbitrium*. In particular, it completely removes the presence of different possibilities of being or not being. This freedom permeates the entire being of the living God, for, if, in general, life is autonomous being and, in this sense, freedom, then the divine life is absolute freedom, for it does not have anything outside itself which could constrain it. But in this it does not differ in any way from that manifestation of the life of divinity which is expressed also in divinity's relation to creation. Freedom as a distinctive attribute of the divine creativity is recognized as belonging to divinity. But, for some reason, freedom is understood here in the bad sense of accidentalism, in the sense of the arbitrary choice between different but equally possible possibilities. Only a single and unique reality exists, which in its own way is not less "necessary" than God's own life in Himself, although this reality differs from God's own life. And if God is Love in His own life, He is Love as the Creator too, and this love contains the entire force of free necessity or necessity in freedom.

Here, one must distinguish the special directedness of God's love in creation, but this does not make love for creation unlove to any degree whatever, but only a special mode of the one divine love. As we have already pointed out, God-Love cannot fail to be the Creator and cannot fail to love creation, for He cannot fail to be Himself, that is, Love. And the manifestation of love in creation necessarily belongs to the fullness of its self-revelation. Love cannot leave unactualized even a single possibility of love, and, in this sense, it needs creation, although it is ontologically independent of creation. On the contrary, creation wholly depends on the Creator. God, the Creator of the world, is also the source of creaturely freedom, which, in a certain sense, belongs to the image of God in man, having also an uncreated principle in itself.

Freedom is personal. It is rooted in the life of the person; it is the disclosure of this life. But, in creation, freedom is *prior to* the person, so to speak, and ascends through various stages of development *to* the person. What significance can we attach to such an impersonal, subjectless freedom, which, however, is included in personal freedom? Such an extrapersonal freedom is, in general, nothing else but *life;* it corresponds to the living principle in creation. God did not create death, and all of God's creation is alive, is created for life that is immediately nonpersonal, or rather pre-personal. But this pre-personal life is capable of being included in all the forms of life, even the highest ones. To be sure, the inorganic world differs from the organic world. However, in the first place, all inorganic substances contain a special, though hidden, breath of life, which is still in a state of slumber, as it were. This is not an absence of life. It is sleep, or a state of unconsciousness. All these substances, each in its own way, represent, so to speak, "a site of life." They participate in life: they enter into the life of living beings and live in them. The inorganic becomes organic, and the whole world must be understood not only as a series of gradations of life but also as a living being, a universal organism. The wall between the inorganic and organic worlds is porous. These are not two alien, mutually hostile worlds, but two different states of one living world (as follows from the Genesis story of the creation of the world). The inorganic world is locked in a state of paralysis, but it is transformed, comes to life (if only partially) by becoming fused with organic matter.

All living things possess a sensitivity and spontaneity that can be called organic freedom as a state of life. But by no means do all living things participate in the personal principle, for this principle is foreign to the entire animal world. However, all living things have a special "organic" spontaneity of movement and a sensitivity, from the dimmest to the highest states of life. The combination of the two expresses *natural* freedom, in contrast to personal freedom. By virtue of this natural freedom, creaturely nature experiences itself, precisely at its highest stages, individually, though not hypostatically (because of the absence of personality). An individual is not a person insofar as it lacks the spiritual principle of personhood; however, in an individual, nature acquires concrete living being, and every animal individual is an independent center of natural life, with its spontaneity and sensitivity.

In this special sense, it is necessary to speak of creaturely freedom *prior to* and *outside of* man, of self-evident freedom in the animal world. The basic difference between animal freedom and human (and angelic) freedom consists in the fact that the former is not endowed with a creative power capable of personal self-determination. Even if it is individual, animal freedom is not personal. In this sense, animal freedom is wholly natural and instinctive. Animal life repeats itself, not manifesting itself by free acts of self-creation. Individual animals can be more or less successful, but they nevertheless repeat one another. The animal world does not have a history in which a creative personal principle is presupposed. "The soul of animals is in the blood," and they have only the life of the blood, lacking spirit.

As we have already indicated, this instinctive solution of life's problems by animals can be more complete and infallible than the effect of free human activity, for in the animal world there operates the wisdom of nature, the creaturely Sophia as the world soul. Viewed independently of the hypostases by which it is to be hypostatized, the world soul has its own freedom, since it is the general principle of the *life* of creation. The world realizes itself in the evolution of life, obeying an obscure instinct and ascending to higher forms of life *freely,* not as a thing but as a living being. It is as the organic world soul that the creaturely Sophia acquires her greatest independence and her greatest elemental power. It is as the organic world soul that she becomes most detached, as it were, from her heavenly prototype in the Divine Sophia. Her reality is expressed most powerfully in this elemental power, which is the most immediate manifestation of creaturely, impersonal freedom. Nature-philosophy very justly felt this freedom of the world soul in its struggle toward free self-realization, in the anguish and chaos of a being that had not yet achieved fullness. This freedom attains a great height first in the animal world, where the fire of life burns clearly, and then it reaches its peak in man, where nature transcends itself and the instinct of natural freedom passes into personal, spiritual freedom.

Thus, the most general precondition of freedom is spontaneity of movement, autonomy of life. Freedom is life diffused through creation and proper to every living being. It is the freedom of the world soul living in each living being, the *psychic* freedom of the "blood," insofar as blood is the soul of the animal world (and, in and through the animal world, of the entire pre-animal world). This world consists of the body, as matter contained in and coming to life in corporeality, *hule,* reality as such, and of the soul, living and vivifying. To this world, together with all the animals, man as a psychic (or natural) being also belongs, in contradistinction and even in opposition to the spiritual man: "There is a natural body, and there is a spiritual body. And so it is written: The first man Adam was made a living soul [Gen. 2:7]; the last Adam was made a quickening spirit" (1 Cor. 15:44-45). In the New Testament, this natural body is also called the *flesh:* "All flesh is not the same flesh: but there is one kind of flesh of men, another flesh of beasts, another of fishes, and another of birds" (v. 39). These different kinds of flesh are sometimes generalized according to the feature of life into a certain general notion of *flesh.* Only in the case of man is the taking on of flesh as a spiritual state considered blameworthy; and he is included in the order of the flesh of all the beings of the animal world who have blood as their principle of life. Man is taken here as belonging to one whole with all the "flesh" of the whole animal world, with "every living creature of all flesh" (Gen. 9:15).

As flesh or living soul, man belongs to the living principle of the world and is united with this principle by the spontaneity of life conferred by the world soul, by the natural freedom of the given. This freedom is the voice of nature itself, natural necessity, though a necessity that is not imposed from outside, like the law of matter in the inorganic, pre-animal world, but is rather the inner voice of life, life's own self-determination. There is no mechanical necessity here, even though such necessity is included in organic life, just as there is no external compulsion. This is the voice of life itself, the world soul, calling creatures and leading them on the pathways of their life. This is their free *amor fati.*

Without this spontaneity of life, its inner free automatism, the higher life of free beings, spiritual freedom, is impossible, this freedom which is correlated, first of all, with psychic, or natural, freedom: first natural, then spiritual (cf. 1 Cor. 15:46). Between rock and man stands the organic world, life in its spontaneity, for life is freedom. Along with this animal freedom, man contains a spiritual principle. He is an incarnate spirit, but a spirit that is inseparably united with flesh. For this reason it is said even about the Incarnation of God: "And the Word was made flesh" (John 1:14). The problem of human freedom necessarily includes this duality of man, the correlation of flesh and spirit.

Freedom in the true sense of the word exists in the life of the creaturely spirit, both in incarnate spirits, that is, in man, and in nonincarnate ("fleshless") spirits. Freedom is not absolute; it presupposes not self-creating, but *created*, given being. Freedom is conditioned, and also limited, by the *given*, which is synonymous with necessity. But this necessity is not a mechanical, outwardly acting force. Rather, it is the proper life of a living being in its spontaneity and conformity to law. It is, first of all, the life of the "flesh," which is not annulled by any freedom and which is *given* to man in his natural condition. This condition is not a dead, leaden mass, but a flexible, changeable, elastic given, which manifests resistance but gives way to force. Freedom is therefore correlative to the given as a task to be realized. What is essential here is that freedom never and in no sense is self-creation *out of nothing*, as something absolutely new, for it always realizes a task on the basis of the given.

In sophiological terms, one can say that the given is the Divine Sophia, as the eternal and absolute foundation of the world, while the task to be realized is the creaturely Sophia, in whom the image of the Divine Sophia is actualized on principles of freedom by the world soul, and then by human freedom. The absolute is actualized in the relative on pathways of creaturely creativity. In this sense, freedom must be understood as correlated with creaturely creativity. On the one hand, man is a living automaton, a "flesh" that receives its life from the world soul, the creaturely Sophia, as the given. But he also determines his life not automatically, but creatively, as a task to be realized, actualizing himself out of himself. In Plato's *Timaeus*, the demiurge creates the world while contemplating ideas, that is, the Divine Sophia, out of different mixtures of being with nonbeing, that is, within the limits of the creaturely world, the creaturely Sophia. This demiurge is, of course, not God, but man; and this image defines the place of man in the world as a creaturely god, who creates *not* out of nothing, but who creates . . . the creaturely Sophia.

In this sense, the category of freedom is identical to the category of (creaturely) creativity in its necessary correlativeness with the given as the condition or material of creativity. Freedom that detaches itself from this correlativeness, although it is not capable of ontologically transcending it, stops being true freedom, but is only a Luciferian pose, which is condemned as emptiness and . . . boredom. It is like a cliff that hangs over an abyss, but which, an illusory mirror, poses no risk of falling, for it does not have reality. For, we repeat, the absolute arbitrariness of *liberum arbitrium* is only a pose, powerless to realize itself even by falling into the abyss of *nothing*, for creaturely freedom cannot separate itself from its creaturely given, which protects it on all sides from the ontological abyss.

Creaturely freedom therefore has an antinomic character: It is connected with necessity, which is both its limit and the condition for its manifestation, the given that allows it to realize its task. The human person is the subject: it is determined by its predicate not passively but actively, by a free, creative effort. If we view the act of freedom from the point of view of the given determining it, we necessarily arrive at the deterministic negation of freedom: Necessity and automatism, although a living automatism, operate in human life; and freedom is only a subjective reflex or ontological illusion. If we look at life from within the creative effort, it presents itself to us precisely as freedom in all the certainty of this life act. The two opposite theses of the antinomy are equally convincing and ontologically justified by the character of creaturely freedom, which unites the task to be realized and the given. This antinomy of creativity is not a logical contradiction, which can and must be overcome. It expresses the very character of creaturely freedom. Freedom as self-determination — from itself, although in the given — is *power*. But, as having before itself the given, which limits and determines it, freedom is *powerlessness*.

Power is the manifestation of freedom as self-determination, and power is capable of increasing. Increasing power signifies man's humanization, his mastering of his own given, or nature, through freedom or creativity. In power, there is a certain synthesis of freedom and the given (necessity), their harmony. Creaturely freedom, or creativity not out of nothing but out of givenness, necessarily has a *theme*, which is sought and found freely. This creative freedom admits different *variations* in the execution of a given theme, but these are only variations, not the theme itself. The theme is written in heaven, in the Divine Sophia, although its execution (of which there are various possibilities) or nonexecution is entrusted to creation in its creaturely freedom.

We have arrived at the question of the image and likeness of God, insofar as they are manifested in man's creaturely freedom. Here, it is necessary not only to explain the resemblance between image and Proto-image but also to distinguish between the two. The freedom that creation experiences is *not* proper to God, for He is above freedom. God's suprafreedom, which is limited by no given and which is perfectly adequate to His nature, can signify in Him only the character of His self-positing by an absolute act. Creaturely freedom is precisely incapable of this absoluteness of self-positing. However, the image of God is preserved in creaturely freedom by the fact that this freedom is nevertheless a self-positing, though not an absolute one, and human life is marked by continuous personal self-creation. The image of God is therefore manifested, first of all, in the person, which is the principle of creativity and freedom. However, because this creativity is not absolute but presupposes a given in human nature, the image of God in man is a task requiring realization, and this is the *likeness* of God.

The image is connected with the likeness the way a task is connected with its realization, the way a question is connected with its answer, the way potency is connected with energy. Between the image and the likeness is the given, which grounds and determines the task to be realized. The given never presents itself in the form of a compulsory necessity, or in the form of a finished, perfect reality, which can only be accepted. On the contrary, the given is like an anamnesis, an infinite series of possible creative variations, but on the definite, absolute theme of the Divine Sophia, realized in creaturely Sophia — by man's creativity and therefore self-creativity.

Likeness is precisely human creativity, which has an "image" for itself. God has Sophia as the divine world and fully reveals Himself in her. Man also has Sophia, although not divinely but creaturally, as his given and the task he has to realize, as likeness that is always being attained. In their inseparableness, image and likeness therefore express man's creaturely and also creative freedom. In human life, there is nothing that does not bear the stamp of freedom or self-positing, and that also is not determined, in the broadest sense of the world, by the given. In this general ontological sense, there is nothing that is not determined. Freedom and determinism are equally proper to man.

The various aspects of this determinism are inexhaustible, from the tragic conflict between freedom and the given to their harmonious interpenetration, where the image of God shines in its absoluteness in creaturely life and the antithesis of freedom and necessity is overcome. On the pathways of creaturely life with its self-creativity, freedom is expressed in an infinite series of different possibilities, among which human freedom chooses. Freedom is free, that is, unmotivated except by itself. In this sense, it is truly *liberum arbitrium,* though only within the limits of particular self-determinations and settings of goals. But, at the same time, human actions are always motivated, which allows the adherents of philosophical determinism to deny the existence of freedom. However, there is a misunderstanding here, for the motivation is effected freely and creatively; the motives are accepted by freedom, however it may be determined by the given and the task to be realized.

Human action is always a *free* and (in this sense) a creative choice, the finding and actualization of *one* of many possibilities, whose number is indeterminate. Precisely this constitutes the freedom and indeterminacy of this choice. Precisely in this sense freedom always introduces something *new,* which is also synonymous with creativity. But this new thing is not absolutely new. It is not creativity out of nothing, but is determined within the general limits of the proto-images of being in the Divine Sophia.

Thus, in relation to image, likeness always moves along a line of possibilities, which fluctuate. The most difficult and painful state of freedom is indeterminacy, or the powerlessness to make a choice. This process is reminiscent of "creation out of nothing"; it is a kind of unconnectedness with or even opposition to the given. The opposite of creaturely freedom is ontological arbitrariness, which does not know its own paths; and liberation from such freedom signifies the triumph in us of true freedom, obedient to and permeated by the given: "Know the truth, and the truth shall make you free" (John 8:32), free from creaturely arbitrariness and in accord with the God-given givenness. Freedom in this sense grows; it knows its ages and paths. But the final limit toward which it strives is its self-revocation, in the image of God, that is, its merging with the natural given. The divine image of being is higher than freedom, even as the prehuman image of being is lower than freedom. The path of freedom in opposition to the given is man's path. This path must be taken to the end in human becoming, in order to achieve the triumph of the identification of freedom and necessity.[2] This once again confirms that freedom is not substantial but modal in character.

There is one more meaning of freedom, one that does not refer to ontology but that is of the greatest practical significance. This is its opposition to unfreedom, to all forms of coercion or pressure from external

2. In the inept language of Marxism this is called "the leap from necessity into the realm of freedom" — Balaam's ass bearing witness to the truth.

necessity (in the sociopolitical and economic domain). Coercion and need appear here as a sort of evil given, pressing on the decisions of our will and our acts. But however strange this might appear, the basic character of freedom as self-determination is not revoked or changed even here. Even our decisions that are most constrained in content remain not less free than any other decisions. External pressure and coercion are still directed at our freedom, and nothing can be accomplished by man without it.

Absence of external coercion does not, in itself, signify a lesser dependence upon the given or a greater intensity of creativity than when it is present. The freedom of human creativity is unassailable in its nucleus, whatever attempts may be made against it on the part of external coercion. In a certain sense, freedom and coercion are not correlative. This means that creaturely freedom is not omnipotence, which is proper only to God. Creaturely freedom does presuppose a certain power, which can be greater or smaller, but it is inevitably limited by powerlessness. But this concerns only manifestations of freedom, not freedom itself. One cannot deny that power is included in the task of freedom, whereas slavery, or powerlessness, is hostile to its actualization. Nevertheless, personal freedom and power (or powerlessness) never coincide. Only divine freedom is also omnipotence; the two are adequate to each other, owing to which freedom loses its independent, separate existence, which it has in creatureliness.

In creation, freedom arises and exists in unfreedom, as power in powerlessness. Without freedom, no power exists, just as no freedom exists without power. If creation were a thing, object, or mechanism, it would contain neither freedom nor necessity, for mechanism or thingness is not necessity, which is a reflex of freedom. Freedom experiences necessity as a certain limit for itself and also as a coercion. Freedom in the sense of omnipotence lies beyond freedom-necessity in their monodualism and inseparableness. To steal power as omnipotence and in *this* sense to become a god is the satanical temptation of "the prince of this world," possible only at the apex of creation, for the first of the created spirits. But such a pretension to omnipotence is, of course, illusory and imaginary, and does not allow creation to transcend freedom and necessity, does not lead beyond the *given,* the arena in which creatureliness is manifested. Even at the peak of attained power, of freedom in the mastery of creaturely nature, *that which* creation possesses does *not* belong to it: creation's natural power is given to it by God; it is a given that it can use. Stirner's utopian *Der Einzige und sein Eigenthum* or the absolute self-willfulness of Dostoevsky's underground heroes remains beyond the limits of what can be realized. Creation does not belong to itself. It is given to itself or created, and, in each act of creaturely freedom, it must bear witness to the *reception* of this gift as talents given and entrusted to it by God.

Like creaturely freedom, creaturely life by each of its acts bears witness to the Creator and the giver of life. "What hast thou that thou didst not receive? now if thou didst receive it, why dost thou glory, as if thou hadst not received it?" (1 Cor. 4:7). Atheism and anthropotheism, the former in stupidity and blindness, the latter in the madness of arrogance and rapaciousness, strive to appropriate this being, which is only given to them, to tear it away from the protosource. This convulsion of imaginary freedom is not able to gain dominion over creation. The pretension of creaturely pride, hubris, at bottom is nevertheless conscious of its created givenness, which it desires to transform into self-positing. This pretension strives to silence the voice of this self-witness, becoming exhausted in the exertions of blasphemy against God and rebellion, this negative devotion to God. But, in its normal state, creatureliness is precisely devotion to God, or more precisely, devotion to Sophia, although it exists *in re*, while *res* itself is manifested precisely in *modo*. For this reason, in our life, *modus* and *res* are often confused and even identified in practice. And this logic of the "practical reason" makes it possible to be tempted by the modality of freedom as a reality, by freedom in the actualization of the given as self-positing. But this is only a temptation, which distorts the normal relationship between modus and thing.

Creaturely freedom actualizes a certain inexorable potentiality, which is grounded in the divine given of creation, by a series of free creative acts. For divine life with its identity between freedom and self-positing as the self-given, the multiplicity of different possibilities does not exist. Only unique, universal, all-encompassing life exists for it. There is no *in one way or another*, no *more or less*. What we have here is the reign of total determinism in total freedom. This is divine freedom, the Pleroma. Therefore, the category of *possibility* does not, in general, apply to divine life, which is unique and absolute.

As we have seen, the application of this category to divinity is, in general, the weak point of Western theology. By contrast, this category of possibility is the determining one for creaturely life and creaturely freedom. It is the actualization of possibilities. Indissolubly connected with this is creaturely creativity, which consists precisely in such actualization, being equally distant from mechanical necessity and divine fullness, which equally annul all possibilities. This actualization of possibilities constitutes the distinctive character of creaturely creativity. The *new* thing that this creativity brings is determined in this actualization, for where there is no novelty, there is no creativity. Creativity, even creaturely creativity, always contains a certain relative novelty for creaturely life, sophianic variations, as it were. But this definition of creaturely creativity as an actualization of possibilities also contains its natural limitation. Possibility cannot be an ontological impossibility; it is limited by the given in which it is realized — within the limits of the world.

Supramundane creativity, absolute creativity "out of nothing," is wholly inaccessible to creaturely creativity. *Nothing* is a negative limit to such creativity, just as the given of the world is its positive limit. Attempts at creativity out of nothing, or at divine creativity, are, in all their diversity, only a satanic convulsion, an impotent grimace, and do not go beyond such a pose. Possibility is always conditioned; it exists only in the presence of a determinate given, a created being. It cannot free itself from this given, cannot transcend it. Therefore, the category of possibility is applicable in general to the creaturely Sophia, is a characteristic feature of the creaturely Sophia, whereas this category is completely inapplicable to the Divine Sophia. In its ontological foundation, the creaturely world is wholly determined, from beginning to end. This *determinism* is the Wisdom of God, the Divine Sophia, who reveals herself in the creaturely Sophia.

However, in the mode of its being for itself, in its own life, the creaturely world is not subject to determinism, but is a possibility that is ceaselessly being actualized, infinite, inexhaustible creativity and becoming. Mixed with *nothing* and herself having become becoming, entrusted to freedom, the creaturely Sophia is *the possibility of possibilities,* the ontological place of the creative freedom of creatures. But this possibility is limited by impossibility, both from above and from below. The upper bound is established by the perfect inaccessibility for creation of the power of the divine creative act, and the desire to attain it only attests to creation's powerlessness and limitedness. The lower bound is relative and always mobile. It passes through the domain of what can be realized in general, *in abstracto,* but what cannot be realized by means of a given creative act. Even though it is not yet an insane pretension, exceeding the bounds of the possible, a problem that is beyond one's powers to solve is nevertheless an error in the evaluation of these powers, whose deficiency makes the objectively possible a de facto impossibility. Creaturely power is always limited and cannot become omnipotence.

Possibility enables *individuality,* which is characterized by unrepeatability and, in this sense, originality. Originality, that is, primordiality, self-belonging, is united here with the given, as the possibility of a given concrete possibility. Creaturely originality is relative and limited, and, in this sense, it must be distinguished from divine originality, which is single and unique, excluding all possibilities. This difference is, in any case, a sign of incompleteness and imperfection. But creaturely originality transcends the uniformity that is proper to instinct and to mechanical necessity with its determining principle: *causa aequat effectum.* In creaturely creativity we have, on the one hand, an inner *causa,* lying in the depths of personal being, a *causa* as the ontological boundary and theme of being. On the other hand, we have in it the free, creative execution of this theme, its "original development," creaturely creativity as the actualization of a new possibility. Creative freedom is the presence of possibilities, while free creativity is the selection, from an indeterminate number of possibilities, of one for actualization. Objectively, *possibility* is a peculiar combination of givenness-*necessity,* within the limits of which it is actualized, with freedom (in this sense, randomness), which is introduced by the modifying act of the free selection of one possibility or another.[3]

Creaturely freedom, as the possibility of possibilities, is, in this sense, an *indeterminacy,* which passes into determinacy by an autonomous act, by self-determination. This constitutes its "contingency," which is neither causelessness nor determinedness. Contingency corresponds to the *multiplicity* of possibilities contained in one general given. Such multiplicity plays a role not only in the different aspects of free self-determination in general, but also in the possibility that these aspects can change in time. This changeability is, as it were, the reverse side of creaturely freedom, which is essentially connected with the limited nature of all the forms of creaturely being, its implenitude and inadequacy to itself, to its proper task. This expresses the general ontological foundation of creaturely being, the relation of the Divine Sophia to the creaturely Sophia: heaven and earth, the eternal foundation and the empirical actualization. This actualization is accomplished on the basis of creaturely freedom in a series of attempts, each of which is, in itself, imperfect and inadequate, but nevertheless belongs to the *path* and is included in the actualization.

---

3. In its logical structure, the relation of free possibility to determined givenness can be likened to the statistical law of large numbers. The general limits of givenness are expressed here in a regularity manifested in the case of a large number of observations, whereas individual deviations from the mean, in which alone the regularity is realized, correspond to concrete cases of modal freedom. The law itself does not constitute a form of mechanical necessity, unchangeable in itself, but is applied to history and sociology. No other type of regularity exists or can exist here.

140

This changeable nature of freedom corresponds not only to the multiplicity of possibilities, the pluralism of creativity, but also to its various degrees, or ages. We have already spoken of the liberation from creaturely freedom as the path of overcoming different possibilities toward the one, higher reality, which is the adequacy of the creaturely Sophia to the Divine Sophia: God will be all in all. This is the path of the clarification of different possibilities and their comparative assessment, the path from randomness to free determinism, from many possibilities to a single possibility, choice being overcome. The Church teaches that, after the trial experienced with the fall of Satan, the holy angels are no longer subject to this changeable nature of freedom, that they have become liberated from this bad freedom, and find themselves on the straight and righteous path. The same holds for human saints beyond this world; for them too there is only a single reality, removing different possibilities, as the highest degree of freedom.

This reality is opposite to the original state of *liberum arbitrium indifferentiae* before the fall. It represents, as the experience of sin has shown, the presence of unlimited possibilities, which in fact was manifested in the fall. We must therefore replace the abstract, formal concept of freedom, as *indifferentia,* with its concrete, living, developing manifestation on the basis of inner determinism, to which a determinate creativity of life corresponds. Even though it is established on the unshakable foundation of the Divine Sophia, the life of the world, or the creaturely Sophia, assumes a character of indeterminacy depending on the presence of freedom. Although the improvisation of freedom is accomplished not out of nothing but on specific themes, this improvisation actualizes a series of different possibilities, in the case of a choice between different paths of life.

These creaturely variations of freedom are also united with the action of divine providence (about which below). This introduces a corrective, so to speak, to this changeability which accompanies the slackness and occasionalism of creaturely freedom, with the multiplicity of its possibilities; and this assures the achievement of the goal of creation. But this divine interference does not remove the presence of different possibilities in the paths of the life of creation. Scholastic theology attributes to God Himself the presence of such different possibilities, admitting here too the possibility of *more or less,* considering the created world not only as one of many possible worlds (and even admitting the possibility of its noncreation) but, in general, as imperfect in itself. To admit this *ex parte Dei,* in relation to God as the Creator, is wholly impossible. God *creates* on the basis of the Divine Sophia all that is "good" (cf. Gen. 1:4, etc.). And He created in exhaustive fullness, after which He "rested from all his work."

But we must recognize the presence of *different* possibilities and, therefore, successes or failures, *better or worse,* on the part of creatures. In the creation of the world, God acts on the basis of the Divine Sophia: "The Lord by wisdom hath founded the earth" (Prov. 3:19). But in the life of the already created world, or the creaturely Sophia, He acts jointly with creation itself, created on the basis of creaturely freedom, and He therefore interacts with creation. This interaction exists already in the supra-temporal act of creaturely self-positing, just as it exists in the temporal process of the history of the world and man. Here, the perfection of creation, "God is all in all," is actually achieved through imperfection, thanks to the limitedness that characterizes every creaturely act. And the life of creation as the revelation of the creaturely Sophia cannot be otherwise.

In this imperfection, caused by creaturely freedom, that which can be called the *kenosis* of the Divine Sophia in the creaturely Sophia is manifested. God's kenosis in relation to creation consists in the fact that God posits, along with His absolute, supramundane being, the becoming being of the creaturely world, and in this becoming being the presence of creaturely freedom, corresponding to his self-determination and correlated with his "will." On the other hand, the kenosis of Sophia consists in self-diminution from fullness to potentiality. The measure of this kenosis even increases with ascent to the higher stages of creaturely freedom. If, in the pre-organic world, "non-living" nature is more or less obedient to the sophianic laws of its being, this obedience decreases with the appearance and affirmation of the spontaneity of life. The dark instinct of the genus is, in this sense, sophianically more conforming to law than the self-determination of individuals, and this conformity to law is hidden even deeper inside when there appears in the world the personal principle with its creative freedom, actualizing out of itself the sophianicity of its own life.

Insofar as it is synonymous with creaturely creative activity or self-creative activity, creaturely life contains an ontological antinomy. If creatureliness is a given, then freedom is the striving to transcend this given, to free oneself of it, to reveal oneself in self-affirmation. Freedom strives to escape the given, but at the same time it actually thirsts for it, like a snake catching itself by its tail and at the same time fleeing from itself. It is not by chance that the "ancient serpent" is a metaphor for rebellious creation, which asserts itself in imaginary absoluteness but which actually possesses only a creaturely freedom and therefore is afflicted by envy. Creaturely freedom is serpentine circular motion, which would be empty and contentless if it did not find support in the fixed base of its own (although creaturely) being, actualized in freedom. It is only thanks to this fixed base that this motion does not come to naught but is a spiral ascent.

"Ye shall be as gods, knowing good and evil," the serpent tempts Eve with the false phantom of absolute freedom, which, of course, does not consist in knowledge of good and evil with their limitedness and relativity. Absolute freedom, insofar as one can speak of it, is free of all given and coincides with divine omnipotence and self-determination. Satan's temptation, deceptive and death-dealing to creation, actually wishes to nullify the freedom of creation, while pretending to remove its antinomy and to make it free *quand même*, independent of all given, free out of itself. That is, it wishes to make creation a fruitless void instead of positive creativity. Antinomy in the life of creation is not a sign of weakness but the fire of life. This antinomy expresses the character of the creaturely Sophia as Divine-humanity, in which two forms of being, two natures, are united without separation and without confusion, in accordance with the Chalcedonian ontology.

But this antinomic duality inevitably puts the stamp of relativity, limitation, and, therefore, imperfection on creaturely freedom. Creaturely freedom has a theme not in itself but for itself, and this theme, even though it belongs to the sophianic cosmos, is isolated from this cosmos and is given into the particular possession of individual freedom, whose task it then is to realize it. But the dialectic of creaturely freedom consists in the fact that, at first, this theme must be received and assimilated as one's own, in all its individual limitedness; then, at the end of the path of freedom, it must merge with the ocean of sophianic being, its singularity participating in fullness, and on the pathways of freedom, overcome individuality for the sake of higher and ultimate freedom, with the acceptance of sophianic determination as the goal.

Thus, freedom as the limitedness of individual being, as well as its ontological fullness, is given as the principle of creaturely life, as a particular creative act of God, calling creation to being. But individual being, positing the principle of creaturely freedom, precisely contains all the relativity of creaturely creativity, all its fateful limitedness. This being cannot attain the chef d'oeuvre that it seeks; it is limited in its tasks and possibilities, and it is thus condemned to commit errors. *Es irrt der Mensch, solang er strebt* [Man errs as long as he strives]. Limitedness and implenitude, leaving room for various possibilities and therefore errors, make the path of creaturely freedom a broken one, not a straight one. This curved, zigzag ascent is a search for oneself, an effort to disclose the unique face of individuality in creation as well as its place in the whole, in the pleroma, in the sophianic proto-image of being. Even when it is submerged in the ocean of universal being, no streamlet of life loses its identity.

Thus, all creaturely creativity is imperfect and error-prone. This holds for the creativity of both men and angels ("Behold, he put no trust in his servants; and his angels he charged with folly [Job 4:18]; "Know ye not that we shall judge angels?" [1 Cor. 6:3]). This is not yet sin or evil, although it is a favorable soil for the latter through a certain limitation of vision. On the contrary, this is a kind of ontological shadow of creatureliness as non-absolute being. This limitation is not insurmountable; on the contrary, it is to be overcome on the pathways of freedom, which will be creation's highest achievement. Only what was directly called to being by God's omnipotence was originally perfect ("it was good"), not what belongs to an even more perfect and higher order of creation, to the free and creative order, namely, to human beings and angels, who bear in themselves the image of God and whose task, in their creative activity, is to realize his likeness in themselves.

This final goal justifies this order's shaky, fluctuating path toward freedom, marked by the fatal implenitude and imperfection proper to becoming. Therefore, the path of the world is a multistep, multistage actualization of possibilities given to freedom in the fulfillment of its tasks. We repeat, imperfection is not sin or evil in itself. The path of freedom is the *good* of creaturely growth, the gift of the Creator's condescension toward the creature. But imperfection is characterized by successive approximations, by a search with inevitable errors and deviations, which nevertheless are to be overcome. On this path, man in his creaturely freedom is not left to his own powers. He is assisted by divine providence (about which below), although this assistance is accompanied by temptations from the evil power, pushing man onto the path of disorganization, selfhood, arbitrariness, and rebellion. In any case, creaturely freedom is synonymous not only with power but also with powerlessness, limitedness, and imperfection, although this freedom, on its laborious and arduous path, belongs to the image of the sought-for perfection.

In summing up this ontological analysis of creaturely freedom, we must note once again that the notion of *liberum arbitrium indifferentiae* is inapplicable to it, in the direct sense. What does creaturely freedom really mean? It is correct to say, on the one hand, that creaturely freedom is always an element characterized by spontaneity, by the absence of causal necessity. Freedom cannot be annulled by coercion. Even when man acts contrary to his own will, out of weakness or coercion, the latter too is introduced into the sphere of his freedom, is freely (and to that extent responsibly) accepted. In this sense, freedom is synonymous with life. This self-determination, this spontaneity in the sense of causelessness, is the very essence of freedom, which is a divine gift of the Creator, who communicates to creatures the image of His creative activity. This is not an illusion but reality itself, *"Ding an sich,"* in man, alongside his empirical causal determinability. Man lives in freedom, creatively, however insignificant this freedom may be in its range in general and in each of its separate acts in particular. Man will be judged precisely according to the deeds of his creative activity in freedom.

However, freedom is inseparably connected with the fact that it is determined and motivated (which, according to Schopenhauer, is only one of the modes of the general law of causality). *Indifferentia* is an empty abstraction, corresponding to nothing in reality. Free will is always and inevitably motivated and, first of all, from within. Creaturely freedom is always actualized within a determinate given; its entire content and its positive possibilities depend on this given. The arbitrariness of *liberum arbitrium* is therefore limited by the acceptance or nonacceptance, the selection or rejection, of different possibilities that arise on the basis of the given. And external coercion, the pressure of necessity or compulsion, takes an inner coefficient in the person, becomes inner self-determination. Therefore, freedom is never the irrational arbitrariness of *sic volo* but is always and invariably motivated with all the power of persuasiveness for each given moment. Freedom lets itself be convinced and compelled; it requires this, because otherwise it would remain a motor without a drive. Freedom is inseparably united with the given, for it is limited and relative. But, as a result, freedom can be diverse and capable of growth and education.

In general, the abstract concept of freedom as a uniform act of personal self-determination actually has a numberless multitude of concrete forms and degrees. But, for all of them, there is but one door leading into personal life. This door is opened by freedom, and except through this door, nothing can enter personal life. This is the necessary foundation of personal life, not only in this age but also in the future age. God communes with the creature on the basis of His own image that is imprinted in it. He communes with the creature through the personal principle, as person to person, as absolutely free and self-positing Subject with creaturely subject, which is limited in the possibilities of its self-positing but nevertheless possesses this divine gift of freedom. And if the creature is called to actualize *in likeness* the divine image imprinted in it, then one of the tasks of this likening to God is to use the modality of freedom in such a way that it will not feel itself to be in conflict with necessity or limited givenness.

CHAPTER 3

Evil

1. Creaturely Limitedness and Imperfection

The world is the creaturely Sophia. It is created by God and is therefore divine in its foundation. The fullness of being is implanted in the world and all the perfection that is possible for creation lies in this fullness. "It was good" to such an extent that God could "rest" from the works of creation that He had made. But how did evil get into the world, and what is evil?

First of all: Does evil *exist,* as an independent principle of being, as a "substance," alongside good? The philosophers of antiquity, the church fathers, and the scholastic theologians all unanimously answered this question in the negative: evil does *not exist* alongside good as an independent principle, a principle that competes with and is parallel to good. Oriental dualism, which accepts two equal principles, the good god and the evil god, the primordial light and darkness, is completely incompatible with Christianity just as it is with any healthy worldview. Evil is not a substance but a *state* of creaturely being. "The prince of this world" is not a god but only a rebellious creature. As it is most commonly defined, evil is an absence of good, *sterēsis, privatio,* an accident, a parasite of being. In the positive sense, only Good, only God and His power in creation, exists. Ontologically, evil does not exist, but is a phantom of nonbeing.

But it is insufficient to expose evil in its ontological nothingness before the face of God; one must also recognize its fatal, destructive force in creation. For if in the higher, divine plane, evil does not exist, it exists in the lower, creaturely plane, as a positive and peculiarly creative force. One must define the place of evil in the world, if only in its parasitic being. If

147

God did not create evil, where did it come from? If evil is not being but only a *state* of being, how did this state become possible?

There is a certain general precondition of evil, which, in itself, is not yet evil, but which makes room for evil, provides an objective possibility for it. This precondition has two aspects, objective and subjective. It refers to the *nature* of creatures and to creaturely *freedom*. Essential to creatureliness is *becoming*, process, in which the fullness, plan, and idea of creation, sketched out in the heavens, in the Divine Sophia, are actualized. This signifies that, even though it enters *potentially* into the whole, every individual part or stage of being is necessarily *limited*, for it is actually separated from the whole. Every individual part of being belongs *to the all* without actually being *in the all*. This state exists as long as there is no fullness, as long as God is not in the all and the all is not in God. This limitedness of *all* being, its fragmented or partial character, also signifies that it is not infallible.

Creaturely being allows the existence of different possibilities, which are not equivalent, even if their integral gives a positive and desired result. The mere presence of different possibilities already signifies that none of them are infallible, or perfect, that all are in a state of seeking. Perfection is what is sought by, not given to, creatures, who do not know the chef d'oeuvre, and this is not only because of sin but primarily because of creatureliness. It is precisely in this sense (in what other?) that Scripture speaks about angels: "His angels he [God] charged with folly" (Job 4:18). The service of the holy angels, free of evil and sinfulness, can contain errors and deficiencies simply as a result of creaturely limitedness and therefore imperfection. This limitedness of creatures and the resulting non-infallible state in the absence of the chef d'oeuvre are also manifested in creaturely creativity, which is included in the plan of the world's creation. This creaturely creativity does not possess divine perfection and fullness, although it is free, for such is the very nature of creativity. Although it creates out of the given and on a given theme, it also has an element of creation out of nothing, which permeates with limitedness all creaturely being in its becoming.

The creative self-determination of creatures is subject to imperfection and error, allows for different paths and possibilities. But imperfection and the presence of different possibilities are not yet evil, just as error is not sin. Rather, they simply characterize becoming as such. Even if evil had not entered into the world, this possibility and presence of creaturely errors and imperfections would have been inevitable. Of course, we have in mind here precisely the *creaturely* aspect of the world's becoming, but the latter is not limited to this aspect. It also includes the divine participation of providence with its infallibility in relation to creaturely errors and limitedness. Thus, from the side of nature, creaturely creativity entails not only the possibility but even the inevitability of errors, which, in themselves, are not yet evil but prepare a place for evil. In itself, the creativity of creatures is the work of God's love and condescension, which entrusts to the limited powers of creatures the fulfillment of God's will "both in heaven and on earth."

Error and imperfection are, in a certain sense, the privilege of creatures, since their relation to the world is neither automatic nor instinctive. If the world were an automaton or a *perpetuum mobile,* it would operate with the precision of a mechanism or with the infallibility of instinct, but then there would be no place in it for creaturely creativity, which is synonymous with life. And the world would then be dead — but God did not create death. If some say that the imperfection of creation is attributable to the Creator, and He is therefore responsible for this imperfection, to this we must answer that the path of imperfection leads to the state of perfection in which God will be all in all. But this could not be the original state of creation. Creation's task is to actualize itself, to find itself by its *own creativity,* this thanks to the fullness of the divine powers implanted in it but despite the limitedness of each individual point of being in actualized multiplicity. God's love and goodness, His "long-suffering patience and great mercy," are manifested precisely in the giving of a relative autonomy of being to creation even at the price of limitedness. God put *everything* into His creation that could be put into it. This gift of the Creator to creation, the given as a task to be realized, contains fullness and perfection to the extent they can be received by creation, which is created out of nothing and permeated by this nothing as its inner boundary. However, the creature receives the possibility of ascending to perfection, of removing boundaries, of overcoming the "individual" as self-isolating, nonuniversal being in the ongoing sophianization of creation.

The imperfection of creation is manifested not only in the spiritual and animate world but also in the kingdom of nature, in prehuman and even inorganic being. The natural world is created by God as "good" (Gen. 1). The original earth, *tohu vabohu,* obediently attended God's creative word and produced out of itself what it was commanded to produce. However, even in this original perfection, the prehuman world was created with man's creative action in mind. The task of man's creative activity is to raise the world, by humanizing it, to the perfection implanted in it, for man was told: "Be fruitful and multiply, and replenish the earth, and subdue it: and have dominion" over the entire animal world (Gen. 1:28). In the beginning "there was not a man to till the ground" (2:5), but after his creation he was put "into the garden of Eden to dress it and to keep it" (2:15). Indeed, he was called to transform the entire world into this garden of God. Thus, even nonhuman nature was to a certain degree entrusted to man's creativity for the purpose of being elevated to perfection and fullness.[1]

All the same, we can differentiate various degrees of perfection in nonhuman nature by establishing a certain general principle for this differentiation: The lower a given genus stands on the organic ladder of life, the more fully it will actualize itself and, in this sense, the more perfectly and, so to speak, infallibly it will express itself. Such is inorganic nature. Such, further, is instinctive life in the organic kingdom, the natural structure of organisms. It is, in general, all the aspects of being in which the action of God's creative hand is manifested. In contrast, the highest form of creation, namely, man, being called to perfect and create himself, is most marked by imperfection and limitation. Therefore, man has a *history,* something that the instinctive and, to this extent, automatic life of animals does not have. The historicism of human existence (which through man extends also to the world of fleshless spirits) attests to man's imperfection in every given epoch, as well as to his being called to perfection through self-creation, which is the high calling of the children of God. God's original blessing already contains this summons of man to history: "Be fruitful, and multiply, and replenish the earth, and subdue it: and have dominion" (Gen. 1:28).

2. Creaturely Freedom as the Possibility of Good and of Evil

The world is created in man and in angels on the basis of the freedom of creaturely self-determination. This refers, first of all, to the supramundane or premundane self-determination of every creaturely spirit (see above). Such is its creaturely *how* with regard to the reception of the theme of its being, given by God. *More or less, better or worse, fuller or more meager, more or less successful* are possible here. This difference of *measure* in the reception of one's own degree of genius that is given by God to every human being (for no human being is created empty, bereft of his own theme) does

---

1. Cf. *The Philosophy of Economy.*

not yet contain evil. Rather, it contains the original differentiation according to talents, which are given (in this sense, it would be more precise to say: "taken") in quantities of five, two, and one for creative application in life. And it is the work of God's wisdom and providence to assist creaturely freedom in increasing these talents to the measure of fullness. But, here, the different degrees of perfection connected with creaturely freedom are determined by acceptance or nonacceptance, obedience or disobedience. Manifested here is the peculiar inertia of the nonbeing, the *nothing*, "out of" which human beings (and the angels) are created. This *nothing* offers passive resistance, for only the uncreated, that is, the Divine Spirit, the *actus purus*, is fully actual. This passive resistance of ontological inertia is overcome in different degrees by creaturely freedom.

On this basis the creaturely spirit can be a more or less adequate or inadequate image of itself. Of course, not one of the spirits called to being by the Creator can be fully unsuccessful with respect to itself, for that would mean that it has rejected its own being, and that God's creative act is unrealized. To speculate about such possibilities of nonbeing, about such phantoms of emptiness, of *nothing*, is a useless abstraction, for only being exists. Nonbeing does not exist. Therefore, for practical purposes, we must conclude that there is no creaturely spirit that would fail to respond to God's creative call, and it can only be a question of difference in the responses. Of course, these differences in the mode of receiving being from God's hands admit a certain imperfection, a certain defectiveness from the very beginning (even apart from original sin). But, in itself, defectiveness is not yet sin, although it is a predisposition to sinfulness. However, sinfulness can also be caused by a relative fullness, if this fullness is not accompanied by a disposition to persevere in the life of the spirit (Lucifer).

The active manifestation of creaturely freedom in life begins only "after" creation, upon the entry of creatures into time. Two possibilities, two paths of life, exist from the very beginning: The first is the path of the direct acceptance of God's lordship, with increasing conformity to God's will, *outside* the opposition between good and evil, outside their tragic collision and antagonism. The second is the path of the appearance in man of such antagonism and struggle. Good and evil, with their opposition, do not exist from the very beginning, but belong to the creaturely and fallen world, in which "the light shineth in darkness." Darkness is the invisible and, in this sense, nonexistent substratum of the light, corresponding to the precreaturely *nothing* (of course, not in the chronological but in the ontological sense). "God is light, and in him is no darkness at all" (1 John

1:5). As darkness, this nothing is actualized in creation, in creation's becoming, which essentially is a combination of light and shadow. Darkness becomes a reality when the equilibrium of this combination is disrupted, and the shadow stops being only a means for the light but opens a path for darkness.

This initially occurs in the creaturely spirit, which, in its limitation and in its freedom, is capable of realizing the nothing as darkness, that is, as evil in its opposition to good. In creation a state free of this opposition exists. Creation begins with and ends with this state. On the one hand, this is the state of childish innocence and inexperience, passive saintliness in the sense of ignorance of sin and evil. On the other hand, it is the state of active saintliness, which defeats and transcends sin and evil. "Whosoever shall not receive the kingdom of God as a little child, he shall not enter therein" (Mark 10:15). Good is correlative with evil, and the two are extinguished in the light of saintliness as the image of God: "ye shall be holy; for I am holy" (Lev. 11:44). Between the saintliness of innocence and the saintliness of active accomplishment lies the path of good and evil, the keeping of the commandments.

The initial naivete, which instinctively, as it were, obeys the inner call of nature in its sophianicity, needs a commandment directed at freedom. Such precisely was God's commandment given in paradise to Adam and Eve, whatever its concrete content may have been. This commandment reveals to man the possibility of the appearance of good and evil in their opposition. This commandment corresponds to the untested, naive state of creatures. But for saintliness in the state of maturity and experience this commandment loses its force. For the righteous there is no law; there is only love. Even though we have no direct knowledge of God's commandments in the angelic world prior to the fall of Satan, we can suppose that the angels knew an analogous situation "under the law," where their freedom was put to the test, a freedom that would cease to exist in the later state of spiritual maturity and experience. The holy angels are now beyond good and evil: freedom as choice has been transcended, for their choice has been made.

Good arises together with evil; it is the reaction of saintliness to sin and evil. Having arisen in creation, evil casts on everything its sinister shadow and evokes the counteraction of good, which, in this sense, is tried and tested saintliness, the opposition to evil. Temptation approached even the Only Sinless One, the Son of God and of man, who entered the world that had become subject to "the prince of this world." The Lord came precisely to destroy Satan's works and to annul his power, by accepting temptation in his battle against evil: "the prince of this world cometh, and hath nothing in me" (John 14:30; cf. Heb. 2:18). Evil is a real and active power in the world, and it is, of course, insufficient to understand it only negatively, as absence of good or imperfection. It is a special kingdom, which has its own "prince." Even though his works are already destroyed and he has been chased away, the prince remains in the world for a time.

The principle of evil in the creaturely world is the fruit of creaturely self-determination and creativity. Evil *arises* in time, just as it has its end in time. One can say that, in a certain sense, evil is created by creatures (both angelic and human), but, of course, not "out of nothing" (which is the character of God's creation). Rather, it is created out of the creatures themselves, who are created by God. In this sense, evil is a parasite of being; it arises in being as its sickness; it gets its strength from being. Actualized *nothing* becomes a reality.

Evil comes from creaturely freedom. The world, created by God as "good" (Gen. 1), is given by God to man and the angels to protect and lead to fullness. Creaturely freedom is thereby implanted in the world's being, and, through this freedom, evil is also implanted in the world. According to Church doctrine, evil appears first (both ontologically and chronologically) in the spiritual world, in the world of fleshless angels. It is here that evil exists in a pure form, not as a misunderstanding, error, or even deception (as in man), but as direct self-determination. Evil arises here directly in the domain of the relation to God, for fleshless spirits see Him face to face. No atheism or half-faith is possible here, according to the direct testimony of a servant of the Lord: "the devils also believe, and tremble" (James 2:19). Evil is direct rebellion against God and hostility toward Him. According to revelation, before Lucifer fell his position was the most elevated in creation (see Ezek. 28:14-15; Isa. 14:12-13). Consequently, a certain period of time elapses *before* the fall, and then during the fall itself (for there are no grounds to conclude that the fall occurred in an instant, and to deny the presence of a certain process and struggle here: cf. Rev. 12:7). As a result of the fall, a self-determination *against* God occurs, which inevitably leads to the expulsion of Satan from the heavens after a spiritual battle with the archangel Michael and his host.

Freedom is without cause. It determines itself on the basis of itself. In this sense, the original sin associated with the fall of the angels is, as a work of freedom, without cause and irrational. It is not subject to any rational explanation. Furthermore, it is irrational and antirational, self-willful and arbitrary. But such precisely is creaturely freedom. Creaturely freedom not only conforms to law in the sense of freely agreeing with the objective law of creaturely being, in its sophianicity, in God. But it is also arbitrary, rebellious, insane. The potential capacity not only for good (i.e., for conformity with objective law) but also for evil (i.e., for arbitrariness and caprice) is the *privilegium odiosum* of creation in its original untested state. And this capacity cannot be taken away from creation even in the face of the terrible danger that is contained in it: satanism. For God's love, manifested in the creation of the world on the basis of creaturely freedom, will endure any sacrifice in its long-suffering patience, and it is ready in advance to redeem and restore the distorted face of creation.

As we already know, there are two aspects of the self-determination of the creaturely spirit: supramundane or supratemporal, and in time. God's thought about creation is fulfilled in time, and creation comes out "good" from the Creator's hands. Therefore Satan too was created as an angel, indeed, as the supreme angel, as "Lucifer, son of the morning" (Isa. 14:12): "Thou sealest up the sum, full of wisdom, and perfect in beauty. . . . Thou art the anointed cherub that covereth; and I have set thee so: thou wast upon the holy mountain of God; thou hast walked up and down in the midst of the stones of fire. Thou wast perfect in thy ways from the day that thou wast created, till iniquity was found in thee" (Ezek. 28:12-15). It is clear from this that Satan too was perfect in his creation, as well as in the free acceptance of the creative plan. There was a time before his fall when he was the highest of the cherubim. But this first supratemporal and temporal self-determination is not the definitive and decisive one for creation. Self-determination in freedom begins together with time for Lucifer too, as well as for the other angels, and it *continues* for all times, revealing the inexhaustible depths of the sophianic foundation of creation and the uncountable possibilities of freedom.

Essential self-determination through freedom refers to the life of the creaturely spirit both in its relation to God (and through this to itself) and in its relation to its own nature. Freedom is arbitrary and a law unto itself. In its *limit*, freedom can be reduced to what Dostoevsky called "living by one's own dumb will." That is, it can be reduced to arbitrariness or willfulness. However, freedom as absolute arbitrariness or willfulness cannot be realized, and creatures as such are not a law unto themselves. They are determined inwardly in the very act of creation; they are *given* to themselves. Freedom can oppose this givenness, can be unnatural or unlawful in the sense of this opposition, this ontological self-disfigurement. But even this self-disfigurement is determinate, although with a negative coefficient. This unlawful freedom is an ontological *revolt* and, in the final analysis, it is the spiritual self-enslavement of creatures, their enslavement by their own nature. This unlawful freedom is determined by an inner disharmony, by a rending contradiction. Even in revolt, creation cannot arbitrarily become *anything it wants to be*. It remains *only itself,* but turned inside out, so to speak. In this sense, the condition of createdness or natural givenness is enslavement for creatures insofar as they rebel against this givenness and against their Creator. In this rebellion, creation is ultimately powerless, for it is barren. By contrast, true freedom from enslavement by the given is achieved only when the given is accepted by a free acceptance of God's thought about us: "ye shall know the truth, and the truth shall make you free" (John 8:32). Therefore, Satan too, as revolt incarnate, is a *slave,* a slave to himself, and the beautiful "demon"[2] is only a pose, a grimace, the mask of the fallen angel.

Thus, creatureliness, the union of freedom and givenness, contains the possibility of revolt and self-willfulness, which tempt us under the masks of pretend genius and self-deification. Creatureliness contains luciferism as a temptation that is to be overcome. Luciferism has its foundation not in an accident or caprice, but in the very character of creatureliness as the union of free self-determination and the natural given. This given must be received as God's gift, but it can also be stolen by self-deifying creation.

This hypostatic self-determination of fleshless spirits with regard to God must be accomplished *in time.* Here, it is first necessary to understand that the hypostatic *reception* of God's creative act, since the participation of creatures in their creation is expressed in this act, is an act of love-humility toward God. Creatures *humble* themselves before God's omnipotence and wisdom, which is manifested in their creation, and by love they answer God's love, which is imprinted in creation. Creation is the work of love also in the sense that the meeting in love of Creator and creation occurs in it, the meeting of giving love and grateful, humbly accepting love. Otherwise, the very act of creation and the original "it was good" of all creation would be impossible. In God, creation is an act of ecstatic love, in which He goes outside the bounds of the Holy Trinity, into "nothing," and there draws out of Himself the "fourth," creaturely hypostases, created in His image, that is, first of all, those upon whom the gift of love has been conferred. A creaturely hypostasis is precisely the fiery tongue of the Spirit, of God's love, igniting in "nothing" the fiery tongue of the answer-

2. This is a reference to artists (notably Lermontov in his poem "Demon") who have romanticized the satanic principle. — Trans.

ing love of creation, and this meeting of love contains the mysterious act of the creation of the hypostases. Therefore *all* the hypostases are created in love; they are created as loving God. That is their ontological point of departure. And just as Satan was created as an archangel by a loving God, the demons were created as angels. Their fallen state is a violation of the original norm of being, a self-disfigurement, opposition to the law of their own life. And it is from this that the inner "eternal" fire of hell is ignited.

How was this violation possible and how did it happen? In other words: Is this trihypostatic love a necessary *given* for creation, a *compulsory* necessity, or is it a freely, creatively actualized possibility, or task? The latter is of course the case. Love is free; it is given and actualized by freedom. This is a self-evident axiom of love. But creaturely love for God must be realized in time, in becoming. If divine love is unchanging and eternal, creaturely love is characterized by increase and decrease. It reflects the changing character of creaturely life. For the igniting or extinguishing of this love no causes can be found except the self-causedness of freedom or causelessness. But it is nonlawful or self-caused even when it is antilawful, when it goes contrary to that which constitutes the inner norm, the law, of a creature's life.

In this sense, that change in the life of creaturely spirits which is the fall of the angels, with their loss of the love for God, is *possible* only because of their perversity in freedom, and this possibility becomes a reality in the fall of Lucifer and his angels. This fall took place in time. There are no grounds to consider it as being instantaneous and to deny that it has duration. In any case, it is completely possible to understand it as a *series* of inner events and self-determinations of creaturely spirits. Only in its termination did this series turn out to be incompatible with the abiding of these spirits in heaven, from which they were in fact expelled.

This extinguishing of love for God leads to the awakening of spiritual self-love, egocentrism, isolation and self-blinding, self-immersion, the seeing only of self, excessive pride in oneself. Satanical pride is a manifestation of the extinguishing of love for God; it obscures the image of God, the image of sacrificial and self-renouncing trihypostatic love, in which each of the hypostases acquires its own personal center not in itself but outside of itself, in other hypostases. Opposed to this humility and altruism of divine love is the pride of satanical unlove, which is incorrectly called "self-love," for this is a contradiction in terms: Love cannot be monohypostatic, egocentric, self-directed. A self-lover has no one and nothing to love in the case of this identity of the subject and object of love. Such an egocentric self-godhood inevitably contains the ineradicable, insurmountable consciousness of all the falsity of these pretensions, of this self-deification. Creatures *know* their creatureliness and, in this sense, their nondivinity or "nothing"-ness. Creatures are conscious of their createdness or givenness for themselves. To attribute *one's own to oneself* is a plundering, which is expressed in a cold fire of envy and a hatred of God to which this envy gives rise. It is expressed in a devouring rivalry with Him, in a madness of despair, in writhings and convulsions of envy. Here, creatures must continuously convince themselves that they are the equals of the Creator and even superior to Him. This is the fatal chain of satanical inflamement: unlove, pride, envy, hatred, despair, the dark flame. St. Isaac the Syrian once expressed the thought that the burning in hell is the torment of love: extinguishing love in themselves, beings created by love, in love, and for love do not stop being tormented precisely by what constitutes the inner law of their being. From the radiant flame of love, they become submerged in the dark, freezing, hellish fire of envy, hatred, malice. Hatred is the negative energy of love, love with a minus sign. But it preserves its "absolute" value, that power of love by which these beings are defeated in their spiritual suicide, which does not know death. The spirit that is in the image of God is a loving being; this spirit is created for love, which determines this spirit's entire life even in a fallen state. Satanical wickedness is the dark infernal face of inextinguishable love, love that has turned into its opposite.

The life of fleshless spirits, even in their fallen condition, remains transcendent for man as an incarnate being. However, with the spiritual side of his being, man touches the spiritual world, and to this extent he is capable of a certain, even if limited, perception of this world. But such a human perception of angels as well as demons inevitably remains limited because of its anthropomorphicity.

Not having their own world, angels are directed by the energy of their being toward God, toward the divine world, or the Divine Sophia, and toward the human world, the creaturely Sophia. The submergence of angels in the divine life constitutes the source of their own life, which is an unlimited deification by grace. But what happens when, on the pathways of its freedom, a fallen spirit turns away from this source, is deprived of life in God, and remains only in its creaturely life? Posited to being by God, this life is indestructible. It exists potentially, but even this potentiality is a *force,* an evil insatiable will seeking to realize itself. The lust for power of "the prince of this world" is a direct expression of this life. This all-devouring lust for power cannot find satisfaction for itself, for it is a pretender to God's grandeur, which is inaccessible to creatures. In the soil of this lust for power grow anger, envy, hatred, and, in general, all the dark traits of insane self-love. The closest analogy to this state is the state of insanity with its frenzy and phantasms. The spirit that has closed itself up in itself, alienated from reality, finds itself in an emptiness that it fills with its own emanations. And an imaginary, "bad" infinity of emptiness is thus created, where metaphysical boredom and a multiplicity of illusory forms reign. Of the past grandeur there remains only a devouring force that is incapable of equilibrating itself, a pure subjectivism whose sole object is the subject itself. This force adorns itself with all the colors of the rainbow in its self-admiration (the peacock's plumage, according to the insight of Mikhail Vrubel').[3] Since all fleshless spirits are hypostatic, have a personal character, and constitute a hierarchy, this hierarchism is also preserved in the fallen state, though now in evil, together with the personal qualities that determine the further fate of the demons. The general character of demonism remains unchanged, but various personal traits appear in it.

Clearly, one can distinguish *degrees* of fallenness, which are different for the fallen angels at different times, for their life too remains subject to becoming, which excludes stabilized immobility. Indirect evidence of this can be found in certain biblical passages, for instance, in Job 1–2, where, together with the sons of God, Satan came to present himself before the Lord, and the Lord spoke with him. In any case, this narrative indicates that the state of cold doubt and slander had not yet taken away from Satan the possibility of presenting himself (and evidently the need to present himself) before God and of being an instrument of God's will, if only by way of his permission. To whatever time we refer this event, it indisputably shows that even Satan could have preserved a certain possibility of worshiping God even after the fall, for God's seed is indestructible (this idea has an enormous significance for eschatology).

The consequences of the fall of spirits could not have expressed themselves only in subjectivism, since the service of the "angels," as well as their very nature, is tied to the existence of visible creation, to the human world and man. The two worlds — angelic and human — are inseparably linked. The supreme angel, together with his minions, was called to become man's first friend, and this service could have been based only on self-renouncing love. When this love faded, its place was taken by the lust for power, fed by envy, for, originally, from his creation, man was placed ontologically higher than the angels, having his own world, which the angels serve. From the guardian angel of the world Satan is transformed into

---

3. Mikhail Vrubel' (1856-1910) was the greatest Russian painter of his time.

"the prince of this world," who wants to gain possession of it. He becomes a conquering predator, governed not by love but by envy and the lust for power, not by truth but by falsehood. The devil "was a murderer from the beginning, and abode not in the truth, because there is no truth in him" (John 8:44). Satan's relation to the world is based upon his all-devouring subjectivism, for he finds for himself a kingdom in which he can rule parasitically, until he is "cast out" (John 12:31). As an angel he retains access to the life of the world and his own place of action in it. As Satan he retains this possibility of action in the world, but he uses it now to *pervert* the world according to his own likeness, to sow his chaff in the world, to poison and ruin the world. As an angel he is not transcendent to the world but belongs to it; as Satan he is hostile to the world. And by this creative capacity of evil, he acquires objective life. If the life of the holy angels is co-human by their positive service, then in the case of Satan too it is co-human, but now only because of parasitic infection. Satan's insane desire to become God's equal and to take God's place in the human world finds a temporary and apparent realization, whence the creative action of evil in the world and the battle for the world with God. The result of this battle is already certain: the hopeless defeat of Satan and his expulsion, which has already occurred in the plane of eternity: "the prince of this world [will] be cast out" (John 12:31). Satanism is an insane wager that has already been lost. But there is no choice; the road will be taken to the end. A catastrophe will then inevitably occur in satanism itself, and a new epoch will begin once the kingdom of the prince of this world is abolished and the true King is enthroned in the world: Christ, come in glory into His kingdom.

The parasitic intrusion of the fallen angels in the life of the world leads to a change in the very nature of the fallen angels. In brief, they are transformed into demons and participate in the life of the human world, through man himself, as well as through the animal world and the natural world in general. The world soul becomes sick with demon possession. The very fall of the angels is already a severe sickness for all of creation, for this sickness does not remain localized but extends to all of nature and to man. The Gospel has a number of passages that directly indicate the relationship between bodily and spiritual sickness on the one hand and demonic possession on the other. To heal the sick soul of the world, exorcism by the cross must be applied to it and the prince of this world must be expelled. This sickness does not destroy the world's sophianicity and is powerless to destroy God's creation. Like every sickness, it exists only by the powers of life, by the creative energy that belongs to the world as the creaturely Sophia. But, in its creatureliness, the world is susceptible to sicknesses and demonic infections, albeit temporary ones. Demons are thus unnaturally implanted in the life of the world. Instead of that angelic service which does not change the proper nature and life of the angels, here we have the parasitic intrusion of fleshless spirits into the life of flesh, their spiritual enfleshing, as it were. They attempt to share the life of the flesh by becoming spiritual carriers of passions and lusts. This is symbolically expressed in the narrative in Genesis 6:2, where "the sons of God" began to choose as their wives "the daughters of men," which led to the birth of giants. One has to think that this refers to a certain excitation of the flesh, a sensual passion implanted into beings who are nonsensual by nature. It is permissible to think that demons are humanized by human passions and lusts, which they themselves excite, and a mutual perversion therefore takes place.

But all this is only a particular case of the general relation that exists between the fallen angels and man. Thanks to this relation, demons can overcome their subjectivism; they can transcend their impotent "I-ness" into objectivity, gaining the ability to create evil and to corrupt. Between the spiritual and human worlds there is no ontological impenetrability; the two worlds are mutually connected by a certain "and." And a wall that would separate the two worlds and make powerless the action of evil in the world could exist only if this relation is annulled, if the very nature of man and the angels in their interrelationship is destroyed or changed. Therefore, after having appeared in the spiritual world, evil inevitably seeps also into the human world. The demons become tempters and the fallen archangel becomes Satan. The ability of evil to be creative and to acquire a certain dominion over the human world is the inner basis of demonic self-assertion.

The history of fallen humanity has a prologue in heaven, and evil in a pure form (and not as a fruit of ignorance, misunderstanding, deception, and self-deception) first appears in the spiritual world. Of course, even here one cannot deny the presence of ignorance and self-deception, and, in any case, of spiritual inexperience, since the idea of the total conquest of the human world is an illusion and fallacy, for it does not take into account God's wisdom and goodness, manifested by the Incarnation. In this sense, satanism is an adventure which will end in nothing. Created by God and belonging to Him, the world will return to God. But before it returns to Him, the world must pass through a long period of fallenness and of the lordship of the prince of this world, who destroys and spoils creation to the extent that this is compatible with its existence.

Nevertheless there is one objective and insurmountable boundary for this creative power of evil: This "minus" of being cannot destroy creation, cannot cast it into pre-creaturely nonbeing.[4] Even Satan himself cannot destroy himself. In the spiritual world the very idea of murder or suicide is nonsense, and Satan is only a "murderer of men." And as a murderer of men, he is also a murderer of the world in the sense that he brings spoilage and corruption into the natural world. To be sure, he does not have the power to destroy the world, for it rests upon an unshakable foundation and "will not move." But to the extent that the angels are assigned the task of guarding the world and therefore of acting upon it, this possibility of action, even though it is limited, is retained also by the fallen angels, as can be concluded from several hints in Scripture (e.g., Luke 13:16; 1 Cor. 5:5; 2 Cor. 12:7; 2 Thess. 2:9; 1 Tim. 1:20). This produces a kind of evil providence of satanic actions in the world, which need to be exorcised (and which are exorcised by all manner of blessings of things, places, homes, and so on, as well as "prohibitions" before baptism). But for the most part these paths of evil will remain unrevealed to us until evil is definitively exposed and thus reduced to an empty, impotent potentiality.[5]

Evil in man is different from satanic evil, although it is connected with the latter. The two differ, first of all, in degree of consciousness and intensity by reason of the complexity of human nature and the existence of a special human world. Satanism is pure evil as direct revolt against God. In contrast, for man, who has, thanks to his corporeality, his own world and his own life in it, God's being is an object of *faith*, which, in a certain sense, goes against the evidence of this world. And the falling away from God in this special human world is therefore not a direct and conscious act, but a complex consequence of a confusion owing to which man has not discerned his proper nature. To some extent this falling away is a fruit of misunderstanding and even deception. Of course, the possibility of evil nestles in the human heart, in the freedom to love or not love God. But all of these complicating elements are added to man's self-determination, as we find in the biblical story of the fall (Gen. 3). First of all, we have the fundamental fact that the fall of man has its beginning not in man himself but outside of him, that it begins with the tempting whisper of the serpent. One may ask: Would this fall have taken place even without such a temptation? One

---

4. See my article "The Problem of Conditional Immortality."

5. Especially mysterious are, of course, psychic illnesses, which have both a spiritual and a corporeal basis. Unfathomable as to their origin, these illnesses are perversions of the image of being.

cannot completely deny this, of course, since creaturely freedom, together with the complexity of human nature, also includes such a possibility. But one can say confidently that an evil limited only to human nature could not have attained the scope that became accessible to it in the fall with the participation of the dark spirituality of the fallen angels.

The temptation of man takes place on the complex path of deception and self-deception, the path of error. Evil first presents itself before man in the guise of the natural world. Given the closeness of man to the animal world, he could "converse" with the representatives of this world. Adam was capable of naming these representatives, that is, of knowing them and distinguishing their special qualities. Especially natural in God's garden is such a "conversation" with the serpent, wiser "than any beast of the field which the Lord God has made" (Gen. 3:1). Adam could at first converse with the serpent even without suspecting that it was a medium for the spirit of evil (this is a clear example of the influence of spirits of evil on the natural world that has remained even after the fall). The beginning of evil in man is therefore connected not with revolt or usurpation, but with misunderstanding, naivete, and ignorance. Our progenitors did not know how to recognize or to terminate the poisonous conversation with the serpent.

The second stage of temptation is also not a conscious evil but is only gullibility and curiosity, which signify that filial love and trust in God have already begun to cool in the heart. Here, the question of the meaning of the commandment not to eat of the fruits of the tree of the knowledge of good and evil arises, clearly, in its allegorical significance. This commandment is, first of all, an immanent norm, a law of human nature. An analogous commandment, as the voice of their nature, was of course received by the fallen angels before their fall. But, to the first man, who was inexperienced and ignorant of the whole depth and complexity of his own nature, God could have given a formal, external commandment ("God said") either through angels, with whom man could then have been in direct contact, or through immediate communication. In any case, the violation of this commandment, the eating of the fruit of the tree of knowledge of good and evil, was not only disobedience to God and thus a sin against love, but also an ontological error. In man is born the thought that through the elements of the world he is capable of ascending to the highest levels of spiritual life and knowledge. His consciousness of his spirituality has grown dim, and the equilibrium between his flesh and his spirit has been disrupted. He has become of the world and of the flesh. He has come to know the pleasures of the flesh independently of its relation to the spirit and has stopped being its master. He has thereby become mortal.

Thus, the deception of Satan was a grandiose ontological provocation, which perverted the correct relationship between the constituent parts of man's being. And from this there follow with implacable logic the spiritual consequences of this perversion, with fatal results for man and all of creation. But this perversion was not and could not have been final and definitive. The opposition of two principles, good and evil, appears in man. In contradistinction to the case of the fallen spirits, good arises in man together with evil. Prior to this duality, which demons do not know, there was a place in human life neither for evil nor for good. Good was dissolved in the natural holiness proper to the creation that came out of the Creator's hands. This untested holiness before the fall, which was not conscious of itself and for which a special path of growth and deepening had been prepared, ceded its place, through the temptation by the serpent, to the agonizing "knowledge of good and evil."

Temptation takes reality as its starting point, but perverts it. Man truly was created to become a son of God and a creaturely god, but this could have and should have been realized on the paths of holiness, leading to perfect deification ("ye shall be as gods"). Satan lured man onto the path of human-divinity and egocentrism. On this path of the cooling of love there was revealed, first of all, the knowledge of evil, which in a pure form, without any good, became the lot of Satan himself. By contrast, in man the knowledge of evil also became the beginning of the introduction of good, a new, special awakening of the principle that constitutes the positive essence of man's being. Good and evil in their opposition appear in the creaturely Sophia as two ontological poles: being and the nothing "out of" which the world is created. This duality launches the historical process as the tragic battle between good and evil. The power of Divine-humanity acts on the side of good, whereas, on the side of evil, the greatest intensity of the creaturely potentiality of *nothing* (the "minus" of being) is attained in satanism, human-divinity, anti-Christianity. Evil is actualized and acquires a creative power precisely in human life and in the human world. Here, evil occupies for a time the neutral, but then malignly neutralized, territory of pure humanity, the natural world as such, outside of God and therefore against God. Possessing the world through fallen man, Satan gains "the kingdom of this world."

In man, evil has many aspects, many stages. It begins with the submergence (a submergence that should not be) of man into the flesh of the world and directly into his own corporeality, resulting in the imprison-

163

ment of his spirit. It continues in the relatively neutral medium of creaturely autonomy, but also of limitation, with the whole multiplicity of human possibilities. The condition and consequence of all this is spiritual self-willfulness and self-deification, with a corresponding weakening of the love for God, opening the way to satanical hostility against Him. On this background of dark, twilight, or falsely illuminated being ("take heed therefore that the light which is in thee be not darkness" [Luke 11:35]; "and men loved darkness rather than light" [John 3:19]) appears the chiaroscuro of the world's being. But in this chiaroscuro there is no place for absolute darkness, for even in the very depths of darkness the sophianic seeds of being shine forth ("And the light shineth in darkness; and the darkness comprehended it not" [John 1:5]). But in this world of semidarkness and in this darkened human nature, there shines "the light of the world," "the true Light" (John 1:9; 8:12; 12:46) that chases away the darkness; and "the people that walked in darkness have seen a great light" (Isa. 9:2).

There is yet another fundamental difference between evil in the spiritual world and that in the human world. The first is personal, although the fallen spirits do gather together to form their special kingdom and their army. The second, on the other hand, is not only personal but also natural and generic. Every man "that cometh into the world" enters into a contaminated medium and assimilates this medium in his own way. This once again brings us face to face in the doctrine of evil with the enigma of original sin and its significance for human destiny.

3. Original Sin

The dogma of original sin is the axis of Christian soteriology. This dogma states that, with the fall of Adam in Eden, the whole human race fell, to be redeemed later by the new Adam, Christ. "Wherefore, as by one man sin entered into the world, and death by sin; and so death passed upon all men, for that all have sinned . . . . if through the offence of one many be dead, much more the grace of God, and the gift by grace, which is by one man, Jesus Christ, hath abounded unto many" (Rom. 5:12, 15). "For as in Adam all die, even so in Christ shall all be made alive" (1 Cor. 15:22). To the unity in Adam's fall, or "original sin," corresponds the unity of salvation in Christ, who received the integral Adam, for "what is not assumed is not redeemed." The soteriology of the Church is based on the following premises of an axiomatic character: (1) the unity of the human race in Adam and his fall from his original state; (2) the commonality of sin-tainted nature inherited by all, together with the personal guilt of every person through his personal participation in this sin; and (3) the redemption accomplished by Christ, with restoration not only of Adam but also of every individual, through the healing of original sin by the sacrament of baptism.

One cannot fail to see the supreme importance of this dogma, since if it is rejected or shaken, the salvific faith in redemption will be shaken (which is why the Church has so zealously defended this dogma since the time of the Augustinian-Pelagian disputes). The Church confesses this dogma in a great many liturgical texts as a doctrine that is religiously self-evident.[6]

Nevertheless, this dogma, viewed historically and theologically, by no means has the universality and indisputability in Christian tradition that could be expected considering its general acceptance from the axiomatic point of view. In any case, its essential elements require theological interpretation, especially in our time, in view of the real or illusory knowledge of the life of the world that our time has acquired and the problematic that follows from this.[7] Here, we limit ourselves to the briefest historical survey of the doctrine of original sin, referring the reader to the exhaustive studies of Williams and of Tennant for the details.[8]

In the Old Testament, the narrative of the fall of Adam and Eve (Gen. 3) is, of course, of fundamental significance. Whatever the critical commentaries to this text, it preserves all its dogmatic significance for the Church. Compared with it, other texts (e.g., Gen. 6:1-5) have only an auxiliary significance. Of course, the full significance of the doctrine of Adam's fall could be revealed only in the light of Christian revelation (as was the case with other fundamental dogmas of Christianity: those of the Holy

6. This self-evidentness of dogma is expressed as follows by Cardinal Newman: "The human race is implicated in some terrible aboriginal calamity, and thus the doctrine of what is technically called original sin becomes to me almost as certain as that the world exists, and as the existence of God" (*Apologia pro vita sua*, c. 5).

7. Completely just is the following statement from a recent study of original sin, which gives an exhaustive exposition of the history of this doctrine: "When we enquire for a clear statement of the irreducible essence of the Fall-doctrine to which historic Christianity as such is committed, we are faced by a remarkable absence of universal authoritative definition. Neither the Nicene nor the Apostles' Creed contains any direct allusion to the subject, nor can any positive and detailed information be gathered from the decrees of the undisputed Oecumenical Councils" (N. P. Williams, *The Ideas of the Fall and of Original Sin*, Bampton Lectures, London, 1927, p. 11).

8. F. R. Tennant, *The Sources of the Doctrine of the Fall and Original Sin*, Cambridge, 1903. Also by the same author: *The Origin and Propagation of Sin*, 1908; *The Concept of Sin*, 1912. Cf. articles about sin in various theological encyclopedias (French, English, German, the Russian *Great Encyclopedia*).

Trinity, the immortality of the soul, universal resurrection, etc.). Although the Gospels do not *directly* address original sin, the New Testament attests to the sinfulness of human nature with a clarity that does not admit doubt, even as it attests to the participation of fallen spirits in the life of the world and of man. A generalizing interpretation of original sin is given by the apostle Paul, who describes with startling power its action in man (see Rom. 8:15-24) in the opposition of flesh and spirit. In connection with this he develops his general doctrine of redemption. A theological doctrine of original sin can be developed on the basis of numerous texts that rely on Paul's interpretation.

However, such a doctrine does not arise in the Church until the fourth or fifth century, primarily in the doctrine of St. Augustine. Prior to Augustine, we have only a series of dogmatic glosses, as it were, on separate aspects of the doctrine of original sin, without any great precision. One should note that, in the East, among the Greek fathers, the doctrine of original sin is not as severe as in the West; and in certain cases it is colored by the personal worldview of the writer. (Among such doctrines we must first mention Origen's doctrine of the fall of spirits as well as St. Irenaeus's doctrine of *anakephalaiosis,* where Christ is the head of the human race, a doctrine that presupposes that its original head was Adam.) Among the Cappadocians the doctrine of St. Gregory of Nyssa is most colored by Origen's allegorism and spiritualism. St. Gregory the Theologian approaches Gregory of Nyssa to some extent. In general, we do not find among the Greek fathers a finished doctrine of original sin and its consequences, which in general are characterized more mildly than in Augustinianism. The true homeland of the doctrine of original sin in all its severity is Western theology, in St. Ambrose, Ambrosiaster, and primarily St. Augustine, who stamped his spirit in this respect on the entire church doctrine (and first of all on the definitions of the councils of Carthage and Orange); indeed, the very term *originale peccatum* belongs to Augustine.[9] His entire anthropology and soteriology are based on the idea of man's loss of original righteousness and therefore freedom of will. Because of this, man is doomed to perdition as *massa perditionis,* from which only the elect can escape by the redeeming power of Christ's deed, by divine grace given to man. This is expressed with particular clarity in Augustine's view of the fate of unbaptized children, who in the case of death bear the entire burden of condemnation. The very event of original sin is viewed as historical, as having taken place at a definite time.

9. *Ad. Simplic.* 1, qu. 10.

How should one understand the fall of *all* of humankind in the person of the *one* Adam? St. Augustine gives only a general answer to this question, and henceforth this answer is repeated in the catechistic formulas as something instructive and self-evident. That is, the propagation of original sin is explained by the sinful heredity that burdens man from his birth (see Ps. 51). Original sin is therefore related not to man's personal self-determination but first of all to the sinfulness of all of human nature. But, at the same time, original sin, according to Augustine, is not only a hereditary disease but also precisely sin as personal guilt. This is the fundamental defect and even contradiction of his doctrine of original sin, which has been inherited from him by future theologians. Is a hereditary disease, like, for example, syphilis, insanity, or tuberculosis, the personal sin of those unfortunates who are born burdened with it, and not, rather, their severe fate? Can the inheritance from the first Adam, hanging over all his descendants, really be imputed to every man as his personal sin? Given this posing of the question of original sin it is too easy to reduce this doctrine to absurdity and to contradiction once it is necessary to admit in one form or another the personal participation in it of all men. But only under this condition does it become understandable that the presence of original sin in us is felt as morally self-evident in some way and that it is unshakably affirmed by the Church theologically and practically (by the institution of the baptism of infants). To be sure, the truth is not shaken by the absence of an appropriate theological explanation. But it does not follow that the dominant doctrine, Augustinianism, is sufficient in this matter. However, neither in the East nor in the West has theology gone beyond this doctrine, the West expressing it in a more severe form, the East in a milder form.

The doctrine of original sin presupposes, first of all, a certain *event*, which occurred in space and time. Thus, according to its accepted interpretation in dogmatics, this event is a historical event; it belongs to history. The story told in Genesis 3 is considered to belong to history in the same sense as other events described in the sacred history. This story refers to a number of facts in the life of this world. This idea is even expressly affirmed against the view that interprets the story of the fall of our progenitors in Eden after the serpent's temptation as a legend or an allegory, or even refers this event to supramundane being, placing it beyond the limits of empirical reality.[10]

---

10. E.g., Origen. An analogous conception is not foreign to contemporary theology. See, for example, Peter Green, *The Problem of Evil*, London, 1920.

To a literal interpretation of Genesis 3, however, is opposed the modern scientific consciousness, which has been brought up on principles of evolutionism. Difficult to accept for this consciousness is the doctrine of the original perfection of man *(status naturae purae)*, from which, in any case, the doctrine of original sin issues. It sees history as a gradual loss of the original perfection, as a fall from it. In other words, history is depicted as a descent from what is higher to what is lower, whereas the evolutionary doctrine, together with the modern science that it has nurtured, sees in history the reverse process of movement from what is lower to what is higher, from the amorphous to the differentiated, from the simple to the complex. Science utterly fails to find traces of this original edenic state of man on earth and therefore considers the very supposition of such a state to be incompatible with empirical data. This conviction is the dominant one in contemporary minds, seeping even into theology.[11] Theology faces then the following alternative: (1) science with its evolution or (2) legend, which claims to replace history and for which there are no data in empirical reality. The aporia that results, the divergence between the data of scientific knowledge and the data of revelation, also has an excruciating and destructive impact upon spiritual life, sometimes leading to disbelief or indifferentism.

But it is possible to see in this apparent contradiction a simple misunderstanding and to affirm both that the biblical story is true and that the scientific picture of the world's development in history has a certain approximate and, of course, relative truthfulness. This misunderstanding is caused both by the imprecise use of the category of "history" and by the incautious, uncritical exaggeration of the significance of scientific data.

In the first case, it should be observed that, when theologians speak of the historical character of the story of Genesis 1–3 (and they speak of it frequently and insistently), they try to establish that the events described actually occurred in the life of creation. However, there is no need to attribute to these events a historical character like that of events of the empirical life of this world, for such events by no means exhaust the entire fullness and depth of being. Can one, for example, equate in this sense, as equally historical events, the creation of light on the first day and, say, the Babylonian captivity, the expulsion from Eden, and the fall of the kingdom of Israel? It is sufficient to make such a comparison to feel the whole difference between

---

11. This is how a contemporary theologian expresses it: "Augustinianism, with its theory of a Paradisal condition of original perfection, cannot possibly be dovetailed into the picture of a gradual ascent from gross and brutish beginnings which is given us by geology and biology" (Williams, op. cit., 1., c., p. 513).

these *types* of events, each of which, however, belongs in its own way to the real history of the world. We distinguish different aeons in this history, so to speak: the state of creation before its sixth day and the appearance of man; its destiny before Adam's fall, and then after the fall, which corresponds to our present aeon; and finally, the life of the future age. All of these are *different* aeons, although they all belong to the *one* reality of this world and in this sense to its history. Therefore, we should not use a single concept of history for events that refer to different aeons of history.

Let us make another comparison: "For, behold, I create new heavens and a new earth: and the former shall not be remembered, nor come into mind" (Isa. 65:17). Or: "the day of the Lord will come as a thief in the night: in the which the heavens shall pass away with a great noise, and the elements shall melt with fervent heat, the earth also and the works that are therein shall be burned up" (2 Pet. 3:10). In a general sense, the events mentioned here, like the building by Solomon of his temple or the Babylonian captivity, belong to the history of the world. But at the same time they are categorially different. The *unqualified* application of the concept of history to such events provokes legitimate doubt. For, indisputably, calling both the Second Coming of Christ and, say, the taking of Jericho — or the creation of the world and the building of Moses' tabernacle — facts of history, even though it may be justified in one sense, appears to be wholly impossible in another sense. In other words, "reality" in the life of the world has different forms which differ to the same degree that life in the Jerusalem of Palestine differs from life in the City of God, the heavenly Jerusalem that is descending to earth. And this reality, which *differs* from the present reality, cannot be expressed or described in the same language of "history." There is in the life of the world, alongside the present history, much that does not fit into this history, although it is connected with and concerns it. This reality can be called, if you will, *meta-history* (or even hyper-history).

The first thing that follows from the existence of these different forms of "historical" being is that they are mutually closed off from each other, although this does not necessarily mean that they are mutually impenetrable. On the one hand, there is the inner, ontological unity of the world, the relation of alpha and omega, beginning and end, in sophianicity. On the other hand, these different forms of the world can turn out to be inaccessible to mutual perception, but the world's being is, in any case, not exhausted by the present, empirically limited state in its becoming. The future age, which is announced in prophecies and postulated by the inner call of the world, is nevertheless unknown to the world at the present time and simply does not exist, as it were, on the paths of "experience." It follows that this kind of reality, or event, belonging to the life of the world and of humanity but transcending the given aeon or its empirical domain, cannot be described in the language of this domain. What is necessary here is the translation from one language into another with due account taken of the existing differences.

Therefore the language of empirical history cannot be used to represent meta-historical events. The language of symbols or "myths" is the appropriate one. These symbols derive from mythologemas that are stored in the memory of humankind as an echo or anamnesis of prehistoric or meta-historic events. A myth, in the *positive* sense of this concept, is a story, expressed in a language not proper to the empirical domain, about what lies beyond this domain, about what belongs to the meta-empirical domain and meta-history. In essence, this being can be conveyed only in the language of myth and symbol.

Such is the language of the first three chapters of Genesis, the story of the creation of the world and man, and of the fall. To assert that these stories are a "history" in the very *same* sense as empirical history is to do violence to their direct meaning, to subject them to critical mutilation, inasmuch as myth cannot be defended as empirical history. But to transform myth, which is a story of meta-empirical and meta-historical reality, into an empty legend is to lack understanding of its high value as a hieroglyph of truth, which is worthy precisely in this capacity of pious understanding. In this sense, although it is a history, the Genesis 3 narrative of the fall is meta-historical in nature; and in this capacity it is a myth, which is grander and more significant in its generalized and symbolical images than any empirical history. Empirical history begins precisely with the fall, which is its starting premise. But this beginning of history lies beyond empirical being and cannot be included in its chronology. From the point of view of form, the history of literature must classify myth as a type of popular art ("folklore"), which, however, can have a profound and even divinely inspired content. Of course, to understand myth, it is insufficient to limit oneself to literary analysis alone, considering it exhaustive (as is the practice of contemporary science).

A second conclusion that can be drawn from the meta-historical character of the narrative in Genesis 3 refers to its content. An event is described that lies beyond our history, although at its boundary. Being connected with our history, this event inwardly permeates it. But this event cannot be perceived in the chain of empirical events, for it is not there. It took place, but beyond the limits of this world: After the expulsion of our progenitors from Eden, its gates were locked, and an angel with a fiery sword protects this boundary of being that has become transcendent for us. But this event took place precisely in this world, or at least for this world.

Therefore, the sacred writer uses symbolic-mythic images to describe both the *place* of Eden and the circumstances and form of the event. This description expresses the general idea that this event belongs to the life of our world. This overcomes in a fundamental way a number of basic misunderstandings that arise in the consciousness of modern man. Modern man finds in this world neither the place of Eden nor traces of man's original perfection. Nor does he find the mysterious serpent that conversed with our progenitors, the tree of life, or the tree of the knowledge of good and evil. Modern man knows in the past only the disharmonious violence of nature and the bitter struggle of men with beasts and among themselves. For modern man, original man appears in a troglodytic state, which he leaves only through slow evolution, perhaps lasting millions of years. In general, our *history* has no place for the original state of our progenitors. The story of this state is therefore often viewed as a legend without any basis in reality.

But this conclusion scarcely has the indisputability that is ascribed to it. It is connected with the arbitrary, unprovable, and incorrect premise that our empirical world exhausts all the possibilities of the life of the world and of man, and therefore what does not agree with this premise is considered as being outside the bounds of reality in general. Of course, if one were to accept this dogma of empirical positivism and limit the reality of the world to its present historical evolution, there would be nowhere to put prehistory, eschatology, man's life after death, or his life after resurrection. This assertion, which is incoherent and full of contradictions although it is considered self-evident, is by no means the only possible one. On the contrary, a wholly different postulate of thought is perfectly admissible here, namely that the life of the world is not confined to or exhausted by its present state. But neither the past of the world when man was without sin nor the new heaven and new earth of the future age can be known from the life of the present age, for they are separated from the present age by a certain *transcensus.* From this point of view it becomes understandable and natural that, on our earth, no traces of Eden or of the edenic original state of man can be found. They are in fact not found in our world, although this does not mean that there were no such traces in the past or even that they do not exist even now — in the depths of the world's being if not in its empirical reality. Adam's fall was a catastrophe that changed the fate of the world. It was an impenetrable wall that separated his original state from his later state, so that in the later state one can no longer find traces of the original state (except in obscure anamnesis, slumbering in the human soul).

The contemporary mistrust of the biblical story is based on yet another prejudice of evolutionism, according to which the world's development is asserted to ascend from the lower to the higher, from the elementary to the complex, not vice versa. The preliminary question of the inner nature of this evolution and of its motive force is usually not addressed. Instead, a bad dogmatism, one that is unconscious and uncritical, prevails here. The sole basis of evolution is all-explaining accident. This absolute occasionalism represents a *de facto* rejection of both fundamental postulates of empirical knowledge, which in positive and negative form express the law of causality, namely: *ex nihilo nil fit* and *causa aequat effectum*. The principle of evolution consists only in the fact that, owing to the coincidence of favorable accidents, new forms of being appear, and develop in ascending complexity, realizing a "progress" that becomes synonymous with evolution. No other principles of evolutionism can be indicated, and this doctrine remains only an empirical generalization that affirms the permanent miracle of the appearance of new forms and states of being.

This occasionalism affects the entire contemporary worldview that rejects the very possibility of *another* being. This worldview also rejects the possibility of another, to some degree opposite, path of development: not ascending but descending. It rejects what is actually the case: the fall and expulsion from Eden of the first human being.

However, subtler minds, dissatisfied with the crudeness of this primitive and dogmatic occasionalism, are seeking ways to achieve an inner, entelechic, dynamic understanding of the world's evolution. They consider the various stages of this evolution not as caprices of chance but as the manifestation of an inner plan, the actualization of the prototypes of the world, or, to use Aristotle's term, entelechies. This conception overcomes the occasionalism that characterizes positivism. In the evolution of the world there is actualized in time and in empirical reality that which *is* at the basis of this reality, that which is above or prior to this reality; more precisely, that which is beyond it.

The modes and forms of being that are actualized in the evolutionary process are not accidents but genuine themes of this being, implanted by God in creation, as the sophianic seeds of being, as its entelechic foundation. This is the creative "let there be": "let the earth bring forth grass" (Gen. 1:11; also see Gen. 1:20, 24). The world soul, or the creaturely Sophia, actualizes this sophianic content of creation in gradual and successive stages, or (what is the same thing) through an *evolutionary* process. Far

172

from contradicting the doctrine of the Six Days of Creation, the idea of evolution in this sense constitutes its unfolding. Positing the "days" of creation as the inner stages of creation, it is perfectly possible to admit their simultaneous and parallel actualization. The sequence of "days" would thus refer not to the chronology but to the hierarchy of being, so to speak. At the same time, it is possible to admit a gradual or evolutionary actualization of all the forms of being. Given such an interpretation, the createdness and preestablishment of different forms of being are completely compatible with the long and difficult process of their empirical appearance. Not having a hypostatic, conscious center but representing only nonhypostatic "nature," the world soul, in its blindness and instinctiveness, in the struggle of elemental forces, both creative and destructive, fulfills, as if groping, the inner plan of being in its possible variants.

From this point of view, there is no difficulty in combining the idea of creation with the principle of evolution. All the same, this principle determines only the "how," not the "what" of creation. And this "how," or the paths of the world, can differ depending on different conditions, the first of which refers to man in connection with his central place in the world, as the "king" and, in a certain sense, the governer of nature.

Moreover, the life of the vegetative and animal world refers also to prehuman being even according to the story of the Six Days. Man comes into the world last, on the sixth day. Prior to and without man, the world evolves toward him. All that is called into being by God bears His blessing, the divine "it was good." But this cannot remove the limited character of the world's proper being. This limited character can be transcended only by man. As long as the sophianic instinctiveness of the world soul reigns in creation, the latter remains unfinished, for it is incompletely humanized. Therefore, the evolution of the world within its proper limits also presupposes its relative imperfection, which by no means contradicts the "it was good" of the divine plan, the sophianic content of being. Geological periods, the "struggle for existence," mortality in the animal world, in which there is no immortality of individuals but only of species,[12] could all have been present to a certain degree (a degree impossible to define with precision) in the world of the six days of creation, prior to man.

12. Revelation does not touch upon the immortality of animals. On the contrary, the divine institution of blood sacrifices indirectly attests to the absence of such immortality. The immortality of individuals is unnecessary for and therefore not proper to the animal world, although the possibility that such immortality can be given through man is not excluded.

Here, we approach the most difficult and radical question in the general doctrine of original sin, in connection with the evolutionary conception of the world process: To what degree is man himself subject to evolution, and is he subject to it at all? Should one begin the history of man with the original perfection of Adam, *status naturae purae,* which already manifests the fullness of the image of God in man, or should one "evolutionarily" seek man in the manlike ape, which, according to Nietzsche, lost its mind and became *homo sapiens?* Modern science knows or thinks it knows only the latter hypothesis, that is, how, from the depths of half-animal, half-savage existence, man ascends to the light of humanity, to the difference between good and evil, to the awakening of thought and creative action; that is, how he ascends from the troglodyte to Prometheus. There is no need to fragment creation into individual "days" conceived as isolated acts separated from the whole. This is even formally contradicted by the very sequence of the days of creation (plants were created on the "third" day; fishes and birds on the "fifth" day; animals on the "sixth" day), which, in any case, attests to their inner connectedness.

In addition, in its achievement, each of these days expresses a whole domain of creation with an endless quantity and diversity of separate but interrelated species. Finally, one must remember that the entire Six Days represent nothing more than an extended tale of the creation of man, who, of course, has his own phylogenesis, for he includes all the forms of the world's being and is truly a world-man. Taking this idea as our point of departure, nothing prevents us from supposing that, both physiologically and zoologically, man's appearance could have been evolutionarily prepared in the animal world, and in this sense the doctrine of evolutionism could also be satisfied. Man does not begin but ends creation. He encompasses creation within himself. His creation is not a separate creative act, wholly isolated in the world, self-enclosed, beginning and ending in itself. Rather, it is organically included in the whole of creation. In other words, in the Six Days, man is included in the ladder of life of the creaturely world; he stands on its highest rung. But this evolutionary connection of man with his animal ancestors does not exhaust the main thing in him, his humanity, which consists in the image and likeness of God, which are *not* proper to the animal world. God "breathed into his nostrils the breath of life" (Gen. 2:7). This means that, although man is phylogenetically connected with the animal world by his animal nature, his origin is not merely an evolutionary achievement, but an express and new divine creative act that is *outside* the evolutionary process. It is something *new* in creation.

174

It is necessary to *distinguish* separate acts of creation according to their character and, in particular, to isolate the act of the creation of man as something wholly new and original. Man's humanity (and, in man, the humanization of the animal world) is attained not as one of the stages of the evolutionary process but as something completely new, a *transcensus*, and even, in this sense, an ontological catastrophe. The divine light was lit in the zoological life of creation; the divine spirit entered an animal soul. From the universal "earth," which contained the whole fullness of creaturely life, God created a body to encompass a divine principle: the human spirit. Evolution is interrupted, and zoology and physiology are surpassed; man is created. Therefore, in the face of this discontinuity, this appearance of the *humanity* of man, new and commensurable with nothing else in the creaturely world, one must tell doctrinal evolutionism: "Hands off!" Man is not a product of evolution; evolution could have produced only a manlike animal.

Man appeared in the world suddenly, catastrophically. Between man's animal nature and his humanity lies an ontological *hiatus,* an abyss that cannot be overcome by any evolution. Man enters as a new and independent factor into the chain of cosmic causality. The basic postulate of evolution, according to which man is the product of a progressive causal sequence, has no validity with reference to his origin; it refers only to his animal-corporeal aspect. From the point of view of evolution, man in his humanity is without cause or above cause, above the world. The appearance of what is human in man is what crowns him with the image of God, and therefore does not refer to the action of the world soul, which realizes the different forms of creation. True, this appearance presupposes the participation of the world soul in what, in itself, is not human in man, but only becomes what is human in man, is included in it through union with the human spirit. But the human spirit is not a product of evolution, for it bears the stamp of eternity. But by his union with creaturely nature, man enters into temporal being. Coming at a definite moment of time, his appearance is included in the world's evolution. The spirit that comes from God inhabits a form of organic life brought to maximal relative perfection.

The following question arises in connection with this: Is this appearance of the *first* man on earth, Adam, marked by a state of original perfection, or is it marked by a primordial imperfection, from which he ascends to a higher (though not the highest) level only in the course of the ages? Modern evolutionists answer yes to the second half of this question, wholly applying the theory of evolution to the origin of man. By contrast, the Church's doctrine of the creation of man and of his original state rejects this position. The appearance of a godlike spirit in man is shrouded in mystery and can by no means be known by empirical knowledge (which therefore often wholly denies the existence of such a spirit). The theory of evolution is incapable of establishing when, where, and how this spirit appears, and man begins. One can even say that, in general, man never begins evolutionarily in the world or by the powers of the world, but appears in it suddenly; his appearance is incommensurable with the world process and the possibilities contained in it.

Man is a supramundane principle in the world, although his manifestation and actualization belong to history. Therefore, it is wholly arbitrary, uncritical, and profoundly unscientific to extend the principle of evolution to the human spirit. The human spirit is a completely autonomous given in the world, which does not depend on evolution. By its existence the human spirit surpasses and delimits the evolutionary process; it surpasses the possibilities of the world soul.

Either the human spirit does not exist and therefore man does not exist, or it proceeds from God and enters the world process in order to hypostatize the world soul. In the latter case, the application of the usual categories of evolutionism is completely unjustified; and all obstacles are removed to affirming that man appears in the world with all the fullness of humanity, *"in statu naturae purae,"* already containing all the possibilities of his being, even if not yet fully actualized. For unprejudiced thought the only possibility is to accept this *fullness,* which has come from God, precisely as the original state of primordial man, since the very being of the human spirit is not subject to evolution. The human spirit either exists or it does not exist, and no evolution can overcome the abyss lying between its existence and its nonexistence. It is then the role of evolution or, more precisely, of history to disclose all the possibilities implanted in the human spirit, in its union with the world soul, or nature. This fullness presupposes not only the complete clarity of the self-consciousness of the human spirit and the corresponding clarity of the knowledge of God (Adam "spoke" with God), but also the harmonious connection of the human spirit with the world, that is, with the world soul, through the human body. Even though the human spirit enters the world from above, from God, and is united with the world soul, not only is it not an alien principle for the world but it presupposes for itself this connection as preestablished. As a hypostasis this spirit hypostatizes precisely the creaturely Sophia, or the world soul, and lives in and with the world soul.

All being that is connected with the world soul, as *natura naturans* and *natura naturata,* is, in a certain sense, subject to evolution, for out of itself the world soul brings forth its forms, ascends to the fullness of its being, actualizes its seminal logoses. Meantime, although the origin of the human spirit does not depend on evolution, the human spirit lives in the world and has its nature in the world. To this extent the human spirit assimilates the evolutionary principle in its unfolding and is therefore subject to history. But this does not mean that, in its origin, the human spirit necessarily was in a dormant, preconscious and unconscious, potential state, which it could leave only by realizing itself evolutionarily. No such dependence of the human spirit on evolution exists. The dormant, unconscious state of the human spirit is not its original state, corresponding to its essence, but a secondary state, connected with its given self-determination. For the human spirit, this unconscious state is only one of the *possibilities,* issuing from its connection with the world; it is by no means the only possibility, even though in historical reality we know only this defective form of its being: the state of the fallen Adam. Primordial here, however, is not this state of the potentiality and meonality, as it were, of the human spirit, into which the latter can fall on the paths of its life, but rather the fullness of self-consciousness. Nevertheless, this fullness must yet determine itself in relation to the world, link itself with the world, and include the life of the world in the proper being of the human spirit. Man as a microcosm is the king of creation, its responsible ruler, including and determining all. To his spiritual fullness must correspond the fullness of life in the world, power over the world, and the spiritualization of the world. And the first self-determination of the human spirit is accomplished on this path of the establishment of relations between man and the world; and this self-determination is connected with its self-determination in relation to God.

Thus, the history of man begins not from below but from above, from fullness and harmony, when the spirit that proceeds from God enters the world. This idea corresponds to the cosmogonic myth according to which man was introduced into the world, set before the face of the world, to "possess" the earth and to "have dominion" over it. To this refers also the intuitive knowing of the world that was expressed in the naming of the animals and that, of course, was a precondition for "dressing and keeping" the Garden of Eden, and then the whole universe. The stumbling block for contemporary thought here is that the history of the world preserves traces neither of Eden nor of the perfection of the original man, which is why the biblical story is considered only a naive legend. The story itself insists that this place is precisely *on the earth* (Gen. 2:10-14). It even

177

describes the features of the Garden of Eden in terms of a certain empirico-mystical geography (see 2:8). What should one's attitude be toward this story in the face of the existing critique?

One can say that the remembrance of an edenic state and of God's garden is nevertheless preserved in the secret recesses of our self-consciousness, as an obscure anamnesis of another being, similar to the dreams of golden childhood and most accessible to childhood. These are distinct, palpable revelations of the world's sophianicity in our soul, although they are usually obscured in the soul by our failure to believe in their genuineness or even in their possibility. But it is important to understand the possibility and reality of the edenic state of the world and of man irrespective of the presence or absence of their traces in our present world. The Garden of Eden is conceived in the biblical story as expressly planted by God so that man would dwell in it (see Gen. 2:8).

Beyond the Garden stretches the whole natural world, which is born in the instinctive exertions of the world soul, of the "earth," which actualizes the creative seeds of its sophianicity. This is the future place of Adam's "expulsion" from the edenic (and as if supranatural) conditions of being into the natural world, full of the "struggle for existence." He is cast into this world by God's determination, which, of course, does not change human nature but only affirms the ontological inevitability of this path of life in the natural world after and as a consequence of the fall. This earth, which had contained the possibility of becoming God's garden through Adam's creative obedience in "keeping and dressing" it, now, because of his disobedience, has become a meager land, bringing forth "thorns and thistles." Only *this* natural world is known to fallen man. In it there is *no* Eden, which for a time is removed, as it were, from the world after Adam's expulsion from it: "Therefore the Lord God sent him forth from the garden of Eden, to till the ground from whence he was taken" (Gen. 3:23). From this earth are emitted the moans of "evolutionary" being, with the struggle for existence, "economic materialism," and death. The first attempt to inwardly overcome this evolutionism did not appear to succeed. Eden was taken from the world as an unactualized and unactualizable possibility. It was removed to the heavenly plane of the prototypes of the world that is known to fleshless spirits, its protectors and servants. And Eden, closed to man, is protected for a time by the flaming sword of the angel.

But what was this earthly and "historical" Eden? First of all, it was an edenic *perception* of creation: Sinless man could not see it except as God's garden. His knowledge might have been incomplete and limited, because in Eden he lived separated from the rest of the world, as, in general, all in him was in a state of preliminary, not final harmony. But Eden, as the express dwelling of man, was possible on the earth only on the condition of this sinlessness, with man's openness to all of creation, which is proper to him as one called to become its king. (This openness finds its expression in his ability to name the animals; Gen. 2:19.) But, in conformity with this ability of man to perceive Eden, it could have appeared on the earth by a special and complementary creative act of God (see Gen. 2:8-9), which nature could have received thanks only to the presence of a perfect creature, sinless man.

Eden was a *preparation* for what was hidden in the recesses of all of natural being. It was a sort of eschatology of natural being: The image of the new Eden sketched out in Revelation 22:1-5, with the river and tree of life, includes what was in the original Garden of Eden. But the original Eden, which appeared on the earth only in connection with the sinless state of man, becomes inaccessible, transcendent to creation, and as if nonexistent after its fall. Eden's trees degenerate and turn wild, while its rivers become those of actual geography and history. Between them there is no longer a place for Eden, for the edenic vision has faded. If, prior to his fall, man could have a habitation only in Eden, in the preliminarily revealed perfection of nature, then after the fall he could no longer contain this perfection, and only the earth of exile became accessible to him, that is, a state of the natural world that was proper to the world prior to and apart from man, outside of his lordly protection and cultivation. And man himself became only natural.

Therefore, in the natural world, one does not find and cannot find traces of Eden as the supranatural illumination of natural being. A rupture has formed in the inner life of nature, owing to which "the creature was made subject to vanity" (i.e., lost its edenic perfection) "not willingly, but by reason of him who hath subjected the same," and "groaneth and travaileth in pain . . . until now" (Rom. 8:20, 22). Two possibilities were marked out in the life of creation: (1) the "evolutionary"-instinctive development of creation before man, but one that later, under man's rule, was to acquire the light of reason and become liberated from the power of nonhypostatic elementalness; and (2) the development of creation *with* man, who was called to become the created god, the protector and cultivator of Eden. But instead of humanizing nature, man himself became the slave of nature and a prisoner to its necessity. And he will be a slave until the new Adam, the "Man from heaven," returns to humankind the kingship that it has lost, and the natural world becomes a new heaven and a new earth, with a new city, the holy Jerusalem (see Rev. 21:1). At the same time that Eden was removed from the earth, or (what is the same thing) Adam was expelled from it, Adam was deprived of God's glory (see Rom. 3:23), and donned the "coats of skins" (Gen. 3:21) of history "to till the ground from whence he was taken" (3:23). That is, he was called to ascend, by a long historical path, to his original state, which he had lost.

Thus, in history, we know neither Eden nor the state of the sinlessness of our progenitors, *in statu naturae purae*. All this belongs to *meta-history*, and one should therefore not seek this in the historical world and time. It belongs to history only as its prologue. Prior to his fall, Adam is the only "progenitor." After the fall, he is one of many progenitors; he belongs to a specific generation and is empirically connected with the whole organic world. And Eve becomes "the mother of all who live," that is, she represents the unitary naturalness of humankind, which is actualized in a series of natural births. One can say that an ontological abyss lies between the meta-history of the first three chapters of Genesis and the history of Adam's race. Even if we accept that the Adam of the initial Genesis narrative is the same person as the Adam of the later chapters (which is not really necessary, since the "adam" of the first chapters is *man in general,* whereas in the later chapters he is a specific individual, with his own name), they are still separated by the threshold lying between meta-history and history. Beginning with the fourth chapter, Adam is a "patriarch," the progenitor of a specific generation, and this is clearly a generation that is by no means unique in history. From the text of chapter 4 it follows that other human tribes, besides the "adamites," are meant here.

We can draw the following general conclusion about the historical and meta-historical Genesis 1–3. On the pathways of the development of life on our planet, on the phylogenetic ladder of man, there appear both the animal species *homo sapiens* and, in this species, an individual capable and worthy of becoming the vessel for the human spirit, of serving for its incarnation. This corresponds to the passages where it is said that "God formed man of the dust of the ground" (Gen. 2:7), from that very same "earth" that brought forth all the species of organic life (so that in this sense even the identification "dust thou art, and unto dust shalt thou return" [Gen. 3:19] became possible). This splendid animal, by its form already prefiguring man, *takes* from God the human spirit and is illuminated by it. Through this act, which transcends the being of the organic world and therefore is not subject to any empirical observation and interpretation, a perfect man arises from this perfect animal. This man is perfect in the sense that he corresponds to the creative design, and he bears within himself the task and potential of the world's humanization. This perfect man issues out of God's hands into the world, into the Garden of Eden that was expressly humanized for him. But, in his fall, man loses his perfect humanity, which remains beyond the limits of history as an unactualized ideal. Human history begins and proceeds in the same "evolutionary" way as the rest of creation, with the difference, of course, that, even in the natural process, man retains the supranatural principle of his spirit.

It has never been and cannot be indisputably proved that the *entire* history of humankind is *only* "evolutionary" in character, that is, that it proceeds from the lower to the higher, and not vice versa. This idea of a linear universal, all-embracing progress (even if there are regressions) cannot be proved because of the absence of the very possibility of such exhaustive experience. This idea is not so much a result of empirical observation as an *a priori*, purely doctrinal prejudice, in the light of which the testimony of the Bible is devalued. If we reject the universality of the principle of evolution, not only can we determine the appropriate role of this principle, but we can also affirm the truth of the original God-revelation in *meta*-history, the light of which has been preserved in the history of humankind in its chosen part, the part that did not fall under the sway of the surrounding paganism.

Thus, two paths of knowledge and life appear: (1) the divinely revealed religion of the Old Testament, entrusted to the "chosen people," and (2) natural revelation, with all its distortions and obscurities. Thus, man's original perfection, like his fall, can and should be understood as a genuine event in the life of the world and man. Although this perfection belongs to meta-history, in its consequences in history it can be understood as a certain *a priori* of history.

In original sin, we distinguish its extension over all of human nature from its extension over all human individuals. Let us begin with the first. Extension of original sin through birth is understood as a severe heredity, since we were all in Adam then. This is considered to be self-evident without at all being so. That which empirically is "heredity" attests to an ontological fact, the existence of a certain reality of the *species* as a mysterious force that acquires a wholly empirical expression. Thanks to this empirical expression, the existence of a species can be self-evidently understood on the basis of "heredity," whose phenomena are accessible to concrete investigation and formulation. Indeed, as a primordial fact or force, heredity does attest to the existence of a species, or (what is the same thing) of "nature," in contrast to an individual. Heredity belongs to metaphysics, or more precisely to meta-empiricism, as a force that acts above or in the depths of visible reality. It cannot be conceived except in categories of ideal being, in terms of Plato's ideas or Aristotle's entelechies, which in fact is the tendency of the advanced natural-science, in agreement with the revelation that clearly teaches that plants and animals were created "after their kind" (Gen. 1:11-12; 1:21, 25). The *kind,* or genus, for each form of being is its sophianic prototype, which ontologically precedes, or preestablishes, its being in the world. This is precisely that fundamental principle in concrete reality which evolutionists contrive not to notice, striving instead to explain the "origin of species" solely on the basis of evolution, whereas what in fact has to be explained is their existence and stability. It is proper to a "species" not only to "come into being" through evolution but also to *exist* after having come into being. A species is an *idea* that becomes a fact. It is a force that determines, or qualifies, the life of individuals.

With respect to his nature man is also a genus or species: the multiunity of humankind. Human nature is completely analogous in this respect to animal and plant species. This unity of human nature is expressed in heredity, which unifies separate individuals in a diverse connection of genera, generations, families, and nations. Heredity is only the empirical expression of a prototype, of a unitary nature. To accept this unity of human nature (which signifies, in the last analysis, that then we were all in Adam) is as natural as to admit changes in this nature, which can be valid for the *whole* genus. The humankind of Adam before the fall, *in statu naturae purae,* and after it, before redemption and after it, remains the same, with one destiny. The original being of the genus is a certain initial *given,* supranatural and primordial (which is something evolutionists are incapable of understanding). This being belongs to the creaturely Sophia and has its proto-image in her, while humankind, as the prototype of prototypes, containing all prototypes, is a "microcosm."

Meanwhile, one must recognize not only this stable being of the genus but also its initial fullness and reality. The error of evolutionism concerning genera and species consists in conceiving them as the sum or integral of an infinite series of differentials, of infinitesimal changes,[13] so that the very existence of the whole or species is rejected in favor of these differentials, none of which contains the idea of the species as such. This is because evolutionary thought tends to reject prototypes, idea-forces. But

---

13. It is characteristic that the rationalist Cohen places the infinitesimally small at the basis of reality.

with this rejection one also rejects the genera of being, which one recognizes only for convenience of classification (just as in ordinary, everyday life we accept the revolution of the sun around the earth even though we know that reality contradicts this).

This original being of humankind as a unity is expressed in the doctrine of the proto-Adam, in whom "all were then found." This formula expresses precisely the unity of human nature, which received its self-determination in the proto- and all-Adam. This manifestation of *all* human nature, of *all* humankind in the one Adam is given in revelation, and it is a postulate of sophianic anthropology. The teaching of revelation, creationism, is completely irreconcilable here with evolutionism. Evolutionism does not know an original and single humankind. It knows only the existence of individual atoms of humankind, out of which, through addition, the single humankind arises. Of course, evolutionism's conception is clearly contradictory even in the formal sense, for atoms are only atoms, and they therefore cannot be integrated into anything. For such integration an atom must be an atom of *something*, and this *something* must exist prior to every atom, just as a whole does not arise from the parts that compose it but exists prior to them. Prototypes, or protoenergies, are indivisible, and, in relation to human nature, the proto-Adam is also the all-Adam, bearing in himself all humankind. Precisely in this sense, with respect to his integral nature, it is true that "all of us were then in Adam." Nature is revealed in multiple individuals, but it is not divided. It is inwardly transparent and has a single destiny. Therefore, if a self-determination in relation to nature occurred in the first man, and a certain damage to this nature occurred as a result, this damage necessarily extends as a *hereditary illness* to all nature and to all human beings. Here, as a result of the exclusive connection existing between hypostasis and nature in the deepest recesses of personal life, in its intimate sources, the *personal* life of all the hypostases is necessarily damaged, takes on a sinister and fatal character, and becomes contradictory and tragic. It is sufficient to remember the whole life of the "body of death," the terrible spasms of sex, and bodily and psychic illnesses, to understand original sin also as a *destiny* weighing upon all humankind.

However, this knowledge of destiny is not yet consciousness of sin. In order for us to become conscious of destiny as sin, we must be conscious of our personal participation in sin. Only in this sense can one speak of original sin as a personal sin with which each man enters the world (which is why the Church has established the baptism of infants). But, given such a situation, only two ways out are possible: either the direct rejection of original sin as such, for a personal sin was committed only by Adam, whereas his descendants undeservedly bear the mark and consequences of this sin even though they personally are not guilty of it (such a supposition clearly implies a rejection of original sin); or the recognition of the *personal* participation in original sin of each one of us, to which an obscure anamnesis attests. But such a personal fall, making us coparticipants in Adam's sin, did not take place within the limits of this world. It took place outside this world, or, more correctly, at the threshold of our entry into the world. (The idea of *pre*-existence in the sense of a *time* preceding our aeon was condemned by the Church in Origen's doctrine and is essentially incompatible with a healthy ontology.)[14] Of course, we cannot have a direct remembrance of this fall outside the world. We can have only an obscure ontological anamnesis of it, since it is for us not an event but a state.

This *personal* fall at the threshold of the world is as much a *postulate* of our self-consciousness as an evident reality attested to by the diversity of personal characters. This diversity appears to be innate or "intelligible"; it cannot be explained by the causality of this world, and this character expresses precisely individuality at its root. This idea must be linked with the more general idea (see above) that man himself participates, in a certain sense, in his own origin, accepting his being from the Creator. And this acceptance is characterized not by monotonous sameness but by the individual qualifiedness of self-determination. Every person pre-enacts Adam's fall (with differences in mode and intensity). Every person repeats this fall, as it were, by his agreement to enter into a world damaged by Adam's sin, thus accepting the infirm human nature, the sick flesh that already bears the seeds of death. This acceptance becomes equivalent here to the acceptance of being in general, for after Adam's fall there is no other world, no world without sin.

But this reasoning leaves unresolved the following difficulty. According to Genesis 2, Adam's fall *is preceded by* a state of original innocence and "glory" (Rom. 3:23) but without choice or self-determination *(liberum arbitrium indifferentiae)*. Adam is brought out of this indeterminacy by the commandment, which he can keep or transgress. In contrast to the supramundane self-determination of all of Adam's descendants, this self-determination takes place in time (Adam's length of stay in Eden

14. In *The Burning Bush,* I expounded the doctrine of a supramundane fall as coparticipation in Adam's original sin. For an analogous opinion (but without sophiological premises) in the theological literature, see Julius Müller's extensive investigation: *Die christliche Lehre von der Sünde,* 6th ed., vol. 2, chap. 4, Bremen, 1889.

before the fall is not revealed to us, but this has no bearing upon the question we are considering here). Adam was created in a sinless state, which, as a result of his self-determination, turned out to be only pre-sinless. Thus, his determination to being includes *both* states: the original state that accords with God's intention and the fallen state that includes the darkening by sins.

Such a division or duality is proper only to the first man, who begins the human race. Our progenitor's state is manifested not only in conclusive self-determination but also in process, in which both dialectical moments are clear: primordial harmony and "the knowledge of good and evil" with enslavement by the element of the world. But the first man, precisely as the *first,* is self-determined not only individually but also universally. The relation of the human spirit to its *nature,* which is one for all humankind, is established in him. For all humankind, all of Adam's descendants, there is now no choice between the world in the state before Adam's fall and the state after it. For his descendants the only choice is *to be or not to be* in this world, which is in a state that should not be; but this acceptance of being, this *to be,* includes an infinite number of individual self-determinations and gradations. This self-determination takes place not in time, as it did for Adam and Eve, but above time; however, it is directed at time and is, as it were, simultaneous with Adam, is in Adam. In entering the world, all of Adam's descendants receive, each personally, the original sin. The temptation in Eden is not repeated for them, for in a certain sense this temptation took place for each of them at the pre-temporal point of their entry into the world (i.e., at the threshold of temporal being) already after the temptation, into the world of the temptation's consequences, after the fall.

Such is the most general meaning of the dogmatic idea that "we were all then in Adam." But this idea is also applicable to the multi-unity of human hypostases. Each human hypostasis is an independent center of creation, hypostatizes creation in its own way. But hypostases are not only a plurality of centers, indifferent to one another and multiplying the number of worlds, as it were. In fact, for all of them the world is one, just as the human hypostases are not a *series* but a *genus,* with an inner multi-unity realized in the unity of nature. This *genus* bears the image of the Holy Trinity, which is hypostatically multiple in consubstantiality. Trihypostatizedness is the perfect manifestation of the divine person, as the Father and the Son and the Holy Spirit. But does not the image of the Holy Trinity in man also represent an analogous manifestation of the principle of multi-hypostatizedness in the unity of nature, so that individual hypostases are different hypostatic aspects of a certain multi-unitary hypostasis of the integral Adam, aspects that are neither identical nor mutually alien, for they are included in the multi-unity of the man Adam?

This multi-unity, not given but only proposed as a task in the multiplicity of hypostases, also becomes a kind of supranatural reality, full of grace: "That they may all be one; as thou, Father, art in me, and I in thee . . . that they may be one, even as we are one" (John 17:21-22). What is divided into individuals in a state of cold indifference or enmity becomes mutually penetrable and transparent in a unity of love. One can therefore speak not only of the unity of humankind but also of the unity of *man,* of the firstborn Adam, in whom — once again and anew — we all were then. In other words, a bond of love or, at least, of the *solidarity* of the generic person exists, out of which one cannot fall completely and definitively.

Once again, from another direction, we encounter the idea of the *fullness* of the finished human multi-unity, of the integral Adam. And it becomes clear why his governing hypostasis, simply as the first, entrains in its fall its co-hypostases, so to speak. Their destinies are inseparable from that of Adam both in the mystery of original sin and in the mystery of the universal salvation that is to come, for we are all Adam; we all bear the name of the all-man.

Certainly, in the new Adam, in Christ, who is the new All-man in our all-humanity, we are all united. We are all included, as it were, in His person. We are "Christians," that is, christs as members of His body. In Him we receive a "new name" (Rev. 2:17), and it is not we who live but Christ who lives in us, by virtue of our love for Him, by which multiplicity is overcome in multi-unity: "A new commandment I give unto you, That ye love one another; as I have loved you, that ye also love one another" (John 13:34).[15]

Even though the power of the humanity of the old Adam is surpassed in the new Adam, it is not annulled. It is precisely this original hypostatic *multi-unity* of man, with one nature, that enables us to understand the fact that the Logos assumed the human nature ("flesh") fully without diminishing it or doing violence to it. But, at the same time, this

---

15. Therefore, the separation of the Mother of God from the human race by the mechanical "privilege" of being free of original sin contradicts this love and, in a certain sense, does not exalt but diminishes Her holiness. The voluntary acceptance of the destinies of the fallen Adam with original sin in the name of sacrificial love prefigures the Incarnation, with the reception not only of human nature but also of the death on the cross.

one hypostasis is the *all-hypostasis,* which is completely analogous to the human multi-unity. Every human person is assumed by the Logos into his humanity not only naturally but also hypostatically, inasmuch as the hypostasis of the Logos is precisely the Proto-image of man in the heavens, which is realized in man as its image. The hypostasis of the Logos contains all the human hypostases capable of being likened to this image, of ontologically merging with it. Of course, this refers only to the ontology of salvation, so to speak, not to the accomplishment of salvation by every man's freedom. But God "will have all men to be saved, and to come unto the knowledge of the truth. For there is one God, and one mediator between God and men, the man Christ Jesus" (1 Tim. 2:3-5). Highly significant here is precisely this juxtaposition: *all* men and the *one* mediator, the *Man,* the all-man, Christ. But Christ's all-humanity in His proper hypostasis is directly analogous to Adam's all-humanity in his hypostasis. This is also the first condition of the Incarnation.

The whole depth and significance of this idea of humankind as a *multi-unity* in the integral Adam, old and new, according to which we were all in Adam just as we are all in Christ, is disclosed to us in different aspects. To the contemporary consciousness this idea is most accessible in its biological aspect as heredity, the organic connectedness of the human race, and in its sociological aspect as the gregarious character of the human race, manifested in economic, legal, governmental, cultural, and linguistic connectedness. An individual does not exist outside this connectedness, which is a kind of common coordinate system for man. But a biological-sociological or generally empirical understanding of this connectedness is clearly insufficient, for it too requires explanation. Even though heredity and gregariousness operate in the whole animal world, which develops "according to its kind," this is insufficient to produce *history* as the combination of the destinies of humankind in its individual diversity.

To understand these destinies it is necessary to postulate a general ontological supra-individual and all-individual substrate of history. By a voluntary self-blinding, positivism rejects ontology and remains satisfied with its surrogates in little-signifying "myths" about heredity and gregariousness, which, of course, are not made less mysterious by the fact that their phenomenology is accessible to empirical observation. The ontology we mean, joining together heredity and sociability in the human race, is the anthropological principle of multi-unity, of the multi-unitary Adam, of the one but multipersonal humankind, one in creation and in fall, in redemption and in resurrection, in Adam and in Christ. Only this idea accords with the actual data, and with the postulate of anthropology in its biological and sociological aspects. The destiny of humankind is multi-unitary. This idea should be employed throughout anthropology (if it is employed, even if insufficiently, in soteriology, it is completely neglected in eschatology, where humankind is simply cut asunder into two unrelated parts; but about this below).

It is also necessary to establish a general distinction between original sin, *hamartema*, or sinfulness, and individual sins, *paraptōmata*, between ontological sin and empirical or historical sin. The difference is that the former belongs to man's pre-temporal ontology, whereas the latter belongs to the empirical realization of this ontology in freedom. The former is completely, ontologically wiped away by the new Adam, whereas the latter is a living bridge between the old Adam and the new Adam in the acquisition of the gift of redemption by human freedom.

What then is the nature of original sin? Is it the direct and pure evil of not desiring the good because of an unlove for God and an insane creaturely self-love? Or is it something complex, where the evil of unlove for God and of creaturely narcissism (which is so completely rejected by the first "beatitude": "blessed are the poor in spirit") is combined with and, to a certain degree, complicated by deception, self-deception, error?

As a result of its complexity compared with fleshless spirits, human nature contains the particular possibility of anthropological error, which is connected with sin, precisely because the proper relation between man's spirit and nature, his soul and body, is not observed. The loss of this equilibrium already contains the seeds of that domination of the flesh over the spirit that makes man a slave to the flesh and "a child of anger" in God's eyes. This loss of equilibrium, of the spirit's domination over nature, is the source of the life of sin, from which man can be delivered only through the new Adam, come "to renew man's fallen nature."

Man did not cause himself to fall. He was deceived and tempted by the serpent, and this in his highest calling, the calling to Divine-humanity: "Ye shall be as gods." The temptation referred not to the goal but to the means, to the falsehood of the path: Deification is not attained by communion with the flesh of this world (the eating of the fruit), through false love of the world, faith in the world, divinization of the world. Of course, this error already contained the seed of sin: the falling away from God, the cooling of love, mistrust, disobedience, and, as a result, the loss of the original, graceful harmony. As a result, unclean lust raises its head, and there begins the path of the knowledge of "good *and* evil," the path of *relative* good through the overcoming of its negation on the part of evil. This knowledge replaces the original holiness, which did not know this connectedness and opposition of good and evil and transcended this opposition.

This inner disharmony results in a disordering of the relations of man to his own body, which has become the body of death, owing to the insufficient power of the human spirit to master it. It also results in a disordering of man's relation to the whole natural world. It is very important to establish that original sin also has a cosmic significance: In man, who was called to be the king of the universe, the cultivator and protector of the cosmos, but who lost this power of his, all of creation turned out to be deprived of the creaturely logos and submitted itself to "vanity." This means that nature was left to its own powers and to the instinct of the world soul, in its sophianic wisdom but also in its nonhypostatic blindness. The hypostasis of the world, man, found itself blindfolded, as it were; it became subject to instinct. It did not completely lose the light of reason, for man's fall only weakened and perverted him, and could not abolish in him the indestructible image of God. Nevertheless, the original power over the world that had been given to man at his creation was replaced by a burdensome and laborious "economic" activity. Creative activity became combined with greed and coercion, while possession was accompanied by enslavement on the sorrowful and tragic paths of history: the era of "economic materialism" began, with the search for ways to overcome it on the paths of history.

History is a broken mirror, which reflects the image of God in man in a distorted and fragmented manner. The universal "apocatastasis" consists in restoring this integral image, in uniting its fragments for its definitive revelation beyond history. The character of this path, broken and with no escape, is determined by original sin, the source of the human tragedy. This tragedy attests to man's high nobility, his divine calling. He cannot be satisfied with anything less, but at the same time he does not have the power to realize this calling. This destiny is symbolically represented by the figure of Prometheus, who stole fire from heaven and brought it down to men in order to humanize them. And this humanization was accompanied by a rejection of the power of the prince of this world, who had fallen away from God. Prometheus symbolizes the struggle with metaphysical "petit-bourgeois" mediocrity, with the self-satisfaction of this world, in the name of the higher principle of life, the kingdom of God. The usual Luciferian "petit-bourgeois" interpretation of this symbol reduces it to the level of a struggle for the immanent empirical values of this world, whereas it actually summons man to a higher vocation, to the kingdom of God. It is this "petit-bourgeois" spirit that perpetuates good *and* evil in their interdependence as the sole path of life and ascent. The fallen state of man with the possibilities that it contains is therefore considered to be the supreme and unique state.

Original sin has an essential significance for the manifestation of human nature with its creative potential. It weakens this nature precisely where the uncreated-created spirit, the very source of freedom and creativity, is joined with the "flesh," with created humankind. The power of the spirit over the body, the force of humanity, is thus paralyzed. The measure of this weakening has been defined in different ways. Since Augustine it has become customary to exaggerate it to the point of the total loss of freedom to do the good, so that even the potential of freedom can be actualized only in evil. This idea received an exaggerated and extreme expression in Protestantism, in Luther's doctrine of *servum arbitrium* and Calvin's predestination. In fact both doctrines signify the loss of the image of God. Not pretending to precision, the Orthodox doctrine (agreeing here with the Catholic doctrine) affirms only a certain *darkening* (not defined with greater precision) of the image of God with the weakening of freedom, although man is seen as preserving the capacity for good in counteraction to evil. Therefore, man's creative power is, in general, preserved.[16]

To be sure, such a doctrine appears incomprehensible and incoherent if freedom is understood not in a modal sense, as self-determination *in* and *from* the given, but in the absolute sense of an autonomous creative principle, as self-determination from the emptiness of *nothing*, which supposedly contains something ontologically new, free from the given. Without mentioning the conceptually superficial, purely negative, and vacuous character of such a self-determination, it leads to a completely atomistic theory of humankind as an indeterminate series of separate, unconnected, and unconnectable centers of personal freedom outside of their general given. Conversely, by recognizing a principle of all-humanity behind individual atoms, one introduces the given in the freedom of self-determination. And freedom thereby becomes merely modal and stops having the absolute character of arbitrary generation from nothing.

16. "We believe that man, who fell by transgressing, has become like the wordless animals, i.e., he has become darkened and deprived of perfection and passionlessness. But he has not been deprived of that nature and power which he had acquired from the all-good God. For, in the contrary case, he would have become irrational and therefore not a man. But he has that nature with which he is created, as well as natural power, free, vital, active, so that, by his nature, he can choose and do the good, and avoid and reject evil . . ." (*Epistle of the Eastern Patriarchs,* chap. 14).

But real, concrete freedom, modal freedom, can be greater or smaller in magnitude, more or less complete. It can decrease or increase. It can ascend from the slavery of sin and the flesh to the freedom of the children of God in the Holy Spirit: "Where the Spirit of the Lord is, there is liberty" (2 Cor. 3:17). Concrete freedom is a positive power and force, as well as a value, which is inseparable from an even greater value, namely individuality. In individuality, the free person is endowed with his proper qualities and included in the integral humankind. If human beings had absolute freedom *outside* of the given, if they were determined from nothing, they would not have individuality as the concrete form of the person; for, determined by nothing, they would remain self-enclosed, with no point of reference, no place in reality. On the contrary, if they were wholly exhausted by their given, if they did not possess modal freedom in assimilating it, they would be things, deprived of all creative relation to themselves and to the world; that is, they would be deprived of the image of God.

But creaturely freedom changes and increases from what is given to what is proposed as a task, from necessity to creative activity, from fact to act, from subordination to possession. In general, freedom is not an abstractly static, negative determination but a concretely dynamic self-positing from fact to act, the two being combined in it in different forms. Original sin was an ontological catastrophe in man, causing in his life an unlawful predominance of fact over act, an excessive dependence on nature, and an attenuation of the power of his spirit, with a general weakening of his being.

This state was not and could not have been unchanging and stable. It included the possibility of an even greater fall (to the level of the "flesh" or satanization, enslavement by demons) as well as the possibility of ascent from power to power, to the holiness of the Mother of God. This capacity for transformation also serves as the basis of the possibility of salvation through redemption, through the acceptance of a power that frees one from the burdensome bonds of the world, giving one new power over the latter.

Original sin has a quantitative influence on man's freedom, for it multiplies his dependence on nature. And, in this sense, it dehumanizes him to a certain degree, transforming him from a king into a slave. Only through a long and laborious process does man escape from this slavery. But this sin also has a qualitative influence, in inwardly subjecting man, in determining the direction of a life enslaved by sin and the flesh, in provoking the tragic contradiction between *velle* and *posse, velle* and *esse*. It is this tragic contradiction that is expressed in the universal-human cry of the apostle Paul: "O wretched man that I am! Who shall deliver me from the body of this death?" (Rom. 7:24).

The original (and even more than the original) freedom is restored to the children of men by the God-man. Only He manifested in Himself the full measure of human freedom, by linking it with subordination to the divine will: this is expressed in the Sixth Ecumenical Council's dogma of the two wills and the two energies, according to which human will "follows," *hepomene,* God's will. This formula applies, in essence, to creaturely freedom, giving it a dogmatic definition and interpretation. The fullness of creaturely freedom is expressed by the commandment of the prayer: "Thy will be done on earth as it is in heaven" as well as by the prayer of the God-man that comes from His human nature: "not as I will, but as thou wilt. . . . Thy will be done" (Matt. 26:39, 42).

As opposition to God's will, original sin extends over the whole surface of human life, which is poisoned by the serpent in the hidden recesses of the will and the depths of the flesh. This sin does not suppress but paralyzes freedom, as it were, making it lose its joyously creative character of growth, tragically weakening it. Nevertheless, however deep the paralysis of freedom and the enslavement of the spirit by the elements of the world, one cannot speak of its total loss or of a *servum arbitrium,* for freedom is the proper element of the spirit, which, above all, is a self-affirmation and a self-determination. The measure of this self-determination can be greatly diminished and become imperceptible. It can be reduced almost to a potential state. Nevertheless, the axiom remains inviolate that the nature of the spirit is freedom. Self-determination is absolute in the Absolute, in divinity; whereas it is relative in the given and on the basis of the given, in creation.

CHAPTER 4

God and Creaturely Freedom

1. Divine Providence with Regard to the World

God posited the being of the world in Sophia. God's Wisdom is the positive principle of the world created out of nothing. The world contains this Wisdom. Wisdom is the power of the world's being, its divinity, about which it is said: "In him we live, and move, and have our being" (Acts 17:28). This positive foundation gives indestructibility to the world: "The world also is stablished, that it cannot be moved" (Ps. 93:1). God's creative words, with the blessing "let there be," resound for all times in the universe. The world was created once, but the creative act continues supratemporally and all-temporally: "My Father worketh hitherto, and I work" (John 5:17). In this sense, the preservation of the world's being with its indestructibility is already included in the creation of the world and does not require a special providence for itself.

Nevertheless, the doctrine of divine providence, its certainty established by revelation,[1] concerns precisely the preservation of creation, in the sense of directing its life. The world is not self-enclosed. It is not shut off from spiritual action, which imparts to it new natural forces,[2] as it were. Rather, its life is directed by divine providence. Sometimes angels (cf. the figures of the Apocalypse) serve as the intermediaries, and sometimes God himself is mentioned in connection with providence. However, in any case, the data of revelation are completely incompatible with the concep-

---

1. See the texts in the dogmatic handbooks: in Metr. Macarius, vol. 1; "Providence," in *Dict. de théol. cath.*, 13, etc.

2. Cf. my work *On the Gospel Miracles*, chap. 1.

193

tion of deism, according to which the Creator abandons the world to its own fate, with God being compared to the skillful mechanic of a *perpetuum mobile*. This comparison is completely unsuitable if only because, in its anthropomorphicity in relation to God, it employs the determinations of time, *before* and *after:* Beginning at a certain moment of time and finishing at a certain moment of time, God creates the world and then completely breaks off His relation to it, dooming it to godlessness and Himself to worldlessness. This conception clearly conceives God's being as changeable (which is impermissible) and attributes wholly extra-divine existence to the world. But, in this sense, the world, being "outside" of God, is for Him a boundary, which is even less acceptable. In general, deism is an extreme form of sophiamachy: since it abolishes the sophianic connection of God with the world, deism is (for all practical purposes) an atheism.

God's relation to the world is not exhausted by His calling it to being through the command "let there be." It is a *positive* correlation in Sophia, Divine and creaturely. It is a certain common life of God in the world and of the world in God, which is expressed in the idea of divine providence with regard to the world. The world, created by God, is for all time sustained in being by this creative act, which has neither beginning nor end, for it issues from divine eternity. God never began to be the Creator, just as He will never stop being the Creator (see above). But this supratemporal and omnitemporal character of creation, as the very being of the world, is accompanied by God's divine watching over of this world in its proper life in time. Such is God's relation to the created world, which has in itself the power to exist and, in this sense, is self-subsistent in its proper life.

For rational thought there is a clear contradiction here, which deism seeks to overcome: either the Creator and only the Creator, or the Provider and only the Provider. *Tertium non datur.* But a revealed doctrine requires precisely this suprarational *tertium:* The Creator is also the Provider, and He is such not according to temporal succession, as naive thought has it. Rather, He is "simultaneously" the Creator and the Provider. The very being of creation consists in its createdess, in the constant process of its being created, which is actualized in its life. To this creation that owes its being to Him, God reveals Himself also as the Provider, and this providential act (or act of acts) has neither beginning nor end. God always provides for creation, has a positive relation to the latter, lives a joint life with it, however imprecise the expression "the joint life of the Creator and creation" may be. The foundation of this joint life consists in the very creation of the world, which, in creation, receives the full power of being, reality for God.

The reality of the world is the reality of the creaturely Sophia, *ens realissimum*. That is, this reality comes from God himself, who cannot diminish it without diminishing His own reality. But the relation of the original reality to the derivative reality is necessarily that of *ens realissimum* to *ens reale*, or that of *ens originale* to *ens derivativum*. There cannot be two equally prototypical realities; that would be ditheism. But there can be and are two unequal realities: divine and creaturely. God is always the Creator; that is, He creates creation and therefore has it for Himself. Therefore, He always maintains a relationship to creation: for creation, He is not only the Creator but also the Provider.

The aforesaid establishes the *formal* possibility, so to speak, of a divine providence based on the existence of a relation between God and the world as two realities that have being for each other. But does such a necessary relation of these realities not make God's very being relative? Does it not deprive God's being of its absoluteness? All doubt regarding this is removed by the fact that these two realities are not equal. Rather, one is derivative of the other and, in this sense, cannot limit it. God is the Creator in His self-revelation for creation, but His own being in Himself as the Absolute lies beyond this distinction and is transcendent for the world. For creation God's own being is therefore felt as an absolute *non (alpha privativum)* or *supra (trans, hyper)* with respect to any ontic determination. Therefore, the very relation between God and the world, between Creator and Provider, is, first of all, the Absolute's own self-determination, His revelation in Himself as divine Love. But creation perceives this relation not with its creaturely originality, which is precreaturely and extra-creaturely nothing, a pure zero, absolute emptiness, but by the divine power implanted in it. In this sense, this relation is divinity's own life in Himself and "outside" Himself, as the Divine and the creaturely Sophia. The creaturely Sophia is God's extra-divine life and being, that is, His life and being in creation.

Thus, the possibility and necessity of God's providence are sufficiently grounded in His creative act, by virtue of which the life of creation exists. But this does not yet determine the form of this providential relation as the "preservation and guidance" of creation. Is not the objection of the deists (and of all those who deny the reality of God's providence) persuasive here? In their objection the deists liken God to an imperfect mechanic who unsuccessfully or unsatisfactorily created the world. If this machine cannot move under its own power without requiring constant correction or maintenance in the form of supernatural interference in its operation ("miracles" of all kinds), then, clearly, either it is the work of an imperfect, limited creator or two beings participated in its creation: one who created and one who damaged and destroyed. Even apart from any special providence, should not all things progress toward what is better "in this best of all possible worlds"?

If one understands the creation of the world as it is usually understood (unfortunately, not only in deism but also in scholastic theology), this objection must then be accepted as unanswerable. The creation of the world out of "nothing" is considered here as the action of God *ad extra,* by the power of His omnipotence and wisdom creating the world, which does not have, strictly speaking, any foundation in His own life. In general, the world is considered to be a product of divine caprice, both in its form and in its being. In this case, it is perfectly legitimate to use the analogy of the mechanic and his machine, although even a machine is not an indifferent object of the mechanic's invention and, in this sense, an external and accidental work. Rather, it has an inner connection with the mechanic. It is his creation, a manifestation of his person, and to this extent it is he himself.

The creation of the world is not only a work of God's omnipotence, which seeks to be manifested and finds this manifestation in one of a multiplicity of possible worlds. It is also a self-revelation of God who is Love. The creation of the world is connected with the Creator by its participation in divinity and in divine life. The world has in itself the principle of divine life and lives by this principle. It lives not only in itself but also in God, not only for itself but also for God. Although the world is called to being out of nothing, creation is not *nothing* before God, because, in itself, it has divine power, its own divinity, so to speak, which is the creaturely Sophia. All that is exists by God's power and, in this (but of course only in this and precisely in this) sense, it is divine. The world is a creaturely divinity, and creation is God's self-positing to extra-divine being. Therefore, the world has in itself its own metaphysical elasticity. The world is *correlated* with God, no longer as a metaphysically empty place, or a pure nothing, but as the creaturely Sophia, as divine life that has issued into nothing and acquired an identity in its own extra-divine being, in the creaturely world.

But in this case another question arises. As the creaturely Sophia, does the world also admit upon itself a special divine action, divine providence, and does it have need of this action? Or does the world have sufficient fullness and perfection in itself (the "it was good," which is complete and has no need for further perfection)? Would not God's providence with regard to the world be, as it were, His providence with regard to Himself (which is clearly absurd)?

But this reasoning is totally refuted by the fact that, in creation, the divine seeds are implanted in nothing, and being is ontologically mixed with nonbeing, is in a state of becoming, which by definition cannot be perfect. "It was good" refers to the divine plan for creation (its entelechic character), and not to its actual state, which by no means is its last word. Creation is imperfect in every one of its states, for it is unfinished; predetermined in its entelechy, it leaves room for different possibilities of its realization, for different variants of being.

Thus, the world receives an independence to follow its destinies. This independence is realized in the world soul as the universal connectedness, the total unity of creaturely being. This world soul (see above) is the creaturely Sophia in her actualization in being. As a nonhypostatic principle (but one that is capable of being hypostatized and called to hypostatization), the world soul actualizes the instinctive and, in *this* sense, blind thirst for and power of being. Her diverse elements sprout to life not only in harmonious agreement but also crowding one another, in a kind of "struggle for existence," according to their elemental nature. And this elemental nature contains not only positive but also destructive forces. This world soul is not only the principle of life but also "Chronos devouring his children." It is not only the Porus of divine abundance but also the Peneus[3] of its own imperfection.

Therefore, in its proper being, the world soul is divided into "heaven and earth," as it were, the world of the angels as bearers of the sophianic prototypes of creation and the world of earth's reality, which has beneath it the seething *tohu vabohu,* the primordial chaos. Creation arises through the elemental forces of the world soul that it contains, but its formation and being presuppose the participation and activity of the angels (as Scripture testifies in speaking of particular angels who are the protectors of the elements [see Rev. 7:1; 14:18; 16:5] and fight battles). This is a manifestation of God's providential activity with respect to the creaturely world, realized through the angels: The elemental life of the world, in its blind instinct, is protected and directed by the hypostatically conscious guidance of the angels, who can be seen as a heavenly mirror of the earthly creation, the helmsmen of this creation. This is, so to speak, the heavenly

---

3. Porus was a king of the Indian provinces east of the river Hydaspes, who offered a formidable resistance to Alexander when the latter attempted to cross this river, 327 B.C. He was of gigantic stature. Because of that, and his valor, his name has come to signify great strength and prowess. Peneus, a Greek god and a river in Thessaly, presumably connotes meagerness and infirmity. — Trans.

(although creaturely) aura of the world soul. The natural world, in its own being, left to its sophianic instinct, contains an inexhaustible abundance of creative energies and vital principles; but it is subject to chaos, to manifested multiplicity. This chaotic character can also lead to collisions of the principles of being, and the world in its natural foundation therefore requires guidance, which is realized through the angels.

This guidance is certainly necessary, first because of the fall that took place in the spiritual world, and then because of man's fall. The fall in the spiritual world could not fail to have repercussions in the natural world, since angels who had formerly been guardians of creation are transformed through the fall into spirits of wickedness in high places, poisoning and perverting creation. Scripture sufficiently bears witness to the potentiality of this evil creative activity.[4] Of course, demons do have an influence on the natural world. We do not have the data to affirm that natural cataclysms (such as earthquakes, catastrophes, etc.) always have their origin not in the elemental chaos but in the wicked activity of evil spirits. The same thing must be said concerning certain phenomena of the vegetative and animal world, such as the existence of deadly poisons, all kinds of harmful plants, predators who exterminate one another, repulsive or harmful animals and insects, and so on. To be sure, all of these assessments are relative, since they are made from a limited human point of view. And, of course, one can doubt whether demonic forces are capable of summoning to existence any species of new being, thereby parodying the Creator and creation. It is more probable that what we have here is only a perversion of the good image of creation, sometimes to the point of unrecognizability. But, in any case, it is clear that such an incessant attack of the forces of evil against God's creation necessitates a defense against this attack. And this defense constitutes part of the general service of the angels who implement God's providential watching over creation.

But the necessity of such providence is also revealed in another aspect. With the fall of man the world loses the one who was called to become its king and guide, as the hypostasis of creation, humanizing it and leading it from chaotic instinct to intelligence. The animal world also turns out to be condemned to savagery by being left in its animal state, whereas animals were called to be man's friends, his younger brothers, as

---

4. With God's permission, Satan tempts Job; the temptations are expressed in a series of natural phenomena (fire from the heavens, winds, sicknesses). Satan binds Abraham's daughter (Luke 13:16). The demons expelled from the possessed Gadarene enter a herd of swine (Luke 8:31-33), etc.

it were. The fall darkened the reason of the world in man; the whole world was damaged in its development and abandoned its proper destiny: "For the creature was made subject to vanity, not willingly, but by reason of him who hath subjected the same. . . . the whole creation groaneth and travaileth in pain" (Rom. 8:20-22).

It follows that the world in its actual state is by no means a perfect and finished mechanism, a mechanism that does not require active care or the guidance of God's providence. To be sure, in its being, the world remains indestructible. But, in its ways, it can be subject to perversion and damage, being transformed from God's garden into an accursed earth. Through this perversion, the world, despite the sophianic roots of its being, can resist the ways of God. It therefore requires protection and guidance. This guidance is accomplished by God through the service of the angels. Because of its blindness and elemental character, nonhypostatic or preconscious nature cannot have a direct relation with God. Its relation with God is accomplished through servant spirits, who by their proper nature are predestined precisely to this service. Even though they are hypostatic spirits, they serve here as natural, though conscious, powers. They are both the consciousness and the ideal sophianicity of nature. They belong to creation but are a superior form of it. They have a specific place in the life of nature. Being open to divine inspirations, they are also conductors of natural energies, accomplishers of God's thought about creation. They implement the sophianic protection of creation; and this is precisely what is called divine providence in nature. "Wisdom reacheth from one end to another mightily: and sweetly doth she order all things" (Wisd. of Sol. 8:1).

God's providence toward creatures is accomplished by the power of sophianicity proper to them. But just as the world's creation has its principle in the Father, "the Creator of heaven and earth," who creates the world by the Son and the Holy Spirit in Sophia, so also providential action with regard to the world is accomplished by the "Almighty" Father, through the Son and the Holy Spirit. The Church teaches that providence is accomplished by the entire Holy Trinity, according to the different characters of its hypostases. In this respect, Scripture testifies that providence proceeds, first of all, from the Father: the Heavenly Father "maketh his sun to rise on the evil and on the good, and sendeth rain on the just and on the unjust" (Matt. 5:45). He feeds the fowls of the air (6:26), clothes the grass of the field (6:30), and concerns himself with sparrows (10:29-30). But what is said here about the Father, the starting hypostasis, represents, in this case, only an abbreviated monogram of the Holy Trinity and of

Sophia, the Wisdom of God. These texts about the Father do not have a limiting significance, which would exclude the participation of the other hypostases in divine providence. (Such an interpretation contradicts the rest of the doctrine of revelation.) The Father is understood here as God in general. Just as the world is created by the Holy Trinity in Sophia, so it is preserved by the Holy Trinity. This is an axiomatic principle of theology.

However, it is important to emphasize once again the difference between creation and providence. In creation, the world receives the determination of its being. In providence, this determination of its being, one and unalterable, is not renewed; but that which was given once and for all is fulfilled and, so to speak, confirmed by God. Nor does providence violate the divine sabbath, which corresponds to the fullness of creation in the Six Days. Rather, it imparts to the sabbath a durational, all-temporal, actual character. Therefore, by no means is providence a new creation, fulfilling and completing what was unfinished. Nor is it ontological violence done to the world, which remakes it, as it were, communicating new possibilities to it.

Although it is by no means foreign to Catholic theology, which generally admits a multiplicity of worlds that could be created and therefore a multiplicity of divine wisdoms, such an idea contradicts the original fullness and perfection of creation. Once it is summoned into being by God, the world is not only the best of all worlds but even the only and perfect world. But it faces the task of becoming itself, of actualizing its perfection in the creaturely Sophia on the basis of creaturely freedom. Therefore, in the life of nature, we have both the shining of the creaturely Sophia, the revelation of paradise, and the seething of the blind element, natural chaos. The first belongs to the angelic side of nature (to the "morning," according to St. Augustine's interpretation), while the second belongs to the "night," to the meonality of creation, to its createdness "out of nothing." Nature follows the path of its sophianization, in which providence is accomplished through the intermediary of the angelic world. But this world does not introduce anything completely new and alien into the life of nature. It only helps nature to become itself, to actualize its proper image, implanted in it by the Creator. Nature is *nascens natura,* the symphony of the world that seeks the harmony of the spheres and to overcome its own dissonances. The relation between divine guidance and creaturely freedom is expressed here as the incessant introduction into the life of creation of its own principles, accessible to but unactualized by it. And freedom here is the instinct of life, the unconscious reception of the life-creating spirit, the unconscious or (more precisely) the preconscious love of creation for itself in its divinely sophianic prototype, the natural eros. In this sense, one can say that God's providence in the natural world is the Divine Sophia herself, acting in the natural world as a force of internal movement, *kinoun hōs erōmenon*, according to Aristotle.

We have thus defined the limits and character of this providential action in contradistinction to new creativity. Nature, not fully *nata* but only *natura*, has an indestructible foundation and content. Therefore, the action of providence, the pressure, if you will, that it exerts on creation in view of creation's own purposes, cannot crush or squeeze out this content. It only appropriately directs a life already given, realizes the immanent goals of the universe.

There is an insurmountable difference between creation and providence here. Ontological miracles are alien to providence. The fundamental and all-embracing miracle is creation itself. Even if providence is accompanied by that higher purposefulness in which we see "miracles," these providential actions must nonetheless be distinguished from new creation. Ontologically, there is no place for new creation in the all-exhaustive fullness of creation, in which God rested from his works. This fullness of creation is nothing else but its sophianicity. There is only one Divine Sophia, who is the foundation of the creaturely Sophia. Therefore, the action of providence stops before this foundation and protects it; its task is to remove the forces of cosmic inertia and chaotic rebellion that are antagonistic to this foundation or restrain its energy. This action unveils the luminous figure of the Divine Sophia in the hostile *nothing* that has received being by the Creator's act.

2. Divine Providence with Regard to Man

Man is a microcosm. In man, the world overcomes its elemental character and acquires a logos. Man is the creaturely Sophia in the fullness of the image of God in creation. In connection with this fundamental relation there again arises the question posed in deism: Does the world have need of the further interference of God in its fate, the special guidance of providence, or is providence superfluous and even contradictory? Does providence not take away from man what is given to him? "The prince of this world" desires precisely such a separation of the world from God and lures man onto the path of this temptation. On the contrary, revelation clearly and decisively teaches that God exercises His providence in the world and that He directs the world.

The general question of the relation between God and man in the life of creation arises. First of all, does man need such divine guidance after he has received from God a created-uncreated spirit and possesses the image of God as his supreme and indestructible reality? Further, is there an ontological basis for some sort of interrelationship between God and man, for what Orthodox theology calls *synergism?* Or was the relation between God and man exhausted by the act of the creation of man in the image of God, after which he was set free as the prince of this world? And this is inevitably followed by a second question: If God's providence exists in the world, how is it realized in relation to creaturely, human freedom? How is the divine omnipotence, which for creatures has the significance of overwhelming necessity, compatible with human freedom? Let us start with the first question.

The image of God in man is not merely a "resemblance" or a "property." It is a higher reality, a spiritual reality, an energy of God-likeness and God-likening. The union of "image and likeness" is the realization of the image in life, the transition from statics to dynamics, from potentiality to energy. But at the same time the character of the *image* creates an indissoluble connection between it and the Proto-image, whose copy it is. The image in this sense is not original but derivative. Its whole reality is conditioned precisely by this connection; the image is this connection itself *in actu.* Man's originality consists precisely in the ontological nature of this connection, uniting divinity and nothing, immersing the "energies" of the divine life in creatureliness. This connection implies a certain inseparability of God and man, which in advance excludes deism's postulate of a radical separation between God and man (together with all of creation).

This idea can be more precisely expressed in sophiological terms. Man contains the creaturely Sophia, is, in this sense, a creaturely-sophianic hypostasis. Man's sophianicity signifies the universal fullness of his being, whereas his creatureliness signifies this fullness only in a state of potentiality. Sophianicity is given to man as a possibility and is only proposed as a reality: his task is to actualize this sophianicity. Creaturely sophianicity is a mixture of the meonal potentiality of becoming with the supreme reality of divine energies. The first is not yet a reality, whereas the second is an abiding power, and the fruit of this union is becoming, the ascent from power to power.

In relation to the Divine Sophia the creaturely Sophia is in this sense a "receptacle" *(ekmageion),* where the Proto-image is reflected. Moreover, this reflection is not a static relation but a dynamics of life, which therefore has times and seasons, can be greater or less, changeable and mobile. It is *life,* uniting in itself the seeds of eternal life and of creaturely temporality.

Creaturely sophianicity presupposes the possibility of unlimited sophianization, the approximation of the image to the Proto-image. But, inversely, creaturely life can also include motion in the opposite direction, the distancing, or separation, of the image from the Proto-image, although this separation can never lead to a complete break, to the complete fading of the image, to the revocation of the *ekmageion,* for this image is indestructible. It bears the stamp of eternity, albeit a creaturely eternity: *aeviternitas* as the reflection of *aeternitas.*

This eternal life is without limit. It is inexhaustible for creation, which is why the the Divine Sophia and the creaturely Sophia converge forever without coinciding; and in this sense this convergence is "infinite life." The sophianization of creation therefore contains infinite possibilities of ascending and descending motion, of deceleration and acceleration. In this sense the sophianization of creation represents, first of all, the unceasing ontological interaction of God with creation: in other words, providence. Creation has need of this providential action, for it is incomplete, dissatisfied with itself; it thirsts for fulfillment, *seeks* God. Theological discourse usually expresses this idea by saying that creation seeks and receives God's *grace.* This reception of grace, or sophianization, follows the path of deification: a union with God that has already been accomplished for all of creation through the union of two natures, divine and human, in Christ, according to the Chalcedonian dogma, and through the descent of the Holy Spirit upon the apostles and all of humankind, according to the dogma of the Pentecost.

Here it is necessary to remove a prejudice that crops up on this path. The sophianization of man by grace, which in a special sense is also called *salvation* (see below), is *not* wholly connected with the fall of man, with "*beata Adae culpa* [the blessed sin of Adam]." It is generally thought that salvation is something extraordinary that comes from outside, that it transcends man's natural vocation, his creaturely sophianicity. Both the Incarnation and the Pentecost, the deification of man, are considered here only in their instrumental significance for our salvation ("soteriologically"). What is not noticed here is that this ontological possibility of "salvation" through deification is predetermined by the very creation of man in the image of God. The fall of man here signifies only deviation from the straight path of his ascent, which leads him to deification, or sophianization, by virtue of the image of God in him. Man's state before the fall does not in any way correspond to the postulates of deism concerning the total separation of man's life from God and the abolition of God's leadership.

On the contrary, the edenic state is distinguished by a special closeness of God to man, which, of course, was expressed precisely in God's "providence" toward man and the interaction (synergism) of God and man. God gives man lessons of wisdom, as it were. God awakens in man his sophianicity, leading animals to him for naming, entrusting him also with Eve, as flesh of his flesh, giving the commandment of the keeping of Eden and of the observance of God's will regarding the forbidden tree. Also, God's judgment after the fall reveals the divine image in man, his sophianicity, through the negative manifestation of its power. The same significance is possessed by God's "covenant" with man in the person of the chosen people of God, by the tabernacle, by the laws, by the prophecies, by the entire path of the Old Testament revelation. And the same thing, though to a lesser degree, must be said about "natural revelation," beyond the limits of the Old Testament church, and, in general, about the religious life of all of humankind.

The action of providence aimed at the sophianization of creation is not limited to this revelation as doctrine. This action also includes the works of providence in the destinies of particular individuals and all peoples. On the paths of this divine guidance, the Incarnation and Pentecost, even though they are central, determining, decisive events, must also be viewed in the general perspective of the ongoing sophianization of creation. This sophianization, which has inwardly already been accomplished in these events, still awaits its manifest accomplishment in the destinies of the world and of humankind beyond the present aeon, in the Parousia. In their inner significance, all of these paths on which God guides us to salvation are determined by the connection between image and Proto-image, between the Divine Sophia and the creaturely Sophia. *In actu*, precisely this connection is divine providence. It is the foundation and goal, the entelechy of divine providence. But as the relation between the Divine and the creaturely Sophia, between God and the world, this connection necessarily is *interaction,* or "synergism." It is ongoing Divine-humanity, which was dogmatically defined by the decrees of the fourth and sixth ecumenical councils.

3. Divine Causality and Creaturely Freedom (The Problem of Synergism)

How should one understand this interrelationship of God and the world once one sweeps away the temptation of deism, which rejects all interaction or synergism between God and the world? This problem first arose in

St. Augustine's development of his doctrine of grace and the freedom (or, rather, the lack of freedom) of man after the fall. To save the remnants of the freedom that he had so zealously defended against the Manichaeans, Augustine had to reduce it to a subjective-psychological state of man, who realizes necessity in such a form. The doctrine of predestination that Augustine was compelled to defend, did not, of course, leave room for actual, creative freedom. In his doctrine, freedom could only represent a psychological illusion on the background of a general determinism. (It is not by chance that Augustine accepts that, if God had so willed, Judas would not have fallen and the apostle Paul would have remained a persecutor of Christ, that is, that they were therefore only instruments, if not puppets, of providence.)

But given its soteriological orientation, Augustinianism did not make determinism the universal principle of ontology, which it was for Aquinas and remains so even for present-day Thomism. As in many other cases, Thomism remains under the influence of Aristotelianism in the doctrine of God and the world. The first principle of ontology for Thomism is *quod movetur, ab alio movetur* (that which is moved is moved by something else). The whole world is permeated with the causal connection, which goes back to the prime mover and the first cause, to God. The mechanism of causal connection expresses the interrelationship of God and the world, as many texts in Aquinas indicate. True, these texts are subject to various interpretations and their meaning is disputed. On this soil there has arisen in contemporary Thomism a complex controversy,[5] in which there are at least two fundamental opposed tendencies, headed by two eminent theologians, Garrigou-Lagrange and d'Alès, with others joining in. We have no need to enter into this controversy within the framework of Thomism itself and its interpretation, especially since, in virtue of the wise restraint of *infallibile judicium* (infallible judgment) concerning this question, freedom of opinion is permitted here after long and unsuccessful attempts to achieve unanimity of thought.

We shall touch only upon the general contours of this problematic. The basic idea of the doctrine of the *motio* or *praemotio physica* (physical motion or pre-motion) consists in the fact that God, as the first cause and prime mover of the world, causally determines everything that takes place in the world, and this is not a moral but precisely a "physical," natural, ontic determination, extending to "free acts." God is the prime mover and

---

5. See the interesting work of J. Stufler: *Gott, der erste Beweger aller Dinge*, Innsbruck, 1936. [. . .]

the first cause, to which all second causes are subordinate in their actions. If one did not recognize the *praemotio physica*, one could not affirm that the origin of causality is in God or that the second causes and their actions are subordinate to the first cause. Thus, the principle of *praemotio physica* consists in recognizing the one, supreme, omnipresent causality of God in the world: "*Dieu déterminant ou déterminé, pas de milieu* [The determining or determined God, nothing in between]," insistently repeats a major representative of contemporary Thomism.[6] If God does not possess this unlimited power of causation, then, argue the Thomists, He turns out to be dependent on and limited by creation.

Great difficulties arise when one tries to precisely interpret Aquinas's doctrine on the basis of his many works. These difficulties lead to endless disputes among the Thomists. The main such difficulty concerns the distinction between the first cause and the second causes. This distinction coincides to a significant degree with the opposition between divine first-causality and creaturely freedom, which Aquinas, like Augustine, does not want to reject. Although the distinguishing characteristic of freedom of actions is their spontaneity, they proceed from the first cause. This distinction and this contraposition of first cause and second cause evidently corresponds to the relation between God and the world. God is not only the first cause *among* others, but also the unique cause in the precise sense, not only the immanent but also the transcendent cause (such also is the idea of the prime mover in Aristotle).

Thomism does not posit a radical and consistent determinism, for it tries to preserve freedom, *liberum arbitrium,* by combining it with and, of course, subordinating it to causality. This is done by distinguishing two types of causal determination: concrete — *ad unum* — determination of the will according to the order of necessity and its absence, *determinatio non necessitans.*[7] Thus, a second cause is introduced in the system of universal determinism at least as a variant: creaturely freedom. However, no place in the system is, in essence, found for it except as one of the forms of causality. In individual cases creaturely freedom is considered as one of the components of the world's causality or of individual acts and personal self-determinations. The severity and exclusivity of determinism are therefore avoided without the open introduction of a *"concursus,"* an interaction — now not of the first cause *and* the second cause, but of two causes acting in

---

6. Garrigou-Lagrange, *Dieu,* 6th ed., op. cit., epilogue. By the same author: "Prémotion physique," in *Dict. de théol. cath.,* 13, 1, 1936.

7. See *Summa Theologica* Ia, IIae, q. 10, a. 4. [. . .]

the world, divine and creaturely. The hidden contradiction of Thomism (as well as of Augustinianism) consists in the fact that a purely *modal* concept of freedom, as a special form of causality, is raised to an ontological value, which enters into a *concursus* with the divine causality. Thus, Aquinas is saved from his own determinism. This recognition of "second causes," alongside the first and universal cause, which is being itself, has become the most vulnerable point in the doctrine of Thomism, as a flagrant contradiction in the system of causal monism.

The first cause acts on the second causes, which receive from it a *complementum causalitas*. But, as Molina (*De Concordia*, p. 152) correctly observes, a fire burns without needing any special *motio* for this, just as, in general, this whole conception of the action of the first cause through second causes is doubtful. But Thomism attempts to get around this difficulty by insisting on the universal causality of God. *Deus determinans, non determinatus* (God is determining, not determined).

But causal monism is a mechanistic system in the sense that it views the world as a continuous chain of causes, proceeding from the prime mover. The energy of the causality of this first cause absorbs, so to speak, the derivative causality of the second causes, and Thomism here involuntarily converges with Spinozism in its doctrine of modi. To free his monism from contradictions, Aquinas is compelled to attribute a character of instrumentality to the second causes. Such a character is also proper to all "free" actions in relation to the true first cause, which is being itself. However, at the same time he attributes an independent individualization of actions to the second, free causes (which they have as "contingent" causes, connected with the nature of the self-determination of the will). To this is connected the possibility of "merits" and, in general, the personal participation in one's own destiny.[8]

In general, the efforts of contemporary Thomists are directed, on the one hand, at protecting their teacher from Jansenism with its determinism *"titulo infirmitatis, non titulo dependentiae a Deo* [by reason of weakness, not by reason of dependence on God]," and, on the other hand, at proving that creaturely freedom is fully compatible with the divine *praemotio*, insofar as "our free act wholly depends upon us as the second cause, and

---

8. Here the obscure notion of *determinatio non necessitans* is applied. By virtue of this, the Virgin Mary, for example, freely and unhesitatingly pronounced her *fiat* (though in the presence of the divine *motio*); the apostle Paul was freely converted on the way to Damascus; the holy martyrs freely remained faithful to their confession in their torments; and even Christ freely accepted his death (cf. "Prémotion physique," *Dict. de théol. cath.*, 13, 1, col. 54).

wholly upon God as the first cause."[9] Here, the relation of the first cause to the existence of evil and sin is divine permission, its *conditio sine qua non*, but not its cause.[10] "*Deus est causa actus peccati, non tamen est causa peccati* [God is the cause of the act of sin, but He is not the cause of sin]" (Ia, IIae, q. 79, a. 2). If God had not permitted Judas's sin, it would not have been possible, but it was committed freely, just as every sin is. It presupposes the positive accomplishment of the fact in its natural being, but only a permission of the act in its sinfulness.

The determinism of the *praemotio physica*, which Thomism expounds inexorably though not completely consistently, encounters a limit in creaturely freedom, which is expressed in the possibility of a certain *choice:* to do or not to do, and how. There is no ontological place in the system of determinism even for this kind of freedom, a conclusion that Aquinas and the Thomists evade terminologically, calling freedom one of the variants of causality (*determinatum aut non determinatum ad unum* [limited or not limited to one thing]), which is far from being satisfactory. If a mountain (Mt. Blanc, say) settles with all of its weight upon a thin nail that enters into a soft tree, it is meaningless to speak of the possibility of resistance or of choice for this nail: the choice of entering into the tree or of resisting. But the relation between the omnipotence of God and creaturely freedom is incommensurable even with the hugeness of Mt. Blanc in relation to the nail: creaturely freedom is simply annihilated.

Such a juxtaposition of divine predestination, *praemotio physica,* and the *either/or* of creaturely freedom contains neither an antinomy nor a dialectical contradiction that is to be overcome, but a simple contradiction that attests to the inconsistency of this doctrine. Therefore, all the efforts of Thomistic theology consist in trying to fill this breach, in persuading oneself that, even despite this contradiction, all is well. In all of modern Catholic theology, no question is more difficult and no controversy is more acute than those concerning freedom and necessity, the nail and Mt. Blanc. Therefore, on the one hand, the frank affirmation of determinism makes a very strong impression, expressed in ecclesiastical interdicts. We have such an affirmation in the teachings of Jansenius,[11] the Jansenists,

---

9. Ibid., col. 69.

10. Ibid., col. 71.

11. In his posthumously published treatise on Augustine, Bishop Jansenius expounds his doctrine as a system of consistent determinism and predestination (for which there is more than sufficient ground in Augustine's works). Jansenius's work represents a whole system of theology, which is, of course, very close to Calvinism and predestinationism in general. It is distinguished by an enormous energy of thought and irreproachable argument.

their precursors, and their successors (Baius, Hermes, et al.). Protestant doctrines of the unfreedom of human will and predestination have an analogous significance. The tendency to reinforce the leaning building of Thomism from the side that is most threatened is therefore natural and inevitable. This reinforcement relies not only on commentaries and interpretations of Aquinas's works but also on attempts to complete his doctrine. We find such an attempt in the doctrine of the Portuguese Jesuit Molina and his followers. A severe (although completely dignified) polemic exists between Molinists and Thomists, even though the two tendencies belong to the same type of causal determinism, differing only as variants. Molina's doctrine[12] is not directed *against* Thomism at all; it is completely based on the premises of Thomism. It seeks to complete Thomism and to liberate it from the contradiction between causal necessity and creaturely freedom that afflicts it.

The paradoxical idea that Molina introduces in the discussion of the question of freedom and necessity is that of *scientia media* in God. The meaning of this expression is clarified by a special doctrine of knowledge in God. According to Aquinas (Ia. qu. 8-9), "God's knowledge is the cause of things," like an artist's plan of action. It is realized if will is added to it; *scientia intelligentiae* then becomes *scientia visionis*. Through *scientia visionis* God knows not only the present, past, and future, but also the possible, what is not, was not, and will not be. He knows this not through *scientia visionis* but only according to *simplex intelligentia*. To these two types of knowledge in God, Molina adds a *third, scientia media*, which refers to a possible future, which, although it does not yet exist, can exist: *futuribilia*. *Futuribilia* come into existence only with the participation of divinely created free will, which transforms them, or not, into reality. The "middle knowledge" is not fully free in God, like that which follows from the free determination of God's will. It is also not fully natural, even though it corresponds to God's omnipotence. It approaches God's omnipotence insofar as it precedes the free act of God's will, and it approaches the free determination of God's will insofar as it is connected with the free act of God's creation.

Through this third knowledge there is introduced into the life of creation the factor of creaturely freedom, which God Himself takes into account in relation to *futuribilia*. On the one hand, as possibilities, they are

---

12. *Concordia liberi arbitrii, cum gratiae donis, divina praescientia, providentia, praedestinatione et reprobatione ad nonnulles primae divi Thomae articulos*, Lisbon, 1588. (I have used the edition of 1876, Paris.)

all known to God, for he *"ex altissima et inscrutabili comprehensione cuiusque liberi arbitrii in sua essentia intuitus est* [has contemplated all free will by the exalted and inscrutable comprehension of his essence]." This assures God's providence with regard to the world. But, at the same time, the actualization of certain possibilities from a general pool of *futuribilia* depends on creaturely freedom. These self-determinations of creaturely freedom are taken into account by providence itself, which enters into interaction with them. The question of the relation of the first and second causes, so acute in Thomism, is decided here by a peculiar synergism of *partialium causarum* [partial causes], where a single effect is achieved by two particular causes: *"totus quippe effectus et a Deo est et a causis secundis, sed neque a Deo neque a causis secundis ut a tota causa, sed ut a parte causa, quae simul exigit concursum et influxum alterius: non secus ac cum duo trahunt navem totus motus proficiscitur ab unoquoque trahentium, sed non tanquam a tota causa motus, siquidem quivis eorum simul efficit cum altero omnes ac singules partes eiusdem motus* [of course, the entire effect is both from God and from second causes, but neither from God nor from second causes as from a whole cause, but as from a partial cause, which brings about the interaction and influx of the other simultaneously: this is no different than when two people drag a ship, and the total motion begins from each of the two pullers, but not as if they were moved by a whole cause, as if one of them had carried out all the individual parts of the same motion at the same time as the other]" (*Concordia*, in qu. 14, a. 13).

This well-known figure of the cooperation of two who pull a single ship illustrates the basic idea of *scientia media*, according to which the second causes are not wholly determined by the first, but are united with the first to achieve a single common result. Creaturely freedom thereby enters into cooperation with God,[13] as Molina declares: *"[C]oncursus Dei generalis determinatur a particulari concursu causarum secundarum* [the general interaction of God is determined by the particular interaction of the second causes]"; and it is not the cause of an act of free will, which, even given this *"concursus,"* can freely will or not will. *Concursus Dei generalis* not only is not the effective cause of acts of the free will but itself depends on the latter (qu. 14, a. 13, disp. 29). It follows that the fruit of this action can be distinguished depending on human freedom. In fact, in the presence of all these conditions, human freedom can act or not act *(potest agere et non agere)* (*Conc.*, qu. 14, a. 13, disp. 11).

Molina's doctrine is a developed treatise, and its basic principle is ap-

---

13. See *Conc.*, q. 14, a. 13, disp. 26.

plied to different particular questions in the doctrine of grace. An examination of these particularities is not part of our task; let us limit ourselves to the basic idea.

Thomism and Molinism collide in modern Catholic theology as two distinct doctrines, and they are opposed with regard to the most essential question, that of freedom. It is considered that Molinism rescues creaturely freedom from the power of predestination at the price of limiting divine freedom. This accusation is rejected by its defenders, particularly by d'Alès, who tries to reconcile the first principles of Molinism and Thomism as much as possible.

We must say that the fundamental difference between Thomism and Molinism has been greatly exaggerated. They differ only in relatively secondary details, not in "what" but in "how." The two converge in what is essential: They both consider freedom as a special form of causality, alongside the first-causality of God; they both recognize these *two* forms of causality; and they both attempt to combine and arrange those forms. In both doctrines, when they are truly grounded, only the first cause is manifested, whereas the second remains indeterminate. What is important is not how their union is understood in its particulars, but the fact that this union, or correlation, of the two causalities is posited as the basis. To be sure, the ontological primacy of the first, or divine, cause is inevitable here, however its interrelationship with the second is interpreted further. Both Thomism and Molinism are variants of one and the same worldview: causal determinism. The second causality through freedom is brought in as contraband and remains in *clair-obscur* whether it is defined as *causa deficiens* (insufficient cause), which determines sin, having its causal being on the basis of the first, or as freedom of choice, which compensates for the absence of *determinatio necessitans ad unum* (determination leading necessarily to one thing). However one construes this relation in its details, even such a measure of freedom is not compatible with universal causality, is a breach in its impenetrability, a hole in the vessel, allowing the liquid to escape.

Thomism and Molinism refer to the inner dialectic of causal determinism, with which no freedom is compatible, and there remains a place only for the stoic principle: *fata volentem ducunt, nolentem trahunt* (fate leads the willing, but drags the unwilling). From this point of view, the difference between Thomism and Molinism, so exaggerated in Catholic doctrine, is purely fictitious, insofar as both are forms of inconsistent determinism, trying to save themselves in different ways from their own inexorability. The dilemma of *Dieu déterminant ou déterminé* (determining or determined God) remains in full force here, for omnipresent causality

211

does not leave a place for *concursus divinus*, for interaction or even co-action of the first and second causes, necessity and creaturely freedom. In general, in this causal monism, there is no room for a relation other than causal succession. Insofar as the fundamental, initial determination of Aristotelianism about God and the world, about eternity and temporality, remains ambiguous (see above), this lack of clarity and ambiguity are reproduced in Thomism and in its variant, Molinism. Strictly speaking, there is a place here neither for the distinction between the first and second cause nor for the distinction (which is the same thing) between God and the world, since God is introduced here into the causal logic of the world and the world is absorbed by God's being. In this monism, there is neither God nor world in their correlation.

It is difficult to understand this theory even as a pantheism (in view of its opacity and ambiguity). Pantheism can be understood only as the idea of a becoming, emerging God, in which case the world process is a theogonic one. In whatever terms this theogony is expressed (in terms of Hegel's logic, the cosmogonic doctrines of the Eleatics, or ancient mythology), it is also a cosmogony. But this process needs a *terminus a quo* and a *terminus ad quem*, a definition of the initial state and the final goal, potentiality and entelechy. A consistent pantheism as a comprehensive worldview is, of course, not possible, for it falls apart in its contradictoriness. Both the beginning and the final goal remain equally transcendent for it, are outside of its frame. It is only a middle, a *durée*, which cannot be determined from itself. Therefore, consistent pantheism necessarily leads to Thomism and presupposes it. Consistent pantheism simply does not exist in a pure form. On the other hand, the mechanical causality of *praemotio physica*, within its proper limits, is not theism, atheism, pantheism, or acosmism. It is, in general, found beyond the limits of theological definitions with their fundamental scheme or relation: God and the world. This causality is a bad infinity, without beginning (for there is no room for it in the "first cause," whose concept antinomically falls apart: see Kant) and without end, in its mechanical deadness. It leads to the "dead end" in which Catholic theology now finds itself on the paths of Aristotelian Thomism.

4. The Problem of Predestination
(Praedestinatio et Reprobatio)

The doctrine of causal determinism, oriented toward the idea of causal connection as a *succession* of causes and effects, defines the relation of God to the world according to the category of temporality, thus bringing Him down into the temporal process. The initial push of the first cause, which begins the motion, propagates wavelike in the cosmic mechanics, being transmitted from what precedes to what follows. The dialectic of determinism inwardly postulates this first wave as the transcendent-immanent principle of motion *prior to* and *for* time, presupposing the continuity of a causal, self-contained series. Therefore, this dialectic leads with internal necessity to the idea of *predestination:* In the cosmic process, God is not only the *first* cause but also the *all*-cause, which determines all. The universality of the first cause is connected, above all, with its initial position in the causal series of the world's being. A purely mechanical conception of the world should supposedly result from this, but it is not valid at its initial point, at the *beginning* of the causal series. The causal chain is suspended in the void; its upper end hangs in the air and is not attached to anything, for there is nothing to attach it to.

However, if the first cause is understood as divine energy, it is capable of placing the "second causes" in their sequential series, in which there naturally is now no place for an effective causality. But in both cases the "second causes" are distinguished by complete passivity in relation to the first cause; they are not effective and do not interact; they only receive, transmitting further the action of the first cause. The whole energy of causality in this causal scheme belongs only to the first cause, in relation to which the whole system of second causes is only a transmission mechanism. Attempts to avoid this inevitable conclusion only complicate and obscure the principle of causality in its purity (which we see in Molinism). The doctrine of determinism implies an anthropomorphic conception of the first cause: it introduces the first cause in the temporal process and defines it according to the categories of this process. The "first" cause therefore becomes the pre-cause or the cause of all causes, so to speak. It is *predestination,* a certain cosmic *fatum.*

Determinism necessarily contains this idea, and its history demonstrates its inner dialectic. It is not accidental, therefore, that St. Augustine, with his denial of the freedom of the will in fallen man,[14] is the progenitor of the most radical doctrine of predestinationism, which has all the features of anthropomorphism (specifically with regard to the application of the category of time to God). In Augustine's doctrine, a distinc-

---

14. In the matter of free will, Augustine attempts to preserve its appearance even in the face of predestination, despite the fact that it clearly contradicts the latter. . . . See *Sermo* 163, c. 11, n. 13.

tion is made between *praedestinato ad gratiam* and *reprobatio ad gehennam*. Augustine directly affirms only the former, with the latter being introduced surreptitiously. The absence of freedom of the will in fallen man makes him not the subject but the object of divine grace, which acts upon the soul with insuperable force *(indeclinabiliter et insuperabiliter)*. God predestines human will to salvation, and this will accordingly is "prepared by the Lord." "The good application of good will" also comes from Him. But this refers only to the elect, who are "predestined before creation" by that divine prevision by which God knew His future works.[15] God's prevision is included in His predestination of the elect, but it differs from His predestination of the reprobate. Even though the latter are called to being by God's power, this power remains passive and as if ineffectual in relation to them, leaving them to their own lot. The elect are saved by grace, which is given or not given according to God's will, and not on the basis of the prevision of good works, which are precisely a consequence of predestination. Those who are not among the elect are condemned to perdition by reason of sinful impotence. They are the *massa perditionis* (mass of perdition). Divine justice is applied to them, and punishes their sin. This idea is most powerfully expressed in Augustine's judgments concerning children who die in early childhood. Those who are the elect among them and worthy of forgiveness participate in eternal bliss, whereas those who are reprobate and deprived of this good are condemned to eternal torments (which, however, are *mitissima* [very gentle]).

The number of the elect is therefore known in advance by God in virtue of his predestination. God could have kept Judas from betrayal by the power of his grace, and by taking it away He could have left Peter in the state of reprobation: *potuit ergo, sed noluit* (he could have, but he did not wish to). Human destinies are therefore wholly determined by God's omnipotence; predestinationism becomes religious fatalism, which is intensified by a tacitly admitted *reprobatio*. Even though *reprobatio* is explicitly rejected, it is, according to the general context of the doctrine, tacitly introduced, of course, as if by a certain permission of God, leaving in sin the reprobate, to whom only justice is done, in contrast to the preference for the elect. To the question, What explains this election of some and the reprobation of others? Augustine responded that he did not know, referring to the unfathomability of the ways of God. The inevitable conclusion that follows and was drawn later is that Christ brought redemption and came into the world only for the elect.

15. [. . .] See *De corr. et gr.,* XVIII, 35, c. 938.

Augustine left the stamp of his spirit on the Western church's doctrine of predestination, both in the positive recognition of predestination to salvation and in the (apparent) rejection of the doctrine of reprobation.[16]

The dogmatic inconsistency (not to say hypocrisy) of this apparent rejection of *reprobatio* with its de facto acceptance was exposed in the eleventh century by the monk Gottschalk (who was condemned at a number of councils). He affirmed *double* predestination, with a plus and with a minus: *"gemina est praedestinatio, sive electorum ad requiem, sive reproborum ad mortem* [predestination is double, being either that of the elect to repose or that of the reprobates to death]." The official doctrine of the Catholic church, however, remained the recognition only of *praedestinatio ad salutem* (predestination to salvation), accompanied by the rejection of *reprobatio*. But this is only a fig leaf covering the nakedness of a systematic determinism, which, when one accepts its initial premise of human passivity and impotence (referred to as the bondage of the will), leads with inexorable logic to the recognition of both types of predestination.

Thomism continues the tradition of Augustinianism in Western theology in the question of predestination, whose doctrine it fully shares with respect to *praedestinatio ad gloriam* (predestination to glory), inconsistently (following Augustine) rejecting *reprobatio ad gehennam* (reprobation to hell). The basic distinction between Augustinianism and Thomism in this question consists in the fact that the former develops this doctrine in the soteriological aspect as a doctrine of grace, while the latter develops it more as a philosophical doctrine of causal determinism, *praemotio physica*, which in a certain sense is its particular application. First of all, Thomism radically separates prevision from predestination and rejects any causal connection between them: *"[P]raedestinatio non est aliquid in praedestinatis, sed in praedestinante tantum. . . . Executio huius ordinis est passive quidem in praedestinatis, active autem est in Deo.* [Predestination does not refer to the predestined but only to the predestinator. . . . The execution of this order is passive with respect to the predestined but active with respect to God]" (qu. 23, a. 2).

<hr/>

16. See the decrees of the following councils: Arausicanum II 529, can. 25 (Denzinger, *Enchiridion,* ed. 13, n. 200, p. 85); Carisiacense I, 853 (contra Gottschalk et praedestinatianos) (ibid. n. 316-19, p. 144-45); Valentinum III, 855 (contra J. Scotum), *de praedestinatione,* can. 1, 2, especially 3 (ibid. n. 320-22, p. 145-48). Cf. "Predestination" in *Dict. de théol. cath.;* B. Lavaud, *La prédestination d'après les docteurs du Moyen Age,* 12, 2, col. 2901-35.

Predestination to salvation is explained by the action of the first cause, predestining human will to this path. "Since an act of free will has God as its cause, it is necessary that what comes from free will also be subordinate to providence. Human providence is included in divine providence as a particular cause in a general one" (qu. 22, a. 2). "God moves will inevitably by virtue of the effectiveness of the motive force, which cannot turn out to be ineffective" (*de Malo*, 9, VI, a. 1, a d 3-m). Given this universal determination, "no distinction is made between that which comes from free will and that which comes from predestination, just as no distinction is made between that which comes from the first cause and that which comes from the second cause." "Insofar as God's love is the cause of the excellence of things, then one thing would not be better than another if God did not want for the one a greater good than for the other" (q. 20, a.3). Consequently, "some goods of life are better than others because God desires for them a greater good. It follows that He loves the better more" (ibid., a. 4).

In this doctrine, differences between human actions are wholly explained by a one-sided act of the divine will as the first and essentially the sole determining cause. This doctrine would appear to lead with inexorable logic (and even with a greater inevitability than in Augustinianism) to the doctrine of the active reprobation of those condemned to perdition. However, Aquinas, like Augustine, does not draw this conclusion from his own doctrine, thus destroying its consistency. Here is how Aquinas discusses reprobation: "Since divine providence predestines some people to eternal salvation, it permits some not to take advantage of this power, and this is called reprobation. . . . Thus, just as predestination includes the will to the transmission of grace and glory, so reprobation includes the will to permit someone to fall into guilt and to bear the punishment of condemnation for guilt. . . . *Reprobatio* is not the cause of what is present, i.e., guilt, but is the cause of the abandonment by God" (qu. 23, a. 3). "From God's goodness issues the cause of the predestination of some and the reprobation of others. . . . For it is necessary that God's goodness, which, in itself, is simple and unitary, be multifariously represented in things . . . and therefore the fullness of the universe *requires different stages* of things, some of which occupy the lowest place in the universe. And for the diversity of the stages to be observed in things, God permits the existence of several forms of evil, in order not to hinder many goods" (qu. 23, a. 4). To these considerations (which anticipate the satanic cynicism of Mephistopheles and Ivan Karamazov concerning the salvific character of the "minus" of being) is added a repetition of Augustine's considerations: "God wished to show his goodness to people, in relation to those whom he predestined, sparing them according to grace and punishing them according to justice." "Why he chose some and reprobated others there is no other reason than God's will" (ibid.). And since predestination is executed in the most precise and infallible way, the number [here Aquinas repeats Augustine] of the predestined is fixed *[est certus]*."

To be sure, this theological masquerade, whose goal is to conceal *reprobatio* as one of the *two* forms of predestination, is even less successful here than before. For if in Augustinianism we had a divine arbitrariness in the dispensation of grace, then, here, God acts as the first cause or prime mover, who causally predetermines everything, and nothing exists outside this determination.

The theological nemesis of determinism appeared in the sixteenth century in the form of Calvinism. Having the courage of consistency, Calvinism took all the horrifying conclusions of predestination to their extreme. Calvin's teaching is not so much a philosophical doctrine as a religious one. It treats the paths of salvation, and the place of *praemotio physica* is therefore taken in his work by God's absolute and unfathomable will, by his power and majesty. Calvin proclaims his doctrine of double predestination, to glory and to perdition, as God's inexorable will (thereby making the Gospel approach the Koran). It is clear that such an absolute predestination completely eliminates the freedom of the will (although good works are retained), election or reprobation being logically considered an inevitable fate (*Inst.* 3, 22, 2). "Whom God does not choose he reprobates." There is an initial inequality in the destinies of individuals, and to affirm election but to deny reprobation is "childishness." *C'est une sottise trop lourde* [It is a very serious folly]." It follows that God desires evil too. "He established with the decree of his will" the fall of the first man (*Inst.* 3, 23, 81). Adam fell because of a divine predestination. "God not only foresaw the fall of the first man, and in him of all his descendants; he willed it" (*Inst.* 3, 23, 7).

There is no need to examine in detail this generally known doctrine. It is sufficient to indicate its main ideas. They inevitably lead to a causal determinism that determines the relation between God and the world. Philosophical abstraction is combined here with religious fanaticism. The doctrine of predestination is accepted, fully or in part, by a number of Reformed confessions.

The logic of Calvinism concerning predestination naturally evoked a reaction of self-defense in Catholicism. But this reaction was not accompanied by a reassessment of previous positions or by new arguments. Instead, it involved only an apologetic divergence from the doctrine of reprobation, as was the case in the ninth century too. And in passing it was necessary indirectly to reject and even condemn certain positions or at least the extreme interpretation of Augustinianism. Such, for example, are the canons of the Council of Trent (Sess. 6, can. 4, 5, 6). In particular, the fifth canon condemns the Augustinian-Lutheran doctrine (of course, without names) of Adam's loss of the freedom of his will in original sin. Canon 17 condemns the doctrine of the abandonment of those predestined to evil without the help of grace. And only indirectly, with shameful concealment and without further development, predestination to salvation (see above) is affirmed in cap. 805. In this sense, even though the Catholic Church maintained its previous dogmatic position, it did not come out victorious in the dogmatic dispute with Calvinism, because in essence it did not accept the battle. This dispute is continuing surreptitiously even in our own time in the argument between Thomists and Molinists. Dogmatically, the Reformation remains undefeated, and it cannot be defeated as long as the dispute is fought on the ground of various types of causal determinism. The dispute can be overcome only if the question is transferred to another plane, that of sophiology.

The Orthodox East remained inwardly untouched by the problems and disputes that arose in the West around the doctrines of Calvinism, Augustinianism, and Thomism; and the corresponding theological doctrine is simply absent in the East. In practical terms, the attitude of the East in the days of the Reformation and afterward was determined primarily by the necessity of defending itself against the attack of Lutheranism and especially Calvinism; and it was natural that in this defense the East relied — sometimes more than it ought to have — on doctrines of Catholic theology. The East shares with this theology the rejection of the doctrine of reprobation, though its rejection is just as theologically ungrounded as that in Catholic theology. The East also borrows from this theology the acceptance of predestination to salvation, and this acceptance is just as inconsistent and unclarified.

The Orthodox doctrine on this question is expounded in the "Epistle of the Orthodox Patriarchs," article 3. In the first part the doctrine of predestination is accepted, though this is a predestination based on God's foreknowledge. "We believe that the all-good God predestined to glory those whom He had chosen from all eternity, and those whom He reprobated He gave to condemnation, not because He wished in this way to justify some and to abandon others and condemn them without cause, for this is not proper to God, our common and unprejudiced Father, 'who will have all

218

men to be saved and to come unto knowledge of the truth' (1 Tim. 2:4). But insofar as he foresaw that some would use the freedom of their will for the good, whereas others would use it for the bad, He *predestined some to glory and condemned others.*" "But that which the blasphemous heretics say, namely that God supposedly predestines or condemns without considering the works of those predestined or condemned, this we account madness and dishonor. . . . To believe, teach, or think in this way we will never dare . . . and upon those who speak and think in this way we place an everlasting anathema, and we consider them the worst of all the unfaithful." This definition first affirms the predestination of those "chosen from all eternity," although at the same time this eternal predestination is considered only as a prevision of the mode in which "the freedom of the will is used," on the basis of which some are predestined to glory, and others to perdition. It is unclear whether this concerns *praedestinatio in praedestinatis* or *praedestinante tantum* (Aquinas). But the same article affirms "free will" with particular energy (although this is not related to a general doctrine of predestination and divine providence) and condemns *reprobatio* decisively (although also without theological motivation). In any case, one can say that Calvinism as well as *gemina praedestinatio*[17] remained foreign to Orthodox theology. It goes without saying that it is also absent in the patristic tradition.[18]

17. In the "Orthodox Confession" (part 1, 30), we read: "Foreknowledge, predestination, and providence differ in God according to their effects. Providence refers to created things. However, foreknowledge and predestination, although they are different, existed in God prior to the existence of all creatures. Foreknowledge is knowledge of the future without determination of the latter in its particulars; that is, it does not determine the existence of one thing or another. But predestination, which depends on foreknowledge, is a particular determination; that is, it determines what must be." (This scholastic distinction precisely corresponds to Aquinas's doctrine of two modes of knowledge in God: *scientia visionis* and *scientia intelligentiae*. The first refers only to possible and conceivable things, the second to things that become reality: Ia, Iae, qu. 14, a. 9.) "Thus, it is fair to say that, according to our mode of representation, foreknowledge comes first in God, followed by predestination, and then by providence with regard to created things." (This anthropomorphic "comes first" and "followed by," representing a direct application of temporal categories to God, can provoke nothing but doubt.) "The Apostle clearly teaches us: Romans 8:29-30. However, these words must be applied only to man. In effect, other creatures (except angels) are not subject to predestination, for they do not have freedom and therefore cannot have any sin."

18. "God foresees all things but He does not predestinate all things. Thus, He foresees that which is found in our power but does not predestinate it. For He does not want vice to appear, but He does not forcibly predestinate to virtue. Therefore, predestination is a work of God's will, based on foreknowledge. According to His foreknowledge, God predestinates that which is not in our power" (*Brief Exposition of the Orthodox Faith*, 2, 30, p. 972). [. . .]

5. God and Creaturely Freedom (Synergism)

As we have seen, if one understands the relation between God and the world on the basis of causality, as between a "first" cause and the "second" causes, in whatever variants, this leads to an aporia without a way out. This aporia is expressed in the inevitable absorption of the second causes by the first cause, that is, in the de facto abolition of the second causes. Here the world is only an outward projection of the first cause, which, by its very definition, cannot be one of two causes, even the primary one, but is necessarily unique (i.e., is no longer a cause). Here, if one wishes to preserve some place for the world, this can be done only by recognizing its identity with the non-world, the supra-world, divinity. Such a worldview inevitably results in a completely non-Christian theocosmism or pantheism of the Spinoza type, and Neothomism diverges from it only by its inconsistency. But at the same time it is an acosmism (or even an anticosmism), for in this relation there is no independent place for the world in its *reality*: the life of the world is simply the life of God as the first and unique cause. This life does not contain second causes; they do not cause anything; and there is nothing for them to cause and nowhere to cause it. All is already caused by the first cause.

A causal conception of the relation between God and the world does not leave a place for the being of the world and is not capable of justifying it. The Mt. Blanc weight of the first cause, settling upon the little pebble of the second cause, simply destroys it, even if we suppose that this little pebble could in some way come into being and exist alongside Mt. Blanc. The world does not exist and therefore man with his freedom and his fate does not exist. There is, in general, nothing that differs from the first cause; the grayness of causal monism is triumphant. Only lack of consistency keeps one from seeing this. The situation is rescued by the fact that, in this system, concepts or categories are introduced that do not belong to it but have a dogmatic origin. Extraneous material is fed into the forge of causality, and one wishes that this material not be melted in the red-hot furnace, but that it even become fused together with this furnace in some way.

This entire doctrine of the first and second causes, the doctrine of God as the *cause* of the world, which acts upon the world but also interacts with it in some way, is only a monstrous misunderstanding, a theological temptation, which replaces the revelation of the living and personal God with the doctrine of an impersonal mechanism of causality. Here, the idea of creation, of the Creator and creation, is replaced by the concept of a well-adjusted mechanism of causes; and into the motion, established from the foundation, of the moving parts, one wishes to inject freedom. In this doctrine, neither man, the image of God, nor God, man's Proto-image and Creator, exists. To be sure, this does not negate the sincerity of the intention and desire to express Christian truths in the language of Aristotle and Laplace, but it attests to the total theological failure of this intention and desire.

In the face of this fundamental misunderstanding there can be no question of any partial corrections or of the advantages of Thomism over Molinism and Calvinism, or vice versa. One must "leave the city," reject this whole insuperable aporia, which follows from the very *statement* of the problem. In this aporia the relation of God and the world is treated as a particular case of the doctrine of causality, by application of the axiom *quod movetur ab alio movetur* (that which is moved is moved by something else) (which is the starting point of Thomism and all its branchings). Against this illusory axiom it is necessary to object with all possible energy that it is *not* causality that determines the relation between God and the world, and that *not* everything that is moved by "another," from outside, is totally deprived of the ability to move itself (though not by a *perpetuum mobile* mechanism). Translating this into the language of causality (with all the paradoxical inaccuracy of such a translation), one can say that the first cause *and* the second causes do not exist, but that, alongside the first cause, there can be a series of second-first causes. However, perhaps it is better not to have recourse to such a translation, which would be capable only of generating new misunderstandings connected with the idea of second-first causes and of leading to further difficulties. In general, the idea of the Creator and creation does not need to be translated into the language of mechanical causality, for it has another category, its proper one, that of *co-imagedness,* since the creature contains the living *image* of the Creator and is correlated with Him.

The tragic failure of Western theology in the most fundamental question of cosmology, the question of whether the world exists or does not exist in its ontological foundation, is a negative argument in favor of the sophiological statement of this question as the only possible statement for overcoming the aporias noted. Having exhausted this negative argument, we must turn to a positive development of the sophiological idea with reference to this question.

Let us first say that God is not the cause of the world, but its Creator.[19] Causal connection is valid only within the *limits* of the creaturely world, as its particular, concrete determination. It cannot be applied outside the creaturely world for determining this world's origin and correlation with the Creator (the causal connection encounters here the barbed-wire barriers of Kant's cosmological antinomy). Moreover, even when applied to the world, the category of causality has a limit, since human freedom and creative activity operate there, interacting with causality.

The world does not have a cause, since it is created; and *God is not the cause of the world and not a cause in the world, but its Creator and Provider.* God's creative act is not the mechanical causation through Himself of the world's being, but His going out of Himself in creation through the positing of the world as the creaturely Sophia. In the creation of the world, God, in becoming the Creator, repeats or doubles his own being beyond the Divine Sophia in the creaturely Sophia. The creaturely Sophia is precisely what Western theologians describe by the term "second causes," which exist alongside or as a consequence of the first cause. In relation to the Divine Sophia, the creaturely Sophia is not a second cause mechanically caused by a first cause. Rather, the creaturely Sophia is the self-repetition, as it were, of the Divine Sophia outside of divine being, in the "nothing" "out of" which or in which God created the world. Having the force of divine being, the creaturely Sophia, in herself, as the "Beginning" of creaturely being, does not need a "first" cause and cannot even have one. But, manifesting divine being outside of God, in nothing, the creaturely Sophia abides in becoming as the true substance, the entelechy and mover of the world, of which she herself is the *immanent* first cause in a certain sense.

One can say that the world belongs to itself: As the creaturely Sophia the world is autonomous, it does not need a cause but is its own cause. The world really does have in itself a creaturely and motive force, which is the entelechy of its becoming, growing its seeds, the logoses of being. We have defined the creaturely Sophia in relation to the world as the world soul, as the world's motive force, which is expressed also in the causal connection of being and in organic life. In this sense, ancient philosophy defined the world as a living being, *zōon* (Aristotle). Broadening this comparison, one can say that this being also has a skeleton, subordinate to mechanical and chemical laws, a sensing body, endowed with an organic

19. It goes without saying that, beginning with Aquinas, all Catholic theologians acknowledge this *dogmatically,* but *theologically* they turn onto other paths, where Aristotelianism plays the role of the guiding idea of Christian revelation.

activity, and, finally, a living soul, the principle of the "blood," with its psychological laws. All of these aspects of being are not caused by one another, just as they are not mutually isolated. Rather, they form the living unity of the cosmic *zōon*, are connected by the world soul. In itself, this unity does not have hypostatic being. It is nonhypostatic, impersonal, and, in this sense, it is unconscious or preconscious, although it lives and possesses a spontaneity, an instinct of self-determination, a kind of impersonal freedom, like every living being.

Defined this way, is the world not an autocosmos, a self-world, which belongs to itself and is self-sufficient, as deism and even pantheism consider it? But it is evident that such an entity stops being the *world* in the precise theological sense, since the *world* is a correlative concept, conditioned by its connection with God.

It was pointed out above that the *connection* of God and the world is grounded in sophianicity. The Divine Sophia is one, although she has two forms of being, in God and in creation. She is one and the same "Beginning" of being, which exists in God's eternity and in creaturely becoming. In and through this "Beginning" the world has its reality, divine in its source but extra-divine and, in this sense, no longer divine in its own being. This connection includes not only the relation of the Creator to creation, that is, the *createdness* of the world, but also the very being of the world as its own life, in which sophianicity acts as the determining force in becoming, in the world process.

In this sense one can say that God's providential activity with respect to the world is its sophianicity *in actu*, ongoing sophianization. Sophianicity is not only the statics but also the dynamics of the world, not only being but also protection and becoming. In this (but precisely only in this) sense, the Divine Sophia is the Guardian Angel of the creaturely world. This is true also in the sense that the divine providence that protects creation and its life is accomplished through the angels. They are the sophianic "heaven" for the world, the creaturely bridge between the noncreaturely, Divine Sophia and the creaturely Sophia, the creaturely medium *(metaxu)* between the Creator and creation. The creaturely world has two aspects: heaven and earth. It is directed toward the divine springs of being and toward itself. But the living can commune only with the living, and the testimony of revelation to the effect that different aspects of creaturely being are entrusted to different angels contains the assurance that the whole creaturely world is a ladder of life, on which the holy angels ascend and descend, not only in their proper being (according to the Old Testament vision of Jacob) but also in the divine-human world, according to the word of the Lord (see John 1:51). Intimate knowledge of this ontic structure of the world is inaccessible to man, at least within the limits of this aeon, as long as the body is not so much a ladder of revelation as a barrier to revelation. However, the very fact of sophianic providence is firmly established in revelation.[20]

A further question arises concerning the sophianicity of providence: In what sense is providence a *hypostatic* act of the Holy Trinity or of its hypostases, about which it is said, "My Father worketh hitherto, and I work" (John 5:17)? Of course, if we speak of sophianic providence, it cannot be understood as existing extra-hypostatically, for, in God, all that is sophianic is hypostatic and all that is hypostatic is sophianic. God's nature *(ousia)* is inseparable from the divine hypostatic triunity, although it differs from the latter. Just as in our discussion of the creation of the world (see the second volume of this trilogy, *The Comforter*) we spoke of the predominantly hypostatic participation of the Father as the Creator alongside the predominantly sophianic participation of the Second and Third hypostases, so in providence, in relation to the creaturely Sophia, we have knowledge of the hypostatic action of the Father as the "Pantocrator" or Provider, and of the predominantly sophianic participation of the other hypostases. Between creation and providential action with respect to the world, there exists a complete correspondence. The Father-Provider is turned toward the world by Sophia, who reveals Him through the revelation of the two revealing hypostases. Therefore, Scripture too attributes providential actions predominantly to the Father (see above). This same doctrine is the guiding one in the patristic tradition as well.[21]

---

20. If the Lord says that "their angels [i.e., the angels of these little ones] do always behold the face of my Father which is in heaven" (Matt. 18:10), this should equally be acknowledged with regard to the angels of the world in its natural life (cf., e.g., Job 1–2). The world has need of the protection of the angels, because, with the fall of Satan and his angels, the power of evil has entered the world; and this power delights in suffering and destruction, sowing chaff in God's world. We are not given to know the extent of this corruption of the world and of individual species of creation, beginning with the serpent of Eden. The instinct of popular wisdom spontaneously links certain types of animals and plants with the action of the power of evil, which does not have the capacity for new creation and, like the slanderer-devil, slanders creatures and corrupts them. In this sense, animals and plants yearn to be healed; some yearn to be changed completely, others to be merely tamed.

21. According to Athanasius the Great, "The Father does all things through the Son in the Holy Spirit, and the unity of the Holy Trinity is thereby preserved, and the Church preaches one God, 'who is above all, and through all, and in . . . all' (Eph. 4:6):

The sophianicity of creation as divine providence is more fully disclosed in the world of hypostatic being, that is, the human world. The extra-hypostatic nature retains its force here, requiring in virtue of its general character the providential protection of the angels. But the hypostatic principle of the spirit is also manifested here. This principle finds itself in a personal relationship with God as hypostasis with hypostasis, divine hypostasis with creaturely hypostasis, Proto-image with image. Creaturely freedom, modal yet authentic within its limits, encounters divine suggestions which graciously flow into it and are "synergistically" united with it. Man wrestles with God, like Jacob, in his freedom, but he also asks for and receives God's blessing, also like Jacob.

Grace pours into the world through human hypostases, insofar as they do not shut themselves off and resist this pouring forth. Theology distinguishes different modes and degrees of grace, but before making such a distinction one must establish the general and fundamental fact of its descent upon man from God. This fact most nearly corresponds to the theological concept of natural grace, given to creation and man as such, by virtue of the very mode of his being: Natural grace is, first of all, creaturely sophianicity, serving as the basis of all being regardless of its form. This includes even the being of the devil, even though he rejects his own sophianicity and battles against his sophianization. This is the grace of creation and of the preservation of creatures.

By their very nature, precisely by virtue of creaturely freedom, creatures cannot receive their being in a purely passive manner. They are endowed with free activity and are individually qualified in the reception of their being. They absorb grace, and this absorption of grace is an ongoing sophianization, the actualization of image in likeness. This absorption of grace gives to man the divine power to become not other than himself but precisely himself in his eternal aspect, since it is incumbent upon man to become a god-man in Christ's Divine-humanity by the power of the Holy Spirit, a son of God and a son of man by the will of the Father in Heaven. Such is the divine determination, *horismos,* not *pre*-determination, *pro-orismos, praedestinatio,* for in God's eternity there is no "pre" (*pro* or *prae*), since there is no time. But Divine-humanity is eternal in God and

---

'above all' is the Father, as the principle and source; 'through all' means through the Son; 'in all' means by God the Father through the Son in the Holy Spirit" (*ad regin. Ser.* 2, n. 51). According to John of Damascus: "God (the Father) creates by thought, and this thought becomes deed, initiated by the Word and accomplished by the Spirit" (*Precise Exposition of the Orthodox Faith,* 2, chap. 2).

supratemporal in creation, whereas in creaturely being it is accomplished in time, is becoming humanity. The Incarnation of Christ and the descent of the Holy Spirit are the given that corresponds to the task of man's sophianization by grace. Man does not remain alone or solitary in his being. He is not separated from God, as deism conceives him. But he is also not fused with or identical to God, as pantheism thinks. He is united in his life with God; he is correlated with God, interacts with Him, as the creaturely Sophia with the Divine Sophia, as a creaturely hypostatic spirit with a divine hypostatic spirit.

By no means does grace as the power of sophianization abolish creaturely freedom in individual manifestations of the latter. Grace does not act *insuperabiliter et indeclinabiliter, fortiter et suaviter, invincibili delectatione, physica praemotione* [insuperably and irresistibly, powerfully and sweetly, by invincible pleasure and physical pre-motion] (as Augustine, Jansenius, Aquinas, and Calvin teach). Rather, it convinces "not by might, nor by power, but by my spirit" (Zech. 4:6), in the end by divine love. The freedom of the person remains inviolable and impenetrable even for God. Voluntarily, by His kenosis of Creator and Provider, He suspends His omnipotence before the person. His omnipotence does not destroy the ontological barriers, as Christ Himself says about Himself: "I stand at the door, and knock: if any man hear my voice, and open the door, I will come into him, and will sup with him, and he with me" (Rev. 3:20). This door is creaturely freedom, the source of the originality and reality of creation in its correlation with the Creator. In creating man, He gives this source to creation to keep as its own property as it were; but at the same time it remains inseparable from God. In the Divine Sophia, God is correlated, as it were, with Himself in the creaturely Sophia, in creation, which is real by this divine reality.

Here, we must consider the question of this relation, which has been so muddled by the anthropomorphic doctrine of predestination that introduces time — "pre" — into the divine life. The fundamental idea of the doctrine of predestination is that, from all eternity, God preestablished all events in time (whether as first cause or as absolute will). This idea implies a representation of the eternity-time relation such that eternity precedes time in some way, is placed at the beginning of time as a kind of pre-time, and establishes the beginning of the causal connection as the first cause. But this idea has neither a metaphysical nor a religious foundation. Eternity and time are not two parts of one temporal process, but belong to two totally different categories. Divine eternity does not precede time, but is its foundation, and by no means can it be situated in the temporal process. The relation of God's omniscience to time cannot be expressed with complete precision in the language of verb forms, which are all determined by time, as present, past, and future, These forms are inapplicable to divine eternity (although in human language the present tense is used as a surrogate to express this supratemporality), and the temporal process with its becoming does not exist for this eternity. The all-seeing eye contemplates the *all* in its eternal unity in one supratemporal act. All of humankind, living, dead, and not yet born, in all of its history, the alpha and the omega, the beginning and the end, the Old and the New Testament, as well as the life of the future age — the whole *fullness* of creaturely-sophianic being is seen in this one act.

Thus, one can and must say that eternity contains all the content of time. There is and can be nothing in time that does not have its foundation in eternity, in the Divine Sophia, who reveals herself in the creaturely Sophia, in the world. This is truly what we can call *determination, horismos,* in the sophianic sense of the word. All the aspects of being have their root in Sophia and are sophianically determined in this sense. They presuppose a sophianic given and task, their own entelechy. But this ontological determination, with creaturely freedom necessarily being present, is something wholly other than the causal predestination from all eternity of that which is to take place in time, where freedom is in fact annulled and eternity is equated with the beginning of time.

In divine eternity there is a *determination* that covers the whole reality of the world and all the possibilities contained in it. All these possibilities are actualized by creaturely freedom, which, like all creative activity, contains something new in this sense. But it is new only for creation, not for God. To admit the contrary would be to abolish the sophianicity of creation, which, by itself, by its creaturely freedom, would thereby actualize a supra-sophianic or extra-sophianic novelty of being. But, in his freedom and creative activity, man cannot tear himself away from his sophianic roots and become a created creator, a self-god. All creaturely creative activity is accomplished on prescribed themes, as it were, as variations of sophianicity. These themes are practically inexhaustible and infinite, and pour into eternal life. But they are sophianically determined precisely in eternity, in the Divine Sophia. But this ontological determination has nothing in common with predestination, which annuls the world's originality and creaturely freedom, and transforms the human world into a world of things. This sophianic determination is accomplished by creaturely freedom, which is included in and inseparable from this determination, just as the Divine Sophia and the creaturely Sophia, united in a

227

single root of being, are inseparable, though not identical. In this sense, one can say that the sophianicity of the world is precisely its determined condition, its law. The world reposes not upon itself and not upon its creatureliness, but is affirmed in God, in whom "we live, and move, and have our being" (Acts 17:28).

This just idea has received an erroneous, helpless expression in the Thomistic doctrine of *praemotio physica*. This doctrine is right in relating all that exists in the world to God as His action and revelation. Its error consists in defining this relation as a causal connection. Such causal monism leads to pantheism (instead of panentheism),[22] and the First Cause, that is, God, appears as a nonhypostatic, impersonal prime mover, who becomes one with the world moved by Him, as transcendentally immanent with respect to it (according to Aristotle). This error is due to the absence of a conscious sophiology in Thomism, although this doctrine is in fact a sophiological one. As in the general doctrine of God in the world, or the doctrine of ideas (see above), sophiology in Thomism is unfinished and underdeveloped, and, in this sense, it is blind. Nevertheless, one should appreciate the fact that Thomism *poses the problem,* but this problem can be defined and solved only in the framework of sophiology. The very idea of *motio physica,* of the sophianicity of creation or of the divine foundation of creaturely being, is reasonable and just, although it is expressed in the language of temporal being as *prae-motio.*

The same thing can be said about Molinism, since it is only a variant of causal determinism, or a special interpretation of Thomism as regards *praemotio physica* or the sophianicity of creation. The specificity of Molinism concerns only the question of creaturely freedom, but the fundamental idea of the divine foundation of creation and its rootedness in divine eternity remains unshakable. There is a helpless expression of the same idea even in Calvinism, where, beneath the mask of despotic divine omnipotence, of universal predestination according to the Creator's will, one dimly senses the same idea of the correlation of eternity and temporality, of the divine substance of the world, whose manifestation is totally determined by God's will. This is a distinctive interpretation of the same idea that we "live, and move, and have our being" in God. Thus, even in Calvinism, the ontological idea is sophiological, although it receives a grotesque expression. Once again, the fundamental problem of the relation between God and the world can be resolved only in sophiological terms.

---

22. Panentheism, as opposed to pantheism, is the theory that being is contained in all things. — Trans.

Thus, the sophiological problem is a determining one for the course of Western theology into the post-patristic epoch, although it is not really mastered there. By contrast, in this problem's true homeland, the East, theological thought, temporarily interrupted, appears to have forgotten its sophiological heritage and the silent legacy that it has received from the classical age of Eastern theology, from patristics. In any case, it turns out now that the East has nothing to oppose to the dim, unconscious sophiology of the West except an evasive and predominantly negative apologetics that casts away the shell without noticing the kernel and that does not give its own answer to the sophiological problem. This answer must consist in the unfolding of a doctrine of the sophianicity of creation as its rootedness in God's eternity. This sophianicity exists for eternity and from all eternity in God as his sophianic mirror, although it is defined erroneously as predestination. "You had scrutinised my every action; all were recorded in your book, my days listed and determined, even before the first of them occurred" (Ps. 139:16; translation taken from *The Jerusalem Bible*).

But besides this extratemporal or supratemporal self-determination of God in His divine life, God also has a relation to the world that issues not from divine eternity but from creaturely temporality. God is the Creator and Pantocrator of creation. He turns His face toward creation and — miracle of miracles of divine condescension! — He Himself lives in time with and for creation. For Himself as well He posits becoming. Abiding in eternity and in the unchangeable fullness of His being in Himself, He lives in the life of creation and with creation. In Himself, God is Absolute, supramundane being, but He is also God for the world. This means that He has a positive relation to the world; He interacts with the world; He establishes a "synergism" with it.

How can one harmonize these two antinomic determinations of the Absolute and of God? This is the ultimate boundary for human thought and knowledge, defended by the fiery sword of theological antinomy. Both of its terms are axiomatically certain; they must both be preserved in all their power, while appearing to mutually repel and even contradict each other. But, strictly speaking, this is not a logical contradiction that results in absurdity and therefore annuls itself when it is fully clarified. Rather, it is an ontological distinction, which is expressed in two determinations that cannot be harmonized in rational thought. One must come to a clear understanding of this boundary of thought together with the unconditional significance of both propositions. In this sense, one must effect a *critical* antinomism of thought, without allowing this criticism to *confuse* the two planes, with thought leaping from the one to the other. Rather, thought must have knowledge of the existence of both planes.

This antinomic self-determination expresses a *kenosis* of the Absolute, which becomes the Creator and God. The Father of eternity voluntarily limits Himself by positing non-absolute being, that is, the life of creation, and condescends, so to speak, to co-participation in its temporality and becoming. The idea of the kenosis affirms with the same power both terms of the antinomy in their conjugacy. The kenosis as such presupposes, not as a chronological precedent but as an ontological premise, the fullness of non-kenotic being in relation to which the kenosis of the Absolute is defined and from which it proceeds. In the kenosis, the Absolute and God as the Creator of the world and Redeemer are united and co-posited. Otherwise, there would be not a kenosis but a change in divinity itself.

The kenosis of the Absolute in the world and for the world is a basic, unifying idea for theology. The creaturely reason is not able to grasp the union of these two initial postulates of theology, each of which is equally grounded and with necessity postulated by thought. The realization of these postulates, their conjunction in being, is totally inaccessible for creaturely experience. This experience is determined only by one of the theses of the antinomy, the postulate of becoming. Kenosis as self-diminution, or condescension, is foreign to creation, which, on the contrary, is oriented toward ascent, deification, becoming. In the fullness of time the two postulates are to be vitally, ontologically united, when God will be all in all, and the whole reality of creation will be preserved. But, in this age, in the depths of becoming, both truths must be observed with equal force: both the truth of God's unchanging eternity and self-sufficiency, and the truth of the revelation of divinity in creation, with divinity living a common life with creation in this sense and to this extent *becoming* in time. Here our thought encounters as ontological problems such events in the life of divinity as the Incarnation, the descent of the Holy Spirit into the world, and the future coming of Christ (the parousia).

It is this general postulate of the superlatively real (and not imaginary) reality of God's revelation and life in the world that renders time real as the form of becoming, and this not only for the world but also for God. More precisely, ontological thought must recognize the presence of divine eternity and all the power of this eternity in each atom and in each instant of creaturely being, in its sophianicity *("praemotio physica")*, as well as the reality of time and becoming. God, whose name is Eternity, lives as the Creator in time as well, *together* with creation. This signifies not that He is limited by time but that He limits Himself by time in order to adapt Himself ontologically to creation. Clearly, time is actualized differently in God's life than in human life (for "one day is with the Lord as a thousand years" [2 Pet. 3:8]). Here, only *via analogiae, negationis, eminentiae* [the path of analogy, of negation, of projection] is theologically applicable, but it is important to understand all the reality of time and temporality. Since, in God, temporality is united with eternity, we speak with Plato about time as the "moving image of eternity," or we use other metaphors to express the conjunction of the two terms of the antinomy — temporality and eternity — in divine being. But, given all this, we affirm with undiminished vigor the antinomic thesis of the reality of temporality for God.

The same thing goes for spatiality, which, of course, is not a property of God's absolute being but is nonetheless kenotically received by the Creator and Provider, who lives also the spatial life with creation. Of course, here too, it is necessary to establish the whole force of the difference between spatiality for God and spatiality for creation; and this we shall do by the same theological methods of thought. In theology, this divine spatiality is usually defined as omnipresence, which expresses the general idea that space is not a boundary for God's being but only His kenotic self-limitation. But such a spatiality, as a relation of God to creation, does not thereby lose anything of its reality. And this reality of temporality and spatiality represents the general precondition for the *mutual relation* between God and creation, or their synergism.

We have seen that the main difficulty and insurmountable aporia of Thomism with all its variants (including Molinism) consist in the fact that Thomism is incapable of safeguarding the originality of creation and creaturely freedom as the "second" cause alongside the "first" cause. In the sophiological statement of the problem, it is a question not of the hetero-onticity or equi-onticity of the first and second causes, but of their homoi-onticity. This problem is resolved by the fact that creation has both its own reality and a divine reality given to it by God: the creaturely Sophia. In his relation to creation God is correlated with Himself, in His proper divinity, which, however, has received extra-divine being as the world. Here, the Divine Sophia is correlated with the creaturely Sophia in that they are ontologically inseparable but also cosmically separate. Therefore, creation has its own ontological elasticity and even resistance, which creaturely reality manifests in relation to the divine reality. Creation has its own indestructibility ("the world also shall be stable, that it be not moved" [1 Chron. 16:30]), which grounds the possibility of God's interaction with the world, the reality of creaturely freedom even in the face of divine government.

This interaction is fully realized only in human beings. Human beings are persons with a hypostatic being that freely posits and determines itself, even if only within the limits of the creaturely given. As a hypostasis, the human being enters into hypostatic communion with God. As uncreated-created spirits that have come out of God, human beings are direct recipients of divine action; they interact with divinity, receiving grace through the angels or directly (in the Church). But even here the human person with his freedom preserves his indestructibility and self-determinability in relation to divinity. Divinity can act upon the person only by interacting with it on the basis of creaturely freedom. God spares the person and protects him even from His own omnipotence. He acts without coercing; that is, He persuades, limiting His power to the measure of creaturely receptivity. This is precisely *synergism,* as the form of divine providence with regard to human beings.

In order to define more precisely this freedom of the person, one must remember that the person is created by God in this freedom (see above), and that this freedom is not an abstract but a qualified one. Human beings are determined, first of all, as members of humankind, by their place in and connectedness with humankind. On the other hand, after being created by God, human beings have their individual determination, their own idea. A human being is not humanity in general, but an individually determined human being with his own theme of being. He receives this theme in freedom, which includes various possibilities of its reception. This self-determination occurs not in time but supratemporally (although it does not occur in eternity, since it belongs, nevertheless, to the life of creation). This self-determination marks the beginning of temporal being, which realizes and reveals this freedom. All human persons thereby enter into the world with their proper self-determinations, although they are not externally *pre*-determined. People are born not as impersonal ciphers but as individually different persons. In connection with this individual supratemporal self-determination in which the person in his freedom receives *in his own way* the God-given theme of his own being, there is also determined his place in the human race, in its history — heredity and environment, the epoch, the nation, and finally, ancestors and parents. (Parents are closest of all to the individuality, since even their name forms part of a person's name.) All of these aspects of personal destiny enter into individual life as a given, as the action of the Creator upon man. However, this given is realized by "intelligible" freedom, by the meta-empirical self-determination of human beings.[23]

It follows that the "second cause," creation, whose peak is man, receives, when it is created, being as a given from God. But, at the same time, creation is a given *for* God as well in this its proper being, with which God interacts synergistically. That which is given and that which is proposed as a task, or necessity and freedom, are interwoven and alternate in human life. Creaturely freedom proceeds from the given; it is applied to and receives its content from the given, while God answers these calls of freedom and its need in the general context of being, which contains an infinite number of elements. The world is an indefinite equation with an infinite number of unknowns that is solved by God's wisdom. It is an axiom of faith here that *God answers the needs of creation with absolute infallibility and purposefulness while preserving freedom within the limits of the world's entelechy.* Creaturely freedom, as a modal freedom, does not create the world with its given. But it informs the world, fulfilling the plan for the world in one way or another, by one path or another, with reference to unchangeable foundations of being.

Divine providence is therefore a dialogue of God's wisdom and omnipotence with free creaturely life. In this dialogue, God's infallible action in the world (with the participation of the holy angels) is accomplished in conjunction with the fluctuating and never infallible action of creaturely freedom. Providence shows absolute skill and inventiveness in correcting and fulfilling the actions of creaturely freedom ("God's Word is supremely clever," it is said in one of the canons), in guiding the world to salvation; but it always respects the originality and freedom of creation. The Lord does not annihilate the forces and bearers of evil. He spares even Satan, the father of lies himself, but he defeats him on his *own* paths, allowing the chaff to grow together with the wheat until harvest. He "permits" evil in order to protect the very foundation of creation: its freedom and self-determination. God's "long-suffering patience" with respect to creation is manifested here. By no means is this divine patience characterized by that impetuousness with which even the apostles asked Christ to bring fire

23. Therefore, *contrary* to Augustine's assertion, Judas, in his apostleship and in his entire destiny, was not the victim of a divine arbitrariness that could have saved him if it had so wished. Rather, Judas followed his own self-determination — of course, on the basis of his personal acceptance of the divine theme of his being. Thus, Judas was called to apostleship, but to an apostleship that was inwardly defective. (See my article "Judas Iscariot: Traitor-Apostle.")

down from heaven, in order to break the stubbornness of the Samaritans who would not let them pass. The relation of the Creator to creation in "synergism" always remains meek and restrained, the kenosis of God in creation. This kenosis is determined by the union of God's omniscience and wisdom in relation to the *paths* of the world, but with the self-limitation of His omnipotence. God waits for creaturely freedom to say: "Behold the handmaid of the Lord: be it unto me according to thy word" (Luke 1:38). And experiencing God's loving long-suffering patience and wisdom, astonished creation confesses: "O the depth of the riches both of the wisdom and knowledge of God! How unsearchable are his judgments, and his ways past finding out!" (Rom. 11:33). However, the foundation and final goal of creation are known: "for of him, and through him, and to him, are all things: to whom be glory for ever. Amen" (Rom. 11:36).

Therefore, although they are unfathomable for creation, the ways of providence constitute a postulate of faith in the Creator. And this postulate is conceived not only apophatically, in learned ignorance *(docta ignorantia* and *credo quia absurdum),* but also kataphatically, for life itself is knowledge, although only "in part" (1 Cor. 13). Of course, this knowledge is powerless to know God's ways as a whole, since they are transcendent for man. But at the same time they are *revealed* for faith, are known in the experience of faith, in the feat of faith. This poses a constant problem for religious life: the problem of *seeking* and doing God's will, and also accepting the divine destinies — which surpass human will and knowledge — as God's will.

In the agony at Gethsemane we have a model for this faith in providence and for this acceptance of God's will: "If it be possible, let this cup pass from me: nevertheless, not as I will, but as thou wilt" (Matt. 26:39). The Lord's Prayer gives us the most general and complete doctrine of this faith and acceptance: "Thy will be done on earth, as it is in heaven." Here, man does not reject God's supreme gift, creaturely freedom; rather, he desires to realize it by a free submission to God's will, according to the image of the God-man, in whom, according to the dogma of the sixth ecumenical council, human will freely "follows" God's will.

Ontologically, man cannot get rid of freedom even if he so desires, for it is the mode of the very being of the creaturely spirit. But creaturely freedom does not have an unchanging content. It seeks this content, being determined on the ways between the given and the task to be realized. Creaturely freedom is naturally afflicted by selfhood, from which it can free itself only by a voluntary self-renunciation, in the death on the cross ("let him deny himself, and take up his cross" [Matt. 16:24]). Therefore, the supreme freedom is the one that is manifested in the obedience of the Handmaid of the Lord: "be it unto me according to thy word" (Luke 1:38). But the voluntary acceptance of what happens to us in faith and obedience to God's will is illuminated for us from within. Through this acceptance we discover this will that acts in the whole life of the world. This faith in divine providence does not paralyze our creative activity in freedom and does not condemn us to the quietistic passivity of fatalism. On the contrary, it reinforces our will to search for the right way to accomplish God's will in us and through us, in true "synergism."

The destinies of the world are only partly revealed to us as the ways of God's providence, His leadership in the life of creation. Thus, despite the meandering of its ways, we recognize that our salvation was being built in the "sacred history" of the Jewish nation, in its historical destiny; we attain a profound knowledge of the "philosophy" of this history, whose fabric is woven of different threads. This can be seen, for example, even in the Gospel genealogy of Christ the Savior, which includes a great human diversity. In the Bible, the veil of the mystery of divine providence is lifted to such an extent that we gain knowledge of the purposefulness of individual human deeds and historical events. In the prophetic book of the New Testament, the Revelation of St. John, we have not so much a concrete revelation of the future as a symbolic and, in this sense, abstract representation of the destinies of the church in the world. But, here too, the higher reason of history is revealed. But the concreteness of prophecy here is not only inappropriate but even impossible, since it is a question not of the past but of the future, not of what has taken place but of what has yet to take place, not of facts but of "tendencies."

This brings us face to face with the general question of the limits of divine knowledge in relation to the actions of creaturely freedom. This question has implicitly been present in the course of the entire controversy over determinism. It asks: What degree of reality can be assigned to human freedom in the face of God, and is this reality only subjective and illusory? This freedom is essentially conceived as illusory in Augustinianism and Thomism. Molina attempted to assert its objectivity under the protection of *scientia media;* however, he combined this with the acceptance of God's foreknowledge and the relatively free acts of man. However, he also shares the general postulate of Thomism that *scientia Dei est causa rerum.* Therefore, he essentially remains on the soil of divine determinism, in which there is no place for free choice.

Both Scripture and tradition testify that "God's grace does not constrain or overwhelm human freedom." Accordingly, "Scripture contains innumerable exhortations, promises, threats to provoke man to be virtuous," while "the holy fathers and teachers of the Church unanimously taught that man freely acts in choosing and accomplishing good works and is not constrained by God's grace."[24] How can one understand and accept the principle of freedom in the face of God's omnipotence and His wise providence toward the world, this *interaction* of the Creator and creation, their "synergism"? In order to accept this principle fully, one must admit the genuineness or mutual reality of both sides in this interaction. This reality is conditioned by the fact that even the Creator Himself cannot penetrate, in some sense, the ontic kernel of creation, creaturely freedom. Of course, creaturely freedom remains limited here by its modal character. However, even within these limits it is characterized by creative self-determination out of itself. Creaturely freedom cannot bring anything ontologically new into the world, but it does have a certain *originality*, proper to all personal life. This constitutes its creative element, as autonomous motivation and individual self-determination.

If we understand this element in the light of causality and predestination, freedom becomes a subjective illusion. It is of this freedom that Spinoza and Kant speak: If an arrow shot from a bow had consciousness, it would consider that it was moving by its own free will. However, the whole force of such an argument relies on the absurd and contradictory hypothesis of an arrow that is conscious of its own motion, for this would not be an arrow. Likewise, motion as a predicate is determined by its subject; it does not determine it. Creaturely freedom must not only be created but also recognized by God; its existence must be respected by Him. The ways of creaturely freedom in the world are the ways of creative activity before the face of God to the extent that this freedom, in its modality, refers not to the ontology but to the history of the world. This history is created by both God and man, in their synergism (it would be more precise to include the angels, who participate in this creative activity in their co-humanity).

Recognition of the genuineness of freedom therefore signifies that man has a certain independence from God, both in the search for the ways of God's will and in the opposition to his will. Thus, God reserves for man his own place in the ways of the divine providence, in the accomplishment of the goals of creation. We repeat that man does not have the power to create the world, whose ways are established by God; but he is given the power to follow these ways — for better or worse, in one manner or an-

24. Cf. Metr. Macarius, *Dogmatic Theology*, 2:193.

other. Man cannot create anything, cannot summon anything to new being, for the power of creation belongs only to God. But man's freedom and creative activity realize creation *together with* God. Without God's will not a hair can fall from man's head; but it is man's task to "do works," to participate in the "common work" of God's salvation of the world. Just as in Christ two wills and two natures act harmoniously without separation and without confusion, so it is given to His humankind to reveal its human condition together and in harmony with Him, which includes the possibility of disharmony.

All this brings us to the central question of God's omniscience in relation to creaturely freedom and its works. Does God know the works of our freedom "before" they are accomplished, on the basis of His omniscience? This question is answered in the affirmative by predestinationism in its various forms. God's knowledge determines being: "For whom he did foreknow, he also did predestinate" (Rom. 8:29). But to say that God knows in advance the works of freedom is a de facto annulment of freedom, its transformation into a subjective illusion. The acceptance of this supposition therefore places all the difficulties of predestination before us.

In order to come to a clearer statement of this problem, one must distinguish the two different planes in which it is posed: that of eternity and that of the history of creaturely being. In God's eternity, where all exists in one extra-temporal act, there are no present, past, and future. Here, all things *super-are* from all eternity, and, of course, there is no limit to God's knowledge; there is only omniscience. Here, God is not the Creator and God for creation; rather, He lives in the inaccessible light of His self-sufficient absolute life that is always identical to itself. There is only *knowledge* here; foreknowledge and ignorance are absent. The latter arise only with regard to the relation between God as Creator and the world as creation.

If God created man in freedom, in His own image, as a son of God and a friend of God, a god according to grace, then the reality of this creation includes his freedom as creative self-determination not only in relation to the world but also in relation to God. To admit the contrary would be to introduce a contradiction in God, who would then be considered as having posited only a fictitious, illusory freedom. And then one would inevitably have to accept Calvin's conclusion that man fell not freely but because God desired it, for only God's will and freedom exist. In other words, God could not or did not wish to create creaturely freedom or, more precisely, its subjects or bearers who presuppose it. Therefore, to unite creaturely freedom with divine omniscience, one must say not that God foresaw and therefore predestined the fall of man (a statement that is sometimes encountered in handbooks of dogma) but that God, knowing His creation with *all* the possibilities contained therein, knows also the *possibility* of the fall, which, however, did not have to occur and can occur only by human freedom. Otherwise, the contrary assertion of Calvinism would be right. Elevating one's thought to the spiritual world, one must say the same thing about the fall of Satan, who, of course, did not have to fall. Otherwise, one would have to conclude that he was created as Satan or, at least, with the inner necessity of becoming Satan.

Let us repeat, *all* the possibilities of creaturely being, having their roots in the Creator's knowledge, are open to this knowledge, since they belong to the world created by Him and are included in this world's composition, not only in the form of "integral wisdom" but also in the form of a distributed multiplicity. In this sense, creation — in both the spiritual and the human world — cannot bring anything ontologically new into the world; it cannot surprise or enrich the Creator Himself. But the very choice and creative actualization of these possibilities, that is, the domain of modal freedom, remain entrusted to creation and *to this extent* are its creative contribution. Although creation cannot be absolutely unexpected and new for God in the ontological sense, nevertheless in empirical ("contingent") being, it represents a new manifestation for God Himself, who is waiting to see whether man will open or not open the doors of his heart. God Himself will know this only when it happens.

The synergism here is a mutual self-determination that has an element of novelty, actualized in different modes for the two sides in the interaction. The ways of the world are therefore *not* predetermined as a *single* causal connection in which there is no place for contingent causes. (According to Aquinas, they are *"non determinatum ad unum* [not determined to one thing].") Otherwise, in the context of causality, all would turn out to be *determinatum ad unum* (determined to one thing). On the contrary, the determination of creaturely freedom must be understood according to a series of infinite variations, actually as *non determinatum ad unum,* but with these variations remaining subordinate to one plan, to one ontological possibility, multiply actualized. To creaturely freedom it is given to participate in the destinies of all of creation and, first of all, in the proper ways of man. If, in God's eternity, the world's being is uniquely and totally determined by the fact that it belongs to God's life, then, in the creaturely world, on the contrary, we have the incompleteness, the under-determinedness, the still-continuing self-determination of the world. Veiling His face, God remains ignorant of the actions of human freedom. Otherwise, these actions would not have their own reality, but would only be a function of a certain divine mechanism of things.

Divine providence does not destroy human freedom but responds to it, acting with absolute wisdom. *God cooperates with creatures according to an infallible purposiveness, while preserving their freedom.* This postulate of faith is unshakably valid. The principle of synergism signifies that creatures are never deprived of the protection of divine providence, whatever may be their proper self-determinations, toward good or toward evil. Here, both the permission and the direction of events remain in God's hands and are accomplished by divine wisdom. No creature is removed from this universal protection of providence, not even Satan and his servants (see the prologue to Job). The understanding of these ways of providence, of this absolute purposiveness of the ways of God, surpasses all capacity of human invention if only because each of us knows and has access to only a negligible segment of time, only a single point of the world process outside of the general connectedness of the present, past, and future in which "wisdom is justified of her children" (Matt. 11:19).

But it is not difficult to understand that this postulate also contains a just interpretation of theodicy, the basic idea of which was expressed by an unbelieving mind in the mocking dictum: "all is for the best in this best of all possible worlds." The stupidity of this witticism consists in the fact that it closes people's eyes to the reality of the freedom with which God honored creation, whereas Voltaire wishes to see in the paths or destinies of the world only the actions of God and blasphemously mocks the broken character of these paths. But one should never forget that God's action in the world is his *synergism* with creation. And with a veil of sin and arbitrariness creaturely freedom obscures the understanding of the ways of providence, leaving them accessible only to the eyes of faith in a state of special inspiration — by virtue of an express revelation. It follows that a *rational theodicy,* which discloses the ways of God in the world, *is impossible.* A true theodicy will be possible only in the eschatological fullness of time, when the ways of the Lord will be revealed: "For we know in part, and we prophesy in part. But when that which is perfect is come, then that which is in part shall be done away" (1 Cor. 13:9-10). The key to the problem of theodicy is precisely *synergism.*

Groping, our thought tries to grasp the constant and the variable aspects of the synergic process. This process includes God's direct action, corresponding to the wise ways of providence. This action is distinguished by the infallibility proper to God's omnipotence with regard to the paths or destinies of the world: God knows His creation. But He knows it in its freedom, and the reality of this freedom cannot be defended by the sophistries to which the adherents of determinism have recourse. They interpret freedom as only a special mode, or particular case, of determination, according to which some of God's predestinations are fulfilled by the force of things while others are fulfilled freely, by the subjectively spontaneous action of human energy, which, however, is united with an insensible divine pressure. Here, of course, synergism is only replaced by a special kind of determinism. But freedom presupposes creative self-determination out of itself, within the limits of creaturely possibilities, and this freedom exists not only for itself but also for God.[25] Therefore, God Himself takes into account these free self-determinations, answering them divinely; and the fabric of history is thus woven of two intertwined threads. History is a dialogue between God and man, and their synergism is a divine-human process. The idea of man as a puppet, moved by the string of necessity, must be rejected as firmly as the idea of occasionalism, according to which history is an unlimited and chaotic improvisation of accidents.

This general idea of the dialectic of synergism is fully confirmed by the sacred history of the Old and New Testaments. The history of Old Testament humankind is symbolized by the personal struggle of Israel with the Unknown (Gen. 32:24-30). This history cannot be understood outside of this God-battling synergism, whose presupposition is creaturely freedom, a certain independence of creation from the Creator, although at its peak creation freely submits to the Creator: "Behold the handmaid of the Lord." This self-determination of freedom should be understood in all its power and genuineness, and thus by no means as a preestablished *deus ex machina*. In the New Testament, the synergism of God and man figures, first of all, in the life of the God-man Himself, in the union in Him of two wills and two energies, with the human will always conforming with and "following" the divine will. The entire path of Christ's earthly service consists in the fulfillment not of His own will but of the will of the Father who sent Him. This is made manifest with particular clarity in the agony at Gethsemane with its "not as I will, but as thou wilt."

In general, it is impossible to understand the course of the *divine-*

25. Metropolitan Macarius asserts the following: "Our acts do not depend on God's foreknowledge. On the contrary, God foresees, or sees, them because we ourselves have decided to commit them, and we do commit them" (*Dogmatic Theology*, 1:126). Here we have a kind of Molinism.

human life except in the light of synergism. But one must immediately qualify or delimit this statement. In the strict sense, synergism presupposes a creaturely hypostasis as the subject of freedom. Such a creaturely human hypostasis is absent in Christ (to assert the contrary would be to follow the Antiochene conception of the doubling of hypostases in Christ). However, we also confess that, in Christ, the human nature does not remain nonhypostatic but that it is hypostatized by the one divine-human hypostasis. In this sense, Christ's humanity properly has that freedom by virtue of which alone He could have offered obedience to the Father even unto death. His whole life can be understood only on the basis of the synergistic relation between His two natures. Synergism in Christ is possible only by virtue of the genuineness of His kenosis. It is from this angle that one must, in particular, consider His "ignorance" and, in general, the fact that He took upon Himself the limitations of humanity during His earthly service. This includes the fact that He did not know the day of the Second Coming[26] (see Mark 13:32), and the fact of His unceasing prayer, consecrating His human nature to God (and, above all, the prayer during the agony at Gethsemane). These human limitations, kenotically accepted by the Lord, represent here the foundation of possible synergism.

But if such is the life of the Shepherd, such also is the life of His flock, beginning with His chosen disciples. This life is unceasing interaction: the invincible power of the Teacher interacts with the freedom to accept or not accept His teaching, as well as Him Himself. And, here, with equal force it is said, on the one hand: "While I was with them in the world, I kept them in thy name: those that thou gavest me I have kept, and none of them is lost, but the son of perdition" (John 17:12); and on the other hand: "how often would I have gathered thy children together, even as a hen gathereth her chickens under her wings, and ye would not!" (Matt. 23:37).

The mystery of God's providence consists also in the fact that God's knowledge of the heart chooses with absolute infallibility the mode and moment of divine action. He permitted Peter's rejection but called to him when the hour was right: "Simon, son of Jonas, lovest thou me?" (John 21:15). He permitted Saul's persecution but also called him when the hour was right, not before and not after, when a light from heaven shined around him. He summoned Judas into the circle of the apostles and allowed him to perform the apostolic ministry, but abandoned him later in permitting his terrible betrayal. The actions of God, as well as His in-

---

26. See *The Lamb of God*, pp. 282ff.

actions and permissions, in relation to every human being are full of this divine mystery.

But this unfathomable mystery presupposes at its basis the divine providence with its omniscience, without which its infallibility would be impossible. The ways of divine guidance are not accomplished outside of creaturely freedom, but they cannot be wholly entrusted to this freedom. Here we once again encounter a union of freedom and necessity. However, this difficulty can be resolved by considering the character of creaturely freedom, which exists only within the limits of the given, with all the possibilities known to its Creator, and contains the themes of creative possibility for creation as tasks to be realized. The destinies of creation are therefore determined without regard to freedom, so to speak, but including it. In connection with this, it is appropriate to pose the question of prophecy: How is prophecy possible and what does it signify? A simple reference to God's omnipotence and omniscience clearly does not suffice to answer this question. Rather, the question must be posed in connection with synergism.

The general concept of prophecy covers different forms of prophecy: natural and by grace, *human* perspicacity and divinely inspired insight. The human reason is given the ability to apprehend the connection of events to a greater or lesser degree, depending on individual talent and capacity. This ability can be defined as a historical and personal perspicacity, as a special sensitivity to the connection of events, depending on the generic character of human beings. This historical sense (the muse Clio) is not limited to the past and present, but also extends to the future.[27] To be sure, this possibility of prevision on the basis of the "laws" that govern things excludes, *ex hypothesi* and by method, the element of human creativity and freedom, as well as variations of events connected with them. Moreover, insofar as these are *minima* about which sociology *non curat praetor* (has no jurisdiction), they can in practice be abstracted. But the very domain of sociological prevision, or prophecy, therefore remains substantially limited. This domain does not extend to concrete *history* in the precise sense but is limited to "tendencies." Sociology is empirically inclined to neglect these individual deviations, despite the fact that they contain the true reality and highest value of life.

---

27. Debates about to what degree it is possible to predict the future on the basis of data of the past and present have frequently arisen in historiosophy and statistics. This question has had a decisive significance for Marxism and, in general, for the entire positivistic theory of progress.

This natural and, so to speak, sociological prevision becomes more acute among the prophets and acquires a supernatural, divinely inspired character. It is marked by a greater clarity, a wider horizon, and relative infallibility. However, a "sociological," abstractly schematic type of cognition and representation of the future is preserved here. This is not so much a prediction of future events as a profound knowledge of the spiritual powers acting in history. Such is the character of Judaic apocalyptics, where kingdoms and nations are symbolically represented as beasts, plants, and phenomena of nature.[28] We find this in the Book of Daniel and, to a certain degree, in the Revelation of St. John.

Much more limited is the sphere of insights or prophecies about specific persons and events, comprising, so to speak, *vetum testamentum in novo*. The Gospels, as does the New Testament in general, often refer to Old Testament prophecies, sometimes with an original application of these prophecies,[29] and sometimes with obvious traces of a *vaticinium post eventum* (prophecy after the fact) in the application of a more or less abstract figure to a concrete event or person. What the prophets saw as something spiritually inevitable in the character of the future in general is applied in the New Testament to concrete events as a prophecy of fact. The prophetic character of such visions (and prefigurations) is not diminished if the truth they contain is combined with highly obscure and abstract predictions. They should not be understood as a mechanical communication, a "dictation" of future and yet incomprehensible facts, a peering into the future over a veil. Such a superstitious conception of prophecies transforms them into a sort of sacred guessing. But prophecy is a divine-human work, which is possible only to the extent that human nature, exalted by grace, is capable of receiving it, without, however, being coerced. Prophecies are human questionings (cf. Dan. 10), to which revelations give answer.

What does the knowledge of the future given by inspiration from above represent? If *scientia rerum est causa rerum,* that is, if God's knowledge causally determines events, then prophecies would be acts of new creation, as it were, effects of divine omnipotence. But that would annul divine providence, which concerns an already existing and complete creation and presupposes that creation has a fixed and stable character. However, divine providence is not *causa rerum* but an interaction between God and

28. See my article "Apocalypse and Socialism" in the collection *Two Cities,* vol. 2.

29. For example, Matt. 2:23: "And he came and dwelt in a city called Nazareth: that it might be fulfilled which was spoken by the prophets, He shall be called a Nazarene."

man. On God's part this interaction is determined by perfect knowledge of existing creation in its entire composition. God knows the plan of the universe and all the elements contained therein. He knows from the beginning of creation all people, both those born and those unborn. For man's creation, unfolding in time in successive births, is supratemporally accomplished by the single act of the creation of the *entire* human race, both as a whole and in its individuals (see above). God therefore knows the history of humankind in its supratemporal plan. Finally, God also knows the sophianicity of creation, with the consequent conformity to law of the latter, as well as with all the possibilities contained therein: God sees the supramundane panorama of cosmic and historical being.

Interwoven into this conformity to law is the variable factor of creaturely freedom, which is combined with divine action (we will not as yet speak of its character) and the resulting interaction. Inasmuch as God knows all the natural and human components of the world, this is a domain of direct divine knowledge. When human freedom and its synergism with God are factored in, we have deviation from law, a certain, though relative, novelty with which God does not interfere in His kenosis with respect to creation. However, this novelty is limited in its possibilities, for creaturely freedom exists not essentially but modally, not in and by itself but in something, in the given in creation; creaturely freedom is not a *what* but a *how*. In this sense, the *entire* panorama of the world's life is accessible to divine knowledge, both in the already accomplished self-determination of freedom and in the self-determination that has not yet been accomplished, for freedom is incapable of changing the general path of the world, although it affects its particularities. The world is governed by God's will, above us and in us, although it is we who must seek, or not seek, God's will and fulfill it, or not fulfill it, in freedom: We must be free subjects, not passive objects. However, the presence of freedom in the not-yet accomplished life of the world makes, to this extent, the picture of the world not yet fully developed, full of shadows, as it were. The basic contours are revealed but not the details.

Prophetic prevision has access only to "tendencies," and their character is more sociological than historical. This also has an inevitable influence on the character of prophecies of the future, in which only what is accessible to knowledge, that is, the existent, is seen, but what has not yet been accomplished is absent. This produces the special language of prophecies, which is usually figurative and schematic, not concrete. However, there are exceptions, when prophecies refer, if not directly to concrete facts or features, then to specific persons or, at least, types. Let us mention the

"Angel" of the Lord, the Forerunner; "the seed of the woman," the New Eve (more prefigured than directly indicated); "the two witnesses"; "the man of iniquity," and so on. All of these persons, known in the ways of God, occupy their proper place in the fullness of pre-temporal humankind, which the prophecies attest to, not as predestination but as knowledge. It is incorrect to think that the appearance of the Mother of God in the world was provoked only by the fall of Adam and Eve and the necessity of salvation through the Incarnation, whose instrument She was. From this one might draw the further conclusion that without this express necessity the Ever-Virgin would not have appeared in the world. But that is not so. From the very beginning and, so to speak, "before" the fall and independently of it, the Most Holy Mother of God is the summit of the human race; and She shone when the times were fulfilled, like other persons indicated in the prophecies. Although this manifestation corresponds to the special goals of providence, it essentially refers to God's knowledge of *all* humankind, both born and not yet born, and to knowledge of each of its members ("Thine eyes did see my substance" [Ps. 139:16]).

A wholly special and exclusive place is certainly occupied by the messianic prophecies (together with their prophetic prefigurations) which refer to God's direct action in the world, to the Incarnation and the descent of the Holy Spirit, which constitute the foundation, from all eternity, of the world, not for its creation but for its deification. Of course, here, we must consider inappropriate all occasionalism, according to which the Incarnation and the sending down of the Holy Spirit could have failed to take place if Adam's fall *("beata Adae culpa")* had not bent God's will in that direction. Such an opinion introduces an anthropomorphism in our representations of God; it supposes that He changes His thoughts not only about man but also about Himself in His relation to the world. Rather, we must recognize that the Incarnation and the sending down of the Holy Spirit represent, as it were, a second creation of the world in God, its deification, which is precisely the main content of the world's life. There is no prophecy about this creation as one of the future events, but there is a divine revelation about this accomplishment as such. Also related to this is divine knowledge of different features of this accomplishment, as a series of events in the chain of earthly being.

Thus, we distinguish different levels, as it were, in prophecies according to their content: God's revelation about Himself in relation to the world; the plan of creation, which is accomplished supratemporally and is being actualized in time; and finally, the ways of providence in relation to human freedom.

Prophecies connected with man's self-determination in freedom have, in general, a *conditional* character, and even must have such a character, if freedom has its proper reality. The Lord says the following: "At what instant I shall speak concerning a nation, and concerning a kingdom, to pluck up, and to pull down, and to destroy it; if that nation, against whom I have pronounced, turn from their evil, I will repent of the evil that I thought to do unto them. And at what instant I shall speak concerning a nation, and concerning a kingdom, to build and to plant it; if it do evil in my sight, that it obey not my voice, then I will repent of the good, wherewith I said I would benefit them" (Jer. 18:7-10). Also, the Lord says the following (to the prophet): "If so be they will hearken, and turn every man from his evil way, that I may repent me of the evil, which I purpose to do unto them because of the evil of their doings" (26:3). "Therefore now amend your ways and your doings, and obey the voice of the Lord your God; and the Lord will repent him of the evil that he hath pronounced against you" (26:13).

Freedom introduces its variants in the flow of events and disrupts or deflects their regularity. These deflections can remain unnoticeable in the basic course of events as it is portrayed by prophecy. And then prophecy remains in full force: it is not subject to verification or correction by freedom. Just as a statistical series encompasses individual deviations, which do not destroy it, so prophecies manifest this internal regularity in a highly generalized, symbolic style. However, when prophecy becomes less abstractly sociological and more individually concrete, its conditionality, which depends on the action of freedom, becomes manifest. We have an example of this in Jonah's prophecy of the destruction of Nineveh, which turned out to be conditional since Nineveh was spared thanks to the prayers of its repentant inhabitants.[30]

Prophecies in general, and eschatological ones in particular, should be understood in the light of this conditionality, which is due to self-determination in freedom. Their goal is not to anticipate the inevitable, but to indicate what is possible and to deflect what should not be, by an appeal to repentance and courage. This basic tendency is not contradicted by texts that supposedly bear witness to "predestination" and are erroneously interpreted fatalistically. (In connection with this, we must examine

---

30. The conditionality of prophecy can also apply to events that did not occur. An example: "Woe unto thee, Chorazin! woe unto thee, Bethsaida! for if the mighty works, which were done in you, had been done in Tyre and Sidon, they would have repented long ago in sackcloth and ashes" (Matt. 11:21). [. . .]

the question of sacred divinings of all sorts, from the Old Testament questioning of the Urim and the Thummim [see Exod. 28:30] to various cases of New Testament clairvoyance. Without touching upon to what degree such questioning might have the character of a temptation, emanating from unhealthy curiosity or from lack of confidence in divine providence, one can also apply the category of conditional prophecy to such cases, insofar as here human freedom confronts and influences the destinies of the world.)

Providence is manifested not only in the care for the world through the holy angels and, in general, through a spiritual causality that can take on a miraculous character in relation to the natural world; it is also manifested in a direct intervention in the destinies of the world. The object of such intervention is, above all, what does not depend on human will but represents the fulfillment of the pre-temporal divine plan. Such are, first of all, the births and deaths of specific persons, established by God's will. Prophecies of these births and deaths are directly communicated by God to individuals who are susceptible to divine suggestions. This immediacy clearly manifests the divine-human character of prophecy, which becomes accessible to the interior hearing of God's words (cf. such expressions in the prophetic books as "a word of God came" and "the Lord said to me"). Here we also have prophecies in the narrow sense, as predictions of facts. Here are a few examples: God's prediction to Abraham and Sarah of the birth of their son Isaac (Gen. 18:10-14); the high priest Eli's prediction to Hannah of the birth of her son Samuel (1 Sam. 1:17, 20); the prophecy of the death and then the recovery of King Hezekiah (Isa. 38; 2 Kings 20).

The concept of *synergism* (a particular case of which is prophecy) extends to a general definition of the relation of creation to the Creator as the correlation of the creaturely and Divine Sophia, or the actual sophianicity of creation. Belonging to itself in freedom, creation is ontologically never separated from its sophianic-divine foundation. Divine power ceaselessly flows in the world and sustains the world's being not only through a single supratemporal and extra-temporal creative act of God, but also through providential action with regard to creation, directed toward its sophianization. Creation and providence are inseparable. In other words, there exists a "natural" grace of creation, physicosophianic, without which and outside of which creation could not exist but would sink into the abyss of *nothing*. This grace is communicated directly to creation through the world soul, prehuman or not yet humanized being, and then through man. *Grace* in the true sense is precisely the power of deification, in which creation surpasses itself in man, transcends the bounds of natural or physico-sophianic being, and acquires the power of new sophianization by receiving the principles of divine life in Divine-humanity.

The Incarnation too can be understood in the light of synergism.[31] Such is its human preparation, from the patriarchs to "the handmaid of the Lord," who in human freedom uttered Her "be it unto me according to thy word." Such is also its realization in the God-man, who harmoniously united in himself divine and human will. Synergism is also manifested in the reception of the gifts of the Holy Spirit: every person receives according to his capacity to receive. The ontology of *prayer* must also be understood in connection with synergism. Prayer is a form of direct synergism, a living meeting of God and man. In prayer as praise, human beings are permeated with life in God and are thus deified through the contemplation of God's mysteries and miracles. In prayer as petition, human beings seek to unite their will with God's will. The domain of synergism expands and is deepened in proportion to the efficacy of the prayer.

The Lord maximally manifested this synergism of prayer in himself: his entire life was an unceasing prayer, united with the fulfillment of the Father's will. And in his disciples as well he instilled this idea of the power and efficacy of prayer: "Ask and it shall be given you" (Matt. 7:7). "And all things, whatsoever ye shall ask in prayer, believing, ye shall receive" (Matt. 21:22; Mark 11:24; Luke 11:9). The Lord bore witness to this in the most powerful manner. To be sure, not every prayer of petition has this efficacy, but only that which accords with God's will and is not madness or delusion, or merely an expression of egotism. But prayer with faith, with devo-

---

31. God's synergism with man has an express significance in the life of Divine-humanity. Christ's incarnation was not limited to a specific place and time: According to his promise, the resurrected and ascended Christ mysteriously abides in humankind "always, now and for ever and for ages of ages," not identifying himself with humanity but not separating himself from it either. Certain writers and mystics express this idea in a highly paradoxical form. Cf. a saying of the Lord in the *Agrapha*: "Split a tree. I am there. Cut a rock asunder. I am there." Augustine expresses this with particular force (see the comparison of texts in E. Mersch, *Le corps mystique du Christ*, Louvain, 1933, vol. 2, chap. 4): "Christ speaks in us, prays in us. He suffers in us *quia et ipsi sunt ego*." "Extend your love to the whole world if you wish to love Christ, for Christ's members extend throughout the whole world" (*In. Epist. Io. ad Parth.* 10; PL 35, 2060-61). "If Christ's members were not He, He would not have said: 'Saul, Saul, why persecutest thou me?' For Paul did not persecute him on earth, but, of course, he persecuted His members, the faithful. However, He wished to say not my saints, servants, or brothers, but 'me', i.e., my members, of whom I am the head" (*In. Joh.* 28; PL 35, 1622). [. . .]

tion to the will of God, is capable of working miracles and spiritually influencing the world's causality (insofar as it accords with God's will, of course). This form of living synergism in prayer expresses the interpenetrability of the Divine and creaturely Sophia. It wholly excludes, of course, the closed self-sufficiency and mechanical regularity of the world, a self-sufficiency inaccessible to spiritual influences. For one who prays, this mechanical regularity, alien to human life, is removed, and human life becomes transparent to God's will that is accomplished in it; and the praying person directly addresses himself to this divine will. Prayer is a miracle of revealed synergism: God listens to the prayer of faith, and its efficacy is self-evident.

But to better understand the operation of providence, one must see in it not only a synergic interaction between God and man but also God's direct action, which for man has the force of necessity, as his fate. In the life of the world, and in human life in particular, not all, and even relatively little, is determined by creaturely freedom in its limited possibilities. Freedom itself is confined within a definite frame of life. We are given to ourselves both outwardly and inwardly; we not only make ourselves, but our destiny is accomplished upon us. We are born in this world in a definite place and at a definite time; our life is determined in its mode and duration, in its events and possibilities. We must postulate that all this has sufficient ground for itself, both in our supratemporal self-determination and in the omni-temporal life of the whole in which we are included. And only a little window remains open for freedom.

In view of all this, perhaps one should speak not of the freedom but of the unfreedom of human self-determination, of its determinedness. The truth of the doctrine of "predestination" consists precisely in the fact that this doctrine attempts to take into account this force of necessity in human destinies. This necessity can take different forms: laws of nature, fate, chance, historical circumstances. But in all these forms it presses on freedom, not only limiting it but in some cases paralyzing it. Necessity is capable of provoking somber fatalism, the phantasms of reincarnation, karma, and fate. God or "moira" (i.e., fate) — these are the alternatives. Only the naivete of positivism can console itself with various self-deceptions and imagine, as a victory over fate, a "leap" from necessity to freedom. The phantom of blind fate can be dissipated only by the power of the religious understanding of life and the feat of faith, which also gives knowledge of freedom.

The action of providence in human life, as a transcendent force, can also be perceived synergically through the free acceptance of what happens to man as God's will, through filial obedience to His will. God acts in the world, and all that happens in the world is the accomplishment of divine plan and government. It can and must be perceived as an ongoing, but not revealed, theodicy, as God's beneficent will. The synergic activity of such an acceptance in the giving of oneself to God's will necessitates an utmost tension; it is a feat of spiritual ascesis. Faith lets a man see. Through faith he freely participates in what belongs to necessity. For him, the iron curtain of causal necessity that shuts off the world's sophianicity falls away. He feels the divine presence in implacable necessity; he comes to know that without God's will not a hair can fall from the head, and that, unless it is God's will, we cannot add even one cubit to our stature. The world's necessity appears to man then as the ongoing sophianicity of the world, as God's providence watching over the world. Necessity is then accepted as God's gift, as God's work upon us.

Sometimes this significance of necessity comes to the surface, becomes explicit, as God's direct assistance and mercy. But sometimes, and much more often, this significance is hidden in the depths of events. There is a special inspiration, a grace of faith, in God's providence: *credo quia absurdum, sed ut intellego* (I believe because it is absurd, but as I understand it). "Now I know in part, but then shall I know even as also I am known" (1 Cor. 13:12). To be sure, such a spiritual orientation is expressed most clearly in the idea of the *cross* and its voluntary acceptance. This can refer equally to an act of will that consists in choosing one's cross and to the acceptance and bearing of an involuntary cross. This gives a providential meaning to our whole life. The commandment to take up and bear our cross is addressed by the Lord to all who wish to follow Him. The cross includes the idea of universal synergism, first, in its subjective significance as reconciliation with fate, which thereby loses its randomness and meaninglessness. But it also has a completely objective significance, for the interaction between the divine will and the human will is realized in it. The cross is a question addressed to human will, and the taking up of the cross is the good answer to this question in the humility of the heart. The cross is the banner of the sophianicity of the world in its ascent to its supreme and final goal: the sophianization of creation.

The Church, History, and the Afterlife

CHAPTER 5

The Church

1. The Essence of the Church
(Ecclesiology and Sophiology)

The most generalized and profound concept of synergism is connected with the idea of the Church in all its diverse meanings. Let us begin with its most general meaning. The Church is the fulfillment of God's eternal plan[1] concerning creation and the salvation, sanctification, glorification, deification, and sophianization of creation. In this sense, the Church is the very foundation of creation, its inner entelechy. The Church is Sophia in both of her aspects, Divine and creaturely, in their interrelationship, which is expressed in their union. This union is a synergism, Divine-humanity *in actu,* in its eternal being and in its creaturely becoming.

On the one hand, the Church was not "founded" and did not appear

---

1. Its main interest being directed at the Church as a salvific institution and organization, patristics did not insist on the primordial significance of the Church as the foundation of creation. However, we do encounter this idea in patristics from time to time, e.g., in *The Shepherd* of Hermas. Hermas saw an old woman, and a youth appeared to him in a dream and told him that this old woman was God's Church. "I asked him why she was old. He told me that she is old because she was created before all things, and the world was created for her" (Vis. 11, 4, 1). [. . .] In Clement's Homily 14:3, the preexistent Church is identified with the Holy Spirit; in Hermas, however, the Spirit, revealed in Christ, acts in the Church. This expresses the essence of the distinction between the hypostases of the Son and the Holy Spirit in the revelation of the Father. Theology usually considers the idea of the eternal existence of the Church to be an accidental phenomenon, an "echo of Gnostic ideas" (Vl. Troitsky, *Essays on the History of the Dogma of the Church [Ocherki iz istorii dogmata Tserkvi],* Sergiev Posad, 1912, p. 105).

in time; it is eternal with the eternity of God, for it is the Divine Sophia herself. On the other hand, the Church shares with creation the destinies of becoming, and in this sense she appears, or rather becomes manifest, in time or in history. The Church is manifested in different forms: the edenic Church, the Old Testament Church, the New Testament Church, and finally the Church of the life of the age (or, rather, ages) to come. The ecclesiological Epistle to the Ephesians (whose ecclesial authority does not depend on how the critical question concerning its author is decided) speaks of the Church as the foundation of creation. This epistle says that the God and Father of our Lord Jesus Christ

> hath chosen us in him before the foundation of the world . . . having predestinated us unto the adoption of children by Jesus Christ to himself, according to the good pleasure of his will, to the praise of the glory of his grace, wherein he hath made us accepted in the beloved. In whom we have redemption through his blood, the forgiveness of sins, according to the riches of his grace; wherein he hath abounded toward us in all wisdom and prudence; having made known unto us the mystery of his will, according to his good pleasure which he hath purposed in himself: that in *the dispensation of the fullness of times* he might gather together in one all things in Christ, both which are in heaven, and which are on earth, even in him: in whom also we have obtained an inheritance, being predestinated according to the purpose of him who worketh all things after the counsel of his own will. (Eph. 1:4-11)

This text expresses the general plan of creation in relation to its divine foundation — Christ, in indivisible union with the Holy Spirit. In his glorification, Christ was given "to be the head over all things to the church, which is his body, the fulness of him that filleth all in all" (1:22-23). The words "the fulness [*pleroma*] of all in all" refer, of course, to the Divine Sophia as the foundation of creation in its perfection. Synergism is the character of this relation: "by grace are ye saved through faith; and that not of yourselves: it is the gift of God: not of works. . . . For we are his workmanship, created in Christ Jesus unto good works, which God hath before ordained that we should walk in them" (2:8-10). This is precisely "the fellowship of the mystery, which from the beginning of the world hath been hid in God, who created all things by Jesus Christ: to the intent that now unto the principalities and powers in heavenly places might be known by the church the manifold wisdom of God [*he polypoikilos sophia tou theou*], according to the eternal purpose which he purposed in Christ

Jesus our Lord" (3:9-11). One cannot more clearly express the sophianic foundation of the world, which is the Church. And the sophianization of the world is accomplished through the redemption given by the Lord Jesus Christ in His incarnation by the Holy Spirit.

This general relation between the divine and creaturely principles, sophianization *in actu,* is defined as *grace* in all the different senses of this term.[2] In this respect, the Church is considered as an organization of gracious life, as well as life itself. The gift of grace, given and received in divine-human synergism, accomplishes our *salvation* as the realization of the entelechy of the world, that is, the sophianization of the world.[3]

In Scripture, the term *church* is used in two senses: (1) in the sense of a local community of believers, that is, in the sense of *churches* in the plural, united by unity of life; and (2) in the sense of the *Church* as this very life, as one mystical essence. In this sense, the Church is described as the body of Christ animated by the Holy Spirit, as His temple, and as the bride of Christ. Let us try to understand the full power of these expressions.

The Church as the body of Christ is considered in relation both to the unity of *multiple* members and to their differentiation in *one* body. And this unity is defined pneumatologically, in relation to the Holy Spirit, who lives in the Church; and christologically, in relation to Christ. The pneumatological aspect and the christological aspect are juxtaposed in 1 Corinthians 6:15, 19: "Know ye not that your bodies are the members of Christ? . . . Know ye not that your body is the temple of the Holy Spirit which is in you, which ye have of God, and ye are not your own?" There is an analogous juxtaposition in chapter 12, in reference to the differentiation of the gifts of the one Spirit of God, as well as that of the members of the one Body of Christ:

> There are diversities of gifts, but the same Spirit. And there are differences of administrations, but the same Lord. And there are diversities

---

2. Scripture uses the term "grace" in different senses (besides goodness in general): (1) love (Luke 1:30; 2:40); (2) divinely revealed teaching, Christ's gospel (Luke 4:22; John 1:16-17); (3) Christ's revelation and election (Rom. 1:5; Eph. 3:8; Gal. 2:9); (4) the work of redemption and its fruits (Rom. 5:15-21); (5) the entire economy of salvation (2 Tim. 1:9; Eph. 1:4-7); (6) benediction (Rom. 1:7; 1 Cor. 1:3; 2 Cor. 1:2, etc.); (7) the gift of the Holy Spirit (Heb. 10:29; 1 Cor. 15:10; 2 Cor. 12:9). See V. Katansky, "The General Doctrine of Salvation in Freedom *(Obshchee uchenie o spasenii v svobode),*" *Khrist. Cht.* 1900, 1, 39 sqq.

3. A three-page excursus on the meanings of the term "salvation" in Scripture has been omitted at this point. — Trans.

of operations, but it is the same God which worketh all in all. But the manifestation of the Spirit is given to every man to profit withal. [An enumeration of these diverse gifts of the Spirit follows.] But all these worketh that one and the self-same Spirit, dividing to every man severally as he will. (12:4-11)

The apostle then directly passes to the doctrine of the body of Christ: "For as the body is one, and hath many members, and all the members of that one body, being many, are one body: so also is Christ. For by one Spirit are we all baptized into one body, whether we be Jews or Gentiles, whether we be bond or free; and have been all made to drink into one Spirit" (12:12-13). The apostle then discusses the differentiation of the members of the body and their connection: "Now ye are the body of Christ, and members in particular. And God[4] hath set some in the church" (vv. 27-28). He then again enumerates the gifts and ministries in the Church (vv. 28-30).

This juxtaposition (apparently in no particular order) of Christ and the Holy Spirit is of great ecclesiological importance. To this is added the doctrine of the differentiation of the members of the body and the corresponding gifts. This general idea of the unity of the body of Christ with the multiplicity of members is also expressed in Romans 12:5: "So we, being many, are one body in Christ, and every one members one of another." In Romans 12:6-8 we again find an enumeration of the diverse gifts and ministries in the Church, corresponding to the differentiation of members, "according to the grace that is given to us" (v. 6). Only here these gifts are not attributed to a single source, the Holy Spirit, as is the case in 1 Corinthians (whose doctrine should, of course, be considered authoritative here).

The eucharistic doctrine of 1 Corinthians 10:17 has an analogous significance with reference to the unity of the Church: "we being many are one bread, and one body: for we are all partakers of that one bread." Finally, according to the doctrine of the Epistle to the Ephesians, this multi-unity of the Church, with its distinctions and cohesiveness, is revealed as the *fullness* of Christ: "[He] hath put all things under his feet, and gave him to be the head over all things to the church, which is his body [*to sōma autou*], the fulness [*to plerōma*] of him that filleth all [*ta panta*] in all" (Eph. 1:22-23). (The use of the article underscores the ontological significance of these concepts). Here the christological aspect is united, as it is in

---

4. "God" (*ho theos*, the hypostatic God) clearly refers here (on the basis of a direct comparison with 1 Cor. 6:8-11) to the Holy Spirit.

1 Corinthians, with the pneumatological aspect. About Christ it is said that He reconciled us with God, "for we are his workmanship, created in Christ Jesus unto good works, which God hath before ordained that we should walk in them" (2:10), "for to make in himself of twain one new man, so making peace; and that he might reconcile both unto God in one body by Christ" (2:15-16). The apostle continues: "for through him we both have access by one Spirit unto the Father.... Jesus Christ himself being the chief corner stone ... in whom ye are also builded together for an habitation of God through the Spirit" (2:18-22). Finally, Colossians 2:19 speaks of the "Head, from which all the body by joints and bands having nourishment ministered, and knit together, increaseth with the increase of God."

In these ecclesiological texts it is first necessary to delineate the idea of sobornost,[5] according to which the Church is an *organism* or a body, or generally a living multi-unity. In the Church, many members are united and diverse gifts are distributed, her living multi-unity being headed by Christ and quickened by the Holy Spirit.

In virtue of this dyadic character of the Church, believers are told that they are the body of Christ and the temple of the Holy Spirit. In effect, one is not possible without the other, and any ecclesiology that is monistic, not dyadic, is defective. Compare once again Ephesians 2:18-22. As the eternal Divine-humanity, the heavenly Church is the life of God, the self-revelation of God, the Divine Sophia. The idea that the Church as the body of Christ is "the fulness of him which filleth all in all" (Eph. 1:23) refers precisely to this definition. What does this *plerōma* signify if not the eternal life of God, the Divine Sophia, who alone is worthy of being called "all in all"? To be sure, this name cannot be given to creaturely being, which is in a state of becoming. However, in this becoming we are "predestined" by God's will "that in the dispensation of the fulness of times he might gather together in one all things in Christ" (1:10). The Incarnation of Christ accomplishes the unification of divine and creaturely life, man's deification, which is precisely the power of the heavenly Church manifested in the earthly Church. The sophiological interpretation overcomes the otherwise insurmountable difficulties posed by applying both the conception of "the fulness of him that filleth all in all" and the conception of the Church's pilgrimage in the world, *ekklesia paroikousa*, to the defini-

5. Sobornost is the idea of inner ecclesial community formulated by the Slavophiles in the nineteenth century. See the translator's introduction for elaboration. — Trans.

tion of the Church. The Church is the unity of the supra-eternal Divine Sophia and the becoming creaturely Sophia. Only this eternal unity of God's life as *ens realissimum* of the Church is capable of explaining all the power and truth of the insistent affirmations of the apostle, constituting the very foundation of church ontology:

> 1 Cor. 10:17: "we being many are . . . one body."
> Rom. 12:5: "we, being many, are one body in Christ."
> Col. 3:15: "ye are called in one body."
> Eph. 2:16: "that he might reconcile both unto God in one body."
> Eph. 3:6: "that the Gentiles should be fellow heirs, and of the same body."
> Eph. 4:4: "There is one body, and one Spirit."

One should not diminish the ontological significance of this unity by transforming it into merely a figure, a simile: *like* a body or *similar* to a body. On the contrary, the apostle speaks precisely about *one* body (Eph. 4:4-6), in direct relation with the unity of God. The Church is not a conglomerate, but a body; and, as such, it is not quasi-one, but genuinely one, although this unity is not empirical, but substantial, ontological. Empirically it as yet only "increaseth with the increase of God" (Col. 2:19).

What is the nature of this unity? It corresponds to the unity of divine life, which is one — not by the unity of emptiness, but by the unity of fullness, of the wholeness of all in all. This fullness is the one revelation of God's trihypostatic life, in which unity exists as triunity. Here, Scripture speaks not merely of the unity of God's life but precisely of the unity of the *body,* the body of Christ, animated by the Holy Spirit. In relation to the Spirit, the body is not its negation, but its self-revelation. As the body of Christ, the Church is a participation in the divine life, this life's self-revelation in the ongoing deification of creation. Therefore, all is one in Christ, for Christ is one and the Holy Spirit is one; and the Church is one as this divine life conferred upon creation.

The affirmation that the Church is the body of Christ, of the God-man, the true God and the true man, contains two ideas: first, that it is proper to God, as well as to man, and therefore to the God-man, to have a body; and second, that the body of the God-man, the body of Christ, is the Church as deified humanity, as divine-human life.

As regards the first idea, it is impermissible to narrow and thus distort the general idea of the body of Christ by asserting that a body is proper to Christ only according to humanity, as the garment of flesh that

258

He, though He Himself is bodiless, puts on for our sake and for our salvation. Such a supposition is ontologically contradictory, for what is essentially bodiless cannot put on corporeality. Church tradition rejected precisely such a conception of the Incarnation: an Incarnation that would be mere appearance, limited to the putting on of an alien garment and not involving the authentic assumption of true humanity. Such an assumption could be possible only in the case of the positive correlation of the two natures, divine and human. Such a correlation presupposes the existence of two corporealities: spiritual or divine corporeality, which is the Divine Sophia or the glory of God, and human corporeality. The existence of the body of Christ is thus a divine-human fact. To fear the idea that corporeality as a principle of the self-revelation of the divine Spirit contradicts His spirituality is a misunderstanding and leads to the negation, or diminution, of the power of the Incarnation.

However, the main difficulty of ecclesiology concerns not unity but *multi*-unity, the multiplicity of forms of this one life, its manifestation in fullness to which both the multiplicity of the members of one body and the differentiation and multiplicity of the gifts of the one Spirit correspond. Ecclesiological thought must unite the whole reality of unity, or integral wisdom, with multiplicity of forms. Each of many persons, while remaining himself in his singularity, is a member of the one Christ and is animated by the one Spirit. But if each member is Christ when he participates in Christ's life, then what constitutes his own life?

The idea of the unity of the Church as the body of Christ, and also as the temple of the Holy Spirit, contains the obvious antinomy of the one and the many, of the identical and the different, of Christ's and not Christ's. In this antinomy, thesis and antithesis must have equal force; between them there is no logical or static synthesis. Such antinomies can be overcome only dynamically, by the churning of life. The paradox of the body and the members ("ye are the body of Christ, and members in particular" [1 Cor. 12:27]) consists in the fact that each member of the body is thereby the body, belonging to the *whole*; and in this sense each member is this whole. But at the same time each member is also different from the whole: "For as the body is one, and hath many members, and all the members of that one body, being many, are one body, so also is Christ" (1 Cor. 12:12).

To be a member of a body is already to be the body, for the members exist only in the body, and to be the body is to have the members, the body existing only in the members, and members that are different: "For the body is not one member, but many" (1 Cor. 12:14; this is followed by an explication of this idea with reference to the foot, the hand, the ear, the eye, hearing). And it is said of all the members that, despite their diversity, they are equivalent, or equicorporeal. But this equivalence is not equality: "God hath set the members every one of them in the body, as it hath pleased him. And if they are all one member, where were the body? But now are they many members, yet but one body" (1 Cor. 12:18-20). The idea of the equivalence of the members of the body is developed in 1 Corinthians 12:21-26.

If one considers that this characterization of the Church as one body with different members refers to the entire multiplicity of humanity as a multi-unity, it becomes evident that the principle of multiplicity refers to human hypostases, while the principle of the unity of the body refers to the unity of humanity, first in the old Adam and then in the new Adam. In the beginning God created man "in our image," "male and female created he them" (Gen. 1:27), and he "said unto them, Be fruitful, and multiply" (Gen. 1:28). And this applied not to new forms of man, or new forms of creation, but to the one man, identical to himself according to his humanity, according to his nature, and at the same time multiple according to his hypostases. Every hypostasis is a personal *how* of the universal *what* and, as such, belongs to the fullness, the pleroma. It is a ray of that divine light about which it is said that it "was the true Light, which lighteth every man that cometh into the world" (John 1:9). Every hypostasis belongs to Christ, who is therefore the *head* of the Church. But the head of the Church is not just *one* of the members of the body, even if the most important one. The head abides *above* all the members. It is the foundation, in which all the different members find themselves as multiple in unity: Christ, the head, is not only a man; He is the All-man. The language that compares the Church with a body is afflicted by imprecision; and one must compensate for this imprecision when trying to grasp the idea being expressed.

But since the Church is a dyadic revelation of Logos and the Holy Spirit, its characterization must include, besides the multi-unity of the hypostatic members of the body, also the multi-unity of the gifts of the Spirit, by the combination of which the Spirit nourishes all humanity, as the same chapter testifies: "there are diversities of gifts, but the same Spirit" (1 Cor. 12:4), and this diversity is produced by that "one and the selfsame Spirit, dividing to every man severally as he will" (12:11). The personal principle, the principle of the individualization of humanity, is thus connected with the biunitary action or self-revelation of the Second and Third Hypostases.

Thus, the doctrine of the Church as the body of Christ comprises a doctrine of humanity in its relation to the eternal Divine-humanity which is its foundation. This presupposes not only the unity of humanity as such but also the multi-unity of human images or persons in Christ as the incarnate Word, anointed by the Holy Spirit reposing upon Him. Here, we once again confront the mystery of how the divine hypostasis of Christ is multiplied and identified in the multiplicity of human hypostases, each of which receives and preserves its proper personal I-ness, while at the same time identifying itself with Christ and individually submerging itself in His person: "yet not I, but Christ liveth in me" (Gal. 2:20).

Such is this antinomy of the one and the many, the proto-image and the images, identical in difference and different in identity, as the many members of one body. Considered rationally, this antinomy leads only to contradictions, but, considered dynamically, it expresses the mystery of Divine-humanity, namely the relation between the Divine Sophia, who belongs to the divine trihypostatizedness, and the creaturely Sophia, who belongs to the multiplicity of images of God, to angels and to human beings, with all these images ontologically transparent for the Proto-image. The same idea is expressed in the Lord's words about the Last Judgment, where He testifies that He is present in every person (and therefore not a single person is excluded from this presence). This is not only a metaphor or a simile, but a testimony about an authentic, although mysterious, reality.

Thus, the doctrine of the Church as the body of Christ, as the temple of the Holy Spirit, has, first of all, an anthropological significance. This doctrine affirms a certain panchristism and panpneumatism, to which no limits are set. In this aspect this doctrine contains the idea that, after the Incarnation and the Pentecost, Christ is the head of humankind and therefore lives in all humankind. The same thing is affirmed concerning the Holy Spirit, and in this sense the apostle Paul's doctrine of the Holy Spirit and His gifts is wholly parallel to Christ's discourse about the Last Judgment.

But, as was his custom, having affirmed this truth as an ontological one, the apostle also indicates its practical applicability to spiritual and moral life. Thus, the doctrine of 1 Corinthians 6 about our bodies as "members of Christ" and temples of the Holy Spirit serves as the basis for a sermon on chastity, and then, in the sublime chapter 12, as the basis for a sermon on mutual love. Depending upon where the accent falls, the main thrust in Paul's ecclesiology is either dogmatic or practical. His ecclesiology attests to that mysterious unity of humanity that is the mystery of the Church and also summons us to accept this mystery as a guide, so that all abide in the union of love. In modern language one could say that this ecclesiology is the doctrine of the sobornost of the Church, understood, both ontologically and pragmatically, as the principle of gathering (Russ. *sobiranie*) and gatheredness (Russ. *sobrannost'*) in love.

Thus, the most important and essential thing in these passages from the apostolic epistles is the fact that, in the doctrine of the Church as the body of Christ and the temple of the Holy Spirit, they provide a foundation for ecclesiology. This doctrine should not be transformed into some sort of decorative ornament that remains in the background while the main attention is directed at the institutional nature and external organization of the Church.

The Church as Divine-humanity, as the body of Christ and the temple of the Holy Spirit, is a *union* of divine and creaturely principles, their interpenetration without separation and without confusion. In this sense, the Church is a *synergism,* where the divine principle descends to penetrate and attach itself to humanity, whereas the human principle ascends to the divine. Therefore, in practical terms, this synergism is a giving and a receiving of divine gifts. Combined, these gifts are *fullness,* whereas in their appropriation by personal reception, in their separateness, they represent different ministries. The growth of the body of the Church (Eph. 4:16), each member receiving his growth, is thereby accomplished. The doctrine of the Church as the body of Christ and the temple of the Holy Spirit is therefore accompanied in the apostle by an indication of these diverse gifts and ministries, with their enumeration (scarcely exhaustive).

This enumeration is characterized, first of all, by the absence of any mention of hierarchy, which, in its present form, appears not to exist at all in the New Testament or in other canonical writings of the Church. All the enumerated ministries have the character of *personal* gifts, missions, inspirations, creativity, which at the same time enter organically into the life of the Church. The Church is manifested here not in the aspect of institutional hierarchism but in the aspect of personal creativity and inspiration, which constitute the content of her life (moreover, as we have already noted, Scripture indicates twice that this free ecclesiality was established by God himself: "that one and the self-same Spirit" . . . "God set the members every one of them in the body, *as it hath pleased him*" [1 Cor. 12:11, 18]). This organic and creative life of the Church ontologically *precedes* the hierarchical principle. In an organized form, this principle appears in the Church only later. This life is the ontological *prius* for this principle (and not vice versa) or, at least, the condition of its being, as its necessary medium.

262

This spiritual and organic character of the Church was forgotten to a significant degree at a comparatively later time and was even obscured by the institutional and hierarchical principle: Hierarchy was advanced as the *prius* of the Church and the corresponding doctrine of revelation was interpreted in the light of this priority. Particularly salient here is Rome's doctrine of the apostolic succession of the hierarchy in the person of the apostle Peter. A similar doctrine is advanced in the East in the form of a collective papacy, where the primacy of the apostle Peter is rejected.[6] It goes without saying that there can be and should be no contradiction between ontological and institutional ecclesiology. However, this can be the case only when one distinguishes these two aspects and respects the correct relationship between them. In any case, the institution should not suppress the ontology, that is, the sophiological doctrine of the Church, as it is represented by various texts of Scripture.

But even more sophiological is the doctrine of the Church as the Bride of Christ and the Wife of the Lamb, the Beloved of the Lover in the Song of Songs. One can also mention the ecclesiology of Ephesians, where once again the Church is spoken of as the Body of Christ. The creaturely aspect of the Church, for which Christ gave Himself, is the aspect that is primarily considered here (see Eph. 5:25). And the union of wife and husband in one flesh, with father and mother abandoned, is interpreted in relation to Christ and the Church as a great mystery (Eph. 5:32). This mysterious and brief yet astonishingly significant text is unique in the apostolic epistles.

However, it has a direct parallel in Revelation, in the most significant (for concluding) words of the last book of the Holy Scripture. In Revelation 21:9-11, the angel tells the seer of mysteries: "Come hither, I will show thee the bride, the *Lamb's wife.*" And that was "the holy Jerusalem, descending out of heaven from God, having the glory of God." In the context, this manifestation which concludes the history of the world, as its ripe fruit, signifies the sophianization of creation and, in this sense, the Divine Sophia (God's glory), who descends from heaven to earth, into the creaturely world. About her it is said (Rev. 22:17): "And the Spirit and the bride say, Come! And let him that heareth say, Come!"

Here we have an intentional doubling of meaning, as it were: Chap-

6. Characteristic for the period of transition is the doctrine of St. Cyprian, who in the treatise *De unitate Ecclesiae* and elsewhere was one of the founders of the Church's clericalization. He accepts Matt. 18:19-20, this unshakable foundation of the Church's life, only in a legal, jurisdictional sense (*De unitate Ecclesiae,* cap. 12).

ter 21 speaks of the bride-wife, who descends from heaven to earth, while Revelation 22:17 speaks of the bride with the Spirit who animates her and lives in her; and she abides in the world and awaits the coming of Christ in the fullness of divine revelation in the world. The Church, as Sophia, abides in the heavens, is the heavenly Jerusalem (about which the apostle Paul speaks in 2 Cor. 5:1-2: "we have a building of God, an house not made with hands, eternal in the heavens. For [this reason] we groan, earnestly desiring to be clothed upon with our house which is from heaven"), which is to descend to earth. And it is by the Spirit that she summons this descent, like the bride (i.e., the earthly, creaturely Church) awaiting her Bridegroom. Heavenly and earthly, the Church is one in ground and limit, in entelechy, but she remains dual in the world process until the end of the world. Therefore, the relation of this heavenly house to the earthly one, or of Christ to the Church, is expressed by help, care, and redemption. The same fifth chapter of Ephesians says that "Christ . . . loved the church, and gave himself for it" (Eph. 5:25), "for no man ever yet hated his own flesh, but nourisheth and cherisheth it, even as the Lord the church" (v. 29). And this union of Christ with the Church, likened to a conjugal union, is the great mystery of the Church.

However, the crown of the mystical doctrine of the Church as love is found not in the Apocalypse of the New Testament but in that of the Old Testament: in the love song of the bride and the Lamb, in the most mysterious (in this sense) and therefore the most New-Testamental book of the Old Testament, the *Song of Songs*. The different parts and figures of this book are even less interpretable than those of the New Testament Revelation. However, it is permeated by such a trepidation of love and sings so marvelously about it that it is a verbal *miracle*. Therefore, we will not try to interpret its individual features. It is sufficient to recognize, in agreement with the whole ancient tradition of the Church, that the Song of Songs represents the relationship between Christ and the Church in the figure of the love between the Bridegroom and the bride, Love itself or Love's hypostasis, the Holy Spirit, being invisibly present.

Here, we have a revelation of the Second and Third Hypostases (the two hypostases that reveal the Father) as a conjugal syzygy, and this becomes a figure for the union of Christ and the Church. The Word and the Spirit bear witness to the Father who abides in the heavens. The Song of Songs is the song of love between God and the world, the Creator and creation, the Divine Sophia and the creaturely Sophia, the Son made incarnate by the Holy Spirit and the Unwedded Bride, His Mother. This relation is love uniting all the aspects of personal and impersonal love, and the mystery of this love is hidden in the heavens, to be revealed on earth. This marvelous and mysterious love clearly presupposes not a psychologism, not an emotion, but an ontology: the reality of the correlation of spiritual realities. This revelation testifies that the Church *is*, that being is proper to her; as *ens realissimum*, she is an object of divine love. In this sense, the Church is represented as a "body" or a wife: "men ought to love their wives as their own bodies" (Eph. 5:28). The Church exists in a multiplicity of hypostases, as the one body of many members. The primary hypostasis of the Church, the Church's personal center, is the Most Pure Mother of Christ, the Spirit-Bearer.

The definitions of Sophia as bride, wife, and body have, since ancient times, served as an occasion for misunderstandings, both in the direction of excessive spiritualism, which annulled the power of this figure and transformed it into an allegory, and in the direction of excessive romanticism, in which poetry, emotion, and even passion came to dominate. To clarify this question it is first necessary to establish the complex of concepts to which the definition of the Church as wife or bride refers, precisely in the aspect of "femininity" (including, of course, the "eternal feminine"). We distinguish a male principle and a female principle in the hypostatic Spirit, since one or the other of these principles characterizes the hypostasis itself. But the figure of the Church does *not* belong to this opposition, or distinction, between male and female in general in the hypostatic sense, in its different aspects. What is meant and opposed here refers not to hypostatic being but to nonhypostatic being, although a being that is called to hypostatization. The heavenly Church, or the Divine Sophia, is precisely such a nonhypostatic principle. However, preserving her proper substantiality as the nature or essence of God, the Divine Sophia is eternally hypostatized in the divine hypostases. Her express hypostasis is the Logos, who, in inseparable and unconfused union with the Holy Spirit, reveals the Father. The nonhypostatic being of the Divine Sophia is determined by the participation of this being in divine love, which unites her with the hypostases and hypostatizes her.

The Church as the creaturely Sophia is hypostatized by the creaturely hypostases. These hypostases are fully united in the hypostasis of the God-man, who is connected with creation directly through the Mother of God, the "Unwedded Bride," overshadowed by the Third Hypostasis. In this sense, the earthly Church is "in-hypostatized" in Christ as the Wife and Bride of the Lamb.

The scriptural doctrine of the Church as the body of Christ, the temple of the Holy Spirit, and the Wife and Bride of the Lamb concerns (as does all of church ontology in general) her eternal foundation in the heavens and her power that is manifested in creation, in humanity. The Church is the general foundation of creaturely being, its beginning and goal. The problem of the Church is posed here outside of historical concreteness, outside of the limits of space and time, outside of specific church organizations. (If certain organizations, e.g., local communities, are in fact named, their inclusion in the Church is understood.)

The question of the *limits* of the Church as an ontological essence does not yet arise here. However, we cannot avoid posing this question, inasmuch as the data required for an answer exist in revelation and follow from the fundamental definitions. The limits of the Church mystically or ontologically coincide with the limits of the power of the Incarnation and the Pentecost; but these limits *do not exist at all.* "And the Word was made flesh" (John 1:14); the incarnation of the Lord as the divine-human person of Christ consisted in the assumption of the *whole* Adam, "perfect" humanity. There are no limits to this assumption, either external or internal. Christ's humanity is the inner human condition of every human being, about which it can be said that *nihil humanum est a Christo alienum* (nothing human is foreign to Christ) (of course, not in the sense of the empirically given, sinful state of humanity, but in the sense of its nature). All human beings belong to Christ's humanity. And if this human condition is the Church as the body of Christ, then, in this sense, *all* humanity belongs to the Church. This mysterious truth is expressed more than once in Scripture.

The angel tells the shepherds on the night of Christ's birth: "I bring you good tidings of great joy, which shall be to *all* people, for unto you is born this day in the city of David a Saviour, which is Christ the Lord" (Luke 2:10-11). And the righteous Simeon praises God for the "salvation which thou hast prepared before the face of all people: a light to lighten the Gentiles and the glory of thy people Israel" (vv. 30-32). "The grace of God that bringeth salvation hath appeared to all men" (Titus 2:11). God "will have all men to be saved, and to come unto the knowledge of the truth" (1 Tim. 2:4). And if the adherents of the doctrine of predestination, from Augustine to Calvin, are led by its logic to conclude that Christ came into the world not to save all of humankind but only a limited number of the elect, this conclusion flatly contradicts the testimony of the apostle, who excludes such a limit.

But the most decisive argument in favor of the universal and all-human power of Christ's Incarnation, as well as of the descent of the Holy Spirit on Pentecost, is the testimony of the Lord Himself in His words concerning the Last Judgment (Matt. 25), where He identifies Himself, His humanity, with all human beings. One should not diminish this testimony by an allegorical interpretation: *All* human beings, present before Christ's tribunal, belong to His humanity, are Christ (this same conclusion can be drawn from other texts as well, e.g., from the parable of the Good Samaritan). It directly follows that no limits exist for the assumption of humanity by the Logos, just as no limits exist for the Holy Spirit who has descended into the world (which is indeed what the apostle Peter says in Acts 2:17 by the words of the prophet Joel: "it shall come to pass in the last days, I will pour out of my Spirit *upon all flesh*").

But this universality must necessarily extend from man and *for* man. Man does not exist separately from the universe. On the contrary, he is its heart and center, a "microcosm," and human nature includes all of creaturely nature. God made man the head of creaturely nature, and by his fall he condemned it to vanity, in which it groans, yearning to be liberated. The natural world is already subject to the power of Christ after the resurrection: "All power is given unto me in heaven and in earth" (Matt. 28:18). The earth of malediction becomes a new earth under a new heaven in resurrection, just as human bodies become bodies of glory. The domain of the power of Divine-humanity coincides with the limits of the Church. More correctly, these limits do not exist at all, for the whole universe belongs to the Church. The universe is the periphery, the cosmic face of the Church.[7]

But this universality (or catholicity) of the Church, which has its foundation in the creation of the world (Eph. 3:9-11), is also manifested eschatologically, at the end of the world, in the parousia, and in what follows the parousia. This removal of the limits of limited being, this catholicity, is manifested first of all in the transfiguration of the world on the "day of the Lord" (2 Pet. 3:7-13), as well as in the judgment of the Lord, to which *all* the peoples will come. And precisely this signifies that limited being belongs ontologically to the Church. The same thing will result after the accomplishment of what is described in 1 Corinthians 15:28: "And when all things shall be subdued unto him, then shall the Son also himself be subject unto him that put all things under him, that God may be all in all." "For of him, and through him, and to him, are all things" (Rom. 11:36).

---

7. Certain icons of the Mother of God express this idea of the cosmic aspect of the Church, where, as the heart and personification of the Church, She is portrayed with various cosmic attributes, e.g., the "Burning Bush," the "Synaxis of the Most Holy Mother of God," etc.

But, in such a definition of the catholicity of the Church, all dissolves in limitlessness. It gives too much, and therefore too little. It must be supplemented or refined. In disclosing the interaction, or synergism, of the divine principle and the human principle, one must distinguish the Church (and the churches) as an institution of grace from the rest of the world that lies outside the Church, "in darkness and in the shadow of death" (Ps. 107:10). Here, the questions of the nature of the Church and her limits are posed in a new way.

2. The Church as a Sacramental and Hierarchical Organization

In the scriptural doctrine of the Church, we do not find any direct indications concerning the Church as an organization. To be sure, Scripture does speak of local churches, to which the apostolic epistles are addressed. They are called "the churches of Christ" (Rom. 16:16), "the churches of Galatia" (1 Cor. 16:1), "the churches of Asia," and the church of "Aquila and Priscilla" (v. 19). But these are not canonical organizations, of course. They are not "autonomous" or "autocephalous." They are merely local communities that feel they belong to the Church. On the other hand, Revelation 1–3 speaks of the "angels" of the seven Churches, who are their spiritual images; and even if they are their hierarchical representatives, they are not representatives of hierarchical charismata and powers but bearers of spirit.

The beginnings of the hierarchical levels that we find in the New Testament are still rather indefinite, and at the same time so different from the church hierarchy in its developed form that they cannot be directly equated with the latter. At most, they are only embryos of the hierarchy that is to develop. There are also no direct indications about the existence of particular sacramental powers that would be connected with definite hierarchical levels (to be sure, the apostolic rank occupies a special place here; however, despite Roman and romanizing theology, it should not be included in this context). Rather, one observes in the New Testament an absence of hierarchical forms. And it is bizarre to seek to overcome this historical fact by the dogmatic postulate of the initial existence of a three-level hierarchy. But that is what is usually done.[8] The apostolic Church

---

8. See my essay "Hierarchy and the Sacraments." The opposite point of view, which is common in dogmatic manuals, is decisively expressed in Troitsky's *Essays on the Doctrine of the Church (Ocherki ucheniya o Tserkvi).* [. . .]

does not know our hierarchical structure, which comes later, beginning with the second century. And we do not have sufficient historical grounds to fill this void on the map of Church history with dogmatic hypotheses. This leads some people to contradict Scripture, which definitely does not contain what they wish to find in it at all costs in virtue of certain dogmatic postulates. Historical facts must be accepted as they are, though they must of course be understood in the light of and in connection with dogmatic teaching.

A vexing hindrance in the history of dogmatics here is the influence of the Reformation and the Counter Reformation with their theological polemic, which posed the question falsely and had an influence not only on Western but also on Eastern theology. Referring to the ecclesiastical organization of the apostolic age and wrongly seeking even now to reconstruct this structure in its entirety without taking into account the power of history, Protestants desire to turn history back two millennia. Hierarchy is rejected completely in the name of this reactionary utopia, and the very appearance of hierarchy is sometimes viewed as a historical fall into sin and an impoverishment of spirit. In contrast, Catholics, in the name of the later history of the Church with its hierarchical structure, reject in a de facto manner the specificity of the apostolic age, seeking there features that appear only in a later period. And they find there a developed hierarchical order, including the primacy of Rome. This idea received a generalized expression in the Tridentine dogma of the direct institution of all the sacraments by Christ. In particular, the hierarchical laying on of hands is affirmed as starting with the apostles, who received the episcopal charisma from Christ.

Such is the interpretation that is given to the "apostolic succession" (of course, first of all as applied to the primacy of the apostle Peter and his successors in the pulpit of Rome). The corresponding doctrine was recently established by a Vatican council. The Tridentine doctrine (with the exception only of the primacy of Rome) was triumphant also in Eastern theology; it was included in the "Orthodox Confession." In the East too, the episcopate began to consider itself as apostolic successors in the Roman sense, that is, as bearers of the *fullness of the apostolic charisma.* But this applied not solely to the archpriest of Rome as the personal successor of the apostle Peter but to the whole episcopate in general.

Thus, the originality of "primitive Christianity" is diminished in a de facto manner by the whole hierarchical Church, whereas the hierarchical Church is rejected by Protestantism in the name of "primitive Christianity." This results in an erroneous antihierarchicalism in Protestantism and in an exaggeration of the historical universality of hierarchical Christianity. Instead of ripping the history of the Church apart into two incompatible parts, would it not be better for both Protestantism and Catholicism to submit humbly to the historical reality as an indication of God's will and to accept the fact that the early Church and the hierarchical Church that succeeded it are the same apostolic Church, unique and identical to itself? And this identity must, first of all, be dogmatically conceived and understood. What, then, can this indubitable difference and this not less indubitable unity and self-identity of the Church signify?

According to the New Testament doctrine, the Church as the mystical body of Christ, the temple of the Spirit, and the Bride of the Lamb is *Divine-humanity,* eternal and historical, heavenly and earthly, divine and creaturely, in the Chalcedonian union of the two natures in Christ. The whole of christology and pneumatology watches over this idea of the Church. In other words, the Church is the Divine Sophia and the creaturely Sophia united (this union signifying not confusion but the penetration of creaturely life by the rays of divinity, their "synergism"). Divinity, or Sophia, is both transcendent and immanent to creation. Sophia is the noumen, *to ontōs on,* the *Ding an sich* of creation, which, nevertheless, preserves its proper empirical or historical form — the phenomenal world. And this union of noncreatureliness and creatureliness, noumenality and phenomenality, also characterizes the Church as the divine in the creaturely, as the eternal and unchanging being of God in the temporal world, created out of "nothing." The divine is unchanging and eternal, while the creaturely is temporal and historical. In this sense, the Church, once again, is a synergism uniting heaven with earth.

It follows that the Church as Divine-humanity is essentially historical, belongs in its creaturely aspect to *history.* The Church has an initial given, which is also her task. All that is human is historical, empirical, phenomenal; yet it is not deprived of ontological content. It is in the light of this radical historicism, inseparable from a noumenal ontologism, that the life of the Church as *church history* must be understood.

It follows that no event, and no single form or institution, of church life can be understood outside of history, deprived of flesh and blood, torn away from place and time. In His human, and thus historical, being the Only Begotten Son of God was connected with this life. The historical concreteness that belongs to phenomenal being is not a deficiency but a necessary mode of being, without which it would disappear into nothingness. But the same thing would happen if this being were emptied of its essential content: "Thou sendest forth thy spirit, they are created. . . . Thou hidest thy face . . . they die, and return to their dust" (Ps. 104:29-30).

The divine and the human are present without separation and without confusion in Divine-humanity. The human, in all its historical forms and phenomenal states, is relative and limited. It is never adequate to and can never wholly express its divine foundation, but it is never separable from this foundation, is never empty. Phenomena are manifestations of the noumenal, its life in us. These general notions of the relation between the noumenal and the phenomenal[9] must be clarified in a doctrine of the Church as Divine-humanity in its history.

From this it follows, first of all, that the Church that we know, the phenomenal Church, also belongs to history, for only through her doors can we — from our creaturely, human being — go out into the spiritual, divine world, the world of grace. In the empirical being of the Church, there is nothing that does not belong to history, that, in itself, is absolute and eternal. This being is necessarily interwoven with divine eternity, but does not fully include it; and because of its phenomenality the empirical being of the Church is not fully adequate to divine eternity. Such is the mystical realism of the Church, her *symbolism*, with all the inseparable interwovenness of the eternal and the temporal. The Church has its divine *Urgrund,* or primordial ground, to which all the negativity of apophatic ecclesiology is applicable, combined, however, with all its kataphaticity as far as the phenomenology of the Church is concerned. It is in the phenomenology of the Church that divine life is experienced and the Sacred is revealed.

Therefore, the Church as a society, an institution, an organization, the "visible" or empirical Church, does not wholly coincide with the Church as Divine-humanity, with its noumenal depth, although the empirical is connected with, based on, and permeated by the Church as Divine-humanity. If one can ask whether there exists an *ecclesia extra ecclesiam,* an ecclesiality outside and beyond the existing ecclesiastical organization, then there is even more reason to ask whether there exists an *ecclesia supra* or *intra ecclesias.* Churches constitute the phenomenology of the Church, the "visible" Church, that is, the Church that is manifested in empirical reality and in this sense is the invisible in the visible. The visible has outer limits, belongs to history, but within these limits the "invisible,"

9. They are characteristic of ancient philosophy, and in modern times they are expressed in the philosophy of Kant, who, however, interpreted them in the spirit of skeptical empiricism and did not put to use the Platonic profundity of his own theory.

noumenal being is revealed. In this sense, churches are the unity, without separation and without confusion, of what belongs to the world and history, the "visible," and of what transcends the world and history, the "invisible."

The Church therefore has a *symbolic* being in the world, as the divine in the human, the invisible in the visible, as Divine-humanity. But in this very same sense the Church and churches, in their interrelationship, represent the one, common sacrament of all the sacraments, the all-sacrament, which contains the mystery of the Church. Sacrament is usually defined as an operation by which an invisible gift of grace is communicated in a visible form, as something noumenal in the phenomenal. And to every sacrament a specific gift is attributed, conferred by precisely this sacrament and in precisely this form. But it is always necessary to remember that one cannot determine the precise limits of this gift, and in particular the limits of its operation. Some sacraments are bestowed for the entirety of life; these include baptism and chrismation, and to some extent marriage and ordination. And, in general, every sacrament opens a way into the depths, into noumenal being, and is therefore indeterminate and inexhaustible in its operation.

There is a certain incommensurability between the inner power of a sacrament and its visible sign or specification, so that even the very differentiation between sacraments is conventional and, so to speak, pragmatic, for "there are diversities of operations, but it is the same God which worketh all in all" (1 Cor. 12:6), and "all these worketh that one and the self-same Spirit, dividing to every man severally *as he will*" (v. 11). And although since the Council of Trent it has become dogma that there are seven sacraments, not more and not less, this pragmatic formula is, of course, powerless to limit the inexhaustible abundance of the spiritual gifts, and in particular the sacramental gifts, given by the Church. Let it suffice to mention that, historically, the number of sacraments has varied,[10] and that, together with sacraments *(sacramenta)*, there have existed *sacramentalia*, which theology considers sacraments of the second rank, as it were, having a lesser efficacy and importance than sacraments in the strict sense. However, the very existence of *sacramentalia* indicates that it is impossible to exhaust or to limit by the number seven the acts of grace of the Church. They are measureless in

---

10. Here one should mention fluctuations in the number of accepted sacraments. For example, monastic tonsure was considered a sacrament in the ancient church, whereas marriage was not included.

essence, for the Spirit "bloweth where it listeth" and "God giveth not the Spirit by measure" (John 3:8, 34).

All this leads to the general conclusion that all the diverse sacraments and *sacramentalia* are based on the sacrament of all sacraments, the all-sacrament: the Church herself as Divine-humanity, the Incarnation and the Pentecost of the Spirit, with their abiding power. And this all-sacrament, which does not have any limits, is accomplished in the world and in humanity upon the whole world and upon all of humanity, always, now, and forever. For the power of the Incarnation is unshakeable, and the descent of the Holy Spirit cannot be revoked. The Church is the mystery of the world, which is manifested as *sacraments.* Therefore, sacrament can be most generally defined as the manifested action of the Church in man. Man is the temple, the sanctuary, the priest, the bringer of sacrifice, and the receiver of sacrifice. The Church herself, the sacrament of sacraments, is not a particular institution, as each of the specific sacraments is. Rather, she is, on the one hand, a sacred fulfillment, the fulfillment of God's original design, of "the dispensation of the mystery, which from the beginning of the world hath been hid in God" (Eph. 3:9). On the other hand, she is the unique and supreme reality of Divine-humanity, revealed by Christ expressly at the Last Supper. She is the sacramental attestation to the Incarnation; the institution of the sacrament of Eucharist is a manifestation of or attestation to the Incarnation. The mystery of the Church, this sacrament of sacraments, precedes and grounds the sacraments. This mystery is the noumen of the sacraments, which are its phenomena, as it were. In relation to the all-sacrament of the Church, the sacraments have a derivative significance, represent its historical institution, but one that has a divine foundation in Divine-humanity.

On the basis of the aforesaid, we can understand the undeniable historical fact that sacraments *arise* in the life of the Church, at different times, as its institutions. By no means does this diminish their power and efficacy, but it does remove the dogmatic fiction imposed on the Catholic Church by the Council of Trent and later adopted by Eastern theology: the fiction that all the sacraments had been instituted personally and directly by Christ and that, from Him, they had been handed down by the holy apostles and through the apostolic succession. For the majority of the sacraments it is impossible to confirm this theory either on the basis of Scripture or on the basis of church history. The sacraments were instituted by the Church at different times, some earlier, some later. This fact led to the dispute concerning the distinction between "evangelical" and "nonevangelical" sacraments; it is solely on this basis that the latter are not accepted as sacraments in Protestantism.[11]

One can even say that, despite the "breaking of bread," baptism, and the apostolic laying on of hands, the primitive Church did not know sacraments in the present canonical sense. This is clearly demonstrated, first of all, by the absence in the primitive Church of the three-level hierarchy as the instituted performers of sacrament. All this came later. The apostolic Church had and dispensed the gifts of the Holy Spirit directly, so to speak, without the special intermediary of a hierarchy. This ancient practice survives today in the fact that baptism can be performed even by the laity, in virtue of the universal royal priesthood. The general fact of a certain undeniable difference between primitive Christianity and the later Church has an enormous fundamental significance, because this difference shows us the nature of the Church as the all-sacrament, which has only a derivative manifestation in sacraments.

The most important truth that follows from this fact is that the hierarchical-sacramental organization is not the adequate or absolute manifestation of the Church, that this organization therefore has a certain relative character. Such a relativization in no wise diminishes the power and significance of the Church as a hierarchical and canonical institution. Nor does it shake the divine foundation of this institution in history. Rather, it indisputably demonstrates that the noumenal or mystical Church does not exactly coincide with its institutional phenomenon. In general, this means that the power of the Church can extend (or rather cannot fail to extend) beyond the institutional Church: *ecclesia extra ecclesias*. This also means that the giving of spiritual gifts, the Pentecost of the Church, is not limited to or exhausted by the "seven" sacraments, but can follow other paths as well, *non*-sacramental ones, which, since apostolic times, has indeed never been denied in the Church.

Hierarchy originally appeared in connection with the performance of the sacraments, and first of all the Eucharist. Certainly, its appearance must have been by divine institution and not due to historical accident or practical convenience. The historical character of hierarchy does not relativize it to the point of depriving it of its character of divine institution in history. It is more correct to say that hierarchy combines both of

11. The Protestant rejection of the nonevangelical sacraments is evidently determined by the Roman Catholic doctrine, according to which only the sacraments instituted by Christ Himself are valid. Protestantism entirely shares this point of view; and while rejecting the Catholic doctrine, it shares its limitations.

these features. On the one hand, it belongs to history in its instrumental emergence, and in this sense it originates *jure humano* or *historico;* but on the other hand, it bears the stamp of divine will and exists also *ex jure divino.* And the one does *not* contradict the other. This double root of hierarchy is also reflected in certain features of its historical being, in its aspirations and prerogatives.

The original priestly, or even sacrificial, ministry of the hierarchy in the celebration of the sacraments is accompanied by the fact that the hierarchy appropriates certain derivative prerogatives, arising from the practical needs of the church community and organization, and these prerogatives acquire a kind of sacramental significance. New features of hierarchical service appear which are understood as special charismatic gifts, connected with the essential function of hierarchy. Thus arose also the doctrine of *charisma veritatis,* from which the doctrine of the exclusive infallibility of the pope of Rome in the West, as well as the doctrine of the collective infallibility of the episcopate in the East, gradually evolved. In parallel, complex canonical relationships between different local churches and their hierarchical heads arose in history. In the West, this resulted in Rome's pretension to direct and universal jurisdiction in the Christian world. In the East, it resulted in the development of a complex system of canonical relationships in the framework of the one ecclesial sobornost.[12] Here, the influence of *jus humanum,* the power of history, is manifested with great force if, of course, such a canonical structure is not dogmatized on the Roman model.

The character of the Church as a multi-unity of sobornost, as the body of Christ, and of the hierarchy as the canonically organized universal royal priesthood is dogmatically unshakeable. However, together with the development of a healthy hierarchism, one notes a certain unhealthy clericalization, both in the dogmatic doctrine concerning the Church and in ecclesial practice. Measure is lost in defining the place and significance of the hierarchy. Bishops, as well as other degrees of the priesthood, are likened to God, Christ, or the apostles (in St. Ignatius of Antioch). The dogmatic fiction of the continuity of the apostolic succession of the hierarchy in the whole Church is established, although examples of this, which are subject to dispute, are presented only for particular cases (Tertullian, St. Irenaeus, St. Polycarp). Ambiguous formulas appear which lead either to an autocratic papism or a collective one, for example, Cyprian's formula *ecclesia in episcopo,* though there is also *episcopus in*

12. See note 5, supra, on sobornost. — Trans.

ecclesia. Even though it has beneficial consequences, the concentration of churches around the bishop for self-defense in the battle against schisms and heresies also leads to a certain hypertrophy of sacramental hierarchism, which disrupts the ecclesial equilibrium. This historical development results in the general conviction that the Church is precisely a hierarchical organization that is adequate to and perfectly realizes the body of Christ. Having the power of the keys, that is, the power of the sacraments, hierarchy is equated with the Church. (This identification becomes firmly rooted in word-usage: the Church is identified with the hierarchy as *pars pro toto* or, at least, as the head, which here replaces the whole body.)

There follows from this a series of further arguments toward the clericalization of the concept of the Church. The idea of the "vicarial" nature of the hierarchy appears: bishops are considered "vicars" of Christ on earth. Hierarchical and sacramental powers are transformed into mystical and organic ones, corresponding to the central position of the head in the organism, by analogy with the doctrine of Christ as the "head of the Church." However, one must firmly remember the distinction that holds here. Christ is not the head of a body to which this head belongs as a part to a whole, even if the most important part. Rather, He is precisely the *head of the Church:* "Christ is the head of the church: and he is the saviour of the body" (Eph. 5:23), that is, of the Church. Here, it is not a question of a head and not even of hierarchical leadership, as it were, for that would be insufficient to define the place of Christ in the Church. He is this very same body in its unity.

The abuse of the idea of the bishop as the "vicar" of Christ is also justified by arguing that Christ is sometimes called the high priest according to the order of Melchizedek, or even simply *archiereus.* But even if the high-priestly "ministry" of Christ effectively justifies the New Testament priesthood, it is by no means identified with this priesthood in the sense that Christ is the *first* high priest of a series of priests. By no means is He first in *this* sense, and by no means is He a member of a series as one of many, even if He is considered the first member of this series (the hierarchical series in Roman theology, from Christ through Peter, is understood in an analogous fashion as *vicarius Christi*).

Christ's high-priestly ministry transcends the New Testament priesthood; and in a certain sense it transcends it to the same degree that it transcends the Old Testament priesthood. It is effectively the basis for the New Testament priesthood, which, however, is not at all the vicariate of Christ, but only a church institution, by virtue of Christ, of course. Unfortunately, this is directly contradicted by the definitions of the councils of Florence and of the Vatican,[13] according to which the Roman high priest *"verum Christi vicarium esse* [is the true vicar of Christ]." Such hierarchical hyperbole, as applied to the whole of the episcopate, is encountered already among the early writers, beginning with St. Ignatius of Antioch, the Apostolic Constitutions, St. Ambrose of Milan, and elsewhere, not, to be sure, as an authoritative dogmatic formula but as a rhetorical clarification of the importance of the episcopal ministry in the Church. Unfortunately, this formula, perhaps not without Latin influences, was included in the Orthodox Confession (1, 58) and in the dogmatic manuals (M. Macarius, 2, par. 174; see infra).

If one examines the full dogmatic significance of the idea that Christ has vicars, whether a single vicar in the person of the pope of Rome, or an indefinite number of vicars in the persons of the bishops of the Eastern church, one gets a heavenly-earthly hierarchy, a ladder between heaven and earth. The aim of this idea is to elevate the earthly hierarchy by uniting it with the heavenly one, but this diminishes the true significance of the Head of the Body, Christ, who, we repeat, is not the head of a body (with which a hierarchy is most comparable) but the Head from, by, and in which the body exists — the Body of Christ. "Know ye not that your bodies are the members of Christ?" (1 Cor. 6:15). "Ye are the body of Christ" (12:27), and from the head the whole body "increaseth with the increase of God" (Col. 2:19), for "the body is of Christ" (2:17), "from whom [is] the whole body" (Eph. 4:16).[14]

Clearly, with regard to Christ as the head in the body of the Church there can be no question of succession or of any kind of vicariate. This is a rhetorical exaggeration which, when taken literally, leads to misunderstandings and even to outright errors, to a hierarchical anthropotheism and even to sectarian exaltation, which indeed constitutes the unconscious mysticism of papism: *vicarius Christi,* Christ on earth. It is precisely against such an inclusion of the God-man in history, by the confusion of different planes of being, noumenal and empirical, that the Lord said: "Then if any man shall say unto you, Lo, here is Christ, or there; believe it not" (Matt. 24:23; Mark 13:21; Luke 17:23).

13. Denzinger, *Enchiridion,* 694, 1832.

14. It is not difficult to see that the scriptural comparison of Christ with the head and the Church with the body has a double meaning: In some cases Scripture indicates the central, guiding significance of the head in the life of the body and its members; in other cases it signifies that Christ as the head determines and contains the body, is the life of the body.

However, the idea of *vicarius Christi* is so hard to swallow that even its authors do not apply it consistently but use it as rhetorical ornament or hyperbole. But alongside this idea, or rather in lieu of it, there is placed another formula, one that sounds more likely: Bishops are the successors of the apostles. In the Roman church, this idea receives a narrow but concrete expression: the true and direct successor of all the apostles in the person of Peter is the bishop of Rome, through whom the apostolic succession of the whole episcopate is linked and confirmed.[15] To this paradoxical but precise formula the Eastern church opposes the more diffuse and historically hard-to-prove idea of the apostolic succession of the whole episcopate. Clearly, in contradistinction to Rome, it is supposed here that all the apostles, in different places, consecrated their successors by the laying on of hands, and that this consecration, proceeding to our own day, is the so-called apostolic succession. Through this consecration the original apostolic hands are laid on all the bishops, as it were, and through this one universal consecration the episcopate arises *in solidum* (St. Cyprian), indivisible, one in its source, and having all its power in each of its members. This idea of the origination of the hierarchy directly from Christ (however, to be consistent, one should apply it to the *whole* hierarchy, not only to the episcopate) can be accepted only in a *general* form, by no means in the sense of the vicariate of Christ or even in the sense of *direct* apostolic succession — in its two variants, Roman and Eastern.

The Lord established such a vicariate neither for the apostle Peter (to think that He did is a mistaken interpretation of Matt. 16:18-19) nor for the apostolate as a whole. The hierarchy in its present form was established by the *Church* and in *this* sense — but only in this sense — it is a historical institution. This means that the Church as the body of Christ, animated by the Holy Spirit, accepted this institution in order to develop and actualize the hierarchical-organic principle proper to her.[16] This hierarchical-organic structure of the Church must be understood in all its fullness, not only in the aspect of hierarchical organization but also in the aspect of that organic connection about which the apostle said:

---

15. As is well known, the Vatican council did not give a precise definition of the episcopate, and this point therefore requires dogmatic clarification. One hopes that this imprecision will turn out to be salvific for a future clarification.

16. See A. P. Lebedev's article "Primitive Christian Hierarchy: Its Origin *(Ierarkhiya pervokhristianskaya: Ee proiskhozhdenie)*," in *The Orthodox Encyclopedia*, 8:673-86. The opposite point of view on its origin is expressed in I. P. Troitsky's article "Hierarchy," op. cit., 6:255-64.

that we . . . speaking the truth in love, may grow up into him in all things, which is the head, even Christ: from whom the whole body fitly joined together and compacted by that which every joint supplieth, according to the effectual working in the measure of every part, maketh increase of the body unto the edifying of itself in love." (Eph. 4:14, 15-16)

This idea can be expressed as follows: in the body of Christ, the hierarchy is not so much a power as a function and a ministry which exists alongside other functions and ministries. Therefore, one must first of all accept that, in this sense, the *whole* church, from top to bottom, is hierarchical, for the chief apostle said: "Ye also, as lively stones, are *built up a spiritual house, an holy priesthood,* to offer up spiritual sacrifices, acceptable to God by Jesus Christ. . . . Ye are a chosen generation, a royal priesthood, an holy nation, a peculiar people" (1 Pet. 2:5, 9). Only on the basis of the principle of universal royal priesthood, of the hierarchism of the *whole* Church, can one understand and accept the *distinction* of the hierarchical functions, and avoid that exaggeration owing to which a clerical absolutism creeps in. This clericalism subverts the very principle of ecclesiastical hierarchism and divides the Church into two parts: the rulers and the ruled, the teachers and the taught, those who command and those who obey.

It is to justify such a conception that dogmatic fictions of the vicariate of Christ and of the "apostolic succession" as power and the organization of power arise, contrary to the Lord's direct testimony:

And there was also a strife among them, which of them should be accounted the greatest. And he said unto them, The kings of the Gentiles exercise lordship over them; and they that exercise authority upon them are called benefactors. But ye shall not be so: but he that is greatest among you, let him be as the younger; and he that is chief, as he that doth serve. (Luke 22:24-26)

For Scripture it is not the institution of the primacy of Peter, or the apostolic primacy of the episcopate, but service, determined by the place of each member in the Church, that represents the fundamental norm of universal priesthood. This is the authentic "apostolic succession" in the Church, and denies any basis for clerical absolutism or "monarchic episcopatism" as manifestations of ecclesiastical hierarchism. Of course, it is not a question of denying or diminishing the rights and obligations of the hierarchical priesthood, but of interpreting it correctly. And the correct interpretation of the hierarchical priesthood excludes the idea of any kind of "vicariate" as the power of Christ *over* the Church and puts in its place the serving of the Church in its *sobornost*.

Even though the Old Testament hierarchism exists within the limits of the chosen people, the people of God, it has a much more rigid and legalistic character than the New Testament hierarchism. The Old Testament hierarchism effectively arises as God's direct institution, as a law given on Sinai. The Old Testament Church is instituted through this hierarchism, whereas, in the New Testament, hierarchism arises in the Church and through the Church. The Roman conception of hierarchy as vicariate, adopted also by the Eastern Church, approaches in its "juridicism" the Old Testament order. The Old Testament priesthood in Aaron and his sons arises by God's direct command, which singles out the tribe of Levites for the priestly ministry: they wear priestly garments, offer sacrifices in the tabernacle, and anoint with sacrificial blood: "I will sanctify the tabernacle of the congregation, and the altar; I will sanctify also both Aaron and his sons, to minister to me in the priest's office" (Exod. 29:44).

By analogy with the Old Testament priesthood the New Testament priesthood also came to be understood as an institution of the law, the instituter being Christ Himself (whence the idea of a legal vicariate). This priesthood thereby became opposite to that after the order of Melchizedek: "without father, without mother, without descent" (Heb. 7:3). Instead, it is proclaimed "after the order of Aaron." But "if therefore perfection were by the Levitical priesthood . . . what further need was there that another priest should rise after the order of Melchisedec, and not be called after the order of Aaron?" (Heb. 7:11). The New Testament priesthood exists by the power of Christ, conferred by the Holy Spirit. It is not the result of a succession from Christ considered as its high priest after the order of Aaron, as is erroneously claimed by the theory of the idea of the vicariate, Christ's vicariate or the apostolic one, the two merging in one common succession. On the contrary, this priesthood exists through a certain identification with Christ in his high-priestly ministry, by virtue of his Divine-humanity. Not only Christ's high priesthood but also the entire New Testament priesthood is given "after the order of Melchizedek," that is, in the image of Christ. This ministry is given by virtue of the Divine-humanity of the Church. It is not an institution but supreme reality itself as the universal royal priesthood.

True, to organize this universal priesthood the New Testament Church too has an established structure, which has arisen in history in the form of different hierarchical levels, with the episcopate at the head. But this hierarchy arises only on the basis of the universal priesthood, in which Divine-humanity as the priesthood of Christ is expressed. The universal priesthood is the *prius* (the first condition) of the episcopate, not vice versa. The episcopate is not a supreme hierarchy which reproduces itself on the basis of a vicariate after the order of Aaron. The succession of laying on of hands, wrongly called the apostolic succession, is the manifestation of an already existing hierarchy, which knows neither an Aaronic nor a Levitical branch but arises "without father, without mother, without descent." Having arisen one day by God's will, on the unfathomable paths of church history, this hierarchy exists preserved precisely in this form. As such an institution, it represents the backbone of the church organism, so to speak; but while supporting the body, this backbone also belongs to and is generated by the body.

In brief, the schema of the Old Testament priesthood is as follows: The very existence of the Church is determined by that of the temple (the tabernacle) and of the priesthood, legitimized by God as a sacred institution, "after the order of Aaron." First the priesthood, then the Church. The schema of the New Testament priesthood is completely opposite: it is not instituted but proceeds from the priesthood of Christ and belongs to His Divine-humanity, which is precisely the Church. It is established as the historical realization of this principle, which is attested to by the fact that the three-level hierarchy (or, more precisely, the four-level hierarchy, counting the laity) appears in history not at the beginning but only in the post-apostolic age. The idea of the vicariate, as an Old Testament conception of the New Testament hierarchy, places the whole virtue of the latter in an instituted succession: in an attribution of power to a new order of Aaron and, through him, to a new branch of the Levites directly from Christ or indirectly from Him through the apostles. The persons thus invested are thereby placed *above* the people of God, are set apart as priests above those who are not of the priesthood and are alien to it. Their role is to sanctify the profane as an organ added to the body of the Church from above but also from outside. Opposed to this is the New Testament idea of the people of God, the royal priesthood, which is the priesthood of Christ and, as such, belongs first of all to the whole Church as the body of Christ. First the Church, then the hierarchy, not vice versa. As the body of Christ and the temple of the Holy Spirit, the Church is the *fullness* from which hierarchical ministry emanates.

The aforesaid, far from diminishing the significance of the hierarchy in the Church, even elevates it, since hierarchy is rooted in the very life of the Church as Divine-humanity, that is, in her sophianicity. This conception overcomes not only the Old Testament and Roman juridicism but also the occasionalism according to which hierarchy is considered as an external, though gracious, appendix to the life of the Church, but nevertheless as a kind of *deus ex machina*. In reality, the Church is totally hierarchical, and the hierarchy is only an organized manifestation of this hierarchicity, which is the very *being* of the Church and not only an institution.

It is important to examine the form of this institution which is usually defined as "apostolic succession" (leaving aside the "vicariate of Christ," an obviously unsuitable conception). In what sense should one understand this "apostolic succession"? What are its power and limits? First of all, it is a *tradition* in the broadest sense, coming from the apostles. This tradition includes not only the "commandments" given to the apostles by Christ through the Holy Spirit (see Acts 1:2), but the whole life of the Church, which began with the Pentecost, with its mysterious and unfathomable depth. This life in Christ by the Holy Spirit has not been interrupted since then and will not be interrupted as such, for Jesus Christ is "the same yesterday, and to day, and for ever" (Heb. 13:8).

This self-identity of the life of the Church, which lies at the base of the unity and continuity of the tradition, is also expressed outwardly in church institutions. But these institutions represent only a secondary manifestation of this unity of tradition. On this basis it is vain to seek institutions of a later origin (although of an indeterminate duration) in any period of history, and in particular in the apostolic age. This holds, in particular, for apostolic consecration by the laying on of hands as a way of communicating specific hierarchical gifts of grace. The laying on of hands is also encountered in the Old Testament, not only in the ritual consecration of sacrifices (Lev. 3:2; 4:4; 8:14; 16:21; Num. 8:12) but also in Moses' laying of hands, by God's commandment, on Joshua the son of Nun, "a man in whom is the spirit" (Num. 27:18-23). In the Acts of the Apostles the apostolic laying on of hands takes place during the election of the seven deacons (Acts 6:6), during the reception of the gift of the Holy Spirit in Samaria (8:17), and during Ananias's laying of hands on Saul that he might "receive [his] sight and be filled with the Holy Spirit" (9:17). And hands are laid on Barnabas and Saul as they are separated from "certain prophets and teachers" in Antioch ("for the work whereunto I have called them"): "And when they had fasted and prayed, and laid their hands on them, they sent them away. So they, being sent forth by the Holy Spirit, departed unto Seleucia" (13:1-4). Also, there is the instance of the apostle

Paul laying hands on the Ephesians, after which "the Holy Spirit came on them, and they spake with tongues, and prophesied" (19:6). That is all.

From this enumeration it is clear that the laying on of hands was not a special rite used for some definite purpose, namely, for the communication of a specific charisma to certain persons. Although, in general, this gift consists in a descent of the Holy Spirit, it does not have a sacramental specificity: It can consist of a sacrament of chrismation, performed through the laying on of hands (in Samaria and Ephesus); a healing (of Paul from blindness); consecration of Paul's departure together with Barnabas for a special ministry; or the consecration of seven deacons. And let us note that those performing the laying on of hands, besides the apostles themselves, include Ananias, "a certain disciple" of the apostles, while among the persons on whom hands were laid, we encounter the apostle Paul himself together with Barnabas. All these data scarcely attest to a rite of hierarchical consecration by the laying on of hands, which supposedly henceforth continued uninterruptedly in the "apostolic succession."[17]

From this one can deduce that the apostolic age knew neither the three-level hierarchy, which was instituted only during the second century, nor a rite of apostolic laying on of hands intended to communicate a *specific* hierarchical gift or to raise to a level of the hierarchy. More specifically, the apostolic laying on of hands can be interpreted as an ordination to the fourth level: the grace-endowed laity, the universal royal priesthood, with full right of entry into the Church (which is what the sacrament of chrismation signifies). The cases of Samaria and of Ephesus approach this.

Therefore, if it is possible to find the foundation of the "apostolic succession" in the direct tradition of the apostolic Church, this is only in the most general sense, not so much in the sense of an articulated hierarchy as in the sense of universal priesthood conferred upon the New Testament Church. The hands of the apostles are outstretched to consecrate all of Christendom as a universal priesthood, although each member of the Church is touched differently by their spiritual touch. For the different levels of the hierarchy this touching is effected by the sacrament of ordination, while for the laity it is effected by the sacrament of chrismation,

---

17. We find a certain indirect, though clearly insufficient, confirmation of this idea in a later text, 1 Tim. 4:14: "Neglect not the gift that is in thee, which was given thee by prophecy, with the laying on of the hands of the presbytery" [*tou presbuteriou*] (variant reading: *tou presbuterou*: of the presbyter). Also 5:22: "Lay hands suddenly on no man." At most, this indicates the general existence of the rite of the laying on of hands, without any explanation of its immediate meaning. Its usual sacramental interpretation depends on historical attraction, so to speak.

which elevates the laity to the rank of universal priesthood, giving the laity access to the sacraments and, first of all, to communion. In the West, the laying on of hands is performed by bishops, whereas in the East it is performed by priests, but with the chrism of consecration by a bishop. Thus, in the East too, chrismation remains an episcopal sacrament, by analogy with hierarchical ordination. The fact that, in a later period, the apostolic laying on of hands is differentiated into the ordination of three priestly levels should not obscure for us the original sacramental amorphousness of this act. It is erroneous to think that, at the present time, "apostolic succession" is proper to the episcopate alone (or together with the clergy) and therefore does not at all extend to the whole body of the Church. On the contrary, this gift is just as universal as the gifts of the Pentecost, which are diverse even though the Spirit is one.

The formation of the hierarchy is connected, as we indicated above, with the institution of the rite of the sacraments and, in particular, of the Divine Eucharist. The Divine Eucharist, which was directly instituted by Christ, did not have a fixed liturgical form in the early Church as regards the mode of its celebration or its celebrators. The Divine Eucharist is simply called the "breaking of bread," which appeared right after the Pentecost (Acts 2:42; cf. 20:7). (The same absence of form, which becomes a state of disorder censured by the apostles, is noted also in 1 Cor. 11:20-22.) Scripture does not say anything about the hierarchical position of the celebrator of the Eucharist. Addressing himself during his absence to the Christians of Corinth (1 Cor. 10:16), the apostle Paul asks them: "The cup of blessing which we bless, is it not the communion of the blood of Christ? The bread which we break, is it not the communion of the body of Christ?" These indications are supplemented by the picture we find in the *Teaching of the Twelve Apostles,* a work that retains traces of the original absence of form of the liturgical rite as far as the celebrator was concerned, since the bread could be broken equally by evangelists, preachers, and prophets.

The conviction that the Eucharist must be celebrated by the bishop, or, in general, by the hierarchy, begins to crystallize only in the second century. This conviction is the object of a particularly insistent sermon of St. Ignatius of Antioch, who clearly considers it something new and far from indisputable, as we can see from the theological imprecision of the definitions he gives for the different hierarchical levels. Later on, this imprecision begins to be replaced by the idea of the exclusive apostolic succession of the hierarchy and its central importance in the Church, until we finally get Cyprian's *episcopus in ecclesia* and *ecclesia in episcopo.* But precisely this course of the historical emergence and development of the episcopate makes clear that the latter becomes, first of all, the organ of the regular, orderly celebration of the Eucharist. This is the *potestas clavium* (or *sacramentalis* in general) out of which, as out of a seed, the entire episcopal-hierarchical system developed. Of course, such a formal constitution of the eucharistic sacrifice was necessary and beneficial on the paths of ecclesiastical history. Like every self-determination of the Church, it is effectuated by the action of the Holy Spirit who leads her. Therefore, the fact that the hierarchy was formed after the apostolic age should not serve as a pretext for antihierarchical affirmations, such as those arbitrary attempts to restore the Church's initial state that were characteristic of the reactionary utopianism associated with Protestantism's notion of "primitive Christianity." Under the pretext of primitive-Christian freedom, Protestantism can, in its own way, produce a clericalization of the Church that is the equal of that produced by the three-level hierarchy. In general, the hypertrophy of hierarchism that may be connected with the character of one historical epoch or another (our own being an example) is an accident. It does not belong to the substantial being of the Church.

Thus, hierarchy comes into being as a function of the regular celebration of the sacraments, and in the first place as a function of the celebration of the Eucharist, which is the "remembrance" established by the Lord himself, "till he come" (1 Cor. 11:26), as *sunkephalaiōsis tes holes oikonomias tode to musterion,* the recapitulation of our salvation.[18] The formation of the hierarchy is thus associated with the formalization of the celebration of the Eucharist, although the latter existed prior to and independently of the hierarchy. Originally, the "breaking of bread" was performed by the Church in the person of the *proestos.* This was not a permanent function of his, but was evidently a task he took on because of his personal authority or position in the Church. In the consciousness of the faithful, it was the *Church* that had primacy, as their gathering. It is precisely this idea that is expressed in Acts 2:42, where the New Testament Eucharist is first spoken of: "in . . . fellowship [*te koinōnia*], and in breaking of bread, and in prayers." The koinonic character of the celebration of the Eucharist, which was virtually forgotten by the later ecclesial consciousness, was, according to the Acts of the Apostles, primordial. The crystallized hierarchical order of the koinonic act came later and was derivative.[19]

18. Theodori Studiti, *Antirr. I adv. Iconomachos,* PG 99, col. 340 c.

19. Gregory Dix speaks justly about this later "clericalization" of the Eucharist in his article "The Idea of the 'Church' in the Primitive Liturgies" in *The Parish Communion,* London, 1937.

One should always remember that, although the Eucharist is one of the "seven" sacraments (according to the present count), it actually has a significance that is greater than that: It is the sacrament of sacraments, the central sacrament of the Church. In the later consciousness, first in the Western Church, primarily in Protestantism, the Eucharist is transformed into the sacrament of communion, and its sacrificial significance is even denied. In any case, the significance of the Eucharist is diminished by the fact that it is conceived dually: as sacrifice and as communion, that is, as two (albeit connected) operations, not as one complex act. (This feature of Western theology has been adopted by Eastern theology to a certain degree.)

The Holy Eucharist is given by the Lord *"in remembrance of me"* (1 Cor. 11:25). First of all, *in sensu realissimo,* the Eucharist is the power of the Incarnation,[20] the realized and abiding Divine-humanity, including all the faithful: "we being many are one bread, and one body: for we are all partakers of that one bread" (10:17). The Divine Eucharist is the abiding of Christ in the world, His connection with the world, *despite* the ascension: "I am with you alway, even unto the end of the world" (Matt. 28:20) by the Holy Spirit, sent by Him into the world from the Father: "And I will pray the Father, and he shall give you another Comforter, that he may abide with you for ever. . . . I will not leave you comfortless: I will come to you" (John 14:16, 18). But this abiding will be mysterious: "the world seeth me no more, but ye see me; because I live, ye shall live also" (v. 19). This mysterious abiding of Christ in the world through the Divine Eucharist[21] lasts "till he come," when the mysterious "remembrance" will be replaced by the new coming of the Lord and the abiding with Him: "and so shall we ever be with the Lord" (1 Thess. 4:17).

Communion with the body and blood is therefore *not yet all* that the Eucharist signifies as the divine "It is finished" (John 19:30), as the sacrificial and abiding Incarnation. It is the sacrament of sacraments, the foundation of all the sacraments, and its accomplishing power is the Pentecost, the coming into the world of the Holy Spirit, who "shall teach you all things, and bring all things to your remembrance, whatsoever I have said

---

20. This idea gets an original expression in Pseudo-Dionysius, the author of the later Church doctrine of the sacraments (*De eccles. hierarchia,* c. III, I). He identifies the sacrament *sunaxeos eipoun koinōnias* as *teletōn telete,* the sacrament of sacraments, the crowning sacrament. [. . .]

21. But it is not exhaustive, for there is also the direct presence of Christ in the world through the blood that poured out of Him and remains in the yet untransfigured world (see my article "The Holy Grail").

unto you" (14:26). "In remembrance of me [*anamnesin*]" and "to bring . . . to your remembrance [*hypomnesei*]" are closely connected, which is expressed in the fact that the "breaking of bread" appears in the life of the Church only after the Pentecost, as the accomplishment of Divine-humanity.

Thus, originally, in the apostolic age, the Divine Eucharist as the basis of all the sacraments was exclusively that which it is as the realization of the body of the Church as the body of Christ. Its essential character was not hierarchical but koinonic. That is, its character was one of sobornost, but this character was replaced as early as the second century by hierarchism, which, of course, did not completely eliminate it, but was capable of obscuring it. How this happened has to be explained by church history. Even today this transition remains an enigma for church history for want of sufficient factual data. (This makes it easy for some to dogmatically postulate the primordiality of the hierarchy, and for others to dogmatically interpret its emergence as the original sin of the historical Church, as a decline of spirituality.) In any case, we already see in St. Ignatius of Antioch the *postulate* of hierarchy as the organ of the sacrament: "Only that Eucharist must be considered *true* which is celebrated by the bishop or by one named by the bishop himself to celebrate it. . . . Without the bishop one is not permitted to baptize or to celebrate the agape."[22]

Neverthless, the reason for this need to organize eucharistic life, the reason for the necessity of a hierarchy and of a liturgical rite, is now clear to us. The Divine Eucharist is a sacrament that must have an ecclesial guarantee for its "authenticity," which distinguishes it from false, emotional ecstasy and anticommunal, non-koinonic ("montanistic") exaltation. The Eucharist could not remain the sole property of the "prophets" but became a ministry of the priests. "Fellowship and the breaking of bread," koinonia as Eucharist, had to produce hierarchical crystals, which later formed an entire hierarchical system. "Sacrament" is precisely characterized by the invisible in the visible, by the gift of grace given in connection with a visible sign. And a specific celebrator is attached to the visible sign.

But this feature was not equally applicable to baptism, even though it was also instituted by the Lord as an "evangelical sacrament." Even at the present time baptism remains much more a sacrament of the universal priesthood (although the words of the Lord were addressed directly to the apostles, the latter are clearly considered here as representing all of

22. St. Ignatius of Antioch, *Ep. Smyrn.*, 7, 8; cf. *Ep. Philad.*, 4.

Christianity). With the appearance and consolidation of the eucharistic hierarchy, baptism too was, of course, regulated by the latter.[23] But even at the present time, baptism can, in case of need, also be performed by the laity if certain requirements are met (even without distinction as to sex, at least in Orthodoxy). In this respect baptism is the first of the sacraments: it gives birth in Christ; it brings the neophyte into the Church as the body of Christ; and the fact that it is a sacrament of the laity makes it the exception among the "seven" sacraments.

This exception is highly significant: it is not a disciplinary or ritual indulgence, but a living testimony to the original, pre-hierarchical state of the universal priesthood of the people of God, out of which an express hierarchy of sacraments had not yet been crystallized. But it is perfectly natural and inevitable that, having emerged as the sign of the "true" Eucharist, the hierarchy should have claimed for itself the exclusive power to celebrate other sacraments too as they appeared and were formally constituted. It would be strange to imagine that side by side there could have existed not one but several hierarchies: one for the Eucharist, another for baptism, a third for chrismation, and so on. Once it arose, the hierarchy became the organ for the celebration of all the sacraments, so that the very definitions of the Church which appeared for the first time (as is highly typical) in the symbolic books of quasi-antihierarchical Protestantism and which penetrated thence into the formulae of other confessions, indicate, among the essential features of the Church, the legitimate celebrators of the sacraments *(ministerium* or *sacerdotium)*.

We will not examine here the history of the individual sacraments or the question of their biblical or patristic foundation. However, one can affirm different origins for each of them. Historically, they arise not at the beginning (according to the Tridentine myth) but gradually, some earlier, others later. They differ in their significance and in their application: some are repeatable (communion, repentance, unction, even marriage), whereas others are unrepeatable (baptism, chrismation, priesthood). Some are universal (baptism, chrismation, repentance, communion), whereas others refer only to particular persons or situations (priesthood, marriage, monasticism). Some can be seen as direct institutions of Christ (baptism, communion, and repentance to some degree), whereas others do not have this privilege (chrismation, marriage, priesthood, unction).

Further, we must not judge the significance of the individual sacraments in the abstract, considering them equal units that form the sacred

23. St. Ignatius of Antioch. See above.

number *seven*. Rather, they are the different concrete organs of a spiritual organism, whose common basis is the Eucharist as the sacrament of sacraments, the sacrament of the Incarnation and the Pentecost, the sacrament of Divine-humanity. One must also affirm as a perfectly obvious fact that to limit the number of sacraments to seven ("not more and not fewer") — as has been done by Latin theology and then by Orthodox theology — is possible neither historically (the seven sacraments in the East as well as in the West date only from the twelfth or thirteenth century) nor in a de facto way, since the sphere of the sacramental life is wider than seven sacraments. It includes an indefinite domain of *sacramentalia*.[24]

All the sacraments and many of the *sacramentalia* are characterized by the fact that *grace* is communicated through them. A legitimately celebrated ecclesial sacrament guarantees the authenticity or objectivity of this gift of grace. In this sense, a sacrament is a divine act, connected with a certain visible sign, *ex opere operato*. The gift is given, and then it is appropriated, *ex opere operantis*, by a personal effort. This dual act, *ex opere operato* and *ex opere operantis*, represents a special form of synergism, proper to the reception of the sacraments: the divine gift of grace is freely appropriated, to different degrees, or it is not appropriated at all by its recipient.[25] This synergic character of sacrament removes the element of *magic* that is sometimes ascribed to it by those who do not understand the free appropriation of the gift of grace. True, this appropriation does not always occur at the exact moment when the sacrament is conferred (as in the case of sacraments conferred upon children: baptism, chrismation, communion). However, even here, the appropriation begins in the original act, although full appropriation is delayed or extended over a period of time.

The same thing can be said about the effect of the gifts of grace conferred by all the sacraments: their divine action is instantaneous, but the appropriation of this action takes place over an indefinite period of time, depending on human freedom. In fact, it essentially takes place over an entire lifetime, as is the case with baptism, chrismation, priesthood, and marriage, which, in general, are sacraments that are celebrated but once.

24. Some of them (tonsure, burial) were originally included among the sacraments. Others (sanctification of the waters of baptism, the consecration of churches, of icons, etc.) must also be included among them. By contrast, in the impoverished mystical life of the Protestant world, the number of sacraments has been reduced and limited, which introduces a new divergence in Christianity, but a divergence whose dogmatic significance is sometimes exaggerated.

25. Does the apostle Paul not attest to this synergism with reference to the sacrament of the Body and Blood in 1 Cor. 11:26-30? [. . .]

And it even takes place beyond life, in eternity. In this sense, although the gift of sacrament has a specific nature, it is not limited to and determined by this nature but generally extends to a person's entire being, transfiguring and guiding him. There is no sacrament whose action does not extend directly or indirectly to the entire life of a human being. The various sacraments are only channels through which the one water of life, divine grace, flows.

Therefore, a quantitative scale, the fullness of their number, cannot be applied directly here in the sense of "the more, the better"; for besides the *opus operatum* there is also the *opus operantis,* different forms of the reception and appropriation of the gift of grace. That is, it is again a question of synergism. The determinacy of the sacramental-hierarchical institutions, as well as of the gifts of the various sacraments, does not yet signify a corresponding determinacy of the appropriation of these gifts and their fruits. The possibility of grace must yet become a reality in a human being's life. God gives and man receives. Whence comes the possibility of cases such as that of Cornelius, upon whom the Holy Spirit poured forth even before baptism (Acts 10:44-47): "The Holy Ghost fell on them, as on us at the beginning" (11:15). And, in this personal Pentecost before baptism, the fullness of the gifts of grace conferred by the sacraments was received.

3. The Limits of Sacramentalism

At the present time the Church is understood, first of all, as a sacramental-hierarchical organization, as the repository of the gifts of grace dispensed by the sacraments as *potestas clavium* or sacramental power. This power is tacitly identified with the Church herself, which in popular usage is frequently equated with the hierarchy. In no wise diminishing the immense value of the gift of sacramental organization, we must nevertheless say that such an identification is illegitimate and does not accord with the truth of Revelation. True, the Church really did institute such an organization and maintains it, but she is scarcely exhausted by it. We already know this from the New Testament doctrine of the Church (see above). As a mystical organism, as Divine-humanity, the Church is the noumen that serves as the basis of the sacramental-hierarchical organization. One cannot reject the necessity and significance of this organization without falling into schism and heresy, the heresy of the pneumatomachians and Quakers. As the repository of the gifts of grace, the Church is a given accessible to all. It is the divinely instituted path of the life of grace. One cannot transcend this path; one cannot montanistically subjectify it, empirically subordinating it to personal merits. Nor can one reject it in the name of personal freedom, which would be individualism. One should appropriately venerate the institutions of the Church. But one should not think that the power of the Church and its action in us are exhausted by "seven" sacraments, "not more and not less."[26]

About what gifts of the Spirit does 1 Corinthians 12 speak (just after the story of the institution of the Divine Eucharist in the preceding chapter)? About the gifts of grace, of course. But does it speak about sacramental gifts? No, not at all, for one would scarcely be justified in speaking of instituted sacraments in the apostolic church. Indeed, to what sacraments do the gifts of the Spirit correspond, the gifts of the word of wisdom, the word of knowledge, faith, the gifts of healing, the working of miracles, prophecy, the discerning of spirits, divers kinds of tongues, the interpretation of tongues (see 1 Cor. 12:8-10)? And does the Church have a hierarchy to which the bestowal of these gifts could be referred? And to what hierarchical levels can one refer this divine institution *"in the church"* of apostles, prophets, teachers, possessors of the gifts of miracle-working, healing, assistance, diversities of tongues (vv. 28-29)? This is not even an exhaustive list, but only one that indicates the diversity of gifts, ministries, actions, and manifestations of the Spirit, who is "one and the selfsame" (v. 11). All these manifestations are not subject to any sacramental regulation, which would constrain "invisible gifts with an external sign." For these gifts the guiding principle is that the Spirit "bloweth where it listeth" (John 3:8), for "God giveth not the Spirit by measure" (John 3:34). Absence of law is the law for such manifestations of the Spirit. The synergistic structure of sacrament appears in these manifestations: the gift of the Spirit and its reception. However, the power of this giving is not conferred upon anyone sacramentally; it remains in the hands of God, as a direct, continuing Pentecost.

If this fact is linked with Christ's "ministries," it refers not to the "high-priestly" ministry but to royal and prophetic inspiration: "The Spirit of the Lord God is upon me, because the Lord hath anointed me to preach good tidings unto the meek; he hath sent me to bind up the brokenhearted, to proclaim liberty to the captives, and the opening of the prison to them that are bound, to proclaim the acceptable year of the Lord" (Isa. 61:1-2). "Verily, verily, I say unto you, He that believeth on me,

26. Cf. St. Augustine, *Contra epistolam Parmeniani*, 2, c. 15; PL 43, 76 [. . .]

the works that I do shall he do also; and greater works than these shall he do, because I go unto my Father" (John 14:12). These *non-sacramental* gifts are in the possession of the prophetic and royal Church,[27] not the hierarchical one. This is the power of Christ, made manifest in Christ's humanity, and it is the breath of the Holy Spirit, illuminating with fiery tongues the prophets chosen by the Holy Spirit.

This aspect of the Church's life can be neither described nor regulated, but it determines a specific content of this life. This breath of the Spirit marks the whole life of the original Church; it is the special mystery of primitive Christianity. But the breath of the Spirit also marks all the heroic periods and all the supreme achievements of the Christian spirit in the history of the Church. It marks Christian asceticism, teaching, and art, all these *opera supererogatoria,* which cannot fit in delimited sacramental-hierarchical forms. These are not sacraments in the strict sense, but operations of the mystery of inspired freedom, expressly protected by the apostle's injunction: "Quench not the Spirit. Despise not prophesyings" (1 Thess. 5:19-20). "The Holy Spirit gives all: it inspires prophecies, accompanies priests, teaches wisdom to illiterates, makes theologians out of fishermen, assembles the Church."[28] Prophecy is dynamics, movement in the life of the church, whereas hierarchism is its statics, its backbone.

St. Seraphim of Sarov said that "the acquisition of the Holy Spirit [i.e., prophecy] is the goal of the Christian life." Inspired illuminations embodied in the works of bearers of spirit attest to this New Testament prophetism, just as the creative achievements of the Christian spirit bear witness to the participation of the Church in Christ's royal ministry. The Spirit breathes here unfettered by the limits of the ecclesiastical organization. A depth of the Church that remains beyond these limits operates here; the partitions of the historical Church do not reach heaven. This lays the foundation for the special being of the Church as an ecclesial reality that is not subject to or regulated by hierarchy. This is the *Una Sancta,* the ever-continuing Incarnation and the ever-continuing Pentecost, the effective presence of God in the world and in humanity. This is the Divine Sophia: the "invisible" Church (that is, the Church that transcends direct knowledge), whose action, nevertheless, is manifested visibly as a mystery that is in the process of being revealed.

This mystery of the Church, this *Una Sancta,* is the prophetic force

---

27. On the enthronement of Christ in the world as the realization of his royal ministry, see *The Lamb of God,* chap. 5, 3.

28. From the Pentecost vespers.

that even now bears witness to the unity of Christ's humankind and draws the churches to return to the Church, to become reintegrated in the ecclesial unity of the Incarnation and the Pentecost, to overcome in the confessions the spirit of confessionalism that supplants the universal unity with ecclesiastical provincialism. Instead of the "mono-ecclesia," this spirit of confessionalism offers "heno-ecclesias." Instead of *Una Sancta,* it offers a "confession": that henotheism that, in the Old Testament and at the lower levels of the religious consciousness, replaced true monotheism.

Thus, there exists the *Ecclesia supra ecclesias,* the *Una Sancta,* as the foundation of *multae ecclesiolae.* It is obvious that there is no place for this idea in the notion of a Church that consists solely of hierarchical organizations, which can be divided and dispute among one another concerning their reality or their substance. Recognizing all the relativity and pragmatic significance of these divisions, we must nevertheless examine them in the light of that supra-empirical, noumenal *unity* of the Church which exists in her prophetic-royal aspect but which also summons us to sacramental-hierarchical unification. In this aspect the Church is turned both toward the contemplation of heaven and toward the distances of history, the horizon where heaven and earth touch. And on this heaven-to-earth, divine-human path of the descent of the Holy Spirit, Christ comes once again in His glory.

This universal character of the Church as the universal-human body of Christ is also confirmed by the fact that Christ, in His own words, will judge "all nations" (Matt. 25:32) at the last judgment; and in all those who are judged, as the basis for the judgment, He will witness His own presence, that is, their participation in the body of Christ. Here the humankind that communes with Christ cannot fit within the limits of even all the Christian confessions put together. Nor can such other New Testament figures of the Church as the woman clothed in the sun, the bride, and the body of Christ be encompassed within the limits of the "confessions." Rather, they refer to the *Una Sancta.*[29]

29. It is typical that, in Revelation, even those of the "seven churches" that are marked by heavy sins related to the doctrine of faith are considered to belong to the supra-confessional *Una Sancta.*

4. Grace

Although the concept of grace is at the center of the doctrine of the Church, it does not have the precision and stability, either terminological[30] or theological, that one would naturally expect. The most general definition of grace connects it with the action of God in man. In this sense, grace is a supernatural gift, divine power and action in creaturely life; and as such, it is a free gift of God's mercy, *gratia gratis data,* as Augustine calls it. Generally speaking, theology has preferred to deal with particular questions relative to different types and applications of grace rather than with grace itself in its essence, with Western theology devoting much more attention to the doctrine of grace than Eastern theology;[31] numerous distinctions and classifications have been developed which have a predominantly pragmatic character. The substantive development of what can be called an ontology of grace has largely remained in shadow. But here we wish to focus our attention on such an ontology, that is, on a sophiological conception of grace.

Two aspects are naturally distinguished in the doctrine of grace: the sending down of grace by God's power and its reception by creation. The *relation* between these two aspects and their effects, as well as the foundation and ultimate goal of this relation, must become the object of a theological (or, more precisely, a sophiological) interpretation.

The doctrine of grace occupies a rather strange place in the system of dogmatic theology. Christology and pneumatology, and even ecclesiology and the doctrine of sacraments, are developed first. And then, as if out of a void, the doctrine of grace appears, as if it had existed apart from the aforementioned categories, as if it were something added on to them, not organically connected with them. Most notably, there is no clarification of the relation between the doctrine of the sacraments, the instituted communications of specific gifts of grace, and grace in general, which appears to exist independently of these gifts. If there is a connection between the two domains, it remains ungraspable and indefinable. One can only say that grace in general is the precondition, as it were, of individual acts of grace, which are the sacraments. The sacraments are the particular in relation to the general, and therefore the significance of the sacraments as the

---

30. In Scripture one can find no fewer than seven different meanings of this word (Katansky, "The General Doctrine of Salvation in Freedom" in *Khrist. Cht.,* 1900, 39 sqq.).

31. See the surveys in the collection *The Grace,* published by the Theological Commission of the Lausanne Conference.

normal but *not* unique paths of the communication of grace is *limited:* they lose the uniqueness and exclusivity that is attributed to them in a de facto manner in theology. If it can be defined at all in terms of sacraments, grace is the sacrament of sacraments, the supernatural action of the Church itself as Divine-humanity, as the body of Christ, in which the Holy Spirit lives. But this "sacrament" *sui generis* does not have *visible* signs or particular agents. It is the path of divine communication, on which the different sacraments are only separate points or episodes. The Spirit bloweth where it listeth, and as it pleases. Grace therefore refers not to the institutional church but to the mystical church. The doctrine of grace therefore cannot be encompassed by the doctrine of the Church as an external, canonical organization.

At the very threshold of the doctrine of grace one encounters the rather unexpected distinction between "natural" and "supernatural" grace. One usually passes by this fundamental distinction, the most essential one for the very notion of grace, as if it were clear and self-evident, whereas it actually contains the crux of the problem.[32] It is not difficult to see that there exists a fundamental difference between grace as a gift of divine life that is communicated to creaturely life and natural grace as a kind of *debitum* of nature (health for the body, talents for the soul, etc.). The first belongs to divine life, while the second belongs to creaturely life. Instead of speaking about natural grace, it would be better to speak directly about creatureliness, not only about its extra-divine being but also about its divine foundation, by virtue of which "we live, and move, and have our being" (Acts 17:28). This divine in the extra-divine, this power of God in creation, is the creaturely Sophia, the ontological foundation of all that exists. It is the world as the Wisdom of God revealed in creation. It is the divine image in man, who is the microcosm linking all of creation with God. It is the world of fleshless angelic powers. It is the whole fullness of creation, the "it was good" of Genesis.

In this connection, one can also speak of God's providence, of God's Wisdom *in actu,* protecting and guiding the world's being. This is the proper life of creation, watched over by God. One can also say that this is

---

32. In Western theology the criterion is the idea of *debitum naturae,* i.e., that which is proper to nature as such according to creation, whereas that which surpasses this refers to grace (see, for example, J. Pohle, *Lehrbuch der Dogmatik,* vol. II, 298, Paderborn, 1921) as *"das specifische Prinzip des absolut übernatürlichen in der Creatur* [the specific principle of the absolutely supernatural in the creature]" (Scheeben, *Handbuch der Kathol. Dogmatik,* 2, 250, Freiburg im Breisgau, 1925). [. . .]

the action of the Divine Sophia in the creaturely Sophia, in their identity and difference, in their mutual connection. This connection is never interrupted, never terminated, for otherwise the foundations of being, unshakably laid by God, the Creator and Almighty, would crumble away. "God understandeth the way thereof [of Wisdom], and he knoweth the place thereof. For he looketh to the ends of the earth, and seeth under the whole heaven" (Job 28:23-24).

Theology does not, in essence, know what to do with the category of "natural" grace. This category satisfies only the needs of scholastic classification. But, in fact, "natural" grace must occupy its legitimate place as the receptacle, the *ekmageion,* of divine grace, as well as the precondition for the ability of creatures to receive the latter. Between "natural" or creaturely being and supernatural grace there must be an ontologically positive relation, without which grace would be a *deus ex machina,* an ontological violence done to creation, and not the elevation of creation to its proto-image. In its sophianicity, creation contains the image, or imprint, of the divine principle of its being. Creation awaits and thirsts for the fullness of its proto-image, its "glory," which is given in the action of grace. Thus, the distinction between natural and supernatural grace expresses, in reality, the relation between the Divine and the creaturely Sophia, between divinity and the world in the process of its deification. In its different forms, grace is precisely this deification, or glorification, of creation, or (what is the same thing) its sophianization.

The existence of "natural" grace is a necessary precondition for the reception of grace in the strict sense. This reception presupposes in creation a *conformity* with divinity that is actualized in deification by grace. "Natural grace" is precisely the humanity that contains the image and likeness of God. In virtue of the divine image and likeness, human beings are called to Divine-humanity, which is the union of the two natures in Christ. Divine-humanity extends to all humankind, which possesses "natural grace" or sophianicity by its creation, and which also receives the divine life in Christ by the Holy Spirit. Grace is not something additional and adventitious. With the Incarnation and the Pentecost, it is Divine-humanity itself *in actu,* realized as deification in many forms and times.

All the aspects of grace and the modes of its bestowal have as their sole purpose and content the elevation of creatures to deification, the imprinting of the image of divinity in the creaturely likeness. Outside of this relation, in the absence of "natural grace," that is, in the absence of the conformity of creation with its Creator, such an imprinting would be an ontological coercion, just as impossible as the transformation of an ape into an angel or a stone into a human being. One should never forget that grace presupposes the synergism of creaturely freedom and divine action. It is not only given to creation; it is also received by creation — *humanum capax divini.* And since Divine-humanity in creation is the Church, grace is identical with the latter. The Church is the life of grace, "gratification," deification in process.

The creaturely image of God in its "natural grace" is characterized by perfection (the "it was good" of Genesis). This image is open to Divine-human life, to the reception of "grace" in the strict sense of the word; but even in its creatureliness it already contains the fullness of the image of God. As such, the creaturely image of God is not afflicted by a *status naturae purae* whose existence would require a certain *donum superadditum supernaturale* for its being, as Latin theology teaches. According to Latin theology, only through the addition of such a gift does *status iustitiae originalis* arise for human beings. But in their creatureliness, human beings are already *in statu integritatis,* in conformity with the creaturely Sophia as their principle, by virtue of which they are open to deification by grace. Catholic theology unnecessarily belittles this fullness of *natura pura* in its sophianicity and even conceives original man as intrinsically deficient and as consisting of two parts: a natural and bestial creature burdened with the flesh and a supernatural, superhuman *donum superadditum,* which balances the defectiveness of the first part. In other words, in himself, in his creatureliness, original man is not yet human but is humanized by an action from outside, by a *deus ex machina.* Moreover, this gift is taken away from him as a consequence of original sin.

This doctrine affirms an impassable chasm between creation as such, *in statu naturae purae,* and its divine proto-image, which participates in divine life. In himself, natural man remains closed to grace unless his nature opens up to it by a special action of God through a *donum superadditum,* this "super" signifying a violence done to the human essence, even if a salvific one. The very possibility of such a gift remains ontologically incomprehensible given the alienation from divine life that is proper to man *in statu naturae purae.* In general, man is a kind of paradox here: Created in an animal and corruptible form, he is immediately called to overcome this form in a supernatural (and therefore unnatural) manner. The action of grace is directed not at the deification of human beings but at the correction and fulfillment of their nature. Only after such a correction is the path to their deification by grace opened. Without need and without sufficient justification (since the biblical doctrine of the creation of man in the image of God does not provide such a justification), a second storey is added to the doctrine of grace. That is, the grace of creation is distinguished from the grace of deification: the gift of grace *during* the creation of man is distinguished as the condition for the gift of grace *after* his creation.

This duality introduces a further complication in the Catholic doctrine of grace, a complication that is expressed in the distinction between *gratia creata* and *increata,* in the recognition of two kinds of gifts of grace. It is asserted that, if grace is divine and if it communicates the gift of the Holy Spirit, then the capacity of creatures to receive this gift is established by a special, *creaturely* sanctifying gift,[33] which is a connection, a *vinculum,* a *gratia unionis.* In Christ, this corresponds to the hypostatic union of two natures, and in creation it is realized through "creaturely grace." This grace is distinct from God while uniting Him with creation, so that "creation becomes the living receptacle of God."

We must first examine this distinction between uncreated and created grace, the ontological essence of which is by no means sufficiently clarified by Catholic theology. The latter chiefly considers the practical significance of this distinction (as preparatory grace and accomplishing grace, as means and goal). What then does this strange notion of *gratia creata* signify, which is distinct from God but which, through a mediating function, realizes the *lumen gratiae?* What is this nonparticipation in the divine life,[34] this nondivine-divine being? This notion finds a place in the general composition of the Catholic doctrine of grace. It is based on the distinction and opposition between natural being and supernatural being, the being full of grace. Their relation is conceived as analogous to mechanical action, as a *deus ex machina,* a kind of ontological coercion. Grace is seen as something added to natural being, this addition already beginning with the creation of man.

Natural man as such, *in statu naturae purae,* does not even appear in the world in his defectiveness. And the very *natura pura* therefore remains only an abstract concept, without any real application in human life. The original Adam appeared in the world already completed by a supernatural gift of grace and therefore *in statu naturae integrae.* After his fall the *donum supernaturale* is taken away from him, and he abides in the state of fallen nature, *in statu naturae lapsae.* Subsequently, reborn by baptism, man again receives a supernatural gift as a kind of *infusio* of grace,[35] because of the merits that Christ acquired by His death on the cross *(causa meritoria).* By

---

33. *Summa Theol.* Ia, q. 43, a. 3.
34. See Scheeben, 1. c. 2, 374.
35. *Conc. Trid.* sess. 7, c. 7: Denz. 800.

virtue of these merits, man receives "not only the forgiveness of sins but also the sanctification and renewal of the inner man."[36] All this is conceived as an external action upon man without connection to him himself, to his proper nature (although *per voluntariam susceptionem gratiae et bonorum* is added). And, in order to establish this connection, to find a foundation for such a gift, a special gift is postulated that is solely intended for this mediation: *lumen gratiae* (Thomas Aquinas), as well as *lumen gloriae.*

We can clearly discern the special motive for establishing such a distance between created and uncreated grace: a middle term is sought between divinity and creation without which they could not be united, for they are considered as being deprived of a direct ontological connection. But a question arises: Is such a middle term sufficient? Is there not repeated here, *mutatis mutandis,* the theological temptation of Arius, who, seeking a middle term between God and the world, had also invented a kind of "created grace" in the idea of the created son? It goes without saying that such a middle term does not mediate anything, for it cannot avoid, at some ultimate point, a direct contact between divinity and creation. Its only recourse is to try to avoid such contact by erecting a multistorey structure of mediation. And to admit the possibility of direct communication of grace to human beings, is this not the same thing as to complicate it with the unnecessary and fruitless postulation of a special grace for the possibility of its reception?

In any case, the concept of created grace, *gratia creata,* is clearly contradictory: If it is a question of grace, a participation in the divine, a contact between creation and divinity, then it is inappropriate to speak of createdness. And if it is a question of natural powers and capacities, then one cannot speak of grace (at least in the supernatural sense). Between creaturely being and divine grace there is and can be no middle term. The very idea of such a middle term is only a misunderstanding, which can by no means resolve the difficulties one encounters when conceiving the connection between divinity and humanity, and half-measures do not help here. One must transpose the question to another plane. That is, one must seek to understand it sophiologically.

The question is as follows: In what way can man be capable of receiving grace, that is, of participating in the divine? What principle of human life makes him receptive to the divine, and what principle makes him closed to divine action or even provokes resistance to such action in him?

---

36. Ibid., 899.

Man's capacity for participating in the divine is the divine image, which is the very foundation of his being. This image is an unceasing call to deification, to the actualization of the power of Divine-humanity, to the sophianization of life, to the identification of the Divine and the creaturely Sophia. This identification has already been realized in the Church, which is the body of Christ and the temple of the Holy Spirit, the life in Christ by the Holy Spirit, the revelation of the Holy Trinity. This is the inexhaustible source of the grace-bestowing power of deification, which leads man from glory to glory.

That which Catholic theology describes by the invented concept *gratia increata* is precisely the image of God in man, man's sophianicity, which makes him open to sophianization, whereas *gratia creata* corresponds here to the creaturely Sophia, the sole difference being that *gratia creata* is not a special gift bestowed ad hoc like *gratia accidentalis,* but the very essence of a human being, his intelligible character *(gratia habitualis).*

It is precisely by virtue of this sophianicity of man, his conformity with God, that it is possible for him to be deified and to receive the Spirit. Sophianicity is the ontological *a priori,* or precondition, of this deification and reception. Man is capable of and summoned to deification; and he himself summons it. This quality of man's is what corresponds to "natural" or "created" grace, which Catholic theology justly seeks, but not there where it is. In the most general sense of this concept, grace is Divine-humanity or the Church, already realized in the Incarnation and Pentecost. Grace has innumerable modes of action and manifestation, and the natural sophianicity of creation constitutes the general condition of its reception.

Even within the limits of the creaturely Sophia, or the domain of "natural grace," one can distinguish these different degrees of its action or manifestation in life. The diversity of measures of natural inspiration is not something mediumistic but corresponds to creative efforts, is the fruit of the synergistic union of freedom and nature. This synergism of nature and grace emerges even more clearly in the life of ecclesial grace. The nature of fallen man *(status naturae lapsae)* has become heavy and has departed far from its original source. Its sophianicity has become dark. And the task of divine grace is not only definitive deification *(gratia sanctificans* or *efficax)* but also the awakening of deification in man *(gratia praeparans).*

To be sure, it is impossible to make a clear demarcation here, for preparatory grace and sanctifying grace have the same source and content. They awaken and renew in man his proper image, "corrupted by passions," and help him in the battle he wages against sin for his spiritual existence. The threshold separating the life of the old man from that of the new man is such acts as the new birth or entry into the Church through the sacraments of baptism and chrismation.

Here for the first time man receives the power to become himself, to reveal his true nature. And his entire new life is actualized on paths of deification by grace, both through sacraments and without them, in multiple and multifarious ways. There is no limit to grace, for it is deification, actualized Divine-humanity, life in God, which is infinitely deep and will never end, not in this age, nor in the age to come. Man is an intermediary, communicating the power of grace to the whole world. Man is the prophet, king, and high priest of creation, leading it to glory, that is, to deification, when "God will be all in all." Therefore, the fundamental axiom of the doctrine of grace must remain its inexhaustibility and indefinability: "The spirit bloweth where it listeth, and thou hearest the sound thereof, but canst not tell whence it cometh, and whither it goeth" (John 3:8).

Grace is Divine-humanity in the process of being accomplished, the Church *in actu*. It is more all-encompassing than any of its manifestations, whether in the sacraments that dispense its separate rays or outside of them. From this alone it follows that the Church, understood as a sacramental institution or organization, does *not* coincide with or exhaust this more general notion of the life of grace. Saul was called by Christ not sacramentally but by a direct action; the gentile Cornelius experienced the appearance of an angel of God; the Old Testament Balaam prophesied outside the Church, as did Melchizedek and all the Old Testament heroes of faith upon whom grace was bestowed (see Hebrews 11).

In the New Testament Church, grace is not a special entering of God's power into the world for the express purpose of being communicated to man. It is only a manifestation and action of this power, which is already fully present in the world, through union with and life in Christ, as well as through the descent of the Holy Spirit into the world and His presence in the world. The treasure of grace as the fullness of life in Christ by the Holy Spirit cannot be increased as such. But the measure of the reception of its gifts differs, as the gifts themselves differ, although the Spirit is the same (see 1 Cor. 12:11).

In theology there arises the question of whether the entire Holy Trinity bestows sanctification by grace or whether it is bestowed only by its hypostases. The prevailing doctrine, in both Eastern and Western theology, is that the sanctification is due to the entire Holy Trinity. This signifies that the deification of creation, Divine-humanity, is accomplished by a trihypostatic action of the Holy Trinity, the participation of each hypostasis corresponding to its properties. The Father, as the hypostasis that reveals Himself while abiding in transcendence, sends into the world the two revealing hypostases: the Son and the Holy Spirit. Their combined action results in the *adoption* of man: "to them gave he the power to become the sons of God" (John 1:12). Having become brothers in Christ, the sons of God become sons, with Christ, of the Father by the Holy Spirit.

A further question arises: Is this deification a hypostatic union with Christ or with the Holy Spirit, or is it natural in character, realized through the participation of a creaturely hypostasis in divine life? Clearly, only a natural union, the participation of the human nature in the divine life, is possible. Otherwise, the creaturely human hypostases would be annulled, and grace would be bestowed according to the mode of the hypostatic union of the natures in Christ. But man's union with Christ, by which he acquires in Him his own hypostatic face, means not the abolition of his creaturely hypostasis but its transfiguration and illumination.

Just as impossible is man's hypostatic union with the person of the Holy Spirit, although some authors allow its possibility. The hypostasis of the Holy Spirit is not in-humanized but only humanizes; it accomplishes the union with Christ, makes man a bearer of spirit, transparent in his human selfhood. By grace it introduces his hypostasis into the trihypostatic love of the Holy Trinity, makes him a "god according to grace." We have a figure of such a work of grace, first of all, in the Mother of God, who in Her resurrection and glorification sits in the heavens "at the right hand of the Son." She is a creaturely hypostasis raised to and thus participating in the life of the three divine hypostases.

If sanctification by grace is not and can by no means be a hypostatic union of God with man, it is necessarily a natural union of two natures, divine and human, in the image of the union accomplished in Christ by the Holy Spirit. This grace-bestowing reception of divine life by man is accompanied by the presence in this life of its proper human hypostasis. This is the hypostasis of the Mother of God, as well as all the creaturely human hypostases in general. The hypostasis of the Mother of God hypostatizes not only *one* of the two natures of the God-man but, in this nature, also the nature of all human hypostases in general. In this is manifested Her significance as the Mother of the entire human race. This hypostatization of the human nature in the Mother of God excludes the possibility of the absorption of this nature by divinity, the possibility of the extinction of the proper hypostatic rays of this nature in the light of the Divine Sun.

But this natural union of man with the divinity of Christ opens the

302

way to deification, that is, to the reception of divine life in human life, to the participation of human life in the Divine. An essential distinction immediately emerges here: In the hypostatic union of the two natures in Christ, the human nature participates, without separation and without confusion, in the fullness of divine life, since "in him dwelleth all the fulness of the Godhead bodily" (Col. 2:9), and upon him the Holy Spirit reposes hypostatically. In creaturely humanity, this union of the divine and human natures, participation in the Divine, is accomplished from power to power and from measure to measure. This is the "eternal life" of creation, which is never exhausted and never attains its fullness. In this sense, it is creaturely eternity *(aeviternitas)* in contradistinction to divine eternity *(aeternitas)*. And because of this imperfection in the communion of creation with divine life, this union of the divine and human natures cannot be accompanied by the hypostatic union with divinity. Rather, it is only the natural, "Chalcedonian" union of the two natures in Christ and through Christ, where human life ("will and energy") "follows" (according to the definition of the Sixth Ecumenical Council) the divine life and is permeated by it from measure to measure.

Although grace, understood as divine-human life, does not signify the hypostatic union of creation with God, it not only does not exclude a *personal* communion with Him, but it even expressly presupposes such a communion. Divinity, or divine life, as Ousia or Sophia is inseparable from the hypostases, is hypostatized from all eternity. Therefore, in striving toward union with the divine life, a creaturely being cannot fail to encounter God *personally,* so to speak; and this encounter is not a hypostatic union of two natures but an encounter or union of hypostases, divine and creaturely. Such an encounter, or union, is accomplished in the life in God and in prayer, linking the action of God in man, the gracious life in God, to the hypostatic source of this life: "not I, but Christ liveth in me" (Gal. 2:20); "we are in him . . . even in his Son Jesus Christ" (1 John 5:20 and elsewhere). Similar things are said about the Holy Spirit: "The Spirit itself beareth witness with our spirit" (Rom. 8:16); "God hath sent forth the Spirit of his Son into your hearts, crying, Abba, Father" (Gal. 4:6). And similar things are said about the Father, before whose face the Son in prayer places — by the Holy Spirit — the sons of God, the sons of man. "Our Father!" In general, all the relations of man to God are *personal,* and this *personal* character, as well as the union of the natures, is embodied in prayer.

However, this hypostatic aspect of the relation of creation and the Creator is not unique and exhaustive. It is not even characteristic of *grace,* by which man comes into contact not with the hypostatic God but with divinity and receives a divine power from the latter. In general, creatures can communicate with God in different ways: in a personal manner and in an impersonal manner (which the Greek language expresses by the presence or absence of the article before God: by *ho Theos* or by *Theos*). To be sure, even in the impersonal case our relation to God does not completely lose a personal character, which cannot be totally eliminated even in theism, but it is deprived of the concreteness that is proper to it when we address the distinct hypostases or the Holy Trinity as the triune God. But beyond this personal relation there is also, so to speak, an indefinite manner of address, directed at God in general, at divinity, or Sophia. This is even more applicable to cases when all of God's creation is impersonally directed toward him, *prior to* or *apart from* man (for example, in the song of the three boys in the Book of Daniel, chapter 3, the noncanonical part, 51-90). In such and similar addresses to God, the inner accent falls not on the person but on the essence, not on a hypostasis of God but on His divinity.

Such precisely is our reception of grace. It is true that grace proceeds from the Father, the Son, and the Holy Spirit, from Unity in Trinity and Trinity in Unity. However, its gift can be un-hypostatized, impersonal, that is, a gift and not the Giver (the failed attempts of certain Catholic theologians to identify this gift with the Giver, the Holy Spirit,[37] only confirm this truth). If we allow that grace is not only bestowed by the Third Hypostasis but in fact is this hypostasis, we abolish this hypostasis by equating it with its own nature, as an impersonal gift. And when we attribute to the Third Hypostasis alone the power to dispense the gifts of grace, which proceed from the divine nature or divinity, we introduce a differentiation in the one divine ousia. But against such a differentiation of the divine ousia into hypostases, one must again affirm the *consubstantiality* of the Holy Trinity and the perfectly equal participation of all the divine hypostases in the one divine nature, which is the sole source of grace (of "energies"), the Divine Sophia. From this point of view it is impermissible for any one hypostasis to possess something that another hypostasis does not possess. To be sure, it is true that each hypostasis has this one nature according to its hypostatic character, and that the gifts of the one divine essence are determined as a function of this hypostatic distinction.

In Divine-humanity as a revelation of the Holy Trinity, the *actualization* of the gifts that God bestows upon creation is proper precisely to the Holy Spirit. The Holy Spirit is the Dispenser, but the gifts bear the stamp

37. See Petau, *Dogm. theol.* 3, *De trinitate*, 8, cap. 6.

of all three hypostases (cf. 1 Cor. 12; Rom. 12:6-8). The Father is revealed in the Son, and life in Christ is actualized by the Holy Spirit. If the content of divine life is defined in the Son, this life becomes a reality for us by the Holy Spirit. One can say that, in this sense, we have Christ by the Holy Spirit, and thereby become children of the Father. We do not know God nonhypostatically, in the separation of the divine nature from the hypostases. In our experience of grace, we most directly know the person of Christ, the God-man. But the grace of deification is, nevertheless, not a hypostatic revelation of God; rather, it corresponds to the nature of God, divinity. In other words, this is the Divine Sophia, the heavenly prototype of humanity, which is being actualized in creation.

Bearing the image of the creaturely Sophia, man finds in this image the call or the postulate of the deification, or sophianization, of his being. Grace is not a divine coercion over the human nature; it is not something accidental, something alien to man, that does not have to be, that exists only as a kind of happy caprice. On the contrary, grace is the actualization of the Divine-humanity of which the seed was implanted in man by virtue of his creation in the image of God and which was accomplished through his communion with God in the Incarnation and the Pentecost. Grace gains this power in the gradual and unceasing approach towards one another of the divine nature and the human nature. In grace, man knows and realizes the foundation of his proper being. "Not I, but Christ liveth in me" (Gal. 2:20), by the Holy Spirit, who unites God with man. Life in Christ is given to man, and it is also proposed to him as a goal; he is a temple of the Holy Spirit.

Thus, *grace* is not something special that is offered to man alongside or outside the Incarnation and the Pentecost. Rather, it is the gift of the Incarnation and the Pentecost. It is Divine-humanity in the process of being accomplished. But Divine-humanity cannot be accomplished by a unique, exhaustive act, as it was on the part of divinity by the descent of the Second and Third Hypostases into the world. As an inexhaustible and eternal principle, Divine-humanity can be realized only a multiple number of times and in multiple forms, in individual gifts and manifestations. One of the most important paths of such manifestation, a path connected with definite forms and external institutions, is sacrament, but this is not the sole path. Furthermore, every gift of grace, even if it is specially qualified by a definite sacrament, has the capacity for growth through the faith and love of its recipient, *ex opere operantis.*

Thus, in relation to Divine-humanity, grace is not a new *what* but only a kind of *how.* The different aspects of the doctrine of grace, its classification, are only a scholastic attempt, imperfect and doomed in advance to fail, to define the paths of this participation in the divine. Nevertheless, such attempts can sometimes have a certain practical utility, both theological and pastoral. But the nature of grace is such that it belongs completely to the one universal sacrament of sacraments: the Sacrament of the Church. There is the Church as an essence, and not only as the "society of the faithful"; and there is grace as the manifestation of this essence.

On this basis, one can resolve the question of the necessity of grace in the dispute between orthodoxy and Pelagianism. The argument between Pelagius and Augustine revolved around the question of whether grace is necessary for salvation. The theological ground for this dispute had not been prepared in advance, since there was no general doctrine of the essence of grace. Each party advanced a deficient, one-sided theory.

Pelagius powerfully affirmed what we considered above as *natural* grace, God's gift to man at creation. This gift essentially consists in the image of God in man, whereas His likeness (likening) is established by human creative activity on the basis of creaturely freedom. The affirmation of the necessity of human creative activity on the basis of freedom does not, in itself, contradict the teaching of the Church. The denial of the necessity of human creative activity would be more likely to contradict this teaching, for, in practical terms, it would mean the abolition of Divine-humanity. The fact that Pelagius so forcefully affirmed human freedom and, as a consequence, the power of personal responsibility and the necessity of asceticism is in complete accord with the orthodox doctrine of *synergism*. Human energy necessarily participates in the work of salvation, that is, in the assimilation of deification, even if the degree of this participation is diminished by original sin.[38] To recognize that human beings, even after the fall, are capable of moving freely toward grace, or of doing the natural good, represents a positive contribution to Christian anthropology.

However, Pelagius's doctrine (which, by the way, we know only from the polemical exposition of Augustine and his followers) appears not to take into account the power of original sin in man. As a result, it does not see the distance between the humanity of the fallen Adam and that of the

---

38. "We believe that, having fallen through transgression, man has been darkened and deprived of perfection and passionlessness. But he was not deprived of that nature and power which he received from the all-good God. For, in the contrary case, he would have become irrational, i.e., not a man. But he possesses the nature with which he was created, as well as natural power, which is free, vital, active; so that, by his nature, he can choose and do the good, and avoid and reject evil. . . . From this it is clear that the good done by man cannot be sin, for good cannot be evil" (*The Epistle of the Eastern Patriarchs*, art. 14).

New Adam; and the meaning of Christ's redemptive act and of the power of the Pentecost is lost. In general, Pelagius's doctrine thereby takes us back to pre-Christian stoicism: the power of human will and asceticism is considered self-sufficient, and the work of Christ has only the significance of an example.

However, one should not forget that Augustine's doctrine is also one-sided, although this one-sidedness is of an opposite character. It is the antithesis to Pelagianism, being polemically dependent upon it. In the first place, this concerns anthropology. Precisely in the polemic with Pelagius, Augustine made the doctrine of original sin all-powerful: original sin is seen as depriving man of the freedom to aspire to the good; it leaves only the freedom to do evil. Although formally Augustine tries to leave an appearance of freedom, it is for him only a subjective experience. Clearly, there is no basis here for synergism, and grace essentially coerces man, acting upon him inexorably and insuperably by an all-conquering delight. From this the doctrine of predestination is consistently developed, with all its fatalism, with all its conclusions, including the conclusion that Christ came to save only the elect (an idea that receives its definitive expression in Calvinism).

If the Pelagian thesis in the dialectic of the doctrine of grace proclaims that humanity is self-sufficient and grace has only an auxiliary significance, then Augustine's antithesis asserts not only the omnipotence of grace but also the complete passivity of man, who is only a plastic material, obedient to his fate. Although Augustine's influence was the key factor in the Church's rejection of Pelagianism, the extremes of his doctrine have by no means been accepted by the Church, either in the East (which at the time was ignorant of the Pelagian dispute) or even in the West. Even though the resolutions of the councils of Carthage and Arles rejected Pelagius's diminution of original sin and the power of grace, they by no means totally accepted Augustine's positive doctrine of the lack of human freedom and predestination. These latter aspects of Augustinism gained an undue power in the West in the post-Reformation theology, in the doctrine of salvation of Luther and especially Calvin. Augustinianism reigns supreme here even at the present time.

This dispute has bequeathed to us the general problem of the relation between freedom and grace and of the limits of the action of grace upon human beings. According to both Scripture and the patristic tradition, the entire life of grace of human beings is realized on the basis of its free reception as well as by virtue of its ceaseless and externally unbounded action. The relation between freedom and grace cannot be defined more precisely. This is understandable if we consider that this is a domain that, on the one hand, depends on human freedom and, on the other hand, is subject to an unfathomable and inexhaustible divine action. This relation has its principle and foundation in the Incarnation and the Pentecost as the accomplished Divine-humanity. Its development consists in the ongoing divinization of man by his participation in the divine and by his reception of grace. Its goal is the perfect deification of humankind, when God will be all in all. But it does not have an end, since deification is *eternal* life in God, which is inexhaustible and without end for ages of ages. But this eternal life in God always retains its initial premises: not only the difference between the Creator and creation, the unpassable distance between them, but also the freely synergistic relation between them. Creation is not abolished, is not consumed in divine fire, does not drown in the ocean of the divine depths, is not annihilated before God's magnificence. It remains in its creaturely identity, for it is posited to being by God and it itself posits itself to being in its freedom. That is the mystery of createdness, God's love for creation, to which creation responds with its own ardent love for God. This is the reciprocity of the love of God and creation, which is also a "synergism."

Personal self-consciousness illuminates the nature of creation but does not completely permeate it. This nature is a dark, hypostatically unilluminated given, an unconscious or subconscious domain which only partially and gradually enters into conscious life. Therefore, the action of grace in human beings not only touches upon consciousness but also takes place outside of consciousness, in the subconscious domain of corporeal and, in general, natural life. Relevant here are such Gospel images as the mustard seed, the leaven and the three measures of meal (Matt. 13), the seed cast into the ground ("the seed should spring up and grow, he knoweth not how" [Mark 4:27]), and so on.

Sometimes this "flame of things," or divine light, bursts out onto the surface of consciousness and illuminates it. This is the light described by St. Symeon the New Theologian and by the hesychasts, the "light of Tabor," the grace manifested to Motovilov by St. Seraphim of Sarov.[39] Even when these illuminations are related to a specific divine

39. Early in the nineteenth century, Motovilov, a Russian landowner who was visiting the monastery of Sarov, saw the "uncreated light" emanating from the face of the great Russian saint Seraphim. Motovilov's eyewitness account is reprinted in Pavel Florensky's *The Pillar and Ground of the Truth,* trans. Boris Jakim, Princeton University Press, Princeton, N.J., 1997, pp. 74-77. — Trans.

hypostasis, to Christ or to the Holy Spirit, they intrinsically remain impersonal; they remain manifestations of divinity, not of the divine hypostases. In this sense, they are sophianic, although, to be sure, divine grace, or Sophia, cannot be completely separated from the hypostases. This distinction between God as a triune hypostasis and divinity, or Sophia, was primarily what St. Gregory Palamas had in mind in his doctrine of the "uncreated energies," which, like lightning flashes of divinity, penetrate into the world. On the one hand, these energies are divine (cf. Palamas's formula: energy is God, *Theos*); on the other hand, they are indeterminately multiple or multiform, since their reception depends on the degree of the recipient's spiritual growth. But according to St. Gregory Palamas these energies remain nonhypostatic and, in general, are not hypostatically qualified. This can be partly explained by the unfinished character of his doctrine, where, in general, the relation between the hypostases in the Holy Trinity and the energies remains unclarified.

But creation's participation in divine life cannot be limited exclusively to this nonhypostatic grace. As a hypostatic entity, who always has a hypostatized natural being, man (as well as the angels) necessarily encounters God personally and receives him personally. It is therefore impossible to eliminate this personal element, entirely replacing it with the subconscious action of grace. Grace is received by a person and personally, although this reception does not exhaust its action. The personal principle cannot be eliminated from human life in general, and in particular it cannot be eliminated from the synergism between God and man that is accomplished in the action of grace.

Here one must underscore the importance of *prayer*, the direct contact between creation and divinity, the sacrament of the Name of God. Prayer is an essentially *personal* relation; it is directed from person to Person; it is built on a personal pronoun. True, despite this personal character of prayer, it is not always hypostatized. Prayer can be addressed not only to the different hypostases of the Holy Trinity or to the Holy Trinity itself, but also to God in general, that is, primarily to divinity, or the Divine Sophia. This only means that, in the consciousness of those who pray, the divine hypostases are never separated from the divine nature, or the Divine Sophia. Prayer is the simplest and most typical case of the action of grace, for in it there takes place an encounter or a union between divinity and the creature in the Name of God. And since true prayer, that of an ardent heart, cannot fail to be heard, this fact of being heard is the simplest form of the action of grace (we must add that the range of the action of grace is extended through the invocation of the saints, who are bearers and therefore intermediaries of grace).

The prayer that is addressed to God not only has a personal, hypostatized character, but it can also refer to a particular hypostasis (the Father, the Son, or the Holy Spirit) or to the Holy Trinity. Such prayer, as well as the grace that it bears, is thus hypostatically qualified. Such, first of all, is the Lord's Prayer, to the Father in Heaven, which the Lord taught His disciples. In this teaching we must distinguish not only the content of this prayer of prayers, which encompasses our whole creaturely being, but also the personal address to the Father, which bears witness that He is accessible to our prayer. This can be said with the same degree of certainty, although in another aspect, about our prayer to the Son of God, the "Prayer of Jesus," which expressly gives us participation in the divine and the gift of life in God. This can also be said, in yet another aspect, about the prayer to the Holy Spirit, who for us is the hypostatically transparent giver of God's grace. Finally, the prayer to the Holy Trinity, for us the most difficult prayer and almost unrealizable, is nevertheless prescribed for us by the Church as an expansion of the praying heart and its elevation to the heavenly abode, according to the Lord's words: "we [My Father and I] will come unto him, and make our abode with him" (John 14:23).

As the special sacrament of the Name of God, prayer signifies the hypostatic bestowal of the gift of grace. It thus differs from the grace of the sacraments strictly speaking with their nonhypostatic character. Prayer is addressed to the divine person or even to creaturely persons (the Most Pure Virgin, angels, saints), where the gift of grace is beseeched. Of course, the sacraments strictly speaking (together with the *sacramentalia*) are always accompanied by prayer, but the gift of grace has a specific character, proper to the given sacrament. Sacramental gifts are not direct actions of the divine hypostases but manifestations of the power of divinity, or the Divine Sophia, who communicates her deifying energy to creation through the creaturely Sophia.

The doctrine of the limits of sacramentalism necessarily includes the question of the *power* and *efficacy* of the sacraments conferred by heterodox confessions, that is, outside of Orthodoxy, which is the dogmatically and hierarchically intact Church and which therefore possesses the full power of the sacraments, *potestas clavium*. Are the sacraments that are performed outside of Orthodoxy efficacious? This question is answered in the affirmative by the practice of the Church, which recognizes that certain of the sacraments performed outside of Orthodoxy are unrepeatable and therefore valid (baptism, chrismation, ordination, marriage). Without going into particulars, we must note the most fundamental principle of this recognition, for to admit this principle at any one of its points is to pose the question of *ecclesia extra ecclesiam* in all its breadth. Even at the present time one encounters people who deny the efficacy of the sacraments outside of Orthodoxy (and who even use blasphemous expressions to describe them, such as "demonic communion"). But this is so incompatible with the view of the Church that it does not even deserve examination. Thus, we must not ask: Do the sacraments of the non-Orthodox have efficacy? Rather, we must ask: What is the degree of this efficacy? Can there be a *more or less* here, or is it necessary either to recognize the full validity of these sacraments or to reject them totally? Neither solution is possible without doing violence to the reality. Sacraments are conferred outside of Orthodoxy too, and not only *ex opere operantis,* being piously received by the faithful, but also *ex opere operato,* in virtue of the divine grace that is bestowed in them.[40] Therefore, one only needs to define the *degree* of the efficacy of the sacraments outside of Orthodoxy as a "confession."

The non-Orthodox view the sacraments as windows open to heaven, through which they in fact perceive it. Heaven is one; only the ways in which it is perceived are different. These different windows are, in practice, opaque for all other confessions, even though the same heaven is perceived through them. To a certain degree this mutual opaqueness has a disciplinary character, corresponding to the separation of the confessions or the "division of the churches" within the one Church. But this separation is a diminution for the confessions in general, since they cannot all be united at one sanctuary, as well as for the non-Orthodox in particular, to different degrees, according to the measure of their infirmity. We have no means by which to measure this diminution in relation to the fullness that is given to the Church, or that rather is a task she must accomplish, the goal being her universal unity. But one does not see any fundamental obstacle to recognizing that, although the efficacy of these sacraments has been diminished, they are nevertheless genuine conductors of the gifts of grace, that they are salvific sacraments, uniting their recipients with the body of the Church. Of course, the actual reception of these gifts by individuals, *opus operantis,* is a mystery of divine providence. But this recognition of the ways of salvation even outside the ecclesiastical organization (so essential for the "ecumenical" movement) has an exceedingly great fundamental significance. If it remains an axiom that *extra ecclesiam nulla salus* (there is no salvation outside the Church), then the idea of *ecclesia*

---

40. We find this affirmation in Augustine. See *Epist.* 89; PL 33, 312. [. . .]

clearly does not coincide here with the notion of a specific ecclesiastical organization but is broader than this notion and refers to the mystical body of the Church.

The problem of defining the relation between the *Ecclesia* and the *ecclesiae* (the Church and the churches) remains unresolved. This is one of the most essential problems of theology, especially in our time, though it must be admitted that Augustine had already struggled over it in his own way and left a number of guiding ideas. These ideas cannot be accepted in their entirety, since they contain a number of obvious contradictions, although, here too, theology has not taken a step forward since Augustine, remaining consciously or subconsciously subject to his exclusive influence. Augustine's point of departure was St. Cyprian's formula that there can be no salvation outside the Church.[41] But even he could not have considered the condition of being outside the Church to signify a total religious void; he did admit the possibility and the reality of faith, of baptism, and of the sacraments "outside the Church" (in the confessional sense of the word). At the same time, and this is a curious and incomprehensible fact, he denied that the gifts of the Holy Spirit and the forgiveness of sins are conferred by these sacraments. For Augustine the reception of a sacrament can result in salvation or in condemnation. But, in that case, what is this faith that does not save, this baptism and repentance that do not free one from sins, this Eucharist that is ineffective even though it is valid?[42]

When applied to the divided Christian world of our own time, this radical contradiction between Augustine's ecclesiology and his soteriology can lead to monstrous conclusions, from which some save themselves by inconsistency, whereas others simply shut their hearts to Christians of all "heterodox" confessions. When they use the word "Church," the Roman Catholics mean only the Church of Rome (they immediately become confused when it is necessary to consider the Orthodox Church, for example). The Orthodox, in turn, have in mind only the Orthodox Church, whereas the Protestant confessions, by reason of their provincialism, usually do not even pose these questions. Not even Roman Catholic theology[43] succeeds in consistently denying the efficacy of the sacraments and, in general, the *ways* of salvation in other confessions. This is possible

41. See *De gestis cum emer.;* PL 43, 695.
42. See *Contra Cresc.,* 1, c. 29; PL 43, 464.
43. We can find an exposition of different opinions on these questions in E. Dublanchy, "Église" (*Dict. de théol. cath.,* 4, 2, chap. 3, col. 2155-75). [. . .]

neither theoretically nor practically, as is demonstrated by the mutual recognition of at least certain sacraments (baptism, chrismation, priesthood, marriage) by different confessions. In defining this relation, one is obliged to introduce the notion of a relative recognition or nonrecognition of sacraments in other confessions, that is, a certain *more or less* (which distinction must first be established in relation to confessions that have preserved the hierarchy of the episcopal consecration or that have not preserved it).

But the same thing must be said about the canonical and jurisdictional boundaries of the Church. Because of its centralism, the Roman Catholic Church does not lend itself to such divisions (although history attests to such a possibility). By the Vatican decree, the Church of Rome made the canon of papal primacy its main dogma. In Eastern theology, one observes a similar tendency to give to ecclesiastical canons a significance that is equal to that of dogmas, which is an obvious exaggeration. Although canonical determinations must have a dogmatic basis, they have only an applied significance: Dogmas express the ontology of the Church, whereas canons correspond to her historically formed juridical organization. The canons have an applied character; and their application to concrete cases is thus not indisputable. From this arises the possibility of canonical and jurisdictional divergences bona fide within the limits of the same local church. These divergences are sometimes so acute and intense that they are capable of leading to the denial of the efficacy of sacraments outside of a given jurisdiction.

An even greater abstention from judgment is appropriate with regard to non-Christians. On the one hand, we know that Christ's Incarnation and the Pentecost are universal. Their efficacy extends to all people without exception; all humankind is the body of Christ. On the other hand, it pleases the Lord to shroud in obscurity the ways of salvation and the eternal destinies of those to whom, in our age, the holy gospel has not been revealed and baptism has not been given, which perhaps is not even their fault but ours. The Church does not judge those on the outside but keeps silent about them, leaving them to God's mercy. Her practical attitude toward them consists of the duty of preaching: "teach all nations, baptizing them" (Matt. 28:19). Also relevant here is "Christ's preaching in hell." The limits and the power of the Church are thereby extended beyond the visible aspect of earthly life. This shows even more clearly how difficult, and even erroneous, it is to try to define the exact boundaries of the Church by making them coincide with the boundaries of the ecclesiastical organization. We must say that, ontologically, these boundaries do not exist at all. To admit them would be to limit and diminish the power of the Incarnation and of the Redemption. The existing boundaries have not an absolute but a pragmatic character.[44]

44. We leave aside here the painful and acute question of *canonical* limits in the life of the Church and of "jurisdictions" — not because we deny their practical importance (which every one of us must take into account in his personal self-determination and conduct in the Church) but because they have no special importance for the problematic of ecclesiology. The canons are forms of ecclesiality, not its essence, as it appears to some who think in an Old Testament manner about the Church.

CHAPTER 6

History

Creation presupposes development, or becoming. In passing from potentiality to actuality, the world discloses the creaturely Sophia in itself. Although the world was fully created in "Six Days," this fullness is not yet a fully actualized one but is still only potential. All the possibilities of the world's being that are to be disclosed and realized are predetermined and included in this fullness. The creaturely Sophia is not only the foundation of the world's being but also its principle of energy. The life of the world is accomplished on the basis of its "laws" or energies; its "evolution" is the dynamic development of its statics. But, at the same time, the world belongs not to itself but to man, who is called to "have dominion" (Gen. 1:26, 28) over it, "to dress it and to keep it" (Gen. 2:15). He is called to humanize this natural world. The world is simultaneously the peripheral body of man, the domain of the psyche, and the arena of human spiritual activity, the object of human creative activity. Man is both a laborer in the world and its "master," as well as its artificer. The logos of the world is also the human logos, and the beauty of the world is also human beauty. Therefore, the world can be understood only through man, in its history. Let us try to define the *boundaries* and general content of this history.

First of all, history is not a bad infinity, a negative eternity, without beginning or end. One cannot apply to history the antinomy of time and eternity that holds for all of creation in its relation to God. History takes place within the *limits* of creation. It belongs to "this age," which is on the threshold of "the life of the future age." History has a beginning and an end. Chasms bound it on both sides: The beginning is bounded by the creation of man; the end is bounded by the beginning of the new time and the future age. In this sense, history is a certain *state* of becoming being that is included in being in a definite way: an additional creation of the world within itself, as it were.

How do we know that history has a limited character? How do we know that it has a beginning and an end? Clearly, neither the one nor the other can become an object of experiential knowledge. In our experience, which refers to the life of the world embraced by history, we can encounter neither its beginning nor its end. No matter how it is decided, this question must remain either an object of ontological speculation or an object of revelation and religious faith.

According to Scripture, the history of the world, as well as that of man, *begins*. It begins "with" the world's creation, or more precisely *after* its creation. That is, the history of the world presupposes the already-existing being of the world.[1] But this history also has an end, to which both the Old Testament and the New Testament eschatologies bear witness. This end is determined by a series of cosmic and historical events associated with the parousia and the transfiguration of the world: "Behold, I make all things new" (Rev. 21:5). The life of the world does not end with history. It is followed by a new aeon: meta-history.

In order to define history it is necessary to pose the question of its subject and its content. The subject of history is all of humankind, both as a multiplicity of individuals with their independent beings and fates, and as the multi-unity of the entire human race. This multi-unity is composed of all the human individuals. Humankind is multi-unitary; it is multiple in hypostases but has one nature and, in a certain sense, one life. Every individual participates in history, but its one subject is the *whole* human race. This one humanity is individually and multifariously manifested in the different human hypostases. It has a certain unity of life, a commonality that can be defined both as the transcendental subject of history and as its transcendental object.

This transcendental subject of humankind, which unites the whole history of the latter in the unity of Adam as a certain universal, all-human *I*, lies at the base of the transcendental functions of humankind. This is, first of all, the universal subject of knowledge, the transcendental gnoseological *I*, which in the particular cognitive acts of individuals realizes the knowledge of the human *race*. The successive accumulation of

---

1. This corresponds to Gen. 2:1-2: "Thus the heavens and the earth were finished, and all the host of them. And on the seventh day God ended his work which he had made; and he rested on the seventh day from all his work which he had made." This is followed by the creation of man, on the basis of whom or in whom human history begins.

thought and knowledge can be understood only on the basis of this all-human unity of Adam, this unity of the human race in Adam. Without this, knowledge would be impossible, for it would scatter into separate cognitive atoms and would therefore not admit common development and accumulation. No transmission of knowledge, education, and training would be possible in the case of such an atomization of knowledge. The stamp of the universal significance of knowledge with its entire logical apparatus and empirical methods lies on all cognitive acts, given the unity of the cognitive object, which is connected with this unity of the cognitive subject. Knowledge is a function of the unity of Adam, of one humanity. The one Adam knows one world. But this unity is realized not only in knowledge but also in man's action in the world. Not only one knowing subject but also one acting subject (the transcendental subject of economy), the common action of man in the world, exists.

Individual acts of will and action compose man's natural being, his dominion over the world. From this arise the pragmatism of scientific knowledge and the establishment of economic goals, the "planned economy." Although the ways of economy, as well as those of knowledge, can diverge in particular cases, these divergences exist only within the framework of one common economic relation to the world, of one common life of the transcendental cosmo-anthropos, of one common transcendental mode of economic activity in the world.

Finally, one common aesthetic function exists for humanity: the creation of beauty, art. Although art is reserved for creatively gifted individuals, it too is rescued from atomistic multiplicity, irreducible to one revelation of beauty, by the fact that it has a common language, that beauty is accessible in the entire multiplicity of its forms. Thus this unity of beauty also presupposes a transcendental subject of beauty, a universal artist, and a common source of beauty: Beauty itself.

All of these aspects of one common all-human life are coordinated to form the unity of history, according to the succession of historical life, the history of culture. Over the whole diverse spectrum of epochs and peoples, the life of humankind as the universal history of the world also presupposes one transcendental subject with one life in history. However this history might be atomized, it is nevertheless the one *book of life* (Rev. 21:27) of all of humankind, which will be judged at the Last Judgment in its totality: "all nations" (Matt. 25:32) will be judged by one judgment.

Without diminishing the significance of multiplicity in the life of humankind in all its aspects (individual, national, group, historical), we must first understand this multi-unity in the transcendental subject of

317

history, in Adam, the generic being. It is evident that this human creative activity is a revelation of humankind gifted with "natural grace." It is a natural humanism, although one that is limited and polluted by original sin and personal sins. The fall of man imparted a particular quality to his vocation and marked his life with ineluctable tragedy, although it did not annul his gifts or abolish his creative tasks. It is incumbent upon man, even in his fallen state, to accomplish the general task of his history; that is, it is incumbent upon him to manifest and actualize his proper humanity, and, it follows, to humanize the world.

This manifestation of humanism concerns the whole fullness and complexity of man in his trine composition. This manifestation does not consist in rejecting or overcoming the fleshly and psychic principle in the name of the spiritual principle. Rather, it presupposes only a specific mode of the coexistence of these principles and a specific mutual qualification. But, first of all, this manifestation represents a combination of different tasks and possibilities: *Homo sum et nihil humani a me alienum esse puto* (I am a man and nothing human is foreign to me). Man must never reject or be ashamed of his humanity; nor must he diminish it. It is this humanity, as the creaturely *debitum,* that contains among its possibilities the image of God and His "likeness," likening or actualization. It is man's sophianicity, the creaturely Sophia, as the reflection of the Divine Sophia in creation. Therefore, this humanity has a specific positive essence, which determines the content of the historical process. The history of humankind is sophianic with the sophianicity of creation. And this is the basis of the humanism of history.

A consequence of this positive content of human history is the fact that the latter is a closed whole. As the image of God, man is inexhaustible as the image of God in its dynamics, in its infinite development and manifestation, in the variations of its themes. But these themes or tasks are determinate and, in this sense, exhaustible in their content. They are a closed circle, a positive infinity, in contradistinction to "bad infinity," indeterminacy, boundlessness, and thus contentlessness, inasmuch as it is deprived of the determinateness of content. This determinate possession of content, the thematics of history, is precisely what makes history self-contained. History cannot arbitrarily or randomly break off at any point; it must end inwardly, mature for its own end. "Now learn a parable of the fig tree; When his branch is yet tender, and putteth forth leaves, ye know that summer is nigh" (Matt. 24:32).

The process of history has a twofold character: organic and creative. First of all, the cosmo-anthropos contains a determinate content of being, in which the world's sophianicity is manifested. This content contains growing seeds of the "Six Days," the creaturely fullness of the creative *let there be*. The world soul is an organic force, which has the instinctive law of its being in its "evolutionary development." In this sense, one can say that the Six Days are continuing. The world is being created into the fullness of its being during its whole life within the limits of this aeon. The time of the coming of the *end* of this creation, beyond which the transfiguration of the world will take place, is known only to God. The coming of the end is a new action of God upon the world, analogous to its creation.[2] This ripening of the world toward its end is described in Scripture in apocalyptic images that express the idea of a cosmic catastrophe, the fire of the world. To be sure, these images should not be interpreted literally; nor should what is real in their content be neglected. They refer to what is as yet transcendent for us, to what is beyond the life of the world. But at the same time they express from this side this vision of what is to come; more exactly, they allow us to perceive the transcensus of the present age into the future age. These images abound in the prophetic visions of both the Old and the New Testament (as well as in the noncanonical apocalypses). They indicate various cosmic convulsions, ontological spasms of the world before its end: "the sun [shall] be darkened, and the moon shall not give her light, and the stars shall fall from heaven, and the powers of the heavens shall be shaken" (Matt. 24:29; cf. Isa. 13:10; Ezek. 32:7-8; Joel 2:31). This fire of the world, in whose flame the old world will be forged into the new, is the express subject of the apostle Peter's prophecy: "the heavens and the earth, which are now, by the same word are kept in store, reserved unto fire against the day of judgment and perdition of ungodly men" (2 Pet. 3:7). "The day of the Lord will come as a thief in the night: in the which the heavens shall pass away with a great noise, and the elements shall melt with fervent heat, the earth also and the works that are therein shall be burned up" (2 Pet. 3:10; cf. 2 Pet. 3:12). "The heavens shall vanish away like smoke, and the earth shall wax old like a garment, and they that dwell therein shall die in like manner" (Isa. 51:6).

The end of this world and its transfiguration are depicted both as God's action upon the world and as the ripe fruit of the world's life, com-

---

2. "For behold, I create a new heavens and a new earth: and the former shall not be remembered, nor come into mind" (Isa. 65:17; also see 66:22). "We, according to his [God's] promise, look for new heavens and a new earth, wherein dwelleth righteousness" (2 Pet. 3:13). "And I saw a new heaven and a new earth: for the first heaven and the first earth were passed away; and there was no more sea" (Rev. 21:1).

parable to a butterfly flying out of its cocoon or a chick breaking through its shell. There is no incompatibility or contradiction here. God's actions correspond to the age of the world itself, the times and seasons of its organic being. But the history of the world and its ripening toward its end are not determined only by its organic development. Human freedom and creative activity participate in this history. The humanization of the world and of man himself, the manifestation of the fullness of powers implanted in his humanity, is man's creative act over himself and over the world.

Man is not a thing or only an object of creation; he is also its subject. Creative freedom is interwoven into the world's being, together with its organic nature. Humanity is the essence, or nature, of the world; creative personality is its multiform hypostasis. The world follows the path of its being together with man, who creatively realizes himself in this process.

Here one can again apply the general idea that man's creative activity is not absolute, that it proceeds not *ex nihilo* but from a natural given to which a task to be realized corresponds. On the pathways of this creative activity there is no place for predetermination, since freedom, albeit a creaturely freedom, a freedom that does not lead to the absolute novelty of ontological autonomy and self-creation, is manifested here. The integral of this activity, its final sum, known by divine providence, is a value that is definite in content, although it can also include variants of personal freedom and creative activity.

In this sense, history as a collective act of free creative activity is not an externally determined, calendar-determined term, but an inner accomplishment. The world ripens toward its end in *different ways* with respect to external accomplishments, although in a definite way with respect to its external result. The modes and degrees of historical creative activity are individual and diverse. There are individuals who are more or less creative, just as historical tasks and situations differ. The organic and the creative are inseparably united in human life; the measure of creativity, like the measure of freedom, cannot be defined in its separateness. These are different aspects of one and the same process, which has its spiritual content and determination, together with its psychic-corporeal, organic being. In man there is nothing purely or abstractly spiritual, nothing that is deprived of "matter," that is free of cosmic psychic-corporeal qualification. The contrary would signify disincarnation, something that is ontologically and in advance impossible for man. Completely false is the conception of spiritual life that views it as the complete rejection of psycho-corporeality and, in *this* sense, as liberation from the latter. On the contrary, spirituality in man is only a special mode of the state of his human createdness in its entirety. In this sense, one can say that every state of man (including the flesh) is also spiritual (as well as psychic-corporeal, of course), that it has a spiritual coefficient. Human creative activity cannot separate itself from the task that is imposed upon it by its natural givenness; it cannot become cosmically empty or acosmic. Man is inseparable from the cosmos.

Although man remains personally qualified in the freedom of his creative activity, the latter is included in the life of the race. This creative activity is not only an activity that belongs to A, B, C, . . . in its determinate form a, b, c, ... It is also universal, all-human creative activity, which determines the life of the world in its one history. This organic whole comprises elements proper to different epochs or nations. Taken separately, these elements can empirically appear to be wholly alien to one another and to mutually exclude one another, to the point of annulling the very idea, possibility, and reality of a universal history. But one should not unquestioningly accept this empirical appearance, which we are not able, for the time being, to overcome by a global vision. The connection of these elements in the one history of humankind remains ontologically irrefragable. The living actualization of this connection belongs to the fullness of history, is revealed at its end, but its contours become more and more distinct as the end is approached, as the universal humankind becomes more visible on the historical surface. Such is the postulate of Christian anthropology.

Thus, the world has a double fullness: through its creation by God, by virtue of which the fullness of its powers and forms as creaturely sophianicity is implanted in the world during the Six Days of creation; and in its history, in which this fullness is actualized. In this sense, history is human self-creative activity in the world. In this activity, there is ontologically nothing new. But without this manifestation creation remains incomplete, unfinished, as it were. The place that in creation belongs to man as a microcosm that extends into the macrocosm determines the significance of human creative activity. Having created man in the fullness of his potential tasks, God entrusts to him their fulfillment. In this sense, the world created by God is completed by man, not as a creator "out of nothing" of course, but as the accomplisher of God's designs. Man accomplishes this mission according to the modalities of creaturely creative activity. Without this accomplishment the fullness of the universe cannot be manifested, and the universe cannot attain its end and its ultimate transfiguration, the passage to the new state of the future age. Therefore, there is, so to speak, a natural preparation for eschatology in history, besides the spiritual preparation. The universe realized in man is the *substrate* of the transfiguration of the world, as its perfect ripeness.

This humanization of the world is the task of all natural humankind, called to dress and to keep the earth. The natural element of human work and creative genius is revealed here. Whatever their manifestations, this work and this genius are an integral part of the common task of humankind, the sum total of the human race. The laborer's hammer blow is included along with the chemist's analysis and the engineer's design, along with Newton's conceptions and Pasteur's discoveries, along with steam power and air travel. Just as this work has a general transcendental subject, it also has a general transcendental object, an integral synthesis of all human works directed at the humanization of the world, its transformation into an anthropo-cosmos.

Of course, to this one can easily object that it is impossible to indicate the measure of God's omnipotence in the world, and that this omnipotence is free to stop the world's life at any moment in order to supply what is lacking and finish what is incomplete — which is why the very idea of such a measure is presumptuous. This is, however, an example of omnipotence usurped by arbitrariness, something which is frequently encountered in theology. The Lord laid the foundation of the world and set aside in it a specific place for man not to direct him partly or fully but to allow him to accomplish his task in the world.

It is indisputable that man himself is not given to know and to define the measure of this accomplishment. Therefore, the end inevitably contains *for man* something unexpected and catastrophic, as Scripture witnesses. But this unfathomability of the end for man, to whom for the time being it is given to know the world only in its temporal becoming, in process, does not signify that the coming of the exhaustive fullness, necessary for the end, does not really exist for God's omniscience. The transfiguration of the world, with the coming of its "end," is, of course, determined not only by its internal structure but also by a direct action of God upon the world, by a new creative act of God. But this act presupposes a preceding divine act in its creation. The passage of the world to another state — the life of the future age — is not a stage of the evolution of the world itself but a creative catastrophe in it. But this is a catastrophe that contains the continuation and fulfillment of the world. One cannot annul this proper life of the world, whose foundation has been laid by God, by conceiving of a kind of divine arbitrariness which does not take into account the proper work of God Himself, who created this world on an unshakable foundation. "Learn a parable of the fig tree" (Matt. 24:32); "let both grow together until the harvest" (13:30).

Man's creative activity in the cosmos also includes the entire domain of culture and civilization. In his creative activity, man is not only the master and a worker in the world but also a thinker and artist. To tear away one aspect or another from the fullness of human creative activity is a mutilation. And — what is even more important — no nations or epochs are excluded from this common human task in the world, for each of them makes its contribution to the fullness.

Moreover, we know from revelation (and this is not inaccessible to our immediate intuition) that spiritual hierarchies participate together with man in the life of the world and its self-determination. They act within the limits of the world and in this sense are its "angels" (or servants). They are "co-human"; they act in the world together with man and through man. Together with man, and within the limits of humanity, dark powers also act in the world. In a certain sense these powers are also co-human and thus are able to act in the world through man.

All this extends the boundaries and the possibilities of the world and makes them even more indefinite and inaccessible for human comprehension, without destroying their reality. When these boundaries are reached, the world does not tarry in its present being but passes, by virtue of God's action, into the life of the future age. Similarly, we also do not know the limits of our own life, beyond which death necessarily comes, as the beginning of the passage into the life of the future age. Death is inwardly inevitable, but the time of its coming is unknown to us. It can come at any moment of our existence.

Creative activity as the actualization of the fullness of man's nature not only has the right to exist but even constitutes the historical duty of humankind. We cannot imagine a human life without any creative activity at all. That would be a pseudo-ascetic acosmism (or rather, anticosmism) of the Buddhist type. It is by no means Christian.

Here we approach the most central problem of the philosophy of history: humanism and its various forms. We are concerned here with the *soul* of humanism or, more precisely, its spirit. Man is a spiritual-psychic-corporeal or spiritual-natural being, and in all his aspects he participates in his creative self-determination, without losing any of these aspects, but diversely manifesting and uniting them. The vital source or material of the creative activity is his indivisible psychic-corporeal nature, this common predicate for his many subjects. But the determining subject, as well as the determined subject, is spirit, uncreated and created, divine-human.

The life of this spirit in its freedom gives the spiritual coefficient, defines the spiritual character of human creative activity. We constantly use such expressions as the spirit of an epoch, of a nation, of a person, which is reflected in their creative activity (civilization and culture) and which defines them. The spirit is the source of man's natural and autonomous creativity, which Christianity does not abolish but raises to its highest state. This spirit determines the direction and achievements, the special gifts and character of different epochs and nations: of the East and ancient Greece, of Europe and Asia, of the ancient world and the modern world, and so on. Insofar as this is natural, rightful "paganism," that is, the human nature in its purity, we must recognize that these branches have equal rights, even though, in spiritual struggle and competition, each affirms itself as unique.

One knows that St. Augustine did not recognize this rightful humanism. He considered the entire pagan world to be a *civitas diabolica*, surrendered all of natural history to Satan, and even viewed the virtues of the pagans as beautiful vices. (Of course, even Augustine could not consistently carry this point of view to its extreme.) This attitude is opposed by the neohumanistic conception of history, a conception characteristic of the Renaissance and of our own time. This conception expresses a falling away from Christianity, a re-paganization, characteristic of our epoch. Of course, the pre-Christian or extra-Christian paganism was much more distant from Christianity than the present de-christianization. If Augustine had written his historiosophical treatise while confronting the Renaissance, he would have had to introduce a new and greater complexity in his speculations, or to regard all human history as a fruit of the fall, making an exception only for the papal hierocracy. But not even Roman Catholicism went so far, even at the time of its greatest triumph in the Middle Ages; nor does it go so far today. Such a historiosophical clericalism would clearly have been compelled to reject completely the natural-human element in its sophianicity and to see in everything that is human only a domain of sin. Such a conception is connected, of course, with the somber aspects of Augustinianism, which, developed consistently, postulate a clerical despotism and a fundamental rejection of freedom. This leads, by way of reaction, to Protestantism with its soteriological fatalism and secularization. Modern anti-Christian humanism is the antithesis of Augustinianism, its black shadow.

However, alongside this religiophilosophical grotesquerie there remains the fateful and tragic question of the contamination and corruption of all human creative activity by original sin and the general sinfulness of life. And this inevitably leads to the question of the measure of this corruption. Is the original sophianicity of creation with its tasks preserved in the sinful world? Or is it completely annulled by sin? Theology has attempted two solutions in this domain: either the total rejection of the power of original sin (in different types of Pelagianism) or the abolition of the sophianicity of creation and the efficacy of the very image of God (in the Reformation). The Eastern Church has preserved a reasonable measure here, recognizing both the effectiveness of original sin and the preservation of the image of God in man, although "corrupted by passions." This corresponds to the antinomian doctrine of Scripture on this question, where one can find sufficient data for both a negative and a positive assessment of natural humanity. Such, for example, is the doctrine of natural revelation to the pagans in the Epistle to the Romans (1:19-21; cf. Acts 17:22-23, 26-29), to which is opposed the affirmation of their sinfulness (Rom. 1:21-32). The very fact that the pagans are called attests that they have a certain measure of goodness, for pious paganism is in its own way a natural old testament. In this sense, Socrates and Plato, as well as other pagan sages, are Christians before Christ or outside of Christianity.

In addition to being afflicted by perversions, paganism has a radically limited character. This cannot destroy the good natural root of God's creation but is capable of damaging it. In general, the pagan world was possessed by the prince of this world and required exorcism. First of all, the pagan religions are limited and therefore susceptible to error and to direct falsehood: *chiaroscuro* and half-truth characterize them. Secondly, the pagan religions are subject to mania and demon-possession. The positive essence of natural humankind with its creative powers is healthy and sophianic, but its state is one of sickness.

Such also is human creative activity in history. In this activity, there is a path common to the whole of humankind, but there are also fetters that are removed only by Christ. And of course, natural humanism's right to exist can be recognized only insofar as it does not imply a struggle against Christianity, where naive paganism is replaced by virulent anti-Christianity. Paganism is a meal that is capable of taking the Christian leaven; it is not a demonic communion that is incompatible with this leaven. It is this leaven that makes humanism Christian.

What does this mean and can there be a Christian humanism? Is this not a contradiction in terms, like a circular square or hot ice? However, where does this prejudice come from? From another, more general, Manichaean prejudice, which gives all human nature over to the power of the prince of this world. It thereby loses the features of the intact divine creation, which clearly bears the sophianic stamp of the image of God. On the other hand, the humanist notion is too much associated with atheistic humanism, or anthropotheism, which was born in the Renaissance and continues to our own time. Such theomachic humanism is a slander against true humanism, whose name is human creative activity.

The true question here is as follows: Can human creative activity be accomplished in the name of Christ; can it be the work of Christ's human-kind? Does it accomplish God's original and unchanging will concerning humanity, or does it consist in robbery and revolt? Is man given his talents for application and use, or is he given them to bury them in the earth, to suppress them? But talents cannot be suppressed; they can only be per-verted (inquisitorial and obscurantist clericalism with its cosmomachy ex-emplifies such perversion). Does the human creative activity manifested in history belong to the kingdom of God, and is it destined for future glo-rification, or is it the domain only of the prince of this world? Is Christ the King to whom all power in heaven and on earth is given? Or does He reign only in the heavens, outside and above this sinful world?

There cannot be two answers to this question: Christ is the King who is to come into the world in the parousia, and His kingdom will be with-out end. This world belongs to Him not only because He is God, one of the hypostases of the Holy Trinity, but also by virtue of His humanization. Having assumed the human nature, the Lord sanctified all the powers and possibilities (except sin) of this nature, and there is nothing human that would not be made divine-human, that would not be redeemed and sanctified by Him. But this enthronement, which was definitively "accom-plished" on Golgotha in the depths of creation, is now being realized in history. Christ's "royal ministry" continues[3] until the end of this age. Instituted by God's power, the kingdom of God is being built in the world on the foundation "which is Jesus Christ" (1 Cor. 3:11), although of differ-ent materials of unequal strength.

The "fire" of the transfiguration of the world at the threshold of the future age will test this strength. Some materials will "withstand," others will "burn," but the new Jerusalem, descending out of heaven from God, is built of earthly materials and has an inscription of angelic and human names (Rev. 21). This building of the city of God in history does not di-minish the significance of God's new creative act in the transfiguration of the world but prepares for the world the material that is the content of

3. For a christological grounding of these thoughts see *The Lamb of God*, the final chapter.

history, its creative activity. The new city is not created out of nothing but is the transfiguration of history. A catastrophic rupture takes place here, but what has been accomplished is not abolished.

Thus, that which, prior to and outside of Christianity, was done blindly, instinctively, and unconsciously, Christianity does as its growing work in the world: the Church acts as a leaven, until all the dough rises. In the "last times," that is, after the Ascension and before the parousia, there is no longer anything neutral in the world, which could remain outside the action of the Church, although this process of the world's ecclesialization in time (positive or negative, with a plus or with a minus) is manifested in complex and diverse forms. The Church's sphere of action does not always coincide with the external forms of its manifestation. Not everything that is done in the name of the Church as a clerical organization is churchly, and vice versa. The old question of "Christians without Christ" remains valid here, in both the direct and the inverse sense, for only the last "day" will test the works of men, when the Lord will judge all the nations. Then there may be those who will say: "Lord, Lord, have we not prophesied in thy name? . . . And in thy name done many wonderful works? And then I will profess unto them, I never knew you" (Matt. 7:22-23). On the other hand, there will be sons who said "I will not" but who went (21:28-30).

The Lord reigns in the world not by virtue of His omnipotence but by the action of the Spirit: "not by might, nor by power, but by my spirit" (Zech. 4:6). "The kingdom of God is within you." However, located "within," in hearts, this kingdom is necessarily manifested in works too, possesses the will, is truly "desired." The figure of the building of the Church, which we find both in the New Testament and in the patristic literature (*The Shepherd* of Hermas), must be interpreted not from the clerical but from the universal and historical point of view. But this process does not consist in the peaceful and harmonious execution of a predesigned plan. It is struggle and tragedy. The kingdom of Christ is opposed by the malice of anti-Christianity and is disputed by the prince of this world.

We return here to our initial conception of human nature and creative activity according to which they not only have a psychic-corporeal potentiality but are also spiritually qualified. In the Christian epoch this spirit is the Spirit of Christ, that is, the Holy Spirit sent by Christ, the power of Divine-humanity. Opposed to this spirit is the satanical spirit that possesses the human spirit, that inspires man to anthropotheism, to satanic-humanity, to *civitas diabolica* (in this sense, Augustine's antithesis remains valid). Just as in the fall the tempting power came not from the human but from the spiritual world, which nevertheless poisoned humanity, so this same power continues to act in the humankind that is redeemed by the blood of the Lamb. It continues to tempt man with the same anthropotheism ("ye shall be as gods"), inspiring human creative activity by this self-deification of the creature, that is, by satanism, with the aim of paralyzing the power of divine-humanity and abolishing the kingdom of God. Therefore, this battle of the forces of Antichrist against the kingdom of God unfolds on the pathways of history.

The Revelation of John views history as the battle of two armies: Christian and anti-Christian. This battle not only takes place in the human world but also includes the participation of the spiritual world. The human world is not closed off; rather, it is permeated by spiritual powers. The human world does not exist in separation from the angelic world; both radiant, angelic forces and dark, satanical forces participate in human history. This battle takes place both in the spiritual world (Rev. 12) and in the human world.

The particulars of the spiritual battle are hidden from us. We can gain some knowledge of it through a special revelation or feel it as the power of evil in general, acting in the world and in man. But the participation of the spiritual world in human history does not change the content of this history as human self-revelation. And this self-revelation of humanism is headed by the humanity of the God-man: this is the kingdom of Christ. He that sits upon the white horse does battle at the head of His army, which wars against the beast and the false prophet and their armies (Rev. 19).

The forces of evil and its inspiration that act in the world are represented by symbolic figures in Revelation. The beast coming out of the human sea stands for the animal, elemental principle in man, which affirms itself as the supreme and unique principle. This is apocalyptic anthropotheism, a challenge from the psychic-corporeal element, the "blood," affirming itself *in place of* the spirit, *against* the spirit. By this self-affirmation it acquires a character of quasi-spirituality or anti-spirituality. As such this is already a force of a spiritual order, the pride of the bestial principle, a power that proclaims itself supreme and acts with all manner of coercion. In modern terms this is the absolute state that does not recognize any principle superior to itself; it is the ideology of force, which tramples the conscience and, as such, is inevitably theomachic in character: "Who is like unto the beast? Who is able to make war with him?" (Rev. 13:4). A certain fullness of historical knowledge of the "beast" in his different aspects has been given to our epoch. But it was early Christianity that was destined to wage the first battle for Christ, against the absolutism of the Roman state, which demanded sacrifices as a sign of recognition; and now an analogous trial is coming.

The second attribute of anti-Christianity is false prophecy, the ideology of bestial power, producing signs and transforming human knowledge into an instrument of spiritual coercion. This significance of the false prophet is figuratively expressed in the words of Revelation 13:15-17: "And he had power to give life unto the image of the beast, that the image of the beast should both speak, and cause that as many as would not worship the image of the beast should be killed. And he causeth all, both small and great, rich and poor, free and bond, to receive a mark in their right hand, or in their foreheads: and that no man might buy or sell, save he that had the mark." And the "number" (name) of the beast (666) is "the number of a man." It is a question here not of the bestialization but of the satanization of humankind, which becomes pneumatomachic and theomachic.

The two principles that are inwardly united in their theomachy and Christomachy, the "beast" and the "false prophet," have the significance, first of all, of historical forces acting in the world. These forces are embodied in personal representatives, "antichrists" (1 John 2:18). These "heroes" of anti-Christianity are legion, of course. However, theological thought and popular tradition eagerly fuse them in the image of a single Antichrist; and the doctrine of a single Antichrist, who concludes universal history with his single combat against Christ, thus arises in the church literature. Much legend and mythology have easily arisen around this figure.

However, one must inquire if this doctrine really has an indisputable foundation, first of all in Scripture and then in dogmatic tradition. If it is certain that Scripture mentions anti-Christianity or, more broadly, theomachy in general, far from so certain is the doctrine of a personal Antichrist. The Old Testament already knows, in a general sense, revolt in humankind against God (see Pss. 2:2-3; 14:1), as well as examples of personal possession by anthropotheism and theomachy in the figures of Nebuchadnezzar and Belshazzar, and especially Antiochus Epiphanes, who are Old Testament prefigurations of the Antichrist (Dan. 11; 1 Macc. 1:10 sq). The figures of Daniel's prophecy clearly inspired certain New Testament features in the depiction of the beast in the Apocalypse.

Leaving aside the exegetical and critical problem of these texts, we must point out differences in the representation of the Antichrist that are of dogmatic significance. First of all, the Epistles of John (1 John 2:18, 22 and 2 John 7) speak not of the Antichrist but of antichrists, and, furthermore, of those who have already come. They are known by their espousal of trinitarian and christological heresies. Thus it is, above all, a question here of dogmatic anti-Christianity, not of a single personal antichrist.

The "beast" of the Apocalypse, like the false prophet, is also not a personal figure but a collective one, a symbol, like the "whore of Babylon," of godless civilization (Rev. 17, 18). Nevertheless, this personification of spiritual powers in Revelation does not contain features so individual that they would allow one to find there a doctrine of the personal Antichrist. One should also note that the anti-Christianity indicated in the Epistles of John does not coincide in its subject with that represented by the images of Revelation. It is a question of *different* aspects of a general anti-Christian movement, which the Gospel apocalypse (Matt. 24), as well as 2 Peter 3:3, Jude 1:18, 1 Timothy 4:1, and 2 Timothy 4:3, characterizes in general terms of spiritual decline and corruption.

Only 2 Thessalonians 2:3-10 speaks directly about a *personal* representative of theomachy: In connection with a universal apostasy, a "man of sin" will be "revealed," "the son of perdition, a lawless one" (this prophecy is complicated by additional, hard-to-interpret features, such as the mystery of "what withholdeth," "the mystery of iniquity," etc.). His activity reminds one of the beast and the prophet in the Apocalypse ("with all power and signs and lying wonders" [2 Thess. 2:9]). Here it is clearly a question of some personal head of theomachy and anthropotheism as a visible *external* sign of the coming of the end, which the Thessalonians awaited with so much fuss. However, this feature should not be considered central and unique; rather, it should be taken in the totality of the eschatological context. And central in this context are anti-Christianity and apostasy.

What is essential here is that, from the beginning to the end of its history, Christianity is accompanied by its black shadow, anti-Christianity. History is a spiritual tragedy consisting in the battle of the prince of this world against Christ and resulting in the institution of Christ's reign. Thus, both in the world soul and in history, a schism takes place, two centers are formed, as it were: the Woman clothed in the sun is opposed by the great whore, who is a mystery, Babylon the great, "drunken with the blood of the saints, and with the blood of the martyrs of Jesus," sitting on a scarlet beast (see Rev. 17:1-6). Thus, one inevitably comes to the conclusion that there is not one but two forms of humanity, and the historiosophical problem of their interrelation arises.

The world of natural humanity cannot be rejected if it is deified, glorified, raised to heaven in Christ. And this deification includes its own phylogenesis, so to speak. That is, it extends to all the stages of being since the creation of the world. The world is one, just as humanity is one, although they are an arena of inner battle. Humanity is a complex of creative potencies, which is united in its psychic-corporeal being but differentiated in its spiritual self-determination. The human heart is a field of spiritual battle, in which one and the same material — human nature — is used to build both the city of God and Babylon, for there are no creative potencies outside of the human nature. The task of Christianity consists not in ascetically deadening the human nature but in manifesting it in the power and fullness of Christian inspiration. Christianity should not be inhuman or extrahuman. Christianity cannot be noncreative and passive in history. All passivity is a capitulation before the enemy, who occupies the place left vacant. We observe this in history in the enslavement of Christianity or, more precisely, of "Moses' seat" (Matt. 23:2) by the pagan state and the powers of this age, by the ruling classes.

One should not limit the power of the Church to the inner world of man, just as one should not see its manifestations only in the external action of the ecclesiastical organization, in the clericalization of history, so to speak. It is wrong to do so if only because not everything that bears the stamp of institutional clericalism is genuinely churchly or even Christian in general (consider the strangling of freedom by *gladium seculare* [the secular sword], the Inquisition, and the persecution of thought and knowledge). The clerical tendency often seems to be a practical, utilitarian application of Christianity, insofar as it strives to use its power, even if for a good end. Humanity is not an *ancilla*, an obedient instrument; rather, in its sophianicity, it is a goal for itself. But, to be sure, despite the limitations noted, the direct influence of historical ecclesiality on the history of culture can inwardly transform the elements of the world. Such a transformation is rarely accessible to direct observation, for it is accomplished inwardly by virtue of an inspiration that deifies creation by the general atmosphere of its thought and life. Therefore, ecclesial humanism needs to manifest its potencies by a creative activity that is accomplished by the gifts of the Spirit, of the Pentecost, and that embraces the whole cosmos: "I will pour out of my Spirit upon all flesh" (Acts 2:17).

Creative activity does not know mechanical automatism. It is accomplished in personal freedom, which qualifies it negatively or positively. But it is for this reason that the domain of creative activity is so susceptible to being corrupted by sin. Moreover, even though creative activity is directly personal, it is not singular in character but universal. It is included in the life of the human race, of the generations, of universal history. It represents not a sum of separate atoms but a historical, genealogical tree, whose life includes all the branches and shoots. In this sense, human creative activity is always the making of history. "I am the vine, ye are the branches" (John 15:5). There are healthy branches, and there are dry and sick ones. In this relationship of genus and individual, we clearly see the character of human creative activity, with all its diverse coefficients.

But creative activity is not something that is merely possible or even inevitable. It is man's *duty*, God's will concerning him. For man is called to "do works" by the power of Christ, by the inspiration of the Holy Spirit. Man has been sent into the world to create. His creativity is not only personal. It is also sophianic; it makes manifest the sophianic face of creation.

Creative activity has always been proper to man, for without it he would lose his humanity. But precisely our epoch in the history of Christianity is destined to understand this vocation of man as emanating from his rootedness in God, as a feature of the image of God in him. Just as other truths of Christianity were understood more fully in the battle against heresy, so a crucial dogmatic question in our own time is the heresy of life in relation to Christian creative activity. Our epoch is characterized by a broad development of creativity "in its own name," by a deluge of anthropotheism, in the form of a luciferian creative intoxication, and by an immersion in dull sensual paganism. These developments cannot be overcome by mere rejection; they can be overcome only by the unfolding of a positive Christian doctrine of the world and creative activity, and by manifestation of its power.

This is only a further unfolding of the Chalcedonian and ditheletic dogma, according to which the fullness of the human nature and the entire power of human creative will and energy in Christ are united with the divine nature, are co-manifested with it and are deified by it. What was accomplished in Christ was pre-accomplished for the whole of humankind. In the light of this dogma, the "cosmos" is not the "kingdom of this world" but God's radiant creation, which is raised by man toward deification. Therefore, the creative tasks that arise before contemporary humankind must be understood in the light of the coming transfiguration of the world, as missions of religious creative activity, according to Christ's commandments: "the works that I shall do [you] shall do also; and greater works than these [you] shall do" (John 14:12).

It is, of course, impossible to enumerate these tasks, for their number is infinite. One of them consists in the mastery of the social element, or the life of the human race, that is, the mastery of sociopolitical organization. This is the social question in the broadest sense. It is clear that the fragmentation of Christianity into different confessions serves as an obstacle to such mastery; for as long as Christianity is incapable of overcoming this fragmentation, it will remain impotent in the task of the social ordering of human life.

Associated with these tasks are the general, inexhaustible tasks of cultural creative activity. It is in this domain that the final battle will be fought between creative activity in the name of Christ and creative activity in its own name, that is, anti-Christian, satanic creative activity. The latter is spiritual robbery, an attempt of the prince of this world to take over God's creation, to steal it from the Lord. But even this black-red or red-black creative activity, intended to build the new Babylon, has its actual source in man with all the riches of the gifts implanted in him. No other source exists. Here one can apply St. Augustine's dictum that even in his fall Satan retains his nature, that of the fallen supreme angel, which is inalienably proper to him according to his creation. Likewise, in satanization man retains his humanity, the fullness of his creative powers, which are directed here toward evil. Therefore, in this double tendency, human creative activity can be defined as "two cities," though within one humankind. At the extreme, at the threshold of the end, the product of the harvest will be manifested: the chaff will be separated from the wheat and burned, and the wheat will be gathered together.

It follows that, despite the unity of humankind and the unique root of all its creative activity, humankind does not know a harmonious conclusion to this activity. On the contrary, its lot is the most agonizing tragedy of the final battle, described in symbolic images in Revelation. History will not end in its immanence but will catastrophically break off, in order to transcend to the new aeon by the power of God. There is no, and will be no, "progress" as the harmony of "bad infinity."

However, although, outwardly, history appears to break off, it will inwardly reach finality in the sense that a fullness of the creaturely manifestation of the human will be attained in it that will *suffice* for the coming of the end and the transfiguration of the world. This ripening of the world toward its end is a mystery of God's omniscience and is known only to the Heavenly Father, the Creator. The culmination and end of the age will consist in a new manifestation of the Church: "the marriage of the Lamb is come, and his wife hath made herself ready" (Rev. 19:7). "Come hither, I will show thee the bride, the Lamb's wife" (21:9). "And the Spirit and the bride say, Come" (22:17). This event, which transcends history, is manifested to the world as the appearance of the "great city, the holy Jerusalem, descending out of heaven from God, having the glory of God" (21:10-11 and sq).

But here it is important to establish that, as created by God ("I make all things new" [Rev. 21:5]), as "descending out of heaven," this *new* thing that enters life not only does not abolish the old, but includes and presupposes it, as in general the past lives and is preserved in the future. That is why it is said: "old things are passed away; behold, all things are become new" (2 Cor. 5:17). This does not mean that the past has completely vanished, but that it lives in the future, the way the Old Testament lives in the New. This brings us to the extremely important conclusion that our present history, on this side, also has an eternal significance — not in its empirical shell but in its inner content.

This eternal element in the temporal belongs to the Church, which is why the Church acts in history as a creative force. The Church is not only Noah's ark, saving those inside it from the flood of corruption. It is also the leaven that leavens *all* the dough. Human history is, first of all, the history of the Church, not only outer and institutional, in the sense of her destiny in the world, but also inner, as the spiritual force that accomplishes Divine-humanity. In this sense, Christian history is, in general, the "last times."

If the history of the chosen people before the coming of Christ is the "sacred history" for us, then after the Incarnation this quality is not limited to one people but is extended to the whole world, which now belongs to Christ and has received the descent of the Holy Spirit and become divine-human. In the Last Judgment, when the final sums will be calculated, when the "books" (Rev. 20:12) will be opened and "all the nations will be gathered," one will see manifested this permeation by the Church of *all* human history as subject to Christ's judgment. The Apocalypse (together with analogous texts of Scripture) is precisely such a revelation of the Church as the inner force and, so to speak, substance of history. The fundamental, guiding idea of this historiosophy is that the history of the Church is not a peaceful "progress" that leads to a harmonious resolution within the limits of this time, but a battle and a tragedy that end in a universal-historical catastrophe and a universal fire. And only out of this is the phoenix of the future age born. And the *whole* of world history consists of the growth in intensity of this spiritual antagonism and combat.[4] This is history growing toward its maturity.

---

4. The spiritual "petty-bourgeoisie," like Marx and the socialists, see in this struggle only an economic content, whereas it is actually fought for ultimate spiritual values.

Can we characterize as pessimism this philosophy of history as the "philosophy of the end"? By no means. On the contrary, it is the most vital and energetic of worldviews. But neither is it optimism, for, *within the limits* of history itself, there is no resolution for this tragedy. It is true that, as the end approaches, the dawn becomes brighter and brighter, illuminating the heavens, and the sensitive ear already hears hymns of victory coming from there. But, down below, the black armies of Gog and Magog amass for the last time, encircling the camp of the saints, preparing for the battle of Armageddon (Rev. 20:8-9). And, in response to this, the armies of heaven and earth gather around the one sitting on the white horse, the one whose name is "The Word of God" (19:11-13), until the arrival of the end of history and the universal resurrection and judgment.

Such a tragic conception of the historical process inevitably leads one to ask whether anything substantial is accomplished and attained in this process that gives to history a positive content necessary for the fulfillment of the times and seasons. The answer to this question must be absolutely affirmative. A widespread opinion — pseudo-ascetic, pseudo-Christian, and truly Manichaean — holds that the life of this world is a kind of purgatory or prison, in which souls must be tormented until a determinate end of the suffering is reached. For such an abstract spiritualism there is no history and no humanity; there are only individual souls yearning to be liberated from their bodies and to leave this world. It therefore becomes incomprehensible why bodily resurrection and transfiguration are necessary.

Such a Platonic-Buddhistic worldview is alien to the Apocalypse as well, insofar as the latter is a philosophy of history. History is a process with a positive content, in which earthly, historical achievements are realized, in which a "progress" is achieved, although a tragic one (but by no means does progress have to be "petty bourgeois" in nature). In history all that can be achieved with regard to the earthly contribution to the construction of the City of God must be achieved. First, we must acknowledge the full importance of the prophecies in Scripture concerning these achievements, both in the Old and in the New Testament. Such prophecies already abound in the Old Testament literature, which is oriented more toward otherworldly values than toward this-worldly values, beginning with God's covenant with Abraham (Gen. 13:15-16; 17:4-8; 22:17-18). There is also the messianic kingdom described by the prophets: Isa. 2:1-4; 11:1-12; 18:3-7; 19:18-24; 25:1-8; 42:1-4; 45:12-25; 60-66; Jer. 12:14-17; Ezek. 16; 39:21-29; 47:22-23; Dan. 2:35; 7:14, 27; Joel 3:4; Amos 9:8-15;

Zech. 8:3, 20-23; 9:9-10; 14:9-21; Mal. 1:11. And compare the "royal psalms": 19, 20, 44, 77, and others.[5]

No matter what attempts are made to diminish or spiritualize their significance, to the point of nullifying their content, all these prophecies attest to certain manifestations of the triumph of the good, to christophanies of a sort in this very world. History manifests not only a growth of anti-Christianity, but also the force of Christianity, the reign of Christ. True, sometimes it might appear (especially if the positive content of the aforementioned prophecies is nullified) that the approach of the end is marked only by a multiplication of vice, of disbelief, of all kinds of perversions (for a depiction of people in the "last" times, see: 2 Tim. 3:1-5; 2 Pet. 2:1-3, 9-22; Jude 8-16). It is marked by a decline of faith (Luke 18:8), by a decline of love (Matt. 24:12), and, in general, by an apparent failure of Christ's work on earth, the duration of the last times being reduced only for the sake of the elect.

But one must recall the general character of the revelation of these somber prospects: it is practical and pedagogical and its purpose is to prevent a state of false, pathological panic, to combat the false yearning for the earthly kingdom, and to summon to patience and martyrdom. We are told to be watchful and to pray, to have patience and faith like that of the saints, to keep our hearts from being scandalized or frightened. And in the face of the last horrors the summons is heard: "then look up, and lift up your heads; for your redemption draweth nigh" (Luke 21:28).

And along with this one hears of the great victory of Christianity, of the fact that it is being preached to the whole world. The prophecies cannot be reduced to external preaching, accompanied by impotence in life, by compromise and collusion with the beast and the false prophet. On the contrary, one must see the victory of Christianity in the life of this world, which is becoming the kingdom of Christ, even before the end of the uprising of Gog and Magog. These new forces of the spiritual conquest of the world and of the institution of Christ's reign in the world, these forces of His new entry into Jerusalem, as it were, are connected with a spiritual event that also refers to the coming of the last times: the conversion of all

5. According to certain theologians (e.g., Schell), the Old Testament kings prefigure different epochs of Christian history: (1) the time of Moses, leader of Israel, friend of God, with the pilgrimage in the desert to the promised land, corresponds to primitive Christianity; (2) the time of David and of his battle against his enemies corresponds to the militant Church of Constantine the Great; (3) the kingdom of Solomon corresponds to the messianic kingdom, which is yet to come.

of Israel. This conversion is solemnly prophesied, as a mystery, by the apostle of the Gentiles (Rom. 9-11). It is a kind of spiritual axis traversing the whole good news, both of the Old and of the New Testament (see Lev. 26:42-45; Deut. 4:23-31; 30; Isa. 6:13; 11:10, 12, 16; 25:8; 32; 35; 43-45; 51; 54-56; 60-62; 66:20-23; Jer. 16:14-15; 23:3-8; 30:22; 31:33 ff; 33; Ezek. 11:16-21; 16:60-62; 34; 36:24 ff; 37; 38-39; Hos. 2:1-2, 23; Joel 2:23; Amos 9:8-15; Mic. 4; 5; 7:7-20; Hag. 2:23; Zech. 9:9-11; 12:10; 14; Matt. 23:39; Luke 21:24).

The resurrection from the dead (Rom. 11:15) of Israel inwardly concludes the triumphant procession of Christianity in the world, "until the fullness of the Gentiles be come in" (v. 25). And if at the beginning the apostolic preaching "went into all the earth, and their words unto the ends of the world" (10:18), at the end of history a new apostolic force of Christianity will pour in through the conversion of Israel. This force will be manifested in everything: in preaching, in works, and in life. This conversion is being prepared by the appearance and preaching of two witnesses: Enoch and Elijah, according to tradition. The Old Testament yearnings for the messianic kingdom merge here with the conversion of the chosen people, of Saul the persecutor, who became Paul the apostle.

This takes us, finally, to the prophecy of the "first resurrection" in the thousand-year kingdom in Revelation 20. In the course of history, this chapter has received different interpretations, which tend to deprive this spiritual as well as church-historical event of its concreteness, to annul it with an allegorical and spiritualistic exegesis; or, on the contrary, to attribute to it an excessively sensuous character, which, to say the least, does not exhaust it and is not adequate to its universal significance. This tendency, corresponding to sensuous representations of the messianic kingdom in Judaic apocalyptics,[6] predominates in the early Christian literature, in Papias, St. Justin the Philosopher, and St. Irenaeus[7] (with references to Isa. 11; 54; 58-59; 65; Ezek. 28, 37; Dan. 7:12; Matt. 26:29, etc.).

Of course, this *realistic* conception of the thousand years, proper to the holy teachers of the Church mentioned above, must, despite certain judaistic features, be considered the Church's original interpretation. This conception was replaced by a spiritualistic interpretation under the influence of the allegorism of Origen and the Alexandrian school, the exegetical ideas of Tychonius, and, finally, the clerical historiosophy of St. Augustine

6. Cf. the essay "Apocalypse and Socialism" in my book *Two Cities*.

7. There is a compilation of these texts in Oksiuk, *The Eschatology of St. Gregory of Nyssa (Eskhatologiya sv. Grigoriya Nisskogo)*, Kiev, 1914, pp. 12-13, 73-78.

and Bishop Andrew of Caesarea. This spiritualistic interpretation continues, even in our own day, to be considered very nearly the obligatory one.

However, in fact, such an interpretation does not have sufficient grounds. It would be correct to say that, in this form, it negates chapter 20 of Revelation and thereby opposes Scripture. One cannot fail to see that in the general context of Revelation the content of chapter 20 is indisputably included in the historical sequence of the events, as *one of these events,* that it is sandwiched between events that precede it (the judgment on the whore, the marriage of the Lamb) and events that follow it: "when the thousand years are expired" (Rev. 20:7); the uprising of Gog and Magog, preceding the end.

What are the main features of the story of the thousand-year kingdom? This kingdom begins in the spiritual world: Coming down from heaven, an angel casts the devil into a bottomless pit and chains him, that "he should deceive the nations no more, till the thousand years should be fulfilled; and after that he must be loosed a little season" (Rev. 20:1-3). This describes a certain event in the spiritual world whose effect is manifested in human history. According to Revelation, human history takes place simultaneously in heaven and on earth (cf. Rev. 5:8-12; 6:9-11; 7:9-17; 14:1-5; 15:1-4).

The main feature of this event is a temporary paralysis of the evil power, which leads to a general change in the spiritual atmosphere, a palpable manifestation of the victorious power of good. But this is accompanied by what Revelation calls the "first resurrection," *he anastasis he prōte* (a *terminus technicus* with an article). As a special form of resurrection, it must be distinguished, first of all, from the universal resurrection in the flesh, about which the Gospels and the apostolic epistles speak. Revelation 20:4 says about "souls" not that they were resurrected (in the flesh) but simply that they "came back to life," *ezesan*. This is resurrection neither in the sense in which the Lord resurrected the dead (the boy, the girl, and Lazarus) nor in the sense in which all will be resurrected by the Lord on the last day (John 6:54). What is evidently meant is a *spiritual* resurrection, which consists in the communication to souls of a special energy enabling them to participate, from that side, in the life of the world and human history. This is expressed in the words: "they came back to life and reigned with Christ a thousand years" (Rev. 20:4; translation based on that in the Russian Bible). To this is added the contrast: "the rest of the dead did not come back to life until the thousand years were finished" (v. 5; translation based on that in the Russian Bible). Further it is said: "they shall be priests of God and of Christ, and shall reign with him a thousand years" (v. 6).

Of course, the souls of all who die in Christ continue their life in Him beyond the grave, even if they are temporarily separated from their bodies (the best proofs of this are in Rev. 5; 7:9-10, 13-17; and especially 6:9-11). They help the life of the world with their prayers (5:8; 8:3-4). But this is their transcendental and external action, so to speak. About those who participate in the first resurrection it is said that "they lived [came back to life] and reigned with Christ a thousand years" (20:4) and "they shall be priests of God and of Christ, and shall reign with him a thousand years" (20:6). Here it is a question of their participation in history, which is, according to the aforesaid, the institution of Christ's reign in the world, by virtue of His "royal ministry." Of course, their *participation* in continuing history is different from the fullness of life of the generations that live on earth during this time. Those who come back to life acquire a special activity not possessed by others who "repose in the Lord," to whom it is said "that they should *rest* yet for a little season" (6:11). Let us not try to divine what is not revealed to us about the special activity of those who have thus come back to life and reign with Christ on earth. Only one thing is clear: the barrier dividing the two worlds, this world and that world, becomes so thin here that the arena of history expands, and history is made not only by the living generations but also with the participation of those who "came back to life."

This general idea must be applied to the dogma of the veneration of the saints and our communion with them. Does the latter, which is accomplished in God and which is essentially due to prayer, not also presuppose this particular aspect, that is, the "first resurrection"? The participation of the saints in our life by their prayer and assistance is an indisputable and permanent fact, which holds for all times. In a certain sense this fact coincides with the fact of the guidance of the world by the holy angels, although at the same time it differs from it. The angels have their special place in the world as cosmic agents of a sort, whereas saints, even those who are glorified and strong by their intercession in prayer, remain outside the world, as it were, in an ontologically defective state through separation from their bodies, a state that will be overcome only in resurrection.

But is it perhaps not appropriate in general to identify the active assistance of the saints, *communio sanctorum*, with their "reign" with Christ about which Revelation speaks, and to ask if this reign is not exhausted by this assistance? However, there is *no* basis for such an affirmation in Revelation, in which the prayers of the saints, rising like incense from censers, clearly differ from their reign with Christ. Although these prayers cer-

339

tainly constitute part of the reign, only the latter has the special fullness of active participation in history that is expressed in a mysterious co-reign with Christ. This co-reign, connected with the return to life (Rev. 20:4) in the first resurrection, communicates such a power and concreteness of this participation that it is *as if* they live on the earth. However, we cannot more precisely define the measure or nature of this participation.

The only indisputable thing is that this "first resurrection" signifies that the saints are specially elected and predestined to salvation: "Blessed and holy is he that hath part in the first resurrection: on such the second death hath no power" (Rev. 20:6). This blessed lot of those resurrected in the first resurrection is opposed to the state of "the rest of the dead," who "live not again until the thousand years were finished" (Rev. 20:5). For history this co-reign with Christ of those who have been resurrected represents an express increase of the victorious power of goodness, corresponding to Satan's enchainment. In brief, this is the final victory of the kingdom of God *on earth*, its anticipation *in history*, as it was prefigured during the earthly days of Christ by the royal entry into Jerusalem. The thousand-year kingdom thus signifies a divinely revealed condemnation of historical pessimism in general and, in particular, of the pseudo-eschatological panic that often marks Christian historiosophy. One is impelled to connect once again this manifestation of the victorious power of Christianity on earth with the "life from the dead" (Rom. 11:15) of Israel and those new powers that will pour into history in connection with this event. Is it not this that is hinted at in the heavenly vision of the victory over the beast and his image, when those standing on the sea of glass "sing the song of Moses the servant of God, and the song of the Lamb" (Rev. 15:3)? To which it is added: "All nations shall come and worship before thee; for thy judgments are made manifest" (v. 4).

It is clear that neither this victory of Christianity on earth nor Christ's royal entry into Jerusalem overcomes or abolishes tragedy within the limits of this world. On the contrary, they represent the most mature stage of this tragedy, the concluding chapter of history: the uprising of the rebellious forces of wickedness, followed by the final catastrophe of the world and the end of this age. Although it has triumphed in the world, goodness will not yet manifest its definitive stability in the last duel with Satan, who "shall be loosed out of his prison, and shall go out to deceive the nations . . . [and] gather them together to battle" (Rev. 20:7-8). This is the ultimate baring of the power of evil that battles against Christ. But the power of the God-man is already manifested here: He "comes in glory to judge the living and the dead," as is sung in the Credo. The Lord shall consume the wicked one "with the spirit of his mouth, and shall destroy [him] with the brightness of his coming" (2 Thess. 2:8).

But here the question of the thousand-year reign arises for us in a new way: Is it sufficient to understand it as an event in time, or is such an interpretation just as one-sided and incomplete as the opposite one? Is one justified in thinking that the millennium signifies, in general, life in the Church, which represents the thousand-year reign itself? This interpretation, however, does not remove and should not remove the other interpretation. Otherwise, violence would inevitably be done to both the letter and the spirit of Scripture. In the Gospel doctrine of the kingdom of God, both meanings are united: The kingdom of God is within us and it also "comes," so that one presupposes the other.

The same thing can be said about eternal life: it is accessible to Christians already here on earth, but it is also an express gift of God. Similarly, the thousand-year kingdom, like the first resurrection, is directed, in different aspects, at both the present and the future. The Church is Christ's reign in the world, which is established in souls and illuminates life. In this sense, one can say that souls sanctified by grace, to whom "belongs the kingdom of heaven," already reign with Christ in the thousand-year kingdom. In this sense this kingdom is an object of mystical evidence, of spiritual experience. But while belonging to eternity, Christian life cannot remain outside of history, closed up in itself. The realization of the kingdom of God illuminates all the epochs of history, but it is especially made manifest only in one epoch, although this too is not its definitive realization, for which, in general, there is no place in this age. Therefore, it is equally true that the "first resurrection" is proper to the Church in all epochs and that it belongs to a particular time. The same thing can be said about the special proximity of the world beyond the grave, *communio sanctorum*, connected with this.

All that has been said in no wise diminishes the guiding significance of the idea of the thousand-year kingdom, which for us is the guiding star of history. This idea is an expression of the Christian notion of progress, where the latter is liberated from its limited naturalistic conception. This idea is proper to Christian humanism, in contradistinction to pagan or anti-Christian humanism. This idea grounds the validity of history with its supreme achievements in this world; moreover, it presupposes and commands these achievements. The end of history is not due to an arbitrary *deus ex machina*, to a divine act of violence that interrupts the contentless bad infinity of human history. On the contrary, a positive goal is set for history: its inner ripening to a good end, although this end comes convulsively and catastrophically. This inwardly overcomes the Manichaean cosmomachy, for which life and history are a void: "Vanity of vanities: all is vanity. . . . The thing that hath been, it is that which shall be; and that which is done is that which shall be done; and there is no new thing under the sun" (Eccles. 1:2, 9).

The idea of the millennium can be the soul of Christian progress, the motive force of Christian humanism, the inspiration of Christian creative activity. There can be and therefore there must be a historical creativity in the name of Christ and with Christ, in the battle against destructive, theomachic and anti-Christian forces in history. This grounds and strengthens our faith in history and our sense of responsibility for it. History is included in the common task of the sophianization of the world in and through man. Thus, historiosophy is a necessary element of sophiology.

Insofar as history is a creative activity, it is a domain of creaturely freedom and of the various possibilities connected with the latter; and conditional prophecy is applicable to it. This leads one to inquire into the general character of the Christian revelation concerning history that we have in the Apocalypse of John. How and in what sense is the Apocalypse possible in general?

This question brings us back to the limits of creaturely freedom and to its relation to the sophianic regularity of creation. Insofar as creaturely freedom has a modal character, creaturely creative activity is not the omnipotence of creation out of nothing but the fulfillment of the sophianicity of creation, although a variable fulfillment. Freedom does not abolish this sophianic regularity but only concretely applies it. The determined character of creative activity is invariably connected with the freedom of its themes and is therefore free of the fetters of determinism. There is room for variants here. The goals of God are unalterable and irrevocable, but the paths to them can differ; and these differences, inessential for the whole, can turn out to be essential for individual destinies and achievements. This leads to the possibility of conditional prophecies and, as Scripture shows, to the fact that they are not irrevocable. The most expressive example is, of course, Jonah's prophecy of the destruction of Nineveh.

One can say that for man all things are accomplished in freedom, both with respect to the acceptance or rejection of his existential theme or task, and with respect to the mode of its acceptance. With reference to the general paths of the life of the world this signifies the possibility of fluctuations of its duration *("mora finis")* in this life. One can say that, consisting of a limited number of elements but admitting an enormous number of their combinations, the world can fully realize the will of God in each of them, although differently. With reference to the general plan of the universe, these variations are the *minima* with which the cosmic order does not concern itself. But for itself each variation is the sole reality, as it were. In connection with this one can pose a general question: namely, how should Revelation as a prophecy about the history of the world and humankind be understood? Are the general laws governing history revealed here, laws that are analogous to those that govern the motion of celestial bodies or other mechanical or physical phenomena? Is there a place here for human freedom and creative activity? Absolutely. Revelation allows freedom and creative activity in a variety of forms.

First, there are the messages to the angels of the churches and, in their persons, to the churches themselves (Rev. 2:5-7, 10, 16, 25; 3:3-5, 11, 18-20). The whole narrative here presupposes the active participation of the armies of Christ as well as the armies of the enemy. However, one must note the distinctive way in which the language of the Apocalypse stylizes events. Most of them are seen from above, as God's actions through angels or through the Lamb Himself, whereas the human side of history, with the reactions proper to it, is only implied. One can therefore get the impression that history is made from above, by divine decrees. But such a view is not compatible with the final sum of history, which is added up at the judgment "according to [each person's] works" (Rev. 20:12). History is nevertheless viewed (as in the Gospel Apocalypse) as the *common work* of humankind. But, to be sure, this creative work not only does not exclude the participation of the divine power but even presupposes it.

History is a divine-human affair: the divine power is combined with human freedom, as the dogma of dithelitism makes clear. As the common work, history is a synergism. And it is this spiritual, divine side of history that Revelation reveals. In the light of Revelation history appears to us as a single tragic act, in which Christ's victory and the institution of His reign in the world are accomplished. In history, humankind experiences in Christ and with Christ a tragic struggle, which is followed by the glorious resurrection. Therefore, on the one hand, one can justly say that the entire Apocalypse does nothing more than exhort us to martyrdom by forewarning us of it. But one can just as justly say that it also calls us to battle and exhorts us to creative action, that it preaches synergism. That is how one should understand the final, summoning words of the Apocalypse: "And the Spirit and the bride say, Come. And let him that heareth say, Come" (Rev. 22:17). For He who is summoned and comes is the "Alpha and

Omega, the Beginning and the End, the First and the Last" (v. 13) — the God-man, who, by His Divine-humanity, is the mover, power, and content of history.

Thus, history does not end naturally but breaks off, as with an ellipsis, which corresponds to its *transcensus* into the life of the future age. In this sense, the millennium is like the line of the horizon, which constantly recedes as one approaches it. This "transcendental" character of the millennium as a moving goal makes it unattainable but always sought.

Thus, we return to the idea that, besides being a specific epoch or episode of history, the millennium is also where the continuous revelation of the Church in history mysteriously abides. In this sense, one can say that the millennium is repeated in history, and this repetition reaches its greatest intensity in history's creative epochs, in their principal themes and creative achievements. In general, the millennium is a symbol of historical creativity. But this does not contradict the idea that all of these diverse goals and achievements lead to a higher synthesis: the thousand-year kingdom in the strict sense. This kingdom makes *possible* the end of history, although it itself is not yet that end, but only its harbinger. The end arrives by a transcendent act of the Father's will.

One thus sees the difference between the idea of apocalyptic culmination proper to Christian millenarianism and evolutionary progress with its immanent achievements of "petty-bourgeois" humanism. One must underscore with particular insistence that it is impossible to unite and to inwardly reconcile the two, even though there are a certain external resemblance and apparent closeness between them. Eschatological progress is a *condition of the end,* while evolutionary progress is a complete *rejection* of the end, and its replacement by bad infinity, which continues on the same historical plane. But there is no common evolutionary humanistic progress, no progress as one humanity in this sense. There is only a succession of generations, which can be united only in the abstract. And this subject of immanent progress is abolished by the existence of death.

On the contrary, it is universal resurrection that synthesizes and really restores *one* humanity as the subject of the achievements of history, although in a different dimension of being. But the idea of this resurrection is completely absent in the evolutionary conception of history. The fact that the ideology of immanent progress forgets death is a striking example of the superficiality and thoughtlessness with which it treats the most essential, decisive problem. There is no progress, for there is no one to progress in the absence of a unique, continuous humanity not subject to a temporal end. *Carpe diem* is the sole conclusion of godless historiosophy.

Before our very eyes, godless historiosophy is inevitably arriving at its total triumph and justification: the idea of the immanent, biological conquest of death by means of natural resurrection. This idea is supposed to plug up all the holes and to overcome the flaws in the theory of immanent progress. Curiously, the idea of immanent resurrection, the "regulation of nature," was born in the fiery Christian spirit of N. F. Fyodorov (although it does have precursors, especially the fantasies of Fourier). For Fyodorov the supreme and most general goal of the "common task" was the resurrection of the fathers by the sons. He forcibly extends the idea of earthly progress to include immortality "by work," so that life itself, this *gift* of the life-giving Lord, becomes a technological achievement. His principle "nothing free" leads him to a hidden Sophiamachy. The "proposed" replaces the "given": man's task is to plunder and appropriate the given, to eliminate the synergism of Divine-humanity. The idea of technological immortality is beginning to tempt the godless progressivists, who hope to use it to decisively overcome the religious worldview and to achieve the triumph of immanentism by assuring the possibility of definitively making oneself at home on the earth.

The tendency of de-godded Fyodorovism (humanistic resurrectionism) is to eliminate eschatology, to make superfluous and unnecessary the second coming of Christ and the final transfiguration of the world. Therefore the "project" of this great elder, which he conceives as the fulfillment of Christ's work on the pathways of the "common task" of humankind, is transformed into the idea of the Tower of Babel, built by theomachic humankind without and against God. Technological resurrection is the supreme and final achievement of "petty-bourgeois" progress, beyond which . . . there is nothing to do. This is the kingdom of insurmountable emptiness and boredom, of mutual cannibalism on the ruins of sentimental love (one of Dostoevsky's nightmares). This is the barrel of the Danaides, an effort to deplete the inexhaustible, despair for the thinking mind and the feeling heart. This is the inner end of the antichrist whom Christ "shall consume with the spirit of his mouth, and shall destroy with the brightness of his coming" (2 Thess. 2:8). "He that sitteth in the heavens shall laugh: the Lord shall have them in derision" (Ps. 2:4). Fyodorov's "project" is a touchstone for godless progress. It leads consciousness to the ultimate question about man himself: does he *really exist,* and *what* is he? If he is only an aggregate of atoms that fall apart only to be collected again, then man does not really exist. There is no one to resurrect and no one to do the resurrecting; there is only the *ewige Wiederkehr* [eternal return] nightmare of Ecclesiastes-Nietzsche. A series of illusions arises, in which repetition is taken to be identity, since the latter cannot be subjectless. Therefore, the de-godded "project" is not the triumph but the total collapse of the theory of progress, an abyss of despair that opens up before man at the end of his path.[8]

The foregoing discussion concerns the idea of immanent, natural, human, technological resurrection. It is clear that this idea disintegrates by an internal contradiction, which also leads to the destruction of the entire atheistic doctrine of progress and historical achievements. But this limited character of immanentism by no means removes the question of the significance of human action and of human participation in the eschatological accomplishments. These achievements can be characterized symbolically as humanity's approach to resurrection through the maximal humanization of matter by the "regulation of the forces of nature." These this-worldly achievements are by no means capable of taking one *beyond* the present state of being. They cannot abolish *transcensus* or render unnecessary the resurrection by divine power that accompanies the transfiguration of the world. The eschatological culmination is a synergistic act, an encounter of God's action with creaturely being that is in a determinate state. It comes "after" history, although it includes and presupposes history as its object.

This is the main idea of the Apocalypse, historiosophical and eschatological: "Write the things which thou hast seen, and the things which are, and the things which shall be hereafter" (Rev. 1:19). The eschatological completion is distinct from the historical one: "And he that sat upon the throne said, Behold, I make all things new. . . . And he said unto me, It is done. I am Alpha and Omega, the Beginning and the End" (21:5, 6). But this new creation presupposes the closed circle of history. "Declaring the

---

8. It would take the art of a Dostoevsky to show the whole depth of this collapse: A mother who, by the regulation of natural forces, gets back her raised son and, by the instinct of a mother's heart, sees in him a deceitful double, not a son but an automaton; a fiance who, instead of his beloved, embraces a robot and knows it is a robot. Mannequins can only mechanically reproduce but cannot creatively unite the past with the future, continuing *one* life. The character of the mechanical repetition that replaces identity is not altered by the fact that "raised" robots are produced not only by a mechanical agglomeration of corporeal or corporealized particles of cosmic matter, but also by an addition of physiological elements, including spermatozoids; for in the living individual the body is only the substrate of the spirit that lives in it. The body is such only in relation to and in union with the spirit living in it, but outside of this union it is a robot. It is theoretically possible to fabricate an indefinite number, a crowd, of robots that repeat one another but that thereby recede farther and farther away from the original.

346

end from the beginning, and from ancient times the things that are not yet done, saying, My counsel shall stand, and I will do all my pleasure. . . . I have spoken it, I will also bring it to pass; I have purposed it, I will also do it" (Isa. 46:10-11).

This connection between history and metahistory, the historical apocalypse and eschatology, is unfathomable for us in this world. On the one hand, a *transcensus*, an act of "new creation," passes between them, although it is based on the original creation. On the other hand, a certain ontological identity exists between them by virtue of the fact that the new creation is based on the original creation. Transfigured history is in fact eschatology: "it doth not yet appear what we shall be" (1 John 3:2). In the world fire all will be melted, and some things will burn ("but he himself shall be saved, yet so as by fire" [1 Cor. 3:15]), but hardly all. And we must conceive this fire as not only a burning one but also as a transfiguring one. This fire needs history as its material. History is, so to speak, the *prius* of eschatology, just as the biography of every human being is not only the material to be judged but also the energy for the life to come (see 1 Cor. 2:9-15).

From here we see and know only history. And we cannot diminish or devalue its significance solely because it will pass through fire. On the contrary, we must discern eternal content in its temporality. The great city, holy Jerusalem, which descends out of "heaven from God," has the heavenly blessing upon it, the "glory of God," but it is not an entirely new creation. The precious stones of the earth are its material, and in general it is an earthly building. Upon it are "written . . . the names of the twelve tribes of the children of Israel" (Rev. 21:12). "The glory and honour of the nations" (v. 26) shall be brought into it, and "the kings of the earth do bring their glory and honour into it" (v. 24). This epilogue of history shows with striking clarity how history, having passed through the divine fire, is transfigured into the eschatological kingdom of God.

Out of this relation come the basic maxims of practical eschatological historicism. First of all, nothing earthly should be absolutized, in the sense of imparting abiding value to it: "here have we no continuing city, but we seek one to come" (Heb. 13:14). All earthly things must be perceived in the light of the coming end, the eschatological culmination. This is the special music of eternity, which is heard near Christian heroes and ascetics. But it is precisely this that gives to earthly works their exclusive significance, placing them in the perspective of eternity. These works do not belong solely to the stream of time (the *panta rei* of Heraclitus and the "vanity of vanities" of Ecclesiastes). They are inscribed in the book of life

347

and "follow" their doers from history into eschatology. This is what gives significance to the creative activity of history, affirms the work of history and the responsibility for this work. This work does not tumble like a house of cards, is not destroyed by the blows of world catastrophe. On the contrary, it is made manifest in its unity, coherence, and reality at the last judgment, before which all the nations will be brought in the unity of their common history.

Man's likeness to God is actualized in historical creative activity. In God's world, man creates his own historical world. This manifested humanness is the historical aspect of the creaturely Sophia, the sophianicity of history, which leads to the humanization and, thus, the sophianization of the world. This humanness is the creaturely substrate for the union of the Divine and the creaturely Sophia, a union which is represented by the figures of the eschatological catastrophe and the transfiguration of the world. This is the final meaning and content of what we have defined as Christian humanism, saving man from self-immersion in creatureliness, in the theomachy of godless or pagan humanism.

A final question remains: Why are the content and theme of creative activity expressed so imprecisely, or represented only by the most general apocalyptic symbols? Why does the unknown, pregnant with all kinds of unexpected things, reign here? And why do the schemata of the Apocalypse refer only to spiritual potencies and not to the absolute values themselves? It is not difficult to answer this: Because creative activity is creative activity, and its distinguishing feature is *novelty*. This constitutes the peculiar interest of creative activity. Although creative activity is creative activity not *ex nihilo* but on the basis of what is given, it nevertheless contains something new, something that is not given but is a task to be accomplished. Since the soul of creative activity is freedom, there is no predetermination here; the two are incompatible. Creative activity is determined only in its possibilities and tasks, not in its concrete reality. This conditions the special joy of creative activity, its *gaia scienza,* this atmosphere of "rebirth": "Life is joyous." Of course, behind this first joyous impulse of creative activity, its implacably tragic aspect is revealed: there is a contradiction between the absoluteness of the impulse and the relativity of its realization. This fatal failure does not allow one to achieve a state of repose, to stop, to achieve "petty bourgeois" comfort and satisfaction, but calls one onward and upward. Thickening into pessimism, this sense of failure colors the following historical epoch. The cry of the vanity of life and of creative activity rises in souls. But the radiant fountain of creative activity once again throws high its jets, which, however, again and again, fall from their heights. . . .

CHAPTER 7

Death and the State after Death

The existence of death, just like birth, shrouds in *mystery* the being of man and of all living things. Man can hide from this mystery only by ceasing to feel or by fleeing from all thought of it, but this is possible only for a time. This mystery is inaccessible to knowledge. It is therefore an object of belief, whatever the content of the latter. Not to believe in immortality is also a kind of belief, impossible to verify within the limits of this life and, in the formal sense, it does not differ from belief in immortality. Of course, a person may be predisposed to the one belief or to the other, depending upon his spiritual state. Therefore, people of the present age, wholly caught up in its life with its vanity, might sincerely be perplexed when they encounter belief in immortality. But on the contrary, this belief can become something self-evident, not admitting even question or doubt, for those who have come to know eternal life within the limits of this world, for those who have encountered God in the life of their spirit, for those who have experienced through love a revelation of death. However, in both cases death represents a *transcensus* into another life, one which remains largely unknown to us.

Scripture gives us some guidance here, some ideas. But these ideas must be clarified and developed theologically. What is most incomprehensible in what can be called the ontology of death is disbelief's assertion that death is the total annihilation of life. It is an axiom for positivism that *ex nihilo nihil fit,* together with the law of the conservation of energy. Positivism therefore rejects the idea of the creation of the world out of nothing and proclaims the eternity of the world, while admitting a spontaneous generation of life. At the same time, positivism easily comes to terms with the transformation of being into nothing, with ontological an-

349

nihilation. And it goes to the extreme of the most radical form of annihilation: not only of the visible forms of bodily life but also of the conscious life of the spirit and of the heart, of creative energy. Therefore, positivism proclaims the ultimate ontological absurdity of a double annihilation: an appearance out of nothing and a return to nothing, a soap bubble that has burst, whose real content is emptiness. In order to avoid accepting the problematic of death, unbelieving thought takes refuge in this ontology of nihilism, in the "outer darkness" of a double nonbeing: *before* death and *after* death.

This shows once again that death can be understood *only in the context of life*, as part of life, and not vice versa: Life cannot be submerged in the nonbeing of death. In this sense, even though death is a parasite of being, it is an act of life. That *nothing* "out of" which God created the world and which in this sense "precedes" the world *does not in fact exist* as such and for itself. Its being consists precisely in nonbeing; its existence is nonexistence. Its positive being begins only in the world and with the world; its autonomous existence in this world, which is a mixture of being and nonbeing, is only relative and derivative, ontologically parasitic. By creating the world out of nothing, God gives a place not only for being but also for nonbeing. He "creates" nonbeing or, more precisely, the possibility of being for nonbeing as a shadow in being or a "minus." However, an autonomous nonbeing that would be identical to absolute death, to the "outer darkness," but that would have the power of being in itself, does not exist at all.

This is proclaimed by revelation (although in a "noncanonical" book): "God made not death . . . for he created all things that they might have their being" (Wisdom of Solomon 1:13, 14). There is no death in the plan of God's creation, in its structure. Death "came into the world through the envy of the devil" (2:24), for "God created man to be immortal, and made him to be an image of his own eternity" (v. 23). Therefore, death has not a substantial but only an accidental being; it can be understood only as a state of life. The mortal nature of life is only its sickness, which is inevitable in the given state of life but not incurable. There was no death and there will be no death. Man was not originally created for death; the natural *possibility* of immortality was implanted in him.

The idea of Catholic theology that man is mortal because of his corporeality and that, therefore, even before the fall his mortality could be overcome only by a supernatural gift of grace, *donum superadditum,* is a blasphemy against God's creation, attributing to the Creator a failure in creation, which can be overcome only by His express action. *Posse non mori,* the possibility of not dying, which, of course, is different from the divine-human power of immortality, *non posse mori,* was given to Adam with his creation. But, like all of God's gifts, it was not only a given but also a task to be realized. Man had to affirm this possibility in himself by a spiritual-creative act, but he could also have annulled it, which is in fact what happened in original sin. This annulment was sealed by a judgment of God, attesting to the change that had taken place: "thou [wilt] return unto the ground; for out of it thou wast taken: for dust thou art, and unto dust shalt thou return" (Gen. 3:19). "Then shall the dust return to the earth as it was: and the spirit shall return unto God who gave it" (Eccles. 12:7). These words of revelation contain an anthropological monogram of death, signifying the separation by God Himself of what was originally united. Death consists in the fact that man's spirit, which originally came from God and in this sense is both created and uncreated, departs the "earth," to which his created nature belongs: a body animated by a soul.

Let us return to the fundamental doctrine of man's sophianicity. The "earth," that is, the creaturely Sophia, is hypostatized by the human spirit, which in its spirituality has the potency of immortality and communicates this potency to its entire complex noncreaturely-creaturely nature. This nature awaits the fullness of its sophianization, necessarily including immortality, in and through the human spirit. Original sin consists in the deviation of man from his path of union with God. It is the beginning of death, which entered the human spirit through sin. To be sure, this deviation cannot lead to the death of the immortal human spirit that came from God (just as it did not lead to the death of the world of fallen spirits). But it was such a weakening of the human spirit, and especially of its power over psychocorporeal nature, that the equilibrium was disrupted: not yet having attained the ontological stability of *non posse mori,* man was pushed in the opposite direction, that of *non posse non mori.* But death, having entered the world, did not annihilate but only weakened life, which was restored by Christ, who trampled death by death.

That which was intended to be united in the tripartite composition of man, spirit, soul, and body, is subjected in death to a temporary separation. The spirit lost the power to sustain a constant connection with its body, and to this extent its strength was reduced. Mortality became the general state of the condition of fallen man. Although it arrives only at a preestablished hour of life, death extends over all of human life from its very beginning. We know this because man can die at any age; all cases of death are only particular applications of the one principle of mortality. All that lives, man, and, with him, all living creatures, begins to die at the beginning of life. Over the whole course of life, the weakening caused by death increases, until life is finally defeated.[1]

First of all, it is necessary to understand the ontological possibility of death, its metaphysics,[2] so to speak. By no means does death signify that the Creator has failed in His work of creation and that He therefore destroys it Himself, as it were; for death is not the annihilation of life but only a particular state of life, and in this sense it is an act of life. True, death did not have to exist, since God did not create it. Nevertheless, the possibility of death is contained in man's complex composition and it has not yet been overcome precisely because of this complexity. Such an ontological complexity does not exist for fleshless spirits. This is why even in the fall they were not touched by death, and Satan and his angels remain just as immortal as the holy angels, although the character of their existence as angels changed. Accordingly, the sophianicity of the angels is limited in comparison with that of man, who is the king of creation, its light and center.

Despite the fullness of his creaturely sophianicity, man is susceptible to death because of his ontological richness, which, at the same time, is complexity. Like all creation, man is an alloy of being and nonbeing; and the latter raises its head and is actualized whenever his ontological equilibrium is shaken. This equilibrium can be definitively established only by the universal absoluteness and fullness of the life revealed in the God-man, who even in His human nature overcame the weakness of creatureliness. Original sin is an actual and universal violation of ontological equilibrium in all of humankind and in each human individual. This equilibrium is restored only in Christ. Therefore, God's judgment upon every individual is not an externally imposed punishment, but expresses the ontological consequence of the violated equilibrium and the bared creatureliness: "dust thou art."

In the fullness of his being, according to God's plan for him, man is not only dust or earth, but God-earth, an incarnate godlike spirit. The fall was accompanied not by a complete rupture between spirit and earth, which would signify an ontological annihilation of man himself, but only by a partial separation, one that is not definitive. The image of God, that

1. This sorrow of the enervation connected with death is expressed in the sorrowful images of Eccles. 12:1-4, 5, 7. [. . .]

2. See my article, still in manuscript, "The Sophiology of Death" (1940). [This article has been published in *Vestnik Russkogo Khristianskogo Dvizhenia*, Paris, 1978, no. 127, pp. 18-41; 1979, no. 128, pp. 13-42. — Trans.].

is, man's original *Divine-humanity*, is preserved. God's plan for creation cannot fail to be realized, but human life, in its pathways, undergoes a pathological interruption, a temporary separation of the soul and body: death. But death is not an ultimate and definitive state, the failure of man's creation. Rather, it is an inevitable stage in man's life.

Death must be understood on the basis of life, as a state of life; not vice versa. Life must not be submerged in death (which is what materialism does). Death is only permitted by God and is therefore providentially included in man's life. Death is not a particular and unexpected event in man's life but a necessary expression of his *mortality*, permeating all of his life. Death is an evolutionarily catastrophic *transcensus*, ripening over the whole course of an individual's life but taking place at the instant of the "hour of death." In this sense, individual death, whatever the form in which it comes, is natural according to the law of mortal life. Originally, however, death is unnatural, since God did not create death, but it entered the world by way of creaturely freedom and sin. This explains the implacable tragedy and insurmountable horror of death, of the open maw of nonbeing. This horror is *ontologically* inseparable from human nature, even in the God-man Himself: "My soul is exceeding sorrowful, even unto death" (Matt. 26:38). "My God, why hast thou forsaken me?" (27:46). The exceeding sorrow of death, the feeling that one is forsaken by God (which, however, is wonderfully combined with union with Christ, who dies together with us), accompanies death like its black shadow. And, in its burial hymns, the Church does not diminish the intensity of the sorrow of death.

That is the spiritual aspect of death. Such also is its bodily aspect: death is the sickness of sicknesses, the suffering of sufferings. But the salvific antinomy of death is also made manifest here. This horror, insurmountable naturally, has *already* been overcome supernaturally, by grace, for the path of death has been followed to the end by Christ and, after Him, by the Mother of God. This path is suffused and illuminated by the fiery tongues of the descent of the Holy Spirit into the world even through the fetters of death. In this sense, the death of the righteous who are pure in heart, who are capable of seeing God, is the joy of joys and the triumph of triumphs. And it is as the coming joy, as the promise of the meeting with Christ ("I . . . [have] a desire to depart, and to be with Christ," says the apostle in Phil. 1:23), that death must be received by the believing soul. All the days of his earthly life, man experiences the antinomy of death. On the one hand, man opposes death with all his being, for at his creation the life-giving Spirit implanted in him love of life as the supreme value and deed, together with its fire. But, on the other hand, sin attacks life with its enervating poison, producing a sense of the weariness of life, so that the immortality of Ahasverus, the wandering Jew, seems like a horrible nightmare and a triumph of hell on earth. Such also would be the kingdom of the prince of this world if it were made eternal by immortality, that immortality engineered by human effort which the ideologues of technological resurrection summon us to. The permitting of death is an act of divine mercy toward creation, for death delivers creation from its fetters: "The corruptible body presseth down the soul, and the earthly tabernacle weigheth down the mind that museth upon many things" (Wis. Sol. 9:15). The burden of life can become unbearable and provoke the temptation of suicide, the flight from life. Nevertheless, God permitted death as an act of His providence, and death, like life, is in God's hands. Only God's wisdom knows the hour and the moment, and at the proper time sends the angel of death. . . .

Death, as we have said, does not abolish the sophianicity of creation, for it does not destroy or abolish creation itself. As a factor in the dialectic of life, death must be understood in the light of the future resurrection, which restores the interrupted life, and in connection with that undying principle in man which continues to live after death (and which not even suicide can destroy). In the tripartite structure of man, death's dividing sickle passes between the spirit and the soul (which are therefore usually combined under the general notion of the soul) on the one hand and between the spirit and the body on the other. It is very important to take into account this indivisibility of the spirit and the soul in death, for it confirms the principle of creaturely immortality in the continuing connection with this world. The soul is an intermediate principle connecting the spirit with the creaturely world. The soul is creaturely, like the "blood" that animates the body: The physical blood dies and decomposes together with the body. But the supraphysical energy of life, whose substratum is the blood, abides (this can also be expressed by the esoteric notion of the "etheric" or "astral" body). It is thus impossible to speak of a complete death in the sense of a victory of nonbeing. This would signify a victory of death over life so complete that it would ontologically exclude resurrection. But resurrection is not only a restoration but also a continuation of life, which supposes a continuous identity and unity of life before death and after resurrection. Once again this compels us to understand death as a state of life.[3]

3. This aspect of the question remains totally unresolved in the doctrine of the "raising from the dead," whence the ambiguity of [Fyodorov's] "project" of raising all people from the dead by means of human action, the project of the "common task." If there is no complete death, there arises the question of the state after death, which must

But the triumph of death would be complete only if the spirit were separated from the soul and body, if the noncreaturely-creaturely principle in man were separated from the creaturely principle, that is, if the spirit were disincarnated. This would evidently signify the annihilation of man himself and a total failure of God's creative plan: Man would be decomposed into his two component parts, the divine principle and the creaturely principle; and he would fall apart into ontological dust. Can one conceive of such a disincarnation of the human spirit? Does the spirit have its own power of being and immortality apart from the body? Is it confined in the body as in a dungeon?

In answering these questions, it is again necessary to reflect upon the meaning of man's uncreated-created, spiritual nature. The human spirit has a divine origin and can participate in divine life. In this sense it is divine, although, in itself, it is not a god with an autonomous source of personal being and nature. Man's personal spirit is also created by God. This means that the personal principle in man is called to being as a repetition or reflection of the Person of God in nonbeing. Although this personal principle has the *simplicity* that is proper to the spirit, it is determinately qualified at its creation. Human hypostases acquired concrete being only in connection with the creaturely cosmos, as its hypostases; and in this sense, they are inseparable from the cosmos. This connection is precisely the corporeality or incarnate condition of the personal spirit.

The human hypostasis does not have a spiritual, supramundane being, nor, in this being, an immortality independent of incarnation. The human spirit is not created a fleshless spirit, like the angels. No human spirit can exist independently of the world. It therefore does not have abstract, nonhuman immortality. Its very being and, therefore, immortality (insofar as it possesses the latter) are qualified by and inseparably connected with the world. This immortality is a human one, whose realization encompasses both death and resurrection. Both the one and the other, accomplished in Christ and, in Him and through Him, in all humankind, have, so to speak, their ontological place in human nature, fully assumed by the Lord in His incarnation. Therefore, the division in this nature which occurs in death would be ontologically contradictory and thus

---

somehow be included in the "project." But it has not been included. In the contrary case, it can be a question not of a raising from the dead, where those raised are identical to the dead, but only of a repetition, which destroys the very idea of the raising from the dead. Here, integral humankind is replaced by a nightmarish collection of robots, whose consciousnesses are similar to their originals, not identical.

impossible if it separated the spirit from the soul and the body, thereby totally destroying man, dehumanizing him. On the contrary, death separates the *human* spirit, which remains connected with the soul, only from the body, that is, from the natural world. Thus, its human energy, the soul, is reduced to a state of potentiality, a shadow state. It loses the fullness of life. But by the power of God manifested in the resurrection of the God-man, it is capable of being restored, of re-creating its body, and thus of realizing its resurrection: "in Christ shall all be made alive. But every man in his own order: Christ the firstfruits; afterward they that are Christ's at his coming" (1 Cor. 15:22-23). Corresponding to this is the image of the grain that contains the whole potentiality of life and awaits only a sign from God to convert it into energy: "And that which thou sowest, thou sowest not that body that shall be, but bare grain, it may chance of wheat, or of some other grain. But God giveth it a body as it hath pleased him, and to every seed his own body" (vv. 37-38).

The human spirit exists as the hypostatic potency of the integral man, who has a body whose energy is the soul. In death, this energy is paralyzed but not annihilated. It remains a quality of the personal spirit. This is why it is so important to understand death not as an annihilation of life but as a dormition, a temporary cessation of the action of the soul upon the body. The soul does not die but is only relatively potentialized. In this sense (but only in this sense), one can refer to the dead as those who are "asleep," and there are different modes and degrees of this dormition.

These general thoughts about death, which are ontological in character, must be dogmatically verified and confirmed on the basis of christology. What exactly does Christ's death represent? Does it represent a disincarnation of the Logos, with the separation of the two natures, divine and human, the divine spirit departing from the human soul and body? This question contains its own answer: the impossibility of admitting such a hypothesis is obvious. The Incarnation of God is eternally inviolable, and death is powerless against it. The apostle Peter applies to Christ's Resurrection (Acts 2:31) the verse from Psalm 16:10: "For thou wilt not leave my soul in hell; neither wilt thou suffer thine Holy One to see corruption." Even in His death the divine Logos remained united with His human nature and was not separated from His human soul even in hell, although He was separated from His flesh. By an act of God, His soul recovered its life-giving power in resurrection. It is in this sense that it is said that Christ rose from the dead,[4] although He was resurrected by the Fa-

---

4. See *The Lamb of God,* the chapter on Christ's resurrection.

ther by the power of the Holy Spirit. Even in the grave the Lord remains the God-man in all fullness. The connection of His divine spirit with His body also remains, as the pledge of resurrection (this is the basis for the dogmatic doctrine of relics).

Just as Christ's death was not a separation of the divine nature and the human nature, nor a separation of the soul and body, so His ascension to heaven in His flesh is not an abandonment of the world but an affirmation and an eternalization of His connection with the world: "I am with you always, even unto the end of the world" (Matt. 28:20). Thus, as an act of life of His human nature, Christ's death does not differ in character from the death that is common to all men. His presence for three days in the grave corresponds to life beyond the grave. This afterlife ministry of Christ consisted in His descent into hell and the preaching to the souls confined there. In the grave, the Lord's body remained in the state of the Divine Deceased, untouched by corruption, for the power of death was limited here: Christ's death was not internally inevitable; He assumed it voluntarily. His communication with the souls of the deceased, that is, His "sermon in hell," attests that, after death, the Lord was in a state that was accessible to the deceased and that, in this sense, was analogous to their own state: being without a body, He remained united with His soul, which nevertheless belongs to this world, since "hell" (sheol) also belongs to it. This connection of the souls of the deceased with the world, as well as among themselves, is confirmed by several parables, notably by the parable of the rich man and Lazarus, whose souls recognize each other in their earthly individuality: The rich man lifted up his eyes and saw "Abraham afar off, and Lazarus in his bosom" (Luke 16:23).

In the church literature, in the lives of the saints and the prologues, in patristic works (e.g., in the works of St. Macarius the Great and St. Cyril of Alexandria) and in some liturgical hymns,[5] death is usually described in an extremely concrete manner. According to these descriptions, death consists in the separation from the body of a kind of transparent shell which has the image of the body and retains its vital life (using a specialized terminology, the occult literature describes something similar, based on the data of visions). The same character is attributed to death in different instances of after-death appearances of the deceased in a transparent image. Uniting these different features, it can be considered, if not a dogma, then at least a dominant tradition of the Church, that, in death,

---

5. All this material has been collected by Bishop Ignatius (Brianchianinov), in "Sermon on Death" (*Collected Works*, vol. 3). Cf. the comparisons in Metr. Macarius, op. cit., vol. 2, par. 250.

an individual is separated only from his body, not from his soul, which continues to live in the "world of the afterlife," that is, in new metaphysical conditions of existence. Abiding in such a shell, in this supracorporeal form, separated from its proper corporeal substratum, the soul preserves its connection with the spirit. Compared with the fullness of life in the body, which life is predetermined for man as adequate to his nature, this infirm life is a "dormition," not a cessation, of the corporeal life. Life *continues* beyond the grave. Its state remains transcendent and largely unknowable for us (which is why excessive curiosity about it is spiritually unhealthy, sidetracking Christian thought into the domain of "spiritual gnosis" or occultism). Nevertheless, we can establish essential features of this life which follow from the fundamental elements of our faith.

First of all, death as the "liberation of the soul from the chains of the body" is a great *initiation*,[6] a revelation of the spiritual world. Having clothed us in "coats of skins" of impenetrable sensuous corporeality, the fall deprived us of spiritual sight.[7] Originally, man had been in a state of natural interaction with the angels, but this was closed to him after the fall. This original state is restored only in Christ: "Hereafter ye shall see heaven open, and the angels of God ascending and descending upon the Son of man" (John 1:51). Therefore, in cases of extraordinary spiritual convulsion, angels have appeared and can appear, by a special divine providence.[8] Heaven was closed and man was expelled from Eden, into which God had come to converse with man before the fall; that is, in Eden, God had been accessible to direct human knowledge. The divine world became hidden in transcendence; it became an object of faith or a problem and theorem for thought. Herein lie the defectiveness and incompleteness of man's corporeal being, and this defectiveness is a fatal one. One can say that, finding himself in a body, man experiences only one domain of life, whereas he is intended to experience life in its fullness. Thus, his earthly experience is a limited one. And if man remained confined forever in the coats of skins of his own body, he would never become fully man, for he was created a citizen of both worlds, for heaven and for earth.

6. We can find inspired pages about this in Schell, *Die Katholische Dogmatik*, vol. 3, part 2, Paderborn, 1893: *Der Tod als Weihe.*

7. Under this name occultists try to pass off their occultistic visions as "spiritual" ones, without distinguishing the soul from the spirit and seeing in them only different levels of one and the same substance, whose lower level is matter and whose higher level is divine spirit.

8. See my book *Jacob's Ladder*, the chapter "Angelophany and Theophany." Also see my book *The Unfading Light*, the section: "Calls and Encounters."

While he himself belongs to the spiritual world, Satan made man subordinate to the earthly world. If man had possessed immortality within the limits of this world, he would have become what the antediluvian humankind destroyed by God was: *flesh* separated from the spirit by a wall of sensuality. And he would have been powerless to break through this wall. But God's love and wisdom found a way to destroy this wall and to fulfill man's being, letting him participate in the spiritual world. This is accomplished through a tragic and catastrophic event in human life: *death*. Temporarily tearing man away from the flesh, death opens for him the gates of the spiritual world, placing him before the reality and the self-evidentness of both the spiritual world's being and God's being. The ecclesiastical literature bears abundant witness to the fact that a dying man can see beings of the spiritual world, angels and demons. The souls of the deceased also approach him. In a further revelation, heaven itself with the One who lives in it can become accessible to him. That which, in our world, is inaccessible to direct experience becomes the dominant reality and even the only reality; confronted with it, it is in this reality that the deceased must live and find himself.

This revelation of the spiritual world in death is the greatest joy and an ineffable triumph for all those who, in this life, yearned for this spiritual world from which they had been exiled. But death is an inexpressible horror, anguish, and torment for those who did not want this spiritual world, did not know it, rejected it. And here one is confronted with this greatest of trials, which makes inevitable one's transformation from a corporeal being into a spiritual being. One who was flesh is forced now to become directly convinced of the existence of his spiritual nature. However, even after death, a human being does not stop being a human being, forever connected with this world by his corporeality. But, for the fullness of spiritual-corporeal being, he is now forced to recognize his spirituality as separated from his corporeality. Death divides human life into two halves, as it were: psychic-corporeal being and spiritual-psychic being, before death and after death. The two halves are inseparably linked; they both belong to the life of the same individual, to his unique life that would have been free of this rupture if it had remained apart from this pathological dialectic of life and death, from the schism of the dual-unity. But this is no longer the case: To achieve fullness of humanization, a human being must go to the end of himself, not only in mortal life but also in the afterlife state, in order to attain the ripeness that makes him capable of receiving resurrection to eternal life in the fullness of true humanity. Understood this way, as an essentially necessary part of human life, death is actually an act of *continuing* life, although life that is affected by "dormition."

This raises a new question: What takes place and can anything take place in life beyond its mortal bound, which is usually understood to be its end? But what can this *end* of life mean? Is it only an interruption, an ellipsis, or is it a *final summation?* It is clearly both the one and the other. Consisting of discrete and changing atoms of time, life is integrated in consciousness after its departure from this earthly time and during its entry into another time, that of the afterlife. In death and after death, an individual sees his past earthly life as a whole, in its synthesis. The latter is, in itself, already a judgment, for it clarifies the general connection, the content and meaning of the life that has passed. Here, there is a clear vision not only of the synthesis but of the truth itself, in the presence of the spiritual world, free of all carnal partiality, in the light of divine justice. This is the self-evidentness of the divine judgment.

This judgment consists, first of all, in self-consciousness and, thus, self-judgment. This judgment is effected, according to divine providence, in the new time of the afterlife as self-knowledge ("trial and tribulation"), self-deepening, and self-verdict. It is necessary to underscore precisely this immanent aspect of human self-judgment, which is the judgment of "conscience," our own judgment, in the presence of God who knows us at the same time that we know ourselves. It is not yet a question of perfect self-knowledge and final judgment, which are possible only in connection with the whole history of humankind. Instead, it is a question of limited and individual judgments, since human life and history have not yet ended, and any accomplished act can be corrected or ruined by others in the future. It is a question of a self-knowledge and a self-definition accomplished in human self-consciousness in the light of divine justice — what theology usually calls "preliminary judgment." It is preliminary both because it is individual in character and because it is not final, since the incorporeal existence in the afterlife does not yet express the fullness of man's being. The "preliminary judgment" is not so much a judgment as an afterlife consciousness of self and the existential self-determination that comes from this consciousness.[9]

Of course, in this final summation, a distinction is established between the innumerable individual human destinies. Much here remains

---

9. One must say that Scripture is quite obscure about the idea of preliminary judgment as such: "It is appointed unto men once to die, but after this the judgment [*meta de touto krisis*]" (Heb. 9:27). *Krisis* is more a consciousness of self than a judicial sentence. [. . .]

unknown to us, including the afterlife fate of infants,[10] both baptized and unbaptized (St. Augustine's agonizing question). A similar veil of mystery conceals the fate of unbaptized nations (which is connected with the question of preaching in hell; see below). Within the limits of Christianity, the differences in the self-determination and self-consciousness of different souls after death are self-evident in any case. In accordance with these differences, one discloses the general schematic contours of these states as determined with a plus or a minus. This schema expresses the general states of "paradise" and "hell" (which are also preliminary in relation to the definitive state of resurrection).

The Catholic doctrine has added to this not only the purgatorial state but also the place of purgatory as temporary, corrective punishment. One cannot argue against the general idea of a purgatorial state beyond the grave, but is it necessary to schematize it as a third place, alongside paradise and hell? The basic notion here, which is proper to Catholic rigorism and also contaminates Orthodox thought, is that a person is definitively and irrevocably earmarked for one of the two states of the afterlife, paradise or hell, even before the universal judgment. But this assertion does not have a sufficient basis, at least in Orthodoxy, which recognizes the efficacy of the prayer for the deceased (see below), for which no limits are set (this is expressed with particular force in the third prayer of the Pentecost vespers). According to Orthodox doctrine, the state of sinners in the afterlife is that of a temporary purgatory rather than that of an irrevocable hell.

It is important to affirm as an indisputable and self-evident truth that, even in his afterlife existence, every individual with his freedom knows a distinct fate and follows his own path of life, just as he does in our world. The difference is that, in the afterlife, the false light and shadows of our world have disappeared and all things are illuminated by the sun of justice, fixed in the heavenly heights, with its beams penetrating into the depths of souls and hearts. The mysteries of the afterlife world are only meagerly revealed by revelation and, certainly, not to satisfy our curiosity but to allow our consciousness to perceive the entire seriousness of

---

10. In the ecclesiastical literature this state is usually explained by comparing it with the life of the holy angels. Without mentioning the fact that here what is unknown is explained through what is unknown, the resemblance is limited to the negative feature of the absence of sin. But deceased infants retain the whole power of their humanity and thereby participate in the universal resurrection. This alone suffices to establish that there is a radical difference between their state and that of angels.

the responsibility we bear for all the works of our life. It is necessary to understand the destinies of man in the afterlife and the preliminary judgment in connection with this continuation of the life of souls without bodies in the afterlife. But does life continue and in what form?

The ecclesiastical and theological literature, both Orthodox and Catholic, insistently and decisively expresses the general idea that, in the afterlife, "the life of action ceases and the time for retribution begins, so that after death neither repentance nor the correction of life is possible."[11] This idea expresses something self-evident insofar as it refers to that *fullness* of life which man has only in union with his body, being thus included in the general creative activity of life. But this idea must be refined and delimited. First of all, it is necessary to eliminate the crudeness this idea acquires from the Catholic theory of merits *(meritum)*, which has entered even Orthodox theology. To be sure, separated from his body, an individual is deprived of the capacity to do "works" and to acquire "merits" that were accessible to him in our world. That is why the preliminary judgment over the past part of life, namely, earthly life, becomes possible. But it does not yet follow from this that this judgment is exhaustive and final. It cannot become such because every individual must yet be judged in relation to all of humankind, and also because his life does not end with his earthly existence but *continues* beyond it, although differently, in a diminished way. It is usually accepted that, after the particular judgment, the deceased remain in a *passive* state, submitting to their fate as the sentence of the tribunal is executed. But such a view contradicts both the nature of the spirit and the data of church tradition and revelation.

The notion of passivity is justly applied to the afterlife when it is used to describe the incomplete character of this life and the inability of the deceased to participate directly in the life of our world. The deceased views our world only as an observer, although he distinguishes in it the light and the darkness of his own past life, its works, "merits," and sins. Nevertheless, the life of the human spirit — clothed here not in a body but only in a soul — continues beyond the grave as well. The spirit *lives* beyond the grave by virtue of its immortality and the divine energy that it has; actuality and freedom and, therefore, creative self-determination remain proper to it. The notions of immobility, unconscious stupor, or confinement in an isolation cell in the afterlife contradict the nature of the spirit and are inapplicable to it. Moreover, new sources and a new knowledge are revealed for the life of the spirit which were inaccessible to it when it was in its earthly shell.

11. Metr. Macarius, *Dogmatic Theology*, vol. 2, 8, par 248. [. . .]

This new knowledge consists in communion with the *spiritual* world of incorporeal beings: first of all, with human souls, communion with whom — in them and through them — is extended to the souls of the whole of humankind (for incorporeal souls cannot be confined in isolation cells); as well as with the angelic world and the demonic world. But the supreme spiritual gift acquired in the afterlife state is a new and *different* knowledge of God, proper to the world of incorporeal spirits. For such spirits, God's being is as clearly visible as the sun in the sky is for us.

To be sure, this communion with the spiritual world is accomplished in an inexhaustible diversity of forms, for a soul only attracts to itself and reveals itself to what it is worthy of or what it is kindred to. But the essential thing here is that this communion with the world of incorporeal spirits is an inexhaustible source of new life and new knowledge. Thus, by no means is the spiritual state of the deceased a static, unchanging one. The deceased assimilate this new life according to each individual's spiritual level. And at the very least it would be risky to assert that this world remains accessible only for contemplation without any participation in its life, once again in conformity with each person's spiritual state. It is also necessary to recognize that this afterlife of an individual in communion with the spiritual world is not less important for his final state than earthly life and, in any case, is a necessary part of the path that leads to universal resurrection. Every individual must, in his own way, ripen spiritually to this resurrection and determine himself with finality both in good and in evil. One must therefore conclude that, even though in resurrection an individual remains identical to himself in everything he has acquired in earthly life, nevertheless, in the afterlife, he becomes *other* than he was even in relation to the state in which he found himself at the moment of death. The afterlife is not only "reward" and "punishment," and not only a "purgatory," but also a spiritual school, a new experience of life, which does not remain without consequence but enriches and changes each individual's spiritual image. We know nothing about the degree or manner of this process. But it is important to establish that, even in the afterlife, human souls experience and acquire something new, each in its own way, in its freedom.

The parable of the rich man and Lazarus confirms this. Unfeeling and egotistical during his earthly life, the rich man turns out, in the afterlife, to be capable of love, which he manifests in caring for his neighbors. The story of this change in the rich man's soul confirms the truth that individuals spiritually continue their earthly life beyond the grave, undergo their fate. But another meaning, totally opposite, can be found in this parable: the afterlife involves repentance and its fruits, consisting in the transformation that begins in the spiritual state of the rich man. But love is not impotent and repentance is not ineffectual. If earthly works have become inaccessible, spiritual works, repentance and efficacious prayer, remain possible. We believe in the efficacy of the prayer of the saints, offered for us here and there, and — heart trembling — we entrust our life to the care of the love and prayer of those close to us.

The Apocalypse reveals in all its profundity this active participation of the deceased in our life through their prayers; and the priceless symbol of the "first resurrection" and of the thousand-year kingdom speaks to us of something even greater. Those who have "come back to life" in the first resurrection, that is, those abiding now with a soul but without a body, are called, like the other deceased, to reign with Christ for a thousand years. Thus, such an interpenetration of the two worlds is *ontologically* possible, even if by virtue of an extraordinary gift of grace. This completely refutes the notion of the passivity of the deceased, according to which their life consists solely of submitting to the verdict of the "preliminary judgment."

Even with regard to the possibility of repentance in the afterlife, we encounter the question of its efficacy, which is already adumbrated in the Gospel parable of the rich man. Of course, the evil caused by the sinner in this world cannot be expunged from the afterlife. However, even "on this side," many kinds of evil cannot be expunged, but repentance in its spiritual fruits is not powerless because of this. Why should it be considered impossible or powerless in the afterlife when all our spiritual knowledge is extended and deepened there? Of course, it is a question of *another* form of repentance than on this side, but it is repentance all the same. Is it the case that we can conceive the state of the repentant Judas only as the frozen, unchanging spasm of suffering caused by his betrayal of his love for the Teacher? And, conversely, was the burning consciousness of sin, the repentance without measure and without end, which was Judas's fall, not inevitable? And if one asserts that late repentance is not accompanied by forgiveness, to whom is it given to measure the depth of the mercy of God, who "hath concluded them all in unbelief, that he might have mercy upon all" (Rom. 11:32)? Repentance has an internal dynamism, a self-moving, self-acting power. Can one in general allow that repentance is ineffective? Therefore, does not the general idea that repentance is powerless and in this sense impossible in the afterlife collide with the opposite idea: the idea of the eternal actuality of the spirit that, in the fullness of this actuality, experiences also the power of repentance?

364

Of course, here too, the fullness of the life of the living is different from that of the dead, and the measure of their repentance is not the same. Clearly, the repentance of the deceased, as a complex inner process of awakening to spiritual life, differs from what takes place in the living. Earthly life is a foundation for the future life, but it is not the only foundation. Earthly life and the afterlife are connected as different aspects of the one life of one and the same spirit. One usually prefers to conceive the afterlife state of "sinners" (but who is free of sin and therefore does not need to repent?) in the juridical and penitentiary form of a sentence served in an afterlife prison, without possibility of pardon or parole. However, it is completely impossible to allow that the spirit could be in a state so static, so frozen in an unchanging spasm or so immersed in passive contemplation of its past actions and deprived of the capacity for further life. If the deceased are no longer capable of participating creatively in the history of this world, at least on this side of being, this does not exclude the possibility of such participation on *that* side — both in relation to the whole world and in relation to oneself. One can consider it an established doctrine of the Church, having sufficient support in Scripture, that the saints act in the world through the power of their prayer and, in general, through their grace-bestowing help, as well as in other ways, yet unknown but immanent to history (the "first resurrection"). But acting thus in relation to others, they also act *upon themselves,* ascend from power to power, from glory to glory. All of these ideas are organically included in the doctrine of the "communion of the saints" *(communio sanctorum).* The more general conclusion necessarily follows from this that the human spirit changes, develops, and grows in the afterlife, despite its temporary separation from the world (there being different degrees and forms of this change).

Concerning this we have the church doctrine, attested to by the apostle Peter (1 Pet. 3:19), on the preaching to the spirits in prison (which Orthodoxy, in contrast to Catholicism, does not limit to *limbus patrum* and which, in general, it does not limit at all). This preaching of Christ, addressed to human freedom, clearly implies the possibility of accepting or rejecting *new* self-determinations, which would be incompatible with a fixed, static condition of the spirit in the afterlife. The same thing can be said regarding the church doctrine on the efficacy of the prayer for the dead. According to this doctrine, the deceased do not have the fullness of life of the living and therefore need the living to pray for them and, especially, to offer the Eucharistic sacrifice, in which the living and the dead are united (symbolically, this is expressed by the immersion in the precious Blood of the particles of bread taken out in the name of the living and the dead).

We must more precisely define the degree of the passivity of the dead. This passivity does not and cannot make the spirit *a mere object,* which receives actions from outside without inwardly transforming them. Just as in the sacrament of repentance the objective element of the forgiveness of sin *(absolutio sacramentalis)* is indissolubly linked with the inner activity of repentance, so the effectiveness of the church prayer for the deceased presupposes a certain answering activity from the deceased themselves. In judging about spiritual states, we must free ourselves from reified representations and apply to them the synergic principle of interaction. The reception of the gift of church prayer signifies an *active* appropriation of this assistance of the Church, of the entire Church without exception, that is, the Church of the living and of the dead. The dead are by no means deprived of the possibility of helping the living through their prayer, and the living unceasingly have recourse to such assistance. To this we must add the idea — expressed by certain spiritual writers (notably by Nicholas Cabasilas) — that the deceased who are worthy of it receive a kind of spiritual communion in connection with the divine liturgy. This also presupposes, of course, a certain spiritual activity on their part.

From all this we conclude that the afterlife state is not death, and not even a stupor of the spirit, but a *continuation* of the life of the spirit begun on earth. Thus, despite the reduced condition of this life which passes outside the body and despite a certain passivity resulting from this, the afterlife state cannot be considered as given once and for all and unchanging, with the total absence of creative freedom. Rather, it is a continuation of spiritual life, which does not end on the other side of death's threshold. The afterlife state is a stage of the path leading to resurrection. The latter is not only an action that God exerts upon man by virtue of Christ's resurrection, but it also assumes a spiritual ripeness, man's readiness to receive it (just as there are inner times and seasons for the coming of physical death).

This connection between life and death, where the latter is included in the general movement toward eschatological culmination and new birth, is usually obscured by a conception that reduces death to a particular judgment, which statically determines the destinies of individuals in the afterlife and deprives these destinies of their proper, independent content. This content consists, on the one hand, of a new initiation that offers contact and common life with the spiritual world, and, on the other hand, of the inner events proper to this continuing spiritual life. Little is revealed to us about this life, and one should not try to gain knowledge of it prematurely. This knowledge will come by itself in the future aeon, by virtue of the developing life of resurrection. But we must know that, for each of us, this life is connected with the state that is revealed in us in the "particular judgment." And this vital self-determination of each of us on earth cannot be only the end and outcome of life; it is also the beginning of a *new* continuation of life.

Having come in the light of the Transfiguration and conversing with Christ, Moses and Elijah reveal a knowledge of Christ and His works that could have been acquired only beyond the grave (or in the special state of separation from the world proper to Elijah, who, taken up into heaven, avoided death). In any case, it is evident that life continues beyond the grave, and here one cannot cite the exclusive election of the two great witnesses of the Transfiguration. They nevertheless remained human beings, and one of them, Moses, experienced a human death. That which is not proper to all human beings cannot be proper to them either. The Revelation of John abounds with examples of the participation of the deceased in the life of the world, which, of course, would be incompatible with the complete passivity of their afterlife state. Examples of this are Revelation 5:8-12; 6:9-11; 7:13-17; 14:1-5; 15:1-3: "And they sing the song of Moses the servant of God, and the song of the Lamb." This is the new song of Moses, which they sing in the afterlife as an expression of the gratitude of "all the nations": Revelation 19:1-6 ("I heard a great voice of much people in heaven") and 20:4-6.

To be sure, depending on the character of this self-determination, the continuation of life beyond the grave can, from the very beginning, be full of agony or, on the contrary, full of bliss, with the infinite diversity of *individual* destinies. The language of the Bible, especially that of the Old Testament, encompasses this diversity in the double schema of hell and paradise (though not without provoking a series of false problems related to the topography of the afterlife, so to speak, to the "site" of paradise and hell, whereas these are only figurative expressions for relations of another spatiality, not physical but "spiritual"). Dissatisfied with this double schema, Catholics add a third element, purgatory. In the medieval worldview (which received its definitive expression in Dante's *Divine Comedy*) this topography receives a fully concrete expression. Eastern theology, fortunately, never achieved such topographic concreteness, although in individual cases it did adopt ancient syncretic representations. We must add that Orthodoxy, together with the traditional double schema of paradise and hell (purgatory being excluded), exhibits a salvific ambiguity in the sense that the boundary between paradise and hell is by no means absolute, for it can be overcome by the prayers of the Church. (This idea is clearly expressed in the third prayer of the Pentecost vespers.)[12] Neverthe-less, theologians view the afterlife mainly as a "retribution": They consider death to be the limit that represents the end of the time of deeds and the beginning of the time of retribution, so that, after death, one can neither repent nor correct one's life. Such is the dominant opinion of theologians, which is passed off as the doctrine of the Church. Here "retribution" is usually taken statically, as an unchanging, passive state, to which it is dif-ficult to apply the notion of *life*. This conception agrees better with the Old Testament figure of the rephaim in sheol, the shades who are also known to ancient paganism (e.g., the shade of Achilles in the *Odyssey*).

But the God of Abraham, Isaac, and Jacob is the God of the living, not of the dead, and the torments of hell are states of continuing life, which not only is patient of these states but also creatively transforms them, which corresponds to the idea of the "purgatorial" state. Of course, this is a reduced form of life, for it is deprived of the fullness of creative ac-tivity, which was proper only to the irrevocable earthly past. "The works of the righteous follow him," to be sure, just as the works of the sinner follow the sinner (this is applicable in general to all earthly works). This must be understood not in the sense of a codex of rewards and punishments, which must be applied without any variation, but in the sense of continu-ing life, for which a determining, but by no means exhaustive, precondi-tion is earthly life with its final summation.[13] Although the terms *retribu-tion* and *reward* are found in Scripture and are even uttered by the Lord Himself, we must understand them not as an external juridical law (which would be contrary to the spirit of Christ's gospel) but as an ontological connection, an internal necessity, according to which an individual suffers to the end all that is inappropriate to his vocation but was committed by him in earthly life: "he himself shall be saved; yet so as by fire" (1 Cor. 3:15).

However, this afterlife existence not only consists in "retribution"

---

12. In John of Damascus there is the following remarkable passage: "If the Church prays for all the deceased who have repented, and her prayers are strong before God and beneficent for them, then all for whom she prays will be saved and none will be deprived of bliss. Let that be so. O if only it could be accomplished! For this is what the all-good Lord thirsts for, wishes, desires; this is what He rejoices in — that none be deprived of His divine gifts" (cited in Metr. Macarius, op. cit., vol. 2, par. 258). From this one can con-clude that, besides the bliss of the saints, only the purgatorial state after death is indubi-table for Orthodoxy.

13. Of interest here is 1 Cor. 3:11-15, which the Catholics apply precisely to purga-tory. [. . .]

but is also a *new* continuation of life: "For we know that if our earthly house of this tabernacle were dissolved, we have a building of God, an house not made with hands, eternal in the heavens. For in this we groan, earnestly desiring to be clothed upon with our house which is from heaven" (2 Cor. 5:1-2). This evidently refers to the glorified body of resurrection, when "we shall be like him" (1 John 3:2). The apostle continues: "If so be that being clothed we shall not be found naked. For we that are in this tabernacle do groan, being burdened, not for that we would be unclothed, but clothed upon, that mortality might be swallowed up of life" (2 Cor. 5:3-4). There is no reason to limit this swallowing up of mortality to the life of resurrection. The life of resurrection itself begins and is prepared over the entire course of an individual's life, both the life on earth and the afterlife, which are interconnected, not opposed.

The doctrine of the afterlife as retribution can be consistently applied only to a limited degree, namely only to Christians, who are capable of being responsible for the fulfillment or nonfulfillment of Christ's commandments. But this doctrine evokes insurmountable doubt where this condition is absent. And that is the case for the overwhelming majority of humankind, that is, for children who die at an early age and for non-Christians: pagans and members of other religions (there are zealots who would put non-Orthodox Christians in the same category). Let us start with children.

The fate of deceased infants has always been an agonizing question in theology (let us recall St. Augustine and his critics), especially as far as unbaptized children are concerned. To be sure, there can be no question of their personal guilt or responsibility. If one takes the penitentiary point of view with regard to the future life, one must inevitably admit, following St. Augustine, that they are condemned to eternal torments, something conscience cannot reconcile itself to. The opposite point of view was indecisively defended by St. Gregory of Nyssa, but in general there is no established church doctrine on this question. Without pretending to have found the key to God's mystery, we cannot fail to see that the problem becomes solvable if we conceive the afterlife not exclusively as a retribution but also as a continuation of earthly life, beginning with the state in which it was interrupted by death. The length of a life, like the hour of death, is determined by God, and, evidently, is generally connected with the individuality and destiny of each human being. One must recognize that, according to the order of the divine purposefulness in view of the fullness of life which is God's gift to every individual who comes into the world, it is proper to infants who die to participate in life only for a moment, to enter the world only to leave it immediately, as a bird grazes a water surface with its wing. Their life unfolds essentially in the afterlife, in which they accomplish an equivalent of earthly life (in a manner unfathomable for us) and in which their souls receive Christ's preaching and ripen for resurrection and immortality. With crystal clarity and indisputably, the afterlife is postulated not as a retribution but as a continuation of life. The inability of theology to solve this problem in connection with the doctrine of retribution only attests to the fact that the problem is stated incorrectly.

This is even more obvious as regards children who have received baptism and chrismation, who have entered into the body of Christ but have died before they have spoken a word. It is obvious that the doctrine of retribution is even less applicable to their fate beyond the grave, both in the sense of original sin, from which they are freed by baptism, and in the sense of personal sins, which they did not have because they were so young. To the extent that it is not a direct absence of consciousness, their life beyond the grave can only be the actualization and continuation of an individual life that barely started on earth. In any case, here one must inevitably extend the doctrine of retribution to make in it a place for the positive growth of life, although in conditions of bodiless existence beyond the grave. Even if this existence is compared with that of angels, this is only a comparison, which does not destroy the ontological chasm that exists between human infants and angels. In any case, the lot of deceased infants is defined by the Church as "blessed" according to the "true promise of the Lord himself."

A similar aporia exists in the doctrine of the afterlife with regard to the mentally retarded, severely handicapped, idiots, and all those whose life is marked by the "karma" of heredity and lack of consciousness. They can be humanized, can enter into the fullness of their human being only by being liberated from the chains of their earthly existence. The mentally ill also belong to this category, at least to a certain extent. According to the conception of the Gospel, they are victims of a satanic violence: after the legion of demons is expelled from him, the Gadarene possessed finds himself at the feet of Jesus and wants to follow Him. Here we once again encounter the mystery of individual destinies. In its enigma, it postulates an afterlife in which the authentic content of the life of those unfortunates will be manifested in an appropriate individual manner. In the face of such questions, we have the revelation of the Savior's words: "In my Father's house are many mansions: if it were not so, I would have told you. I go to prepare a place for you" (John 14:2).

Going from the simple to the complex, we finally confront the mystery of the fate of the pagans and that of the withered fig tree of Israel. Until now the majority of humankind remains in ignorance of Christ, lives as if He had never come. If this majority, too, is subject to the "particular judgment" after death, can one really say that the same judgment will be applied to it as to Christians, who, in their life, knew Christ and His gospel? Evidently not, since this majority, by a permission of God (which, of course, has sufficient grounds, although we do not know what they are), remained without knowledge of Christ and Christianity in its earthly life. But it is just as impossible to suppose that it will always remain without this knowledge. Christ's universal judgment on all the nations directly contradicts this supposition: All the nations, including the pagan ones, will be prepared for it and be capable of attending to it. It is therefore necessary to postulate such a preparation of the pagans in the afterlife. This postulate corresponds to the fact of the preaching in hell, which (contra the assertion of Catholic theology) is not limited to the Old Testament patriarchs *(limbus patrum)* but extends to all the nations. In the afterlife, non-Christians recognize Christ, attend to His preaching, and receive it in different ways, in accordance with the freedom of self-determination of each of them during His earthly life. It must be concluded that the "preliminary judgment" on them will also be Christ's and Christian. They will see themselves and understand their life in the light of Christ, "which lighteth every man" (John 1:9). They will see their religious beliefs as a preparation, as their "Old Testament," through which the Christian truth was seen as through a glass, darkly. They will come to know this truth in themselves and through themselves, and it will judge them, for there is no other judgment than the judgment of the truth, than Christ's Truth. One must further conclude that this revelation of Christ's Truth, or this "preaching in hell," that is, in the afterlife, will be existentially assimilated during the entire further course of the afterlife.

All of this inevitably leads one to pose a general question: To what extent is the power of the Redemption — Christ's incarnation, passion, and resurrection — manifested in the afterlife? The answer is given not only by the dogma of Christ's preaching in hell but also by numerous patristic texts concerning the victory over death and hell (which are crowned by the homily of St. John Chrysostom, which is the sermon read at the Easter vigil). Christ's resurrection illuminated hell by its victory over death. This event should be conceived not as momentary or of short duration, but as permanent. In the afterlife, there is no place for anything that is not Christian, even among non-Christians, although, of course, each individual receives the revealed redemption differently, depending on his freedom. It is necessary to add to this the power of the Pentecost, the descent of the Holy Spirit, reposing upon the Son during His earthly life and in His resurrection, and annihilating hell by the "radiance of divinity." The doors of hell are powerless to impede access to the "rushing wind" (Acts 2:2) of the Pentecost and the appearance of the "tongues of fire."

By ways unknown to us, the power of the Pentecost, the grace-bestowing action of the Holy Spirit, breaks through the walls of hell. This must, in any case, be recognized as far as the righteous of the Old Testament are concerned; nor is one justified in rejecting it with regard to all those who are not prevented by spiritual embitterment (the "blasphemy against the Holy Spirit") from receiving in the afterlife the grace of the Holy Spirit. Is not the help that is given to the souls of the deceased by the prayers of the Church a direct effect of this grace (received synergistically, of course, i.e., with the free participation of these souls)? Here, the Holy Spirit's power to break through the doors of death is affirmed only with reference to the members of the Church. But can this power be limited only to them? Should one not extend it to the whole of the afterlife? Of course, the ways and forms of this action of grace are unknown to us, and we rely upon the promise that "God giveth not the Spirit by measure" (John 3:34).

Thus, the general revelation concerning the afterlife includes the mystery of the destinies of non-Christian humankind, of the "barren pagan church," in connection with the revelation of Christ's Church. In any case, these destinies presuppose a spiritual movement and a series of accomplishments both in the non-Christian and in the Christian world. One cannot consider the afterlife destinies of humankind only from an individualistic point of view, only as a personal "retribution." If, at the terrible hour of death, a person experiences the solitude of abandonment by God, this solitude continues into the afterlife. But the connection of all individuals, the unity of humankind and of its destinies, is also revealed here. Risking imprecision of expression, one can say that, in a certain sense, the afterlife also includes the unfinished, still continuing part of the history of the world and humankind, the uncompleted part of its creative activity, the part of the path to universal resurrection that still remains.

The only conception of the afterlife history of humankind that an individualistically penitentiary worldview can have is one according to which this history consists in passive waiting, each individual waiting in solitary confinement for his final fate in resurrection. Resurrection will take place only when an appropriate number of souls are born and die, or, in general, when God's omnipotence decides to accomplish it. However, the universal resurrection, which depends on God's power, is being accomplished synergistically, that is, in connection with the historical ripening of the world and man, which is taking place not only on this side but also on that side of earthly life. History continues in the afterlife, in connection with what occurs here on earth; the two are intertwined.

On the basis of the actual nature of the spirit, one must conclude that, after the experience of the afterlife, an individual becomes *other* than he was at the moment of his death. His readiness, or ripening, for the life of resurrection partly depends on this experience. The state of the resurrected individual is a summing-up, so to speak, of the two sides which make up his life. With regard to the life of resurrection, the usual view of man virtually ignores the experience of the afterlife: he is considered to remain exactly the same as he was at the moment of death. But, of course, this is not so and cannot be so. This directly contradicts the doctrine of the Church which supposes changes in the course of the afterlife existence, both in individuals and in the whole of the human race. The changes in the afterlife refer not only to an individual's personal spiritual self-creative activity but also to the destinies of all of humankind, for these destinies continue to be experienced on both sides of the grave and to be integrated into the destiny of the individual. We find an astonishing example of this in Scripture: the destinies of God's chosen nation. In the apostle Paul, as in numerous other prophecies about the destiny of Israel, we observe a distinctive antinomism. On the one hand, as the nation that has rejected Christ and taken His blood upon itself, Israel is the withered fig tree, rejected by God. On the other hand, the apostle of the Gentiles prophesies that "all Israel shall be saved" (Rom. 11:26); this universality of salvation is opposed to the "remnant" that exists "at this present time" (v. 5). When, where, and how will this salvation of *all* Israel take place, of this Israel which is destined to be united with the "holy remnant" and to "obtain mercy" (v. 31), if one does not conceive of the earthly path of salvation as continuing in the afterlife?

But one must not forget that humanity does not follow this path in a uniform manner that depends only on the time of birth and death. By an unfathomable divine fate, this occurs for every human being personally and in his generic being in accordance with his particular spiritual needs and capacities. There clearly exists a kind of equivalence between all these different paths and destinies, for God does not know favorites. This equivalence includes not only the different ways in which the afterlife can be lived. It also includes a way in which it is not lived at all: a certain mysterious *change* takes place on the path to universal resurrection (see 1 Cor. 15:51-52; 1 Thess. 4:16-17). This necessity of preliminary change again attests to the nondefinitive and unfinished character of earthly life in relation to the life of resurrection. The path to the parousia and the universal resurrection passes through the valley of death and the afterlife, or through an equivalent "change": "we shall not all sleep, but we shall all be changed . . . for the trumpet shall sound, and the dead shall be raised incorruptible, and we shall be changed" (1 Cor. 15:51-52).

The two parts of life, earthly life and the afterlife, are independent; however, only in mutual connection do they express the fullness of the life of fallen man. Of course, if there were no original sin and its consequence, death, this same fullness would be realized in another way, without the painful separation of the soul from the body that takes place in death. The revelation of the spiritual world that is acquired by those who pass into the afterlife would be accomplished in a direct way. The shell of the body would not be a barrier to such revelation, as it is now, but would be transparent for the phenomena of the spiritual world, and human beings would not be separated from one another by death. But that which was lost through sin is restored in a certain sense through the separation by death. In this sense, this separation is a salvific gift of the God of Abraham, Isaac, and Jacob, the God of the living, not of the dead. And, in this sense, in Scripture death takes its place among God's other great gifts: "the world, or life, or death, or things present, or things to come; all are yours; and ye are Christ's; and Christ is God's" (1 Cor. 3:22-23). Such is the hierarchy of God's gifts, and death is placed on the ladder of the life of creatures.

Therefore, it is wholly insufficient to understand death only as retribution, as a certain punitive appendix to earthly life. It goes without saying that the "particular judgment," as a self-determination realized in earthly life, as the *state* in which the dying person passes into the afterlife, accompanies him there and is, so to speak, the point of departure for his continuing life. However, to understand death *only* as retribution, as reward or punishment, is, in any case, insufficient for all the reasons mentioned. Theology primarily tends to occupy itself with penitentiary questions of hell and paradise, to which Catholics add purgatory. To this is added the question of the corporeal aspect of these states, the question of the bliss of paradise and of the burning in hell (Catholic theology[14] at-

14. See, for example, the systematic exposition in "Feu du purgatoire et de l'enfer," in *Dict. de Théol. cath.*, vol. 5, 2.

tempts to develop a doctrine of the various forms of fire, in purgatory and in hell, while Eastern theology follows, with a great deal of uncertainty, the Catholics). But it is clear that the state of disincarnation after death does not admit corporeal sensations. It admits, at most, only certain spiritual symbols or equivalents of these sensations. We do not know if these states are related to the future life of the bodily resurrection. We can only conclude in general that, in the after*life* as such, the entire fullness of the possibilities of this life will be realized for each individual according to his rank and state. Excessive curiosity in this matter must be considered unhealthy and, in any case, untheological.

The main significance of the afterlife consists in the living out of the fullness of life to the end as a preparation for the universal resurrection and a contribution to the fullness of the sophianicity of creation. Man's sophianicity is manifested not only in life but also in death, in the world on this side and in the world on that side, as the general and unique theme of his being. Theologians usually exclude the afterlife from the makeup of human life; they attribute to it only the episodic significance of a retribution, in a passive waiting for resurrection and the parousia, whereas it is perhaps an even more active path to the latter than is the life on this side. Such a deficient understanding is due to the rationalism of theology, which tries to stuff all the fullness of life into this-worldly schemes, excluding in advance the principles of sophiology and replacing them with categories of criminal law. But life is one here and beyond the grave, as a manifestation of human sophianicity.

There remains a final perplexing question, that of freedom, which is an inseparable part of the actuality of the spirit.

The face of earthly life is turned toward death. Death is an object of horror, about which people try to forget; terrible is the hour of death and the "preliminary judgment." But despite this and above this, death is a joyous hour of initiation or new revelation, of the fulfillment of the "desire to be delivered and to be with Christ," of communion with the spiritual world. In practical terms, death, as what awaits us on the immediate horizon, blocks for us what is more distant: the resurrection to come, which seems abstract compared with the immediate concreteness of death. But in the afterlife, all this has changed, for the prospect of death and its revelation no longer menaces us: Death has come and its revelation has been accomplished. The place of death is taken by universal resurrection, which naturally becomes an object of fear and trembling for some and of joyous hope for others, while for many, if not for the majority, it becomes an object of fear and hope at the same time. In any case, in contrast to the world on this side, the spiritual sky in the afterlife shines with the hope of resurrection, and the prayer "even so, come" (Rev. 22:20) has an unfathomable power for us there.

To be sure, as a work of God upon the world, the universal resurrection constitutes on this side too an object of faith and hope, but whose accomplishment is merely awaited (for "ye know neither the day nor the hour wherein the Son of man cometh" [Matt. 25:13]). But even if here on earth we have received certain indications concerning the approach of the times and seasons, which include calls for us to be active in history, why should we consider that the souls of the deceased, at least of the elect, are deprived of a knowledge and foreknowledge about this that they had even on this side? Why should we think they are deprived of activity in this waiting, since such activity is generally proper to the souls of the deceased? If the deceased are given the power to participate in their own way even in earthly life and history, then even greater must be their power to participate by love, thought, and act in the cosmic prayer for resurrection, uniting heaven, earth, and hell:[15] "Even so, come, Lord Jesus!"

15. The Church bears witness, in the paschal canon, to the participation of the world of the afterlife in the joy of the celebration of resurrection: "Let the heavens make merry and the earth rejoice. Let the whole world, visible and invisible, celebrate" (first ode, second troparion). "At present all is filled with light, heaven and earth and the *netherworld;* let every creature celebrate the resurrection of Christ" (third ode, first troparion). "Those who are *held by the bonds of hell,* in seeing your bounty, go towards the light, O Christ, on joyous feet, praising the eternal Easter" (fifth ode, first troparion).

Eschatology

CHAPTER 8

Parousia, Resurrection, and the City of God

1. Introductory Comments

As the doctrine of *ta eschata*, of the final accomplishments, which transcend the present world, eschatology naturally has particular features that are absent in the other branches of theology. On the one hand, being an integral part of the whole system of theology and concluding this system, as it were, eschatology refers to all the dogmas of theology. It is the last word of Christian ontology and can be expounded only in connection with the latter. On the other hand, its content referring to what is new, to what has not existed previously (to *de novissimis,* according to the Catholic terminology), eschatology is based, more than the other domains of theology, on the revelation given in Scripture and scattered among various sacred texts. There has as yet been no dogmatic summing-up of all of these data of revelation. The Church *has not established a single universally obligatory dogmatic definition in the domain of eschatology,* if we do not count the brief testimony of the Nicaeno-Constantinopolitan Creed concerning the second coming ("He will come again in glory to judge the living and the dead, and His kingdom will have no end"), as well as concerning the resurrection of the dead and the life of the future age. These dogmas of the faith, attested to by the Creed and based on the express promises of the Lord, have not, all the same, been developed by theology. They are considered to be self-evident for the dogmatic consciousness, although that is not, in reality, the case. All the rest, referring to various aspects of eschatology, has not been defined dogmatically; it is an object of dogmatic doctrine that has yet to undergo free theological investigation.

If it is maintained that the absence of an ecclesial definition is compensated by the existence of a firm ecclesial tradition, patristic and other, one must call such an assertion inaccurate or even completely erroneous. Aside from the fact that this tradition is insufficient and disparate,[1] the most important thing here is *the absence of a single tradition*. Instead, we have at least *two* completely different variants: on the one hand, a doctrine originating in Origen and stabilized in the teaching of St. Gregory of Nyssa and his tacit and open followers; and, on the other hand, a widespread doctrine that has had many adherents but none equal in power of theological thought to those mentioned above. (Perhaps in this group we can put Augustine, the greatest teacher of the Western Church, but the originality of his worldview sets him apart in general, especially for Eastern theology.) As regards both particular patristic doctrines and the systematization of biblical texts, an inquiry that would precede dogmatization has yet to be carried out.

Given such a situation, it would be erroneous to maintain that the dogmatic doctrine expounded in the scholastic manuals represents the authoritative and obligatory dogmas of the Church, and to demand subordination to them as such. In response to such a demand it is necessary to establish decisively and definitively that this is an exaggeration and a misunderstanding. The doctrine expounded in the manuals can by no means be accepted without inquiry and verification. It only expresses the opinion of the majority, corresponding to the current status of theological thought on this subject, not more. Characteristic of a specific period of the past, this doctrine is losing its authority more and more at the present time and at the very least requires revision. There is insufficient justification to accept theological opinions as the dogmatic definitions of the Church, especially when these opinions are proper to only *one* type of thought. Eschatological theology remains open to inquiry even at the present time. To be sure, this does not hold equally for all the aspects of eschatology, but it does hold for its most fundamental and crucial aspects. The present chapter, devoted to sophiological eschatology, represents an attempt at such an inquiry and at a revision of the eschatological doctrine (which has already been undertaken and is being undertaken in our time by various authors; among the Russians, we can mention Professor Nesmelov, Father Pavel Florensky, and Berdiaev[2]).

1. A survey of the Russian literature on various eschatological doctrines in patristics can be found in Oksiuk's monograph, *The Eschatology of St. Gregory of Nyssa: A Historico-Dogmatic Investigation*, Kiev, 1914. Cf. V. Nesmelov, *The Dogmatic System of St. Gregory of Nyssa*.

2. Viktor I. Nesmelov (1863-1937) was a Russian Orthodox philosopher and theologian who in particular wrote on philosophical anthropology. Pavel Florensky (1882-

On the basis of the objective situation in Orthodox theology it is at least *possible to debate* about whether crystallized dogmatic definitions in the domain of eschatology exist in Orthodoxy. Therefore to deny that they exist does not, in our opinion, represent a violation of *regula fidei*. Only Catholic doctrine, which tends to issue dogmatic decrees concerning all questions, declares itself to be competent in eschatology too, and it has thereby infected Orthodox theology with this dogmatic maximalism, which is not natural to this theology.

Eschatological theology is, in general, characterized by two features that make it particularly inadequate to its goal: *rationalism* and *anthropomorphism*. Rationalism seeks to capture the object of thought by means of rational schemata, which suppress all contradiction and assert their self-sufficiency for thought. Thus, rationalism delimits in advance the domain of thought by conceiving the final destinies of the world on the basis of the four logical laws (identity, contradiction, the excluded middle, and sufficient reason). Rationalism either completely excludes from the domain of being all that does not fit into this framework, or (which is even worse) it forcibly adapts to its schemata that which clearly does not fit into them. But, by its essence, eschatology deals with a domain of being that transcends the present world and is not measurable solely by the measure of this world. Those of its definitions that are antinomic combine features that the language of rationalistic thought reduces to logical contradictions, or absurd propositions. Rationalism seeks to eliminate, simplify, coarsen these contradictions; in a word, it seeks to rationalize them.

Rationalism totally rejects antinomic thought, which is characteristic of eschatology. This also removes other possibilities of being than those which are accessible to its present state; that is, being's mystery, which transcends its present state, is rejected. But it is precisely the premise of this mystery that lies at the basis of eschatology. Such a two-dimensional thinking also manifests itself in eschatological exegetics, in which it suppresses the antinomism of eschatological texts. It adapts these texts to the life of this aeon, translates them into the language of our world, lays them on the Procrustean bed of a thought that is inappropriate to its object. Owing to such a translation, eschatology is made to approach the empirical being of our world, but it loses its force and acuteness.

1937), an innovative Russian Orthodox theologian, is perhaps the twentieth century's greatest polymath. Nikolai Berdiaev (1874-1948) is perhaps the greatest Russian existentialist philosopher. — Trans.

But rationalism is nothing but anthropomorphism in thought. In contrast to the true anthropological principle, anthropomorphism in theology consists in the application of the limited human measure to the divine domain. This is particularly the case in the doctrine of judgment and punishment. Thanks to this anthropomorphism, eschatology stops being what it is and what it should be, the ontology and anthropology revealed in the final destinies of man. The ontological statement of the problem is replaced by a juridical one, and the mysteries of God's love are measured according to the penal code.

This deformity of anthropomorphism certainly prevents one from conceiving sophiologically the destinies of the world and of man. The mystery of the depth and richness of Divine Wisdom is reduced to a manual of instructions for organizing an exemplary prison where the confinement is without end. These and similar pseudo-dogmas, which anthropomorphism unhesitantly includes in dogmatics as the sole and final word, are the product of a meager theological reason and of a dry, egotistical heart. Insofar as it is revelation and prophecy, eschatology must see as its task an authentically ontological exegesis of the relevant texts, a search for their inner coherence and theological meaning. To be sure, this essay in exegesis must take into account all the traditional doctrines, which are to be understood not in their letter but in their spirit and in the fullness of their historical context. Nevertheless, eschatology remains a domain of theological inquiry on the pathways to a future dogmatic definition, which will be realized in the life of the Church when divine providence decides. But such a requirement is not an absolute one; for there are mysteries of the future age, unfathomable destines and untraceable paths of God (Rom. 11:33), that are perhaps not destined to be fully revealed in this age. Of course, by way of practical guidance, there remains God's injunction and promise: "Ask, and it shall be given you; seek, and ye shall find; knock, and it shall be opened unto you" (Matt. 7:7). But one must also make a place for God's mystery.

2. The End of This Age

"I await the life of the age to come," proclaims the Nicaeno-Constantinopolitan Creed as the last word of its divinely revealed wisdom. But the beginning of the life of the age to come presupposes the end of this age, in which we live, and, with it, the end of the whole world. The creation called to being by God is indestructible and endless, and in this sense the world does not know an end, is "eternal." But the image or mode of being that became proper to the world after the fall at the beginning of our time or this age is transitory and has an end: the image of this world passes away (cf. 1 John 2:17). And it is precisely in *this* sense that it is a question of the end of this world and the end of the age.

The sense of the end is widespread in humankind. Humankind has an instinctive knowledge that the world will end, just as a man dies. Paganism expresses this knowledge in its mythology; and only the spiritual meagerness of contemporary positivism allows it to completely avoid this question or to drown it in notions of infinite progress, which remove the truly catastrophic character of the world's being.

In contrast, revelation both in the Old Testament (in its apocalypses and apocrypha) and in the New Testament clearly and insistently proclaims the end of the world and of history, the catastrophic ellipsis that will end the book of earthly life. Representations of the last day, the day of the Lord, abound in Old Testament prophecies (the Psalms, Isaiah, Joel, etc.), in the Revelation of John, and in the "eschatological discourses" of the Lord (especially Matt. 24), and in the New Testament in general. The fire of the world and the convulsion of the elements are symbolic images of the unimaginable, since the end of the world lies beyond the world's present being, transcends it. The idea that the cosmos is transformed, not abolished but transfigured, is expressed in images of the destruction of the old heaven and old earth and the "creation of a new heaven and a new earth."

This is not a new "six days of creation," a new creation out of nothing: this creation cannot be repeated. Rather, it is a renewal of the created world. It is a creative action of God upon the world, an innovation with respect to the world under the effect of a supracreaturely force that transcends the world. This force cannot be explained on the basis of the life and energies of this world; it does not flow from the "evolution" of the world but transcends this evolution. It is as if there is a breakdown of cosmic causality (which, however, was never continuous, inasmuch as a spiritual causality acts together with physical causality in the world), and supratemporal, divine power enters into the life of the world. But this divine power does not annul the world's proper being, just as it is not annihilated even in the catastrophe or end of this sinful world.

A sort of "synergism" is manifested here between the originally created world and the divine power that renews it. This renewal enters the life of the world as a principle transcendent to the world, but with the original fullness of the world preserved. This is a mystery of God's creative omnipotence, which, from here, is completely inaccessible to humanity. Nevertheless, the reality of this synergism follows from the fact, attested to by revelation, that God's action takes place only in the case of a certain state of the world, its maturity and even old age. The catastrophe of the world is not like a new day (the seventh or eighth) in relation to the Six Days of creation. It remains within the limits of the Six Days while representing a passage to a state transcendent to the present one. A favorite figure for expressing this idea is that of a fire that melts, purifies, and transforms the elements of the world's being but that destroys only what is corruptible and perishable. (See, on the one hand, 2 Pet. 3:10: "the heavens shall pass away with a great noise, and the elements shall melt with fervent heat, the earth also and the works that are therein shall be burned up"; and, on the other hand, the image of the heavenly Jerusalem descending from the new heaven to the new earth, in which "the kings of the earth [will] bring their glory and honour into it" [Rev. 21:24]).

An ontological connection is thus affirmed between our world and the world to come. They are one and the same world in its different states. However, the evolutionary transition from the one to the other is excluded; they are separated — or united — by a chasm, a *transcensus.* The same thing holds for the times and seasons of this accomplishment: When will this be and will it be at all? — are questions that in the past provoked (and even now provoke) doubt and uncertainty (cf. 2 Pet. 3:4-10). The universal catastrophe, turned toward the world, will take place within the world's limits but at its very boundary and in this sense *outside* its time: "the day of the Lord so cometh as a thief in the night" (1 Thess. 5:2). It will be transcendent to earthly time, independent of any calendar date. The calendar will even be abolished, and the connection of time will fall apart. (Remarkably, this image of the "thief in the night" is applied by the Lord to His second coming [Matt. 24:43] in an analogous sense; see below).

But this very same supratemporality in time, and therefore calendar indeterminacy, of the end of the world applies not only to the natural elements of the world but also to human history. Here, this transcendent heterogeneity of the end in relation to earthly time is expressed in different images, but with an analogous meaning. The Lord's eschatological discourses indicate various signs of the approaching end of the age, and the faithful are called to observe them attentively (some attempt to define this end in terms of years and events). Nevertheless, Scripture affirms that the moment of the end is unknown and that the end will come suddenly.

The images of the Gospel indicate that the end will not be encompassed by our time with its seasons. The net of time is torn, and a supertime suddenly shines through it — not as a calendar event but as something that transcends our time. The difference, the incompatibility, between the time of this age and that of the "future" age is underscored by certain New Testament texts. "For as in the days that were before the flood they were eating and drinking, marrying and giving in marriage, until the day that Noe entered into the ark, and knew not until the flood came, and took them all away; so shall also the coming of the Son of man be" (Matt. 24:38-39). Human life is connected by its *yesterday* and *tomorrow*, between which *today* is suspended, but the last day of the world will not have a tomorrow and will not become a yesterday. It will, in general, put an end to *this* manner of computing time. It is outside of it, in another temporality; it will never be in this time. Whence the *suddenness* of its coming, which is a *transcensus*: "as the lightning cometh out of the east, and shineth even unto the west; so shall also the coming of the Son of man be" (Matt. 24:27). The verses of Matthew 24:42, 44 have a similar meaning: "ye know not what hour your Lord doth come . . . for in such an hour as ye think not the Son of man cometh"; therefore, "watch" spiritually and "be ready."

This does not mean that the second coming will nonetheless take place in *one of the hours* of life of this world, or on one of its calendar dates, even if an unknown one. On the contrary, this means that that day and that hour cannot, in general, be known, for they do not belong to the time and life of this age, but are beyond its limits. The end is like death: on this side, for those remaining in the world, death occurs in a given place and at a specific time, whereas for those who die it occurs not in this time but beyond it, beyond the grave, where there are other times and seasons. But at the end of the world, no one will remain to perceive it as an event of this time. The latter is extinguished, to flare up in another way, in a new way.

Thus, we know about the end that "it is near, even at the doors" (Matt. 24:33), and that we must always be "vigilant," "be ready," even though we cannot know at "what hour the Lord will come," for such an hour does not exist in the time of this world. It comes beyond the limits of the world. This hour will not enter into the series of historical events, such as the fall of Rome, the Crusades, the Great War. It is not in history, because it lies *beyond* history. Therefore, the end is essentially an object of faith *par excellence,* and thus it is so easy and natural not to believe in it, to remain self-sufficient in the life of this world. It was thus in ancient times too, for there were always those who said: "Where is the promise of his coming? For since the fathers fell asleep, all things continue as they were from the beginning of the creation" (2 Pet. 3:4). But "the Lord is not slack concerning his promise, as some men count slackness, but is long-suffering to us-ward. . . . The day of the Lord will come as a thief in the night; in the which the heavens shall pass away with a great noise, and the elements shall melt with fervent heat, the earth also and the works that are therein shall be burned up" (2 Pet. 3:9-10). "The day of the Lord" is accompanied by the world fire, by the destruction of the world and its time.[3]

The end of this age is God's business, a determination of the Father's will: "Of that day and hour [it is said in the anthropomorphic language of our time] knoweth no man, no, not the angels of heaven [neither the Son, according to Mark 13:32], but my Father only" (Matt. 24:36). "It is not for you to know the times or the seasons, which the Father hath put in his own power" (Acts 1:7). This means that the end of the age is due to a creative act of God, which depends on the power of the Father, the Almighty, the Creator. Although, as we pointed out above, this act has a synergistic relation to human history and freedom, it includes the Father's creative action upon the world. Therefore, in relation to the world's proper life, it is something new and transcendent. To seek an evolutionary explanation for this act in the natural life of the world and to find a natural necessity for it (as even theologians sometimes do in apologetic zeal) is not to understand its transcendent character and to diminish its creative significance.

The direct dependence of this act upon the Father's will and its transcendence for the world in this sense are related to the fact that its times and seasons are unknown, that it is independent of the life of the world. Here, we are dealing with the action of God's omnipotence, which is revealed in a new day of creation, as it were. The idea of the transcendent end of the world and of this age must be accepted in all its force. As such, this idea can only be an object of religious faith. Only God Himself, through his prophets, can reveal the end to us. Christ, as the God-man, bore witness to it in accomplishing His prophetic, humanly kenotic ministry, in the course of which He Himself, in His self-diminution, did not know the time of the end (Mark 13:32), although, after His glorification, He already knew it. The Apocalypse powerfully bears witness to this: "The revelation of Jesus Christ, which God gave unto him" (Rev. 1:1). Nevertheless, both the determination of the end and the principle of the creation of the world belong to the heavenly Father.

3. The apostle uses anthropomorphic language to express the idea that our time is incommensurable with divine actions: "one day is with the Lord as a thousand years, and a thousand years as one day" (2 Pet. 3:8).

3. The Parousia

The end of the age arrives not in isolation, as a separate event, but in an eschatological context.[4] On this background the central accomplishment is the parousia, the second *coming* of our Lord, Jesus Christ, promised by Scripture and dogmatically proclaimed by the Creed: "[He] comes again in glory." What is the parousia? What does it signify?

One must first consider all the features that, according to revelation, characterize the parousia. In its literal sense, the parousia is the *coming* of the Lord into the world. It is defined in that way in a number of texts: "the Son of man shall come" (Matt. 16:27; 25:31; Mark 8:38); "coming in the clouds of heaven" (Mark 13:26; 14:62; Matt. 24:30; 26:64). In contrast to the first coming (which, according to the Creed, was a "descent from the heavens") is the *second* coming, a return into the world. It is connected with Christ's departure from the world in the Ascension, according to the promise given to the apostles through the angels: "this same Jesus, which is taken up from you into heaven, shall so come in like manner as ye have seen him go into heaven" (Acts 1:11). The Ascension already presupposes the future parousia, just as the latter presupposes the accomplished Ascension. This relation is expressed by the apostle Peter: "the times of refreshing shall come from the presence of the Lord, and he shall send Jesus Christ, which before was preached unto you, whom the heaven must receive until the times of restitution of all things" (Acts 3:19-21). The same idea emanates from a juxtaposition of the following two texts: "Our homeland is in heaven, and from heaven comes the Saviour we are waiting for, the Lord Jesus Christ" (Phil. 3:20; translation taken from *The Jerusalem Bible*), and "the coming of the Lord draweth nigh" (James 5:8).

The parousia is thus the *return* from the heavens into the world of the Lord who has ascended: "at the coming of our Lord Jesus Christ" (1 Thess. 3:13); "the Lord himself shall descend from heaven" (4:16); "unto them that look for him shall [Christ] appear the second time" (Heb. 9:28).

The parousia is also described as the *appearing* of the Lord Jesus Christ, which is one of its most fundamental definitions in Scripture:

---

4. This context is as follows: "But the day of the Lord will come as a thief in the night: in the which the heavens shall pass away with a great noise, and the elements shall melt with fervent heat, the earth also and the works that are therein shall be burned up" (2 Pet. 3:10). "Looking for and hasting unto the coming of the day of God, wherein the heavens being on fire shall be dissolved, and the elements shall melt with fervent heat" (3:12). That is how "the day of the Lord" will come — "the day of the Lord Jesus" (1 Cor. 5:5).

"waiting for the coming of our Lord Jesus Christ" (1 Cor. 1:7; 2 Thess. 1:7; 1 Tim. 6:14; 2 Tim. 1:10; 1 Pet. 1:13; 2 Tim. 4:1: "at his appearing and his kingdom"; Col. 3:4: "when Christ, who is our life, shall appear, then shall ye also appear with him in glory"; 1 Pet. 4:13: "when his glory shall be revealed"; 1 John 2:28: "when he shall appear . . . at his coming"; and Rev. 1:7). Worthy of note is the identity of the terms used to describe the parousia and the earthly appearances of the Lord after His resurrection (see Mark 16:9, 12, 14; Luke 24:34; John 21:1, 14); compare, finally, the apostle Paul's testimony (1 Cor. 15:5-8) concerning the appearances of Christ. Parallel with "Jesus appeared" we have "Jesus came" (Matt. 28:18; John 20:19); "drew near" (Luke 24:15); "stood in the midst" (John 20:26); and "they saw him" (Matt. 28:17; John 20:14, 18, 25). The parousia is therefore a manifestation of the Lord that is accessible to the senses, to sight, hearing, touch. This manifestation has all the features of earthly concreteness.

Finally, a constant feature of the parousia is the coming of the Lord *in glory*, which is usually combined with and to a certain degree is identical in meaning to the appearance of the Lord on the clouds of heaven (cf. the appearance of glory in the Transfiguration and in the Old Testament doxophanies), as well as upon a throne: "when he shall come in his own glory, and in his Father's, and of the holy angels" (Luke 9:26); "he [will come] in the glory of his Father with the holy angels" (Mark 8:38; cf. 13:26); "they shall see the Son of man coming in the clouds of heaven with power and great glory" (Matt. 24:30); "when the Son of man shall come in his glory, and all the holy angels with him, then shall he sit upon the throne of his glory" (Matt. 25:31; cf. 26:64; Mark 14:62). The second coming is therefore the manifestation of His glory (see 1 Pet. 4:13). This coming is as sudden and transcendent as the end of the world. It will be universal: "For as the lightning cometh out of the east, and shineth even unto the west; so shall also the coming of the Son of man be" (Matt. 24:27; Luke 17:24). This coming will be unexpected and its transcendence will pierce through the earthly everydayness (Matt. 24:37-44; Luke 17:26-30). It will be mercilessly evident: "then shall appear the sign of the Son of man in heaven: and then shall all the tribes of the earth mourn, and they shall see the Son of man coming in the clouds of heaven with power and great glory" (Matt. 24:30).

After this preliminary survey of the biblical doctrine of the parousia, let us turn to the dogmatic exegesis of different aspects of this doctrine and, first of all, to the most essential one: What is the parousia as the second coming, the return of Christ into the world that He left in the Ascension? Here, we must return to the fundamental propositions of christology,[5] and in particular to the dogma of the Ascension, in connection with the entire complex of the dogmatics of the Incarnation.

In the absence of a generally accepted doctrine of the Ascension, naturally there cannot be a clear doctrine of the parousia, for the two are indissolubly linked as two sides of one and the same dogma. In order to measure, so to speak, the power of the parousia as the return of the Lord into the world, one must more precisely determine the power of the Ascension as His departure from this world. First of all, one must reject the idea that He completely abandoned the world, terminating all connection with it; that is, that He was disincarnated and that His "descent from the heavens" to assume human flesh was only a brief episode in the life of the world, terminated by the Ascension. To be sure, this idea is a blasphemous dogmatic absurdity, which contradicts the Lord's own promise: "I will not leave you comfortless: I will come to you. Yet a little while, and the world seeth me no more; but ye see me: because I live, ye shall live also" (John 14:18-19). "I am with you alway, even unto the end of the world" (Matt. 28:20). By His incarnation the Lord "forever united the things of earth with the things of heaven."[6] This connection is indissoluble and indestructible. It is actualized, first of all, by the *spiritual* presence of Christ in the world in virtue of the Pentecost: the descent of the Holy Spirit brings Christ back spiritually, as it were, makes His presence accessible, vitally palpable: "yet not I, but Christ liveth in me" (Gal. 2:20).

When it attains a great intensity, this spiritual life in Christ, the action of Christ in man, can, by a special design of God, even be expressed in heavenly appearances of Christ, although they have nothing in common with the parousia. Among these, let us mention, first of all, the appearance of Christ to Saul on the way to Damascus, about which he himself spoke, comparing it with the appearances of the resurrected Christ before the Ascension: "and last of all he was seen of me also, as of one born out of due time. For I am the least of the apostles" (1 Cor. 15:8-9). But in the Acts of the Apostles we do not find a complete identification of this special appearance with the appearances prior to the Ascension.[7] Similar is the heav-

---

5. Concerning this the Church attests: "He will never be separated from us; He will always be with us" (Hymn of the Ascension).

6. See *The Lamb of God*, pp. 420-27.

7. It is described in the third person in Acts 9:3-4, 7: "suddenly there shined round about him a light from heaven: and he fell to the earth, and heard a voice saying unto

enly appearance of Christ to the first martyr, Stephen, whose spiritual character is fully attested: Stephen, "being full of the Holy Spirit, looked up stedfastly into heaven, and saw the glory of God, and Jesus standing on the right hand of God" (Acts 7:55). Saints such as Seraphim of Sarov had analogous visions.

All this constitutes evidence of the spiritual co-abiding of Christ with the Church, even accompanied by a certain vision of Him.[8] He is also present in the Eucharist, which involves not a vision of Him but a sacramental knowledge of His power (even apart from the sacrament, Christ is present on earth through the water and blood that poured out of His side on the cross: the Holy Grail).[9] Christ's presence in the Sacred

---

him, Saul, Saul, why persecutest thou me? . . . And the men which journeyed with him stood speechless, hearing a voice, but seeing no man." This passage speaks of light and a voice, but it does not say that Paul saw Christ Himself. Paul's companions heard only the voice. We find the same thing in Acts 22:6-7. In this passage Ananias speaks the message: "The God of our fathers hath chosen thee, that thou shouldest know his will, and see that Just One, and shouldest hear the voice of his mouth" (Acts 22:14). However, the context leads one to interpret the "light" and the "voice" as a vision of the Just One Himself in the proper sense. This is confirmed by Paul's speech before Agrippa: "At midday, O king, I saw in the way a light from heaven, above the brightness of the sun, shining round about me and them which journeyed with me. And when we were all fallen to the earth, I heard a voice speaking unto me, and saying in the Hebrew tongue, Saul, Saul, why persecutest thou me?" (Acts 26:13-14); "I was not disobedient unto the heavenly vision" (26:19). None of these texts say that Paul saw Christ in the same way that the other apostles did when He appeared on earth after His resurrection. Rather, they say that he experienced a *heavenly* manifestation of light and heard a voice, which, by the way, was also accessible to his companions. The Acts of the Apostles also mention other visions: "Then spake the Lord to Paul in the night by a vision, Be not afraid" (18:9). However, this is not so much an "appearance" as a dream, though it has the character of a divine revelation in the spirit. The following passage has the same significance: "And the night following the Lord stood by him, and said, Be of good cheer" (23:11).

8. A special place is occupied here by the heavenly vision of John the Divine, who "was in the Spirit" (Rev. 1:10). Although Revelation is full of heavenly visions, notably the appearances of Christ, they differ completely from the appearances of Christ on earth to his disciples as well as from the parousia, which comes after them (20:11). These visions have precisely the same spiritual character as those of the apostle Paul. Of course, these are manifestations of Christ — but of Christ as sitting at the right hand of the Father and living in the Church by the Holy Spirit, and not as present on the earth or in the Second Coming.

9. See Bulgakov's article "The Holy Grail," available in Boris Jakim's English translation in *The Holy Grail and the Eucharist,* Lindisfarne Books, Hudson, N.Y., 1997, pp. 23-61. — Trans.

Gifts that He gives for communion has an ontological significance, of course. Accessible to the senses and certified spiritually, this presence of Christ in the flesh remains mysterious or even mystical. In this presence one sees only the matter of this world, sacramentally transmuted into the Body and Blood of Christ, though inaccessible to sense perception. The presence of Christ in the eucharistic elements is both visible and invisible, mysterious. His departure from the world is thus overcome, for the communion establishes a living union (John 6:54), which is a eucharistic bridge between heaven and earth, as it were. Christ becomes accessible to the world in His flesh, in His glorified body. But this takes place sacramentally through communion, whereas His own life remains hidden in the heavens.

The Divine Eucharist is a gift and fruit of the eternally abiding Incarnation, which the Ascension does not annul. However, the Eucharist does not abolish the Ascension, for, in it, Christ does not return to the earth as He was during the days of His earthly ministry, or as the angels promised on the mountain of the Ascension. Although the eucharistic presence of Christ on earth does have an element of the parousia, not only does it not annul its future accomplishment, but it even summons it. The fullness of the promise to return refers to a presence of Christ "with you in all the days" that is not only sacramental and hidden but also evident. The prayer "even so, come" was born of the ardent eucharistic feeling of the early Christians. One can say that the Eucharist and the parousia are linked in this sense as the promise and the accomplishment of Christ's coming into the world.

However, the *mysterious* presence of Christ on the earth, which is not hindered by but corresponds to His presence at the right hand of the Father, does not exhaust all the possibilities of encountering Christ after the Incarnation. It only limits them in a sacramental and, in this sense, spiritualistic manner, which does not know, as it were, Christ's second coming, a presence of Christ on earth that is fully accessible to humanity. In this sense, this presence is lesser than that enjoyed by those who surrounded Christ on earth before His death and resurrection,[10] or by those who sur-

---

10. This is precisely what the Lord told His disciples: "For I tell you, That many prophets and kings [in Matt. 13:17: righteous men] have desired to see those things which ye see, and have not seen them; and to hear those things which ye hear, and have not heard them" (Luke 10:24). "That which was from the beginning, which we have heard, which we have seen with our eyes, which we have looked upon, and our hands have handled" (1 John 1:1).

rounded Him after His resurrection until the Ascension.[11] As the Lord's return into the world, the parousia is therefore, above all, His manifestation, His *visible* appearance. This is precisely what is expressed by the words of the angels at the Ascension: "this same Jesus, which is taken up from you into heaven, shall so come in like manner as *ye have seen him* go into heaven" (Acts 1:11).

But evident to us in advance is the radical difference between the parousia and Christ's appearances in His earthly kenosis, and even after His resurrection, when even those who were near to Him and loved Him (Mary Magdalene, Peter and John, the two disciples on the way to Emmaus) could see Him but not recognize Him at once. In the parousia, His appearance will be universal and blaze like lightning. It will be impossible not to see and recognize it. When "the sign of the Son of man in heaven" appears, "then shall all the tribes of the earth mourn, and they shall see the Son of man coming in the clouds of heaven with power and great glory" (Matt. 24:30). "Behold, he cometh with clouds; and every eye shall see him, and they also which pierced him: and all kindreds of the earth shall wail because of him" (Rev. 1:7; cf. 2 Thess. 1:10). One can say that, just as in the afterlife it is impossible to deny God's existence, which has become self-evident, so here too the descent from the heavens of Christ, the Son of God, the Son of man, will be self-evident. Therefore, Christ's first coming, His coming in kenosis, made it perfectly possible not to notice Him, and even to despise and to hate Him; but the second coming, the coming "in glory," completely excludes such a possibility. Here Christ comes as He is, the Lord in the flesh.

The Lord's departure from the world in the Ascension has not a final but only a providential significance for the salvation of the world through the Incarnation. The ascension of the Lord in the flesh signifies, first of all, the end of His kenosis and His glorification in the human essence, through His presence at the right hand of the Father. Further, it signifies the completion of the work of salvation through the sending down of the Holy Spirit on Pentecost, after the ten days in heaven. But we ask ourselves: for the Son of God who sits at the right hand of the Father, is this

11. It is clear that, in another sense, eucharistic communion is more inner and more complete than any visual and tactile (or, in general, merely sensuous) perception of the appearance of Christ on earth. All those who surrounded Him in earthly life, enemies of His, those indifferent to Him, those of little faith, and even "those who followed Him," had such a perception. In this case this distinction is connected with the kenotic character of His appearance on earth.

work completed even by the Pentecost? Does His working of our salvation not require yet new times and new seasons? Can it be the case that, even despite the abiding in glory and the overcoming of the kenosis, there remains something unfinished in Christ's work, something that is yet to be done and that therefore depends on new times and seasons? To this audacious question, we have a clear answer in Revelation, which attests that the eternal life of Christ in the heavens, at the right hand of the Father, that is, in all the power of His divinity, remains unfathomably and antinomically linked to the times and seasons of this world, whose duration is now fixed: It extends from the Ascension to the parousia.

Thus, we become aware of a new meaning in the prophetic words that the angels address to the disciples after the Ascension: Jesus "shall so come *in like manner* as ye have seen him go into heaven" (that is, still within the limits of earthly events). We already know the apostles' testimony: "The times of refreshing shall come from the presence of the Lord; and he shall send Jesus Christ, which before was preached unto you; whom the heaven must receive until the times of restitution of all things" (Acts 3:19-21). This text clearly indicates a new time, now in heaven. It can be more precisely defined as the time from the Pentecost to the parousia, the new descent of Christ from the heavens. This time is determined by an accomplishment not only in the world, into which the Lord comes, but also in the heavens, whence He comes. We are ignorant of what precisely happens with regard to the Lord who sits in the heavens at the right hand of the Father. Nevertheless, revelation affirms that something happens. The Lord's mysterious words in His parting conversation with his disciples also bear witness to this: "if I go and prepare a place for you, I will come again, and receive you unto myself, that where I am, there ye may be also" (John 14:3).

His coming takes place by the will of Father, who "shall send Jesus Christ, which before was preached unto you" (i.e., at a definite time). The Father knows "the day and hour" of the Second Coming, for He Himself determines them, sending the Son, who, here too, does the Father's will. But the Son is not only sent; He Himself comes into the world, just as, resurrected by the Father, He Himself resurrects, and, raised to heaven by the Father, He Himself ascends. Here, both the Resurrection and the Ascension presuppose the accomplishing action of the Holy Spirit, who reposes upon the Son. And we must affirm the same thing with regard to the parousia. Although the Son Himself comes into the world, in the parousia He is sent by the Father, by the action of the Holy Spirit, "the Spirit of Glory, the Spirit of God," where the glory of Christ is revealed (1 Pet. 4:13).

Therefore, it is first necessary to establish that the parousia, like all the events of the Incarnation (nativity, baptism, resurrection, and ascension), is the work of the Holy Trinity, according to the character of each of the hypostases; that it is, in this sense, a trinitarian accomplishment. Excluded in advance is the possibility of supposing that, sent into the world by the Father, Christ in the parousia is not united with the Holy Spirit, who, having already been sent into the world, abides simultaneously in the heavens and in the world. Christ thereby reveals Himself as the divine path from heaven to earth, a path initiated by His descent from heaven for the Incarnation and completed by the Ascension and the Pentecost. In general, trinitarian theology does not know the purely dyadic action of the Father and the Son without the participation of the Holy Spirit. Therefore, theological thought must, in general, present the parousia as a new revelation of the Holy Trinity in creation: the Father sends; the Son comes; the Holy Spirit has already been sent and meets the Son in the world.

The essential characteristic of the parousia is the appearance of Christ in glory, in direct contrast to His first coming into the world in humility. In His first coming, He was born, virtually unknown and unnoticed, in a manger in Bethlehem on a winter night. But now He comes on the clouds of heaven, seen by all the tribes of the earth. In His first coming, only the angels in the heavens praised Him, but now He comes in glory, surrounded by all the holy angels, visible to all people. One must remember that this meeting with Christ will take place beyond death or "change," that is, in "clear sight" of the whole spiritual world. And so, the presence around Him of the angels, as well as, of course, of the saints, "Christ's at his coming" (1 Cor. 15:23), will be evident to all. Also evident to all will be the flaming sign of the Son of God, which is also the "sign of the Holy Trinity," the Cross.

One can thus establish a distinction between the earthly appearances of the Lord and His appearance in glory in the parousia. He lived in this world among people, as co-human to us; Him "we have seen with our eyes, . . . have looked upon, and our hands have handled" (1 John 1:1), while remaining in this world, in our proper corporeality. The Lord's kenosis was so profound and the veil of flesh covering His divinity was so impenetrable that our nature was not shaken by His coming, which did not surpass human powers. Only the elect were deemed worthy to witness the "appearances" of the glorified Christ after His resurrection (see 1 Cor. 15:5-8). These appearances differed, of course, from the seeing of the Lord that was accessible to all during His earthly ministry. They were precisely appearances of the Resurrected Christ, attesting to His resurrection, through which He had already risen above the world and become detached from it, before being totally separated from it in the Ascension. These appearances of the glorified Lord serve as the intermediate step, as it were, before our meeting Him in glory in the parousia. In these appearances, Christ becomes visible for all in the radiance of divinity in glorified humanity: God in man and Man in God, the God-man, drawing to Himself all the tribes of the earth ("I, if I be lifted up from the earth, will draw all men unto me" [John 12:32]).

The appearance of Christ in the parousia does not know any limits. It is universal, omnipresent, and omnitemporal. He is seen by those who rejoice in Him and by those who tremble in fear of Him, by those who love Him and by those who hate Him. This universality has an absolutely compelling evidentness, analogous to that of the existence of God and of the whole spiritual world in the afterlife. This appearance of Christ is described, in anthropomorphic symbols, as His coming on the clouds of heaven. All of these expressions that link His appearance with a definite place and time are obviously inadequate, since this temporality and this spatiality are other than our own, if indeed it is at all appropriate to speak of temporality and spatiality here. Christ's appearance in the parousia takes us, in general, beyond the limits of this world: it is metaphysical or metacosmic. This "meta" eliminates the threshold between the two states of the world's being. In the parousia, Christ will not appear within the limits of this world; He will not appear beneath this sky and upon this earth and before this humankind. Humankind will see Him in a new world, and this appearance will already constitute a radical *change* in the relation between God and the world.

This change consists, on the one hand, in a new approach of God to the world through the parousia and, on the other hand, in a new approach of creation to God. Our present life is separated from the parousia, but it is also approaching the parousia through death and the afterlife state, or through a "change" equivalent to death, followed by resurrection. The latter consists not just in the revivification of the dead in their bodies but also in their change in conformity with the glorified state of Christ's humanity. Scripture expresses this in symbolic language: "the Lord himself shall descend from heaven with a shout, with the voice of the archangel, and with the trump of God: and the dead in Christ shall rise first. Then we which are alive and remain shall be caught up together with them in the clouds, to meet the Lord in the air: and so shall we ever be with the Lord" (1 Thess. 4:16-17). This passage speaks of being "caught up," which is equivalent to the *transcensus* of death and resurrection, of the meeting with the Lord "in the air" and the being with Him for ever. This universal change extends to the entire natural world, so that, in general, the parousia takes place not in this world but upon a new earth and under a new heaven. The present world, this heaven and this earth, will not see Christ again. The parousia is therefore not an event in the life of this world, and even less is it *one* of this world's events. Rather, it is an accomplishment that entirely transforms the life of this world as well as that of the humanity that passes through resurrection.

The appearance of Christ in heaven, His descent from it on clouds accompanied by angels and saints, seen simultaneously in all places by all of humankind, is, of course, only a symbolic figure of what the helpless language of our spatiality and temporality cannot describe or express. This only means that the entire world and all humankind will be penetrated by the appearance of Christ; it will be visible and palpable to them. Let us add that He will appear not only to humankind but also to the angels, including, *in their own manner*, the fallen spirits, for whom the Lord's coming will signify, first of all, the expulsion from the world of the prince of this world as well as their own expulsion. It will signify for them their accusation and judgment. In other words, the panorama of the parousia is indescribable; it serves only to express the general idea that the Lord will be manifested and that He will be accessible to *all* creation, which will become transparent for his presence.

Besides this *universal* character of the parousia it is necessary to indicate what we can call its most fundamental feature: the coming of Christ *in glory*. What does *glory* mean in this case? It is clearly opposed to kenosis, to the coming of Christ in humility. The time for kenosis has passed. In response to His humility, "God . . . hath highly exalted him, and given him a name which is above every name" — the Lord Jesus Christ "to the glory of God the Father" (Phil. 2:9, 11). After the Ascension, Christ is already glorified near the Father "with the glory which I had with thee before the world was" (John 17:5). This supra-eternal glory of the Logos also became proper to the God-man in the union of His two natures, divine and human; and it accompanies Him when He appears to the world. In anticipation, this glory was manifested as the shining of the transfiguring light on Mount Tabor. But this was only a manifestation of glory, not Glory itself. What is Glory?

Glory in the Holy Trinity corresponds to the revelation of the Third Hypostasis in the dyad of the Father's self-revelation: the Word of all words, the Truth of all being, actualized by the Holy Spirit reposing upon the Son. The Son and the Holy Spirit as the self-revelation of the Father are united without separation and without confusion. Resting upon the Son as the hypostatic Glory of God, the Holy Spirit is precisely the glory to which He attests: "Father, glorify thou me with thine own self with the glory which I had with thee before the world was" (John 17:5). John 17:24 is equivalent: "that they may behold my glory, which thou hast given me: for thou lovedst me before the foundation of the world." "Before the foundation of the world" is a figurative, anthropomorphic expression, which, of course, cannot be understood literally, with reference to a succession in time: it cannot be understood as meaning "before" the being of the world or "after" its foundation. That would introduce time into the divine being. Rather, this phrase expresses a relation between God's proper life in Himself as the Absolute and His revelation in the world as the Creator, a relation between the immanent and the economic Trinity.

The kenosis of the Son after His descent from heaven presupposes the removal of the Glory, not, certainly, in "heaven," in the "immanent" Trinity, but in the world. It presupposes that He will appear in the world in the humble form of a man. However, His earthly ministry also becomes His glorification: the inglorious earthly state is overcome and becomes one that corresponds to the heavenly glory: "I have glorified thee on the earth: I have finished the work which thou gavest me to do" (John 17:4). In response, the Father glorifies Him. This glorification is expressed in a succession of events: The first glorification takes place at baptism by the descent of the Holy Spirit. The second takes place at the Transfiguration, when the overshadowing of the Holy Spirit is visible as the transfiguring light of Tabor. The third takes place in the resurrection, when the Lord assumes His body as already glorified. The fourth takes place at the Ascension and by the sitting at the right hand of the Father, invisible and inaccessible to the world: the Lord raises into heaven His spiritually energetic body of glory, the body of the Ascension. These latter stages complete the kenotic path of His glorification: even in His Divine-humanity, He receives the Glory He possesses from all eternity, "before the foundation of the world." That is, He receives the fullness of the union with the Holy Spirit reposing upon Him.

In the kenosis of the Son according to Divine-humanity, the dyad without separation and without confusion of the Son and the Holy Spirit, underwent a kind of inner, mutual kenosis consisting of a certain separation, as it were. The Son's glory was removed in His kenosis, and the Holy Spirit separated itself from the Son in its own kenosis. The Holy Spirit thus limited the fullness of its gifts and reduced the degree of its repose upon Christ, so to speak. The two kenoses are parallel, but their paths partly coincide and partly diverge. In particular, in the Ascension the kenosis of the Son, which began when He descended from heaven, is overcome. The kenosis of the Holy Spirit also began with its descent from heaven (although, according to its hypostatic character, the Holy Spirit does not leave heaven but unites heaven and earth). In itself, this descent of the Holy Spirit is a kenotic act as such, for its action in the world remains limited by the measure of creaturely reception: the world cannot experience the full force of the Holy Spirit's action without melting and burning up. In the kenosis of descent into the world, this force limits itself and is diminished, as it were: the synergism of grace with creaturely freedom leads to such a self-limitation.

By contrast, the parousia, the coming of the Lord in glory, brings into the world, first of all, the cessation of this kenosis of glory, that is, of the Holy Spirit, which began at the Pentecost. "The Spirit of glory and of God" (1 Pet. 4:14), which already abides in the world, becomes explicit in the appearance of Christ's glory (v. 13). The *glory* that accompanies the parousia not only belongs to Christ but is also communicated through Him to the world in which the Holy Spirit already abides kenotically. The parousia must therefore be understood not only with regard to Christ Himself but also with regard to the dyad of the Son and the Holy Spirit, and further with regard to the entire Holy Trinity. The appearance in glory, the parousia, is also the palpable appearance of the Holy Spirit who reposes upon the Son and abides in the world. Christ, who in ascending to heaven sends down from the Father the hypostatic Holy Spirit into the world, also brings, when He comes in the parousia, the revelation of the Holy Spirit as glory. One can say that He once again effectively sends the Holy Spirit into the world. In this sense, Christ's Second Coming is also the parousia of the Holy Spirit, which only begins with the Pentecost and is concretely accomplished together with Christ's parousia.

Let us once again mentally survey this path from heaven into the world and from the world into heaven. Christ's descent from heaven in the Incarnation is prepared and accomplished by the preliminary descent of the Holy Spirit upon the Virgin Mary, the Spirit-Bearer, at the Annunciation. It is the mode of the Lord's descent from heaven: the reception and birth of God. Further, the Lord Himself, as the God-man and Spirit-Bearer, unites heaven and earth by the power of the Holy Spirit reposing upon Him and by His own ministry. But when the full measure of His kenosis was reached, He ascended, by this same path of the dyadic union of the two revelatory hypostases, from the world into heaven in order to send down the Holy Spirit in its proper hypostasis. This fully restored the connection between heaven and earth; creation was deified; and by its grace the Holy Spirit spiritually reveals Christ on earth.

However, this spiritual revelation of Christ is not definitive, just as the revelation of the Spirit is not definitive. Christ had appeared on the earth incarnate and in-humanized; but then he ascended to heaven, and deprived, so to speak, the world and humankind of that which they had received and known. Likewise, having flared out brilliantly in the Pentecost, the fiery tongues of the Holy Spirit were dissipated in space as if extinguished, and the Spirit's tumultuous breath became silent, as if dissipated in the air. However, for the fullness of the new accomplishment there remains the parousia: Christ again appears in the world, but this time in glory. That is, not only does He Himself once again become visible and accessible to the world, but the glory itself becomes visible, the glory of the Pentecost, the Holy Spirit. *The parousia signifies the power not only of the Incarnation but also of the Pentecost, of Christ in glory and glory in Christ, the appearance in Him, with Him, and through Him of the Holy Spirit.*

In the parousia Christ comes into the world such as He abides in heaven, where He "sits at the right hand of the Father," in the fullness of divine glory. The veil of kenosis no longer covers His divinity, which shines with the eternal light of the Holy Spirit. It is precisely to manifest Himself thus in glory that Christ is sent by the Father and comes down from heaven to abide on earth, while certainly abiding in heaven eternally in the Holy Trinity: "and so shall we ever be with the Lord" (1 Thess. 4:17).

But how can man withstand this appearance of the Lord in glory without becoming blind, without being burned by the light of divinity? How is the parousia *possible* for the world? Can the world withstand it? To Tabor the Lord summoned only His three closest disciples, and limited the appearance of His glory to this mountain. But what would have happened if even then the beams of light of the Transfiguration had reached the darkness swirling at the foot of the mountain and if they had illuminated the crowd gathered in fear and powerlessness around the man possessed by demons? The fact that this did not happen demonstrates that this was unnecessary and impossible. Therefore, the manifestation was visible only to the apostles (to the degree they were capable of seeing it, as the Hymn of the Transfiguration says) and only to the three chosen ones. But in the parousia this appearance becomes accessible to all. How will this become possible? Only one answer can be given to this question: Christ's glory, revealed in the parousia, enters the world and illuminates humankind,[12] so

---

12. Catholic theology has a doctrine of *lumen gloriae,* which represents a precondition for the vision of glory, the *visio beatifica.* In itself this distinction is arbitrary and unedifying, but what is true here is that the very capacity to see Christ's glory already presupposes a preliminary inner action of this glory in the seer himself, a kind of entering into a cloud (Luke 9:34) when seeing the Lord's Transfiguration.

that the whole world meets Christ coming in glory. Christ shines with this glory, which was already in the world without yet being manifested in it. This is the Holy Spirit, come down on Pentecost, his power and revelation.[13]

The kenosis of the Holy Spirit that has descended into the world consists in a limitation of its gifts, in an attenuation of its energy. The natural world retains its unchangingness in creaturely being; it remains in its unrealized and unfinished state. The fullness of its realization, its transparence for the Spirit, its appearance in glory, or glorification, are yet to come. This glorification depends not on a new coming of the Spirit, since the Spirit is already in the world, but on the fullness of its action. This fullness is the transfiguration of the world in connection with the parousia; it is the new heaven and new earth into which Christ comes.

In Scripture, the parousia is accompanied by the fire of the world, the destruction of the world, followed by its transfiguration, but this does not signify a succession or coincidence in time of two parallel events. It is one and the same event: the coming of Christ in glory and the revelation of glory to the world correspond to the action of the Holy Spirit. This fire — in which the present heavens and earth will be consumed on the day of judgment (see 2 Pet. 3:7), when "the heavens shall pass away with a great noise, and the elements shall melt with fervent heat" (v. 10) — signifies the passage of the world through the Pentecost. The Pentecost's fiery tongues become the flame of the world fire, not consuming but transmuting the world.[14] This figure represents a hieroglyph of the cosmic Pentecost. If the parousia is the second coming of Christ in the world, this time in glory, it is also the new revelation of the Holy Spirit, of God's glory, upon Christ and in the world. It is not a new coming of the Holy Spirit, for having come on Pentecost, the Holy Spirit does not leave the world but is hidden in it for a time, as it were. The symbolic language of Revelation describes this by the image of Holy Jerusalem, coming down from God out of heaven: "I saw no temple therein, for the Lord God Almighty and the

---

13. In the light of these ideas one can attribute a dogmatic significance to Motovilov's narrative about how St. Seraphim showed him the action of the Holy Spirit in a brief transfiguration of the world in glory. This is the glory that will become universal in the appearance of Christ and in connection with this appearance. [See note 39 of chap. 5. — Trans.]

14. It is true that the apostle Peter says that "the earth . . . and the works that are therein shall be burned up" (2 Pet. 3:10). However, this should not be understood to mean the earth's destruction, for immediately after this it is said: "we . . . look for new heavens and a new earth" (3:13).

Lamb are the temple of it. And the city had no need of the sun, neither of the moon, to shine in it: for the glory of God did lighten it, and the Lamb is the light thereof" (Rev. 21:22-23).

The burning and destruction of the elements, the death of the old world, its catastrophe, should not be understood as a physical effect of forces belonging to this world, an effect that is produced in an evolutionary manner in virtue of its immanent development, though with a catastrophic result. (The world has already known such cataclysms in its history.) The end of the world is not physical but metaphysical. In reality, the world does not end but is transfigured into a new being, into a new heaven and a new earth. The changes that will take place in it will not be limited to a new combination of the same cosmic elements and the action of the previously existing cosmic forces. Rather, a new supercosmic force will enter the being of the world and transform it. The introduction of this force will affect the entire physical structure of the world, but it will be preserved in its natural being. However, the latter will open up to receive a new element of being: "glory." And this appearance of glory, the glorification of the world, will inwardly change all the elements of its being, will impart a new quality to them.

We know that the "physical" world, its matter *(hule),* is not closed off from nor alien to the spirit. Created out of nothing, the world receives its reality, matter, and elements from the Holy Spirit, so that its most material elements are, at the same time, its most spiritual ones by virtue of their reality. Further, the diversity of the world, its *all,* its universality, in the sense of the presence of all its aspects, ideas, or words *(logoi),* together with their inner interpenetration according to a "logical" order, becomes real by the Holy Spirit, who is the reality of the "cosmos," of universal being. In this aspect the world participates in the spirit by the fact that it is real. Finally, in its life, in its organic causality, the world does not exist solely as material, as self-enclosed in its cosmicity. It is open to the spirit; it is materially spiritual.

In its causality, the life of the world normally includes not only cosmic and natural elements but also a "spiritual causality."[15] And only the self-blindedness of materialism considers the world to be merely material in nature. In fact, it is spiritually material. This spiritual causality enters into the natural world through the spiritual world (for it is in the guardianship of the holy angels) and through its connection with man. However, man himself, together with the spiritual world, is open to the action

15. See my essay "On the Gospel Miracles."

of grace, of the divine spirit, who always, although imperceptibly, acts upon the world with a spiritually transfiguring power. Through this link with the spirit the world is saved from its deistic isolation from God, from self-enclosedness and self-sufficiency. The world has doors that are open to the spirit, to a superphysical action, which, in relation to the limited laws of this world alone, is *miracle*.

By no means does miracle signify an abolition of the laws of the world or the destruction of the world. On the contrary, miracle is included among the postulates of cosmic being. The world awaits and thirsts for miracle, which is a superphysical action upon the natural, physical world, which discloses its fundamental structure with its duality. Miracle loses its miraculousness; it even represents the sole law of the world to the extent that the latter becomes spiritual and transparent for the spirit. Its proper physical being ceases to be alienated from the spirit and even becomes its direct revelation. Every content of this being is transparent here; the ideas of the world shine in matter, so that the whole world really is present in the harmony of the cosmos, that is, in beauty. The transfiguration of the world in glory is its appearance in beauty.[16] Thus, the metaphysical structure of the world is changed or rather revealed by the Transfiguration, without any change in the physical nature of the world, whose foundation was unalterably laid during the Six Days of creation. In its transparence and inner self-evidence, the world becomes harmonious with its idea and, as such, is clothed in beauty. This extends both to the natural world and to man, according to the property of each.

Before undertaking a special examination of these changes, let us try to express dogmatically the basis of this transfiguration. How is the "glory" of the world possible? How can it enter the world? And what does this signify? This can be understood only sophiologically. The world, with man at its head, is the creaturely Sophia. This means that the ontological foundation of the world's being is sophianic. It is a divine energy submerged in creaturely being, in the world created out of nothing but on the foundation of creaturely freedom. This foundation includes the "all" to which is imparted the power of reality and which is "good" (see Gen. 1). This foundation is indestructible in creation. But it is still in a state of becoming, of self-actualization on the basis of creaturely freedom. The

---

16. Revelation expresses this idea by saying that the heavenly Jerusalem, descending out of heaven, has "the glory of God" (Rev. 21:11), although it is made of earthly materials. But these have acquired the transparence of beauty, precisely as precious stones and gold (21:18-21).

creaturely Sophia is, in this sense, also the becoming Sophia. Creation follows a path toward the fullness of its sophianization, toward glory. On this path, man is the leader as the living image of God, as the hypostatic bearer of the creaturely Sophia.

Sophianization had to occur in man. It was his role to lead creation from extradivine being to God, "into the glorious liberty of the children of God" (Rom. 8:21), together with our own "adoption, to wit, the redemption of our body" (v. 23). But man fell on the paths of creaturely freedom, seduced by the devil, and, with him, creation also fell, "was made subject to vanity, not willingly, but by reason of him who hath subjected the same in hope" (8:20). In this fall, "all have sinned, and come short of the glory of God" (3:23), which was proper to creation at the beginning in a preliminary way. The restoration of the sophianicity of creation refers not to its foundation, which is indestructible, but to its state, to the return of glory and, in this sense, salvation. This was the work of the Second Adam, God made man, in union with the Holy Spirit, by virtue of Divine-humanity.

This restoration contains the fullness of the salvation or sophianization of the world, its raising to glory, not only the glory lost by man but also a glory greater than that — the divine glory: "the glory which thou gavest me I have given them" (John 17:22). In Divine-humanity, through the incarnation of the Son and the descent of the Holy Spirit, the world and man have received the fullness of sophianization. The Divine Sophia has united with the creaturely Sophia; creation has been completely deified in the union of the two natures in Christ by the Holy Spirit.

This event takes place in two directions. The first is the kenotic direction: God descends from heaven to adopt the "form of a servant." The second is in the opposite direction: through glorification. The latter is accomplished in a series of events: the Resurrection, the Ascension, the Pentecost, and the Second Coming of the Lord, this time in glory, in which He brings glory to the world and deifies it by the energy of the Holy Spirit. We know how the glorification of Christ was accomplished until the point when He received anew, in the sitting at the right hand of the Father, the glory that He had before the foundation of the world, in order to glorify His human nature as well. But this glorification of Christ, potentially containing the glorification of all creation, had to be realized in the latter as well.

One can say that Christ left the world in His ascension to heaven also because the creaturely world was incapable of receiving and encompassing His presence in glory. But His departure was temporary, and the world had yet to ripen to receive Him anew. But, of course, such ripening could not be achieved solely by the power of the world that had subjected itself to vanity. It could not be achieved solely by the power of man who had fallen away from God. In order to save the world and man, "the Word was made flesh" (John 1:14). Christ "went to look for the sheep that had strayed and, carrying it on his shoulders, he brought it back to the Father," as the liturgical hymn says. He laid the foundation of a new humanity and a new world. In order that this principle could grow, the Holy Spirit was sent into the world by Christ from the Father. The world had always contained the power of the Holy Spirit by virtue of its (albeit creaturely) sophianicity, but, by itself, it would certainly have been incapable of receiving and encompassing the descent of the Holy Spirit. However, the path for the Spirit was opened by the Incarnation. The Holy Spirit comes into the world this time as the "other" Comforter, bringing with Him Christ the Comforter. "He dwelleth with you, and shall be in you. I will not leave you comfortless: I will come to you" (John 14:17-18). The Holy Spirit accomplishes the sanctification of the world, the work of Christ, upon whom He reposes. In this sense, by its *fruits*, the Pentecost is the continuing Incarnation.

The Incarnation is accomplished in the Church and through the Church, the body of Christ in the world and the temple of the Holy Spirit. However, prior to the parousia this sanctification and deification remain incomplete and preliminary, for the action of the Holy Spirit is as yet kenotically limited. But this kenosis of the Holy Spirit ends with the parousia; the whole power of the Pentecost is revealed to the world. The world is sanctified, deified, and glorified by the power of the Holy Spirit, and the parousia arrives by virtue of this action of the Pentecost. It is impossible to say what comes before and what after, for this is a single act that occurs both in heaven and on earth, signifying the end of God's kenosis and the beginning of the world's deification. The Father sends the Son into the world and, secondarily as it were, He sends with Him the Holy Spirit for the joint accomplishment of the parousia and the transfiguration of the world. The Son wills again to carry out the will of the Father, this time by a conclusive and universal act, in order to accomplish the salvation of the world and to "unite the things of earth with those of heaven," as the liturgical hymn says. Meanwhile, the Holy Spirit accompanies the descent of the Son from heaven, surrounding Him with glory, which is the same both in heaven and on earth and which existed before the foundation of the world and is now proper to Him. The world is now ready to receive this glory, for it has already received and has Christ and the Holy Spirit who reposes upon Him.

Prior to the parousia, the Holy Spirit acts in the world only by virtue of the spiritual presence of Christ in it. After the parousia, with the new coming of Christ into the world, there are no longer any limits for this action, because Christ, present in the world, receives for the latter the fullness of the Holy Spirit. Therefore, the parousia also signifies, *as it were*, the second coming of the Holy Spirit into the world — the reign of God come in power. In one of the variants of the Lord's Prayer, the phrase "thy kingdom come" is replaced by "let the Holy Spirit come," that is, it refers directly to the parousia of the Holy Spirit. But since, in the parousia, the coming of Christ is inseparable from the appearance of his glory, that is, the Holy Spirit, the prayer for the parousia refers *both* to the Son and to the Holy Spirit. This leads to the important conclusion that this phrase from the Lord's Prayer is *equivalent* to the early Christian prayer: "Come" (Rev. 22:17), or "even so, come, Lord Jesus" (v. 20). And although this latter prayer no longer has a direct, christological resonance, it does not fail and cannot fail to resound in the Church, even if in a hidden way.[17] This prayer in the name of the spirit-bearing Church is thus expressed by revelation: "And the Spirit and the Bride say, Come" (v. 17).

The reign of God is expressly related to the appearance of the power of the Holy Spirit, which completes the revelation of the entire Holy Trinity. Characteristic in this sense are the texts that refer to the Transfiguration, which, as the appearance of Christ in glory, is the preparation for the parousia, a particular parousia, so to speak, before the apostles on Mount Tabor.[18] "For the Son of man shall come in the glory of his Father. . . . Verily I say unto you, There be some standing here, which shall not taste of death, till they see the Son of man coming in his kingdom" (Matt. 16:27-28). This is followed by the account of the Lord's Transfiguration. The phrase "some standing here" clearly refers to the three apostles who were on Tabor, while the announcement of the Transfiguration is preceded by a mention of the parousia. And the two appear to be identified in a certain sense. To this is added the indication that the Son of man will come in His kingdom, which is identified with the glory and

17. The request in the prayer to the Holy Spirit, "come and dwell in us" *(Veni Creator Spiritus),* therefore also has an eschatological significance and refers to the parousia.

18. "You were transfigured on the mountain, Christ the Lord, having shown your glory to your disciples to the extent they could perceive it. Let your everlasting light shine also upon us sinners" (troparion of the Transfiguration Feast). "You were transfigured on the mountain, and your disciples saw your glory to the extent that they could" (kontakion). These hymns present the Transfiguration as a vision of the glory or (which is the same thing) of the everlasting divine light.

with the parousia.[19] The Transfiguration of Christ is therefore a revelation of the kingdom of God and also of the glory, of the Holy Spirit. In this event of Christ's life, the Holy Spirit, reposing upon Him, is also revealed. This is a revelation not only of the Second but also of the Third Hypostasis, proceeding from the Father. The Transfiguration is therefore a feast not only of the "Lord" (according to the Orthodox classification) but also of the "Holy Spirit." The parousia has a similar significance: It is the appearance of Christ in glory, that is, in the light of the Holy Spirit reposing upon Him, and also of the Glory itself, that is, of the Holy Spirit, as the transfiguring and everlasting light. This is the accomplishment of Christ's high-priestly prayer: that He be given the glory that He had before the foundation of the world, that is, the fullness of the manifestation of the Holy Spirit.

This dyadic character of the parousia is obscured to some extent by the fact that the Third Hypostasis does not have a *personal* revelation. In its transparence, it appears to dissolve and to hide in the two other hypostases: it is a question of the glory of the Father and the glory of the Son, in which or with which He comes in the parousia, not of Glory itself. One is tempted, first of all, to understand glory as an attribute or a "property" of the Father and of the Son, which belongs to both of them, individually or jointly. But this temptation must be decisively rejected. It is totally inadmissible to interpret as an attribute the manifestations of Glory that we find in the doxophanies of the Old Testament (in Moses, Isaiah, and Ezekiel) and in Gospel narratives. Glory is not a quality or a property that can be present or not be present. It is the divine essence itself, to whose reality divine eternity is proper. Glory is the Divine Sophia, Divinity as such.

But this Divinity is the revelation of the Father in the bihypostatic

19. The variants are also significant. Mark 9:1 says: "there be some of them that stand here, which shall not taste of death, till they have seen the kingdom of God come with power." This is preceded, in Mark 8:38, by mention of the parousia. As a manifestation of glory, the Transfiguration is "the kingdom of God come with power," i.e., a manifestation of the Holy Spirit. We find the same thing in Luke 9:26, with mention of the parousia ("in his own glory, and in his Father's, and of the holy angels"). The use of the phrase "in the Father's glory" (or, expanded as we have here, "in his own glory, and in his Father's") confirms the pneumatological idea of the Third Hypostasis as the hypostatic, as well as trihypostatic, glory; for, according to its place in the Holy Trinity, the Third Hypostasis, as the "conclusive" one, glorifies the entire Holy Trinity. And in this sense the Third Hypostasis is the glory of the Father and of the Son, whom the Father glorifies by bringing down upon Him the Holy Spirit, the hypostatic glory itself.

Dyad of the Son and the Holy Spirit. In relation to the Son, Divinity is Wisdom; in relation to the Holy Spirit, Divinity is Glory. If Christ is the hypostatic Wisdom of God, its hypostatized manifestation, then the Holy Spirit is hypostatic Glory. But in contrast to the *explicit* hypostatization of Wisdom in Christ, Glory remains hidden in its hypostatizedness, for the Holy Spirit does not have its hypostatic manifestation as such. In the parousia of the Holy Spirit in the world, we have a parallel to the Pentecost, which, consisting in the sending down of the *hypostatic* Holy Spirit into the world, manifests it in the form of tongues of fire, that is, nonhypostatically: The hypostasis of the Holy Spirit is hidden. Similarly, in the parousia, the hypostasis of the Holy Spirit is hidden in Glory, which, at the same time, is also the *Glorifier* (which is why it is blasphemous to interpret this hypostatic Glory merely as a property, quality, or accident proper only to a given event in the life of Christ, especially since such an interpretation is excluded by the Gospel when it speaks of Glory as the Glory of the Father and the Son).

The Glory as the kingdom come in power reveals as the *King* the One who comes in glory, that is, the One who brings the revelation of the Holy Spirit reposing upon Him, His radiance: "then shall the King say" (Matt. 25:34). The Holy Spirit is the giver of the kingdom but, remaining hypostatically hidden, it is the *kingdom* (as well as the Glory). Receiving the kingdom from the Holy Spirit, the Son is the *King*, the One who reigns. This is a supra-eternal depletion of the Second and the Third Hypostases in their mutual love: the Son receives the Glory from the Holy Spirit, while the Holy Spirit receives the Word from the Son. As "the prophets have said," He will "bring all things to your remembrance, whatsoever I have said unto you" (John 14:26). Therefore, the Glory is most spoken of precisely with reference to the Son: "Now is the Son of man glorified" (13:31).[20]

As the manifestation ("coming") of the two revealing hypostases, the Son and the Holy Spirit, the parousia is the perfect Divine-humanity, the image of God manifested in man. In the revelation of glory in Ezekiel 1, the image of man is included in the manifestation of cosmic glory. The fullness of Divine-humanity is the Dyad of the Second and Third Hypostases which is disclosed in the human image as the creation of man in a

---

20. However, in rare cases Scripture does emphasize the relation between the glory and the Holy Spirit: "But he [Stephen], being full of the Holy Ghost, looked up stedfastly into heaven, and saw the glory of God, and Jesus standing on the right hand of God" (Acts 7:55).

dyad: "God created man in his own image. . . . Male and female created he them" (Gen. 1:27). As a manifestation of heavenly humanity in Divine-humanity ("No man hath ascended up to heaven, but he that came down from heaven, even the Son of man which is in heaven" [John 3:13]), the parousia is the revelation, in Christ in glory, of the Dyad of the Son and the Spirit. As a manifestation of Divine-humanity, the parousia is the manifestation of Christ in the Church and with the Church, the body of Christ, in which the Holy Spirit lives.

One can ask: If Christ comes with the Church, to whom and where will He come? What is the domain of this coming, so to speak? One must distinguish two things: on the one hand, that which can abide in union with Christ in His glorified Church even before the judgment; and, on the other hand, the entire net that catches both the good and the bad fishes, or the entire field where not only wheat but chaff grows. Just as in the particular judgment a certain preliminary determination is made after death, so in the entire body of the Church there are members whose condition already makes them worthy of participating in Christ's parousia, of being illuminated by its spirit-bearing glory in an exceptional sense. But this does not change the fact that all people without exception, including those who come with Christ or who meet Him in the clouds, will stand before His terrible judgment, together even with the angels. Concerning this, Scripture gives us certain indications, which are obscure but sufficiently impressive. Thus, 1 Corinthians 15:22-23 says of the universal resurrection that "in Christ shall all be made alive. But every man in his own order: Christ the firstfruits; afterward they that are Christ's at his coming." To this one must apparently add: "and then all the rest." We find a similar indication in 1 Thessalonians 4:16-17: "the Lord himself shall descend from heaven . . . and the dead in Christ shall rise first; then we which are alive and remain shall be caught up together with them in the clouds, to meet the Lord in the air." Apparently, it is implicitly understood here that there are others who will not share this blessed lot. We find a similar distinction in the general context of 2 Thessalonians 1:10: "when he shall come to be glorified in his saints and to be admired . . . in that day." (Here it is apparently a question not of the last judgment but of the parousia. One can also mention the presence on Tabor of the elect of God, Elijah and Moses, in anticipation of the parousia in the Transfiguration.)

Let us also note the indication (repeated in all the eschatological texts that refer to the parousia; see above) that Christ will come with all the holy angels. To be sure, this accompaniment by heavenly powers ("with great power" [Mark 13:26]) can also be understood as a manifestation of glory proper to God's majesty. In any case, it has this meaning as well. But its more essential meaning consists in the fact that, in their totality ("all" of them, as Matt. 25:31 says), the holy angels constitute the heavenly Church. After the casting down of Satan and his angels, the angelic Church no longer knew diminution owing to sin and, in this sense, was always open to "glory." Therefore, the glory of the parousia does not extend to the angelic Church as her proper glorification. But the holy angels do participate in the universal glorification of the human world, with which they thus establish a new relation, more direct and more complete than even in the afterlife. The destinies of the human world which the holy angels serve are thus also their own destinies. Therefore, after the parousia, their separateness from the human world, which now is natural, would be a defect, both for their own being and for man's being. The angels will be judged by God and by man for the manner in which they served the world, but they will also be the necessary witnesses of its life and destinies. Standing before the Lord's throne, the holy angels constitute God's creaturely glory, and therefore they will necessarily participate in the manifestation of God's glory as the triumph of the heavenly Church.

But in pursuing further our inquiry into the meaning of the parousia, we stop in reverent perplexity: The Lord comes in glory with all the holy angels and with the saints, with all that is holy on earth and in heaven. But where is *She*, the Most Pure and Most Blessed One, raised into heaven in Her Dormition and sitting "at the right hand of the Son"?[21] Can it be that She, the Spirit-Bearer, is diminished and cannot enter into the glory of Her Son? Or can it be that She remains in heaven during the Second Coming of Her Son, whom She did "not leave even in the Dormition"? Or will She too cross the threshold of universal resurrection in order to ascend with the saints to the meeting of Christ?

However, was She not resurrected by Her Son in Her holy Dormition? As soon as one asks these questions, one sees that the Mother of God cannot be separated from the glory, or be left in heaven, to await a new resurrection. She will come into the world; She will come into the world with Her Son in His glory, in the parousia. For the parousia of the Son is also necessarily the parousia of the Mother of God, for it is She who is the creaturely glory of the world, the glory of Christ's humanity. She is His hypostatic humanity. She is the Spirit-Bearer, the living gates for the

21. On the doctrine of the glorification of the Mother of God see *The Burning Bush*, chap. 4.

parousia of the Holy Spirit, through which the Holy Spirit comes into the world.

But how do we dare to assert this? Where does Scripture or even Church tradition say this? It is true that Scripture says nothing about this. But does not Scripture fail to mention much else about Her which the Church contains in its doctrine? Does Scripture say anything about Her birth, Her presentation in the temple, or Her dormition, resurrection, and ascension? And does not human blindness not condemn on this basis the whole of the Church's veneration of the Mother of God? And have we not already known for a long time and has it not even become habitual for us that holy silence crowns the *humility* of the Lord's Servant, who is more venerable than the cherubim and incomparably more glorious than the seraphim, as the liturgical hymn says? And here, in the revelation of the parousia, we find the supreme attestation of this triumph of humility: She abides at the right hand of Her Son, where Her Assumption has placed Her. She is forgotten and set aside neither by the holy angels nor by the saints, for She is the highest and saintliest of all creatures. Will the archangel Gabriel come with Christ among the heavenly hosts, but the one to whom he was sent to say, "Hail, thou that art highly favoured, the Lord is with thee" (Luke 1:28), be absent? Will St. Sergius and St. Seraphim be among those following Christ, whereas the one of "whose kind" they are will be absent?[22] In short, what we find here is a silent dogmatic self-evidence, which manifests itself as soon as we pose the question of the Mother of God. But Scripture is silent. . . .

However, this time, the tradition which informs us about the life of the Most Holy Mother of God on earth and after death also appears to be silent. But this silence is not complete, for it is broken by an iconographic gesture: On icons of the Last Judgment, the Mother of God sits at the right hand of Her Son, without Herself being judged. She implores Him to extend His forgiveness (this idea of the Mother of God as interceding at the Last Judgment is confirmed by a number of liturgical texts). This testimony is sufficient. It contains the seed of a dogmatic doctrine which we must now elaborate.

First of all, what does this doctrine consist in with regard to the parousia, the coming of Christ in glory, that is, in the Holy Spirit? The manifestation of Christ, the incarnate God, is visible and tangible,

---

22. It has been told that, when St. Seraphim of Sarov once saw in a dream the Mother of God surrounded by angels, She pointed to him and said: "he is of our kind." — Trans.

410

whereas the manifestation of the Holy Spirit is tangible but invisible as such, for the hypostasis of the Spirit does not become incarnate, but reveals itself only as Christ's glory. However, this glory is not only Christ's proper glorification but also the already glorified Church, heavenly and earthly. Who can represent this Church, its heart, if not the Mother of God? Having given Her Son to humankind, the Most Pure Mother of God is, of course, both the hypostatic body of Christ *par excellence* and the temple of the Holy Spirit as the Spirit-Bearer. This place at the head of the Church belongs to Her not only after the universal resurrection, from the very beginning of the latter, but even, so to speak, *before* the universal resurrection. Here, She precedes the resurrected humankind, for She was resurrected in Her Dormition, and She is already expressly glorified by the Son in Her sitting in heaven at the right hand of Him who raised Her to heaven and glorified His humanity ("flesh") as the hypostatic humanity.

This express glorification of the Mother of God in heaven completes the series of gifts of grace She receives from the Holy Spirit, beginning with Her conception,[23] and including the entry into the Holy of Holies, the Annunciation, and the Dormition. As the temple that the Holy Spirit came to inhabit at the Annunciation, She is the Spirit-Bearer, the transparent human image of the revelation of the Holy Spirit, who, according to His hypostatic property, does not became incarnate but makes incarnate and glorifies. Alone of God's creatures found worthy of being inhabited by the Holy Spirit, She is the human hypostatic image of the Holy Spirit. One can say that, in this sense, She is the Holy Spirit not incarnate but manifested in a human hypostasis. There is no, and can be no, greater and fuller manifestation of the Holy Spirit. Thus, after the ascension of Christ and the assumption of the Mother of God, there exists in the heavens, with the "Heavenly Man" (1 Cor. 15:47-49), a human image of the Holy Spirit, not according to incarnation, which cannot be, but according to a perfect spiritual conformity with Him.

We thus conclude that, in the parousia, which presupposes the revelation of both hypostases, the Spirit-Bearer (that is, the Mother of God), the image of the Third Hypostasis, returns into the world together with the God-man, the incarnate Logos. In this sense, the parousia should be understood as the return of Christ *and* of the Mother of God into the world. Even in Her Dormition the Mother of God does not stop belonging

---

23. It goes without saying that, even if we do not accept the Catholic dogma of the "immaculate" conception, we must confess that the Mother of God is entirely full of grace.

to the world ("She has not left the world," as the liturgical hymn says) and returns into the world in the parousia.

Her abiding "in the heavens" is, of course, different from that of Christ. Even after the parousia the Lord sits supra-eternally at the right hand of the Father; He abides in heaven and on earth, just as the Holy Spirit does. The presence of the Mother of God in heaven corresponds to Her perfect sanctification and deification, in which She will be followed by humankind in the glorified Church. "The kingdom of God"[24] "will come" into the world, and not the reverse; it will not be ravished from the world "to heaven." In other words, the world will become the place of the kingdom of God: "And there shall be no more curse: but the throne of God and of the Lamb shall be in it; and his servants shall serve him: and they shall see his face; and his name shall be in their foreheads . . . and they shall reign for ever and ever" (Rev. 22:3-5). And this center of the kingdom of God on earth, the throne of the Lamb, will be the Most Holy Mother of God. Her "Dormition" includes, of course, the entire fullness of accomplishments, that is, not only Her blessed dormition but also Her resurrection and Her assumption. However, all this in its combination does not ontologically constitute a "leaving of the world." The Most Holy Mother of God in all Her glory does not stop being a creature connected with the entire world, which is glorified in Her and by Her (cf. Her cosmic icons, e.g., that of the *Burning Bush*). She is the glory of the world.

This inevitably leads to a further question, one that is almost without answer: When does this parousia of the Mother of God occur? It is probable that it occurs, in any case, *not later* than the parousia of Christ, since, according to revelation, the glorified Church, the angels and the saints, accompanies Christ who comes in glory. However, there is no evidence that contradicts the possibility that it may even precede the parousia of Christ. After the Ascension, the Mother of God remained in the world alone, so to speak, without Her Son; and by coming into the world first and alone, She can anticipate His coming into the world if that is necessary for humanity, which has need of the vision of Her face to soften its heart. This is suggested by certain Prologues and Vitae of saints, which contain the idea that the Mother of God's descents into the world, Her appearances in it, attest that She did not abandon the world.

---

24. The "kingdom of God" and the "kingdom of heaven" are terms identical in meaning (Matthew's "of heaven" corresponds to the "of God" of the other Evangelists). But in no wise does this mean that the world is abolished in its own being and raised, so to speak, into heaven.

By reason of that general approach of heaven to the world which pre-cedes the parousia, a particular manifestation of the Most Holy Mother of God in the world before the parousia becomes conceivable. Is it not to such a possibility that the following prophetic vision refers: "The marriage of the Lamb is come, and his wife hath made herself ready. And to her was granted that she should be arrayed in fine linen, clean and white, for the fine linen is the righteousness of saints. And [the angel] saith unto me, Write, Blessed are they which are called unto the marriage supper of the Lamb" (Rev. 19:7-9)? And further: "Come hither, I will show thee the bride, the Lamb's wife. And he carried me away in the spirit to a great and high mountain, and showed me that great city, the holy Jerusalem, descending out of heaven from God" (21:9-10). And finally: "And the Spirit and the bride say, Come" (22:17). The saintliness of the saints, the heavenly Jerusalem, in relation to the Unwedded Bride — does Revelation's symbolic language not refer to the appearance in the world of this Spirit-bearing Bride, preparing the way for the Lord? At present, this remains hidden under the veil of holy mystery. But this veil will fall away when the "times and the seasons" approach and the call of the Bride, "Come!" becomes accessible to vigilant hearing and the vision of the Bride Herself becomes accessible to penetrating sight. . . .

It should also be noted that the personal destiny of the Most Holy Mother of God places Her *outside* the action of the parousia, for this action was already accomplished in relation to Her in Her Dormition. According to the Church's belief (which admittedly is not supported by scriptural evidence but which is affirmed as certain by liturgical tradition), the Lord Himself came down from heaven at Her Dormition to receive Her holy soul, to resurrect Her holy body, and to raise Her into heaven for life in communion with Him, and, through Him, with the entire Holy Trinity (although, of course, not in the interior of the Trinity). It is there, in heaven, that Her maximal deification is accomplished and the supreme goal of creation, its theodicy, is fulfilled. The presence of the Mother of God in the parousia and at the Last Judgment is therefore *essentially different* from the presence of all the other participants, without any exception: from that of the human beings and even of the angels, for all of them find themselves on this side of the parousia and the Judgment. All of them, even the angels, will yet be judged. But the Most Holy Mother of God will not be judged; yet neither does She judge, for She is not God but only the Mother of God. It is Christ who judges as the God-man, to whom the whole judgment is delegated by the Father. Without judging, she bestows mercy, like a Mother. Upon Her reposed the hypostasis of love, the Holy Spirit, who also does not judge but is itself the judgment of the world. This particular aspect of the presence of the Mother of God at the judgment contains a new mystery concerning Her works of love after the judgment toward the judged. But here, in truth, "it is best for us to observe silence." . . .

The return of the Mother of God from heaven into the world after the resurrection signifies the beginning of the universal resurrection, for it would be inappropriate for Her, an already resurrected and glorified creature, to live in the world that has fallen away from God, in the midst of humankind burdened by flesh. Human beings themselves must liken themselves to Her, in order to live in the same world with Her. Her coming into the world as the "Woman clothed in the sun" is already a sign of the resurrection, as is the sign of the Son of man in heaven, the holy cross. The latter, bearing the "trihypostatic image of the Trinity" (as the hymn of the Erection of the Cross says), is therefore the sign of Glory, supra-eternally proper to the Holy Trinity, while in the creaturely world it is proper to the Son of God, the Son of man, come into the world to be crucified. The death on the cross is the way to glorification and the sign of glory. And these signs of resurrection, the appearance of the Cross in the heavens and of the Mother of God on earth, are attested to by the archangel's trumpet, awakening the world from its sleep of death.

The appearance of the Mother of God signifies the beginning of the resurrection of the dead, because She, who is resurrected Herself, can appear only to resurrected humankind together with the resurrected Lord (who, though He appeared on earth after resurrection and in a glorified body, did not then yet appear in glory). The abiding of the Mother of God in heaven evidently does not signify the same thing as the presence of the Lord at the right hand of the Father. He abides in the heavens as "One of the Holy Trinity" (as a troparion says), as God in the interior of the Trinity. But since She is a creature, the Most Holy Mother of God does not ascend into this heaven of heavens. Christ faces Her in His humanity. As the highest of all the creatures, She abides *at the boundary* of heaven and creation. She is the peak of the world, which touches heaven. She is sanctified by the entire power of the Divine Sophia, of the revelation of the Holy Trinity. But She Herself remains the creaturely Sophia. This presence of the Mother of God in the heavens can be defined as the creaturely heaven directly illuminated by the divine heaven.

In the parousia, one therefore finds conjoined in Christ and the Mother of God the manifestation of Divinity itself, of the Divine Sophia, in Christ, and Her manifestation in creation. This attests to the accomplished Divine-humanity, the Incarnation of Christ and the deification of

414

creation. The power of deification is further extended to all creation, which is penetrated by the divine light of transfiguration.

Where is the place of the Forerunner? "Among them that are born of women there hath not risen a greater than John the Baptist" (Matt. 11:11; cf. Luke 7:28), with the exception, of course, of the Mother of God. Where is the place of this angelic man and the "close friend of Christ"?[25] Of course, he is where it is natural for him to be — in the most immediate proximity to Christ, together with the Most Holy Mother of God. The Church iconographically bears witness to this in the icon *Deisis,* in the Novgorod icon of Sophia, and elsewhere. He occupies the same place on icons of the Last Judgment: at the head of the angelic order (as the first angel, replacing the fallen Lucifer, as it were), higher than the apostles, the prophets, and all the other human orders. However, there remains a difference in degree between the Forerunner, the first son of the Church, the head of the angelic order and of the human race — and the Mother of God, the Spirit-Bearer, the Queen of heaven and earth, the personification of the Church as Christ's humanity. Despite his primacy, the Forerunner belongs to the Church, whereas the Mother of God is at the head of the Church; and in heaven there is no one who stands closer than She to Christ (not even the beloved disciple John, from the height of the cross given to Her as a son, who nevertheless remains only one of the apostles). Another difference between the destines of the Forerunner and the Mother of God is that the Forerunner is resurrected only with the entire human race, whereas for the Mother of God death had already been vanquished in Her Dormition, through Her resurrection, assumption, and heavenly glorification.

The Forerunner, the "Friend of the Bridegroom,"[26] the Baptist of Christ, the angelic man, has a unique place in the human race, however hard it may be to define dogmatically. He also accomplishes a special service in the afterlife, where he "announces to those in hell God revealed in the flesh" (from the troparion of the Feast of the Forerunner). This puts him, both in the afterlife and in the resurrection, in an exceptional position relative to the rest of humankind.

A further dogmatic consequence follows from this with sufficient certainty: The Forerunner is present at Christ's judgment with all humankind, but he himself is not judged. The angelic man is therefore superior even to the angels, who, by contrast, will be judged, according to the apostle, and even with the participation of human beings (1 Cor. 6:3). Although

---

25. From the Prayer to the Forerunner.
26. See my book *The Friend of the Bridegroom.*

415

he shares original sin with all human beings, the one who was called "to touch the top of the head of Christ the King" in order to baptize Him is free of personal sin. How else can one understand Christ's testimony that the Forerunner is the greatest of those born of women, a testimony, moreover, that was given on the eve of the Forerunner's martyrdom in prison? With this personal sinlessness the Forerunner approaches the Most Pure Mother of God, although the further path of sanctification that he follows distinguishes him, of course, from the One who is more venerable than the cherubim. She is present at the Last Judgment as the merciful Mother, the Intercessor for mercy, representing the compassionate human essence. If the Judge, the Son, is Truth as Justice, She is the Comforter's Comforting. But this unique gift is not given to the Forerunner; it does not correspond to his ministry. However, he indisputably belongs among those about whom it is said that they do not come to judgment, for they have everlasting life, having "passed from death unto life" (John 5:24). This does not release them from having to be present at the judgment, or even from being personally subject to judgment. But it is clear that they will be ultimately justified. And having at their head the greatest of those born of women, *together with* the merciful Mother, gives them the boldness to pray for mercy at Christ's Dread Tribunal: The fetters of love binding humankind are not abolished and cannot, should not be abolished even by the final trepidation before the judgment of Righteousness in person. And love must not make concessions to the ego's fear for its fate.[27]

Thus, even though he does "not come to the judgment," the Forerunner is present at it at the head of the praying communion of saints *(communio sanctorum)*, angels, and human beings,[28] which never ceases and

---

27. Is this idea not confirmed by the parable of the rich man and Lazarus, where, confronted by his own perdition and experiencing torment, the rich man (who till now has loved only himself) becomes full of loving care for the fate of his brothers, "lest they also come into this place of torment" (Luke 16:28)?

28. Nineteenth-century Catholic theology has developed the doctrine of the primary place of Joseph, husband of Mary, and of his resurrection and assumption. There is no basis for these dogmatic fantasies, which have already crystallized into dogma and devotional practice (see my book *The Friend of the Bridegroom*). Orthodoxy silently places the righteous Joseph among the patriarchs and ancestors of the Savior, where he is, of course, distinguished by his genealogical proximity to him. Nevertheless, in the genealogy (Matt. 1:1), the Lord is called "the son of David, the son of Abraham," whereas Joseph is called "the husband of Mary, of whom was born Jesus" (1:16). Also, Luke 3:23 refers to Jesus as "being (as was supposed) the son of Joseph." The very terminology used should guard against dogmatic hyperbole.

is present everywhere, forming the "synaxis of the Forerunner" (the office celebrated the day after Epiphany). But this synaxis draws its authority and power from a superior synaxis: that of the Mother of God (celebrated the day after Christmas). Such is the relation of the two who "stand before" Christ in the *Deisis,* praying for all of creation.[29]

4. The Transfiguration of the World

Scripture connects the coming of Christ in the parousia with the death and transfiguration, or new creation, of the world (Rev. 21:5; Isa. 45:8; 45:17). They are considered two different aspects of the same event. This connection is not only temporal and chronological but also inner and ontological: "Immediately after the tribulation of those days shall the sun be darkened, and the moon shall not give her light, and the stars shall fall from heaven, and the powers of the heavens shall be shaken. And then shall appear the sign of the Son of man in heaven" (Matt. 24:29-30). The Lord's eschatological discourse establishes a direct relationship ("immediately . . . then") between the cosmic catastrophe and the parousia, which relationship signifies the inner unity of this event — the end of the aeon. Clearly, the symbolic language of the images that describe this event cannot be interpreted literally. In general, it conforms to the language of the apocalypses of this period. It expresses the fundamental idea that the world will undergo a catastrophic *transcensus:* on the one hand, it will perish in a cosmic fire; on the other hand, it will be transformed inwardly. The world becomes new, a "new heaven and a new earth" (this contrast is particularly drastic in 2 Pet. 3:7-13).

The first aspect of this event, the cosmic catastrophe, fills hearts with an ineffable natural terror *(terror antiquus),* for it is the gates of death, not only personal but also cosmic, through which all of creation, the "world soul," passes. By contrast, the second aspect fills hearts with the joyous hope of resurrection. The figures used to describe the cosmic catas-

29. To this one should add another feature characterizing the Forerunner as the angelic human being, leader of both the angelic world and the human world. The angelic world, both in its luminous and in its dark part, is subject to his tutelary prayer. Therefore, the restoration of this "dark" part is accomplished through the express intercession of the Forerunner in prayer, as well as, of course, through the intercession of the Queen of Heaven and Earth, who prays without ceasing. Here we approach the holy, unrevealed mystery of the future age, about which one "should keep silent," although that does not mean that one should deny this mystery or remain insensitive to it.

trophe indicate that the event has not only a physical but also a metaphysical or at least a meta-empirical character: "The heavens shall pass away with a great noise, and the elements shall melt with fervent heat" (2 Pet. 3:10). One can find physical and historical signs to explain these catastrophes ("rumours of wars . . . famines, and pestilences, and earthquakes, in divers places" [Matt. 24:6, 7]), but this is only "the beginning of sorrows" (v. 8), not yet the end (v. 6). On the contrary, all this is situated on *this* side of cosmic being. In effect, it is still possible to believe that this world is stable: "For when they shall say, Peace and safety; then *sudden* destruction cometh upon them, as travail upon a woman with child; and they shall not escape" (1 Thess. 5:3).

In other words, in conformity with the depth of the cosmic catastrophe, the end will arrive not only in the physical plane. It will not be limited to *changes* of cosmic being within the framework of cosmic evolution. The end transcends these limits. It presupposes a meta-empirical change of cosmic being, announced by the apostles and prophets, and by our Lord Himself. In theologically interpreting the end, we must inquire into the meaning of this transfiguration of the world in its two aspects: that of the destruction and that of the resurrection of the world.

The end of the world must first be understood *in connection with* the parousia and even in a certain sense *as* the parousia in its cosmic aspect. The earth and the world are not only the physical or geographic (cosmic) place of the parousia in a purely external sense, but also its metaphysical receptacle. This place must conform to its purpose: It must be worthy of meeting the Lord in glory. For, in its present state, the world cannot encompass the parousia. The world catches fire from the approach of the parousia, melts in its fire. In this sense, the *present* world *will not see* the coming Lord; His coming in consuming glory will not occur on this earth. The parousia must first occur *inside* the world itself. The world will be illuminated by the lightning of the parousia, which will blaze out from the east to the west. The world will not remain in a state indifferent to the approach of the coming Lord; all of creation trembles at His coming. And this trembling of creation will be its burning.

In which of its aspects will the parousia be turned toward the world during its transfiguration? The parousia is not only the coming of Christ in glory but also a trinitarian epiphany: The Father sends the Son, who comes in the glory of the Holy Spirit. But in relation to the transfigured world the parousia consists in the express action of the Holy Spirit, glorifying and transfiguring all of creation. Here, we must remember all that we know about the action of the Third Hypostasis at the creation of the world.[30] The life-giving Spirit clothes the Word, by whom all things were made, in being and reality; and it thereby clothes the world in beauty: "Let it be" and "it was good." This is the illumination of the creaturely Sophia by the Divine Sophia, the manifestation of God in creation.

However, this illumination of the creaturely Sophia has a limit: the limited nature of creaturely being in its selfhood, connected with the fact of its reality. Once created, the world was to be glorified, or sophianized, in connection with man, who was to raise it, together with himself, to a new being. However, the fall interfered with this process and, together with man, "the creature was made subject to vanity, not willingly, but by reason of him who hath subjected the same in hope, because the creature itself also shall be delivered from the bondage of corruption into the glorious liberty of the children of God" (Rom. 8:20-21). For this reason "the whole creation groaneth and travaileth in pain together until now" (v. 22). This deliverance was pre-accomplished in the new Adam, and then He completed it by sending down, from the Father, the Comforter, "comforting" and renewing creation. The fiery tongues of the Pentecost blazed in the world. The glory of the world is already present by the Holy Spirit who descended into the world and is abiding in it. But this glory of the world is not yet manifested, and the "creation groaneth and travaileth in pain together until now." This is connected with the kenosis of the Holy Spirit, who actualizes His renewing and transfiguring power only to the extent that creation has the capacity to receive it.

Both this reception and the sending down of the Holy Spirit into the world depend upon the Incarnation, upon the profound, radical transformation of the world's natural being: The flesh of the world became the flesh of Christ in His humanity. Therefore, the world became capable of bearing the Pentecost, of receiving the fire of the Holy Spirit without being consumed by it. However, just as in His earthly ministry Christ followed to the end the path of humiliation and glorification, so the world, having become His flesh, is continuing to follow the path of this kenosis of the Spirit, which appears to be inactive in the world. The kenosis of the Spirit in the world is the continuing kenosis of Christ, although, for Him, His kenosis has been overcome by His most glorious Ascension.

However, despite this kenosis of the Spirit, the world receives the Spirit's sanctifying power through the Church and, through her sacraments, is sanctified in man. The world invisibly moves toward its transfiguration. The action of the grace of the Holy Spirit prepares the world to re-

---

30. See *The Comforter.*

ceive the parousia, which also presupposes the world's glorification. The coming of the Lord in glory, that is, in all the power of the Holy Spirit, is the transfiguration of the world. As long as the Lord was kenotically present in the world, the action of the Holy Spirit reposing upon Him was limited and was manifested only by the working of miracles during His earthly ministry. The resurrected and glorified Christ no longer reveals Himself in the world except in "appearances" to disciples and the elect. And in His ascension in glory, He takes this glory of His out of the world, as it were. The state of the world conforms to His former kenosis, and this determines the measure of the action of the Pentecost in it. The world which Christ left in the Ascension and in which He is present only spiritually, by the Holy Spirit, remains deprived of His glory. "Heaven must receive [Him] until the times of restitution of all things, which God hath spoken by the mouth of all his holy prophets since the world began" (Acts 3:21).

But, in the parousia, Christ comes into the world in glory, and this means that the world too enters into the glory of Christ. The world passes through the fire of the transfiguration, but it is not consumed, for it has acquired a certain resistance to this fire. It is not consumed, for Christ is present in it; and if Christ is in glory, the world too is in glory. But this glorification and transfiguration of the world signifies nothing else but the cessation of the kenosis of the Holy Spirit. From this moment on, the Holy Spirit acts in the world with all its power. This action "without measure" of the Holy Spirit is its parousia, accompanying the parousia of Christ. Having descended on Pentecost but remaining incompletely manifested, the Holy Spirit appears in the parousia in power and glory, not in separate tongues of flame on the heads of the apostles but in the fire of the world's transfiguration.

When speaking of the end of the world, Scripture uses the figure of *fire*: "the heavens and the earth, which are now, . . . are kept in store, reserved unto fire" (2 Pet. 3:7). "The elements shall melt with fervent heat, the earth also and the works that are therein shall be burned up" (v. 10). This figure is frequently encountered in the most diverse senses, literal or figurative (such as God's anger). Texts referring to theophanies and doxophanies, to the appearances of God and of His glory, have a particular importance here: for example, the Burning Bush (Exod. 3:2; 19:18) and Ezekiel's vision of glory (Ezek. 1 and further). The figure of the *cloud* is analogous (see Gen. 9:13-14; Exod. 14:19-20; 19:9; 34:5; 40:34-38; Num. 9:15-19; 1 Kings 8:10). These manifestations of divinity in fire and cloud are more precisely clarified in the New Testament as pneumatological, as actions of the Holy Spirit. One can be guided here by the Forerunner's preaching about the One Who Comes: "He shall baptize you with the Holy Ghost, and with fire" (Matt. 3:11; Luke 3:16). We find the same identification in Christ's words about the Pentecost: "ye shall be baptized with the Holy Ghost" (Acts 1:5). Analogous to this is the manifestation of Christ's Transfiguration in the light of heavenly fire and in cloud, that is, in the energy of the Holy Spirit. Finally, the descent of the Holy Spirit in the form of tongues of fire clearly attests that the divine fire is identified with the action of the Third Hypostasis.

This outpouring of the Holy Spirit in the first Pentecost has a predominantly ecclesiological effect and is expressed in the foundation of the Christian Church on earth. But it also has an eschatological significance, which refers to the end of the age and to its accomplishment in the natural and human world. It is significant that the prophecy of Joel (2:28-32; Acts 2:17-21), applied by the apostle Peter to the Pentecost, has, in its second part, a clearly eschatological character: "And I will show wonders in the heavens and in the earth, blood, and fire, and pillars of smoke. The sun shall be turned into darkness, and the moon into blood, before the great and the terrible day of the Lord come" (Joel 2:30-31). The figures used in this text differ from those of the "Little Apocalypse," where the Lord says that "the sun [shall] be darkened, and the moon shall not give her light, and the stars shall fall from heaven, and the powers of the heavens shall be shaken" (Matt. 24:29). But the two texts are identical in eschatological content. It is essential to note, however, that Matthew 24 connects this convulsion of nature with the approach of Christ in glory, with His parousia, whereas Acts 2 (= Joel 2) connects it with the realization of the Pentecost, with the first parousia of the Holy Spirit. It is precisely the Holy Spirit who accomplishes the transfiguration of the universe: the energy of the Holy Spirit destroys the sinful, imperfect old world and creates a new world, with the renewal of all creation. This is the power of the Fire that burns, melts, transmutes, illuminates, and transfigures.

The paradoxical, antinomic character of these figures is manifested here in all its force. This antinomic character is particularly salient in Matthew 24, 2 Peter 3, and Revelation 21. First of all, the heavenly Fire sets the world on fire and melts it. That is the first action of the Holy Spirit in the world in its parousia. The Third Hypostasis gives life to and affirms the world in its being. But, at the same time, the heavens and the earth, which "are kept in store" by the Word of God, that is, which contain the fullness (the "all") of the divine forces (or ideas) of the Word, are "reserved unto fire against the day of judgment" (2 Pet. 3:7). The life-giving fire becomes a consuming fire. To be sure, this state of "being reserved" refers, first of all, to the kenosis of the Holy Spirit: the Holy Spirit gives life to the world in its work of creating and protecting it. The Holy Spirit kenotically limits the power of its action in the world so that creation can receive it without being reduced to cinders. The world can withstand only a limited degree of heat, so to speak. When the temperature of the world rises above a certain level, it melts.

But this initial measure of the foundation and preservation of the world by the action of the Holy Spirit is not definitive: it is kenotically limited. True, this measure is even further reduced by the fall of man and the consequent infirmity of all creation that subjects it to "vanity." But with the Pentecost this power becomes potentially present in the world in all its fullness through the hypostatic descent of the Holy Spirit. The Pentecost includes not only what in a certain sense can be called the apocatastasis of creation, its liberation from the vanity of original sin, but also its glorification and transfiguration. Just as the future resurrection of all humankind was pre-accomplished in Christ's resurrection, so the universal transfiguration of the world was pre-accomplished in the descent of the Holy Spirit on Pentecost (according to the prophecy of Joel as applied by the apostle Peter). But both the one and the other remain hidden in the ontological depths of being and await their manifestation in it. Through the outpouring of the Church's gifts, the world is being prepared, is ripening for the meeting with the Pentecost in all the fullness of its power, even though the latter is until now being attenuated by the kenosis of the Holy Spirit. This kenosis ceases only in Christ's parousia, which is also that of the Holy Spirit.

We ask: How was the "first" Pentecost of the Holy Spirit possible? How did the world withstand the descent of the Holy Spirit? Why did the world not burst into flame from the fiery tongues of the Holy Spirit? Why did the universal fire not start then, the fire that is to come at the end of the world?[31]

---

31. Scripture repeatedly attests that creatures cannot withstand the vision of the Glory, that is, the nonkenotic manifestation of the Holy Spirit. Even concerning Paul's vision on the way to Damascus, it is said that Paul "could not see for the glory of that light" (Acts 22:11). This shows that, even in the New Testament, the vision of the Glory could not be borne *before* the parousia. True, on the mountain of the Transfiguration [Matt. 17] the apostles saw this glory "to the extent they were capable of seeing it" (as a hymn of the Transfiguration Feast says), but it is possible to think that this vision was limited and preliminary inasmuch as "Jesus was not yet glorified" (John 7:39). For a special reason ("so that, seeing you crucified, they will understand your voluntary suffering," according to the above hymn) the apostles were given this *preliminary* appearance of

The Pentecost became possible only in connection with the incarnation of Christ. It is on this (ontological) basis that Christ implores the Father to send down the Holy Spirit and that He Himself sends the Holy Spirit from the Father. The Holy Spirit eternally rests upon the Son in the Holy Trinity, and since after the Incarnation the entire world becomes Christ's receptacle, belongs to His humanity, there is already a place in the world for the Holy Spirit's descent and presence. This place is the incarnate Son Himself, the world as the body of Christ, which, in the Pentecost, also becomes the temple of the Holy Spirit. But having ascended in glory to heaven, Christ left the world in a certain sense. Although, spiritually, by the action of the Holy Spirit, He did not "leave" the world, this merely spiritual and mysterious presence of His in the world deprives it of his glory, manifesting Him as if He were still in a state of kenosis. The apostle Paul describes this antinomism between the life in the glorious resurrection and the life in humiliation in the following way: "If ye then be risen with Christ, seek those things which are above, where Christ sitteth on the right hand of God. . . . For ye are dead, and your life is hid with Christ in God. When Christ, who is our life, shall appear, then shall ye also appear with him in glory" (Col. 3:1, 3-4). Resurrection and death, hidden life in Christ and the manifestation in glory, are united here for Christians. All this indisputably corresponds to Christ's continuing kenosis on earth in those who are Christ's (cf. 1 Pet. 4:13; 2 Cor. 1:5; Gal. 2:19-20).

As we have said, this kenosis is accompanied by the kenosis of the Holy Spirit. If the descent of the Holy Spirit became possible by virtue of the Incarnation, then Christ's glory, that is, the Holy Spirit, is hidden in

---

the glory (according to the special order of *gratia luminis*, as Roman theologians would say). In Exod. 33:18-23, the Old Testament declares without reserve that mortals cannot withstand the vision of God's glory. Characteristic here is the vision of the glory that God shows to Moses: "Thou canst not see my face: for there shall no man see me, and live" (Exod. 33:20). God puts Moses "in a cleft of the rock" and covers him with His hand as He passes by: "thou shalt see my back parts: but my face shall not be seen" (33:22-23). These correlative images of the face and of the glory attest, in any case, also to the relativity and incompleteness of the manifestation of the glory, which is separated as it were from the "Face of God." (Analogous is the appearance of the glory to the prophets Isaiah and Ezekiel.) It is remarkable that, on Tabor, the same Moses sees not only the glory but also the face of God manifested now in the flesh. The glory illuminates Christ in the form of a cloud, which moderates and kenotically veils, as it were, the fullness of the manifestation of the glory. But it is only in the New Testament that the *personal* appearance of the glory becomes possible.

the heavens and therefore is not manifested on earth. This Glory acts in a mysterious manner in and through the Church, leading the world to and preparing it for its end and glorious transfiguration. This is its maturity, when the "branch" of the fig tree becomes tender and puts forth leaves, and summer is near (Matt. 24:32), the season "which the Father hath put in his own power" (Acts 1:7). The parousia of the Son is accompanied by the parousia of the Holy Spirit. By His coming in glory Christ brings this glory to the whole world.

Glory, that is, the fullness of the action of the Holy Spirit, comes into the world because Christ comes into it. He receives glory for the *whole* world. He thereby protects the world from the consuming fire, which becomes a "joyous light, a meek shining of Holy Glory," according to the vespers hymn. This highlights a new aspect of the procession and sending down of the Holy Spirit from the Father through the Son and thus upon the Son. With the parousia of the Son the kenosis of the Holy Spirit ends. The world becomes the kingdom of God, in which the power and glory of the Holy Spirit are revealed. The light of Christ's glory spreads its glorifying and transfiguring power over the entire world. It is in this sense that it is said about Christ that "our vile body . . . may be fashioned like unto his glorious body" (Phil. 3:21).

Revelation distinguishes two aspects in the transfiguration of the world: the combustion, melting, and destruction of the world by the fire of the final catastrophe; and the formation of the awaited new heaven and new earth: "For behold, I create new heavens and a new earth: and the former shall not be remembered, nor come into mind" (Isa. 65:17; cf. Isa. 66:22; 2 Pet. 3:13). All the things of the world that are unworthy of being eternalized, all that is illusory and nonsophianic in it, will burn up; and its sophianic image will shine forth in such a way that the creaturely Sophia will become the perfectly transparent revelation of the Divine Sophia and will become identified with the Divine Sophia in this unity of image, while preserving forever her creatureliness and her proper extradivine being. This means that, with reference to the creaturely world, "God will be all in all."

This burning up and this new creation (or re-creation) correspond to human death and resurrection, where all that is mortal and nonsophianic dies and is abolished, and that which remains, the sophianic, is resurrected. Applied to the world soul, this idea means that this soul, as the substance of the world, loses its instinctive and psychical character, and acquires spirituality through man, is humanized in him. Compare what Scripture says about the body as corporeality (which in this case coincides with the world soul): "It is sown a natural body; it is raised a spiritual body. There is a natural body, and there is a spiritual body. And so it is written, The first man Adam was made a living soul [Gen. 2:7]; the last Adam was made a quickening spirit. Howbeit that was not first which is spiritual but that which is natural; and afterward that which is spiritual" (1 Cor. 15:44-46). This spiritualization of the psychic (or natural) corresponds to what the same apostle says about the world soul: namely, that "the creature itself also shall be delivered from the bondage of corruption into the glorious liberty of the children of God" (Rom. 8:21). While preserving its reality and its identity, the world soul will stop being closed to the spirit. It will even stop having a certain dominion over the spirit, but instead will become obedient to it, transparent to it. It will conform to the spirit.

But the world cannot accomplish this passage from the psychic to the spiritual by its own powers. This passage presupposes a new creative act of God, not a new creation though, but a re-creation, a transformation by the Holy Spirit of what already exists.

This new creation is connected with man as the bearer of the world soul and the master of the world. The new creation is in conformity with man, and in this sense it has a human character. If at the present time "we ourselves groan within ourselves, waiting for the adoption, to wit, the redemption of our body" (Rom. 8:23), this body of ours is not separated or isolated from the world. Rather, it is connected with it, for the world is the peripheral body of man. This change is not a physical but a metaphysical act: the substance of the world is brought into a new state by the Holy Spirit and is joyously liberated from vanity, the bondage of corruption, nonspirituality.

In this sense, even the action of the Spirit upon the natural world is a synergistic act. The fire of the Spirit is not only a consuming and destructive fire but also a transfiguring one, because creation is already ripening toward its own transfiguration. The latter comes not early and not late, but by the all-penetrating wisdom of God, together with Christ's parousia, which is accomplished by the parousia of the Holy Spirit. The Holy Spirit abides in the world in virtue of the *creation* as the creative "let there be" — by the Word by whom all things are made. The Spirit abides in the world by the power of the *Pentecost*, which, by the hypostatic descent of the Spirit, lays the foundation not only for the world's being but also for the world's deification through the penetration of the creaturely Sophia by the Divine Sophia. The Pentecost, which presupposes the Incarnation, lays the foundation for this penetration or deification of the world ("God will be all in all").[32] However, this transfiguration that is in the process of being prepared is hidden and delayed by the kenosis of the Holy Spirit in creation. In the continuing deification this power of the Holy Spirit that already abides in the world is manifested in its action upon creatures, in which God's omnipotence is manifested, although without destroying them during the new creation: "I make all things new" (Rev. 21:5). For this new creation is not without foundation in the old creation; it is included in the old creation. The new creation does not abolish the old world; nor does it do ontological violence to it *(deus ex machina),* producing something foreign to the world, something that could not be included in it. On the contrary, this new creation accomplishes precisely what is proper to the world and already given to it, although by kenotic anticipation. But, at the same time, this creation surpasses the possibilities of the life of the world and, in this sense, is the omnipotent action of God *upon* the world, although it is ontologically anticipated by the world.

The transfiguration of the world is therefore simultaneously immanent to and transcendent to the world. The new, second creation is the completion of the first. The new creation acts inexorably and irreversibly as God's action in the world, without doing violence to the world. In order to understand the principle of this new or second creation, one must connect it with the first; one must see in it the completion of the first. God created the world so that it could have autonomous being as an extradivine creation, but He did not intend it to be separate from Him. Rather, He intended that it be united with Him without losing its identity.

The path of the world to the fullness of its being is marked by three events: its *creation* by the Father through the Son in the Holy Spirit; its union with God through the *Incarnation* of the Son sent from the Father, accomplished by the Holy Spirit through the union in Christ of the two natures, divine and human, and, in the latter, of the entire world, which man contains microcosmically; and finally, its *transfiguration,* that is, its definitive deification, where the Divine Sophia is made perfectly transparent through the Holy Spirit sent by the Son from the Father. These three acts of God upon the world — creation, the union with the world in the Incarnation, and the transfiguration by the Holy Spirit — are actions of the God who is in the Holy Trinity. However, they differ according to the hypostatic character of the Person of the Trinity who specifically acts upon the world: In the *creation,* it is the Father, as the transcendent God,

---

32. *Panta en pasi* can mean both "all in *all*" (in the neuter) — in the world, in creation — and "all in *all men*" (in the masculine), about which below.

positing the world "outside" Himself, creating it "out of nothing." In the *Incarnation,* it is the Son, the Hypostasis of the Word of all the words of the world, of the world's entire creaturely content (by Him all things were made): the world ontologically contains and repeats by and in itself, as it were, these words of the Word, while the Word unites in Himself the world and also repeats it, as it were, in connection with His human nature. And finally, the Holy Spirit, by giving life, clothes with being the words of the Father's Word and makes the life of the world a receptacle of divine life. Of course, all these three actions of the Creator in creation cannot be separated from or opposed to one another. All of them are triune acts of the triune God, but they are also clearly qualified by the character of the Hypostasis involved. It is precisely this hypostatic specificity that constitutes the *newness* of each of them: the absolute newness of creation for itself; the newness of its being as the body of God, the flesh of the Son (John 1:14); and finally, its renewal by the Holy Spirit.

Even though the parousia of the Holy Spirit as the manifestation of the power of the Pentecost has a synergistic character, since it acts upon a creation that has its own nature and life, it is, like Christ's parousia, inexorable and unavoidable, acting with compelling force. If, in His parousia, Christ becomes visible for all, both for those who love Him and await Him and for those who do not love Him and reject Him ("then shall all the tribes of the earth mourn, and they shall see the Son of man coming in the clouds of heaven with power and great glory" [Matt. 24:30]), then, in the parousia of the Holy Spirit, the melting and transfiguring fire acts in the world as a metacosmic, supernatural power. To be sure, there is a fundamental difference: Christ's parousia is visible first to human beings, and, through them, to the world. By contrast, the parousia of the Holy Spirit is not visible but rather is felt by creation as the power of spirituality that has dominion over psychic being. However, this property of spirituality is also connected with the being of man as the head of creation, and it is perceived by all creation that groans because of man: all creation rejoices in the Holy Spirit.

In connection with this reception of transfiguration by creation, we must recall what we know about nonhypostatic love, that is, the love of creatures for their Creator and the praise of the Creator to which they are called by Scripture. The transfiguration of the world by the power of the Holy Spirit, the hypostasis of love, will represent a new explosion of the glorifying love of creation for its Creator. Then it will be an evident reality that "the heavens declare the glory of God, and the firmament showeth his handywork. Day unto day uttereth speech, and night unto night showeth knowledge. There is no speech nor language, where their voice is not heard. Their line is gone out through all the earth, and their words to the end of the world" (Ps. 19:1-4). And then the invocations of the three young men in the song they sing in the furnace will be fulfilled in all their power (Dan. 3:57-81). These invocations are addressed to all creation, animate and inanimate, but equally spiritualized: "All things the Lord has made, bless the Lord, give glory and eternal praise to him. . . . The heavens . . . , all the waters above the heavens . . . , all the powers of the Lord . . . , the sun and the moon . . . , the stars of heaven . . . , showers and dews . . . , winds . . . , nights and days . . . , light and darkness . . . , ice and frost . . . , frost and snow, lightning and clouds . . . , mountains and hills . . . , seas and rivers . . . , sea beasts and everything that lives in water . . . , birds of heaven . . . , animals wild and tame . . . give glory and eternal praise to him."

The entire order of the universe that is created in the Six Days is called here to praise the Lord, to know and love Him.

To the fullness of the transfiguration of the world, expressed in different forms, we must add the image of the "great city, the holy Jerusalem, descending out of heaven from God, having the glory of God" (Rev. 21:10-11). This city, its materials, its precious stones, and its structure are described (vv. 11-23). It is measured "according to the measure of a man, that is, of the angel" (v. 17). The descent out of heaven of this city, which clearly has an earthly purpose and even origin, cannot be understood literally, of course. This figure signifies the transfiguration of the earthly, human, historical city ("the nations of them which are saved shall walk in the light of it: and the kings of the earth do bring their glory and honour into it" [v. 24]). This text has in view the historical achievements of human creative activity, which will be liberated and separated from the works of the already fallen Babylon and its riches (18:2-21), and which will participate in the transfiguration in the glory of God. They will also participate in the universal transformation, for, unlike Babylon, they have not merited destruction; but, at the same time, they have need of heavenly light to continue their existence in the future age, in the kingdom of glory. They thus also achieve a certain deification, which extends to the entire world. "And the city had no need of the sun, neither of the moon, to shine in it: for the glory of God did lighten it, and the Lamb is the light thereof" (21:23; cf. 22:5; about the city of God, see below, section 7).

5. The Universal Resurrection

The parousia of Christ is the coming of the Resurrected One in the power and glory of the resurrection. But this manifestation cannot be accomplished in this corruptible world, which is therefore transfigured, and for this corruptible humanity, for "flesh and blood cannot inherit the kingdom of God; neither doth corruption inherit incorruption" (1 Cor. 15:50). "For this corruptible must put on incorruption, and this mortal must put on immortality" (v. 53). Thus, only humanity that has been resurrected and that has been made incorruptible, that has been clothed in immortality, can meet Christ and receive His manifestation. Therefore, even if "we shall not all sleep [die], . . . we shall all be changed" (v. 51), having become incorruptible and immortal. The resurrection of the One is also the universal resurrection, hidden until the "last day" (John 6:39) and revealing the power of Christ's resurrection: "Christ is risen, and life lives. Christ is risen and no dead are in the grave, for Christ rose from the dead, the first-fruit of the deceased."[33]

In Christ's resurrection, together with His humankind, that which is His, the whole human race was pre-resurrected, receiving the power of resurrection: "Christ is risen from the dead; he has destroyed death by death and given life to those in the grave," as the Easter hymn says. Death has lost its force, although it continues to reign in this world, since the latter remains under the power of its prince. But mortality is only a temporary state of the world, not its essence. "Christ is risen from the dead, and become the firstfruits of them that slept. For since by man came death, by man came also the resurrection of the dead. For as in Adam all die, even so in Christ shall all be made alive. But every man in his own order: Christ the firstfruits; afterward they that are Christ's at His coming" (1 Cor. 15:20-23). The God-man is the all-man, and his resurrection is ontologically the universal resurrection, which, however, will be realized only on the last day, in Christ's parousia. "If we believe that Jesus died and rose again, even so them also which sleep [are dead] in Jesus will God bring with him" (1 Thess. 4:14). According to this revelation the parousia *is* also the universal resurrection, and the universal resurrection is the parousia: the two are identical and inseparable.

We already know that Christ's resurrection is both resurrection and the raising from the dead: Christ is raised by the Father by the power of the Holy Spirit and He Himself resurrects, for it was not possible for death

---

33. From John Chrysostom's Easter homily.

to hold Him (see Acts 2:24). His resurrection is a synergistic act,[34] in which human self-determination corresponds to God's action by a perfect accomplishment of God's will and by a redemptive reconciliation with God of the entire fallen human nature. Thus, the universal resurrection also manifests the power of the *redemption* of humankind in Christ. It is evident that if "God," in this case the Father, raises Christ, then in Him all humankind is raised. The raising of all humankind is thus a transcendent action of God in creation. This conclusion is directly confirmed by Scripture: "He that raised up Christ from the dead shall also quicken your mortal bodies by his Spirit that dwelleth in you" (Rom. 8:11). "He which raised up the Lord Jesus shall raise up us also by Jesus" (2 Cor. 4:14).

It might thus appear that, as a new creation, the resurrection of the dead is accomplished by the *Father* through the Son by the Holy Spirit, in the same way that He created the world. But the resurrection is not a new *creation* in the strict sense, but only a restoration (apocatastasis) of the original creation, which is raised to its highest and ultimate being. Therefore, the Father acts here not as the Almighty Creator but as the Provider through the hypostases of the Son and the Holy Spirit, who act, according to their relation that is appropriate in the given situation, in the world in the Divine-humanity that has already been accomplished through the Incarnation and Pentecost.

Here, it is necessary to establish that, although it is the Father who "will resurrect us by his power," He will accomplish this through the Son, according to the Lord's word: "For as the Father raiseth up the dead and quickeneth them; even so the Son quickeneth whom he will" (John 5:21). "The hour is coming, and now is, when the dead shall hear the voice of the Son of God; and they that hear shall live" (v. 25). "This is the Father's will which hath sent me, that of all which he hath given me I should lose nothing, but should raise it up again at the last day . . . and I will raise him up at the last day" (6:39-40). "I am the resurrection and the life" (11:25). In comparing these two series of texts, in one of which it is the Father who raises whereas in the other it is Christ who raises, we must first establish how they are correlated, excluding in advance any possibility that they are in-

---

34. See *The Lamb of God*, pp. 411-17. Here are the relevant texts attesting that "God [= the Father] raised Him" (Christ): Acts 2:24; 3:15, 4.10, 5:30; 10:40; 13:33, 34; 17:31; 26:8; 1 Pet. 1:21; Col. 2:12; Rom. 4:24; 8:11; 1 Cor. 6:14; 2 Cor. 1:9; 4:14; Gal. 1:1; Eph. 1:20; 2:6; 1 Thess. 1:10. The following texts testify that the Son raises mortals from the dead: Matt. 16:21; 17:9, 23 (= 20:19); 27:63; Mark 8:31; 9:9; Luke 18:33; Rom. 4:25; 6:4, 9; 8:34; 14:9; 1 Cor. 15:4, 12, 20; Col. 3:1; 1 Thess. 4:14, 16.

compatible or contradictory. They can be harmonized if we understand that Christ's own resurrection is primordial and fundamental, whereas the universal resurrection is secondary and derivative: The dead are resurrected "in Christ," "Christ the firstfruits; afterward they that are Christ's" (1 Cor. 15:22-23). If Christ is not only raised but resurrects, then in His resurrection He already *co-raises* all who are raised in Him. He is the resurrector of those co-raised with Him. After the Incarnation, the Father acts in the world by and through Christ, especially in the universal resurrection. The latter is the fruit of His resurrection and is included in Him.

However, the proper relationship of the Hypostases is preserved: The principle of the resurrection is nevertheless the "will of the Father," while the raising itself, as the fulfillment of this will, is the work of the Son. And let us not forget the corresponding action of the Holy Spirit, addressed in Romans 8:11. The life-giving Holy Spirit is the life of God. Nevertheless, about this life it is said: "as the Father hath life in himself, so hath he given to the Son to have life in himself" (John 5:26); "as the Father raiseth up the dead, and quickeneth them, even so the Son quickeneth whom he will" (v. 21). This text has, first of all, a general trinitarian sense, for it refers to the eternal procession of the Holy Spirit from the Father and the reposing of the Holy Spirit upon the Son. It also has a christological sense, for the Holy Spirit is communicated to creation and sent by the Son in His glorification. Finally, it has a pneumatological sense, for the Spirit is Life, the power of "quickening" and "raising"; it is resurrection itself. The christological formula according to which the Son quickens and raises can be fully unfolded into a trinitarian formula: according to the will of the Father, the Son sends the Spirit of Life. Resurrection is thus explained as the action of the entire Holy Trinity: the Father is the principle; the Son is the accomplisher; the Holy Spirit is the power and essence of the accomplishment.

This idea can also be expressed in the language of the theology of Glory. Since the parousia of the Son is, in the sense indicated above, also the parousia of the Holy Spirit (and, united, the two constitute the coming of Christ in glory according to the Father's will), the universal resurrection is both the manifestation and the action of this glory in the world. In the parousia, glory cannot be limited solely to the illumination of Christ; its light and force spread throughout creation and raise the dead in glory. "The Spirit of glory and of God" in the revelation of the "glory" of Christ (1 Pet. 4:13-14) raises the dead in glory: "It is sown in dishonour; it is raised in glory: it is sown in weakness; it is raised in power" (1 Cor. 15:43). Incorruptibility is equivalent to glorification. Coming in glory,

Christ communicates this glory to His entire humanity, and this glory, first of all, is resurrection. It corresponds to the general transfiguration of creation in the human world as the manifestation of the entire power of the parousia. Besides being the second coming of Christ, the parousia is also the manifestation of the glory of the Holy Spirit, of the divine Dyad.

The raising of the dead as a manifestation of the power of the parousia is a transcendent action of God in the world, and it is therefore sudden. This means that its power is *not* contained in the life of the world itself (which excludes in advance all naturalism of Fyodorov's type). Nor is it the result of a cosmic and historical evolution. Rather, it is a direct action of God *upon* man (although this does not exclude synergism). One can express the same idea by saying that the universal resurrection is a result of Christ's resurrection, is included in His resurrection. The transcendent aspect of the universal resurrection takes it beyond time, beyond historical continuity. The universal resurrection is outside or above earthly time. With the universal resurrection, a new time begins: the "future age." Scripture expresses this in a number of figures, the most common of which is the "sound of a trumpet," the summoning trumpet of the archangel, announcing God's will: "And he shall send his angels with a great sound of a trumpet, and they shall gather together his elect from the four winds, from one end of heaven to the other" (Matt. 24:31). These words of the Lord are seconded by the apostle of the Gentiles: "Behold, I show you a mystery:[35] We shall not all die, but we shall all be changed, in a moment [*en atomōi*],[36] in the twinkling of an eye, at the *last trump:* for the *trumpet* shall sound, and the dead shall be raised incorruptible, and we shall be changed" (1 Cor. 15:51-52). We find the same image in 1 Thessalonians 4:15-16: "For this we say unto you by the word of the Lord[37] . . . the Lord himself shall descend from heaven with a shout, with the voice of the archangel, and with the trump of God: and the dead in Christ shall rise first." The images of the trumpet of God and the sound of a trumpet are found repeatedly in Revelation as well, with reference to the expression of God's will (see Rev. 4:1; 8:6-8, 10, 12-13; 9:1, 13-14). Analogous to the trumpets are voices and thunders (see Rev. 10:3-7; 16:1, 17; 18:1-2).

35. "Mystery" (*musterion*) indicates here the expressly revelatory character of what is being communicated, corresponding to the divine transcendence of the event.

36. *En atomoi* can refer both to suddenness in time and to the meta-empirical character of a change in relation to the being of the world in its matter — to a change, evidently also transcendent, in the primary, "atomic" structure of the world.

37. This expression is equivalent to "I shew you a mystery" (1 Cor. 15:51), as an express revelation of the action of God over the world and transcendent to the world.

The trumpet that announces a "command" (a military signal) is a figure taken from military life. Here it expresses an action of God that, in its transcendence, is *sudden* for the world (and in this sense catastrophic). This announcement of the universal resurrection is attributed to the angels or to an archangel, without, of course, revoking the fundamental truth, proclaimed by revelation, that the raising of the dead is a work of God. Scripture adds only the idea that the angels participate in the raising of the dead by accomplishing God's will. This corresponds to the general service of the angels in ministering to and watching over the world. This service is clearly not limited to the life of this age but extends to its passage into the future age (where the angels participate as "reapers" in the last separation; see Matt. 13:39-41). On this side of death and resurrection, the form and the degree of this participation are not revealed to us; they surpass our present understanding.

The resurrection of the dead is universal (John 5:28) and simultaneous: "the dead shall hear the voice of the Son of God: and they that hear shall live" (v. 25). The universality of resurrection corresponds to the universal power of the Incarnation, in which the Lord assumed the entire human nature without any restriction or exclusion; and in His glorious resurrection all humankind is raised.[38] "For as in Adam all die, even so in Christ shall all be made alive" (1 Cor. 15:22). Certain questions might arise in connection with particular biblical passages. It is first necessary to clarify a misunderstanding caused by what the Book of Revelation says about the first resurrection (Rev. 20:4-6). From the point of view of the universal resurrection *in the body,* the "first resurrection," that of the righteous, of those who only "came back to life" (however we interpret this), is not a resurrection at all, insofar as it is not a question here of bodily resurrection.

But some texts have other indications: they appear to indicate certain differences as far as the time and form of the resurrection are concerned. Consider, first of all, the Lord's words in Matthew 24:31: "And he shall send his angels with a great sound of a trumpet, and they shall gather together *his elect* from the four winds, from one end of heaven to the other." Does this mean that only the elect will be resurrected, or at least that they will be resurrected first? This idea seems to be even more strongly asserted in 1 Corinthians 15:22-23: "In Christ shall all be made

38. On the rabbinical doctrine of resurrection of the righteous alone, see Iv. G. Troitsky, *The Talmudic Doctrine of the Afterlife State and the Final Fate of Human Beings (Talmudicheskoye uchenie o posmertnom sostoyanii i konechnoi uchasti liudei),* Saint-Petersburg, 1904. Cf. my article "The Problem of Conditional Immortality."

alive. But every man in his own order: Christ the firstfruits; afterward they that are Christ's at his coming" (although the same chapter, verse 52, speaks of unrestricted "change" and resurrection "in a moment, in the twinkling of an eye, at the last trump"). First Thessalonians 4:16-17 belongs among these texts: "the Lord himself shall descend from heaven . . . and *the dead in Christ shall rise first.* . . . Then we which are alive and remain shall be caught up together with them in the clouds, to meet the Lord in the air, and so shall we ever be with the Lord."

However, none of these three texts contradicts the idea of the universal resurrection according to which "all that are in the graves shall hear his voice, and shall come forth; they that have done good, unto the resurrection of life; and they that have done evil, unto the resurrection of damnation" (John 5:28-29). No distinction is made here as to the time of the resurrection of the two groups. Therefore, the texts presented above should be understood not in the sense of temporal sequence but in the sense of a certain qualitative distinction, although one that is expressed in terms of time. The idea here is that those who are Christ's receive the summons to resurrection differently and are resurrected differently from those who are not Christ's: On the one side there are the holy prophets, the apostles, the martyrs, the righteous whose entire life was only a waiting for the coming Christ, with Christ's Forerunner at the head. On the other side there are the indifferent, those immersed in the life of the world, and, then, Christ's enemies, the persecutors, the blasphemers, the godless. If the first are resurrected actively, so to speak, the second are merely subject to the inevitability of resurrection. Synergism is revealed even in resurrection. The first are co-resurrected with Christ, spiritually and of themselves; whereas the second resist passively, so to speak, and do not go out to meet resurrection or await it. For the first, this necessity is a supreme freedom in the joy of the "resurrection of life"; for the second, it is a "condemnation." These differences are expressed in the juxtaposition: first Christ, then Christ's.

Together with resurrection the apostle also speaks of a "change" in the living, which is equated with being raised from the dead. In an instant that cannot be measured — *en atomōi* — the power of death and of resurrection is manifested, on the basis of the fruits of both earthly life and of the afterlife, which will make the living capable — more or less, in one way or another — of receiving resurrection. However, outside this theological postulate, indisputable in its self-evidence, we cannot get any real idea of this event, for we are on this side of death and resurrection. Like the death that is equivalent to it, this "change" separates those who experience it from this world. This "change" gives to those who experience it an analogous knowledge of the spiritual world and frees them from the dust of the earth, making them ready to enter into the new life of resurrection. Besides this theological postulate we cannot say anything more about this.

Let us now turn to the fundamental question: What is the resurrection, the preaching of which constitutes the fundamental content of primitive Christianity? About the apostles it is said at the outset that they "preached through Jesus the resurrection from the dead" (Acts 4:2). In Athens the apostle Paul "preached . . . the resurrection" (17:18). Before the Sanhedrin he says: "It is for our hope in the resurrection of the dead that I am on trial" (23:6). Before the governor Felix he bears witness to his faith "that there shall be a resurrection of the dead" (24:15, 21). He bears witness to the same thing before Agrippa and Festus (26:8). In 1 Corinthians 15:13-14 (cf. vv. 16-17) he confesses as the fundamental truth of our faith: "if there be no resurrection of the dead, then is Christ not risen: and if Christ be not risen, then is our preaching vain, and your faith is also vain." The goal of the Christian life is to "attain unto the resurrection of the dead" (Phil. 3:11), and "as Christ was raised up from the dead by the glory of the Father, even so we also should walk in newness of life" (Rom. 6:4). "He which raised up the Lord Jesus shall raise us up also by Jesus" (2 Cor. 4:14).

According to the Christian faith, resurrection is first of all the quickening of the body and its union with the spirit. It is *bodily* resurrection. "He that raised up Christ from the dead shall also quicken your mortal bodies" (Rom. 8:11). Resurrection consists in the fact that "God giveth it a body" (1 Cor. 15:38). In this sense, resurrection is an apocatastasis; a human being is re-created in his original form, consisting of a soul and a body. The postmortem state of bodilessness and, in this sense, disincarnation, is not natural for human beings; it does not correspond to the fullness of life. On the contrary, ontologically it can be considered only episodic, since God did not create death. It entered the world by sin and was vanquished by Christ's resurrection. The first effect of the power of resurrection therefore consists in restoring the fullness of man in his spiritual and bodily composition. On one side, we have a graveyard with dead bones; on the other side, we have bodiless souls, awaiting the restoration of their integrity through reunification with the body.

Here one must decisively reject Platonism's conception of the body, according to which it is only a temporary prison, fetters for the spirit that are to be removed. One must reject just as decisively the theosophical idea of the metamorphosis of human beings in a series of reincarnations, which obliterates the very distinction between spirit and body and dis-

435

solves the concrete integrity of the first man, Adam, as well as of the New Adam, Christ. The idea of resurrection is best expressed by the concrete and massive figure of the quickening of bones that we have in Ezekiel's vision (chap. 37); or in the simplicity of the Gospel's expression, "they that hear shall live" (John 5:25); or in the descriptions of Christ's resurrection: the sepulchre was empty, "and the napkin, that was about his head, [was] not lying with the linen clothes, but [was] wrapped together in a place by itself" (John 20:7). In this sense the resurrection is, first of all, the victory over death: the dead receive their bodies as quickened, while those who are "changed" know a new state of their bodies.

The resurrection is also communion with eternal life, which excludes the very possibility of a new death *(non posse mori)*. This is the power of Christ's resurrection: "in Christ shall all be made alive" (1 Cor. 15:22). In this sense, the universal resurrection is essentially different from the miraculous raisings described in both the Old and the New Testament, and even from those accomplished by Christ himself. These raisings did not bestow immortality: neither the children raised by the prophets Elijah (1 Kings 17:21-23) and Elisha (2 Kings 4:33-36), nor the son of the widow of Nain, nor the daughter of Jairus, nor even Lazarus, the friend of the Lord, nor Eutychus, nor Dorcas, raised by the apostle Peter, received immortality, but died again when the time came. However, in the kingdom of God, on the other side of resurrection, the resurrected do not know death, for "Christ . . . dieth no more; death hath no more dominion over him" (Rom. 6:9). "Then shall be brought to pass the saying that is written, Death is swallowed up in victory. O death, where is thy sting? O grave, where is thy victory?" (1 Cor. 15:54-55).

What is the significance of this extension of the power of Christ's resurrection to all the dead, to all humankind? We already know that the raising of the dead is an action of the entire Holy Trinity, in which the Father wills and the Son actualizes by the Holy Spirit His resurrection as that of all humankind. The universal resurrection is not a new creative action of God in the world, a new fact in the life of the world. Rather, it is the accomplishment of something that has already been pre-accomplished, precisely by the resurrection of Christ. However, it has remained and remains as if without effect during Christ's absence from the time of the Ascension until the parousia. This is expressed by the apostle Paul in the following words: "The times of refreshing shall come from the presence of the Lord; and he shall send Jesus Christ, which before was preached unto you: whom *the heaven must receive until the times of restitution of all things,* which God hath spoken by the mouth of all his holy prophets since the world began" (Acts 3:19-21). "Unto you first God, having raised up his Son Jesus, sent him to bless you" (v. 26). The Son sent His disciples to preach, and this "restitution of all things" continues, in the heavens and in the world, until His Second Coming. Only after this restitution will the Lord come again, now in glory, into the world. But this glory will be completely incompatible with the power of corruption and death in the world and in humanity. And just as the entire world is transfigured in glory, so all humankind is resurrected to meet Christ when He comes again.

But if the Father raises Christ by the Holy Spirit, the Son raises humankind from the dead according to the will of the Father by the Holy Spirit in the revelation of the glory: "He that raised up Christ from the dead shall also quicken your mortal bodies by his Spirit that dwelleth in you" (Rom. 8:11). The Spirit raises humanity precisely by the power of Christ's resurrection. Until the Second Coming of Christ the action of the Holy Spirit come down into the world is providentially limited by its kenosis. After the Second Coming this kenosis cedes its place to the resurrecting action of the Holy Spirit. Having resurrected Christ according to the will of the Father and reposing upon Him hypostatically, the Holy Spirit descends with its power on the dry bones of the dead and gives life to them. "Thus saith the Lord God unto these bones: Behold, I will cause breath [*Spirit* in the Russian Bible] to enter into you, and ye shall live: and I will lay sinews upon you, and will bring flesh upon you, and cover you with skin, and put breath [Spirit] in you, and ye shall live" (Ezek. 37:5-6). But this "putting in of Spirit" is possible only because this is Christ's humanity, upon which the Holy Spirit reposes. Therefore, resurrection is also the definitive manifestation of the power of the Incarnation, as well as of the Pentecost. In *this* sense, the resurrection is an action of the parousia of the Holy Spirit, as is the transfiguration of the world. But it is accomplished in conjunction with the parousia of the Son, apart from whom the Holy Spirit does not act, according to its hypostatic character. "For he shall not speak of himself" (John 16:13). "He shall glorify me: for he shall receive of mine, and shall show it unto you. All things that the Father hath are mine: therefore said I, that he shall take of mine, and shall show it unto you" (John 16:14-15). These words of the Lord, which express interhypostatic relations, signify, with reference to the resurrection of the dead, that the Son raises by the power and will of the Father (John 5:21) and by the action of the Holy Spirit. This action is included in the general glorification of the world with the cessation of the kenosis of the Holy Spirit and the beginning of the "kingdom of glory."

The resurrection of the dead is a direct action of God's power. We have previously noted in the resurrection the human aspect of synergism, according to which different people await it and are prepared for it to different degrees. Moreover, the parousia comes only after the end of history, in the fullness of times. But this synergistic aspect of the accomplishment of the resurrection does not, contrary to Fyodorov, signify any human participation in it. It refers only to the reception of resurrection. Resurrection results from an approach of God to creation of the kind we have in the Incarnation and the Pentecost, or, in general, in the accomplished Divine-humanity. In a certain sense, universal resurrection appears natural for humanity as assumed and pre-resurrected by Christ. But, at the same time, it is, in itself, a supernatural, transcendentally creative act of God: God "will . . . raise up us *by his own power*" (1 Cor. 6:14). The resurrection is therefore an object of faith, as something totally *new* for our present life, about which one can speak only with the apostle's words: "It doth not yet appear what we shall be: but we know that, when he shall appear, we shall be like him; for we shall see him as he is" (1 John 3:2). Further, since it is merely *spiritual* even that joy of resurrection that we experience as such a miracle during the Paschal vigil is not yet this joy of *spiritual and bodily* resurrection. In this age, the resurrection from the dead remains transcendent for us. As a miracle of God, it will remain a mystery for us until it happens to us.

This action of God *upon* man is not limited by our human infirmity; nor does it take individual properties into account. It is therefore universal: All human beings will be resurrected without exception, for the universal resurrection is a work of God. In *this* sense, all are resurrected equally, by God's will, not by arbitrary human will. To be a human being and therefore to belong to Christ's humanity is the sole basis for resurrection: *homo sum et nihil humani a me alienum esse puto.* This same human nature is, by virtue of Christ's Incarnation, also divine-human. That is why *all* are called to the joy of the Resurrection, for "the Savior's death freed all of us" (according to the Easter homily of John Chrysostom).

While remaining a mystery of God, the resurrection of the dead is explained to a certain degree by its effects, and to this extent it can be understood on the basis of revelation. St. Paul compares it to sowing and germination:

That which thou sowest, thou sowest not that body that shall be, but bare grain, it may chance of wheat, or of some other grain: but God giveth it a body as it hath pleased him, and to every seed his own body. All flesh is not the same flesh: but there is one kind of flesh of men, another flesh of beasts, another of fishes, and another of birds. There are also celestial bodies, and bodies terrestrial, but the glory of the celestial is one, and the glory of the terrestrial is another. There is one glory of the sun, and another glory of the moon, and another glory of the stars; for one star differeth from another star in glory. So also is the resurrection of the dead. (1 Cor. 15:37-42)

Two fundamental ideas are expressed here. The first idea likens the power of resurrection to the germinative energy of a seed. The second notes the difference between seeds and therefore between their bodies.

The germinative energy itself, proper to a creation of God, is a natural mystery, whose effects are accessible to our observation. A distinction is made between the quality of the seed and its energy: the "bare grain" and "to every seed his own body." The seed is correlative to the earth as to some reality without qualities or containing all qualities, which gives to the seed a body according to its germinative energy. The "grain dies" in the shell it is given, but this does not destroy its qualitative energy, idea, or entelechy. In the germinative process we have only *repetitions* of totally similar growths. But we cannot say this about human resurrection, although, here too, there is a qualitatively determinate grain in the individual form of the deceased, so that, in a certain sense, resurrection is analogous to germination. But it differs from germination in that it contains the energy of immortality and also preserves the energy of its proper individuality. The analogy must therefore be limited: it can be applied only to the character of the restoration of life in resurrection.

On the one hand, we have a qualitatively determinate germination from the grain, that is, a person already present in creation and only now being resurrected. On the other hand, we have the germinative energy of the grain, inherent to the restoration of life. If one translates this image, which belongs to the life of the vegetative world, into the language of anthropology, one arrives at the affirmation that, in resurrection, a determinate spiritual personality receives, or rather regains, the germinative energy that it needs to restore the fullness of its life, not only spiritual but also corporeal, or more precisely, spiritual-corporeal. Death consists in the fact that the body, which expresses a human being's incarnate condition, his belonging to this world, is separated from his soul and spirit, which remain inseparable even after death, in the afterlife. The soul becomes incapable of maintaining its connection with the body and of quickening it, which brings the soul itself into a state of potentiality.

But, in resurrection, the soul will once again receive from God the

439

energy of the "grain," the quickening power; and, by God's command, it will once again form for itself a body that is proper to it. The matter of this body is taken from the natural world, to which it belongs. Resurrection is therefore not a new creation but only fully restores what has already been created. Through the energy of his soul, every human being receives his proper body, which he had previously (although he receives it in a changed state, about which below). It is important to understand that this body is formed not by the human spirit, which is incapable of this kind of "objectification," but by the soul, which is obedient to the will of God ("the dead shall hear the voice of the Son of God, and they that hear shall live" [John 5:25]). In resurrection, there is therefore no place for human freedom, which is proper to the spirit. Rather, a kind of natural necessity operates here, with the soul finding itself in a passive state. Here, the soul does not receive a new power but only has restored to it the power that had been proper to it before death, when the human being lived bodily.

One can also say that this passive and, in this sense, feminine, substance is, with reference to the universal human multi-unity, the world soul. In other words, the resurrection of the dead is accomplished by an action of God precisely in the world soul, or the whole of "groaning" creation, which is quickened in the victory over death. This action of God is applied not only to every individual human soul but also to the integral Adam, and even to the whole of creation, in which, together with transfiguration, the universal resurrection is triumphant. For resurrection to occur singly for individuals, without that inner connection that unifies the entire human race, would contradict the multi-unity of the latter, in both the Old and the New Adam.

But this multi-unity does not abolish the multiplicity and qualitative diversity of human persons. This is shown by another aspect of St. Paul's doctrine of resurrection, namely in the teaching that "all flesh is not the same flesh" (1 Cor. 15:39). Individual differences exist among creatures from the moment of creation; and they have their imprint in the whole, in the world soul. These differences are fully realized in resurrection. The world and humankind are not a monotonous monolith of uniform repetitions. Rather, they constitute an organic symphony of diversity, which resounds both in the whole, in the world soul, and in every creature: "there is one kind of flesh of men, another flesh of beasts, another of fishes, and another of birds" (1 Cor. 15:39). And, of course, every human soul is individual, in conformity with the individuality of the personal spirit, while participating in the universal world soul. In the universal resurrection, every soul constitutes, by the power of God, that body that is proper to it from creation.

In connection with this a question arises that was much debated in the patristic literature (by Origen, St. Gregory of Nyssa, St. Ephraem, St. Augustine, and others): In what state, at what age, and in what appearance is the body of a resurrected individual restored? To what degree does it retain the individual features that distinguished it in earthly life? The main difficulty here is that the body of the resurrection must possess fullness, perfection, and permanent stability, whereas the earthly body does not have these features. St. Gregory of Nyssa asked, If the goal is fullness, will there not be a whole crowd of bodies for each resurrected individual, with different ages and bearing the traits of these ages? If the goal is the exact repetition of earthly bodies, with what bodies will children, the sick, the handicapped, and so on be resurrected? Let us skip the details of the dispute, all of which reduce to a single general question: Will the resurrected body be an exact as possible reproduction of all the empirical states proper to it in this world of sin and death, or will it be their general adequate form that fully and perfectly expresses the ideal image of a human being as a person and that therefore does not have an exact physical correspondence with his different aspects? Clearly the latter. It is a vain exercise to inquire into individual aspects of this perfection, both because there is an absence of data and because of the audacity of such curiosity.

From this series of questions, one can perhaps identify the question of gender as the most substantial. Some of the holy fathers (notably St. Gregory of Nyssa) teach that gender is abolished in resurrection, not only with regard to bodily differences but also spiritually, since the very appearance of gender is due to the fall and the loss of the original androgynism (J. Boehme). Such an opinion can be considered astonishing, especially among church writers. Is it not evident that the Incarnation simultaneously eternalizes and certifies in their originality both the male gender, assumed by the Lord in His human nature, and the female gender, glorified and sanctified in the person of the Mother of God, who was resurrected and raised to heaven in Her flesh? In general, to deny the original two-gender nature of human beings, which imprints in them the fullness of the image of God (Gen. 1:27), would be to damage a whole series of dogmas of the Christian faith (we have sufficiently discussed this in the two preceding volumes of our trilogy, *The Lamb of God* and *The Comforter*).

Only one aspect of this opinion finds support in Scripture, which says: "meats for the belly, and the belly for meats: but God shall destroy both it and them" (1 Cor. 6:13). One can also mention the Lord's words that "they which shall be accounted worthy to obtain that world, and the resurrection from the dead, neither marry, nor are given in marriage" (Luke 20:35). Clearly, the "abolition of the belly" and that which is below the belly signifies, in the first place, the abolition of the function of maintaining life through food and procreation, which lose all meaning in the future age, where human life is immortal. But here it is unnecessary and vain to ask how far such a change of the body will go and in what precisely it will be expressed, for we are, in general, ignorant of the state of the body after resurrection. We must hold firmly here to only one principle: that the resurrected body is identical to its grain, that is, to the body of the deceased, whose individual form can therefore be recognized (analogously to how the same person can be recognized at different ages and in different states). In other words, the individuality of the body, corresponding to the entire individuality of a human being in its uniqueness, is preserved in resurrection.

Should this be understood in the sense of an exact physical identity between the particles of the buried body and those of the resurrected body? Is there not a continuity of the human body in its earthly life, in its decomposition after death, and in resurrection? In one of the variants of his doctrine of resurrection, St. Gregory of Nyssa was close to such a solution of this problem. He affirmed that the soul puts its imprint *(ekmageion)* on the particles of its body, and, in the universal resurrection, it selects precisely those particles for restoration. This doctrine obviously cannot be accepted in this form if only because, in its earthly life, our body is not stable and unchangeable, but is rather like a flux of particles, entering and exiting, constantly being renewed by assimilation from the matter of the world. In this cosmic circulation, the same particles can enter into the composition of different bodies, human, animal, and vegetable (as occurs during the eating of food). In this respect, the universe is more like a store of different materials of corporeality than like a storehouse of specific bodies, preserved for the last day.

Therefore, it is necessary to narrow and delimit the general idea that individual particles of bodies are specifically marked by the stamp *(sphragis)* of the spirit living in them. This idea refers not so much to the matter of the body that is in flux as to the individual form, to the connection of the soul with the corporeal matter of the world, with the body of bodies.[39] This connection can also be conceived more concretely as the ex-

39. In this sense, in virtue of its unity and general coherence, the universe is man's peripheral body. On this subject see my book *The Philosophy of Economy.*

istence in the universe of a seed "atom," which belongs precisely to a given body and forms its grain or bodily crystal around which corporeality is crystallized. This atom does not have to be understood in the sense of a material particle. It is a sort of energy or energetic center situated in the universe and serving as an intermediary between the soul and the body, as matter of the world. As such, this center that belongs to the soul remains indestructible even in death; it is immortal even as the soul is. And it is precisely to this center that the action of the soul is applied when in resurrection it acquires a new power enabling the restoration of the body and the reestablishment of its own connection, as well as that of the spirit, with the world. That is precisely what resurrection consists in.

The same question is illuminated in a special way by the dogma of holy relics.[40] They represent a special state of bodily remains, retaining a connection with the spirit of the one "reposing in the relics." They are the place of this spirit's presence. Although the holy relics are called incorruptible, physical incorruptibility in the literal sense is not essential here. "Repose in the relics" is expressed in a special connection between the remains and the spirit of the deceased. In this capacity the holy relics anticipate the resurrected body in some sense. In them, the souls of saints are enabled to remain on the earth in a special sense. (To a certain extent an analogous feeling ties us to the graves of loved ones, to their ashes.) This connection of spirit with flesh establishes the relics' distinctive character, which is therefore preserved in the different portions even when the relics are divided. The presence of the saints in their relics is therefore not only a spiritual but equally a corporeal phenomenon. In any case, it cannot be taken to mean that each spirit remains connected with each particle that returns to the universe. The fullness of incorruptibility is proper only to the body of the Lord in the tomb and to that of His Most Pure Mother, the bodies of the Resurrection. The state of the holy relics corresponds to the state of passage through death to resurrection.

The foregoing leads to another question: If the resurrected body does not represent a direct restoration of the body of the deceased but is something new, then what is the relation of the resurrected body to the former body? In particular, what body do resurrected infants receive, or those who were sick and disfigured by sickness (and the process of dying, let us note, produces such disfigurement)? This question belongs among those that cannot be answered. However, if we free ourselves of the idea that resurrection is a literal reproduction of the body of the deceased and

40. See my study "On Holy Relics" (in manuscript).

begin to view it as the process by which the soul regains the power to re-establish the appropriate body for itself, this appropriateness must precisely consist in the fact that every human being actualizes his *proper* bodily form in all its fullness and integrity.

Some patristic writers have thought that resurrection abolishes differences of age and even makes all bodies correspond to the Savior's earthly age. We see no grounds for going so far and denying the possibility of differences of ages as certain spiritual types of growth even in resurrection. For does not every moment in the life of the Savior manifest such a fullness, at least within the limits of His earthly existence?

The restoration of all bodies fully and adequately to their ideal image is a kind of self-evident postulate of the doctrine of resurrection. The resurrected body therefore becomes the perfectly transparent artistic image or form for the spirit living in it. The body is precisely such a form, not an abstract but a concrete form, not a blueprint or schema, but a living image. And insofar as each human being realizes his idea, or his "word," he also possesses his proper form. This image is never fully or adequately realized in individual moments and states of his life (which, moreover, are disfigured by sin, sickness, and mortality) but appears for the first time only in resurrection.

However, for eyes that can see, no state of the body in earthly life is totally deprived of its ideal image (otherwise, it would not be the body of this image). Having conceived this universe of forms of the human multiunity, the divine artist has the power and the wisdom to manifest it in creation, to reveal the riddle of every human being in his outwardness and his inwardness. In such a formulation the question of the identity of the particles of the body of the deceased and those of the body of the resurrected individual loses all meaning. The matter of the resurrected body is taken directly from the "earth," out of which man was formed and to which he returns. This is, of course, a "new earth" under a new heaven, which once again annuls the question of the identity of the particles.

One should rather postulate a universal human corporeality, which is the entire natural world. The mutual impenetrability and repulsion that characterize different bodies in the present natural world is not their final and unique property, which will accompany them even in the transfigured world. Rather, the opposite is the case, as we can conclude from the Lord's entering and leaving through "shut doors." (Is it not this that is attested to by the eucharistic transmutation, which is expressed in the bodily presence of the Lord — *praesentia realis* — in the eucharistic elements of the bread and wine, with the mystery of the transmutation consisting precisely in this co-presence?) Is it therefore not more correct to conceive the relation of resurrected bodies not as a divided multiplicity but as one, common corporeality, proper to the integral Adam and assumed into His humanity by the new Adam?

To be sure, this conception completely removes two questions that preoccupied patristic thought: (1) as to the manner in which the resurrected body will find and reintegrate the particles of the decomposed body and (2) as to their state. But this common corporeality does not exclude the fact that each human person will possess it in his own way, according to his own image. Thus, this unity and universality of humanity's corporeality, as the universal peripheral body, is associated with the multiplicity of individual bodies in which it is realized, each body receiving this corporeality according to its own image, both as its proper body and as the generic, common body of all humankind. Not pretending to have insight into this physics and physiology of the future age, we must nevertheless recognize this postulate as a certain theological hypothesis, which does not exclude points of attachment in this universal body of humankind for individual bodies, in their seed atoms.

Another theological postulate is that, in resurrection, individual bodies are forms of bodily being that express with perfect clarity the idea of each person. These forms contain all the features that make it possible to distinguish and recognize each individual. In other words, resurrected individuals will know one other not only by virtue of their spiritual communication but also according to their bodily form, which has come out of the hands of the Artificer of the universe. In the present life we recognize one another only with difficulty, with much imprecision, imperfection, and error; but in the world of resurrection each individual is accessible to being known in his own image. Individuality is not abolished but is manifested in all its fullness, in the fullness not only of the soul but also of the body.[41] The "spiritual body" is the icon of the spirit (an icon "not

---

41. A vulgarized doctrine of the Origenists, attributed to Origen, which was supposedly condemned at the fifth ecumenical council (though, in fact, it was not considered at this council), contains the idea of the abolition of corporeal individuality in resurrection: "Anyone who asserts that the body of the Lord, after the resurrection, became ethereal and assumed a spherical form, and that all intelligent creatures will be clothed in such bodies after resurrection; anyone who asserts that, just as Christ disposed of His earthly body, so all intelligent beings will not have real bodies after resurrection, let an anathema be placed upon him." Condemned here are both the spiritualistic depreciation of corporeality to the point of its abolition and the depreciation of the individuality of bodies, which are reduced to formless uniformity.

made with hands") — not in the form in which it realizes itself now but as it is conceived and created by God.

Of course, in this case too, it is necessary to take into account the action of synergism: like our entire life, our resurrected body is a resultant of free human creative activity and grace. By his life, a human being creates, to a certain degree, his body, which in resurrection is clothed in glory and immortality by the Lord. St. Paul's words can be applied here:

> Now if any man build upon this foundation gold, silver, precious stones, wood, hay, stubble; every man's work shall be made manifest: for the day shall declare it, because it shall be revealed by fire; and the fire shall try every man's work of what sort it is. If any man's work abide which he hath built thereupon, he shall receive a reward. If any man's work shall be burned, he shall suffer loss: but he himself shall be saved; yet so as by fire. (1 Cor. 3:12-15)

Synergistically, our "building" enters into the composition of the resurrected body, in accordance with its material and quality. Or, being consumed by fire, it is reduced to nothing, and then the glory of resurrection is given by God without human participation, even contrary to man: "he himself shall be saved, yet so as by fire." But all will receive this divine glory of bodily resurrection, even if in different ways. "For we know that if our earthly house of this tabernacle were dissolved, we have a building of God, an house not made with hands, eternal in the heavens" (2 Cor. 5:1), "if so be that being clothed we shall not be found naked" (v. 3). We see here the same idea of a difference in the reception of God's gift, a gift "not made with hands," eternal, but before which one can remain "naked."

This general idea of the glory that clothes resurrected bodies is powerfully expressed by the same apostle in 1 Corinthians 15, which contains an express theology of resurrection: "It is sown in corruption; it is raised in incorruption: it is sown in dishonour; it is raised in glory: it is sown in weakness; it is raised in power: it is sown a natural body; it is raised a spiritual body" (1 Cor. 15:42-44). "Howbeit that was not first which is spiritual, but that which is natural; and afterward that which is spiritual. The first man is of the earth, earthy; the second man is the Lord from heaven. As is the earthy, such are they also that are earthy; and as is the heavenly, such are they also that are heavenly. And as we have borne the image of the earthy, we shall also bear the image of the heavenly" (vv. 46-49). "But we all, with open face beholding as in a glass the glory of the Lord, are changed into the same image from glory to glory, even as by the Spirit of the Lord" (2 Cor. 3:18). These texts proclaim — in the most decisive form and without any limitation or exclusion — the universal resurrection of spiritual bodies in power and glory, in the image of the glorious body of the resurrected Christ, with which they are even identified, so that all resurrected humanity is included in the glorified body of Christ. (Here we must recall what we said above about the unity of the universal body of resurrected humanity.)

The question of the relation between the spiritual body and its glory arises here. First, what is meant by the "spiritual body," in contradistinction to the natural (or psychic) body? In a certain sense, this opposition coincides with that between corruptible and *incorruptible* bodies, between "earthy" and "heavenly" men (see 1 Cor. 15:47-48, 53). Since the spiritual world is usually conceived as incorporeal and corporeality as opposed to spirit, is not the notion of a *spiritual body* contradictory, a contradiction in terms? However, one must distinguish different nuances when comparing the spiritual with the psychic, the fleshly, or the corporeal. Although the Platonic opposition of spirit and body (which is considered as fetters or a prison for the spirit) often seeps into Christian asceticism, it does not conform to the principles of Christian anthropology. The latter takes as its point of departure the definition of man as an incarnate spirit united with a soul, which is the intermediate link between spirit and body. It also does not conform to a healthy ontology, according to which the true substance of matter as universal reality is spirit.[42] The incarnatedness of the spirit is therefore not an ontological contradiction but rather its manifestation in reality, a living revelation. The being of the "spiritual" world of "fleshless" powers can be understood only on the basis of its connection with the fullness of creation, especially the human world, which presupposes angels as its servants.

Thus, spirituality in the sense of the incorporeality of the "fleshless" powers is not an absolute state but only a relative one; it is a special state or part of universal being. Therefore, the idea of the "spiritual body" is, in itself, by no means an ontological absurdity, but must be understood in the specific context in which the apostle Paul places it. He juxtaposes it with the idea of the psychic, or natural, body, or with the synonymous notion of the earthy man. The psychic body and the spiritual body are only *different states* of human corporeality in its relation to the spirit. Taking as our point of departure the tripartite composition of man, which this differentiation

42. See *The Comforter,* chap. 4, b.

does not abolish, there is no basis to eliminate from the spiritual body the psychic element, the soul, which forms the body and thus unites man with the world. It is their relative energy that changes. Originally, before the fall, man was in a state of pre-established harmony of body, soul, and spirit. But this state was only a preliminary one (like preliminary immortality: *posse non mori* but not *non posse mori*). The spirit had to actively master the soul and the body on the basis of its freedom, thereby acquiring power over them. The spirit was still in the state of a "living soul," whereas in the last Adam it was destined to become a "quickening spirit" (1 Cor. 15:45). In this sense, "that was not first which is spiritual, but that which is natural [psychic]; and afterward that which is spiritual" (v. 46). "The first man is of the earth" (v. 47). After the fall, the spirit lost its power over the soul and thus over the body. For the soul, and therefore for the entire human being, there began the state of "corruption," that is, of mortality, "weakness," and "dishonour" (vv. 42-43). His body became "natural," having stopped being "spiritual," as it was before the fall, though only in a preliminary way. And with the growing weakness of spirituality, in the fallen state, man becomes fleshly: "for he . . . is flesh" (Gen. 6:3).

Thus, the spirituality of the body signifies, first of all, the power of the spirit over its soul and its animated body, the transparence of the body for the spirit and its obedience to the latter. In general, it signifies the adequacy of man to his idea or proto-image. But this proto-image can be revealed not at the beginning but only in the fullness of times. This restores the hierarchy of the human tripartite composition that was disfigured by the fall of man, "corrupted by passions." And the animated body becomes the direct manifestation of the spirit, its mirror, its transparent image and glory. The psychic body, by contrast, is a darkened and distorted image, and the psychic man is diminished to enslavement by the flesh and the loss of his human image. He can be freed from this slavery only by death and resurrection, by the power of Christ.

If by resurrection the Lord "shall change our vile body, that it may be fashioned like unto his glorious body" (Phil. 3:21), the character of the resurrected bodies can be deduced from this. They are characterized, first of all, by transparence for and obedience to the spirit, where they overcome the fleshly weight of the psychic body and are liberated from its constraints and limits. The body is freed, first of all, from the purely fleshly needs of stomach and sex that keep the psychic man in bondage. Resurrection in incorruptibility and immortality bestows this freedom. Life in the body with its sensuousness is not abolished but becomes innocent and immaculate, a holy life together with nature, which becomes a source of joy and an object of admiration. This can include the partaking of natural gifts, communion with the flesh of the world. When the Lord institutes the new food and drink, which are His Flesh and His Blood (see John 6:55), does He not say at the Last Supper: "I will not drink of the fruit of the vine, until the kingdom of God shall come" (Luke 22:18)? Did the Lord not partake, in the presence of His disciples, of "a piece of a broiled fish, and of an honeycomb" (24:42) even after the Resurrection? And does Revelation not speak of the pure water of life and the fruits of the tree of life in the New Jerusalem (Rev. 22:1-2)? But the nature of this partaking changes radically, for it is not "meats for the belly" (1 Cor. 6:13), which God will abolish, together with the dependence upon it of life itself. This kind of partaking becomes a manifestation of the sinless life of the body in this world, just as human labor in the world stops being done "in the sweat of thy face" (Gen. 3:19) but becomes the creative dressing and keeping of "Eden."

This spiritualization of the body also liberates the latter from its weight and impenetrability; emblematic of such liberation is the Lord's passage through a "shut door." It is evident that the general character of spatiality and extension changes. It is in this that liberation from the "bondage of corruption" will be realized for all of creation, which is tormented and groans, awaiting the revelation of the sons of God. But, here too, in the absence of appropriate experience, only abstract postulates are accessible to us.

However, we cannot pass by in silence the fundamental, guiding idea that is contained in revelation regarding the universal resurrection, namely, that it will be accomplished *in glory* and is thus included in the general manifestation of glory that accompanies the parousia. If the world receives glory in its transfiguration, man receives it in the universal resurrection (or by a corresponding transformation). Thus, human corporeality too receives the glory that the Lord had before the creation of the world and that He recovers in His glorious resurrection, to give it first to His disciples (John 17:22) and then to all of creation. Various texts of Scripture insistently attest to the resurrection in glory, first, in the most general form: "It is sown in dishonour; it is raised in glory: it is sown in weakness; it is raised in power" (1 Cor. 15:43; v. 53 has the same sense, even if the language is different: "for this corruptible must put on incorruption, and this mortal must put on immortality").

Further, as if in confirmation of the promises of Christ's farewell discourse and of the high-priestly prayer, the apostle Paul explains this idea in the sense of the conformity of the universal resurrection to Christ's glorification: "As is the earthy, such are they also that are earthy; and as is the heavenly, such are they also that are heavenly. And as we have borne the image of the earthy, we shall also bear the image of the heavenly" (1 Cor. 15:48-49). The same idea is confirmed in Philippians 3:21: "[Christ] shall change our vile body, that it may be fashioned like unto his glorious body, according to the working whereby he is able even to subdue all things unto himself." This conformity of the "vile" human body to Christ's body is the power of the Incarnation by which the Lord assumed the fullness of human nature and glorified it in Himself; whereas in the Second Coming He communicates His glory to all humanity. But, despite all the conformity of our "vile" bodies to Christ's body of glory, creaturely humanity receives this glory only in a creaturely manner, that is, in becoming, in ascending from glory to glory: "We . . . are changed into the same image from glory to glory" (2 Cor. 3:18).

This applies, we repeat, to *all* humanity without any exception, for the Lord, having become the new Adam, assumed humanity in its entirety:[43] "As we have borne the image of the earthy, we shall also bear the image of the heavenly" (1 Cor. 15:49). The image of the heavenly will shine upon all resurrected human bodies, clothed in *glory*. This brings us back to the general doctrine of glory, the manifestation of the Holy Spirit, the Holy Spirit's action and revelation in creation. As such, glory clothes creation in beauty by a universal transfiguration. But this idea can be expressed definitively and fully only sophiologically. The natural beauty of creation and, in it, of man is creation's sophianic prototype, the creaturely Sophia. The fullness of creation participates in this prototype, and every human person belongs to the integral Adam, the creaturely image of God.[44] Every person has his own proto-image, which corresponds to his personal idea. Originally, every human being is a living work of art, the artistic image of a personal spirit that comes out of the hands of the Divine Artist, the Creator of creation. It is in the image of these proto-images that our bodies will be resurrected.

Creaturely sophianicity, whose seal is imprinted in the original man, is in a state of becoming, like all creation. Although the Holy Spirit illumi-

---

43. Some find limits to this universality of glory in the Lord's words: "then shall the righteous shine forth as the sun in the kingdom of their Father" (Matt. 13:43). However, these words of the parable of the tares contain not a denial of the universal glorification of bodies in resurrection but only an indication of the special glorification of the righteous (see below).

44. Here it is appropriate to remember the considerations of St. John of Damascus in his apologia for the veneration of icons. See my article "The Icon and Its Veneration."

nates creation, thus manifesting the sophianicity of the latter, this manifestation is incomplete and preliminary even in the original Adam himself. Although the "fallen image, corrupted by passions" preserves its sophianic foundation even after the fall, before being renewed by Christ, it manifests this sophianicity only obscurely. But this foundation *does exist* in man; it is known by and visible to his Creator. The Incarnation, in which all human beings are co-resurrected in glory together with Christ, makes this sophianic proto-image of every human being transparent and clear. Resurrection in glory is therefore the definitive sophianization of man through the manifestation in him of his proto-image. In this sense, resurrection in glory is the manifestation of the Divine Sophia in the creaturely Sophia, the completion of creation. One cannot suppose that the image of the resurrected human being is wholly new, that it is imposed on him from outside, as it were. On the contrary, it is his proper eternal image in God, hitherto hidden and obscure, but manifested in its power and glory in resurrection.

Since the transfiguration of the world is in general due to the power and action of the Holy Spirit outside of its kenosis, this kenosis (as the voluntary self-limitation of the Spirit's action) ceases here, and the Holy Spirit pours forth in glory upon all resurrected humanity. Christ, who comes in glory, is God's power and wisdom. And the Holy Spirit, the Spirit of power and wisdom, by its action manifests them in creation. In resurrection, man appears in the light of the Divine Sophia, in the sophianicity by virtue of which and for the sake of which he has been created. This sophianization in resurrection is, as it were, a new, second act of the creation, in which man is born "in incorruption, power, and glory." This new act became possible when it received a foundation for itself in Divine-humanity, in the union of the two natures in Christ by the Holy Spirit.

Since the Incarnation has, as a result of man's fall, the significance of redemption, resurrection is also the salvation of the human race from death. But redemption does not exhaust the work of the Incarnation. Through the union in Christ of the divine and human natures, the Divine and the creaturely Sophia, redemption is also the sophianization and glorification of creation. It is inconceivable that, even if there had been no fall, man would forever have remained separated from God, as even the original Adam had been, since between the Creator and creation there is a chasm the latter is incapable of crossing. Only the Creator can cross this chasm, by uniting Himself with man. He thereby completes creation, enabling it to realize its supreme goal, giving man the power to manifest the image of God not only in anticipation but in the fullness of life, by becoming a "god by grace." This is accessible only to man resurrected in incorruptibility, immortality, and glory. This is in fact what God told him: "God standeth in the congregation of the mighty; he judgeth among the gods. . . . I have said, Ye are gods; and all of you are children of the most High" (Ps. 82:1, 6; cf. John 10:34). Can the creaturely Sophia remain unrevealed in the fullness and glory of the Divine Sophia? Can the sophianization of creation in resurrection fail to be accomplished to the degree where "God may be all in all" (1 Cor. 15:28), to the point of the total sophianization of creation?

But new difficulties await us here. Scripture affirms the universal resurrection in glory so unshakably that it should be considered a dogma of the Church. And it is in fact indisputable in the sense that incorruptibility and immortality are given to *all* resurrected bodies. If that were not the case, we would be led to speculations (of occult and Talmudic origin) on a conditional, that is, not universal, immortality.[45] This universality of resurrection, which is unconnected with the personal qualities of those resurrected, is due to its transcendent character: The resurrection of the dead is an action of God's power upon human beings, analogous to creation. To this extent it is independent of the qualities or merits of a human being; it is wholly a gift of God. Resurrection is based not on a self-determination of human freedom and action but on the divine determination of creation in its original sophianicity. Only God has the power to give life and immortality, the fullness of His image to every human being, who has His proto-image in the Divine Sophia.

In resurrection, every human being is clothed in this image according to the divine sketch. This signifies that he is clothed in beauty. The bodies of the resurrected will be resplendent: "The resurrected body will be spiritual and miraculous, such that its quality cannot be adequately explained."[46] And angels and human beings will see one another as beautiful: God created the world as "good" (see Gen. 1). He did not populate the kingdom of glory with cripples, deformed people, or lepers, since pathological defects and monstrosities refer not to being but to states, not to divine creation but to creaturely freedom. Not the arbitrary defectiveness of creatureliness but the fullness of creation will be manifested in resurrection. Nevertheless, certain authors have extended this creaturely defectiveness to the very form of the resurrection, contending that the bodies and

45. Cf. my article "The Problem of Conditional Immortality."
46. St. Cyril of Jerusalem, *Catech. bapt.*, 18, 18; PG 33, 1040 A.

images of sinners will reflect their inner deformity.[47] But apart from the fact that such ideas directly contradict the testimony of Scripture, they also presuppose the ultimate failure of God's creation, the impotence of God's image in man, man's loss of his original sophianicity.

Nevertheless, it is natural to ask what this power of immortality and incorruptibility is based upon and whether it can be proper to beings who are ontologically empty, devoid of divine power. Are not the adherents of "conditional immortality" therefore more consistent? In answer, we must affirm the dogmatic postulate of *universal* resurrection in incorruptibility and glory: the resurrected will appear in the form in which they exist in God's eyes. And it is as such that the righteous will see them, to the degree that each of them will be capable of perceiving God's creation.

Regarding the immortal and incorruptible bodies of resurrection one can admit only those differences that are grounded ontologically and belong not to a state but to the very hierarchy of creaturely being: differences that exist also in the angelic world and go back to the origins of creation. It is precisely of such differences that the apostle speaks:

> All flesh is not the same flesh; but there is one kind of flesh of men, another flesh of beasts, another of fishes, and another of birds. There are also celestial bodies, and bodies terrestrial; but the glory of the celestial is one, and the glory of the terrestrial is another. There is one glory of the sun, and another glory of the moon, and another glory of the stars: for one star differeth from another star in glory. So also is the resurrection of the dead. (1 Cor. 15:39-42)

This hierarchy forms the universal harmony of creation. The meaning of "celestial bodies" and "bodies terrestrial" is uncertain. The scriptural text puts the difference between them in the same series as the purely natural difference between different kinds of bodies and kinds of flesh. But this text also mentions that the kinds of glory and the modes of glorification differ.

Apart from this text, Scripture says nothing about the transformation or transfiguration of celestial bodies or about their different glory,

---

47. That is the opinion of St. Ephraem the Syrian among others: "All will receive bodies in conformity with their works. The bodies of the righteous will shine forth seven times as bright as the light of the sun, whereas the bodies of sinners will be dark and full of a foul stench. Some will be like the light, others like the darkness" (*Sermon on the Judgment and the Resurrection,* part 3).

that is, about their glorification in transfiguration. Since their state is, in general, connected with the earthly world and accompanies the world in its catastrophe (Matt. 24:29; cf. Isa. 13:9-10; Ezek. 32:7-8; Joel 3:15), this state is also transformed: it becomes the *new* heaven that accompanies the new earth, and receives its glory. The Old and New Testaments are geocentric, but this geocentrism is not exclusive, for the earth belongs to the cosmos. The future unity of the life of the universe is therefore a postulate of Christian cosmology and eschatology. If some of the church fathers thought that, in a certain sense, stars are the "bodies" of angels, they did not thereby deny, to be sure, the bodilessness of angels. But they connected in a certain way the hypostatic "images" of angels with the images of stars, which, moreover, "differed in glory." Such is the new connection of the human and angelic worlds that will ensue in resurrection, when human beings will abide "as the angels of God in heaven" (Matt. 22:30). This relation will extend to heaven and earth, to "celestial bodies" and "bodies terrestrial."

We now confront the greatest difficulty in theology: the problem of how to reconcile the sophianicity of creation in its being with the nonsophianicity of its state in freedom. It is necessary to introduce here the problem of synergism, of the union of the divine and human principles, a synergism not only of harmony but also of conflict. The problem reduces to the different modes in which creatures experience their resurrection. These modes inevitably lead to the ultimate separation of the "last judgment." In its revelation of the "last day," Scripture unites the transfiguration of the world, the resurrection of the dead, and this judgment that separates the sheep from the goats, the wheat from the chaff, the righteous from the sinners. These two apparently so different and even opposite events should be conceived as two aspects of the end of the present aeon, with the passage from the kingdom of grace to the kingdom of glory.

6. Judgment and Separation

"And He will come again in glory to judge the living and the dead, and His reign will be without end," proclaims the Creed, conjoining and apparently identifying the coming in glory and the universal judgment as two aspects of the same event. Scripture conjoins them in a similar way: "For the Son of man shall come in the glory of his Father with his angels; and then he shall reward every man according to his works" (Matt. 16:27; cf.

25:31-46 and numerous other texts). The resurrection and the judgment are conjoined in John 5:28-29: "All that are in the graves shall hear his voice, and shall come forth; they that have done good, unto the resurrection of life; and they that have done evil, unto the resurrection of damnation." Thus, it is necessary first of all to understand this connection of the judgment and the coming of the Lord in glory with the universal resurrection in incorruptibility and glory.

It is insufficient to juxtapose externally the judgment and the resurrection as if they were independent of each other. It is also necessary to grasp their inner and necessary connection, as the Old and the New Testament establish it: the identity of the manifestation of *glory* and of the Judge in glory with the Lord's judgment.

Sometimes, especially in the Old Testament, the manifestation of glory is described using such figures as "throne," "fire," and "flame of fire." (Even in Matt. 25:31 we read: "When the Son of man shall come in his glory, and all the holy angels with him, then shall he sit upon the throne of his glory.") Similar images, particularly expressive ones, can be found in Ezekiel (1:4-5) and in Daniel (7:9-10), with a description of the Last Judgment.

It is necessary to understand that the parousia, the coming of Christ in glory, that is, in the manifestation of the Holy Spirit, is, as such, already the judgment. The parousia cannot be an external and mutually indifferent encounter between God who has come into the world and man who remains in his isolated state of being, as he was before this encounter. On the contrary, man too is clothed in glory and incorruptibility, and the creaturely Sophia becomes transparent for the Divine Sophia. This changes man's very being. This encounter with God, this entering into the realm of the divine fire, is not something optional for human beings. It is inevitable. For some this is the time of liberation ("look up, and lift up your heads" [Luke 21:28]). For others it is a time of fear and horror: "then shall all the tribes of the earth mourn, and they shall see the Son of man coming in the clouds of heaven with power and great glory" (Matt. 24:30). No one can avoid this encounter, for it is not an outward encounter but an inward one. For many this will be an unexpected and undesired transformation of their being, for the transfiguration, the light of glory given to human beings, can do more than illuminate. It can also consume in fire.

What is this fire that burns the chaff? And how is the judgment accomplished? The Judge is the Son of man, to whom the Father has given the power to judge those whom "he is not ashamed to call . . . brethren"

(Heb. 2:11, 17; cf. Ps. 82:1: "God standeth in the congregation of the mighty; he judgeth among the gods"). About this judgment, which is the baptism of the world by fire, the Forerunner of the Lord says: "He [Christ] shall baptize you with the Holy Ghost, and with fire" (Matt. 3:11; Luke 3:16). This baptism by fire refers not only to the Pentecost of Zion, which opens up the kingdom of grace and serves as the precursor of the Pentecost of the world, the kingdom of glory in the parousia. This baptism is in fact the glory as the manifestation of the Holy Spirit. Christ enters the world in an evident manner for every human being by the power of the Holy Spirit. The parousia manifestly clothes every human being in Christ by the Holy Spirit.

It is precisely in this sense that the parousia is also the judgment. And Christ, as the Judge (John 5:27), judges by the Holy Spirit. Human beings are clothed in Christ, who is the Truth and the Life, by the life-giving Holy Spirit, who is the Spirit of Truth. This means that every human being is inwardly confronted with the truth about himself. Every human being sees himself in the truth, by a vision that is not abstract but living, like the consuming flame of a fire from whose light one cannot hide, *for* all will become visible: "for judgment I am come into this world" (John 9:39), says the Lord. "Now is the judgment of this world" (12:31). But this judgment will be accomplished by Christ through the Comforter: "when he is come, he will reprove the world of sin, and of righteousness, and of judgment. . . . Of judgment, because the prince of this world is judged" (16:8, 11).

The manifestation of God's glory in the world is also the manifestation of the truth itself, as well as the abolition of falsehood and the power of the father of lies (John 8:44). No falsehood, no self-deception, no error will have a place in the kingdom of truth, and this "exposure" by the Spirit of truth is already the judgment. By virtue of the truth this judgment becomes for everyone a self-judgment, a shedding of the veils of falsehood and self-deception that cover emptiness. The enthronement of Christ in the world, the reign of God come in power, is the Holy Spirit that fully, without any kenosis, pours forth upon all flesh. Christ's revelation in the Holy Spirit has an irresistible force, which is manifested both in the universal resurrection and in the transformation of the world, with a transfiguration and glorification that extend to all flesh. This illuminating and transfiguring power is expressed in the image of *fire,* not natural of course but "spiritual," which will penetrate the "spiritual" body and the spirit itself. The fire of the future age consumes, but it also transfigures, illuminates, gladdens. These two definitions, light and fire, are applicable to both hypostases: to the hypostasis of the Son ("I am the light of the world" [John 8:12]; "who is close to me is close to fire" [from the apocryphal Gospel]; "I am come to send fire on the earth" [Luke 12:49]) as well as to the hypostasis of the Holy Spirit manifested in the form of fiery tongues. The difference is that the Son is "the serene light of the Holy Glory," while the Spirit is a fiery flame.

All resurrected bodies will rise incorruptible and spirit-bearing. But how is this spirituality realized with regard to human creatureliness and creaturely freedom? Does the principle of synergism operate here? Yes, it does, and the judgment and the separation are accomplished precisely through this principle.

In his new state, resurrected and incorruptible, the state that is proper to man in his earthly life and that is manifested and confirmed in the afterlife is not abolished. It is transformed. Incorruptibility and glorification are given to him by God in resurrection *ex opere operato*, so to speak, and enter into life as an irresistible force, as a higher reality from which man cannot hide. But the manner in which every human being receives this incorruptibility and glorification remains proper to him, corresponding to the *ex opere operantis* of the sacrament.

Here too, in this conjunction of the divine given and of its personal, creaturely reception, there is manifested the synergism of man's divine-creaturely, divine-human being. Man's state of incorruptibility and glory, his manifested sophianicity, is not added from outside but impregnates from within the proper humanness of every human being. Just as on the pathways of salvation in earthly life the hidden life in Christ is united with natural humanity, so in resurrection all human beings are clothed in Christ by the Holy Spirit in connection with each proper creaturely human life. But, to be sure, creaturely limitedness here does not limit the power of divine action in the manifestation of the divine image in man. A human being is saved by this action, though only in connection with what he himself is. These forms of salvation differ depending upon what foundation a human being has built upon. It is possible that he himself will be saved "yet so as by fire" (1 Cor. 3:15); and he will be naked, for his work will be consumed.

The judgment and separation consist in the fact that every human being will be placed before his own eternal image in Christ, that is, before Christ. And in the light of this image, he will see his own reality, and this comparison will be the judgment. It is this that is the Last Judgment of Christ upon every human being. In this judgment, the "books" are opened, for the Holy Spirit gives the power to read them clearly. Human

457

life in all its fullness and connectedness is manifested in the implacable, inwardly irrefutable light of justice. This is a global vista, referring to man not only as a personal being but also as a generic one. Both man's life and his responsibility are conditioned by and linked with the destinies of the whole human race. He is judged or rather he judges himself in Christ as belonging to all humankind, to the whole history of "all the nations," in the total concreteness of all-human, universal being. He now knows this being as the life of Christ's humanity, which He assumed in His double nature.

The figures that are used to describe the last separation, or judgment, and that are borrowed from the language of human jurisprudence should not lead us into error concerning the inner, *immanent* character of this judgment. Inwardly and immanently, it has a self-evident character. The proper self-determination of every human being in his creaturely freedom presents itself here as a certain self-evident reality, and not only as an external judgment upon him. This means that the Father left the judgment to His Son, who Himself is the Son of man, and, in His humanity, every human being finds himself and the judgment upon himself. This judgment is therefore not transcendent but immanent. In every human being, his own unreality or nakedness, his failure to wear a wedding garment at the wedding feast, is clearly distinguished from Christ's reality.

Just as the Holy Spirit manifests Christ in glory, so it reveals Christ's presence in every human being. The judgment is the theophany to the world of the Son sent by the Father in the Holy Spirit. Resurrection in incorruptibility and glorification is precisely the Last Judgment, in which creation appears before the face of God and sees itself in God. For the image of God, given to man at his creation, is also the judgment upon man in relation to his likeness, which is the realization of this image in creaturely freedom. The "likeness" is the book of life opened at the judgment. God's image will be revealed to every human being by the Holy Spirit as inner justice and judgment for creaturely life. This judgment of Christ is also every human being's own judgment upon himself. It consists in each person seeing himself in the light of his own justice, in the light of his proto-image, which he perceives in his resurrection under illumination by the Holy Spirit. The Judgment is the judgment of every human being in his true image upon himself in his "likeness." As such, the judgment is self-evidently persuasive. This genuine image for every human being is Christ: The judgment consists in the fact that the light has come into the world (see John 3:19). "For judgment I am come into this world" (9:39).

Is it possible to reject this ontological self-judgment upon oneself as inappropriate and unconvincing? No! It is not possible, for one is judged by one's own being, by one's own truth. St. Isaac the Syrian says that the torments of hell are the burning of love for God, the burning fire of this love (we will encounter this idea again when we consider the burning in hell). This idea is also applicable to man's relation to his divine proto-image: being aware of how distant he is from his proto-image in his given state or likeness, a human being nevertheless recognizes himself in this image as he could and should be according to God's thought. He loves this image of himself, judges himself by it, compares himself to it, does not and cannot retreat from it inwardly.

This proto-image is Christ. Every human being sees himself in Christ and measures the extent of his difference from this proto-image. A human being cannot fail to love the Christ who is revealed in him, and he cannot fail to love himself revealed in Christ. The two things are the same. Such is human ontology. Love is the Holy Spirit, who sets the heart afire with this love. But this love, this blazing up of the Spirit, is also the judgment of the individual upon himself, his vision of himself outside himself, in conflict with himself, that is, outside Christ and far from Christ. And the measure and knowledge of this separation are determined by Love, that is, by the Holy Spirit. The same fire, the same love gladdens and burns, torments and gives joy. The judgment of love is the most terrible judgment, more terrible than that of justice and wrath, than that of the law, for it includes all this but also transcends it. The judgment of love consists of a revolution in people's hearts, in which, by the action of the Holy Spirit in the resurrection, the eternal source of love for Christ is revealed together with the torment caused by the failure to actualize this love in the life that has passed. It is impossible to appear before Christ and to see Him without loving Him. In the resurrection, there is no longer any place for anti-Christianity, for enmity toward Christ, for satanic hatred of Him, just as there is no place for fear of Him as the Judge terrible in His omnipotence and the fury of His wrath. The Lord will come as He was on earth: meek and humble in heart, though now in glory. But this meekness and humility will burn hearts by their love and their judgment. God-Love judges with love the sins against love.

There is another judgment of love besides that of the God-man, Christ. This is a human judgment and therefore completely immanent, before a human hypostasis filled with the Holy Spirit: Mary the Spirit-Bearer. The sacred silence that veils Her presence in the kingdom of resurrection does not permit us to forget the power of this presence in the light of the love that emanates from it. The image of the Mother and Ever-Virgin irresistibly penetrates into every human heart by virtue of a holy humanity transparent to the manifestation of the Holy Spirit. Only satanic dementia remains, for a time, insensitive to the Most Pure One, who is the "many-sorrowed wound of the demons" (Akathistos, ik. 2), the "fall of the demons" (ik. 6). But for the human race, She is the living bridge that connects it to Her Son and God, "conducting to heaven those who are on earth" (ibid.). It is not by chance that the blasphemy against the Holy Spirit, including, of course, the blasphemy against the Most Pure Spirit-Bearer, is the most serious sin, bearing witness to an exceptional corruptedness and hardness of heart. This sin remains an unhealable wound and sickness, and it will be forgiven neither in this life nor in the future one. But its shadow does not weaken the manifestation of the Most Holy Mother of God in glory, in Her motherly love and holiness. The appearance of the "Servant of the Lord" awakens in us knowledge of ourselves in our sinful corruptedness and egotism; and it also awakens our repentance. The Ever-Virgin is the living conscience in human beings.

The figures of the angels and saints who surround the Lord in His glorious coming possess a similar, though lesser, significance. The first among these is the greatest of those born of woman, the Forerunner, who on the icons of the Deisis and the Last Judgment stands, with the Mother of God, closest to the Savior, closer than the angels.

In company with the angels, who become known to man in the after-life, Christ's entire saintly humanity demonstrates to every human being the untruths of his path and opens for him the book of his sinful life. In this regard, Scripture says that, first of all, the holy apostles participate in the judgment: "In the regeneration when the Son of man shall sit in the throne of his glory, ye also shall sit upon twelve thrones, judging the twelve tribes of Israel" (Matt. 19:28). As do the saints: "Do ye not know that the saints shall judge the world?" (1 Cor. 6:2). It is even the case that "we shall judge angels" (v. 3), just as the angels will judge us, separating the wheat from the chaff. For it is said that "the angels shall come forth, and sever the wicked from among the just" (Matt. 13:49). It is remarkable that here, as in similar texts that attest directly to the participation of angels and human beings in the judgment, there is complete silence about the Mother of God in Her humility (and only iconography breaks this silence).

The judgment and the verdict constitute an inner, immanent, personal act accomplished by each human being upon himself in the light of Christ's justice, by the Holy Spirit. But this act is also accomplished upon all of humanity that is present before this judgment of justice. The inner character of this judgment does not make it subjective. On the contrary, it is characterized by the greatest objectivity and the power of a divine work. This work is expressed in a symbolic language, suitable for the human understanding, of concrete images describing an external event. Nevertheless, this event must be understood in its inner meaning. Such images are used in the Lord's discourse in the form of a parable in Matthew 25:31-46, as well as in a number of texts of similar character: the Lord "will judge the world" (Acts 17:31; cf. Rom. 2:6; 14:10; Acts 10:42; 2 Tim. 4:1; 1 Pet. 4:3-5). In connection with this, a number of images refer to retribution. For instance, Scripture speaks of "the day of wrath and revelation of the righteous judgment of God, who will render to every man according to his deeds" (Rom. 2:5-6). It says that "we must all appear before the judgment seat of Christ, that every one may receive the things done in his body, according to that he hath done, whether it be good or bad" (2 Cor. 5:10; cf. 11:15; Gal. 6:7-9; Jude 15; Matt. 12:36-37; 1 Cor. 4:5). Other texts more clearly indicate the personal responsibility of every human being for his life (Luke 12:47; Matt. 25:14-30; Rom. 2:11-12). Finally, still other texts speak of the separation of the tares from the wheat and their burning, of the gathering of "all things that offend" and their casting into "a furnace of fire" (Matt. 13:41-50). In their terrifying tragic seriousness, all these images impress upon every human being that he is responsible for his own life. They speak of God's implacable justice, which, nevertheless, is also love. But this love has as its object not slaves or things but the free children of God, who will be judged by an appropriate judgment. But for a sinful human being this judgment is also a dread judgment.[48]

How can one ontologically understand this judgment, which is expressed in the separation of the wheat from the tares, which are burned in the furnace of fire and cast into the outer darkness? First of all, such images should by no means be understood in the sense of annihilation,[49] according to the theory of conditional immortality. Resurrection in incorruptibility and in glory is neither annulled nor limited by the separation that follows the judgment. Spiritual "death," or any other defect, is inseparable from immortality. According to the apostle Paul, "If any man's work shall be burned, he shall suffer loss, but he himself shall be saved; yet

---

48. These figures are powerfully employed in liturgical texts, e.g., in the office of Sunday of the pre-Lent feast.

49. See a comparison of texts of this nature in my article "The Problem of Conditional Immortality."

so as by fire" (1 Cor. 3:15). There is no place for evil and sin in the kingdom of God, but sinners, with their incorruptible image, abide in the kingdom, though they bear within themselves the principle of the torment of death, of the undying worm and the inextinguishable fire. This combination of incorruptibility and glory with the casting into the outer darkness, the judgment with its double sentence, cannot be grasped by our understanding. It is one of the fundamental antinomies of the kingdom of Glory.

Nor should one diminish the *universal* significance of this antinomy. True, in the form of a parable, the discourse on the Last Judgment applies this final separation to different objects: to sheep and to goats, to those who go on the right and to those who go on the left. One could deduce from this that human beings are separated into the sinless and those who are subject to sin. But no one is perfectly sinless except the "Sole Sinless One" and the Most Pure Mother of God, just as no human beings are so utterly sinful that no trace of good can be found in them. In the fall of man in Adam, we know elements of error and delusion, which, without erasing the fall, somewhat soften it.

The same thing is applicable to every person in his creaturely limitedness. Whatever may be the differences between different individuals as far as their personal sinfulness is concerned, this sinfulness always has an element of delusion and error, of acts accomplished in the name of an imaginary good. Pure evil for the sake of evil, satanical evil, is something not proper to man, who bears the principle of good. In individual cases, evil can decidedly predominate, but, in the final separation, evil itself is known only in conjunction with, even if in conflict with, good. In this sense, hell is a function of heaven, and evil is the shadow of good, not only in the world in general but also in every human being in particular. It follows that the separation into sheep and goats is accomplished (of course to different degrees) within every individual, and his right and left sides are bared in this separation. To a certain extent all are condemned and all are justified. A condemnation that would be the final casting into the outer darkness (nonbeing) is metaphysical death. Even to be rejected, a human being must have in himself the power of being; that is, he must find support in the image of God given to him. Thus, the *judgment* and its sentence introduce into the life of every person an antinomic separation that consists in participating in glory and incorruptibility and, at the same time, in burning in the fire of divine rejection. The difference between the two states can here be only a quantitative one.

The judgment condemns in every person that which deserves con-

462

demnation, that which is incompatible with glory. The judgment is inwardly executed by every person's sophianicity, which is the ontological norm of his being. His sophianicity judges his proper creaturely self-determination, convinces him that it does not correspond to this norm. His sophianic image in incorruptibility and glory is his true reality, which is recognized by him as such. On the contrary, that which seemed to him real in his earthly life is condemned as unreal, as illusory: "He himself shall be saved, yet so as by fire" (1 Cor. 3:15); we desire to be clothed, so that "we shall not be found naked" (2 Cor. 5:3).

It is precisely to this ontological condemnation, which is also the metaphysical annihilation of what is condemned, its transformation into a phantom, into a nightmare vision, that the Scripture's pitiless words about death, perdition, annihilation, destruction, and disappearance refer. They refer not to personal being, not to every human being's immortal life, but to his mortal, illusory content, which is consumed by the divine fire. The inner division of every human being, his separation into mortal and immortal parts, with the dying, the burning up of what is corruptible, that is the fundamental fact of the life of resurrection, the judgment of God. This judgment is not the execution of any external laws and norms, whose violation entails punishment. That is only a figurative, anthropomorphic manner of expressing the idea that the life of immortality is in conformity with man's divine, sophianic image. Everything that is not in conformity with this image falls into the outer darkness, into nonbeing, which also manifests itself as a minus of being, as the nonexistent in the existent. This is the "eternal fire." In the light of resurrection there is nothing and can be nothing that is ambiguous and unclear. What should not be is also nonexistent, and all that is existent is unalloyed good. The spiritual sword cuts a human being asunder to his very depths.

This partial nonbeing, the dark shadow of being, is experienced as fire, torment, punishment, immersion in the lake of fire. For every human being, such a transformation into nonbeing, the burning up of that which had constituted his life, is a metaphysical dying, a perishing, an eternal torment, a judgment of justice, a seeing of himself in the light of justice. Every human being experiences this in his own way, in conformity with his wrong state and to the degree it is wrong. These torments clearly have an absolutely individual character for every human being. But it is necessary to indicate again, with maximal force, that which constitutes the very essence of the judgment and of immortal life: "Annihilation" is *not* spiritual death, and it does not extend to the entire being of a person. It is a separation or a spiritual amputation, so to speak, but not death by execution. In other words, the very possibility of this separation presupposes a person's participation in eternal life and therefore in its bliss, but it also presupposes his burning in hell. Union in separation is an unfathomable (for the present moment) mystery of the judgment and of the life of the future age. How can one life contain the union of joy and sorrow, of bliss and the torment of terrible remorse and late repentance, of a vision of the divine proto-image of creation and the dead form of one's own (even if only partial) nonbeing? But the question arises: Is this not something more than a logical contradiction? Is it not also a contradiction of life? Does the joy of bliss not require *fullness* for itself? That is the natural question that arises to perplex us. However, it becomes clear that, in this case, the logic of our present being, where we are guided only by its criteria, is insufficient. Fullness can be conceived not only extensively, as the complete filling of consciousness, but also intensively, qualitatively, in the sense of a revelation of divine proto-images. Hell necessarily presupposes the knowledge of heaven, of lost bliss, just as the torments of hell are, according to the formula (already cited) of St. Isaac the Syrian, the torments of love for God.

Certain analogies can arise in connection with this question. The Church's teaching affirms that the Golgotha sacrifice was real not only on Good Friday, when it was offered, but that it is also real at all times and on all altars. Furthermore, according to the insistent teaching of certain holy fathers (especially Augustine) Christ is suffering even now in His humanity,[50] to which He Himself attests by the questions and answers at the Last Judgment, while sitting at the right hand of the Father in glory. To be sure, such an analogy does not signify the equating, or identification, of the life of the God-man with that of creation. Nevertheless, it permits one to conclude that Christ's heavenly glory and His earthly suffering are not incompatible or mutually exclusive. In the case of the Mother of God, one can even more forcefully affirm the absence of incompatibility between Her heavenly bliss and Her earthly sorrow: "In your Dormition, you have not abandoned the world," says the hymn of the Feast of the Dormition. In the vision of Her Protection, where she covers humanity with Her veil, the Mother of God weeps for the world even in Her heavenly glory and descends into it in Her "way of sorrows." It should also be remembered that, on the basis of the doctrine of the Last Judgment and of the final separation, we must, or at least can, conclude that the personal bliss of the righteous is fully *compatible* with the sorrow they feel for their condemned

50. See my essay "The Holy Grail."

brothers. To be sure, it is absolutely inadmissible to think (although, astonishingly, it is done all the time) that the "righteous" are capable of egotistically and unfeelingly forgetting about the "sinners," as if the latter did not even exist for them. The separation that takes place within humanity is, in any case, a source of affliction, although it is compatible with heavenly bliss. Otherwise, hell would be universal and heaven would be impossible.

We must therefore conclude that the very separation into heaven and hell, into eternal bliss and eternal torments, is internal and relative. Every human being bears within himself the principle of the one and the other, depending upon the measure of his personal righteousness. Since no human being is without sin, there is no one who does not have the burning of hell within himself, even if only to a minimal degree. Conversely, there is no human being whose soul is not illuminated by the light of paradise, even if only at a single point or by a distant reflection. "One star differeth from another star in glory" (1 Cor. 15:41), and this is a difference not only in the intensity of the light but also in the ratio of light to shadow. Of course, this difference is not only a quantitative one, so to speak, but also a qualitative one. This difference determines the general life sum, the properties and size of the "star," as well as its color, which is complex, consisting of the compounding and mixing of different shades.

Here, one can also ask why Scripture speaks of heaven and hell, eternal life and torment, precisely in their opposition. But this opposition in no wise removes the complexity of the life situation: Does the Lord not say that it is necessary to cast off the offending eye or hand? "For it is profitable for thee that one of thy members should perish, and not that thy whole body should be cast into hell" (Matt. 5:30). There can therefore be a difference between an intact body and one that is deprived of one of its members, such a deprivation corresponding, in this comparison, to a spiritual infirmity.

Hell and heaven are, above all, a summation of life not only in its fullness and complexity but also in its diversity of forms. It is not by chance that the Lord speaks of the *many* mansions in His Father's house, which signifies first of all the diversity of their forms. And this diversity can be composed of different combinations of hell and heaven, life and death, incorruptibility and perdition in one and the same human destiny. This union of opposites is the fundamental *postulate* of eschatology, although we are incapable of grasping it by a concrete representation. But this postulate follows necessarily from the very foundations of sophiological anthropology, that is, from the union in man of the Divine

465

Sophia (the proto-image) and the creaturely Sophia (the "likeness"), divine creative power and creaturely freedom.

It is this postulate, this antinomic idea, contained in a homily of St. Isaac the Syrian, that we put at the basis of eschatology, as its initial proposition. Here is the pertinent passage: "I say that those tormented in gehenna are struck by the scourge of love. And how bitter and cruel is this agony of love, for, feeling that they have sinned against love, they experience a torment that is greater than any other. The affliction that strikes the heart because of the sin against love is more terrible than any possible punishment. It is wrong to think that sinners in gehenna are deprived of God's love. *Love is produced by knowledge of the truth, which (everyone is in agreement about this) is given to all in general.* But by its power love affects human beings in a twofold manner: It torments sinners, as even here a friend sometimes causes one to suffer, and it gladdens those who have carried out their duty. And so, in my opinion, the torment of gehenna consists in repentance. Love fills with its joys the souls of the children on high."[51] But love is God, just as knowledge of the truth is knowledge of God. St. Isaac recognizes that both are proper to both the righteous and sinners in the life of resurrection. We shall yet return to the content of this postulate.

7. The Eternal in the Temporal
(On the Eternity of Bliss and Torments)

In order to fully understand the ontological nature of the judgment and separation, we must take a further step in the analysis of the initial definitions. In particular, we must try to clarify the concepts *eternity* and *eternal,* which have a fundamental significance in eschatology. We must first say that these concepts are *by no means* clear and self-evident. On the contrary, they have many meanings and must be continually defined anew. The basic preliminary question here is whether eternity is one of the determinations of temporality, one of its dimensions, so to speak, even if a negative one (precisely as the absence of an end), or whether, on the contrary, it is incommensurable with time — whether it is situated outside of and above temporality and in general is not time at all.

In the popular conception, which — alas! — has become the dominant one in theology as well, eternity *is* a measure of time, that is, it ex-

---

51. *Ascetic Discourses,* 19 (at the end), according to the Russian translation, Moscow, 1854; 3rd ed., 1911.

presses the infinitude of time. And it does this, curiously, not in relation to the beginning, which would make it synonymous with beginning-lessness (in this sense, eternity is applicable de facto to God), but in relation to the end: Eternity is understood as an infinite duration of time (as "bad infinity," according to Hegel's expression). Higher mathematics uses the concept of infinity in its own way, but this methodological, auxiliary concept is eliminated in the final result, which is expressed in finite and concrete quantities. Its application in theology, however, has nothing like the logical rigor of its application in mathematics. In theology, it signifies an indeterminate duration as such, without an end but with a beginning. As a further derivative feature, it also signifies unchangedness and unchangeability. However, in this sense eternity can be applied only to God's absoluteness (in which there is no place for change) but not to the life of creation, which has a beginning and, in essence, is in the process of *becoming*. Here we have the fundamental distinction between divine eternity and creaturely eternity *(aeternitas* and *aeviternitas)*. But, ontologically, creaturely life and even creaturely eternity are nevertheless temporality, becoming, but without end and continuing for ages of ages. Therefore, eternity understood as infinite becoming or infinite temporality is the direct opposite of divine eternity, the unchangeability of fullness, which is transcendent to time and knows neither beginning nor end. But eschatological discussions constantly confuse these two incompatible notions of eternity. Moreover, the main conception of eternity that is accepted as self-evident in these discussions and is not held to require further clarification is its most meager conception, that of one-sided, bad infinity. Biblical sayings concerning eternity are also usually understood in this sense.

But, exegetically, it is first necessary to establish that such an interpretation does not accord with the word usage that can be considered dominant in the Old Testament. Here, eternity is ascribed to facts and institutions whose temporality and limited duration are self-evident: for example, eternal law, eternal priesthood, and suchlike expressions are even put in God's mouth. One could think that the Old Testament, which expressly had a temporary and preliminary significance, had been instituted for all time, which clearly contradicts reality. Thus, a natural question arises: Is it necessary to see here only a stylistic *lapsus calami* (which would be impious and in any case could not be considered a satisfactory method of exegesis, at least for a large number of cases), or should one consider that the word is used in a special sense and seek to determine what this sense is? If we follow the latter course, it would be necessary to reject in ad-

467

vance the conception of eternity as infinity in time and, in general, as a temporal determination, and to affirm a wholly different conception of eternity: the idea of eternity as a particular quality. Such institutions, which attest to direct indications and actions of God's hand in the life of humanity, have a sacred and, in this sense, divine character. Taking into account its different nuances, "eternal" is used here as a synonym for "divine." "Eternity" is synonymous with God's activity, manifestation, or energy. It is the ladder between heaven and earth.

Turning to the New Testament, we are assured in advance by a number of contemporary interpreters that the word "eternal" *(aiōnios)* signifies "infinite" in the sense of bad infinity. The tendency of this interpretation consists in the desire to exegetically prove the infinity of "eternal torments." But the ontological sense of the word *aionios* cannot be decided by purely philological considerations. The context plays the dominant role here, as we have just seen in the case of the Old Testament texts. In any case, there is no doubt that the New Testament too contains a number of texts in which the significance of infinite time is not ascribed to the concept of eternity. Such, first of all, is the Johannine doctrine of eternal life, which is revealed in temporal life and therefore can in no wise signify bad infinity (see John 3:15, 16; 4:14, 36; 5:24; 6:27, 40, 47, 54; 10:28; 12:50; 17:2-3).

In these texts, "eternity" signifies spiritual being, a determinate qualitative character of the latter. We must attribute the same significance to eternal life in the Synoptic Gospels: Matthew 19:16, 29; Mark 10:17, 30 ("he shall receive . . . in the world to come eternal life"); Luke 10:25; 18:18, 30. A similar meaning should be attributed to this expression in the following New Testament texts as well: Acts 13:46, 48; 1 John 1:2; 2:25; 5:11, 13, 20 ("this is the true God, and eternal life"); Jude 21; Romans 2:7; 5:21; 6:22-23; and 1 Timothy 1:16. All of these cases of the usage of the word "eternal" certainly do not refer to temporal determinations.[52]

These different texts exclude an automatic interpretation of the concept of eternity in the sense of bad infinity. In these texts, eternity clearly means *good* infinity, that is, eternal life in God, which has no end, for it is

---

52. According to E. B. Pusey (*What Is of Faith as to Everlasting Punishment,* 1880, 1. c. 38-9) the word *aiōnios* occurs seventy-one times in the New Testament. It modifies the nouns life (forty-four times), God (three times), the kingdom of Christ, redemption, the blood of His Covenant, the Gospel, salvation, Christ's dwelling in heaven, the glory given to us, our inheritance, our consolation, our participation in eternal life, the eternal fire (three times), punishment, judgment, and destruction (four times).

inexhaustible. But, here too, infinity in time is not the unique and fundamental meaning of the concept of eternity, but only a concomitant and derivative meaning. Eternity does not receive here the meaning of one of the determinations of temporality or time. With regard to time, eternity is not a quantitative but a qualitative determination. It is God, divine life revealing itself to humankind that lives in time and thus entering into the *content* of time: "this is life eternal, that they might know thee the only true God" (John 17:3). The patristic interpretation of this text sees in it a promise of eternal life not only in the future but also in the present age. Eternal life is life in God, in His Church, the touching of divinity, God's revelation to humanity. But this character of eternal life that reveals itself in time also includes good infinity in time.

We must mention once again that all creaturely being is becoming being, which is submerged in time. But besides the fluid and changeable *panta rei,* the inexhaustible depths of eternity are revealed in this being. *Aeternitas* is revealed in *aeviternitas,* and this for always, for ages of ages. Creation cannot have an eternal life that is free of temporality, because it would then become identical to the Creator; it would have the fullness of eternity. But creation infinitely encompasses eternity, and thus lives by eternity. In this respect, creation has eternal life. Eternal life therefore acquires an ontological, not a chronological, sense. Moreover, the life of our age differs from that of the future age by a different experience of eternity in time. In the present age, we are immersed in temporal becoming to the point where direct knowledge of God as the source of all life is inaccessible to us apart from a special revelation of eternal life. But, in the age of resurrection, *all* resurrected human beings, clothed in the glory of incorruptibility, will know eternal life, though in different ways, each in accordance with his state. Ignorance of God and total separatedness from eternal life are impossible: All know God; His eternity is revealed to all, and, in this sense, eternal life is given to all. Thus, eternal life, or eternity, is a special quality of the life of the future age, which will pass not apart from and in isolation from God, as our age does, but in His knowledge, as life in God.

We must now turn to the question of this *difference* in the perception of eternity, that is, as eternal life and eternal torments. Leaving aside for the moment the abstract character of this schema, we must put in brackets, so to speak, the common feature of eternity that is attributed to two such different categories. The chronological conception of eternity that is dominant in theology and that applies to both cases interprets eternity as an infinite duration, and all attention is concentrated on this. Eternity is taken not in a qualitative but, exclusively, in a quantitative sense. From this it is concluded that heavenly bliss and eternal torments are equally eternal: If bliss does not have an end, neither do the torments of hell. This argument is encountered even among such church fathers as St. Basil the Great and St. Augustine, and, following them, others repeat it as well. Eternal life in God and the torments of hell therefore turn out to have the same eternity. But such an identification encounters an insurmountable obstacle in certain Gospel texts. One such text says: "inherit the kingdom prepared for you from the foundation of the world" (Matt. 25:34), while another speaks of the "everlasting fire, prepared for the devil and his angels" (v. 41).

These are two wholly different forms, two different qualities of eternity. If the kingdom of God is the ground and goal of the creation of the world, its supramundane foundation in God, then can one say that the being and eternity of hell were included in the world's fullness at its creation? Did God create hell — if not in its immediate reality, then at least in its potentiality? Or is hell a creation of Satan and his angels, as well as of the free creatures who have fallen under his influence? That is, is it the case that hell has no being but is only a state (that it is "prepared for Satan and his angels," in direct opposition to "the kingdom prepared from the foundation of the world," i.e., of course, by the Creator Himself)? Hell is clearly *not* an original creation of God. It appears in creation as a result of the fall of Satan and his angels. And if one speaks of "eternal torment" in parallel with "eternal life," this only indicates the essential difference between these two kinds of eternity. They cannot therefore be abstractly identified as forms of equally infinite time. This is a striking example of that one-sided and erroneous conception of eternity as time, precisely as bad infinity, which transforms it into an empty and abstract form, independent of its content. Just as abstract, qualityless time does not exist, so abstract, qualityless eternity does not exist. Eternity is defined as a function of its concrete manifestation.

Therefore, it is necessary to pose the central question of eschatology as regards eternity: What does the attribute of *eternity* actually signify with reference to creation? And, here, one must first completely exclude the conception of eternity as time and temporality. Let us state more precisely that time and eternity are by no means related in the way that is usually postulated, because eternity is not a temporal but a *qualitative* determination. And one must not forget this. In this sense, *eternity does not have any relation to time,* and such expressions as eternal bliss, eternal torments, eternal perdition, eternal fire, and their synonyms do not signify infinite time. There is simply no question of time here, just as there is no question of it in John 17:3: "This is life eternal, that they might know thee the only true God, and Jesus Christ, whom thou has sent."

Time and the temporality of life can mean two things: First, they can signify the changeability, corruptibility, and mortality proper to the present age, to our mortal life that is limited by times and seasons. They are the sign of the transience and changeability of life: All is in flux and all passes. In this sense, time is essentially connected with death. Second, in a more general sense, time is synonymous with becoming, with creatureliness in general. God alone possesses the fullness and unchangeability of eternity; growth, or becoming, is proper to creation. Creation can never have access to the divine fullness of eternity. For creation, the assimilation of eternal life is a process that extends to all times: "now and forever and for ages of ages." God cannot be wholly encompassed by the life of creation; otherwise, creation itself would become God. The victory over death in Christ's resurrection and the universal resurrection in incorruptibility do give a new, different experience of time compared to mortal life, namely, the experience of its infinite duration. But this is precisely only temporality, not eternity, with which the infinity of time is erroneously identified. Time and eternity remain separated by an ontological chasm, though they are also connected, as a flow of waters is connected with its source. If eschatology speaks of eternal life and the eternity of different states of life, this signifies neither the abolition of the temporality of creaturely life (and, in this sense, the abolition of time in general and its submergence in the immobility of eternity) nor the identification of time and eternity. Even in the future age, the life of creation continues in time, remains a becoming, and is accompanied by growth, by ascent from glory to glory "in infinite life."

What, then, does *eternity* signify as a determination of the life of the future age in its different states? Eternity qualifies immortal, infinite life, precisely when this life is turned toward God and is permeated with God's light. Eternity is the being of this life in God, which is proper to it as a creation of God. Originally, God created the world and man in it in order to reveal Himself to man as the Creator, in the divine foundation of the world, in the sophianicity of the latter. As the creaturely Sophia, the world in man was to know God in the world, eternity in time. God came to man to converse with him in Eden. Eternity was accessible to man, both by the immanent revelation of God in the world and by His transcendent revelation above the world (the conversation in paradise). Creation was incapable of overcoming this distance between the transcendent and the immanent. Nevertheless, life in God and, in this sense, eternal life was the supreme goal for creation. But this goal was a task to be accomplished, not a given. The fall caused an essential change: it broke man's direct connection with eternity and cast his life wholly into temporality. It did this not only by allowing death to enter his life, owing to which time became synonymous with corruptibility and mortality, but also, and especially, by shutting him off from heaven and making him an inhabitant of "this" world.

The eye of eternity in man became unseeing, and his life began to measure itself according to the elements of the world, not only outwardly but also inwardly. Breakthroughs into heaven, or into eternity, became the achievements of just a few chosen ones, in brief moments of their lives. Rays of eternity illuminated the life of the world only to show it its temporality and relativity — by reminding it of heaven. Nevertheless, this connection of the Creator with creation remained indestructible, to be sure, for the very life and being of the world consisted in this connection. But this connection was obscured for man by the veil of temporality. In Divine-humanity, through the Incarnation and the descent of the Holy Spirit in the Pentecost, the distance between heaven and earth was overcome thanks to the union of the two natures, divine and human. Although this was accomplished for all of creation, it remained hidden. Resurrected in glory, Christ ascended from earth to heaven in order to return from heaven to earth through the descent of the Holy Spirit and through the parousia. The parousia, the coming in glory, is God's definitive action directed toward the sophianization of the world. In Sophia, God becomes the immediate and dominant reality for the world and humanity. *All* human beings who are resurrected in incorruptibility and glory recognize themselves in Christ and, by the Holy Spirit, come to know themselves in their sophianicity, in the glory prepared for them in Christ before the foundation of the world.

While belonging to the creaturely world, all human beings are, so to speak, obliged by God's love to live in divine life, in glory and deification. This is God's inalienable gift to creation, the completion of His work on the world. Here, man loses his creaturely selfhood and mundaneness, which hide him from God "amongst the trees" (Gen. 3:8). Man sees himself before the face of God, in the light of divine eternity. This directedness toward God, which renders all life transparent to the divine light, is in fact the *eternity,* or the eternal life, about which the eschatological texts speak. This is the most general quality of eternity, based on the new relation of creation to God, on the proximity to Him which is given and acquired by the Incarnation, by the presence of Christ in the world in virtue of His humanity in every human being, and by the abiding of the Holy Spirit. The life of all human beings, of the righteous and of sinners, in heaven and in hell, passes in the light of God's face, in the illumination of divine love, caressing or burning (once again, according to St. Isaac the Syrian).

Thus, as the general quality of the life of the future age, eternity is the state of glory and incorruptibility, manifested sophianicity, the power of the resurrection. It is the vision of God's face, life by God, in God, and before God ("The God of all grace, who hath called us unto *his eternal glory* by Christ Jesus" [1 Pet. 5:10]). But it is here that the real problem arises: the problem of eternal life in creaturely temporality, of the union of creaturely humanity and the divine image, in other words, the problem of the *synergism* of the divine and human natures in the life of incorruptibility and eternity.

The creaturely nature of human beings with its freedom is not annihilated even when it encounters God's eternity and is thereby immersed in eternal life, in the light of God's face. This encounter takes place for every human being in accordance with the state of his creaturely being. It corresponds to what Scripture calls judgment and verdict: a human being sees himself in the justice of eternity, in his supra-eternal aspect as God conceived him (this is the measure of the talents given to him). All self-evaluations are accomplished by him in the light of this eternity. He is thus his own judge; the excruciating separation and judgment that result from this confrontation are produced in him himself. It is in this sense that Scripture speaks of "eternal judgment" (*krimatos aiōniou;* Heb. 6:2). All the vital self-evaluations that a human being performs acquire a quality of *eternity,* without reference, for the moment, to time. It is in this sense that one should interpret not only Matthew 25:41, 46 but also a number of other expressions in which the epithet "eternal" is used in combination with "life," "perdition," "fire" (Dan. 12:2; Jude 6-7; 2 Thess. 1:9; Matt. 18:8: "eternal fire"), as well as such synonymous expressions as "unquenchable fire" and "undying worm" (Matt. 3:12; Mark 3:28-29; 9:43-48; Luke 3:17). There are other expressions that imply the same thing without actually using the epithet "eternity": death, perdition, corruption, destruction, and so on (see above). Clearly, condemnation to death, perdition, and annihilation should not be understood literally here, for that would contradict resurrection in incorruptibility and immortality. They indicate only the special character of the sufferings of sinners in the state of glory.[53]

The fundamental idea of the judgment consists in the fact that, de-

53. A roughly two-page excursus on the fate of sinners after death according to the New Testament is omitted here. — Trans.

spite the glorification by the resurrection, which is a work and gift of God, synergism, particularly a human being's self-determination in his creaturely freedom, is fully preserved. This self-determination is accomplished as a result of his encounter with his proper sophianic proto-image in God; and this encounter involves a judgment and a separation, resulting in perdition or salvation. A human being's free ontic self-determination is the sum total of his entire life in earthly time, in this aeon. God as the Creator and Resurrector gives all to man, but He does not thereby deprive him of his creaturely freedom of self-determination, just as He does not give him what belongs to him himself and what he must acquire by himself. On the threshold of the life of the future age, of the new immortal life, this self-determination is not a singular act in time but a sum total that represents the synthesis of times, the "book of life." A result of God's wisdom and justice, this sum total is, of course, individual for every human being. One must not forget that there are myriads of human beings who predominantly remain in a state of passivity; such, first of all, are those who died in infancy, before reaching the age of maturity or even consciousness. There is also an infinite diversity of *destinies,* which are independent of the free will of human beings and determine their freedom, but without abolishing it. To be sure, the divine judgment, whose sentence constitutes the sum total in question, knows the entire force of this "predestination," which concerns both what a human being has done and what he has not done in his freedom.

Judgment as separation expresses the relation between image and likeness, which can be in mutual harmony or in antinomic conjugacy. Image corresponds to the heavenly mansions in the Father's house, to the edenic bliss of "eternal life." Likeness, by contrast, corresponds to that excruciating division within the resurrected human being where he does not yet actually possess what is his potentially; whereas his divine proto-image is in full possession of it. He contemplates this image before himself and in himself as the inner norm of his being, whereas, by reason of his proper self-determination and God's judgment, he cannot encompass this being in himself. He cannot possess part (and this part can be large or small) of that which is given to him and loved by him in God (cf. St. Isaac the Syrian); and this failure to possess, this active emptiness at the place of fullness, is experienced as perdition and death, or rather as a perishing and a dying, as "eternal torment," as the fire of hell. This ontological suffering is described only in symbolic images borrowed from the habitual lexicon of apocalyptics. It is clear that these images should not be interpreted literally. Their fundamental significance lies in their description of the torments of unrealized and unrealizable love, the deprivation of the bliss of love, the consciousness of the sin against love.

Is there a place in the fire of hell for theomachy, for a satanical hatred of God with its demented and fanatical blasphemy? Is atheism or anthropotheism possible there? Does it not appear that all this has become impossible, for it belongs to the past age, when the world existed far from God? Even in the afterlife there is no place for atheism, even though, just as in the present world and for the present humanity, God's being might not appear there with triumphant, all-conquering evidence. In the future age, on the other hand, it is in general impossible not to know and love God. This love is the law of being there.

But this love for God is also the source not only of bliss but also of the burning in hell, since the sin against this love is manifested precisely in this burning. A human being experiences the vanity and impotence of the love to which he is called by his own being that is revealed to him. The revelation of the Divine Sophia in a human being himself as his proto-image, the manifestation of the Ever-Virgin as the fullness and perfection of love in human form, and the Eternal Eye of the Dread Judge Himself, whose judgment is love and truth, penetrate into the most hardened souls, making them malleable by fire. The divine love that is revealed to creation is also the judgment that is experienced by creatures as their proper ontological consciousness. And this judgment mysteriously combines calling and rejection, blessing and damnation, which can refer to one and the same person but in different aspects of his being.

How can damnation and blessing go hand in hand? Or how can the one who was sent "into the world not to condemn the world; but that the world through him might be saved" (John 3:17) pronounce with love: "depart from me, ye cursed, into everlasting fire" (Matt. 25:41)? God's love, it must be said, is also His justice. God's love consumes in fire and rejects what is unworthy, while being revealed in this rejection. "For God hath concluded them all in unbelief that he might have mercy upon all. O the depth of the riches both of the wisdom and knowledge of God!" (Rom. 11:32-33). The one not clothed in a wedding garment is expelled from the wedding feast, about which it is said: "if so be that being clothed we shall not be found naked" (2 Cor. 5:3). This *nakedness,* this absence of that which is given and must be present, *sterēsis,* as the original definition of evil, is fundamental for the torments of hell. It is the *fire* that burns without consuming. One must reject every pusillanimous, sentimental hope that the evil committed by a human being and therefore present in him can simply be forgiven, as if ignored at the tribunal of justice. God does not tolerate sin, and its simple forgiveness is ontologically impossible. Acceptance of sin would not accord with God's holiness and justice.[54] Once committed, a sin must be lived through to the end, and the entire mercilessness of God's justice must pierce our being when we think of what defense we will offer at Christ's Dread Tribunal.

The mystery here, which, as usual, bears the stamp of an antinomy, is that the very distinction between heaven and hell exists only for our limited earthly condition. But since every human being sins, the two states inevitably coexist in one and the same person. One state does not abolish the other, but one or the other is dominant. Hidden from us are God's judgments, which can compensate or even abolish our sins in the definitive verdict, according to His mercy. But the opposite question can also be asked: Are good works that precede the fall also annulled, or is their existence a supplementary burden? Does Judas the Apostle intercede with his apostolic ministry for Judas the Betrayer? Does the apostle Peter, who, contrary to his apostleship, renounced Christ, bear the torments of punishment for this renunciation? The *mixture* of good and evil that is proper to the overwhelming majority of human beings compels us to postulate not a simple but a complex sum total of God's judgment, which unites blessing and condemnation. This mystery of the life of the future age surpasses our understanding.

Clearly, the torments of hell are, first of all, a *spiritual* state of human beings. However, is it possible to limit the life of resurrected human beings to spirituality alone, disincarnating them, so to speak? This refers to suffering and to bliss in equal measure. One should not fall into spiritualism, for the latter contradicts the nature of human beings as incarnate spirits. If the fullness of human life in this age is connected not only with the spirituality but also with the corporeality of man, the same thing should hold for the life of resurrection. Everything that we know about the appearances of the resurrected Lord leads to this conclusion. By these appearances He proved to His disciples that He was not a spirit, "for a spirit hath not flesh and bones, as ye see me have" (Luke 24:39). The same conclusion must be drawn from His mysterious presence in the Eucharistic Body and Blood as well as from the resurrection of the dead in the flesh, in connection with the resurrection of Christ (1 Cor. 15:16-17). If those raised from the dead live in their incorruptible and glorified bod-

---

54. The forgiveness and remission of sins in the sacrament of confession does not signify a reconciliation with sin, for this sacrament presupposes active contrition, to which the Lord responds with His redemptive sacrifice.

ies, these bodies are called to share with them joy and sorrow, bliss and suffering. To be sure, we must not forget that the resurrected bodies are spiritual, that they possess a corporeality that is different from the present one, a corporeality that is transparent for and harmonious with the spirit. We do not have empirical knowledge of this kind of corporeality, but we do know that it is more closely connected with the spirit than our own is. We are therefore justified in speaking of the participation of the body in both the bliss and the torment of resurrected humanity, particularly of its burning in the "fire of hell." To be sure, these earthly images should be used only to express the general idea of spiritual corporeality in the life of the future age, to confirm this anthropological principle. Attempts to give a greater concretization to this principle lead only to superstition.[55]

The recognition of the corporeal character of the torments of hell leads to a further question, which follows from this postulate: If spiritual bliss and suffering can be combined in the same person, we must conclude the same thing about his corporeal state, which combines the joy of spiritual corporeality and the suffering of its darkening. In the framework of the ontological harmonization of opposites, we must also accept the idea that the bodies of *all* human beings have a glorified image, are clothed in beauty, but at the same time they appear in a corrupted form for those who suffer. Only one thing cannot be admitted: that the image of glory is *totally* engulfed by the image of hellish degradation.

Thus, the fundamental antinomic postulate of eschatology is that the eternal life of incorruptibility and glory can coexist with eternal death and perdition. Both, to different degrees, are included in being. When it is conceived statically, this antinomy becomes a direct contradiction. When it is conceived dynamically, it can be grasped livingly. In general, all eschatological determinations must be understood not statically but as the "eternal" dynamics of the life of the spirit. One must therefore completely reject the conception of eternity as bad infinity: as a *qualitative* category, eternity is wholly inapplicable to time and its terms, or rather to termlessness or infinity (moreover, this infinity would be a one-sided one, with a beginning but without an end). Creatureliness presupposes becoming, or temporality, which effectively begins in the act of creation, but it

---

55. Catholic theology considers with particular gusto the question of the nature of the infernal fire as such, and in contradistinction from the purgatorial fire. See, for example, the extensive article of A. Michel in *Dict. de Théol. Cath.* 5, 2:1. "Feu de l'enfer"; 2. "Feu du jugement"; 3. "Feu du purgatoire" (col. 2196-261). Biblical and patristic data are gathered here.

does not have an end, since God's creation is indestructible. Only in this sense can one speak of creaturely eternity, *aeviternitas,* in contradistinction to *aeternitas,* God's genuine eternity, which surpasses all becoming. Creaturely, or temporal, eternity (becoming eternity) and divine eternity are not only different but opposite. This does not prevent time, which has its foundation in eternity (and, according to Plato, is "the moving image of eternity"), from meeting eternity, from being able to encompass the revelation of eternity. But, in this meeting, temporality does not lose its fundamental quality, namely, becoming and changeability. Nor does eternity lose anything of its immobility and unchangeability. The two categories are antinomically united in the concept of the "eternal life" that is bestowed upon creation.

For a correct understanding of this creaturely eternity it is necessary to remove yet one more fundamental misunderstanding, which distorts the entire eschatological problematic. *Creaturely* eternity is usually identified with *divine* eternity, that is, with unchangeable immobility in the fullness of the absolute, whereas, in fact, creaturely eternity *never* attains and does not encompass such divine fullness and unchangeability. Creaturely eternity is becoming, growth, ascent from glory to glory. In this sense, revelation gives a clear, unambiguous definition: "we all, with open face beholding as in a glass the glory of the Lord, are changed into the same image *from glory to glory,* even as by the Spirit of the Lord" (2 Cor. 3:18). Growth, that is, becoming, in the change from glory to glory is directly affirmed by this text. It thus excludes the immobility and unchangeability of creaturely eternity. The same general idea is expressed by a formula that is frequently repeated in both Scripture and liturgical texts: *in ages of ages.* Infinite stages of eternity, an unending ladder of ascent from earth to heaven,[56] are introduced here.

---

56. True, this idea of the continuous infinity of ascent appears to be contradicted by texts that speak precisely about the fullness of revelation. Examples of such texts are 1 John 3:2: "Beloved, now are we the sons of God, and it doth not yet appear what we shall be: but we know that, when he shall appear, we shall be like him; for we shall see him as he is"; and 1 Cor. 13:10, 12: "when that which is perfect is come, then that which is in part shall be done away. . . . Now we see through a glass, darkly; but then face to face; now I know in part; but then shall I know even as also I am known." These texts speak of a new revelation of God, which is connected with the immediate divine vision of the *parousia* in the most general sense, that is, the manifestation of Christ in the glory or in the Holy Spirit. A radical change of the relation of creation to the Creator takes place: knowledge becomes "as . . . I am known," that is, sophianic. But this parousian revelation in no wise excludes further ascent from glory to glory within the limits of this new knowledge.

By no means does the revelation of "eternal life" abolish the nature of the creaturely spirit, the constant creative movement in which this spirit's life is expressed. The life of the spirit is constant creative activity and spontaneous mobility. Both the stupor of immobility, which is taken for eternity, and inert thingness are alien to this life. The spirit is actual and perpetually dynamic. Therefore, the spirit also receives actually and in becoming the new life that is revealed to it in God as "eternal life." In "eternal life," the spirit *lives* by the entire fullness of its *creaturely* life in the likening to its proto-image, in active sophianization, which knows no end. The bliss of the righteous, or, more precisely, the bliss that is accessible to a created being in the form of and in proportion to this being's righteousness, is different for every individual ("in my Father's house are many mansions"). It is different not only in its fundamental, initial determination, but also in its manifestation in life. Here, it is important to establish the very presence of such a path. Eternal life is a path, not a way station, not a stagnation in some nirvana. It is creative ascent in the reception of divine life and its revelations. "Many mansions" is not only a qualitative but also a quantitative definition of this ascent, a measure of its different stages. One should also not forget that the determination of this measure also depends on how right and left, righteousness and sinfulness, fullness and emptiness, are interrelated in each human being, since no one is perfectly righteous.

Eternal life, or eternal bliss, is deification, the reception of divine life, actualized sophianization: "God will be all in all." But this marvelous gift of God's love does not abolish this "all," that is, the proper creaturely nature of the recipients. God is the positive *content* of eternal life, but this life is the creative assimilation of this content. It is a synergism. The relationship between God and human beings, between grace and creatureliness, is not excluded in any one of the successive states of human life, not even in this ultimate *all in all,* where the divine *all* encounters and fills the creaturely *all.* For this divine fullness is received from measure to measure, from the temporal being of creation to eternity. Eternal life consists in being continuously present before the face of God and continuously seeing oneself in God's light, from which one cannot hide.

Does the dogma of the veneration of the saints and their canonization not exclude the notion of the relativity and compatibility of heaven and hell, even if in different forms and compoundings? This question can be answered by another question: Does human saintliness signify perfect sinlessness, and does canonization presuppose precisely such a conception of saintliness? We think that the testimony that canonization gives concerning saintliness has a somewhat different meaning, that of a sum total, in which sinful infirmities are submerged in a general saintliness. And this sum total is different in each individual case. It is not by chance that the Church distinguishes between major and minor saints, and that their liturgical veneration distinguishes among saints of the "sixth order," the "eighth order," the "tenth order," and so forth. To this we must add saints who are not glorified but are venerated among "all saints." There are also local saints, who are not venerated universally. Finally, besides canonization, general and particular, we can also personally semi-venerate those near to us who "repose in the peace of the Lord." (A grateful son can semi-venerate his mother; a mother can semi-venerate her "blessed" infants, and so forth.)

The forgiveness of sins does not mean they are forgotten. It even presupposes the contrary: their special remembrance in the full awareness of God's mercy. There is no reason to think that the apostle Peter could forget, in this age or the future one, his renunciation of the Lord. According to tradition, he remembered this renunciation all his life, and its memory is preserved forever in the holy Gospel. But this does not nullify the great saintliness of the first apostle, to whom the Lord said on the same day, "Thou art Peter," and then, "Get thee behind me, Satan" (Matt. 16:18, 23). Peter is by no means an exception among all the saints, whose saintliness supposedly signifies freedom from all sin. On the contrary, this is what the prayer of the Church says about all human saintliness: "there is no man who is alive and does not sin. Thou alone art without sin," for "every man [is] a liar, as it is written, That thou mightest be justified in thy sayings, and mightest overcome when thou art judged" (Rom. 3:4). Every human being has need of forgiveness and redemption by the Blood of the Lamb. In other words, the saintliness glorified by the Church signifies not sinlessness but righteousness as the sum total of pluses and minuses, experienced as a synthesis of bliss and suffering. This confirms that, for human beings, there is neither absolute heaven nor absolute hell.

It is sometimes asked whether a new fall that is similar to the first one is possible in the future age on the pathways of creaturely freedom. This question must be answered in the negative, but this is *not* because eternity (even creaturely eternity) is unchangeability and immobility as such. On the contrary, creaturely eternity is the free actuality of the spirit in its creative growth and, therefore, continuous evolution. But this evolution cannot imply a lapse back into a sinful state: on this pathway of growth the possibility of a new fall has been overcome forever. Man outgrows this lower level of freedom of choice between good and evil, between the acceptance of God and the rejection of God. In the state of the world and of humanity in which God will be "all in all," His being will be the dominant and triumphant reality. For the righteous who are worthy of this revelation or, more precisely, for that part of a person which is turned toward God, his being will have such a "sweet irrefutability" that it will be inwardly impossible to fall away from it. After the expulsion of the prince of this world from the world, evil loses its attractiveness. It is exposed and rendered powerless; it is lived to the end and loses its savor, as it were. To this we must add that the righteous experience eternal bliss not in isolation but in the communion of love, in ecclesial union with all humankind. The kingdom of Christ becomes the kingdom of all-conquering universal goodness, which grows toward eternal life not only by personal effort but also in the union and sobornost[57] of the universal Church. Thus, for creation, *eternity* does not signify the abolition of temporality with its becoming. Eternity is not an inert immobility but an inexhaustible source of creative life.[58]

For those in whom Christ has been imaged, this growth cannot be limited. It necessarily extends not only to growth in good but also to the expiation of evil by the experiencing of it to the end, since even the righteous are not free of it and must overcome it with its infernal fumes. If good is originally accompanied by evil, as light is accompanied by darkness, this inner division and sundering of life cannot remain unchanged but is overcome. The spiritual wounds are healed over an indeterminate period of time, in ascent from glory to glory. The measure and the mode of this growth differ depending upon every human being's spiritual state. Using the language of Catholic theology, we can speak of a kind of "purgatorial" state and of a purifying fire that burns the tares remaining in the wheat and destined to be thrown into the unquenchable fire by the reaper

---

57. See the translator's introduction for a discussion of sobornost. — Trans.

58. Is this growth, which begins at the very threshold of "eternal life," not symbolized by that new self-revelation of Christ in His humanity which is already contained in the first questions and answers of Matthew 25:34-46? The Lord calls "the blessed of my Father [to] inherit the kingdom prepared for you from the foundation of the world," for having shown Him active love, for love in general. But the righteous answer him: "Lord, when saw we thee an hungred . . . thirsty . . . a stranger . . . naked . . . sick, or in prison?" And to this the King gives his own answer. One asks: what does this question of the righteous signify? Does it express only their humility or does it also express ignorance and creaturely limitedness, which require an express revelation in order to be overcome, and receives it in such an astonishing form? And is this first revelation not the first act of growth in eternity which the resurrected humankind awaits?

angels. "There remaineth therefore a rest to the people of God" (Heb. 4:9). For every human being, there remains, to different degrees, something to overcome, to expiate, in himself and with the people of God, that is, with the Church, with the Divine-humanity.

We now arrive at the most "accursed" question of eschatology, that of the eternal torments of sinners. Those who understand eternity as temporal infinity (i.e., theologians of all confessions) attempt to affirm the infinity, or "eternity," of the torments of hell in all manner of ways — apologetically, patristically, exegetically. They attempt to prove the justice of the infinite duration of punishment even for temporal sins and the conformity of this punishment with God's wisdom and love. A whole theodicy of eternal torments is thus constructed. Of the great mass of judgments of this kind,[59] of special interest are the opinions of Origen and especially St. Gregory of Nyssa, who are virtually the only ecclesiastical writers (besides Augustine with his rigorism) who made questions of eschatology an object of special inquiry. The Church has not issued a precise determination on this issue, although the doctrine of scholastic theology attempts to pass itself off as such a determination. But, actually, this doctrine only expresses the "opinion" of one of the two tendencies that have opposed each other and continue to oppose each other in theology. Even the definitions that condemn Origenism, which previously had been attributed to the fifth ecumenical council, have been shown by recent historical inquiry not to originate in this council.[60] Even if they had so originated, they would still require interpretation and very careful commentary. In any case, they require a special inquiry.[61]

These definitions are based on a juridical and penitentiary conception, according to which God's relation to the world is determined only by the principle of retribution, contrary to what the Lord Himself said: "God sent not his Son into the world to condemn the world; but that the world

---

59. Among Orthodox authors see Fr. Malinovsky, *Orthodox Dogmatic Theology*, 4:206; Metr. Macarius, vol. 2, par. 271; Bishop Sylvester, *Essay on Orthodox Dogmatic Theology*, Kiev, 1902, vol. 5, par. 219-20. Among numerous scattered affirmations, see those contained in Bishop Theophanes' *Letters* (Moscow, 1893), as well as those of Bishop Mikhail.

60. F. Diekampf, *Die origenistische Streitigkeiten im VI Jahr. und das fünfte allgemeine Konzil*, Munster, 1899.

61. M. Oksiuk, in *The Eschatology of Gregory of Nyssa*, p. 649, justly concludes that the fathers of the fifth ecumenical council "did not condemn the opinions of St. Gregory of Nyssa. And how could they have condemned them if, even before the third ecumenical council, this bishop was recognized by the Church as a saint?"

through him might be saved" (John 3:17), and "I came not to judge the world, but to save the world" (12:47). Thus speaks the Lord Himself, to whom the Father "gave the power to judge." Between judgment and even condemnation on the one hand and the salvation of the world on the other there is therefore no contradiction or incompatibility. A consistently developed penitentiary conception is most vulnerable from the side of theodicy. This conception accepts that, from eternity, God introduced hell and eternal torments in the creation of the world and gave them a power of being equal to that of the kingdom of God, prepared from the foundation of the world. The final accomplishment therefore includes an ontological failure, precisely in its dualistic character: alongside the eternity of the kingdom of God, one affirms the equal eternity of hell. The world is therefore a failure. God's Wisdom has stopped impotently before an insuperable boundary set by creaturely freedom. The sacrifice of Golgotha has turned out to be incapable of triumphing over hell, a triumph proclaimed by both the Old Testament prophet and Christ's apostle: "O hell, where is your victory?" (Hos. 13:14 = 1 Cor. 15:55).[62] The sophianicity of the world has encountered a limit to itself in the antisophianicity of hell, in which the outer darkness in the absence of God's light, the dark antisophia, reigns. Either God's omnipotence or His wisdom is impotent here. And another principle of being raises its head, a principle that even God cannot render powerless or (which is even less comprehensible) that He Himself has instituted.

Such are the stupefying conclusions to which penitentiary theology leads. But a negative critique is insufficient to disclose all the violence such a conception does to thought, conscience, and faith. The *positive* principles that render this conception powerless must also be disclosed here. However, one must first remove a fundamental misunderstanding of a practical nature. Since the time of St. Augustine, who facetiously called his opponents *misericordes,* the "pitying ones," it has become customary to see a kind of moral libertinism, a tendency toward personal irresponsibility and false sentimentalism, in those perplexed by an eternity of torments. One must say at the outset that this genre of condemnation, which is proper to criminological pedagogy, must be excluded in advance here. An examination of the final events and their problematic demands sincerity and courage. To frighten theologically is a fruitless and inappropriate activity. It is unworthy of human beings, who are called to the free love for God.

---

62. This is a literal translation from the Russian Bible. — Trans.

One must indisputably admit the full validity of the axiom that every evil of which a human being is guilty must be fully and totally expiated by him,[63] even if he is forgiven. Sin cannot be remitted *for free*, without suffering, for that would not be mercy but a denial of justice. God's justice does not tolerate sin. Sin cannot be merely permitted and forgotten; it must appear before the face of God's justice. This does not establish a "self-justice," according to which a person is supposedly saved by his own power. For, here too, it is God's power that saves, the redemption by Christ's blood, the forgiveness of the sin. But the ability to receive such a redemption presupposes repentance.

Therefore, the idea that one can avoid with impunity the consequences of sin is insane, craven, and false. Every person must appear before Christ with faith in God's love, invoking God's mercy, but also delivering himself over to the tribunal of His justice. Every person bears within himself the principle of gehennic burning, which is ignited by the power of the parousia of Christ in glory. It is a question here not of divergence from God's justice but of its Christian understanding. And let us boldly say that reason and conscience do not accept the doctrine of the eternity of torments, in the sense of *infinite duration*, of an unchanging stasis. Psychologically too, this doctrine of terror applied to sinners is, of course, totally incapable of achieving its pedagogic goal. Even when it is inclined to panic, human imagination is incapable of concretely grasping the idea of eternal torments as a static infinity in time. And even less can it grasp the gradually increasing intensity of these torments, which can result only in the total annihilation of those in hell and of hell itself. This idea, designed to terrorize souls, does not attain its goal, because it is abstract and therefore powerless. But, at the same time, striking sensitive hearts with horror, paralyzing filial love and the childlike trust in the Heavenly Father, this idea makes Christianity resemble Islam, replacing love with fear. Salvific fear, too, must also have its measure, and not become an attempt to terrorize.

But, fortunately or not, such terror is no longer effective. What is real for human psychology is not abstractly infinite suffering but immediate, concrete suffering. In itself, such suffering is sufficient to break a hardened heart, striking it with the salvific fear of God. According to this fundamental idea, every human being will bear responsibility for his evil

---

63. Of course, this does not in the slightest contradict forgiveness of sins in the sacrament of repentance, which already includes this experiencing or expiation to the end, with the application of the power of Christ's redemptive sacrifice.

thoughts, works, desires, known sins, and even those that are unknown in the consciousness but present in the subconsciousness. *Every* human being will expiate his sins to the end not in the abstract and imaginary infinity of "eternal torments" but in the concrete suffering that they will cause. The prevalence of the pedagogy of fear in eschatology, which perhaps was characteristic of and effective in the psychology of past ages, is ineffective and tends to be shocking in our own time. This is a simple and evident psychological fact. By no means does this signify that we have lost the fear of God and stopped being conscious of the implacable responsibility that we bear for our lives. Rather, it signifies that the modern consciousness does not accept the idea of infinite punishment and torment for finite and limited sins.

The idea of the Last Judgment has as its content the fact that responsibility exists fully, together with the punishment immanently implied by it. And this punishment is an authentically "eternal" torment for every human being, the fear inspired by these torments being the fear of love, the fear of God. Although "perfect love casteth out fear" (1 John 4:18), the fear of God is the inevitable path of love. This idea of the responsibility for sins and of God's wrath directed at sins is a healthy spiritual salt that is more beneficial for the soul than the terror of infinite torments, which neither reason nor conscience can accept, even before a human tribunal.

And was it not for *all* the sins of *all* humankind that the Son of God tasted the agony of Gethsemane and the death on Golgotha, in which was concentrated the entire redemptive fullness of the "eternal" torments, that is, the entire intensity of the suffering caused by being abandoned and rejected by God under the burden of the all-human sin that weighed upon Him? However, the profound "eternity" of these torments was concentrated and experienced in a determinate period of time, from the Nativity to the Passion, or from "Let this cup pass from me" to "It is finished," but not in eternity as infinity in time. That would have been unrealizable. Understood in *this* sense, redemption simply could not have taken place, contrary to the direct testimony of Christ Himself, as well as of the entire New Testament. This is clear proof that, when applied to punishment for sin, "eternity" signifies not the infinite duration of time but the infinite intensity of time's content. And that is what constitutes the cross of Christ.

Thus, setting aside pseudo-pedagogy and the penitentiary psychology, let us consider the fundamental question of what eternity means with reference to the notion of eternal torments (and its metaphorical synonyms: eternal fire, gehenna, and so forth). We already know that eternity does not signify time (not even time of infinite duration) and that creaturely eternity *(aeviternitas)* signifies the infinite revelation of eternity in time and time's rootedness in eternity. Applied to the eternal bliss of the kingdom of God, prepared before the foundation of the world, this notion meets with no difficulty. It signifies the infinite ascent of creation from glory to glory, the actual identification of the creaturely Sophia and the Divine Sophia, the sophianization, or deification, of creation. God's depths are unfathomable, and the ocean of divine knowledge is given for infinite life. Good, that is, life in God, is characterized by inexhaustibility and infinity. But all these questions have a completely different character when they are raised in connection with the eternity of torments, which is the eternity of evil and suffering.

"Eternal torment," as the supreme measure of punishment, infinitely surpasses all the measures of punishment meted out on earth. Eternity of torments in this sense also signifies both an eternity of suffering and an eternity of evil. But can evil and suffering be considered eternal in the sense of the infinity that is proper to good, and what principle permits us to assert this? St. Gregory of Nyssa's answer was a mighty No! And his arguments have never been refuted.

Those who proclaim the infinity of torments also necessarily affirm the eternity of evil and its coeternity with good, as well as the invincible fury of the hatred that sinners direct toward God. This question is examined by St. Gregory of Nyssa in the general context of the problem of evil. He understands the latter in the spirit of Platonism as the absence of good, *sterēsis,* as not having its proper being, as a parasite that has not been created by God but that has entered the world by reason of creaturely freedom. Thus, evil does not have eternity; the latter is proper only to good.[64] On the contrary, evil is destined to be "annihilated." The assertion of the infinite presence of evil in the world is a kind of Manichaeanism.[65]

St. Gregory of Nyssa also indicates that evil does not have the creative power of eternity and therefore cannot extend into infinity. On the contrary, it is confined within definite limits. In other words, evil is incapable of infinite self-creative activity. If it did have that capability, it would be equal in power to good, and that would be another form of dualistic Manichaeanism. Therefore, "beyond the limits of evil, good prevails." Evil

---

64. Oksiuk, op. cit., 510 sq.

65. Saint Augustine, who at one time had overcome Manichaeanism on his path to the Church, partly returns to it in his eschatology, which consists of a series of contradictions between its overall sophiologism and this dualism.

has an end. Finally, the third, or ontological (essentially sophiological), argument of St. Gregory, his theodiocy, consists in the fact that "the world and man, as God's beautiful creation, are brought into being for an even greater beauty, and the goal of creation must be brought into harmony with divine nature."

Having briefly outlined St. Gregory's argumentation, let us turn to a substantive sophiological examination of the question. *Eternal* fire, *eternal* torment, *eternal* perdition and other synonymous expressions have no relation to *time*. They are not temporal but qualitative determinations. They express the general idea of suffering before the face of God, in God, in God's love. They have a *sophianic* significance in the sense that, having come to know himself in his sophianic *form*, the glorified human being will thereby also know himself in his own *deformity*, will be horrified by himself. And this deformation of his likeness in relation to his proto-image is for him the scourge of love, the burning fire of love. This deformation has its particular aspect in each case: If there are many mansions in the Father's house, and many proto-images, there are not fewer deformities, perversions, monstrosities. But however many such deformities there may be, their character remains the same: nakedness, the absence of a wedding garment, the excruciating disharmony between what has been realized and what remains a task to be realized. This is accusation and reproach, open arms that cannot embrace, a thirst that cannot be satisfied, an emptiness that cannot be filled, anguish of separation combined with joy of theophany, "death and hell" and the "lake of fire." About this it is said: "depart from me, ye cursed, into everlasting fire" (Matt. 25:41).

Does the exile of sinners far from the face of God, into the outer darkness, signify that His face is completely hidden from them and that they are completely separated from those who see God? Does it signify that they are able to commune only with those who, like them, are rejected? Yes and no. Certainly, God's word does not miss its mark, even if heaven and earth cease to be. There is the inexpressible sorrow of one's emptiness, which separates one from God; there is the ineffable pain of this separation. But this sorrow and pain already signify the seeing of God, even if from afar, from the abyss, from the grave, from the lake of fire. But this (let us once again remember St. Isaac the Syrian) is the sorrow of love ignited by Christ, by the vision of Him and His Most Pure Mother. And this love irresistibly pierces the heart with its sweet spear even in the outer darkness. Even hell cannot be deprived of this vision. Hell itself consists of unfulfilled love for God, which, because of spiritual limitation, is expressed in enmity toward Him, theomachy, or in spiritual sleep. The state of hell is, in essence, antinomic, because it combines the revelation of God and the abandonment by God; and it is this antinomic character that imparts to hell an eternal character. God Himself does not reject creation. It is creation that, in its desolate emptiness, rejects God. The image of sophianicity shines in all its glory above every creature, even "in hell." Spiritual beauty, which in the future age will also be corporeal beauty (the beauty of the "spiritual body"), judges and saves the world. The image of God in man judges its own likeness as a poor likeness, a deformed image.

In discussing heaven and hell, one should remember that, although this judgment is personal, is rendered upon every person, it is also universal ("all nations"), for Christ's humanity is one, and the destiny of everyone is connected with the destiny of all; everyone is responsible for all. One certainly cannot accept the incongruous and monstrous idea that, having received and become absorbed in their "reward," the righteous immediately forget their brothers suffering in hell. Can it be that the revelation of the God of love will cause their hearts to freeze in self-love and make them lose even that degree of mutual love which they had before the universal resurrection? On the contrary: this banishment into the outer darkness strikes all human beings in a certain sense, though in different ways and to different degrees. The righteous, too, in their edenic habitations suffer from the hell of sinners. It is true that Gospel expressions and figures that refer to personal responsibility and contain warnings to individuals about this responsibility do not mention this idea. Nevertheless, Christ's universal redemptive love indisputably and sufficiently attests to it. Salvation not only concerns everyone individually, but it is also the business of the love, prayer, and effort of all humanity, both of its healthy members and of those who are sick and need healing. Hell is therefore an affliction of all humanity.

Here, we approach a mystery of the future age that is perceived by our consciousness only as an antinomic postulate: the mystery of universal participation in the life of heaven and in the life of hell, with the two being compatible. The Mother of God, who is also the Mother of all humankind, pleads at the tribunal for universal *mercy, not for the forgiveness of sins* (which is impossible, for sins must be completely expiated and suffered through) but for mercifulness to sinners. The existence of hell is surrounded not by the cold of an egotistical indifference but by the radiant cloud of the caring love of saved humankind, that is, of the Church which abides for ages of ages in its sobornost as one, holy, and universal. In the Church, the one humankind is not divided into two and is not reconciled with the severing of one of its parts — hell — but sorrows over this part. We repeat: this sorrowing should not be interpreted as a sort of earthly slyness through which, spiritually, one avoids paying what one owes; for sin must be suffered through and expiated to the end. The debtor must not be released from his dungeon until he has paid "the uttermost farthing" (Matt. 5:26).[66] But — this must be said without circumlocution — heaven does not exist in its fullness as long as and insofar as hell exists. Hell is the inner limit for heaven, as it were. And the idea of the eternalization of this separation between hell and heaven, with our comfortably accepting this eternal separation, is a strange aberration of thought and feeling. Some have deduced from this the notion of "conditional immortality," in which this separation is overcome through the annihilation of hell by death.

The eternity of God's presence, the eternal sun of justice, Christ, are revealed equally in heaven and in hell, in both the bliss of the called and chosen and the torments of the called but rejected. But creaturely life passes in time, and therefore there nevertheless remains the question of how one can harmonize this eternal life with temporality. If one commits the error of conceiving eternity as only an infinite time, one purely and simply annuls the problem of the vital *correlation* between eternity and time, the problem of the participation of the latter in the former. This conception is obliged to equate eternity with *unchangeability* (which is proper only to God's grandeur) and, moreover, to attribute it not only to the heavenly state but also to the state of hell, bestowing upon the latter an unchangeable eternity that only God's being possesses. This is one of the principal contradictions of scholastic eschatology.

Temporal eternity, the revelation in time of eternal life in God, does not present difficulties for the understanding, since it is an ascent from glory to glory. This postulate captures the basic truth of the actuality of the human spirit, to which immobility is alien. The human spirit is in constant movement and growth, according to the manifestation in it of the image of God. Remaining essentially temporal, the life of the spirit realizes eternity in itself, as its content, by an infinite becoming.

But what about hell and rejection? Is hell an unchanging condition of the spirit, in which it abides in a state of permanent stagnation? Is it a frozen convulsion of torments and a continuous wail of curses, the bites of the "unsleeping" worm and the burning of the "inextinguishable" fire? Does creaturely life possess a capacity for suffering so inexhaustible that

---

66. Catholics apply this text solely to their own notion of purgatory, and not to that to which it refers — i.e., to hell.

even death, annulling everything in this age, cannot put an end to it? Or, as St. Gregory of Nyssa asked, does the power of evil have an energy of infinite life, of limitless creation, of "eternity," equal to that of heavenly bliss? The hypothesis of such a petrified infernal grimace must purely and simply be rejected, since it clearly contradicts the very essence of the life of the spirit, which does not know such petrifaction. Such an "eternity" would in fact lead to the extinction of life.

But it is even more difficult to admit the eternity of evil, attributing to it an inexhaustible creative activity, at least without a clear acceptance of Manichaean dualism. Evil is negative; it is the minus of being. Evil has a bottom; and if it appears bottomless or poses as bottomless, this is only a deception or a self-deception. The minus must be placed next to something that has an absolute value. As an independent, ontological minus, evil is only a pose. Most importantly, evil is empty and impotent; it is finite. Its creative activity in the world is parasitical, because it lives in symbiosis with being, is nourished by shadows of being, is a semi-being. Evil loses the very foundation of being after the *separation* of good and evil. Evil is not eternalized as a result of this separation but, on the contrary, is ontologically annulled in the parousia. "The prince of this world will be cast out" means that he will remain in his proper emptiness, impotent and sterile, incapable, as a parasite, of creative activity, condemned in his illusory nature.

When the sense of bad infinity is attributed to eternal torments, the preceding considerations inevitably lead one to ask how things stand with this illusory eternity of evil or with this infinite existence of hell. On the one hand, we have the absolute postulate of the changeability and mobility of the creaturely spirit as a manifestation of its life. This postulate prevents us from accepting that immobility of the creaturely spirit in hell that must necessarily be assumed if "eternal torments" are to be admitted. Since it is alive, the creaturely spirit cannot fail to change; and "eternal," that is, infinite, change is possible only toward good, on the pathways of man's deification. An eternal, unlimited creative activity of evil is inconceivable. Eternal creative activity is proper only to good, only to life in God, not to life outside of or apart from God. Therefore, heaven and hell cannot be *equally* eternal: The "eternity" of hell signifies something completely different from the eternity of heaven, for the eternity of hell is finite and self-exhausting. Heaven is the inexhaustibility of divine being, which reveals itself in time, whereas hell is the exposure of nonbeing before the face of divine being. Hell is an illusory eternity (and that is how this eternity is experienced by those abiding in hell). Inasmuch as hell *is not* a creation of God but a product of the self-determination of the prince of this world and of those enslaved by him, it does not have being in itself, nor, therefore, its proper eternity; its "eternity" is only a temporary state of life. These ontological arguments oblige us to deny the infinity of hell; in the ages, hell dissolves into *nothing*, which is its genuine foundation.

But perhaps one must assert a dark eternity of hell, as a counter-eternity opposed to God's eternity, precisely by reason of creaturely freedom and self-determination? Perhaps if this minus is placed in front of genuine eternity, it can indeed establish this sort of counter-eternity? Here, we return to the question of creaturely freedom. Does this freedom have an intrinsic, extra-divine foundation of being, or is it only modal in character as a state of the creature, the self-determination of the creature within the limits of its being? We have already considered this question in chapter 3: the idea of an absolute, extra-divine freedom as original being and unlimited possibilities was exposed there as a fiction and illusion. Freedom is relative: its being is entirely grounded in creaturely being; the task it is to accomplish is based on what it is given. Therefore, on the pathways of theomachy, both human and satanical, freedom cannot be self-sufficient. It rises only to fall; it is overcome and surpassed on the pathways of creaturely life toward its deification. Freedom is not an independent power in itself; it is impotent in its opposition to divinity: "Ye shall know the truth, and the truth shall make you free" (John 8:32). The truth is ontological; evil is mediumistic and deceptive.

One should not confuse evil with suffering, which, in itself, is not evil but can be either good or evil. A conclusion that is supremely important for all of eschatology follows from this: If, in the parousia, God's being is the dominant, all-conquering certainty, as "all in all," then militant atheism and theomachy become impotent here, have their ground removed from under them. Theomachy, blasphemy, and demonic possession no longer have a home in man. There is no place for the revolt against God, for, in the parousia, He is revealed as triumphant truth, all-conquering love, irresistibly attractive and salvific beauty. In the future age, God is the universal and absolute given: in general, there is only God, and there is nothing outside of God, against God, apart from God. This is not contradicted by the proper being of creation, since it is grounded in God and exists in Him. Therefore, Scripture says about sinners that they "shall be punished with everlasting destruction, from the presence of the Lord, and from the glory of His power; when He shall come to be glorified in His saints" (2 Thess. 1:9-10). The punishment here consists precisely in appearing before the face of God. Therefore, the former activity of evil can no longer be ontologically proper to the state of hell. The revolt of evil has exhausted itself. Hell is love for God, though it is a love that cannot be satisfied. Hell is a suffering due to emptiness, due to the inability to contain this love of God.

But, here too, we must be guided by the idea of divine-human synergism. We must define the role of creatureliness in its encounter with divine being and protect its freedom. The theophany in the parousia has all-conquering power and irresistible persuasive force. Nevertheless, it represents not coercion but a manifestation of power, not compulsion but persuasion. God definitively defeats man here by *persuading* him of His truth and power. Job's dispute, as Israel's opposition to God, exhausts itself here. God is so irresistibly persuasive for man because man receives God into himself, in his sophianic proto-image. In this image, man perceives the Divine Sophia, attains a self-knowledge so lofty and clear that it frees him from creaturely freedom as the faculty of choice between different and contradictory possibilities. Man transcends this freedom by a *free necessity*. Therefore, a new falling away from God is now and forever impossible for man, just as it is for the holy angels. The dispute between the Creator and creation inevitably ends for creation when it recognizes that it is defeated.

Such an exhaustive experiencing, or living out to the end, of extra-divine, creaturely freedom by demonstration of its harmony with the divine will ("Thy will be done on earth as it is in heaven"), in conformity with the dithelitic dogma, presupposes an indefinitely long process whose result is given ontologically: "When all things shall be subdued unto him [the Father], then shall the Son also be subject unto him that put all things under him, that God may be all in all" (1 Cor. 15:28). We must understand the torments of hell, too, in the spirit of synergism, not only as passive suffering but also as the spirit's actual, creative effort, which does not stop even in hell (consider the rich man in the Gospel). The torments of hell are a longing for God caused by the love for God. This longing is inevitably combined with the desire to leave the darkness, to overcome the alienation from God, to become oneself in conformity with one's revealed protoimage. However paradoxical this may seem, the state of hell includes not only the torments of love because of unlove, because of the impotence of love, but it also includes a creative activity of love. One who has sinned against love smashes again and again with his entire being against the void, and falls down groaning and gnashing his teeth, to rise again and repeat all this in an "eternal repetition."

But is this torment really eternal in the sense of an infinite series of repetitions, where all human suffering and effort plummet into a tartarus of "eternal" repetitions? Or is it the case that this unchangeability is not proper to the nature of life, which contains the force of the life-giving Spirit? Is it the case that it does not correspond to the actuality of the creaturely spirit, which keeps constantly changing in virtue of the creative energy of its life? However we might try to understand the torments of hell in the sense of eternal repetition or unchangeability, such an understanding encounters an obstacle in the conception of man as a self-creative, self-determining being. In general, this idea of the torments of eternal repetition in an evil eternity and frozen immobility is a satanic nightmare. Not even hell, as a state of hunger for love which transfigures those languishing in it, is such a nightmare. This is also a self-evident postulate of eschatology.

"Eternal torments" occur in creaturely temporality. They are not only a "punishment," since they are the ontologically immanent consequences of sin. They are also *continuing* life and therefore the *living through to the end* of what can and must be lived through, expiated. Even those who are in hell are not deprived of the image of God, of human sophianicity, that is revealed to them there: negatively by the torments and positively by the growing knowledge of themselves in God.

Is there an end and limit to this growth? Is there a limit to the sophianization of man even in the depths of hell? There is none. Or, more precisely, a limit can be ontologically set only in terms of what man *is* according to his creation. Man is saved by the Divine Sophia, who is the foundation of his creaturely being. He is saved by Divine-humanity, whose power is manifested in the likening of man to His proto-image. He is saved by the Cross of Christ and the Holy Spirit, which "bloweth where it listeth," penetrating even down into the depths of hell. Definitive salvation from the depths of hell is accomplished thanks to the actuality of the human spirit, which freely accepts and assimilates the divine principles of being.

Here, sinners experience to the end and fully expiate the evil they received into themselves, this expiation excluding remission "for free." But this no longer leaves a place, in the final accomplishment of the world, for the dungeon of eternal imprisonment and eternal torments, even if it were to coexist alongside the heavenly habitations (such coexistence would amount to the failure of creation for the overwhelming majority, where many would be called but few chosen). About such a world it would be impossible to say that "Wisdom is justified of her works" and that "God will be all in all." Therefore, this is not the ultimate but only the penultimate stage of the world and man. In this stage, Christ, come in glory, still suffers and is crucified in rejected humanity. And the Holy Spirit still experiences a kenosis, though in another sense than before the parousia. God's wisdom and love extend beyond the future age, for ages of ages until the expulsion of the prince of this world. This truth, which is attested to by certain church fathers, is grounded in healthy theology. Otherwise, the idea of eternal hell would forever remain an unbearable burden for man. He can silence in himself this voice of justice and love in the name of obedience to faith, but this obedience is the obedience not of a son but of a slave. He can allow himself to be hypnotized with fear. But there insistently arises the question whether God is pleased by this zeal of Job's friends, God's advocates, who are actually His accusers, for "God hath concluded them all in unbelief that he might have mercy upon all. O the depth of the riches both of the wisdom and knowledge of God!" (Rom. 11:32-33).

This appears to be contradicted by texts that speak of torments "for ever and ever," that is, of their unlimited duration in "bad infinity." On the whole, the Old Testament does not know this idea. Such expressions are especially encountered in the Book of Revelation, with its hyperbolic figures that make no claim to theological precision. Moreover, they refer not so much to persons as to false principles of life: to Babylon, the great whore (Rev. 19:2-3) and to the "beast and false prophet" (20:10), who will be tormented together with the devil in the "lake of fire and brimstone . . . for ever and ever." Without mentioning the figurative character of this expression, which does not admit a literal interpretation, we must remember that the "beast and the false prophet" are not individuals but false principles of life that have power over souls, and the condemnation refers precisely to these principles. This consideration can also be applied to the interpretation of Revelation 14:9-11, which speaks of those who have worshiped the beast and his image, and have received a mark on their forehead or hand: "[they] shall be tormented with fire and brimstone . . . and the smoke of their torment ascendeth up for ever and ever: and they have no rest day nor night." All this also refers, first of all, to the beast and the false prophet, and then to their victims, before whom (Rev. 13:16-17) the falsity of these principles (the totalitarian state, the atheistic civilization) will be exposed. The eternity of condemnation refers to the principles of life themselves, not to their victims. One must also take into account the features of the language of the apocalypses in general. Here, it is appropriate to recall the words of the Savior: "except those days should be shortened, there should no flesh be saved: but for the elect's sake those days shall be shortened" (Matt. 24:22). This refers not only to the flight from Jerusalem but also to the last times of the world, in view of the general doubling of these images of the "Little Apocalypse."

Over many centuries, the conception of the eternity of torments as unchangeable and infinite in duration appeared to offer the most appropriate and effective means to strike the souls of sinners with the fear of God, to conquer their wickedness and spiritual laziness. But at the present time, this pedagogy does not attain its goal. Not terrorization but God's love, manifested even toward those in hell, most effectively touches the soul and awakens it from spiritual sleep. And by no means is it a question of a wicked and craven desire to free oneself from just punishment (which, on the contrary, must be experienced to the end). Rather, it is a question of the impossibility of recognizing "eternal torments" as compatible with God's justice and love, of the inability of the human consciousness even to entertain this notion. The means of pedagogy are changeable and relative, but the pedagogy of St. Gregory of Nyssa and his followers, which has not been condemned and which, in any case, is permitted by the Church, is, even today, more appropriate and more convincing than the pedagogy of terrorization. To be sure, "the fear of the Lord is the beginning of wisdom" (Ps. 111:10; Prov. 1:7), but not its end, for "there is no fear in love, but perfect love casteth out fear" (1 John 4:18), and "herein is our love made perfect, that we may have boldness in the day of judgment" (v. 17). It was love, not fear, that engendered the prayer of the early Christians: "Even so, come, Lord Jesus." At the present time this prayer has grown silent in hearts overwhelmed by fear, but it must radiantly sound again to call for His coming. Over many centuries, this prayer has been growing fainter, and is now almost completely silent. Liturgically, its place has gradually been taken by images of terrorization which express only one side of the parousia and are completely silent about the other side: "look up, and lift up your heads, for your redemption draweth nigh" (Luke 21:28). Of the two sides of the parousia, fear and joy, only fear remains. The time of the manifestation of joy is approaching, this joy which distinguished primitive Christianity.

If the eternity of eternal torments does not exclude but rather presupposes the indefinite, even infinite, duration of time, it thereby also implies a just as indefinite and unlimited changeability, which makes every particular experiencing of eternal torments, as well as of eternal bliss, change with time. Otherwise, this experiencing could not be conceived as occurring in time. The entire vehemence of the champions of the eternity of torments is associated with the assertion that these torments are unchangeable. But this unchangeability is unacceptable, for it contradicts the actual nature of the creaturely spirit. If one excludes this unchangeability, which is proper only to divine eternity, one must inevitably recognize that the state of the tormented ones changes continuously. Revelation is silent about this change, but this does not mean that it does not exist. Revelation does provide an indication of *qualitative* thresholds of time and of their multiple character: Scripture speaks not only of the past, present, or future age, but also of ages, and even of *ages of ages,* that is, of multiple, innumerable stages of time. It would be an exegetical violence done to the text to see in this only a hyperbolic expression, an *epitheton ornans* (with the exception of individual cases, when precisely such a meaning is clear from the context). Such violence must be specially justified in every individual case, but in certain cases it is completely inadmissible.

Thus, the life of the future age, Christ's "reign without end," is not only of indefinite duration but also consists of different periods, or cycles, different "ages" marked by the growth of life. According to the erroneous conception of eternity that transforms it into a passive immobility, "eternal life" is a sort of sclerosis of human activity, where human beings lose what had belonged to them from their creation and had been unfolding in their earthly life: their *creative* principle. But it is clear that such a diminution of human beings does not correspond to the fullness of the divine image that shines in them. The life of the human spirit is creative activity, and every self-determination and state of the human spirit is a free creative act, even in hell. Glorified and rendered incorruptible, human nature does not lose this its humanity nor the creative growth that is proper to it. Even the reception of edenic bliss, the joy of communion with God, is, from the human side, a creative act of ascent from glory to glory.

The dogma of two harmonious wills in the God-man is expressed in "eternal life" as well, namely, in man's synergistic, free and creative deification. Freedom of choice between different possibilities ceases to exist in the future age, but freedom as creative power, as a free reception of the divine gifts of grace, remains intact. Man receives these gifts not passively but creatively. Heavenly bliss includes human creative activity, in knowing and doing, where not only personal gifts ("talents") but also the universal humanity, the Church, will be manifested.

> Behold, the tabernacle of God is with men, and he will dwell with them, and they shall be his people, and God himself shall be with them, and be their God. . . . And he that sat upon the throne said . . . I

will give unto him that is athirst of the fountain of the water of life freely. He that overcometh shall inherit all things; and I will be his God, and he shall be my son. (Rev. 21:3, 5, 6-7)

On the "sabbath" of the people of God, "God shall wipe away all tears from their eyes; and there shall be no more death" (Rev. 21:4), "and there shall be no more curse: but the throne of God and of the Lamb shall be in it; and his servants shall serve him: and they shall see his face; and his name shall be in their foreheads" (22:3-4). "And the Spirit and the bride say, Come. . . . And let him that is athirst come. And whosoever will, let him take the water of life freely" (v. 17). These figures express the synergistic character of the bliss of the future age, where the one athirst is called not only to receive but also to *take* as a "gift" (of grace) from the "fountain of the water of life."

This promise contains in a hidden manner yet another feature. Justification and condemnation, heaven and hell, cannot be considered utterly distinct and mutually exclusive states, since there are no perfectly sinless people. Those who are justified are not without contamination by sin and bear the sorrowful memory of sin even after resurrection, inasmuch as they too *freely* receive from the source of the water of life, by the mercy of God. They are saved, but they fully expiate this sinfulness, and the suffering caused by it is annulled only by a special act of God's grace: "And God shall wipe away all tears from their eyes, and there shall be no more death, neither sorrow, nor crying, neither shall there be any more pain, for the former things are passed away" (Rev. 21:4). However, this gift of divine mercy presupposes that it be received actively, that a creative effort of the human spirit go out to meet it. Inadmissible is the idea of the automatic, or mechanical, reception of this gift, where the spirit is completely passive and lacks the intensity appropriate to it. And that which the prophet's figures symbolize as an instantaneous accomplishment, as a single act, extends over "ages of ages."

But this possibility and even necessity of experiencing hell's dark reflections to the end, even in the heavenly state, in the city of God, is connected with a more general and fundamental question: the question of the *bringing of souls out of hell* through the inner experiencing of hell to the end. "Bring my soul out of prison, that I may praise thy name: the righteous shall compass me about, for thou shalt deal bountifully with me" (Ps. 142:7). That which is possible in the *small,* namely, the experiencing of hell to the end even in the heavenly habitations, is possible also in the *large,* that is, in the state where the torments of hell predominate. If no one is

497

perfectly righteous, there are also no perfect sinners, sinners in whom the power of the sophianic image of God is totally annulled and who are completely incapable of good. A more general question arises: Is the state of hell accessible to the action of God's grace? Can God's grace pass through the gates of hell? According to Scripture this is possible at least before the Last Judgment. Christ's preaching in sheol was addressed not only to the righteous but also to those who were "disobedient, when once the long-suffering of God waited" (1 Pet. 3:20). It is also impossible to exclude the action of the Holy Spirit in the entire subheavenly sphere, even in hell. The image of God in man, God's glory, illumines man in the coming of Christ from the "God of all grace, who hath called us unto his eternal glory by Christ Jesus" (1 Pet. 5:10). Before the name of Jesus shall bend "every knee . . . of things in heaven, and things in earth, and things under the earth," and "every tongue [shall] confess that Jesus Christ is Lord, to the glory of God the Father" (Phil. 2:10, 11). The mercy of the Mother of God, the Spirit-Bearer, makes even the sinners in hell accessible to the action of the Holy Spirit.

In other words, hell's torments of love necessarily contain the regenerating power of the expiation of sin by the experiencing of it to the end. However, this creative experiencing is not only a passive state, in chains imposed from outside. It is also an inwardly, synergistically accepted spiritual state (and also a psychic-corporeal state). This state is appropriately perceived not as a juridical punishment but as an effect of God's justice, which is revealed in its inner persuasiveness. And its acceptance as a just judgment corresponds to an inner movement of the spirit, to a creative determination of the life of the spirit. And in its duration ("in the ages of ages"), this life contains the possibility of a creative suffering that heals, of a movement of the spirit from within toward good in its triumphant force and persuasiveness. Therefore, it is necessary to stop thinking of hell in terms of static and inert immobility, but instead to associate it with the dynamics of life, always creative and growing. Even in hell, the nature of the spirit remains unchanging in its creative changeability. Therefore, the state of hell must be understood as an unceasing creative activity, or more precisely, self-creative activity, of the soul, although this state bears within itself a disastrous split, an alienation from its prototype. All the same, the apostle Paul defines this state as a *salvation*, yet as by fire, after the man's work is burned. It is his nakedness.

Such a state is as unnatural for man as the torments of hell. The glory of the proto-image, given to man as the foundation of his being, turns out to be inaccessible to him, is an unattainable object of hunger and thirst. But if the hunger and thirst for justice that one experiences in this age will be sated in the future age, will this not also extend to all human beings in the ages of ages? Creative human effort will be needed to livingly overcome human perversion and the emptiness of hell by experiencing them to the end. This overcoming will be aided by the Church, thanks to the prayer of all glorified humanity, which in its bliss has not lost the most precious property of the image of God: compassion, that is to say, love.

Different are the degrees of hell's torments, and different are the ways in which they are experienced: "That servant, which knew his lord's will, and prepared not himself, neither did according to his will, shall be beaten with many stripes. But he that knew not, and did commit things worthy of stripes, shall be beaten with few stripes. For unto whomsoever much is given, of him shall be much required; and to whom men have committed much, of him they will ask the more" (Luke 12:47-48). In the parable of the talents, this notion that there should be a conformity between requirements and gifts (talents) is expressed even more severely: "Take therefore the talent from him, and give it unto him which hath ten talents, for unto every one that hath shall be given, and he shall have abundance; but from him that hath not shall be taken away even that which he hath. And cast ye the unprofitable servant into outer darkness: there shall be weeping and gnashing of teeth" (Matt. 25:28-30). These texts reveal to some extent the mystery of the judgment, which requires from all human beings that they do their duty. A duty not done is done by others, and one who has not done his duty is deprived of his gift and cast into outer darkness. He must then overcome his emptiness by expiating it, by experiencing it to the end. But this is only the beginning, the initial determination of his destiny and path, not the end. The weeping and gnashing of teeth in the outer darkness nonetheless bears witness to the life of a spirit that has come to know the entire measure of its fall and that is tormented by repentance. But, like all repentance, these torments are salvific for the spirit. And who can affirm that the breath of the Spirit of God will not come in response to these torments?

One of the dogmatic presuppositions of the doctrine of eternal torments understood as unchangeable and infinite is the assertion that repentance is impossible in the afterlife as well as after the Last Judgment. But this impossibility is clearly contradicted by the efficacy of prayers for the deceased; nor does it have a biblical justification. For the *reception* of the assistance of prayer presupposes that the souls of the deceased actively receive this prayer, in accordance with the general reality of the energy of the spirit, which is characterized by an uninterrupted continuation of life and new self-determinations that arise thence.

It is true that, in the afterlife, human beings lose the capacity for action of the earthly type, which includes the participation of the soul and the body (*opera meritoria,* according to the Catholic doctrine) and direct participation in the making of history. But the disincarnation in death does not suppress the activity of the spirit. This is clear from the fact that saints participate with their prayers in the life of the world and in human history, as revelation shows (Rev. 7:9-17; 8:1-4; 14:1-4; 15:1-4; 20:4-6) and the Church believes. This activity of the spirit can also be concentrated upon repentance in the afterlife, which is facilitated by the prayers of the Church without the possibility of being concretely realized in earthly life. Nevertheless, the afterlife is a continuation of earthly life.

Thus, the Last Judgment does not put an end to the changeability of creaturely being. Nor does it replace the temporality of this being by static divine eternity. Rather, the Last Judgment marks the beginning of a new time, of new ages, of a new becoming. This separation between heaven and hell corresponds to the different qualitative states of individuals, with the *prevalence* in them of different principles, in all the diversity of their combinations. However, one should not see them as two distinct *places.* And if one nevertheless applies the term "place" to conditions of life homogeneous in character, one must speak of a multiplicity of such places, which, however, pass into one another or replace one another.[67] Heaven and hell are therefore abstractions to a certain degree. Let us not forget that, besides the sharp distinction between light and darkness, heaven and hell, there exists a series of indeterminate intermediate states corresponding to the state of the souls of children (the "limbos" of Catholicism), of pagans uninitiated into Christianity, and, in general, of non-Christians, the mentally ill, severely retarded, and so forth. Truly, "in my Father's house are many mansions." And not less important is the fact that this is not a static but a fluid multiplicity, with transitions from one state to another.

The essential question remains: Is the eternity of hell preserved in this unchangeability, or is hell dissolved in the ages of ages? Opinions about this differ. On the one hand, there is the doctrine of St. Gregory of Nyssa and his followers, who are not so few as might appear; on the other hand, there is the overwhelming majority of his opponents. In our view,

---

67. Quite expressive in this regard are ancient pictures of the Last Judgment which portray a poor soul waiting in trepidation to be sentenced and not knowing himself as it were — this living possibility of heaven and hell, with all the transitions between them.

the eternalization of hell would signify that the Divine Sophia, the ground of creation, is powerless to overcome the inertia, infirmity, and antagonism of creation. It would also signify either that good has a vindictive character or that evil is equal to good in power.

It is a bizarre conception of the parousia to limit its power to a judgment whereby heaven and hell are separated and hell is eternalized. What virtue and justification would the parousia have if part of humanity turns out to be unprepared for it? In that case, the parousia would not attain its goal, or it would even attain the opposite: the establishment of an eternal hell. But does this justify the parousia? A separation can be accepted only if, in the final analysis, it nonetheless attains the goal of the universal salvation or the sophianization of creation. Otherwise, creation would appear to be an error or failure, since it would end with the eternity of hell, even if this were accompanied by the eternity of heaven. An eternal separation of humanity into the elect and the reprobate is clearly not the *final* meaning of creation. One must therefore suppose that this separation has an inner proportionality of grace that assures a positive final sum of all the pluses and minuses of history, a universal harmony, total and beautiful. In other words, the judgment that separates the sheep from the goats and good from evil, both in humankind in its entirety and in individual hearts, is not the definitive conclusion of eschatology. It is only the first event of eschatology, the beginning, not the end. Both the judgment and the separation must be understood not as a static unchangeability but as a dynamic striving beyond their limits, on the pathways to universal deification or salvation. Only deification is capable of justifying creation. It is the only theodicy.

But the main misunderstanding that persists in eschatological debates has to do with the conception of eternity in relation to temporality. It is true that both the torments of sinners and the bliss of the righteous are eternal in a certain sense, since both are caused by life in God, by the presence before His face, in the light of divine love, gladdening or burning. But it is also true that both belong to creaturely temporality, which presupposes changeability and becoming. Therefore, the essence of the question is by no means grasped through the opposition of temporality and eternity as mutually exclusive things. On the contrary, only their appropriate combination corresponds to the correct statement of the question, not as "either/or" but as "both-and." Both torments and bliss are eternal and temporal at the same time, eternal in one sense and temporal in another.

There remains yet one more question concerning sinners: What is their relation to the fallen spirits? Here, we are guided by Christ's condemnation: "Depart from me, ye cursed, into everlasting fire, prepared for the devil and his angels" (Matt. 25:41). Are sinners condemned here to a compulsory commerce with demons, a commerce that would be proper to them in the afterlife? Although that is the most widespread opinion, it encounters many difficulties. First of all, does this mean that sinners are deprived of the glory of incorruptibility that is proper to resurrection? The partisans of this theory hold that the resurrected bodies of sinners are entirely deprived of a radiant image, are dark and monstrous, and destined for direct commerce with demons. But nothing directly supports such an opinion. The "everlasting fire, prepared for the devil and his angels," is a *state* of sinners that has the character of the torments of hell that the demons are also subject to. But this does not mean that demons will be given access to the kingdom of glory, to the kingdom of God, and that humankind will remain subject to their attacks in this kingdom. On the contrary, the judgment and the last separation presuppose the liberation of the world from demonic coercion and perversion, according to the Lord's clear testimony: "Now shall the prince of this world be cast out" (John 12:31); "the prince of this world is judged" (16:11). First, the great dragon, the ancient serpent, was cast down from heaven and came down in great fury to those living on the earth and on the sea. He was bound and cast into a bottomless pit for the "thousand years" of Christ's reign (Rev. 12:9-12). He was then "loosed a little season" (20:1-7) until the moment of his final expulsion from the world. What does this expulsion mean? How and into what place is the prince of this world expelled?

This expulsion cannot signify that a considerable part of creation has come under the power of the devil, has entered his domain, as would follow from the theory of the partisans of infinite torments. For them, such a domain would be the kingdom of hell. But this would be equivalent to the establishment of hell as the kingdom of the devil parallel to the kingdom of God, or heaven. Recognizing the eternity of hell as the kingdom of Satan would be tantamount to submerging hell in its own element (Swedenborg's idea) and eternalizing it in this element. But that, by definition, would be directly contrary to expulsion.

True, a certain difficulty arises in the exegesis of Matthew 25:41. What does the "preparation" of the "everlasting fire" for the devil and his angels mean? We must completely exclude the conception of hell and the fire of hell as a *place* for the habitation of demons. The eternal fire is not some place in creation but only a *state* of a certain part of creation, a state reserved for human beings, although they share it with demons. However, this state of hell is that of human beings who have a place *in the world,* whereas the prince of this world will be expelled precisely from it. Therefore, the characterization of eternal fire as "prepared" for the devil *after* his expulsion from the world is only an analogy with the state of the fallen spirits. It is not identical with their state.

The judgment pronounced on human beings consists in the separation of the wheat from the tares, with the "burning" of the latter, that is, with the exposure of all the illusoriness, nothingness, and falsity of the kingdom of sin and evil. Whence the excruciating state of nakedness, emptiness, and unfulfilled love. The fire of hell is a state of creation, one that is connected with resurrection. For this reason alone, it cannot be fully equated with the state of the fallen angels; it can only be compared with this state. Thus, the general conclusion that sinners in hell will also be tormented by commerce with evil spirits applies only to their afterlife state *before* resurrection, not after it, when Satan will be expelled from the world and activity there will have ceased.

This consideration is important for humanity that is resurrected beneath a new heaven and on a new earth, where truth lives and demons lose their poisonousness and power; it is important for the spirits of evil themselves. The expulsion of the prince of the world by the manifestation of God's glory in the parousia signifies the definitive victory of good. The expiation of sin and evil through their experiencing to the end that is accomplished in the torments of hell, for all human beings to the extent of their participation in sin, and especially for the most hardened sinners, has significance for their healing and for their positive assimilation of the principles of heavenly being. This experiencing leads to final stability in goodness, where all return to evil is overcome.

The arrival of Christ's thousand-year reign at the first resurrection (however this is to be understand) is connected with the thousand-year enchainment of Satan and therefore, in some sense, with his temporary expulsion from the world. How can one understand this enchainment of Satan that precedes the establishment of Christ's thousand-year reign with His saints? It clearly anticipates the definitive expulsion of the prince of this world. This first expulsion does not have the finality of the definitive expulsion that signifies the total separation of good from evil with the condemnation of the latter; and in general, it is not connected with judgment. It is, however, a question of a certain paralysis of evil, with a corresponding strengthening of good on the earth; a grace-bestowing change is produced in the entire spiritual atmosphere. In this respect, the first resurrection is already a sort of anticipation of the parousia; it is the first approach of the Coming Christ and precursory tidings of the expulsion of the prince of this world. We do not have the data for a more precise definition of the power of this event, which is represented in the symbolic images of the Apocalypse and refers to the spiritual world. But this thousand-year cosmic exorcism already signals Christ's victory and the approach of His reign. *A fortiori,* the arrival of this reign, which "will have no end," implies the expulsion of the sources of evil from the world. In themselves, evil human beings (and one cannot emphasize this strongly enough) represent a mixture of good and evil, heaven and hell, incorruptibility and corruption in a living ontological conjugacy, and therefore they are incapable of total satanization and identification with the devil.

It is true that Revelation 19:20 and 20:10 seem to contradict this: "And the beast was taken, and with him the false prophet that wrought miracles before him . . . both were cast alive into a lake of fire burning with brimstone." Then: "and the devil that deceived them was cast into the lake of fire and brimstone, where the beast and the false prophet are, and shall be tormented day and night for ever and ever." However, for precision of the exegesis one must keep in mind that "the beast and the false prophet" are by no means specific human individuals. Rather, they are false principles of life, which are subject to judgment by fire together with the "father of lies," who begets and inspires them. In general, these passages depict the final events of the universal historical tragedy that precedes the end of the world and the parousia (Rev. 20:11-12). Only after this do the universal resurrection and the judgment follow: "And death and hell delivered up the dead which were in them: and they were judged every man according to their works" (v. 13).

The expulsion of the prince of the world signifies his complete separation from creation, to which he still had access as an angel, though a fallen one. This metaphysical state is described by apocalyptic images borrowed from the physical world, such as the "outer darkness," which is outside of being, or the "lake of fire burning with brimstone" (Rev. 19:20). The angels were created to serve the world, the connection with which is the foundation of their being. The fallen angels abused this service; they made it into an instrument to rule and corrupt the world. Nevertheless, for the fallen angels too the world remains the only possibility of life. When they are "cast out," they are deprived of this foundation, just as they deprived themselves of another foundation of their being: the presence before God's throne and the life in God. The fallen spirits remain in a state of yawning ontological emptiness and darkness, as if in an airless space. True, they preserve the energy of undying life that was given to them by the Creator, but they do not have the possibility of creatively actualizing this life. The expulsion of the demons from the world does not at all mean that they stop being creatures and in *this* sense stop belonging to the world. This would mean that they are doomed to annihilation and will definitively lose their being.

Even in exile, demons remain God's creation and therefore preserve the indestructible power of being implanted in them by God who created them. It is the *content* of their life that disappears: it departs from them in their "eternal" dying. This is a state of absolute rejection, in relation to both God and the world. This state cannot be ontologically commensurate even with the torments of hell, for hell is a human state and never exists in a pure form, totally separated from heaven or from being in general. Rather, it continues to participate in the latter to a certain extent.

What can we, human beings, for whom such a state is ontologically alien, say about it? How can we fathom it? Here, we have *pure evil*, without any mixture, error, misunderstanding, or infirmity, whereas these are elements that are *always* contained in human sin. Here, we also have conscious theomachy, the enmity, envy, and hatred of creation toward its Creator. There is no place here for doubt, God-seeking, or error. "The devils . . . believe and tremble" (James 2:19) — not out of love, however, but out of fear, hatred, and malice. Here, the state of the prince of this world and of his kingdom is still immeasurably weighed down by all the evil caused by him in the world, the chief of the evils being the murder at Golgotha. If the Lord lifted upon Himself the sin of the world in order to redeem the world, it is precisely this sin that weighs down the fallen spirits, which they themselves provoked by seducing creation. Human language has no words and human nature has no feelings to express this degree of fallenness and alienation from God.

However, in the deep past, Origen and St. Gregory of Nyssa asked whether redemption extends to demons. We cannot give a negative answer to this question, because that would be to limit divine love and the power of redemption, which have no limits. Nevertheless, to answer in the affirmative, it would be necessary that this limit not be set and asserted by rebellious creation itself, by demonic revolt, but that it be abolished "synergistically" in creation. If, in general, sin has its source in creaturely freedom, then in man this freedom is complicated by a series of factors related to his limitedness, infirmity, and misunderstanding. But there is no place for misunderstandings in the spiritual world, and evil will manifests itself there in a pure state: This will is ready there to engage in an unlimited creative activity of evil, which is dreamt of by the partisans of the eternal torments of hell, although they do not think it through to the end. The very possibility of such a creative activity of evil has been abolished by the "casting out" of the prince of this world. This "casting out" also eliminates the possibility of "eternal torments," that is, the unending, inexhaustible creative activity of evil for demons. Instead, one finds enthroned here the emptiness of nonbeing, a total contentlessness of life, a self-devouring subjectivism. This is not death in the sense of annihilation. Rather, it is life that consists of spiritual dying.

The question of the final destiny of Satan becomes exceptionally acute in the problem of theodicy, the justification of God in creation. Origen and especially St. Gregory of Nyssa posed this question in their theology. Here, it is a question of whether evil is invincible in creation. It might appear that, even though God condemned Satan to expulsion from the world, He could not, or did not want to, create a world that is free of evil, but rather one that defeats it even if only in the end, so that it therefore forever remains the outer boundary of the world, as it were. Translated into the language of cosmology, this question signifies: After repenting, will Satan with his kingdom be "saved" after passing through an inconceivably long period of "eternal fire, prepared for the devil and his angels"? Or is such a possibility completely excluded by the nature of things or by the will of God?

Penal-law eschatology is, of course, more insufficient here than anywhere else. For this eschatology, "eternal torments" correspond to the application of the pertinent article of a penal code in virtue of a sentence rendered unilaterally by a tribunal, which excludes in advance all possibility of healing, forgiveness, or restoration. To justify such a conception, it is necessary to demonstrate the impossibility of the salvation or repentance of demons. But we must not forget that the fall of the demons and their abiding in evil, that all the creative activity of evil in the kingdom of the prince of this world, are manifestations of creaturely *freedom in its pure form,* with evil as the objective. The fall of Lucifer and of his angels was a fully conscious act, an act of freedom uncomplicated by any misunderstanding, of freedom that is absolute arbitrariness in the sense of the absence of any possible motivation for it. This freedom is self-willfulness taken to its ultimate extreme and therefore total insanity. It cannot be explained, justified, or even rationally understood. This freedom, in which creatureliness asserts itself as supreme and unique absoluteness, already includes this element of ontological insanity; at the same time it is a pose, emptiness that pretends to be fullness.

For a time this freedom camouflages itself as the rapine of the kingdom of this world by leading the rebellious creaturely selfhood in active battle against the Creator. But this freedom of rebellious self-willfulness cannot be rooted in itself, because, in itself, it is nonetheless emptiness, a minus of being, a force of repulsion, acquiring through this a sort of illusory reality of being. In this sense, this freedom is an ontological illusion that is not yet conscious of itself. One can set forth the paradoxical thesis that Satan exists only because God, his Creator, exists. Hating Him, Satan would like to consider Him as not existing in order to have his own being wholly in himself. But at the same time he cannot get away from God's being and cannot do without it, for it is the only objectivity in his subjective world. To exist, the satanical *I* needs to oppose itself to divine being. It is, as it were, the black shadow of divine being in the world. But this powerlessness to be in himself begets the cold fire of hatred and, as a negative expression of the law of love, it produces an ontological perversion.

God is love. He is love in Himself and in creation, which breathes by this power of love. In the spiritual world, this law of being is incomparably more transparent and more evident than in the human world. But creaturely love in creaturely limitedness, which is also creaturely freedom, also contains the possibility of unlove, which is the true source of satanism. Unlove, envy, hatred, all this is a cold flame, but one that is nonetheless lit from that one divine Love which is the sun of the world. But love is free, and God does not desire compulsion in love; He desires only persuasion. And He created free beings not as things but as self-determining personal centers. And the most profound self-determination to evil that has ever occurred occurred in Satan, and extended to his angels.

If that is the essence of satanism, if this essence is rooted in creaturely freedom, then it is the latter that determines the possibility or impossibility of the "salvation" of Satan, of his spiritual healing. Insofar as unlimited freedom is without bottom or support, satanism is the infinite rebellion of malice and hatred. The pseudo-creative activity of evil is rooted in this emptiness, which determines the *pose* of the "prince of this world," who pretends to be the absolute center of creation. For a time there exists the possibility of such an illusion here and even a place for the authentic creative activity of evil, as long as the kingdom of this world exists. The world here is in some sense stolen from God, who permits this on the pathways of creaturely freedom. But this trial of freedom has its limit; it can and will be experienced to the end. And the end of the trial will come by the power of God, in the parousia, when Satan, *despite* his solipsistic affirmation, will be expelled from this world, will remain void of being, in the pose of a metaphysical charlatan, no longer deceiving anyone, not even himself. Satan will not stop being a creature of God, for, outside of this, only annihilation would await him. But God does not annihilate His creatures. With hatred and against his will, Satan knows that he is a creature of God, but he does not find joy in this, for he hates God precisely owing to this consciousness of his creatureliness. This consciousness of self is for him the primal source of the burning in hell, of the hatred of God as the source of life, of ontological envy.

But after the expulsion of the prince of this world, Satan's duel with God begins. Can we, human beings, know anything about this duel?

As regards freedom that is understood as pure I-ness, self-determination from oneself, negative willfulness and autonomy that finds all givenness repellant, there is a radical difference between the spiritual world, that of the holy angels and of the fallen spirits, and the human world. It is not given to human beings to know freedom as negative willfulness and autonomy in the relatively pure form in which it is known by the spiritual world. This is because, in practice, in concrete life, human freedom is inextricably intergrown with its natural givenness, namely, with all of human nature that is connected with and immersed in the world, and with all the co-humanity of humankind that is present in every human individual. Modal human freedom, the individual *how*, therefore manifests itself only in the complex of the givenness. Therefore, the pretension to absolute pre-creaturely or extra-creaturely freedom as the arbitrariness of absolute creativity is, in general, a Luciferian pose, which imitates the fleshless spirits. All this is a kind of imaginary number, a pure negativity of abstraction.

By contrast, this freedom of arbitrariness can be realized to a greater extent by the fallen spirits, who do not have in themselves the given of the world as their own given, who, at the same time, have cast themselves out of divine life by a free act, and who, finally, do not have a generic life (for the angelic choir does not form an angelkind). But, in its pure negativity and emptiness, this freedom, in seeking a content for itself, involuntarily slides down into a domain inferior for spirits: that of natural being. The fallen spirits become *demons,* and Lucifer becomes *Satan,* parasite of the human world, draped in the toga of the "prince of this world."

Therefore, it is a certain progress in self-consciousness, a kind of regeneration, if, after the expulsion of Satan from the world, the fallen spirits stop being demons in fact and, expelled from the world, return to their original spirituality. Torn away from the world, they are condemned to carry out to the end their experiment of absolute freedom as self-godhood and arbitrariness, to plumb the illusory depths of this freedom, to assert themselves outside of any connection with being, divine or creaturely. And here it is revealed that freedom as absolute arbitrariness is nothing but emptiness, a minus of being, a bottomless boredom whose only positive content is the rebellion against God.

But this pseudo-freedom turns out to be a life in God and for God (even if a negative life), as well as a negative life in the world and for the world, in envy and malice. Satanism is clearly exposed as a zero exalting itself above all being, especially divine being, while existing only by virtue of this being. Freedom as a supramundane and self-subsistent being, as a being alongside and on an equal footing with God, is a pure illusion. It is a shadow of being cast *post factum* of its appearance, though it proclaims itself as existing *ante factum*. It is a kind of "transcendental illusion," a reified fantasy, a supra-reality. Let us recognize, however, that freedom as arbitrariness is realized in the world of the fallen spirits much more fully than in any form of creaturely being that is inseparably linked with the given of the world or of human beings. However, for Satan and his kingdom, which is without any relation, direct or indirect, to this given, an evil eternity of emptiness, the ontological convulsion of the latter, begins. This contentless *not* in relation to the all is asserted as absolute content. It is an eternity, or absoluteness, turned inside out.

How can this emptiness that is left by the "casting out" be filled? How can this spasm accompanied by a pose be resolved? Can this caprice of self-willfulness find in itself a positive power, and how? For if this caprice is suspended in emptiness, can the latter be infinite and (if only in this sense) eternal? The nature of the creaturely spirit is characterized by creative activity, which is its life — as self-creative activity. As long as Satan was the "prince of this world," of God's creation that he had stolen, he was characterized by a parasitical pseudo-creative activity of evil, whose material and content, whose given, taken from the world, were "stolen goods" from the ontological point of view. But when, in the parousia, God takes possession of the world and Satan is expelled from the latter, he will be compelled to see that he is nothing, that his pseudo-creative activity has no content and creates nothing. Can the life of the spirit ground itself in such emptiness except by a gyration in eternal repetition? Can even creaturely freedom be realized in such objectless emptiness? But such a possibility would signify a subject without object or nature, a life without the content of life, the burning fire of the thirst for life without any satisfaction, an absolute dead end. Such is satanical eternity. When freedom is arbitrary and irrational, it contains all possibilities, in particular the bad infinity of satanism as the only stable existence of the now-powerless anti-god.

509

But another thing is much more important: Is there another possibility here, the possibility of Satan's returning to the path of true freedom, prescribed for creation, where, disenchanted in his satanical path of rebellion, he would abandon this stage-prop of a throne of selfhood? This would already be the beginning of Satan's repentance, of his turning to God. It is impossible for human experience to measure the ages of ages of torments of hell necessary to exhaust satanical selfhood and malice. Nevertheless, there is a basis for such a conversion in Satan's nature, for he too is a creature of God and does not stop being such. He continues to possess the energy of reality, which cannot be supplanted or annihilated by the selfhood's arbitrariness. The infinite number of circles of eternal self-repetition in emptiness that constitute the life of Satan after his expulsion from the world include an equally infinite number of repetitions of the consciousness of his createdness, which is his participation in being, whose force is divine being.

Such a self-accusation, such a condemnation of satanism by Satan himself, is capable of producing a crack in the insanity of his selfhood, of planting a doubt in him, a doubt which is already the beginning of a new consciousness of self. Of course, on these pathways he will encounter new satanical torments of pride: the fallen first angel will fight to retain his imaginary primacy in being, to defend his metaphysical self-love. But this self-love begins to doubt itself. Rays of the light of positive being pierce its cast-iron armor, and self-verification begins in the depths of total self-assertion. Once it has begun, this verification cannot stop. It is the first step on the path of return to positive being, on the path to overcoming metaphysical selfhood, which is the real reason for Satan's expulsion, a subjective possibility that has become an objective fact. This overcoming of selfhood can be accomplished only thanks to God's mercy, full of lovingkindness and salvific, suffering long and pitying without end.

In connection with this, we must ask to what extent the power of incorruptibility, after the resurrection and the transfiguration of the world, applies to the angelic world, and if it also applies to the fallen spirits. It does apply to the holy angels, though only indirectly. In their presence before God's throne, they are already illuminated by His glory, which they accompany in the parousia too: "The Son of man shall come in his glory, and all the holy angels with him" (Matt. 25:31). For the holy angels, the glorification of the world signifies only that it establishes direct communion with glorified humanity in the kingdom of glory. In this reflected fashion the power of redemption extends to them as well: "that in the dispensation of the fulness of times he might gather together in one all

510

things in Christ, both which are in heaven, and which are on earth" (Eph. 1:10).

For the fallen spirits, by contrast, this manifestation of glory signifies precisely the "casting out" of the prince of this world and the destruction of his entire kingdom. The existence of the latter was based precisely on the mixing of good and evil in the world, and only this mixing made the presence and activity of the spirits of evil possible in the world. But the light of the glory dissipates the shadows and penetrates the crevices and abysses. The glorified world becomes inaccessible for demons; it no longer has an ontological place for them, for all has become "good" (Gen. 1:4).

It is erroneous to think that, in the separation of the last judgment, the demons have received a special *place* in the world, even if this is only in "hell" together with the sinners, since hell is not a place but a state of the world, and a subjective one to boot. This state corresponds to the suffering caused by the expiation of sin, whereas genuine, objective being is already clothed in sophianic glory. Hell consists in the subjective experiencing of a lack of glory, though not its total absence, for even those who abide in hell are not deprived of it. Therefore, the "expulsion from the world" throws the demons into a state other than hell, a state of unnatural emptiness and rejection. Upon being created, as angels, they were called to *serve* the world. But, in their fall, they desired to *possess* the world, corrupting it. In their expulsion from the world they remain in emptiness, condemned to sustain themselves in objectless solipsism, in envy and anger. They find themselves turned toward the premundane *nothing*, which does not even exist in a pure form, since it is forever covered by being. And if this demonic situation is also "eternal," a bad eternity because it is bottomless and insatiable, it is nonetheless only a subjective state, in which there is *no* positive power of eternity. This state is grounded only in the arbitrariness of creaturely freedom, with its irrationality. And all the energy of this state consists only in self-immersion, in obstinate concentration on oneself.

But by no means does such a state have a positive foundation in itself for infinity. It is suspended in a void of airless space, where a sort of metaphysical obstinacy makes it move endlessly in a circle. Of course, it is theoretically conceivable that this circular motion, this infernal wheel of existence, will never stop, and that "eternal torments" will continue forever (which will satisfy their apologists). But, this arbitrariness, which by nature is contingent and deprived of ontological basis, has no necessity that could ground its unchangeability. On the contrary, one could say that this arbitrariness is a sort of ontological absurdity and accident: in the presence of divine being and creaturely being, it is an immersion in pure subjectivity, in the emptiness of the givenless, contentless I, by a self-blinding, which has its inspiration not even in atheism or acosmism but in antitheism and anticosmism.

The entire energy of such a state consists in the icy ring of unlove and proud obstinacy that separates the demons from the fullness of being in God and His world. At the same time this subjectivity is an ontological absurdity, for the subject, as pure I, requires a given in order to posit itself owing to the fact that it is created. *I* looks into the mirror of *non-I;* the subject needs a predicate and a copula. To assert one's being only in and by oneself, while denying one's createdness and one's Creator, is, besides the obstinacy of self-willfulness, to exhibit an ontological superficiality that has not yet exhausted itself. In this infinite circular motion, there is not only an eternal self-repetition *(ewige Wiederkehr)* but also a positive process of deepening into self, which brings it to its end: *satanism exhausts itself;* it itself finds its end. Having been cast out of the world, the kingdom of being, satanism arrives, by an effort of its will, at a new self-knowledge; but this conversion is already the beginning of an ontological repentance. And this leads to the possibility of the end of satanism, the terrible judgment with presence before God's face, the immanent punishment of the sin against love, "the eternal fire, prepared for the devil and his angels." But this is also the beginning of a life whose path passes through ages of final restoration, of resurrection from the eternal spiritual death.

This is an ontological postulate, a mystery that is totally unfathomable for us and therefore cannot be discussed further. But, in accordance with this ontological postulate, this pathway can end only with the filling of the void that appeared in heaven as a consequence of the fall, with the return of the fallen angels, the "lost sheep," to the fullness of the kingdom of God, where God is definitively all in all *without any limitation or exception,* and creation is without any failure or even minus: "He shall have put down all rule and all authority and power. For he must reign till he hath put all enemies under his feet" (1 Cor. 15:24-25). Here, our theological contemplation can only follow the path of *postulates,* which become harder to understand in proportion as the mysterious depths of eschatology become opened to us.

However, even the very existence of the problem we are considering must be specially justified. Historically, it is easy here to hide under the authority, if not of Origen (whose opinion was condemned by the emperor Justinian), then at least of St. Gregory of Nyssa, who openly and firmly included the final salvation of the demons in the general idea of the apocatastasis. Nevertheless, it is considered dangerous even to touch upon this question. Indeed, as long as the prince of this world and his armies do battle against Christ and all humankind in this world, a sentimental attitude toward the enemies of the name of Christ would constitute an utterly false pity. The Church severely rejects and condemns such false sentimentality under the pretext of love. The Lord Himself not only chased away demons, forbidding and annulling the works of their malignity, but also addressed the words of His holy indignation to them: "O faithless generation, how long shall I be with you? How long shall I suffer you?" (Mark 9:19; Matt. 17:17; Luke 9:41). The Book of Revelation is full of such holy wrath, which is a manifestation of God's love for creation. And, in general, *before* the expulsion of the prince of this world, during the state of battle with him and his continuing power, there can be no reconciliation with him. It is as if a *limit* to love were erected in the hearts of people and even in the Church itself.

But is this limit absolutely uncrossable? Eschatologically, it is lifted at the end of this age, when Satan is expelled and cast "into the lake of fire and brimstone" (Rev. 20:10). But this signifies only the cessation of this age, the conclusion of the historical and cosmic tragedy (the "beast" and the "false prophet," i.e., human, historical potencies, are cast into the lake of fire with the devil). But are the heart of the Church and her love closed off by this circle of fire? St. Isaac the Syrian, seer of the mysteries of the judgment to come, answers this question in terms that echo his discourse on the scourge of love (see above). He speaks here of the *loving, or pitying, heart:* "This is a blazing up of the human heart *with regard to all creation, with regard to people, birds, animals, demons, and all creatures.* By a great and powerful pity that embraces the heart, by a great patience, the human heart becomes a loving or pitying one, and it cannot tolerate or hear or see any harm or any small pain endured by creatures. And also for wordless beings, and for enemies of truth, and for those who do him harm, such a one continuously prays with tears that they be safeguarded and that mercy be granted to them. And for creatures that creep upon the earth he prays with great compassion, which is excited in his heart without measure until there is a likening in this to God."[68]

In St. Isaac's words one hears the voice of ecclesial love itself. That which is the dilettantism or even the sinful sentimentalism of spiritual mediocrity is, at the summits of the spirit, the movement of the loving, or pitying, heart, in the image of the long-suffering and infinitely merciful

---

68. *Ascetic Discourses*, op. cit., 253-54.

Lord. Cast out of the world and having lost all ground of being, Satan, with his angels, is not only insane but also pitiful in his unmasked pretension, in his stupid pose. The ancient serpent, "more subtle than any beast of the field" (Gen. 3:1), turns out to be insane and pitiful in his delusion of grandeur. His being is hallucination and delirium.

These scant but golden words about the *loving, or pitying, heart* contain a series of theological indications in different directions. They refer, first of all, to the final separation of hell and heaven, of the righteous and sinners. The conclusion that is drawn from what is usually said about this separation is that, in the ages of ages, sinners are rejected and separated from the righteous. But the true meaning of this idea must be determined by placing it in the context of the *entire* Christian teaching. We have already seen that a literal and unqualified interpretation of this idea nullifies the unity of humankind assumed by the Lord as the Body of Christ. To consider, as is usually done, that, having entered paradise, the righteous completely forget about the condemned sinners and are separated from them by the ice wall of this forgetting — is to completely contradict the Church's entire teaching on salvation and redemption. In itself, such a forgetting would be the greatest of sins, capable of leading to the perdition of those guilty of it even after justification at the Last Judgment. This sin would consist precisely in that for which the sinners were rejected: the absence of love for suffering humankind and, in this humankind, for the suffering Christ.

Humankind in its entirety is Christ's, for it has entirely been assumed into His Divine-Humanity. And if Christ suffers for and in humankind *before* the judgment, is it possible to think that He stops suffering *after* the judgment in relation to the lost drachma, the lost sheep: "If a man have an hundred sheep, and one of them be gone astray, doth he not leave the ninety and nine, and goeth into the mountains, and seeketh that which is gone astray?" (Matt. 18:12)? Redemption is conceived as the acceptance and compassionate experiencing to the end of the sins of the entire world, and this suffering of the Lord "for all people and for all things" (as the anaphora says), the redemptive sacrifice brought on Golgotha, extends to all times, as long as this sin and this suffering remain. The Lord does not deprive sinners of His redemptive love. He suffers with them and for them in this redemption that *continues* because of the existence of hell. The angry words of God's justice addressed to sinners, "depart from me, ye cursed, into everlasting fire" (Matt. 25:41), are said, nonetheless, by the Savior. They are words of love, punishing but not expelling even sinners from His humankind, for "it is not the will of your Father which is in heaven that one of these little ones should perish" (Matt. 18:14). Even those banished by Christ remain in His love, are embraced by His universal redemptive sacrifice.[69]

And since redemption is accomplished not only by the sacrifice of the Son sent by the Father, but also by the Holy Spirit, healing the sores of creation, the Holy Spirit continues its work of healing and restoration as long as that which is unhealed and unrestored remains. And the Holy Spirit can penetrate even the doors of hell.

The heart of the Mother of God, the Spirit-Bearer, is pierced by the sword of hell because of Her compassionate love; and Her maternal intercession is effected starting with the Dread Judgment, which is the beginning, not the end, of the judgment. And the "Mother of God's way of sorrows," revealed to the vision of the Russian people, continues. Just as Christ's love extends also to the damned and rejected (more precisely, to those who have damned and rejected themselves), so the maternal love does not cease either, which perhaps tries even harder for them and feels an even greater compassion for them, for it is love that damns and rejects them. There can be no final rejection of creation by God's love, just as there can be no final abandonment of creation by the "pitying heart" of the Church's love.

Let us remember, first of all, that the Church is not divided into two parts and that some completely dead part is not cut away from her. The separation of the sheep from the goats, with their final destinies, is a figure that refers not to individual persons or groups of persons but, above all, to their inner state. The possibility of hell and heaven is present in every soul, although to different degrees. This is a horizontal division, which passes through *all* humankind, not a vertical one, which would separate it into two mutually impenetrable parts. For the righteous, that which is "damned" is absorbed and made powerless by that which is "blessed." But, in the darkness of damnation, sinners only see reflections of blessedness cast into the night.

Therefore, the idea of two humankinds, divided and separated from each other at the Last Judgment, does not correspond to the fullness and connectedness of reality. Humankind is one. It is one in Adam and one in Christ, one in his Body, in the Church: "so we, being many, are one body in

---

69. In *The Comforter* I have already touched upon the question of the eternity of the Eucharist in the future age as well. The Eucharist signifies the accomplished Divine-humanity, the life of creation in God, but for those cast out "for ages of ages" the Eucharist is also a redemptive sacrifice, for as long as this reprobation continues.

Christ, and every one members one of another" (Rom. 12:5). This unity is expressed in love. "Whether one member suffer, all the members suffer with it; or one member be honoured, all the members rejoice with it" (1 Cor. 12:26), "for we are members one of another" (Eph. 4:25), "members of his body, of his flesh, and of his bones" (5:30). Can it be that this law of love will lose its power after the Last Judgment? Can it be that not only the sickness but even the spiritual death of many members will cease to provoke the compassion of active, praying love on the part of the healthy members? No! is the answer that must follow from a clear statement of the question. In that sense in which one can speak of them, the torments of hell inevitably extend not only to those who are condemned but also to the entire Church, to all humankind.

We can forget that all are saved with all, just as all are condemned with all and all are responsible for all, only if we understand eschatology exclusively from the criminal-law point of view, and *especially* if we understand salvation individualistically (if not egotistically). Is it possible to accept that the righteous are capable of forgetting their rejected brothers, of being indifferent to them? Do not Moses and the apostle Paul offer a model of love when they declare themselves ready to be rejected for the sins of their people, together with their people? Such a forgetting, if it could occur at all, would be sufficient to sentence the righteous themselves to the torments of hell for the great sin against love. How could a mother remain indifferent to the perdition of her son or a son remain indifferent to the fate of his mother? Can the diverse personal ties of love that connect humankind be frayed to the point where our very memories of one another are lost? Such a picture of mutual annihilationism in love is a terrible nightmare, a blasphemous slander against the God of love and the Church. On the contrary, the existence of a hell with eternal torments affects all humankind, the whole body of the Church like a common malady. The presence of hell becomes a reality for all creation. Therefore, even for the righteous, heavenly bliss comes only *after* the expulsion of hell from the world. "For he [Christ] must reign, till he hath put all enemies under his feet . . . that God may be all in all" (1 Cor. 15:25, 28). All perish and are saved together, although differently, by Christ's redemptive sacrifice, which creaturely sin can neither negate nor limit. And, like the pitying heart of the Mother of God, the Church's love also does not know any limits.

The partisans of "eternal" torments, who without difficulty accept the amnesia of the righteous with regard to the sinners, would also no doubt consider it natural for the holy angels to be indifferent to those who are cast down. The battle of the archangel Michael and his armies against the dragon and his angels manifests their love for God ("they loved not their lives unto the death" [Rev. 12:11]); and the casting down from heaven of the rebels was salvific for all. But would it not be more natural for those who are cast down, for the condemned and banished enemies, to expect — from those very same holy angels with Michael at the head who had cast them down from heaven as well as from the whole praying and pardoning Church — spiritual assistance toward their restoration, which cannot be accomplished except at the cost of inexpressible and — for human beings — unfathomable torment? We do not dare go beyond this speculation, which, however, appears to us to be an inevitable consequence of the Church's love. The one who, by an insane pride, thought himself to be "like the most High" (Isa. 14:14) must, in the depths of his fall, pass through humiliation to humility — to love. The Lord, who knows his creature, gave him being not only for eternal death and sterile torment.

As for creaturely freedom as willful arbitrariness (Dostoevsky's "underground") there can be no direct foreknowledge of the rectification of its ways or of the repentance of Satan. But Satan's very being, his createdness by the omniscient God, is, so to speak, an ontological proof of the inevitability of his future salvation. Even Satan in his madness does not have the power to overcome the fact of his own being, its divine foundation, that is, the sophianicity of all creation, by virtue of which "God will be all in all." Satan cannot fail to be convinced by his own nature of the insanity of seeking freedom in self-willfulness rather than in knowledge of truth, which alone can give true freedom. "Liar and the father of lies" who "abode not in the truth" (John 8:44), he will end by subordinating himself to the truth, and evil will thereby disappear completely from God's creation.

This alone concludes the disclosure of the universal power of Christ's redemptive sacrifice, offered "for all people and for all things," without any limitation or exception. This *universality* of sacrifice that the High Priest offers to the Father by the Holy Spirit precisely signifies the universal "apocatastasis." The Lord redeemed all sin by His blood that "at the name of Jesus every knee should bow, of things in heaven, and things in earth, and things under the earth" (Phil. 2:10). Although the power of the Incarnation seems to refer directly only to all flesh, that is, to the human world, it also extends to the world of the angels, which is connected with the human world, for the angels minister to the human world and thus live one life with it.

517

Another question arises in connection with this: the question of the limits of the Pentecost. Does Pentecost extend to the spiritual world? Did the Holy Spirit also descend upon the angels? It is clear that this question too cannot be answered in the negative: The "Spirit of God bloweth where it listeth," and, of course, the power of His approach to the human world also extends to the incorporeal angelic world, though differently, of course, than to beings clothed in flesh. And the power of the Holy Spirit, which is life-giving, sanctifying, and salvific, cannot fail to touch the fallen spirits who are conscious of their fall. These spiritual corpses are gathered and resurrected also by the action of the Holy Spirit. Such is the Christian *hope*, which is inalienable from our faith, for it is rooted in the fundamental principles of the latter. In this sense, Christian hope is a theological postulate. The perfect Divine-humanity includes and presupposes not only angelic-humanity, that is, the union of heaven and earth, of the human and angelic worlds, but also divine-angelhood, that is, a new deification of the angels through humanity, and thanks to this deification the regeneration, in the ages of ages, of that sick, withered branch of the Lord's vineyard which Christ Himself had condemned to wither. But He came to redeem and save what had perished. We are powerless to describe, even schematically, this path of universal salvation; but we perceive its necessary principles.

Among the eschatological prophecies we find apparent contradictions and divergences. These apparent divergences can be explained by the fact that different prophecies treat different aspects or moments of the final culmination. It is the business of theological exegesis to unite these different aspects. There is a unifying, generalizing text that, in our view, must be placed at the basis of eschatology and that is also its last word: Romans 11:29, 32-36 and 1 Corinthians 15:24-28. This text bears witness to the mystery of the divine economy, which, through all sorts of trials and deviations, leads creation to a good end. Here are these golden words:

> For the gifts and calling of God are without repentance. . . . For God hath concluded them all in unbelief, that he might have mercy upon all. O the depth of the riches both of the wisdom and knowledge of God! how unsearchable are his judgments, and his ways past finding out! For who hath known the mind of the Lord? Or who hath been his counsellor [Isa. 40:13]? Or who hath first given to him, and it shall be recompensed unto him again [Isa. 40:13-14]? *For of him, and through him, and to him, are all things.* To whom be glory for ever. Amen.

518

This marvelous hymn is affirmed and generalized by the prophecy: "Then cometh the end, when he shall have delivered up the kingdom to God, even the Father; when he shall have put down all rule and all authority and power. . . . And when all things shall be subdued unto him, then shall the Son also be subject unto him that put all things under him, that God may be all in all."

8. The City of God

The ultimate accomplishment of the judgment and separation refers, above all, to man's inner world, to his life in God, to his vocation and his rejection. But this does not exhaust this accomplishment, for it also necessarily includes a new relation to the world in its renewal, to the "new heaven and new earth." Not only is the world not abolished as something unnecessary (as it might appear to some), but it even enters into its glory and preserves its original connection with man, who retains his dominant place in the glorified world. The end of the world does not lead to acosmism or anticosmism with the disincarnation of man and his separation from the world. On the contrary, the glory of resurrection and the power of incorruptibility extend to the world too, and man becomes definitively rooted in it as a domain of the kingdom of God after the expulsion of its false prince. When He was parting with His disciples, the Lord told them at the Last Supper: "Verily I say unto you, I will drink no more of the fruit of the vine, until that day that I drink it new in the kingdom of God" (Mark 14:25), that is, until His return to the new earth under the new heaven, in His second and glorious Coming. This symbol expresses the new communion with the world as the kingdom of God that begins with the resurrection. Scripture bears witness to this world only briefly but with astonishing power (Rev. 21-22) in a language of symbolic figures (see below). It follows from these figures that man does not depart from the earth to heaven. On the contrary, heaven bends down to earth, and man's vocation and creative ministry in the world are therefore not abolished but are raised to a new, higher state.

Therefore, although the future age is separated from the present one by a universal catastrophe of being, this catastrophe does not rupture the continuity between them. Human history is included in the life of the future age, continues beyond its proper limits, into meta-history. All that has been accomplished in human history thus acquires a new significance in the *single* stream of life flowing from the Lord. If to justified and pardoned man it will be given to see the Lord and to know Him, this does not abolish his love for and rootedness in God's creation, his cognitive and creative attitude toward creation, to which he was originally called by God. Man will continue to live in the garden of God. Man's proper creative activity continues in meta-history. He does not become an honored "pensioner" of the new world, passively contemplating it. He remains a creative artificer of the world.

To be sure, we can express this idea only in the form of a general eschatological *postulate* relative to meta-history, without trying to disclose what is for now insufficiently knowable for us. Nevertheless, one must firmly establish the basic content of this postulate: the postulate that man is irrevocably rooted in a world that has become the kingdom of God. Ontologically, man is not simplified or impoverished in the life of the future age. On the contrary, for himself and for the world, he will be revealed in the fullness of his humanity, as the creaturely god of the world, as its logos and spirit. For man, the life of the future age will consist in creative activity in the world, creaturely praise. The latter will be similar to angelic praise, which constitutes the creative content of the proper life of angels with reference to the world, bestowed upon man but entrusted to angelic care. The human world together with the angelic world will constitute the powerful choir of creation praising its Creator: "Of him, and through him, and to him, are all things: to whom be glory for ever" (Rom. 11:36).

The main difficulty here is that the life in God that is bestowed upon glorified humanity appears to be incompatible with life in the world, in creation. Is not life in creation extinguished in life in God? Is the direct vision of God compatible with love for the world? In answering this question, we must remember that the world has its center in man, that it is essentially human. It is also clear that love for God in Christ necessarily includes love for man (as well as love for angels); and the second commandment is "similar" to the first, that is, identical with it in this case. One cannot love God without loving man — first of all, in the God-man Himself, in His holy humanity, as well as in His personal humanity, that is, in the Mother of God; and then in the saints, in His Church, the body of Christ and the temple of the Holy Spirit. Further, one cannot love humanity while separating it from the world; one cannot love it apart from the world. To love the saved world is therefore to contemplate God's works, to see the revelation of God in the world. Love of the sinful world and of man burdened by personal and original sin is enmity against God (1 John 2:15). But, in itself, the world is beloved by God, who sent His Son in order to save it (John 3:17). And if the heart of fallen man does not encompass the full measure of love for God and for the world, to love both God and creation is nevertheless the ontological measure of human love.

Himself being a creature, man cannot renounce his creatureliness, which is not a denigration but the determination given to him by God Himself. For man, to assume one's creatureliness is to love it, that is, to love the world and oneself in one's God-given nature. The new creation, the new heaven and new earth, demands a new love in God, in Christ and the Holy Spirit, in the Divine Sophia. The sophianicity of creation, which is the living and permanent self-revelation of God in creation, is in fact this foundation for the unification of love for God and love for the world in the unity of the Divine Sophia and the creaturely Sophia. This corresponds to the apostle Paul's words: "of him, through him, and to him are all things" (Rom. 11:36): *of him* in the Divine Sophia, *through him* as creation based upon her, and *to him* as the union of the Divine and the creaturely Sophia. This will be God all in all, the divine *all* in creaturely being, the Divine Sophia in the creaturely Sophia.

Beyond these postulates nothing can be said from history about metahistory. All that is accessible here to our knowledge is expressed in Revelation chapters 21–22 (as well as in certain Old Testament prophecies). Revelation speaks, first of all, of "the holy city, new Jerusalem, coming down from God out of heaven" (Rev. 21:2). This city is identified with the Bride of the Lamb (vv. 9-10), that is, the Church. It should be emphasized here that this descent from heaven is combined with features that establish the connection of this "new Jerusalem" with the earthly city Jerusalem. Built of earthly materials (gold), the "New Jerusalem" is measured by a human (as well as angelic) measure and is adorned with precious stones of earth. It has twelve angels at twelve gates, and has inscribed upon it the names of the twelve tribes of Israel and of the twelve apostles. This indicates the earthly character of this city. At the same time, it bears the glory of God (v. 23). Also, "the nations . . . which are saved shall walk in the light of it, and the kings of earth [shall] bring their glory and honour into it" (v. 24). This directly indicates that this heavenly-earthly glorified Jerusalem contains the sum-total of universal history as well as the matter of the creaturely world.

Without claiming to interpret the details of this picture (for instance, the precious stones, the measures, and the numbers), we can say that it represents the glorified world, in which there is no place for "any thing that defileth" (Rev. 21:27). The descent of the heavenly Jerusalem coincides with the continuing judgment and separation, in which "he that overcometh shall inherit all things; and I will be his God, and he shall be my son. But the fearful, and unbelieving, and murderers, and whore-mongers, and sorcerers, and idolaters, and all liars, shall have their part in the lake which burneth with fire and brimstone: which is the second death" (vv. 7-8). These apocalyptic images describe the rejection of different categories of sinners, whose fate is the same as that of the "beast and false prophet" (20:10, 14). Of course, such an equation attests to the summational character of this condemnation, which, in general, signifies abandonment *outside* the holy city. But, in accordance with our previous discussion, it is impossible, in a certain sense, to consider this condemnation as final. (Here, more than in other texts, one feels the influence of the apocalyptic language of the epoch.)

The descent from heaven of the "holy Jerusalem" does *not* signify a new creation that takes the place of the old. Such an interpretation is excluded by the whole combination of the individual features of this figure, but it does signify the transfiguration of the world. What is remarkable is that this transfiguration applies not only to the natural world (the "new heaven and new earth") but also to the human, historical world, for the "new Jerusalem, coming down from God out of heaven" (Rev. 21:2), contains features and materials of the earthly Jerusalem. The new Jerusalem represents the synthesis of universal history, which therefore continues beyond this age into metahistory: "The kings of the earth [shall] bring their glory and honour into it" (21:24). This connection between the heavenly and earthly Jerusalems, between meta-history and history, is underscored by a juxtaposition, which is also an opposition, with the earthly city *in malam partem*, Babylon, the great whore, the kingdom of the beast and the false prophet, "that great city, which reigneth over the kings of the earth" (17:18). This kingdom of this world, which does battle with the Lamb, and the fall of this kingdom are depicted in detail in chapters 17 and 18 of Revelation: "that great city Babylon [shall] be thrown down, and shall be found no more at all" (18:21). This destruction of the false kingdom, the false culture, and the godless civilization does not signify the abolition of human creative activity and earthly history. Rather, the latter will become a divine-human revelation: "God . . . will dwell with them [human beings], and they shall be his people" (21:3), and "the throne of God and of the Lamb shall be in it; and his servants shall serve him: and they shall see his face; and his name shall be in their foreheads . . . and they shall reign for ever and ever" (22:3-5).[70]

---

70. Prophecies concerning the new Jerusalem are already found in the Old Testament, particularly in Isa. 62:1-3 and 65:17-19.

This juxtaposition of the earthly city, Babylon, and the heavenly Jerusalem is represented by other figures as well: on the one hand, sitting upon a beast, a woman upon whose "forehead was a name written: mystery, Babylon the great, the mother of harlots and abominations of the earth" (Rev. 17:5); on the other hand, the "woman clothed with the sun," who is pursued by the dragon (chap. 12). The Church is opposed to the anti-church.[71]

Thus, the figure of the new Jerusalem signifies the transfigured and glorified world, which contains the principles of the natural world and the synthesis of human creative activity in history. It is already the meta-cosmos, which in meta-history raises the achievements of this age to the highest level. Principles of being that could have no place in the sin-corrupted world enter into the structure of the new world. And the world's connection is reestablished with the paradise planted by God, with all that grows in it, including the mysterious tree of life and the tree of the "knowledge of good and evil." But the time for such knowledge is past, for good and evil in their duality and state of struggle have been transcended, and there is no more evil. There is also no more good, in its relativity. In the kingdom of God, only the tree of life remains, which has vanquished death, together with the water of life, which restores, as it were, the river that went out of Eden to water the garden (Gen. 2:10): "And he showed me a pure river of water of life, clear as crystal, proceeding out of the throne of God and of the Lamb. In the midst of the street of it, and on either side of the river, was there the tree of life, which bare twelve manner of fruits, and yielded her fruit every month: and the leaves of the tree were for the healing of the nations" (Rev. 22:1-2). This signifies that the earth is no longer accursed, and that the economic enslavement of man to the earth has passed. However, although immortal life does not depend here on food and the stomach, man maintains his good connection with the natural world by partaking of its fruits. By no means is man taken out of the natural world; rather, he is eternalized in it. In the aspect of his psychic-corporeal composition, he remains "earth" as he was by his creation.

In compact and powerful images, an answer is given here to the question of incomprehensible human suffering, to God's apparent impotence in the face of such suffering.[72] This answer, as in the Book of Job, is given by God Himself: "and God shall wipe away all tears from their eyes;

71. For analogous oppositions between the wife (Sophia) and the whore (anti-Sophia), see Prov. 1, 2, 3, 6.

72. Cf. the epilogue to my book *The Comforter*: "The Father."

and there shall be no more death, neither sorrow, nor crying, neither shall there be any more pain: for the former things are passed away" (Rev. 21:4). How and in what sense this takes place is a *mystery* of the future age, but we have here the promise of a full theodicy, the promise of a vitally satisfying and reconciling answer to the "sorrow of the world" and the "accursed questions." The process of the world in human history reaches such ripeness that such an answer becomes possible. Although it is given by God, this answer reaches the human consciousness and is therefore divine-human. Comfort to the world is given by the Comforter: There shall be "neither sorrow nor crying" and "God shall wipe away all tears."

To this we must add that the figure of the new city is presented schematically, statically, so to speak. But the living human spirit does not know immobility; this is only the sign of the *beginning* of meta-history, which has its own *"ages of ages,"* inaccessible to our present knowledge. Meta-history *continues* in the future age, which is not static, but a new life. (The presence of the lake of fire and of those burning in it indirectly attests to this; this is not a definitive, unchanging state but only an initial separation, which will end with the union of all in universal salvation.)

But what chiefly distinguishes the holy city from all earthly cities and even from paradise, into which God came only for conversation with man, is the presence in it of the God-man Himself. Revelation speaks of this repeatedly and with astonishing power. First, one hears "a great voice out of heaven saying, Behold, the tabernacle of God is with men, and he will dwell with them, and they shall be his people, and God himself shall be with them, and be their God" (Rev. 21:3), "for the former things are passed away" (v. 4), and "I make all things new" (v. 5). The perfect Divine-humanity, which, finally, appears in all its visibility, is then spoken of: "It is done. I am Alpha and Omega, the beginning and the end. I will give unto him that is athirst of the foundation of the water of life freely. He that overcometh shall inherit all things; and I will be his God, and he shall be my son" (vv. 6-7). (This is followed by a passage about those excluded from the holy city.)

About the city itself we read: "I saw no temple therein, for the Lord God Almighty and the Lamb are the temple of it. And the city has not need of the sun, neither of the moon, to shine in it, for the glory of God did lighten it, and the Lamb is the light thereof" (Rev. 21:22-23). "The throne of God and of the Lamb shall be in it; and his servants shall serve him: and they shall see his face; and his name shall be in their foreheads. And there shall be no night there; and they need no candle, neither light of the sun; for the Lord God giveth them light: and they shall reign for ever and ever" (22:3-5). Such symbolic figures express the perfect revelation of God and the perfect communion with God. This is no longer a restitution (apocatastasis) of what has been lost, but the accomplishment of the new by the transformation and glorification of the old: The city has "the glory of God" (21:11); "the glory of God did lighten it" (v. 23), by the action of the Holy Spirit. God Himself will dwell with men (v. 3). There is therefore no longer need here for a special temple, since the whole world is God's temple.

The parousia of the Son and the parousia of the Spirit are the revelation of the Father. But the parousias of the Son and of the Spirit are inseparable from that of the Mother of God. This is the most mysterious and significant aspect of the holy city. The great city, the holy Jerusalem, descending out of heaven from God, the tabernacle of God with men, is insistently and repeatedly also called the "wife" or "bride of the Lamb": "The marriage of the Lamb is come, and his wife hath made herself ready. And to her was granted that she should be arrayed in fine linen, clean and white, for the fine linen is the righteousness of saints. And he [the angel] saith unto me, Write, Blessed are they which are called unto the marriage supper of the Lamb" (Rev. 19:7-9). And the angel said, "'Come hither, I will show thee the bride, the Lamb's wife.' And he carried me away in the spirit to a great and high mountain, and showed me that great city, the holy Jerusalem, descending out of heaven from God, having the glory of God" (21:9-11). (A description of the city follows.)

In the final words of the final book of the New Testament, one hears again the heavenly sounds of the Old Testament Apocalypse, the Song of Songs, the song of the sister-bride-wife, the Unwedded Bride. What does this mean? Why do we hear precisely here this revelation of the Church, which we also find in some of the apostolic epistles (Ephesians, Corinthians)? Do we not see an inappropriate agglomeration in these conjoined images of the city "prepared as a bride adorned for her husband" (Rev. 21:2)? Does this agglomeration belong to the eastern style of apocalyptic, or does it express the great, final mystery of Christ and of the Church, and then of Christ and of the Mother-Virgin, the Unwedded Bride, in the revelation of the final accomplishment and of the glory of the world? But is not the entire world in its humanity the kingdom of love, which embraces the natural and human world? In this world, everyone finds himself with all and in all, in creation and history, in the kingdom of grace and glory, in the body of Christ and the temple of the Holy Spirit.

This is the most general and complete revelation that we have of the Church as humanity in Divine-humanity. And if this is the case, then is not the Most Pure Mother of God Herself in Her glory this personal head of the Church, the personal humanity of Divine-humanity? Is She not the Heavenly Jerusalem, which returns to earth from its heavenly home in the parousia of the Mother of God, in order to become here the spiritualized tabernacle of God with men? Is She not Sophia herself, creaturely but entirely deified, the peak of all creation, more venerable than the cherubim and incomparably more glorious than the seraphim? Is She not the glory and the joy of the saved peoples at the marriage feast of the Lamb? Is She not that perfect union of the divine and the human in which all creation, both the angelic choir and humankind, rejoices? She, the Spirit-Bearer, is *Spirit and Bride,* manifesting in Her very being the image of the hypostatic Spirit of God. And about Her it is said in the final words of the New Testament:

> "And the Spirit and the Bride say, Come.
> And let him that heareth say, Come!
> **Even so, come, Lord Jesus!**"

Index

Christ, 98-100, 107-9, 111, 159, 164-66,
187, 226, 230, 233, 248, 266-67, 269,
281, 292, 298, 301-2, 305, 307, 325-
26, 328, 333-34, 338-39, 342-43, 355,
358, 365, 370-71, 373, 386, 390, 403-
4, 419, 423, 434, 438, 448, 451, 476,
481, 485, 487-88, 496, 498, 503, 514-
18, 520, 525; ascension, 357, 389;
body of, 255-62, 279, 287, 293, 295,
313; and the Church, 254-55, 263-64;
and death, 351, 353, 356-57; and the
Eucharist, 391; high-priestly ministry, 276; and Holy Spirit, 327; and
judgment, 456-61, 464, 484;
parousia, 387-89, 392-96, 398-400,
405, 408-9, 411, 414, 417, 420, 422,
424-25, 427, 429, 432, 437, 472, 484,
494, 504; resurrection of, 356-57,
394, 422, 429-32, 435-37, 449, 472;
and synergism, 241; Transfiguration
of, 367, 399, 405-6, 421; vicars of,
276-78, 280
Chrysostom, St. John, 371, 438
Church, 99-100, 164, 254-56, 270-72,
275, 301, 311-13, 327, 334, 366, 380,
424, 488, 496, 500, 517, 525-26; as
body of Christ, 257-62, 266, 282,
287, 515; as Bride of Christ, 263-65;
and canons, 314n.44; glorified, 408-
9, 411; and grace, 294-95, 300-301,
306; as hierarchical organization,
268-69, 274-83, 285, 290, 293; limits
of, 266-67; as sacrament of sacraments, 273, 306; as Sophia, 253, 258,
264-65, 270; as *Una Sancta,* 292-93
City of God. *See* Jerusalem, new
Creation, 7-8, 36-37, 51, 55-57, 62-63,
70, 75, 78, 87, 104-5, 112, 142, 198,
315-16, 425; of I, 94; of man, 89,
175-76, 197; new, 426; out of nothing, 6, 22, 38, 43, 79, 117, 126, 196;
and providence, 201; Six Days of, 53,
64-65, 67-69, 71, 83, 108, 173-74,
319, 321, 384, 402, 428; and time, 58
Creativity, creaturely or human, 139-40,
144, 148-50, 237, 315, 318, 320-21,

323-24, 326, 331-33, 348, 496; in
hell, 498-99; and history, 342-43
Creator, 46, 49, 51, 54, 58-59, 62-64,
66, 68-70, 73, 75, 87, 112, 116-19,
130, 144-45, 149, 155, 194-96, 201,
222, 229, 232, 234
Cyprian, St., 263n.6, 275, 278, 284, 312

Dante, 367
Death, 349, 351-52, 355-60, 366, 368,
372, 374-75; and God, 350, 353-54
Deification, 203, 247, 296-98, 300-302,
305-6, 308, 332, 414-15, 425, 472,
479, 486, 496
Deisis, 415, 417
Deism, 194, 204
Divine-humanity, xi, xvii, 14, 97-98,
123, 188, 204, 225, 248, 253, 257,
262, 267, 281, 289, 295-97, 300-301,
304-5, 308, 327, 334, 344, 345, 352,
397, 403, 407-8, 414, 430, 451, 472,
482, 493, 514, 515n.69, 518, 525-26;
and the Church, 270-73, 282, 290;
and creaturely Sophia, 143; and the
Eucharist, 287; and human-divinity,
163
Dostoevsky, Feodor, 137, 154, 345,
346n.8, 517; Ivan Karamazov, 216
Dualism, 4-6
Duns Scotus, 58

Economy, 317
Eden, 177-81, 185, 358
End of the world (age), 382-83, 387,
418
Ephraem the Syrian, St., 453n.47
Eschatology, 379-82, 466, 506
Eternal torments, 470, 474, 482, 484-
87, 492-93, 495, 499, 501, 506, 516
Eternity, 56, 104, 107, 226-27, 303, 466-
73, 482, 485-86, 489-90, 496, 501;
creaturely, 203, 478, 480; of the
world, 103, 121
Eucharist, 284-89, 291, 391, 392n.11,
444, 515n.69
Evil, 147-49, 151, 190, 490-93, 505-6,
509; as darkness, 151-52; and final